Living to Learn

INVENTORY PRESS

Living to Learn

Art & Education for the Common Good

Edited by Noah Simblist

Introduction

Noah Simblist

In the history of education, there is a fundamental tension between liberation and discipline that crystallizes in times of crisis. As I have been working on this book I have spoken with artists, educators, curators, and other cultural workers who all agree that now is such a time. There is a collapse of belief in museums and universities in areas of the world lucky enough to have such institutions, and an exhaustion of resources felt by grassroots organizers who have created alternatives to them. The pressures that produced this crisis are both economic and political—and often a combination of the two. These tensions also vary from region to region.

My process of gathering contributions for this book overlapped with the war in Israel-Palestine and Lebanon, a time when we have seen the utter destruction of an education infrastructure within Gaza and the violent interruption of learning throughout the region. This context, whose latest swell of violence started in 2023 and, despite some fragile ceasefires is effectively ongoing, underlined the radical stakes at the heart of learning.

One of the roundtables included here, about art education in the Middle East, was rescheduled constantly to account for Israeli attacks in Palestine and Lebanon. This was poignantly illustrated by a story that professor Gregory Buchakjian, who teaches at ALBA, an art school in Beirut, told about a student. He said, "The other day, I saw a student who lives in a neighborhood that was bombed. She was sitting on a chair. She couldn't think. She couldn't say a word, her face was completely white, she was completely traumatized. She wanted to stay. The students want to come because otherwise they are stuck at home, and they feel they are going mad. So this young woman who didn't sleep at night was exhausted.

She didn't want to go home because the campus is a safe space and outside of the war arena." Sometimes the stakes of schooling are life itself, where classrooms become not only spaces for learning but potentially spaces for care.

This book, *Living to Learn: Art & Education for the Common Good*, addresses contemporary art as a site of learning. It builds on the ambition of education as a civic service for the common good, but when it intersects with art, the compound *art & education* encompasses different modes of address to a public, not just as a methodology but also as a subject. As I'll outline later, learning, as opposed to teaching, was the operative word for both the educational turn and the radical pedagogies that inspired it. Learning was thought to be a more ethical operation, one that doesn't presuppose hierarchies and thus is more connected to the liberatory dimensions of education. The title of this book links living to learning to imply that learning is not circumscribed to one's childhood in the form of school but rather is a mechanism to apply curiosity and openness as a practice in everyday life. Furthermore, it connects to the social dimension of education, and, as it applies to art, the ways in which art and life can be connected.[1]

The "educational turn" emerged in the early twenty-first century as a form of art and exhibition making that proposed a radical shift in the ways that we assume art's role in society. These art practices were radical in several ways. One has to do with an intervention into normative expectations of the form of art. Drawing on the dematerialization of Conceptualism, the educational turn decentered the art object and focused instead on discourse.[2] Another had to do with a more political intention, aligning art practice with critiques of society. To shift the focus of an exhibition from objects to discourse could be seen as anti-capitalist, since it elided the production and exchange of commodities. But as I'll describe later, capitalism has a way of engulfing everything, even practices built in opposition to it.[3] One central argument within the educational turn was that education is essential to produce and develop a public, as defined by egalitarian principles, and by bringing that to an art practice, the cultural sphere could be reinvigorated as a truly public sphere.[4]

In the twenty-first century, *art & education* had to contend with the tensions between pedagogy as a process to serve democracy, decolonization, and the public sphere and the ways in which it could be used as a tool to reinforce systems of oppression. The educational turn in the twenty-first century produced small, often artist-run, alternative education institutions, as well as new kinds of artistic and curatorial practices and radical changes in universities and museums. This book will chart these developments, with particular attention to the Americas and the Middle East. It is not intended to be a definitive survey of global practices in this field. There are many more examples than this book can hold. But it is intended to be

1 The "living" in *Living to Learn* is inspired by Nato Thompson's survey of social practice, *Living as Form: Socially Engaged Art from 1991–2011* (MIT Press, 2012). Linking the notion of the "common good" to ideas about art and the public is inspired by the 2016 anthology *Public Servants: Art and the Crisis of the Common Good* (MIT Press, 2016), edited by Johanna Burton, Shannon Jackson, and Dominic Willsdon.

2 Lucy Lippard, *Six Years: The Dematerialization of the Art Object from 1966–1972* (University of California Press, 1997).

3 As artist Andrea Fraser put it, "L'1% C'est Moi," *Texte zur Kunst* (September 2011): 114–127.

4 See Jurgen Habermas, *The Structural Transformation of the Public Sphere: An Inquiry into a Category of Bourgeois Society* (MIT Press, 1991), and Hannah Arendt's notion of the "space of appearance" in Hannah Arendt, *The Human Condition* (University of Chicago Press, 1958), 219.

decidedly global, as it covers a period when globalization became a defining characteristic of contemporary art.

My focus on these two regions is based on considerations that are both institutional and personal. One is that I and the Institute for Contemporary Art at Virginia Commonwealth University, the academic museum producing this publication, are based in a US context, and thus part of a larger flow of political economies that move through the Americas. I also have worked with artists and institutions in Latin America and the Caribbean from my position in the US, taking students to visit some of the initiatives included in this volume such as SOMA and Capacete. Secondly, VCU has a campus in Doha, Qatar, part of a dramatic development of universities and museums in the Gulf region. Also, for two decades much of my work as a writer and curator has focused on the Middle East. Both these areas have been significant centers of alternative organizations and artistic practices during this time.

5 Horace Mann, *The Republic and the School: Horace Mann On the Education of Free Men* (Teachers College Press, 1957).

6 Gabriela Ossenbach and María del Mar del Pozo, "Postcolonial Models, Cultural Transfers and Transnational Perspectives in Latin America: A Research Agenda" *Paedagogica Historica: International Journal of the History of Education* 47, no. 5 (2011), 579–600 and Walter D. Mignolo and Catherine E. Walsh, *On Decoloniality: Concepts, Analytics, Praxis* (Duke University Press, 2018), 135.

7 Akkari Abdeljalil, "Education in the Middle East and North Africa: The Current Situation and Future Challenges," *International Education Journal* 5, no. 2 (2004): 144–153. The artist Alia Farid curated an exhibition at the Swiss Institute in New York in 2021 that also touched on this history in the Middle East. *The Space Between Classrooms* took as its starting point the prototype for schools that Swiss architect Alfred Roth designed for Kuwait's Ministry of Public Works during the late 1960s.

8 Wendy Brown, "The End of Educated Democracy," *Representations* 116, no. 1 (2011): 19–41; Henry A. Giroux, *Schooling and the Struggle for Public Life: Democracy's Promise and Education's Challenge* (Paradigm Publishers, 2005).

Education and Democracy

Ideas about education in the Global North emerged in the late eighteenth and early nineteenth centuries alongside the development of democracy. In France, the secretary of education François Guizot established a law that secular primary education be accessible for all citizens. In the United States, Thomas Jefferson and later Horace Mann and John Dewey advocated for a similar notion—that a democratic society requires an educated citizenry.[5] In Latin America during this same period, a postcolonial era of nation-building was also influenced by these models, especially European ones.[6] In Egypt, President Gamal Abdel Nasser advocated for free public education as a part of its own decolonial process.[7]

Wendy Brown and Henry A. Giroux, writing in the early twenty-first century and responding to neoliberal disinvestments to education, lamented the break from this history, forcing education from the public to the private sphere.[8] But the ideals of the Enlightenment era, replacing the church and the crown with a democratic public, were also fraught with a series of power relationships that made assumptions about who could have access to, or participate in, this public. The ideals of democratic republics in Europe and the Americas often failed to live up to their stated principles.

Paulo Freire, the Brazilian educator and philosopher and a central figure in twentieth-century radical pedagogy, argued that education could be a path to the liberation of the oppressed within these republics, that despite the limitations of early forms of education in nascent democracies, it still could be used to overcome those challenges.[9] Similarly, bell hooks argued that education could be a model for undoing many of the structures that reproduce inequality in society.[10]

Formal modes of education in Europe and the United States developed in the nineteenth century relied on lectures, memorization, and mastery, whereas more experimental forms of education, developed in the twentieth century, included more active engagement and participation.[11] In the language of theater, noting the performativity of education, the fourth wall is broken, allowing a more porous relationship between performer/teacher and audience/students. This shift in forms of teaching produced new architectures for the physical embodiment of these ideas.[12]

Similarly, the traditional understanding of art in the nineteenth century was that it entailed objects for passive contemplation. In the twentieth century, various modernist experiments produced models for participation such as Conceptual art, performance art, and Fluxus. These forms broke the fourth wall between art and spectator; they came about for many reasons but one might argue that a certain degree of freedom was at stake. The ways artists broke the fourth wall shared a democratizing impulse with a similar break in education. Redistributing authorship between artist and spectator modeled a similar redistribution of power and authority.

Radical Pedagogy and Its Legacies

Many of the artistic movements that inspired art & education practices were themselves influenced by a cluster of theories subsumed under the term *radical pedagogy*. Philosophers Michel Foucault and Louis Althusser argued that schools were mechanisms that reproduced power and ideology through structures of discipline, much like the army or the police and despite their appearance as soft power.[13]

Following this, Austrian philosopher and theologian Ivan Illich argued that traditional models of education were structured so that the pupil was "schooled" to receive the instruction of a teacher for the purpose of grade advancement and acquiring a degree. He argued instead for the "deschooling" of a schooled society and to replace teaching with learning. This sentiment is echoed in curator Miguel Lopez's interview with artist Patricia Belli included here. Illich proposed "learning webs" made up of networks such as skill sharing, peer matching, and resource libraries for self-directed modes of education.[14] Illich worked with these ideas throughout the Americas, including stints in Puerto Rico and Mexico.

In a similar vein, philosopher Jacques Rancière argued for an "ignorant schoolmaster" to interrupt the power dynamic between teacher and student.[15] As you will see in his contribution to this book, curator Manuel Borja-Villel cites this notion as an influence on his educational programming

9 Paulo Freire, *Pedagogy of the Oppressed* (Continuum, 1970).

10 bell hooks, "Theory as Liberatory Practice," *Yale Journal of Law and Feminism* 4, no. 1 (1991): 1–12.

11 See Ruth Erickson, "A Progressive Education," *Leap Before You Look: Black Mountain College, 1933–1957* (Hammer Museum and Yale University Press, 2015).

12 See Beatriz Colomina, Ignacio G. Galán, Evangelos Kotsioris, and Anna-Maria Meister, eds., *Radical Pedagogies* (MIT Press, 2022) and the 2021 exhibition *Education Shock: Learning, Politics, and Architecture in the 1960s and '70s* at the Haus der Kulturen der Welt in Berlin.

13 Michel Foucault, *The Archaeology of Knowledge* (Routledge, 1972); Louis Althusser, "Ideology and Ideological State Apparatuses," *Lenin and Philosophy and Other Essays* (Monthly Review Press, 1971), 127–188.

14 Ivan Illich, "Why We Must Disestablish School," *Deschooling Society* (Harper & Row, 1972), 1–23.

15 Jacques Rancière, *The Ignorant Schoolmaster: Five Lessons in Intellectual Emancipation* (Stanford University Press, 1991).

at the Museu d'Art Contemporani de Barcelona (MACBA).

In his influential 1968 book *Pedagogy of the Oppressed*, Freire argued against what he called the traditional "banking" model of education, in which students are treated as empty vessels to be filled with information. Instead, he argues for students to engage in dialogue and become active political subjects. This educational model, based on the value of equity, can lead to them identifying the conditions of their oppression and creating a framework for their liberation.[16] A work by the Brazilian artist Jonathas de Andrade was inspired by Freire's educational models and is included in this book. bell hooks wrote about the potential for education to provide a pathway for liberation from systemic oppression. In her 1994 book *Teaching to Transgress*, she argues that after school desegregation in the United States, classrooms became highly politicized spaces to negotiate intersectional racial politics and that politicization activated their potential to make education a place for freedom.[17] Two artists included in *Living to Learn*, Kameelah Janan Rasheed and Steffani Jemison, cite hooks as inspiration for their approaches to teaching.

In many cases institutions such as universities or museums have been rife with inequality and oppression, and one approach to radical pedagogies like deschooling is anti-institutional. In her essay reproduced here, art historian Beatriz E. Balanta asserts that "it is easier for a camel to go through the eye of a needle than for a person of color to inhabit academia." In his essay, artist and architect Yazan Khalili describes struggles with freedom of speech and the ways that both the law and cultural funding resist it.

16 Paulo Freire, *Pedagogy of the Oppressed.*

17 bell hooks, *Teaching to Transgress: Education as the Practice of Freedom* (Routledge, 1994).

The impulse for artists to self-organize many of the projects tied to the educational turn produced a radical alternative to and also a critique of institutions, asking them to evolve and help dismantle these systems of oppression. But sometimes the claims of radicality did not match the forms and structures these initiatives took. It prompts the question: Do we abandon institutions as hopeless power structures or work to reform them? Put another way, while smaller alternative institutions and artist interventions are necessary, should we give up on the potential for larger institutions to care for the common good? As curator and educator Dominic Willsdon argues in his contribution to this book, there *is* something valuable about institutions caring for the public. Reversing our perspective, if we invest in alternative structures, how can we ensure that they are not only financially viable but also ideologically sustainable? Beatriz Santiago Muñoz, an editorial advisor and contributor to this book, describes her work with the Puerto Rican space Beta Local, founded on Illich's principles, and the ways in which that work began to be conditioned by the requirements of foundation grants—as opposed to the intentions of its founding. The radicality of the alternative is often tamed to meet the requirements of nongovernmental administration.

* * *

In the twenty-first century, the notion of radicality has itself been turned on its head. As I write this in the first months of the second Trump administration, two interpretations of revolution and liberation are being invoked in American political discourse.

First, the Tea Party during the Obama administration, developed not just as an opposition to those in power but also the governing logic of the incumbent. This new form of conservatism, sometimes called the alt-right or the new right, assumes that the government and all aspects of the elite that control contemporary society are guided by liberal values that must be overthrown with the zeal of the American revolution. In this case, the Tea Party was not against British colonial occupiers but a liberal American elite. This has evolved so that when Trump and other Republicans today speak about "the deep state" or "the administrative state" that seeks to control the freedom of the American people, it is iconoclastic, a call to tear down institutions not only within the US government but also NGOs, universities, and cultural institutions. The penultimate manifestation of this movement was the attack on the US capitol on January 6, 2021, by Trump supporters. This inspired supporters of the outgoing Brazilian president Jair Bolsonaro on January 8, 2023, to storm the capital in Brasília, revealing that this way of thinking was not unique to the United States.

Secondly, these notions of freedom—and the use of disruption as a method to achieve it—have been amplified by a coalition of conservatives in the US that has built a new network of alliances across the globe. The COVID–19 pandemic accelerated this process. As public-health agencies advocated for sheltering in place, vaccines, and masking as measures to protect both individuals and communities, there was a severe backlash. Opponents of these measures saw them as government control, an overreach into their civil liberties. Suddenly the phrase "my body, my choice," previously associated with feminist abortion-rights advocates on the political left, was now the rallying cry of a libertarian right. When Althusser was writing about the ideological state apparatus as a mechanism of control, he assumed a conservative hold on power. Similarly, the politics of radical pedagogy assumed that marginalized voices were progressive. When Foucault wrote about skepticism of the intentions of education or medical establishments, it was based on the assumption that power had been transferred from a feudal king to a conservative administrative state. But that same logic has now been turned on its head, and the alt right sounds like Foucault voicing skepticism about the scientific method and the intentions of educational institutions.

Nowhere was this ideological battle more apparent than in the sphere of education, especially for K–12 students. Education in the US became politicized, and formerly quiet school-board meetings became highly charged political spaces to air these debates. Not since the movement to desegregate schools in the 1950s had we seen such venom. This charged atmosphere was compounded by the murder of George Floyd in May 2020 and the widespread response led by the Black Lives Matter (BLM) movement. Suddenly, Critical Race Theory (CRT) and Diversity, Equity, and Inclusion (DEI) initiatives were brought into broader social awareness, and mostly white conservative parents accused schools of not only brainwashing their children about COVID but also making them feel bad for being complicit with white supremacy. The conservative activist Christopher Rufo fanned these flames and galvanized these isolated moments into a movement that was invited into the establishment by the second Trump administration, whose educational and cultural policies have been guided by this ethno-nationalist backlash.

As queer and trans students started to become more visible in mainstream society and the use of chosen pronouns and gender-affirming healthcare became more common, a related backlash arose. In 2016, North Carolina's House of Representatives passed Bill 2, which requires anyone in a public facility, including all public schools, to use the bathroom corresponding to the gender they were assigned at birth. Gordon Hall's essay "Gender, Sculpture, and Relearning How to See," reprinted here, references this bill and discusses how an object, like a body, is legible. As I write this, federal agencies have been instructed to dismantle DEI and LGBTQ-friendly policies, including those that allow for the inclusion of trans people in public-education spaces.

Education and art play a particular role in polities defined by democracy and the rights and representation of the citizen subject, like the United States. They are also ways to critique the hypocrisies of liberal and neoliberal societies and their claims of inclusion.[18] But now, as a new, increasingly ethno-nationalist social contract emerges, there is a radical undoing of established precedent. Now the challenge for people invested in progressive forms of art and education is deciding whether we defend the flawed institutions, letting go of the impulse to critique them, or build new alternatives on their ashes.

The Educational Turn

So what *was* the educational turn? One might begin with the premise that every artwork is a school, as one of this book's contributors, curator and art historian Sarah Rifky says, and we could think of the educational turn as a shift in a way of thinking about how any artwork functions. In that sense, it would be more interpretive than proscriptive. But the educational turn was more literal than that. As outlined by theorist and curator Irit Rogoff, the educational turn was not a "reading strategy" like the linguistic turn of the 1970s, which was a way of thinking about either art or education. Instead, she argues that the educational turn was an active movement responding to urgencies within the field of education.[19] One of the most impactful of these was the Bologna Accord, which sought to standardize education in Europe by creating systems of outcomes and accountabilities and was modeled on a similar system in the United States. Rogoff and her colleagues were alarmed by this pressure, which treated knowledge production like many other forms of production in a capitalist society and turned ideas into commodities and treated teachers and students as workers in a factory, alienated from their labor.

Even though this book does not include contributions from others, like Rogoff, who participated in the European examples of the educational turn, I think it's useful to give a short summary of this activity as context for what is included here.

Based in London, and teaching at Goldsmiths College, Rogoff was deeply engaged in the discourse of the educational turn in Europe. In 2006, Rogoff co-organized A.C.A.D.E.M.Y. at the Van Abbemuseum in Eindhoven, The Netherlands, a project that asked the question, "What can we learn from the museum?" It included a series of exhibitions and events with collaborators that also explored how learning can be applied to institutions.[20] Two terms that she introduced to this effort are *potentiality* and *actualization*. She says that there was a

18 Sara Ahmed, *On Being Included: Racism and Diversity in Institutional Life* (Duke University Press, 2012).

19 Irit Rogoff, "Turning," *e-flux Journal* (October, 2008), http://www.e- flux.com/journal/turning/.

20 Angelica Nollert and Irit Rogoff, eds., *A.C.A.D.E.M.Y.* (Berlin: Revolver Press, 2006).

desire to reintroduce the potential for failure and risk-taking into an education discourse that was becoming more bureaucratized and homogenized. In Berlin in 2007, she co-organized the conference Summit: Non-Aligned Initiatives in Education Culture, along with the Witte de With Center for Contemporary Art, Goldsmiths, and unitednationsplaza.

Biennials began to expand their reach beyond exhibition making, revealing the conversations that often make up a curator's research as public platforms. Rogoff refers to the discussion forum 100 Days—100 Guests at Documenta X (1997, curated by Catherine David), which hosted one hundred talks during the exhibition, and to the four discussion platforms across the globe prior to the opening of Documenta XI (2002, curated by Okwui Enwezor et al.), as important moments in this development.[21] In addition to discussions, these platforms also were significantly inclusive of art practices, and by extension political contexts, outside of Europe and the United States. For example, David included several Lebanese artists who had developed practices in the wake of the Lebanese civil war, which had ended in 1990. Enwezor, born in Nigeria, was the first non-European artistic director of Documenta, and centered postcolonial narratives told by non-European subjects.

But some attempts at using dialogue to bring different political subjects together revealed that such conversations could be high-stakes. unitednationsplaza grew out of a perennial exhibition, Manifesta 6, which was set to take place in Nicosia, Cyprus in 2006. Nicosia is a capital divided between Turkish and Greek control. According to the Manifesta website,

> The self-composed collective consisted of German curator Florian Waldfovel, American Russian Anton Vidokle, and Egyptian Mai Abu ElDahab, who worked together with General Coordinator Yiannis Toumazis and Director Hedwig Fijen on a pre-biennial research model called the Manifesta 6 Coffee Breaks, which took place 5 months before the opening of the school in 2006 in the Northern territories of the city of Nicosia. Fifteen artists-in-residence organizations from all over Europe and US were invited to share their ideas about a new living and working space in Manifesta 6 to be positioned on both sides of the Green Line.[22]

The organizers of Manifesta 6 intended to turn the traditional biennial into an experimental art school to promote dialogue between European artists. Their website says,

> The Manifesta 6 School was envisioned as a postgraduate, transdisciplinary program for approximately ninety participants from many parts of the world, lasting about twelve weeks, selected based on an Open Call. Inspired by historical examples, such as Black Mountain College in the US and the Bauhaus in Germany, the Manifesta 6 School would have been a meeting ground for cultural producers in the region and beyond, as well as a platform for collaboration, discussion, and co-production.[23]

In keeping with the notion of open dialogue, the organizers intended on locating this school on both the Greek and Turkish sides of the border. This intent inflamed tensions with the Greek Cypriot authorities and Manifesta 6 was cancelled by the President of the Greek part of Cyprus, who froze its bank accounts. Curator Anton Vidokle took the plans for the cancelled Manifesta 6 project and turned them into a new project

21 Nollert and Rogoff, *A.C.A.D.E.M.Y.*

22 "Manifesta 6 Nicosia, cancelled," https://www.manifesta.org/editions/manifesta-6-nicosia/about

23 "Manifesta 6 Nicosia, cancelled."

called unitednationsplaza, in collaboration with theorists, artists, and curators Boris Groys, Jalal Toufic, Liam Gillick, Martha Rosler, Natascha Sadr Haghighian, Nikolaus Hirsch, Tirdad Zolghadr, and Walid Raad. unitednationsplaza was first launched in Berlin in 2007 and then traveled to Mexico City and to New York's New Museum in 2008.

This history of Manifesta 6 is significant not only because it was a foundational example of the educational turn applied to a biennial but also because it shows how the principles of dialogue and engagement were at odds with a geopolitical situation predicated on separation.

In 2008, curator Paul O'Neill and artist Mick Wilson organized a panel at the ICA London, "You Talkin' to Me? Why Art Is Turning to Education," as a part of the Nought to Sixty Salon discussions. This was preparation for a 2010 book also edited by O'Neill and Wilson, *Curating and the Educational Turn*. In 2009, Steven Henry Madoff published *Art School (Propositions for the 21st Century)*.[24] In 2011, Felicity Allen edited an anthology about education for the MIT Press/Whitechapel Documents of Contemporary Art series.[25] Over these few years the particular conversation in Europe and the United States around education as an art practice covered a lot of territory.[26] This publication builds on that work but does not seek to recapitulate it, instead expanding its scope beyond what was traditionally referred to as the educational turn to include practices that are adjacent to its focus.

Education vs. Research

Rogoff suggests that the aesthetics of pedagogy that have characterized many of the projects in the educational turn—think of rooms with a chalkboard, a library, a set of chairs—might have become too ossified in their own formal expression to continue the urgency and dynamism that originally characterized the project of education as a form of art and exhibition making. In this sense, the aesthetics of pedagogy grew out of Conceptualism's aesthetic of administration.[27]

Even the physical layout of alternative spaces started to resemble one another. Organizations included in this book such as Beta Local, lugar a dudas, Capacete, and SOMA all have a kitchen, a library, and a space for a projector or blackboard together with a table and chairs. In his contribution, Sean Dockray talks about the importance of a large square table at the center of The Public School, the Los Angeles–based organization that he ran. But perhaps the spatial aesthetics of the educational turn aren't a tired exhibition style but more akin to a paradigm of encounter on par with the white cube or the black box.[28]

Often this pedagogical aesthetic resembled artistic practices, predicated on research, that might use an archive as the basis of the work. One question that has come up for me: When is a practice centered on education and when is it giving form to research? When artists center their practices on researching a given subject and then

24 Steven Henry Madoff, *Art School (Propositions for the 21st Century)* (MIT Press, 2009).

25 Felicity Allen, ed., *Education* (MIT Press and Whitechapel Gallery, 2011).

26 See also the 2023 exhibition *The Educational Web* at the Kunstverein Hamburg and Sam Thorne, *School: A Recent History of Self-Organized Art Education* (Sternberg Press, 2016).

27 Benjamin H. D. Buchloh, "Conceptual Art 1962–1969: From the Aesthetic of Administration to the Critique of Institutions," *October 55* (1990): 105–43.

28 I'm indebted to curator and writer Gavin Kroeber for this point.

share what they learn, is that a form of education? In some cases, yes. In others, no. I believe there is an overlap between research-based practices and education as a medium of knowledge exchange. But if education is not embraced as an intrinsic model, then these practices rely on preexisting structures to use as methodologies to present that knowledge, or, as Paulo Freire would say, it relies on a banking model of education.

There has been ample work done by curators, critics, and scholars to address research-based practices, including Paul O'Neill and Mick Wilson's *Curating Research* (2015) and Tom Holert's *Knowledge Beside Itself: Contemporary Art's Epistemic Politics* (2020).[29] For curators, the centrality of research does not just help them and a viewer interpret a work of art, or produce a thesis that binds together a set of artworks. Research, as a model of work for curators, allows for the project they produce to engage learning as an ongoing process that the viewer/audience/user participates in. Holert points out that while we might recognize the forms archive-based art take, what is often at stake is, following Michel Foucault, the power struggles over the ownership, representation, and reproduction of knowledge.

So, when Documenta 15, curated by ruangrupa, included The Black Archives, Asia Art Archive, Fehras Publishing, and Chimurenga, it was to present archives of marginalized knowledge as an intervention into normative structures of knowledge in the Global North. But one thing that I have encountered in archive projects like these is that the viewer/audience/user must come to the archive with the preexisting knowledge about how to navigate it. If we take education into account, it's like teaching someone by handing them a book without ever unpacking it in a classroom discussion.[30] Education is a way to make an archive more accessible and more transparent, yes, but also to challenge its authority, its structure, and the assumptions that might be embedded in it by putting it into dialogue with different points of view. Perhaps the best way to address this is to ask whom this work is meant to engage. ruangrupa set up a network of collectives included in Documenta 15 that they referred to as a *lumbung*, a community of interdependence. Perhaps those collectives were prepared to function as learners, but a general audience seemed less so.

Research as a practice for artists and curators rose to prominence in parallel with the knowledge-based economy. This transition to a post-Fordist political economy seemingly dematerialized labor alongside a shift from mechanical to digital production. The twenty-first century is the so-called information age, and the ways in which we find, store, and transfer data seem to supersede the manufacture of tangible things, at least in the Global North. So, as artists decenter the materiality of the object in favor of discourse and the organization of knowledge, it can follow the progressive politics of representation by presenting otherwise marginalized forms of knowledge. On the other hand, the obsession with knowledge and information as the basis of artistic practice seems to follow the most hegemonic of belief systems and power relations in an information-based economy. In this sense, research-based practices run the risk of following the same neoliberal

29 Paul O'Neill and Mick Wilson, eds., *Curating Research* (Open Editions, 2015); Tom Holert, *Knowledge Beside Itself: Contemporary Art's Epistemic Politics* (Sternberg Press, 2020).

30 There is a huge body of work on the archive and art, but two useful sources are Charles Merriweather, ed., *The Archive*, Whitechapel Documents of Contemporary Art (MIT Press, 2002) and Okwui Enwezor, *Archive Fever: Uses of the Document in Contemporary Art* (International Center for Photography, 2008).

patterns as the rest of the world, or as Buchloh would put it, a new aesthetics of administration.[31]

The potential conflict is this: The new aesthetics of administration in an information economy pronounces social exchange as one of ease and fluidity. It's guided by the principles of reducing user friction and maximizing efficiency, like the sleek lines of an iPhone, flexible hot desks, and hybrid work environments. On the other hand, the affective nature of this aesthetic is about maximizing user engagement through friction, enflaming rage as clickbait, driving up user numbers by harnessing base desires. Museums and universities use community engagement, feedback forums, or research exchanges to illustrate connection and fluidity and responsiveness. Some forms of activism against these institutions manifest as rage against the machine. But the truth of educational endeavors is that they are really hard and really slow. Art & education projects take more labor and resources to sustain than exhibitions in museums or university curricula. True education cannot take place as either fluid ease or carnal rage. It is guided by the principle that, as writer Sarah Schulman says, conflict is not abuse.[32] Learning spaces are defined by students recognizing things that they don't know about the world or about themselves, and that often produces a feeling of discomfort. This realization is often encountered as conflict, with a teacher, another student, or even their conception of themselves. The work of transformation, of growth, is moving through that discomfort to not only build something new but also to maintain the discomfort. Sustaining this mode of working has been difficult for institutions large and small.

31 Buchloh, "Conceptual Art 1962–1969."

32 Sarah Schulman, *Conflict Is Not Abuse: Overstating Harm, Community Responsibility, and the Duty of Repair* (Arsenal Pulp Press, 2016).

Education as Socially Engaged Art: Participation and Collaboration

Another node in the Venn diagram of art & education is socially engaged art practices. Here it might help to explain a term that I used above: viewer/audience/user. Following relational aesthetics and other forms of conceptually based performative art, socially engaged art practices privilege the social, the gathering of people together, as their primary medium. As such, they often do not assume that the primary work exists in visual terms, so the "viewer" is a metaphor for someone who might engage with the work. Similarly, since this work is social, it is rare for there to be a single person to whom the work is directed. It is more often an audience. But, as I mentioned above, this kind of engagement often breaks the fourth wall in Brechtian fashion, so the audience is not an autonomous entity that passively consumes the experience. Instead, the borders between artist and artwork and audience are blurred—so much so that the ones who engage the work might be referred to as users, to borrow a term from the information economy.

Art historian Claire Bishop's study of socially engaged practices, especially her 2006 anthology *Participation* and her 2012 book *Artificial Hells: Participatory Art and the Politics of Spectatorship*, emphasizes the importance of participation for social practice and includes some pedagogical projects as examples.[33] Participation, for Bishop, has its origins in the twentieth century through Dada, theorist Walter Benjamin, and Brecht, who saw participation as a political activation of art's potential. This dovetails with art historian Grant Kester's writing, most notably his 2004 book *Conversation Pieces*, where he outlines something that he calls "dialogical aesthetics," a formal structure for conversation.[34] But Bishop and Kester famously debated whether socially engaged art practices should engage with ethics.[35] A more recent book, *Art as Policies for Care: Socially Engaged Art 2010–ongoing*, doubles down on the ethical demand, centering care as a model for art and encouraging artists to contribute to the public sphere and rethink the commons.[36]

Social Media and the Digital Commons

What does the *social* of socially engaged practices mean today? It's notable that the social as a subject, medium, and methodology of art practice, predicated on embodied human contact, emerged at around the same time as social media.[37] This was also a moment of relative social isolation, when activities like shopping, dining, and movie-watching moved online. The public sphere shifted from the museum or the theater or the coffee shop to online forums. Some have lamented this symptom of the internet age, while others like Legacy Russell have advocated that digital spaces have given rise to new social formations. In these spaces, one can code switch through avatars and screen names, shifting out of identity markers that make it harder in a mode that she—eliding the more traditional term IRL—calls AFK, away from the keyboard.[38] Even the medically advised isolation of shelter-in-place policies in response to the COVID–19 pandemic produced a fluency in online lectures, discussions, and collaborative work solutions, and with it a tension between physical separation and a greater potential to be connected to communities around the world. The idea of open-source software, tied to the start of the internet, might seem quaint in a time when tech billionaires use the social dimension of their platforms to surveil, control, and commodify us. But concurrent with the rise of a high-tech corporate hegemony has been the use of these same technologies for mutual aid and knowledge-sharing. For instance, during the height of the Black Lives Matter protests in summer 2020, syllabi and reading lists on Black Radicalism and African Diasporic history and theory circulated widely online. Artist and writer Andrew Woolbright's essay on Dark Study, an online platform launched in 2020 by artists Caitlin Cherry and Nicole Won Hee Maloof, highlights how they leveraged digital space for knowledge-sharing as a more accessible form of learning.

One social mode of art & education is collaboration, an aspect of group formation that emerges from both the classroom and the artist-run institutions that often produced alternative models of pedagogy. After all, a class is a group that includes the teacher and the students, but how this group functions has a lot to do with different ideas of group work. Musician and writer Ethan Philbrick describes the ambivalence of group work as a product of a neoliberal condition in which our capacity to form groups is often put to work.[39] The twenty-first century also

33 Claire Bishop, ed., *Participation*, Whitechapel Documents of Contemporary Art (MIT Press, 2006) and Claire Bishop, *Artificial Hells: Participatory Art and the Politics of Spectatorship* (Verso, 2012).

34 Grant H. Kester, *Conversation Pieces: Community and Communication in Modern Art* (University of California Press, 2004).

35 See Grant H. Kester, "Another Turn (2006)" and Claire Bishop, "Response to Grant Kester (2006)," both in *Education*, ed. Felicity Allen (MIT Press, 2011).

36 Martina Angelotti, Matteo Lucchetti, and Judith Wielander, eds., *Art as Policies for Care: Socially Engaged Art 2010–ongoing* (Nero Editions, 2024).

37 Facebook (2004), Twitter (2006), the iPhone (2007), Instagram (2010), TikTok (2016).

38 Legacy Russell, *Glitch Feminism: A Manifesto* (Verso, 2020).

39 See Ethan Philbrick, *Group Works: Art, Politics, and Collective Ambivalence* (Fordham University Press, 2023), 16.

produced a resurgence of interest in forms of collective art making and institution making, such as art historian Blake Stimson and artist Gregory Sholette's anthology of texts about collectivism.[40] Much like the shift from objects to the social in the educational turn and socially engaged practices, collectivism shifted the assumption of a singular author to acts of commoning.[41]

The Historical Context

While not all educational projects that emerge from art practices are inherently activist, or even explicitly political, there is a history of the intersection between activism and socially engaged education. Most notable is the relationship between the Situationist International and the student uprising in May 1968 in France.[42]

During the May 1968 protests, a slogan emerged—"beneath the pavement, the beach"—that referred to student protesters who were picking up cobblestones from the city streets and throwing them at the police barricades.[43] The gap created by this lifted brick revealed the sand of this imaginary beach. The phrase implies that through action there is also political speculation, and hopeful speculation about the future often underlies the act of being a university student. It also implies that actively engaging with the built environment of a place, one can build a new future. Scholar and curator Claire Doherty linked the term *situation* with discourses around site specificity and art in the public sphere.[44] One dimension of site specificity implies its contemporary political reality and the ways in which that is related to an historical context. In this sense, there is also a temporal dimension to site specificity, one that artist Tania Bruguera would call a project's timing-specific nature.

Much of the state of education is tied to the state of the world. We are in *catastrophe time*, as Gary Zhexi Zhang, a contributor to this volume, says, in a state of ecological and political crisis and economic collapse, brought about by a financially unsustainable form of neoliberal privatization, leveraged through student debt and real-estate debt and endowments tied to the markets.[45] But what political markers of the twenty-first century, especially with regard to the Americas and the Middle East, set the stage for art & education projects that served a common good?

Geopolitical events had a huge impact on art & education. George W. Bush first heard about the attack of September 11, 2001, while reading to an elementary-school class. The effects of consequent invasions and occupations of Iraq and Afghanistan and the enthusiastic violence of American imperialism can be felt to this day throughout the Middle East. At the same time, the Gulf exploded as a growing center for museums, biennials, and universities located in spectacular cities of steel and glass that were rising from relatively modest built environments. Two examples of this are included here: a conversation with Zeina Arida, director of Mathaf in Doha, Qatar, and one with Noora Al Mualla,

40 Blake Stimson and Gregory Sholette, eds., *Collectivism After Modernism: The Art of Social Imagination After 1945* (University of Minnesota Press, 2007).

41 See Michael Hardt and Antonio Negri, *Commonwealth* (Harvard University Press, 2009).

42 T. J. Clark and Donald Nicholson-Smith, "Why Art Can't Kill the Situationist International," *October 79* (Winter 1997): 15–31.

43 McKenzie Wark, *The Beach Beneath the Street: The Everyday Life and Glorious Times of the Situationist International* (Verso, 2011).

44 Claire Doherty, ed., *Situation*, Whitechapel Documents of Contemporary Art (MIT Press, 2009).

45 Gary Zhexi Zhang, *Catastrophe Time* (Strange Attractor Press, 2023).

director of learning and research at the Sharjah Art Foundation in the United Arab Emirates. The sheer labor to build these urban centers provoked protest from artist groups like Gulf Labor. The Arab Spring, which began in late 2010, also provoked massive change throughout the MENA region. Sparked by the self-immolation of Mohamed Bouazizi, a Tunisian street vendor, its effects included regime change in Egypt and a civil war in Syria, which, as of this writing in 2025, has arrived at a fragile peace. The turmoil in Syria and Iraq, in particular, led to a huge refugee crisis that rippled through Europe.

In Palestine-Israel, the second Intifada broke out in 2000, leading to a brutal clap back from Israel including an apartheid wall, housing demolitions, checkpoints, and a spike in settlements. Throughout the twenty-first century, the United States has sent Israel billions of dollars in military aid every year. One project described here by researcher and curator Rasha Salti and artist Khaled Hourani is *Picasso in Palestine*, which highlighted these conditions by turning a school into a museum. Lebanon encountered tremendous political upheaval, even in the relative peace after its civil war concluded in 1990. In 2004 the prime minister of Lebanon, Rafic Hariri, was assassinated and, in 2006, Israel launched its largest attack since 1982. A conversation between sociologist and art historian Pelin Tan and curator Christine Tohme about the Beirut-based Ashkal Alwan illustrates the complexity of culture work in this context. After the Hamas attack on Israel on October 7, 2023, a war broke out between Israel and Palestine that has also spilled over to involve Lebanon, Iran, and Yemen. As of this writing there is a fragile ceasefire but, as I have been working on this book, this conflict has had a very strong ripple effect on universities, museums, biennials, and many other areas of the art & education sphere, as several texts in this volume make clear.

Meanwhile, in Latin America, the twenty-first century has been characterized by what has been called a *pink tide*, as many governments became more leftist. There was tremendous hope when Luiz Inácio Lula da Silva served as president of Brazil, for the first time, from 2003–11. Hugo Chávez was elected president of Venezuela in 1998 and Evo Morales served as president of Bolivia from 2006–19. While it's difficult to make sweeping generalizations about this region over the last twenty-five years, there were swings back and forth along the ideological spectrum. Following the end of the Cold War, attempts at US-style privatization in combination with foreign investment led to tremendous income inequality and neoliberal debt pressures. In many Latin American countries this led to the more leftist governments that sought to soften the blow to the working classes. But in places like Brazil, Lula was eventually followed by Jair Bolsonaro, who, like Donald Trump in the wake of Barack Obama, worked to undo many of the protections that had been instituted by the progressive government. In a conversation included here, Thiago Gil de Oliveira Virava, formerly the director of education of the São Paulo Biennial, discusses how the institution responded to these changing conditions through education. In the case of Venezuela, the policies implemented by Chávez and then his successor Nicolás Maduro produced a financial crisis and then a refugee crisis that rippled throughout the region. Additionally, instability in Central America led to an immigration crisis that pushed northward toward the United States.[46]

Immigration from the Middle East to Europe and north from Central America was caused by the instability of these regions' political economies but also by radical shifts in climate change. These immigration crises contributed to a rise in isolationism and ethno-nationalism in both the United States and Europe. The election of Donald Trump as president of the United States in 2016 and the withdrawal of the United Kingdom from Europe through Brexit in 2020 are instances in which isolationism accelerated.

The 2008 financial crisis, otherwise known as the Great Recession, was felt globally. Rooted in the collapse of the United States housing market and related areas of banking and insurance, it led to austerity measures that were acutely felt in both art and education. In these pages, philosopher Brian Holmes alludes to the ways these developments affected public universities in the United States. The Great Recession produced a reckoning with growing income inequality and class disparity through Occupy Wall Street, which centered on Zucotti Park in downtown Manhattan. Interestingly, 16 Beaver, a small alternative space that engaged with modes of discourse and pedagogy, was located just a few blocks away. 16 Beaver hosted seminars related to Occupy as well as sessions related to the wars in Iraq and Afghanistan and the Arab Spring. In the collaboration between Campus in Camps and Grupo Contrafilé included here, architect Sandi Hilal notes that, for Palestinians, the term *occupy*, in the Occupy movement, made them uncomfortable and notes that you can only occupy something that isn't yours. She prefers the term *return*.

In 2013 the hashtag #BlackLivesMatter sparked a movement protesting the killing of Trayvon Martin, Eric Garner, Michael Brown Jr., and other Black people, many of whom were shot by police. The murder of George Floyd by Derek Chauvin, a Minneapolis police officer, reignited this movement, which spread beyond the borders of the United States, galvanizing a global conversation around racism. For example, artist Helmut Batista, the founder of Capacete, an alternative art space in Rio de Janeiro, talks about stepping back to let a more diverse leadership take over. Echoing this shift, for the first time, the curatorial team of the 35th São Paulo Biennial, presented in 2023, was majority Black.

In 2017 the hashtag #metoo sparked a global movement against sexual assault and sexual harassment. Sexual-assault survivor Tarana Burke began using the term in the 2000s, and it went viral in 2017 when American celebrities began using it in reference to their own high-profile assault cases. This also shaped the context of the first Trump administration's early days, which included the 2017 Women's March protest in Washington, DC, and dozens of global cities. In Argentina, a "green wave" of abortion-rights activism spread to other Latin American countries protesting against femicide and for family-planning rights.

Of course, intersectional conversations around race, gender, and sexuality had their roots in twentieth-century civil-rights struggles and the culture wars of the 1980s and '90s. But social media and a rapidly changing political landscape brought these issues to the foreground in new ways that had profound effects on art and education in the twenty-first century. In 2015, the

46 For a great summary of the political, social, and economic contexts of socially engaged art in Latin America during the 1990s and early 2000s, see Bill Kelley Jr., and Grant H. Kester, eds., *Collective Situations: Readings in Contemporary Latin American Art, 1995–2010,* (Duke University Press, 2017).

Supreme Court of the United States made same-sex marriage legal and, over the course of the twenty-first century, that right was enshrined in hundreds of countries around the world. Conversations around queer and trans rights and representation also grew during this time.

In 2020, the COVID–19 pandemic broke an already fragile public sector in the Americas and the Middle East. Aside from straining public-health efforts and other social services, it accelerated a decrease in European aid to Latin America and the Middle East. Furthermore, through the isolation of stay-at-home orders, social engagement through participation and collaboration was even more difficult. As you'll see from the discussion around the Latin American school Secue_LA included in this book, art & education initiatives made inventive attempts to use digital spaces for collaboration.

The 2020 pandemic coincided with a resurgence of Black Lives Matter, as critic and curator Anuradha Vikram's essay "Unstable Connections: University Teaching in a Time of Protest and Quarantine" describes. The public-health crisis revealed severe limitations to public infrastructure and to the government as an agent that could care for the public. At the same time, George Floyd's murder and the consequent racial-justice uprising made clear that the law, and the police as its enforcing body, were structurally incapable of caring for the whole public, with some members afforded more privilege than others. From a progressive standpoint, that moment revealed on two fronts how "the public"—as it has been imagined within American democracy—might not exist. But now, in 2025, during a second Trump administration that is intentionally destroying the government because it is perceived to only serve a liberal elite, the public, as an imaginary construct, is being put into question by the political right. If the public is attacked as an illegitimate concept from both the left and the right, how do we address the notion of public education as a common good?

Student activism

As schools became sites of ideological battles, they also became, quite literally, more violent spaces. Over the course of the twenty-first century there was a huge uptick in school shootings in the United States. Building on a long-standing debate about guns in American culture, advocates on the right have advocated for the freedom of American citizens to bear arms as protected by the Second Amendment while opponents argue that students should have the right to attend school without fear of being shot. Artist Cara Benedetto's project in this book speaks to this condition, once again reminding us, like that terrified student in Beirut, that the stakes of schooling are life itself.

One of these school shootings was in Parkland, Florida in 2018, when nineteen-year-old Nikolas Cruz killed seventeen people. The students that survived became activists for gun control. Starting with the hashtag #neveragain, they organized the March for Our Lives in Washington, DC, the biggest youth-led protest since the Vietnam War era, then founded a political action committee that has influenced elections and related legislation. A major theme in this activism was the political power that the National Rifle Association had amassed through hundreds of millions of dollars spent lobbying Congress. The challenge for these student activists was not just how to advocate for what they believed to be right, but how to confront an edifice of such staggering financial power.

Students, in high school or university contexts, have often advocated for political or social change, and just as often have been met with the force of state violence and repression. In addition to the students in Paris in May '68 mentioned above, a famous example of this is the October 1968 Tlatelolco massacre in Mexico City, during which Mexican military forces attacked students from the National Autonomous University of Mexico, killing hundreds. Artist and writer Sean Dockray links a 2013 crackdown on student protesters at the University of São Paulo with the clearing of a Occupy-related protest camp at the University of California, Davis that same year.[47] Dockray describes these both as indications of not only the increasing militarization of campuses but also a desire on the part of political leaders and university administrators to prevent the kinds of protest culture that characterized the 1960s and '70s.

I have included two essays that emerged from student activists in the twenty-first century. One, by Brian Holmes, relates to the University of California system protests that Dockray references. Students and faculty there were responding to neoliberal pressures on universities to privatize and to assert austerity measures, which they recognized would lead to fewer resources and more student debt. They saw this as connected to the larger political economy, within which the public sector was shrinking and class disparity was growing. The second text, written by an anonymous Harvard senior and entitled "Why I Protest," emerged from an encampment movement in 2024 protesting not only the war in Palestine-Israel but also US foreign aid and the complicity in that conflict of the university through its endowment investments. Following the principles of the Boycott, Divestment, and Sanctions movement, these student-led Palestinian-solidarity encampments challenged their universities to reconcile the humanistic claims of their mission statements with their complicity in the political economy of war. Art historian Ariella Aïsha Azoulay's text included here, "The University Struggle to Unlearn Zionism," shows how universities as institutions learned—and are still learning—to go through a deschooling process that is akin to decolonization.

47 Sean Dockray, "Openings and Closings," in Tim Ivison and Tom Vandeputte, eds., *Contestations: Learning from Critical Experiments in Education* (Bedford Press, 2014), 32.

Debt, Indebtedness, and the Future

I have come to believe that the most pressing issues facing art & education at this moment can be ascribed to the political economy of debt and indebtedness. In the United States a neoliberal disinvestment in the public sector began in the 1980s. With this withdrawal of public support came an increase in mechanisms to justify the limited resources left. Under the Bush administration in the early 2000s, the No Child Left Behind Act tied budgets to test scores, a policy that continued during the Obama administration. As Irit Rogoff outlined, the educational turn was a response to neoliberal forces such as the Bologna Accord in Europe, inspired by the US model, which emphasized capitalist structures of maximizing output through a restructuring for institutional efficiencies. This was a tension between the goals of public and private enterprises, nonprofit versus profit-based structures. This tension has also been felt by artists and alternative spaces seeking resources from wealthy individuals, foundations, or nations through a system of patronage that demands clear goals and outcomes for any investment. While education is for the common good, it is often tasked to fit into a capitalist system that is run by a different logic than the speculative spirit of learning. We are required to pay into a system that doesn't acknowledge the currency of emotional labor or ideas that don't have measurable outcomes. Thus our balance sheet is almost always in the red. I would argue that debt is the most common way that the gap between these two systems is filled.

One consequence of the 2008 financial crisis, and Occupy Wall Street as a response to it, was that student debt became an increasingly important issue as the cost of education ballooned. A few texts included in this volume address these developments. The artist-run group BFAMFAPHD published a report that accounted for the problems of student debt in 2014. Writer and filmmaker Astra Taylor helped cofound an organization called The Debt Collective that took the approach that if corporations and nations are allowed to restructure obligations, then students should be able to as well. The Debt Collective abolished over thirty-one-million dollars in student debt using the principles of collective bargaining. Another outgrowth of Occupy was the collective Occupy Museums. Its project DebtFair presented a 2015 artwork that illustrates student debt, titled *Stress, Fear, and Anxiety Bundle*, in the 2017 Whitney Biennial.

Given this discussion around student debt and the increasing financial pressures faced by educational and arts institutions large and small, established and alternative, how can we approach the question of debt more broadly?

One of the Debt Collective's initiatives is the Rolling Jubilee Fund, established to address debt related to public education. This fund was named after the ancient practice described in the book of Leviticus, in which every fiftieth year is a Jubilee year during which all debts are forgiven. The late David Graeber, an anthropologist and a co-organizer of Occupy Wall Street, refers to debt as the oldest form of currency and notes that economic life was traditionally rooted in social currency, which was meant to "create, maintain, or sever relations between people, rather than purchase things."[48] One might feel indebted to one's parents, one's community, or one's god, and might show appreciation through various offerings or gifts. Graeber argues that the notion of indebtedness that characterized older human economies has transformed into something much more violent; debt, he says, is not the problem, but instead the form that it has taken. Graeber relates a conversation that he had at a party with someone who argued that, as a moral principle, everyone must pay their debts. But, he notes, it is clear that in today's economy that such a moral principle is inconsistently applied. The Great Recession pushed many financial institutions and other companies into bankruptcy, and some were bailed out by the United States government through the Troubled Asset Relief Program. While companies could be relieved of their debts during this difficult time, individuals who could no longer pay their mortgages often lost their homes. He notes the similarity to the International Monetary Fund insisting on restructuring the economies of developing countries so they can pay back their debts.

48 David Graeber, *Debt: The First 5000 Years* (Melville House, 2012), 158.

One issue with debt is its relationship to time. The Great Recession brought to the foreground a complex network of finance and insurance predicated on risk and investment in relation to the future. But scholars Paula Chakravartty and Denise Ferreira da Silva argue that the risk associated with home ownership is also compounded by the past. They point out that the subprime mortgage, at the center of this financial crisis, became racially signified because banks systematically questioned the creditworthiness of borrowers of color. This was based on much longer histories of oppression, including redlining and other forms of segregation and dispossession that limited the building of generational wealth among Black and Latinx families. And when we consider the fact that the funding of public education in the United States is determined largely by real estate, with wealthier families in more expensive homes enjoying wealthier school districts, we must also acknowledge that it is deeply tied to this arc of history and racialized risk.[49]

Furthermore, Chakravartty and Ferreira da Silva argue that there is a biopolitics of the house. While a house may be property, it is also a framework for the home, as in the family, and the domestic private sphere. So when that house, that home, is financialized and furthermore linked to the financialization of education, a housing crisis impacts much more than property or money—it impacts one's life. The risks to one's life get written on the body, since the racial logic of global capitalism has historically treated different bodies differently, despite the professed equality of the marketplace. This is a condition not only in the United States but has been applied to the Global South as the legacies of colonialism continue in postcolonial times, as developing countries remain indebted to the developed world.[50] Latin American alternative education organizations discuss this postcolonial legacy later in the book. And curator Sarah Rifky's essay also tells a story of how the introduction and withdrawal of European and American patronage through various cultural-development projects affected alternative education projects in Egypt.

As exemplified by many of the vibrant practices in the so-called "Third World" described in this book, these places are often a space of innovation that far outpaces the pedagogical creativity of supposed centers in the Global North. In "A Third University is Possible," la paperson (a.k.a. K. Wayne Yang) argues that just as Third Cinema, a political film movement in Latin America in the 1960s and '70s, invented new paradigms that not only incorporated first- and second-world sources but also reinvented them into something entirely new and unique, a Third University could do the same.[51]

The essay also outlines the history of land grant universities and how they embed real-estate speculation and colonization into the bedrock of the university. In 1862, Abraham Lincoln signed the Morrill Act into law, giving states federal lands that had been taken from Indigenous people so that they could sell portions of them to fund the building of universities, which would, in turn, create an infrastructure for industry through research. Thus the practice of university real-estate speculation that continues to this day is an extension of

49 Paula Chakravartty and Denise Ferreira da Silva, "Accumulation, Dispossession, and Debt: The Racial Logic of Global Capitalism—An Introduction," *American Quarterly 64,* no. 3, "Race, Empire, and the Crisis of the Subprime" (September 2012): 361–385.

50 David Harvey, *A Brief History of Neoliberalism* (Oxford University Press, 2007), 5–38.

51 la paperson, *A Third University Is Possible* (University of Minnesota Press, 2017).

American settler colonialism.[52] Real estate is also an investment tool, part of an investment portfolio. The two sides of investment in an American university are student tuition, most commonly paid for via debt, and real-estate speculation, also realized through debt in the form of mortgages. Both the students and the university are bound by unpayable debts.[53]

In 2013 theorists Fred Moten and Stefano Harney published *The Undercommons*, a critique of higher education with a chapter that focuses on debt.[54] This incredibly influential text, written in prose that combines theory with poetry and wordplay, differentiates study from learning for "credit," for a degree paid for by tuition. Study is something that produces the mutuality of non-commodified indebtedness that Graeber identified.

In the summer of 2020, as a part of their labor organizing around affordable housing, immigration precarity, and policing, a group of UC Irvine graduate students hosted Moten and Harney for an online discussion of their writing on the university and the undercommons. The intergenerational solidarity of the event was remarkable: Moten and Harney suggested tactics for surviving academia to a group of younger scholars. The undercommons is similar to the Third University in the sense that it is imagined as a space for marginalized people to come together for study, for organizing, or other forms of mutuality. It is not so much a space outside of the university but outside of the university's logic, which is one that the authors refer to as an experience economy.[55]

As I mentioned earlier, in 2024, Palestinian-solidarity encampments popped up on campuses in the United States and around the world in response to the genocide in Gaza. Aside from being an example of student activism, they highlighted the economic conditions of the university. One of the most prominent sites of these protests was Columbia University. Adam Tooze, chair of the university's history department, is represented here by a sketch of his attempt to map the political economy of the university. As he reminds us, in addition to tuition, public and private universities rely heavily on endowments to fund themselves. These are built with private gifts and invested like any other fund in the market. The students were demanding, in keeping with the Boycott, Divestment, and Sanctions movement, that Columbia's funds divest from companies that are tied to Israel. In this, the students' demands are like those of Occupy Museums; in both cases, the Palestinian-solidarity movement was questioning the ethics of the money that supports the institution.

We have now reached the point where we can see clearly that education and capitalism are inextricably linked. Similarly, the notion of indebtedness and exchange that Graeber notes as an ancient form of human economy are related to the principles of collaboration and participation employed by the many artists who use education as a medium. It is when ownership—of land, or homes, or bodies, or ideas—is invoked that education slips into a situation of unpayable debt that, by definition, works against the common good. In this book, educators in universities, museums, and alternative arts organizations all describe

52 la paperson, *A Third University Is Possible*, 25–29.

53 Denise Ferreira da Silva, *Unpayable Debt* (Sternberg Press, 2022).

54 Fred Moten and Stefano Harney, *The Undercommons: Fugitive Planning and Black Study* (Minor Compositions, 2013)

55 Moten and Harney extended their ideas of the undercommons in a text that they circulated online in conjunction with this Zoom convening with the UC Irvine students. The piece, dated July 9, 2020, is entitled "the university: last words." In it they expand on the notion of the professor as a worker in an experience economy.

the current conditions as a crisis. The violent and carceral logic of debt has displaced the communal mindset of indebtedness. One dimension of this is, of course, how capital is tied to power and ideology. But can we imagine another system? The Debt Collective, the Third University, and the Undercommons are all examples of such propositions for change, and several initiatives included in *Living to Learn* point to yet more possibilities.

* * *

I have divided this book into five sections: Alternative Arts Organizations, a collection of practices that emerged to attend to various needs within the civic spaces of the Americas and the Middle East; BFAMFAPhD, a survey of formal accredited art schools and universities; Practices, focusing on education as a medium and a subject for artists and curators; Museums and Biennials, a survey of the ways institutions have addressed pedagogy; and Sustainability, a section that addresses ecological, economic, and programmatic strategies for sustaining art & education practices into the future. In addition, artists' projects are woven between these sections to show, rather than tell, a story of living to learn.

The sustainability section brings together examples of initiatives that have been innovative and hopeful despite the challenges of this moment. Artist Hope Ginsburg's *Meditation Ocean* links questions of ecological sustainability with mindfulness practices and an engagement with different audiences through a range of pedagogical models. Astra Taylor describes the solidarity work of the Debt Collective. Designer and curator Prem Krishnamurthy and curator Sam Rauch describe their Department of Transformation, which has initiated collaborations between independent artists and cultural workers and public universities. I also include conversations among those involved in the Dakar-based RAW Académie residency at the Institute of Contemporary Arts in Philadelphia, which produced really deep, intersectional conversations about how radically different institutions can challenge one another to grow through collaboration. Gary Zhexi Zhang's contribution to this section describes financial worlding.[56] He contends that investment, like debt, is predicated on the future. We can speculate on possible futures and that speculation is a way of building our current world. While optimism can sometimes be cruel,[57] Zhang helps us see that if we understand world making as a form of belief, then we don't have to be held hostage to some notion of fate; instead, we can create a new world predicated on the futures we want to see.

I began this essay by invoking the necropolitics of a terrified student learning in a warzone. But no matter what is at stake, it is often tough to find hope and to believe in a sustainable future. This is especially true when considering debt and indebtedness, and how unjust political economies are both communal and personal. Given how entrenched universities, museums, and NGOs are in the violence of financialization, political ideology, and the relationships between the two, how can we believe that things will change for the better? When I have my own doubts, I look to the ways that the late scholar José Estaban Muñoz describes a queer utopia:

56 Originally published in Gary Zhexi Zhang, "On Financial Worlding," in *Catastrophe Time* (Strange Attractor Press, 2023).

57 Lauren Berlant, *Cruel Optimism* (Duke University Press, 2011).

> Queerness is a structuring and educated mode of desiring that allows us to see and feel beyond the quagmire of the present. The here and now is a prison house. We must strive, in the face of the here and now's totalizing rendering of reality, to think and feel a *then and there*. Some will say that all we have are the pleasures of this moment, but we must never settle for that minimal transport; we must dream and enact new and better pleasures, other ways of being in the world, and ultimately new worlds.[58]

Queerness is a subaltern state in a heteronormative world, just like education pushes against the hegemony of debt, choosing indebtedness instead. Education is often thought of as training for the future, but even when it's considered in less transactional terms it still implies some form of growth or transformation, either of an individual (a student) or a group (a class). If we can change how we imagine our futures, then perhaps we can meaningfully change our present and build a better world for the common good.

58 José Esteban Muñoz, *Cruising Utopia: The Then and There of Queer Utopia* (New York University Press, 2009), 1.

Educação para adultos (Education for adults), 2010

Jonathas de Andrade

Digital offset print on paper in sixty parts, each 13 3/8 × 18 1/8 in. (34 × 46 cm).

This project started from a series of twenty educational posters printed in the 1970s and used by the artist's mother when she was working as a teacher in the '80s and '90s. The approach to pedagogy these posters exemplify is influenced by Paulo Freire's method of literacy, combining education with social consciousness. Freire had been invited by Brazilian President João Goulart's government in the 1960s to organize the National Literacy Campaign. The military coup of 1964 interrupted the project, and Freire was persecuted, arrested, and exiled.

Using the concepts and procedures of Freire's alphabetization method, Jonathas de Andrade's posters were the basis for a monthlong series of daily meetings that the artist conducted with a group of illiterate women. Each day's conversations became photographic subjects for new posters created by the artist. At the end of this process, Andrade created a work that includes sixty posters that mix important historical moments—1964, 1971, 1980, 1990, and 2010—presented without specific reference to which image corresponds with which date. The collection speaks to the pedagogical process that de Andrade and his mother engaged in and the larger context of Freire's influence on learning as a mechanism for emancipation.

Eight posters are excerpted here.

brasil—brazil

colônia—cologne

dinheiro—money

enxada—hoe

faca—knife

fogo—fire

riqueza—wealth

saque—sack

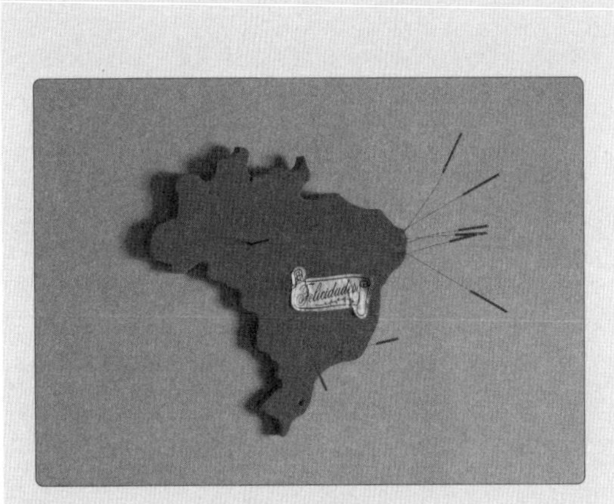

brasil

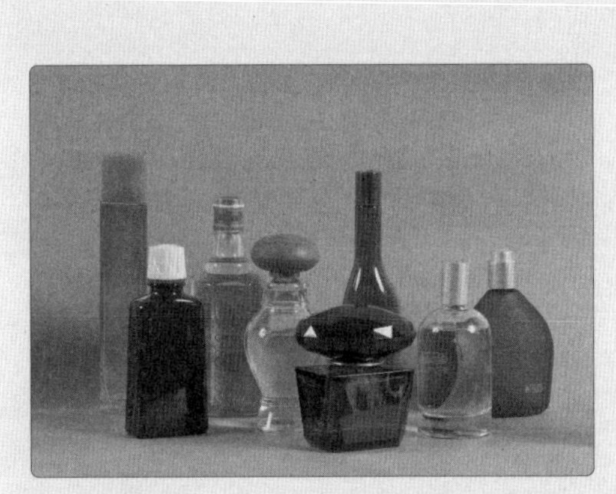

colônia

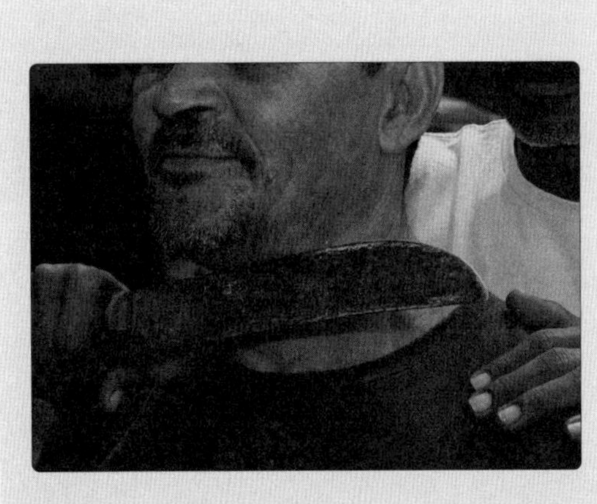

faca

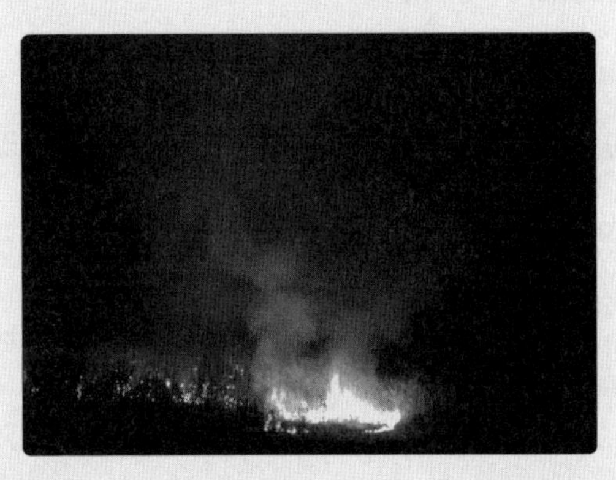

fogo

Educação para adultos (Education for adults), 2010

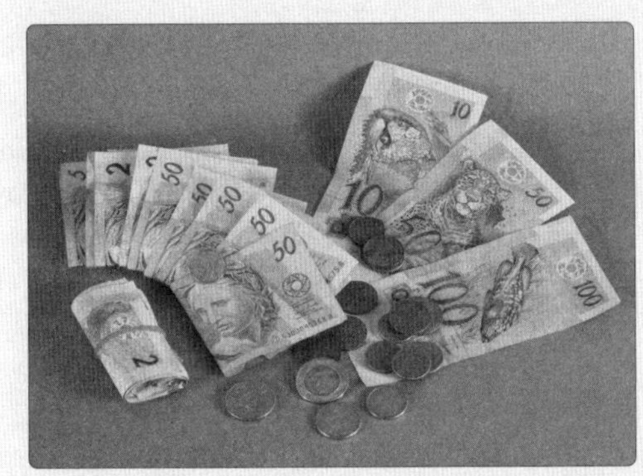

dinheiro

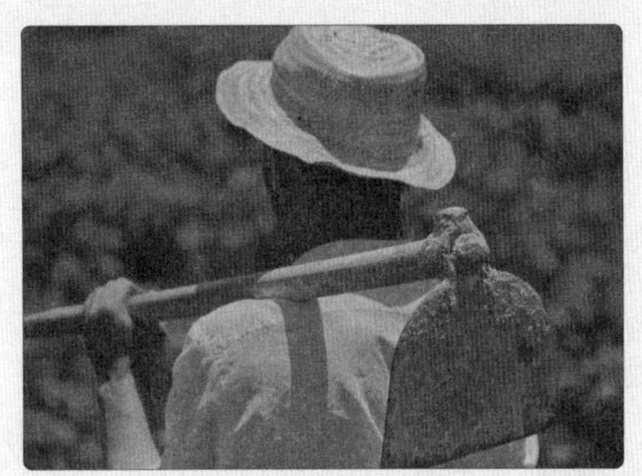

enxada

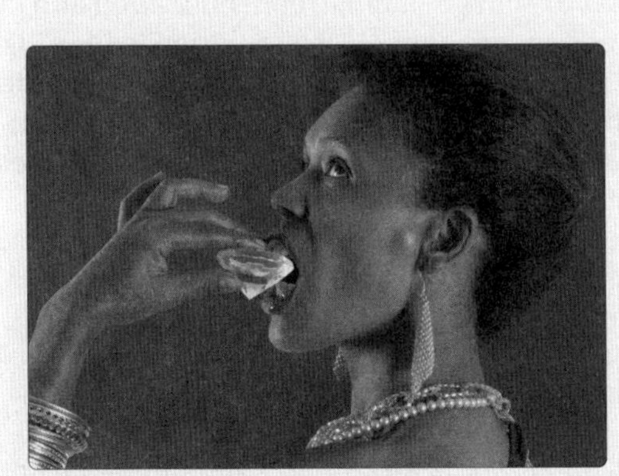

riqueza

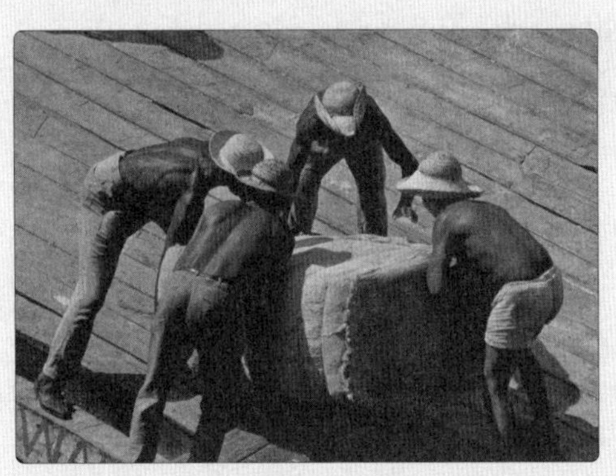

saque

I.
Alternative Arts Organizations

Recently formed alternative arts organizations are at the heart of the art & education initiatives described in this book. The organizations featured in this section worked in the Caribbean, Nicaragua, Colombia, Mexico, Egypt, Palestine, Lebanon, and the US and offer a snapshot of some prominent practices in the Americas and the MENA region.[1] Others, most notably Secue_LA, are included in the sustainability section of *Living to Learn.*

Researcher and curator Engy Mohsen offers case studies from the Middle East, noting a reliance on European and American funding and the irony of a postcolonial, neoliberal, NGO-development culture that echoes colonial paradigms. But these organizations also helped catalyze an alternative to a set of aesthetic and political institutions that are relatively conservative.

This brings up the larger question about these organizations: an alternative to what? Is it the cost of mainstream education and its consequent debt? Is it a stale curriculum? Is it political constraints? It's important to note the different contexts of each of these initiatives. For example, when Kim Córdova writes about SOMA, she describes its founding in response to the particular circumstances in Mexico. It was an antidote to the lack of contemporary art in local MFA programs. But it also created a new creative ecology for the local art scene. The alternative is not so much in relation to the institutions *as schools*, but in offering a different model of professionalization after graduation.

In some ways this is similar for Ashkal Alwan in Beirut, as described in the conversation between founding director Christine Tohmé and sociologist and art historian

1 For more examples of these kinds of organizations, see the 2023 exhibition *The Educational Web* at Kunstverein Hamburg and Sam Thorne's anthology *School: A Recent History of Self-Organized Art Education* (Sternberg Press, 2016). See also the partial list of alternative arts organizations at the end of this book.

Pelin Tan. While the city has established universities and alternative spaces,[2] Ashkal Alwan provides an opportunity for rigorous sustained learning combined with more freedom and a commitment to site-specific attention to the region. The political instability of a particular regional context is something that Ashkal Alwan shares with lugar a dudas, based in Cali, Colombia. While the regions' political economies are different, there is something in their stories that rhymes. Artist Oscar Muñoz and cultural worker Sally Mizrachi tell the story of founding lugar a dudas at a moment in the 1990s when the drug war was grim. While Ashkal Alwan grew out of the post–civil war reality, it has continuously had to navigate political, social, and economic instability. So has lugar a dudas.

Nonetheless, these organizations repeatedly describe gathering people together to create new forms of collectivity. Artist Pablo Guardiola is a codirector of Beta—Local, a Puerto Rico–based organization cofounded by fellow artist Beatriz Santiago Muñoz. Guardiola writes here about RAY | RAYO | RAYON, an initiative, also cofounded by Santiago Muñoz, that brings together artists from across the Caribbean for an itinerant school. It offers opportunities for dialogue and connection by focusing on the fractured archipelago of the region.

In some cases, technology has enabled this convening. Artist and writer Andrew Woolbright's essay on Dark Study describes an innovative online alternative to MFA programs that emerged in 2020 during the COVID-19 pandemic. Similarly, writer and curator Miguel A. López speaks with Nicaraguan artist Patricia Belli about an influential television program about contemporary art that her organization produced.

Many threads connect these stories, and I encourage the reader to find points of connection not only between the projects described here but also between them and other practitioners and organizations referred to throughout the book. What should unfold is a constellation, predicated on commonality and separated by the particularities of context, that cares for communities through opportunities to learn.

2 See the conversation about art education in the MENA region in the BFAMFAPhD section of this book.

Intended Missions, Adjacent Outcomes: A Reflection On "Art Schools" in the Arab World

Engy M. Sarhan

My participation in "independent art schools" between 2018 and 2023 left me with more urgent questions than answers: What conditions led such schools to emerge in the first place? What were their desired outcomes? What were we producing in them? I took part in the Roznama Studio Program (Cairo, 2018), MASS Alexandria (Alexandria, 2018–19), Artists for Artists (online, 2020), and the School of Commons (Zürich, 2022 and 2023). These schools were the entry point for me into contemporary art. On many occasions, I tried to actively question how this type of school is formed and functions. These questions eventually turned into a meta-discourse, a critique of the situatedness of my practice and how it became undetachable from the educational initiatives it leans on.

What—or, more accurately, who—is being produced in these art programs, and what is the expected outcome? What I mean by "production" lies in the essence of the creation process itself, and how this applies to different subjects—for example, artists or curators—in these closed environments. Was the intention of these programs to produce a form of shared knowledge? Or to consciously shape what art theorist Thierry de Duve called "the attitude" of artists?[1] Or was it merely to make artworks palpable and stage them in an exhibition space toward the end of the program period?

While the outcome often manifests as an exhibition, it also creates an archive of the program. Value, as drawn from anthropologist Julia Elyachar's analysis, reflects not just material outcomes but also control over what is considered important.[2] This raises

1 Thierry de Duve, "When Form Has Become Attitude—and Beyond," in *The Artist and the Academy: Issues in Fine Art Education and The Wider Cultural Context*, ed. Stephen Foster and Nicholas deVille (John Hansard Gallery, 1994).

2 Koray Çalişkan. "Book Review: *Markets of Dispossession: NGOs, Economic Development, and the State in Cairo*," *The Arab Studies Journal* 14, no. 2 (Fall 2006): 163–65.

questions about what is more critical: fully developed works, theoretical foundations, or practical career opportunities. The value of these programs hinges on the contributions and roles of each player—participant, instructor, founder—in navigating the complex ecology of these institutions.

The emergence of alternative and independent art schools in Beirut, Cairo, and Ramallah over the past two decades represents a significant shift in the landscape of art education in the Arab world.[3] These schools distinguish themselves from formal art institutions and position themselves as an alternative to their inadequacies. They do so by designing curricula that are more aligned with contemporary art practices and critical thinking. The deficiencies of formal art institutions cut across the region, which suffers from outdated course curriculums, separation of departments by medium, exclusion of theory-based study, undereducated and underpaid faculty and staff, bureaucracy, and learning environments that stifle critical thinking and academic freedom. The suffer from anachronism, rigidity, and disconnection from current contemporary global art discourses.

"Traveling Theory" and Defining Flow

In his 1983 essay "Traveling Theory," Palestinian American philosopher and literary critic Edward Said expands on cultural exchange, hybridity, and disseminating intellectual concepts across geographical and cultural boundaries.[4] To demonstrate how theory can take different forms as it "travels" from one region, discipline, or discourse to another, Said's essay lends itself to analyzing each of the schools that I will discuss as case studies. Said argues that a recognizable pattern exists in the movement of ideas, typically encompassing three or four standard stages. The third stage involves "a set of conditions—call them conditions of acceptance or, as an inevitable part of acceptance, resistances—which then confronts the transplanted theory or idea, making possible its introduction or toleration, however alien it might appear to be."[5]

By viewing these alternative art schools through the lens of Said's traveling theory, especially what he calls the conditions of acceptance and resistance that confronted some discourses while being translated into their immediate social, political, and economic contexts, we can better understand the complex interplay between global educational approaches and local practices. This interaction has forged a practice of art education in the Arab world that responds to specific needs and urgencies.

Intended Missions, Adjacent Outcomes

While independent art schools claim to fill gaps in formal art education, I argue that their unstated and unaddressed outcome is the impact they have on participants' subjectivities. Rather than bridging the gap, the broadening of participants' intellectual and social access, perception, and understanding of a global art world, instead, creates a rift that further foregrounds the separation between their stated missions and adjacent practical outcomes.

3 I would like to borrow the definition of the term "Arab World" from *Mophradat*, an art and funding institution based in Belgium: "a loosely defined geography that is called home by people of diverse ethnicities, gender identities, religions, ideologies, and languages." https://mophradat.org/en/who-we-are.

4 Edward Said, "Traveling Theory," in *The World, the Text, and the Critic* (Harvard University Press, 1983), 226.

5 Said, "Traveling Theory," 226–227.

Independent art schools aim to expand participants' perceptions and understanding of their social and cultural contexts beyond mere professionalization. This broader educational objective aligns with the Uruguayan German artist Luis Camnitzer's concept of "true education," which, as highlighted by art critic and educator Brian Kuan Wood, emphasizes the negotiation of social relations and the pursuit of collective betterment.[6] Camnitzer argues that proper education transcends mere training; it involves critical engagement with the world and fosters an environment where social and political issues can be explored through art.

The Imaginary School Program (Cairo, 2014–15)[7]

The Imaginary School Program (ISP) was a cross-disciplinary, practice-based theory initiative for twelve participants. The school comprised workshops, lectures, field trips, reading groups, and other hybrid activities. The program's primary focus—as they described it—was the study of institutions and forms of organizing, particularly within Cairo's cultural landscape, culminating in a collective publication and a collateral exhibition. It aimed to inspire political imagination and novel forms of social organization and to reflect the urgency of and dynamic changes in Cairo's political and cultural environment after the 2011 uprisings.

The open call for the program was published on the Contemporary& and Beirut art space websites. Its stated mission was broken down into seven questions that address different aspects of the program.[8] One of the primary questions listed is, simply, "Why the ISP?" The answer preempts the first question an applicant might ask. The language used in the school description asserts its position within the larger fabric of civic society, employing concepts that triangulate "civic responsibility," "social justice," and "alternative infrastructure." This choice of terminology suggests that the school aims to play a significant role in shaping and reinforcing these ideals within the community and its immediate surroundings.

While the school's stated mission emphasized scrutinizing some of the existing organizations around it, ISP resonated in a completely different manner within the context in which it operated in Egypt. The framing of a school as an institutional clinic implied a certain distancing from the surrounding institutional landscape. However, the school could only perform this role through self-identification within said landscape. This, in turn, required a certain degree of code-switching, which the school used as a strategy to negotiate presence in public space and still engage politically. Borrowed from linguistics, the term *code-switching* describes alternating between two or more languages within a conversation or discourse, often based on the social context or conversational setting. (I will explain more thoroughly how I see code-switching differently from translation later in the essay.) Code-switching is used to navigate different cultural or linguistic environments and convey specific social or cultural identities. This could be seen through the lens of Said's traveling theory. This process of code-switching is what he

6 Brian Kuan Wood, "Foreword," *Luiz Camnitzer: One Number Is Worth One Word* (Sternberg Press, 2020), 6.

7 See the Imaginary School Program on the Beirut website, http://beirutbeirut.org/en/projects/535d21725562-7576a7180000.

8 "Call for Applications: The Imaginary School Program." *Contemporary And*, n.d., https://contemporaryand.com/exhibition/call-for-applications-the-imaginary-school-program.

refers to as the fourth and final phase, which is how the transformed idea starts to occupy a new position, time, and place.

On the one hand, the school adopted a specific universal language to situate itself on a broader scale. On the other, there was a disconnect when this language was applied to its specific local context, revealing that the school's practical outcome was on an adjacent trajectory. In an online exchange with curator Sarah Rifky, we exchanged ideas to define what role ISP might have played within its neighborhood.[9] What enabled the space to exist is the fact that Rifky is not foreign to the street, area, or neighborhood; it is a family-owned space built by her great-grandparents, and where she used to live. Even though she was aware of those factors, she admitted that she never articulated it that way.

Spaces like the ISP can only exist in that form and shape due to their specific social and cultural contexts. The way they engage with particular questions is facilitated by what I refer to as a "social passport." This concept is crucial because it draws from the social connections embedded within the community and the relationships people have with their environment. It allows for introducing new and unconventional ideas that are socially acceptable, relying on a network of trust and familiarity within the built environment and previous connections. This "social passport" is not merely about social capital in the traditional sense; it is a form of community-building where relationships of trust are forged. This network of trust and shared understanding enables the school to negotiate its presence on the street and neighborhood level and allows it to engage in politically charged discourse effectively.

The same can be said about the set of relationships that define the roles of people involved at the ISP. Rifky noted that she had been friends with Jens Maier-Rothe, her cofounder, and that Habibaa Effat, office manager at *Beirut* and one of the participants in ISP, was her first cousin. When discussing relationships such as friendship and family in a specific place, there is often a disconnect between what these relationships signify and how they function in practice.

In various Black or lesbian communities, comradeship, friendship, and intersectional solidarity form a fundamental political foundation.[10] Furthermore, the French philosopher Jacques Derrida wrote about the concept of friendship and its political implications, both historical and future, to envision a radically new form of friendship that fosters a deeper and more inclusive democracy.[11] He argued that there is a paradox in friendship, as it is typically perceived as a private relationship yet often carries significant political implications.

Similarly, in Egypt, as exemplified here by Beirut and the Imaginary School Program, friendship is a significant political formation, although we lack the conceptual language to discuss it more explicitly. These relationships are deeply embedded in our daily lives, yet their cultural significance remains underexplored and unnamed in societal discourse. This is akin to the experiences of cultural workers who navigate complex social and political landscapes where personal bonds are not just social connections but also crucial support systems and sources of solidarity. These relationships, while often perceived as private, inherently carry political weight.

9 Sarah Rifky, interview via Zoom, May 30, 2024.

10 Alexandra Kollontai, *Red Love* (Seven Arts, 1927); bell hooks, *Feminist Theory: From Margin to Center* (South End Press, 1984); Pat Parker, *Movement in Black: The Collected Poetry of Pat Parker, 1961–1978* (The Crossing Press, 1978).

11 Jacques Derrida, *The Politics of Friendship* (Verso, 2020).

They facilitate collaboration, foster mutual aid, and create support networks essential for sustaining cultural and political work in challenging environments.

Discursive and cultural concepts often require code-switching, revealing varying awareness and intention across individuals and communities. This is particularly evident in spaces like the ISP, where social relationships, such as friendship and family, play crucial political roles by fostering trust and building community. Despite their impact, these relationships lack clear terminology and remain under-discussed. Addressing this gap can illuminate the nuanced forces shaping social relationships and their influence on political structures. Moreover, making power dynamics more visible and reducing the opacity of these relationships can significantly affect participants' subjectivities and the accessibility of such spaces.

The School of Intrusions (Ramallah, 2019–24)[12]

The School of Intrusions (SoI) is an educational practice in occupied Palestine. It uses informal gatherings to engage with urban and rural spaces, treating them as common areas for mutual learning and collective action. Initiated in 2019 by curator Lara Khaldi and artist Noor Abed, who are both Palestinian, SoI uses "intrusion" or "direct intervention" into public sites as its core strategy. It challenges traditional education by integrating it into daily life and exploring community-based, experiential knowledge. As the name suggests, "intrusions" is a play on words that hints at the potential of being politically playful and thought-provoking.

In an interview, Abed mentioned that one of the founding pillars of the school was the Brazilian educator and philosopher Paulo Freire's *The Pedagogy of Freedom*, and especially his description of education as "[a form] of intervention in the world."[13] Unlike its counterparts, the SoI does not formalize a process of admission and selection of participants, and the cohorts' names are not announced at the beginning of each edition. Its structure assumes no space, walls, or institutional affiliation.

I came across the most recent description of the school on the website of Neither on Land nor at Sea, where Abed and Khaldi were invited to give an online presentation about the school via Zoom on May 14, 2023.[14] As it's described, "School of Intrusions is a collective practicing informal ways of gathering in and around specific urban and rural sites. The members of the group change and fluctuate. It grew from a conversation about education, art schools, collectivity, and the city as a shared space in Palestine."

According to the text, the school describes itself using language and discursive terminology—like "commons," "collective," and "gathering"—nowadays somewhat ubiquitous in contemporary critical theory; especially as these terms relate to "public space," the school occupies a particular "social and political imaginary." While considering the broader factors at play, these terms are commonly used yet lack precise definitions in application, and they are connected to many of the notions

12 See the School of Intrusions's Instagram account, https://www.instagram.com/schoolofintrusions.

13 Klara Czerniewska-Andryszczyk and Noor Abed, "Intruding in istory and Space" (2020). https://u-jazdowski.pl/en/programme/residencies/conversations/intruding-in-history-and-space-

14 *Neither On Land nor at Sea* is a research project initiated and curated by UNIDEE Residency Programs at Cittadellarte—Fondazione Pistoletto by Chiara Cartuccia, the visiting curator for 2022–24. https://neitheronlandnorat-sea.art/public-programme.

and concepts that aim to describe this field of practice. The lexicon of SoI (as well as some of the other schools) relates to common terminology of contemporary art and curatorial practice, including "happenings," "site-specific art," "dialogic art," "socially engaged art," "participatory art," "social practice," and the art of "social cooperation."[15] In this way, the school lends itself a certain legibility that translates into value because it is easily understood and comprehended within a global network.

Despite deploying a particular terminology and discursive formation, the school resonates in a completely different manner within the context in which it operates in Palestine. While there is a borrowing of a specific language to situate the school on a more global scale, there is a rift in which this language applies on the ground. This, in turn, requires a certain degree of code-switching, in which the school is used as a strategy, as an invisibility cloak, to be able to negotiate presence in the public cultural sphere and still act in a politically engaged manner. This is similar to the first case study, the ISP in Cairo, using code-switching as a strategy. SoI's use of code-switching is subtly different, though. ISP was more concerned with using the translation process to navigate the intricacies of social relationships. Inversely, SoI is primarily concerned with different power dynamics as the participants engage with a public space.

Following this hypothesis, framing the group's work as a school can be seen as a strategy to "intrude" into public space (as well as into the traditions of institutional art education). In turn, this allows us to consider the possibilities of making this association on the ground. For example, framing their activity as a "school" is less dangerous than framing themselves as guerrilla activists. The weight of framing changes significantly if a group uses guerrilla tactics to force themselves into a space and call themselves a school that aims to engage with discursive content. By positioning the group as a school, they can pursue their practice and goals using a framework for dialogue and education rather than political confrontation, making their approach non-threatening and potentially more effective in permeating public spaces.

The history of the Palestinian resistance tells us that this reading is not a wild stretch of imagination, and experience has shown us that employing such strategies is necessary and urgent. During the First Intifada in 1987, which was mainly led by women, activists organized economic cooperatives, mobile health clinics, and underground schools to sustain and strengthen the insurrection.[16] In some cases, women organized "classrooms" in their homes and in open areas like grassy fields to defy the Israeli-imposed closure of Palestinian schools.[17] In the documentary film *Naila and the Uprising* (2017), activist Naima Al-Sheikh Ali explains how "publicly,

15 Allan Kaprow, *Essays on the Blurring of Art and Life*, ed. Jeff Kelley (University of California Press, 1993); Miwon Kwon, *One Place After Another: Site-Specific Art and Locational Identity* (The MIT Press, 2003); Grant H. Kester, *Conversation Pieces: Community and Communication in Modern Art* (University of California Press, 2004); Pablo Helguera, *Education for Socially Engaged Art: A Materials and Techniques Handbook* (Jorge Pinto Books, 2011); Claire Bishop, *Artificial Hells: Participatory Art and Politics Spectatorship* (Verso, 2012); Maria Lind and Nato Thompson, "Returning On Bikes: Notes On Social Practice," in *Living as Form: Socially Engaged Art from 1991–2011* (Creative Time and MIT Press, 2012), 46–55; Tom Finkelpearl, *What We Made: Conversations On Art and Social Cooperation* (Duke University Press, 2013).

16 This is not to be confused with the Great Revolt in Palestine (1936–39), which is referred to as the "First Intifada" in some historical accounts.

17 Sarah Aziza, "Palestine's First Intifada Is Still a Model for Grassroots Resistance," *The Nation*, December 8, 2017, https://www.thenation.com/article/archive/palestines-first-intifada-is-still-a-model-for-grassroots-resistance.

the women's committees were known for their social work. But in reality, and covertly, it was all political organizing. Nurseries, sewing workshops, teaching women how to knit, cook, and so on. All that was window dressing."

In studying the SoI, I posit that there is a certain degree of translation at play. What I mean by translation is that there is flexibility in moving between languages depending on the audience, whether participants or the general art public. This involves liberties in how terms and strategies are employed. It is essential to differentiate this from code-switching, where conversation shifts between languages while accommodating both—assuming the recipient's familiarity with each. This also does not negate that the artists behind it are entirely aware of this act of code-switching between widely understood terms and local particularities. However, the critical part about this practice is that it is not divulged. In her essay "Qalqalah: The Subject of Language," Sarah Rifky speculatively asks, "[I]s a political paradigm shift possible through a rediscovery of other languages? Is speaking more than one language a form of treason masked as knowledge?"[18] By practicing this translational code-switching, they are not acknowledging the impossibilities and the paradoxes of said translation process. Some of the impossibilities of translation include presenting the school to an international art audience that does not factor in the enforced restrictions on the freedom of movement of Palestinians in the West Bank, where the school primarily took place, and how that affects access to public space in rural and urban areas. Conversely, there is also the challenge of presenting knowledge embedded in a global art context to local participants, which might seem detached from its application on the ground.

Since the pilot edition of SoI took place in Palestine, in the West Bank, predominantly in and around Ramallah and Jerusalem, I was curious to find out from Abed and Khaldi whether they believed that the specific political context in Palestine played a role in shaping the school, mainly when it came to reclaiming both private and public sites or "treating [them] as commons," as mentioned in the project description.

In reflecting on Abed and Khaldi's statements, it becomes clear that the political context in Palestine, particularly after the Oslo Accords, significantly shaped the School of Intrusions (SoI). Both emphasized how the rapid shift from communal to privatized spaces impacted their work. Abed highlighted the role of neoliberal policies in transforming public and private spaces, explaining how cities like Ramallah created an illusion of freedom despite ongoing colonialism. Khaldi echoed this sentiment by recounting how, during the First Intifada, private spaces became public out of necessity, while the post-Oslo period saw a retreat into privatization. Both noted that SoI's work involved reclaiming these spaces, not only physically but also symbolically, by challenging economic and spatial boundaries.

Home Workspace Program (Beirut, 2011–)

Launched by Ashkal Alwan in Beirut in 2011, the Home Workspace Program (HWP) is an annual eleven-month arts study program designed for participants from Lebanon, the Arab region, and the world.[19]

18 Sarah Rifky, "Qalqalah: The Subject of Language." *Qalqalah 1* (2020): 109, https://qalqalah.org/en/histories/qalqalah-the-subject-of-language

In general, every iteration of the program was informed by the prior years, with the possibility for total restructuring. This way, new elements could be developed to meet the program's needs.

A generic description of the program can be found on Ashkal Alwan's website. Each year, the text changes slightly at the discretion of the newly assigned professors, who are invited to rethink the program and revamp its curriculum. This mainly highlights the motive behind the program while stating that a primary factor for its initiation was providing a solution for the "privatization" of art education. It reads:

> HWP is an annual arts study program that invites participants to develop their formal, technical, and theoretical skills in a critical setting and provides enrolled fellows with feedback and resources to facilitate and support their art practice. HWP was initially developed to explore interdisciplinary, critical models of art education in Lebanon and beyond, where education is mostly privatized. Moreover, it aims to include a wide range of professors, all the while addressing geopolitical particularities in art and the educational landscape.[20]

The text suggests that the program strongly emphasizes professionalization. Designed for young artists, it claims to prepare and equip them with all the necessary tools, whether practical or theoretical, to launch their artistic careers. The text also highlights another important factor, the economic setting in which it exists; most art education in Lebanon has become privatized. In response, HWP can open up opportunities for those wishing to participate, as it is free of charge.

Upon reviewing the profiles of the lead professors and the overarching thematic focuses, I could observe a noticeable tendency to prioritize theory over practice, particularly during the earlier years of HWP. In an interview with sociologist and art historian Pelin Tan, Ashkal Alwan's co-founder, Christine Tohmé, addressed this polarity by emphasizing the importance of being rooted in practical work, which can be applied on the ground to better understand the surrounding environment rather than merely reproducing theory or stultified and stilted forms.[21] She further explained that HWP is not outcome-oriented but instead focuses on forms of exchange that create a dialogue with the local context.

Tohmé stated that HWP works in a traditional way, where it maintains a fixed structure with seminars and group critiques. However, it sustains a fluidity in the refusal to replicate entrenched ideas of a recurring "faculty" or curriculum and the liberties given each year to visiting artists and professors to reshape it. Agency is given to those who join to create their own projects and extend beyond the local network. They consistently come back and contribute through teaching, participating in group critiques, or joining as guest artists, ensuring they remain integral to HWP's expanding community.

19 Ashkal Alwan, The Lebanese Association for Plastic Arts, is a nonprofit organization based in Beirut, Lebanon's capital city. It was founded in 1993 by its current director, Lebanese curator Christine Tohmé, alongside Lebanese artist Marwan Rechmaoui. It is considered one of several influential institutions and projects that emerged across the city in the wake of the Lebanese civil war. 20 See the Home Workspace Program on Ashkal Alwan's website, https://www.ashkalalwan.org/program.php?category=3.

20 See the Home Workspace Program on Ashkal Alwan's website, https://www.ashkalalwan.org/program.php?category=3.

21 Pelin Tan, Magnus Ericson, and Christine Tohmé, "Home Workspace Program," Urgent Pedagogies, November 2020, https://urgentpedagogies.iaspis.se/home-workspace-program. See also pp. 44–51 in this volume.

Instead of focusing on apparent dichotomies of practical vs. theoretical and structured vs. fluidity, I wonder if the HWP can be read through different lenses. Here, I am not proposing to overlook contradictions in professed and materialized goals but to offer a third and adjacent reading. I believe that while HWP claims to fill gaps and complement formal art education in Lebanon, its more material outcome is how it increases participants' intellectual and social access, perception, and understanding of art, mainly through the expansion of the artists' networks: the connections made between the participants and visiting advisors and professors as well as among themselves.

In a conversation between Tohmé and curator Rachel Dedman, a participant in HWP during 2013–14, the former mentioned that "here is a network that you build, friends you make, collaborations that you form, that [are] very important." Dedman responded that the takeaway from that formative year was the network and how people connected between the gaps of the institution. The spaces in which things coalesced among people were exciting for her. The human dynamics that play into such structures were seen as the most exciting aspect by far.[22] As scholar Ilka Eickhof describes in her essay "Class and Creative Economies: The Cultural Field in Cairo," "[t]he pressure of neoliberal labor turns networking into an investment and connections to different social actors into precious symbolic capital."[23]

This network of different actors was especially enabled by the international nature of HWP. The students and instructors were much more diverse in background and types of practice than the two other case studies, the ISP and the SoI. Thinking back to Said's idea of "traveling theory," I tried to determine if it was clear to the participants whether some ideas or theories brought about in the context of HWP were more accepted and taken up, while others were rejected or not as embraced. I spoke with Egyptian writer and curator Sara El Adl, a PhD candidate in visual culture at Goldsmiths, who took part in HWP in 2016–17.

El Adl reported that many practice-based artists complained about the required reading and the lack of hands-on practice. There was an expectation that bringing artists with studio-based practices into the program would expand that part of their practice. However, some artists felt their studio work hit a theoretical plateau. Additionally, she noted that the institution explicitly demanded finished work from each artist by the end of the year for the open studio. This contradiction left El Adl thinking that the experience was not what she has expected. She remarked that these represented two different types of people the program aimed to bring together, and finding both would be challenging, as participants would likely come out only half-satisfied with what they encountered.

While the school's stated mission focuses on interdisciplinarity and merging technical and theoretical skills, it seems that students with either theory-based or studio-based practices could only fit into one aspect of the curriculum, namely the proposed seminars and workshops or the culminating open studios. Here, I posit that there is a lack of transparency or clarity. As El Adl mentioned, the program seemed to struggle with confusion about what it wanted from participants, resulting in flat interactions.

22 Rachel Dedman and Christine Tohmé, "Present Continuous," *IBRAAZ*, May 6, 2016. https://www.ibraaz.org/interviews/188.

23 Ilka Eickhof, "Class and Creative Economies," in Richard Jacquemond and Félix Lang, eds., *Culture and Crisis in the Arab World: Art, Practice, and Production in Spaces of Conflict* (I.B. Tauris, 2019), 206.

From Promise to Practice: Reflections On "Art Schools"

I keep going back to where these schools can take us next. There is a need for them to expand, offering more people diverse methods of learning and valuing knowledge through practical application. Unlike their official counterparts, these schools strive to provide alternative ways of knowing—knowledge that is not state-mandated. We can think of it as subversive or insurgent knowledge. Clearly, we need different spaces for learning that challenge conventional education. Here, I am considering the extent to which independent art schools like the Imaginary School Program, the School of Intrusions, and the Home Workspace Program uphold their stated missions. Instead of arriving at concrete answers, I find myself with open conclusions.

I realized that I had the enormous task of collating official narratives and personal accounts—which more often than not refuted one another—to reconstruct a narrative. Through conducting these interviews, I also realized that most practitioners are part of the diasporic community, predominantly in Europe and North America. By describing the Arab art community as "transnationals," the lawyer and scholar of locally-driven development Nadia Cherif remarks that "[m]ore than 62% of them [artists applying for grants from their country of origin] have experienced migration to locations outside the Arab world or present a transnational aspect in their life, making the mobility/transnational parameter much more prevalent than it first appeared."[24]

When we speak about our diasporic experiences, I wonder if a direct link can be drawn to how those schools have contributed to our educational and artistic biographies. Christine Tohmé says HWP "has acted as a passport for young local artists, some of whom had no prior formal training in the arts, to continue their studies and/or produce abroad."[25]

Said exemplifies this, arguing that "[c]ultural and intellectual life are usually nourished and often sustained by this circulation of ideas." This can happen through those who act as vessels. I intended to tackle and analyze the concepts of language to understand terminology and metaphor. This is useful as it allows us to read into things and not take them at face value. I tried to inspect what is presented across three different schools, locations, and active years rather than how they were described. Across all of them I saw a productive space in misunderstanding, rereading, and distorting the supposed facts that we were presented with.

There is value in being politically playful, using camouflage, switching strategies, occupying future imaginaries, borrowing terminology, moving between translations, code-switching, leaving room for charitable interpretations, and crafting our understanding of what a postcolonial liberation in the field of para-institutional art education requires.

This essay is adapted from a dissertation submitted in June 2024 to the Department of Cultural Analysis and Mediation at Zurich University of the Arts and titled Knowledge Flows: A Study of Para-institutional Art Schools in the Arab World.

24 Nadia Cherif, *Read the Room #2: Transnationals: Who Are They and What Do They Want?* (Mophradat, 2021), https://mophradat.org/en/library/read-the-room-2-by-nadia-cherif-2021.

25 Pelin Tan, Magnus Ericson, and Christine Tohmé, "Home Workspace Program," *Urgent Pedagogies* (November 2020), https://urgentpedagogies.iaspis.se/home-workspace-program. See also pp. 44–51 in this volume.

Home Workspace Program

Christine Tohmé interviewed by Pelin Tan and Magnus Ericson

Ashkal Alwan, The Lebanese Association for Plastic Arts, is a nonprofit organization based in Beirut. Since its founding in 1993, the association has dedicated itself to promoting contemporary artistic practice, fostering critical thinking around social realities, and engaging in community-based projects.

In 2011, Ashkal Alwan launched the Home Workspace Program (HWP), a free arts study program that invites fellows to develop their formal, technical, and theoretical skills and provides them with resources and feedback.

HWP was initially developed to explore interdisciplinary, critical models of art education in a context in which education is mostly privatized. Moreover, it aims to include a wide range of professors, all the while addressing geopolitical particularities in art and the educational landscape.

In response to the ongoing pandemic and political and economic collapse in Lebanon, which continue to threaten cultural and educational infrastructures, HWP has gone online, and remains open to anyone wishing to attend and free of charge.

Pelin Tan Can you tell us how and why the Home Workspace Program was initiated and organized as an academic program within Ashkal Alwan?

Christine Tohmé Throughout the early 2000s, friends and I had been consistently talking about establishing a model of education that could complement traditional educational structures in Beirut. However, we were keen on having that model act differently to academia—in particular its stultifying frameworks and codes—and avoid having it replicate its structures. Home Workspace Program (HWP) thus started out as a program aiming to respond to prevailing shortcomings in critical arts and humanities studies in the region and has sought, over the years, to be attentive to the shifts in the educational system available for young artists. It was also a way for Ashkal Alwan to extend the Home Works Forum[1] in time and space, ensuring that the debates and issues discussed within its realm every three years, and for a limited period, could continue to be engaged with and explored. We were prompted to consider moving into a physical space that would act as a communal ecosystem for artists, scholars, activists, and cultural practitioners.

Today, Home Workspace Program is an arts study program open to artists from Lebanon, the Arab region, and the world over to develop their formal, technical, and theoretical skills in a critical setting. The program provides fellows with feedback and resources to facilitate and support their art practice. It has now run ten successful editions.[2]

The people I had started to work with at first—Joana Hadjithomas, Walid Raad, Lina Majdalanie, Gregory Sholette, and Khalil Rabah—all became part of the program's Advisory Curriculum Committee, allowing us to gather and think together about the knowledges and pedagogical forms of exchange we want to bring forth and infuse into the program for each edition. This committee, which is also integral in the selection of fellows, rotates every three years, and has since included Natascha Sadr Haghighian, Tony Chakar, Joe Namy, Iman Issa, and Zeynep Oz.

HWP is organized annually around workshops, seminars, lectures, group critiques, and studio visits. Visiting Professors (VPs) and their invited guests organize workshops and seminars based on their practices. Alongside the work of the VPs, the curriculum includes a series of seminars, offered by guest professors, to complement the fellows' theoretical and art historical knowledge. Advisors follow the fellows' work throughout the year, organizing group critiques and one-on-one sessions. Each year an invited guest organizes a preface to the program. In these first three weeks, fellows introduce their work, are introduced to the HWP program, and are oriented to Lebanon's urban and cultural geography through site visits and talks. Since the program's first year in 2011, we have collaborated and exchanged with many institutions and collectives who initiated similar programs, such as MASS Alexandria's studio space and study program, RAW Material Company's residency program in Dakar, WHW Akademija in Zagreb, and Kem in Poland.

1 Initiated in 2002 and taking place every three years in different venues across Beirut, Home Works: A Forum On Cultural Practices brings together performances, exhibitions, screenings, and discursive programs around a common set of urgent questions. The work of the forum's participants endeavors to create methods of critical inquiry and aesthetic form capable of conveying those questions meaningfully—and proposing possible solutions.

2 This is how the program was structured throughout the years:

Year 1: Emily Jacir (Resident Professor) + Amal Issa (Program Coordinator)

Year 2: Matthias Lilienthal (Resident Professor) + Rewa Baassiri (Coordinator X-Apartments) and Amal Issa (Program Coordinator)

Year 3: Amal Issa (Director) + Anton Vidokle and Jalal Toufic (Resident Professors) + Rewa Baassiri (Program Coordinator)

Year 4: Amal Issa (Director) + Curriculum Committee: Kader Attia, Joana Hadjithomas & Khalil Joreige, Walid Raad, Khalil Rabah, Lina Majdalanie, Gregory Sholette, and What, How, & for Whom (WHW) (Resident Professors) + Moritz Fingerhut (Program Coordinator)

Year 5: Ghalya Saadawi (Resident Professor) + Haig Aivazian (Resident Advisor) + Moritz Fingerhut (Program Coordinator)

Year 6: Ghalya Saadawi (Resident Professor) + Joe Namy (Resident Advisor) + Lara Saab (Program Coordinator)

Year 7: Roy Samaha, Joe Namy, and Haig Aivazian (Resident Advisors) + Lara Saab (Program Coordinator)

Year 8: Joe Namy (Resident Advisor) + Lara Saab (Program Coordinator)

Year 9: Joe Namy, Haig Aivazian, and Daniele Genadry (Resident Advisors) + Lara Saab (Program Coordinator)

Year 10: Open Year (conceived and managed by Ashkal Alwan team: Thourayya Kreidieh, Edwin Nasr)

In December 2020, and in response to the political and material urgencies in Lebanon that continue to threaten cultural and educational infrastructures, we launched the tenth edition of HWP in an open-year format, available to anyone wishing to attend. The selection committee has been put aside in favor of welcoming all those interested in registering; no applications are therefore required anymore. More than 350 participants from Lebanon, the broader region, and internationally took part in five chapters and four skill-based workshops. We were thus overwhelmed by the public's unprecedented enthusiasm vis-à-vis this edition of HWP, and are convinced that, amid precarious conditions, interdisciplinary forms of learning and exchange remain matters of great importance.

HWP 2021 was divided into five chapters unfolding over the course of six months from January until June 2021. Each chapter lasted three weeks and was organized by a Lead Professor who (1) designed a curriculum responding to a set of theoretical and aesthetic concerns and (2) invited up to four Visiting Professors to each lead a seminar, workshop, or collective reading session. Chapter 1, led by Adrian Lahoud and Lawrence Abu Hamdan with invited guests Walid Sadek, Dread Scott, and Susan Schuppli, expanded on the idea of a "scene" in a criminal event to better understand the collective preconditions of testimony. Chapter 2, led by Rasha Salti with invited guests Mahasen Nasser-Eldin, Mila Turajlić, Mohanad Yaqubi, Jihan El-Tahri, and Kader Attia, explored the question of restitution and the materiality of photographic and audiovisual archives that amplify the north-south chasm and resurrect the unresolved specters of colonial history. Chapter 3, led by Marwa Arsanios with invited guests Catherine Malabou, Lama El Khatib, Natascha Sadr Haghighian, and Ashkan Sepahvand, engaged with and through the works of scholars and artists to think about new tools for action and praxis within our current political condition and its impasses. Chapter 4, led by Pelin Tan with Dima Srouji, Rojda Tuğrul, Hera Büyüktaşciyan, and Zainab Bahrani, created room for and brought forward collective critical thinking by focusing on memorizing lands, de/archiving artefacts, enacting nonhuman cycles, and engaging with poetics of exile. Chapter 5, led by Zeynep Öz and Daniel Blanga Gubbay with Arzu Sak Seyhun, Nazlı Pişkin, Otobong Nkanga, Long Litt Woon, Ibrahim Nehme, and Farid Rakun (from ruangrupa), asked: How can we raise awareness about human and more-than-human networks of labor and collaboration that exist in a landscape, in a practice, and within art-related processes? In parallel to the chapters, HWP offered four skills-based workshops that were also free and open to all those who pre-registered: coding with Leen Charaffedine, urban mapping with Monica Basbous, video editing with Carine Doumit and Nour Ouayda, and sound with Tarek Atoui.

Magnus Ericson What has been the role of the program when it comes to engaging with a local context and for creating communities?

CT Home Workspace Program provided many artists and cultural practitioners with an opportunity to produce and think alongside peers from the region and beyond. HWP was and still is a vibrant, urgent energy of people meeting and affecting each other, and being affected by the city, the political situation, the institutions, to be continuously "present." And if it instigates and shapes communities, I would say it is due to the structure of the program, which isn't result-oriented, and relies instead on forms of exchange to sustain continuous dialogue amid a localized context, that is, Beirut, where fellows are, from the get-go, immersed in particular dynamics and asked to respond to and operate within everyday situations with a sense of collectivity in mind. In addition to forming relations among and beyond one another, fellows also end up engaging in forms of community making with the city's civic, cultural, and academic sectors, as well as with the actors—scholars, journalists, NGO workers, activists, lawyers, environmental policymakers—that comprise and compose them.

Creating a continuous platform for the fellows takes an enormous amount of work and perseverance. It becomes a year-round space of doing, thinking, and happening and a space for people to take time off from the stress of production and art-market pressures. HWP has acted as a passport for young local artists, some of whom had no prior formal training in the arts, to continue their studies and/or produce abroad. HWP continues to work like a traditional course in that it has a solid structure with seminars and group critiques. However, its fluidity lies in its refusal to reproduce calcified notions of a recurring "faculty" or curriculum and its openness to the visions of visiting artists and professors each year. HWP provides agency to those who have joined it to create their own projects and expand beyond the local network. They continuously return and engage in different ways either by teaching, being part of a group critique, or by joining as guest artists. They always remain part of HWP's growing community.

Throughout that process, and to this day, Ashkal Alwan has been invested in redefining the function and scope of its public mission, exploring how publicness can be deployed and experienced, and toward which parameters the public sphere can be expanded.

PT Can you outline the current situation in Lebanon and Beirut for us to further understand the changing role of Ashkal Alwan, its program, and the space itself?

CT Lebanon started grappling with three different crises unfolding simultaneously: (1) an unprecedented economic and financial crisis characterized by the ongoing devaluation of the local currency and an impossibility of the state to pay its gargantuan public debt; (2) a crisis of political legitimation initially wrought by the October 17 uprisings and the protesters' call for dismantling over thirty years of systemic corruption, sectarian power-sharing, and neoliberal austerity policies; and, as of March 2020, (3) a sanitary crisis in conjunction with the emergence of the ongoing COVID–19 pandemic on a global scale.

On October 17, 2019, protests broke out across Beirut—later leading to a national uprising—and coincided with the opening night of Home Works 8; as a result, the entirety of its programs and exhibitions were either postponed or cancelled. The circumstances that led to the postponement of Home Works 8 were rather particular and raised questions pertaining to our work and the context in which we operate. The first couple of days of the program (October 17 and 18) witnessed unexpected popular uprisings that swept the entire country and were to continue for weeks to follow. Roads leading to the airport were blocked and most highways were closed off; and while both the army and security forces intervened on the streets, protests seemed to be increasing in intensity by the hour. For the first weeks of the uprising, we actively participated in mass protests and general strikes, closely monitored the situation as it was unfolding, and consulted with friends and colleagues from the legal, academic, journalistic, and artistic-cultural sectors to decide on the best way forward. Our conclusion was to indefinitely postpone our discursive (talks, panels, and readings) and performance (music, dance, theater, and lecture-performances) programs and events. Our artistic, intellectual, and organizational energy were meant to be redirected toward the achievement of our hopes and aspirations, the possibility of which was and still is being granted to us by a momentum that should have been seized at any cost.

The logistics of cancelling the forum after two years of organizational, promotional, and artistic work was no small feat. Additionally, and for the first time since its launching, visas for international and regional fellows participating in HWP had been rejected by the Ministry of Interior and Municipalities, signaling a new era of cultural isolation and severed relations between the state and the nongovernmental sector. Though the fellows' residencies were eventually secured, the incident cast a cloud of uncertainty on the educational program's continuity and sustainability. Due both to the emergence of COVID–19 pandemic as well as the culmination of Lebanon's economic and financial crises, the institution's challenges became manifold. The banking sector's capital controls on international wire transfers and foreign-currency transactions resulted in a sector-wide incapacity to meet financial obligations, including the payment of salaries, contractual fees, rents, and so on. With most of our resources either locked or made to disappear, we were and continue to be incapacitated to continue our operations or plan for the future. We have also been pushed to discontinue and/or manage alternative routes for our ongoing projects with artists outside of Lebanon, as well as our financial support to local community members who depend on aid to carry on with production-related tasks or studies abroad. Furthermore, on March 30, 2020, the ninth edition of Home Workspace Program was discontinued due to our inability to secure the health and safety of our fellows during their stay in Beirut. Fortunately, most of the seminars, workshops, and one-on-one sessions we'd planned for the 2019–20 edition were moved online.

On August 4, 2020, a large amount of ammonium nitrate, stored at the port of the city of Beirut, exploded, causing at least 220 deaths, 6,500 injuries, US$10–15 billion in property damage, and leaving an estimated 300,000 people homeless. As a result, Ashkal Alwan directed its efforts to repurposing its facilities and accommodating artists, cultural workers, and activists in Beirut who lost their spaces and incomes due to the unfolding simultaneous financial, political, and sanitary crises. We were convinced that, by focusing our efforts toward making our space available and open to the public, we would be able to help the artists operating within our ecosystem reclaim their material and intellectual agency, push their practices, and retrieve part of their losses. It goes without saying that these crises haven't only affected the cultural sector but are also actively threatening its very existence.

As we continue to face the most acute form of precarity since Ashkal Alwan's inception, we are being pushed to experiment with new methods and forms and to challenge conventional ways of going about institution-building. This has, again, led to a succession of trials and errors whereby the porosity of our space served as a blueprint to think through potential configurations that would best fit our communities. Over the last couple of years, Ashkal Alwan has focused on repurposing its two-thousand-square-meter venue. In January 2020, the Community Studios Project was initiated as more and more practitioners, collectives, and nomadic institutions were losing their workspaces. In parallel, Ashkal Alwan was rethinking HWP's structure. The program eventually needed to grow and evolve together with existing platforms, not against them, as current circumstances had rendered artistic production increasingly inaccessible.

ME What is your view on Ashkal Alwan as a possible space for resilience?

CT The question of imagining, building, and sustaining an art institution that not only responds to shifting material conditions but also reconfigures itself as a result has been a concern of Ashkal Alwan since its inception. As an institution, Ashkal Alwan was born in and around "crisis" in the mid-1990s, at a time when the postwar reconstruction project in Beirut was materializing. Ashkal Alwan was then responding to the expropriation of public spaces within the city of Beirut and, also, the imposition of a state-sponsored form of "collective amnesia" in relation to the civil wars and the injustices that had unfolded throughout its occurrence. It is important that we think past the term "resilience" and its supposition that one has to persevere despite and not against the conditions that have been imposed on them. We have long sustained and fed the discourse of "resilience" in Lebanon as artistic-cultural institutions who have always been imbricated within larger civil-society networks and as inhabitants of a country where the state of exception has become the norm. The absence of state structures has exposed us to mass precarity. Rather than conceiving strategies of resilience, we should seek to engage in oppositional politics.

Today, Ashkal Alwan faces different challenges that are not only related to its local context but expand toward operating as a regional and international platform. We're undergoing a specific crisis in Lebanon that's producing its own set of morbid symptoms: currently, the Lebanese government, following decades of neglecting and marginalizing local artistic-cultural institutions, is consciously attempting to suffocate the sector by imposing draconian tax measures and doubling down on forms of policing and censorship, which includes having General Security reject visa applications from incoming artists and cultural practitioners wishing to join HWP. This continues to affect the work and programs we do at Ashkal Alwan. A new era of cultural isolation is being ushered in, and it is now up to us to determine the tools that enable us to engage with the battle to come. We have long been committed to alternative modes of cultivating friendships and networks of solidarity. But what do you do when the artists, cultural practitioners, thinkers, and activists that compose your community are either leaving or being driven out of Beirut and stripped of their ability to dream? My sense is that fragmentation is among the most significant challenges we will be facing in the coming years.

PT Can you finally tell us how you have developed an archive in relation to Askal Alwan and its different programs?

CT In 2015, and in line with our apprehension of publicness and accessibility, our efforts to consolidate Ashkal Alwan's archive began. Over the span of three decades, we have been accumulating a large and diverse audiovisual archive containing magnetic and digital tapes, DVDs, and digital files. This material largely comprises films and performances, recordings of previous editions of the Home Works Forum, the Home Workspace Program lectures, and numerous seminars and talks. Having been dispersed across several media, all materials were collected on an open-source media-archive platform called pan.do/ra, which we set up on-premise in December 2015. This platform came to host the organization's entire audiovisual archive but was only meant to be accessible from the Ashkal Alwan space in Beirut. Later in the process, we decided to migrate the centralized archival unit to exist on the cloud. So, Ashkal Alwan established its archive as an open-access online platform, making available terabytes of digital recordings to the wider public. The archive was launched in March 2020, coinciding with the first imposed international lockdown as a result of the ongoing COVID–19 pandemic.

For me, this archive is a living testament and a material witness of history—not as a succession of past events, but a continuous process of meaning-making. I consult my archive on an almost daily basis to situate myself, my curatorial practice, and Ashkal Alwan's institutional activities within broader political developments. It helps us understand where to locate our current tasks and interests. It also, in a way, allows myself and my colleagues at Ashkal Alwan to monitor the ways in which our work might have helped shape a civic discourse in Beirut, or whether we've succeeded in forming networks of alliances with regional institutions or committed individuals working in the artistic-cultural field. This accumulation of past activities—what was uttered and produced within their occurrence, what was deemed as a glitch, and what succeeded in starting a conversation—imposes a path forward for future institutional activities.

In fact, and in response to a growing refiguration of its public mission amidst an age of social distancing, we ended up moving most of our programs—including HWP—online. Perpetual Postponement,[3] an online publishing platform, comes as the logical continuation of our commitment to participating in the conception of openly accessible digital and online platforms. It also responds to a lack of platforms in the region that promote politically engaged and experimental writing in Arabic as well as interdisciplinary arts initiatives. Within its first year, the platform hosted short- and long-form textual essays and interviews, sound pieces, as well as short films, video montages, 3D renderings, and drawings by artists, scholars, writers, and activists based in the Arab region and invested in different disciplines, geographies, and contexts.

Furthermore, as of October 2021, Ashkal Alwan is launching its Archive Residency program, offering artists, researchers, and scholars the opportunity to engage with and research its audiovisual and archive of artistic and cultural practices with a view to developing their own projects. The program will take place over a period of three months at the Ashkal

3 Perpetual Postponement is an online publishing platform launched on June 20, 2020; see www.ashkalalwan.org/program.php?category=5.

Alwan library. The library houses a growing collection of books, catalogs, periodicals, and ephemera and includes material on art history, theory, education, architecture, photography, film, media, theater, performance art, comics, philosophy, critical and political theory, literature, poetry, and cultural policy. The final, and public, outcome of the residency can take different formats and should be determined by the selected residents and Ashkal Alwan. Residents will be granted a shared studio space and a monthly honorarium.

This conversation took place online between Beirut; Mardin, Turkey; and Stockholm on November 5, 2020, then was transcribed and edited. It was originally published in Urgent Pedagogies, November 2020. https://urgentpedagogies.iaspis.se/home-workspace-program.

Urgent Pedagogies is an IASPIS project and platform for inquiry, sharing knowledge and experience on how socially engaged critical spatial practice may act in relation and response to the urgencies of social justice and equality, contested territories, and conditions of conflict, and though strategies and settings for learning, un-learning, thinking together, and alternative forms of producing and sharing knowledge. The project is developed and pursued by Magnus Ericson, Head of Applied Arts, IASPIS and Pelin Tan, sociologist, curator, and professor in the Fine Arts Faculty of Batman University, Turkey.

On Divergent Art Education: A Case Study in Dark Study

Andrew Woolbright

We cannot say what new structures will replace the ones we live with yet, because once we have torn shit down, we will inevitably see more and see differently and feel a new sense of wanting and being and becoming. What we want after "the break" will be different from what we think we want before the break and both are necessarily different from the desire that issues from being in the break.[1] —Jack Halberstam

A wave of writing on radical education appeared in the wake of the 2008 financial collapse and surfaced again three years later during the Occupy protests. Both moments rehearsed our current one: increased economic inequality, dramatic disinvestment in public goods, and an accelerated dependence on debt to access education. These inequalities, while addressed polemically, were rarely addressed materially. Voyeuristic appraisals of programs like AltMFA, The Black School, Mountain School of Arts, and Bruce High Quality Foundation University often positioned these radical alternatives more like novelties than a serious replacement of the established art education system and, in turn, regulated a cruel optimism of that system and its promises.[2] Much of this writing was sensory, first-person, and romantic: the reader might be informed of what a seminar room smelled like but not what the students did there nor how they came to education, let alone any discussion of the institution's pedagogical ideology. The establishment crowded

1 Jack Halbertsam, "The Wild Beyond: With and for the Undercommons," in Fred Moten and Stefano Harney, *The Undercommons: Fugitive Planning and Black Study* (Autonomedia, 2013), 6.

2 Lauren Berlant describes cruel optimism as "a relation of attachments to compromised conditions of possibility whose realization is discovered either to be impossible, sheer fantasy, or too possibly, and toxic." The cruelty of this false desire "is that the subjects who have x in their lives might not well endure the loss of their object/scene of desire, even though its presence threatens their well-being because the continuity of its form provides something of the continuity of the subject's sense of what it means to keep on living on and to look forward to being in the world." Lauren Berlant, *Cruel Optimism* (Duke University Press, 2011), 24.

out the alternative and cast these schools in narrow terms of opposition rather than as possibilities to serve the artists that traditional institutions often excluded. The MFA, then and now, perpetuates professionalization, offering access and art-world visibility for considerable debt-backed fees instead of an education that empowers artists to challenge the system's fundamental inequities. This exchange was commonly accepted and influenced what was written about and how, what was seen, and what was buried.

Critical attention confers legitimacy, and while a lack of a sincere engagement with the alternative is not the only problem faced by radical programs, it contributes to keeping new, divergent forms of education suspended between launch and long-term viability. For radical and utopic models to develop, they need a new kind of evaluative writing, one that enables prospective students to understand the definitions of an education that encourages a deep, investigative, and expansive art practice. This writing must be material rather than idealized; embodied rather than voyeuristic; and focused on subjects (the students and their work and the teachers' articulated pedagogies) rather than subjectivities. It ought to answer not only how but what and why. Most importantly, it must be patient, rigorous, and observant. As Fred Moten and Stefano Harney outline in *The Undercommons*, their collaborative exploration of a divergent space for study and the development of a new, free commons within society, "we owe it to each other to falsify the institution.... We owe each other the indeterminate. We owe each other everything."[3] Significant criticism of the MFA system certainly exists, but for all the signaling, why have no divergent programs established themselves as a serious replacement of high-debt higher education?

Enter Dark Study. Developed by Caitlin Cherry and Nicole Won Hee Maloof, Dark Study is a new para-institution launched in January that operates beyond the traditional structures of education to counter the inaccessibility and weaknesses of art school that make it an unrealistic, even inhospitable, place for so many artists to make their work. Conversations about Dark Study began last winter, before COVID, between Cherry, Maloof, and Nora Khan amid their disappointment with the limitations imposed by discipline-centric pedagogy, unresponsive curricula, and the accelerating precarity of adjuncts. When the first COVID lockdown was initiated and education went from in-person to online, the founders' idea of a decentered, radically interdisciplinary alternative to the MFA found form. Exceeding medium specificity and technical training, Dark Study offers an education in cultural and media theory and empire and capital's roles in the development of contemporary art. The program addresses the problems and traumas Cherry and Maloof encountered in their own education experiences—both as students and as professors—and challenges pre-existing forms of education in legacy institutions that prize results-oriented evaluation on a limited timeline in a discrete space. Because it is free, Dark Study dismisses the contract between art world success and debt. It offers an immersive space of study, one that is responsive to the students' needs, and seeks to fulfill education's capacity for community-building through shared growth rather than individualized participation in a system designed to satisfy the demands of capital.

Running a free program that stands a chance of shifting power away from traditional institutions comes with countless obstacles and requires a combination of intellect, critical strategizing, and organizational

3 Fred Moten and Stefano Harney, *The Undercommons*, 20.

skill. As both practicing artists and educators, Cherry and Maloof offer unique perspectives from which to deliver a potential undercommons in art education. Cherry's hybridized practice involves virtual reality and installation situated with painting to question the role of the market and its presence in the reification of art as a commodity. She can as readily and easily discuss Alexander Galloway's *Protocol: How Control Exists after Decentralization* as contemporary figuration. Maloof uses printmaking, bookmaking, and video to explore folkloric and personal narratives and representations of labor and, over the past year, has led an underground and international Marxist theory book club. Cherry teaches painting at Virginia Commonwealth University School of the Arts and Maloof at Sarah Lawrence College. Together, they have assembled a roster of visiting artists and advisors—Sondra Perry, Jesse Darling, David Xu Borgonjon, Che Gossett, and Serubiri Moses—who bring with them experiences and pedagogies grounded in the overlaps of the fields of art, technology, and culture.

Dark Study received 180 applications from its first call, a testament to artists' readiness for an alternative. In the Instagram announcement, Cherry and Maloof kept Dark Study's pedagogy and intentions deliberately vague to resist "the call to order," a strategy adapted from Moten and Harney's *Undercommons*. Due to this intentional abstraction of their process, the applicant pool was impressively heterogeneous, interdisciplinary, and diverse across ethnicity, age, class, education, and professional experience. The application-making process was carefully considered. The school's portal states:

> Community-building in schools is often talked about as if the process begins on the first day of school—a group of students happens to find themselves in the same space, at the same time. However, the community formed in the classroom is engineered long before the group gathers; its shape, the conversations it will likely have, is rooted in the application form. An application form is a subtle form of gatekeeping. If a school truly wants to give opportunities to those who have been locked or forced out of higher education, then the usual signs of access and training embedded in the application must be reassessed. Using the same old "natural" markers of "success" can only reproduce the hostile conditions that exist in society at large, undermining any attempts at creating an inclusive community before the first day arrives.[4]

When Maloof and Cherry evaluated the applicants, the ideology of the school was put to the test. "We had a stated aim for the school. We had to make sure that the way we were assessing people actually matched that goal," Maloof says. "It's easy for those things to not match up, which is a criticism we have of institutions, and how they are able to keep people out while they proclaim this 'welcoming of diversity.'" Some applicants were artists with MFAs or doctorates from elite institutions and others were musicians, gallerists, physicists, robotics engineers, or artists who had an established exhibition record, perhaps thinking that Dark Study more akin to a cultural think tank or postgraduate program like the Studio Museum Residency or the Whitney Independent Study Program than an MFA. Maloof explained the way they handled these expectations within the application process: "Some people with multiple postgraduate degrees applied, some with master's degrees, and some enrolled in PhD programs. We did tend to weed out

4 https://www.darkstudy.net/.

people who had an exceptional amount of education, because it was clear they could, through their own means, access such programs on their own and afford them. It didn't seem like we would do them a service, and they would be taking up a space from someone who doesn't have access to those higher institutions of education, and that's who we were really targeting. We weren't biased against individuals with lots of access, but that signaled to us they had tools in place to find access on their own." Art speak also proved a dead end with them. "If we sensed too much of that intellectual posturing in their applications, which often is rewarded in art schools, it was a red flag."

Cherry and Maloof insisted on the application being free and avoiding the exorbitant fees of Submittable and SlideRoom, which proved to be a challenging administrative problem. "Our application was essay heavy. We had to tell ourselves, 'We have to slow down, spend more time with each application,'" Cherry says, "and that to thoughtfully consider each candidate would take time." Dark Study did not require transcripts or letters of recommendation, traditional signals in the application process that vet applicants with better connections. One especially helpful prompt for applicants was to provide an "Alternative Story," a biography of failures, a negative CV made up of rejected applications and barriers that withheld access. To demonstrate the transparency and inclusivity that traditional institutions often only speak to, the founders provided their own versions as examples on Dark Study's website. In her bio, Cherry writes:

> I didn't come from a creative family. My mother was a secretary and my father worked most of his life as a worker on an automotive assembly line. Growing up in Chicago, I lacked any particular motivation to do anything but sports and art. My GPA and ACT scores would have hardly gotten me into a decent state school, I certainly wasn't Northwestern-bound. It took me a while to become "good at school." My parents supported my ambitions the best they could. I spent a year at a community college before I was able to attend the School of the Art Institute of Chicago.[5]

Having narrowed the applicant pool, Cherry and Maloof interviewed twenty-five finalists to get a sense of the kind of cohort they could assemble and decided to accept all of them based on their level of work, an assessment of their need, and the founders' critical self-evaluation of what needs they could reasonably meet and address through teaching. Attending class from Oklahoma, Kentucky, California, New York, Ghana, Mexico, and China, among other places, the first twenty-five students are diverse in ethnicity and gender identity. "The reality is it takes risk, vulnerability, and time," Cherry says. "If you put these candidates in front of a different panel, you'd get a different program."

One of those candidates was Lela Welch. She dropped out of college in 2008 as her struggles with addiction became unmanageable, and although she was able to finish her bachelor's degree in 2018, the path back to school proved difficult. Between 2008 and 2018, Welch worked at homeless shelters, a start-up, and in addiction treatment, and is now a temp administrator at a psychiatric office in San Luis Obispo, California. Though Welch has the lived experiences that MFA programs often suggest they want in a candidate, her location, schedule, and educational history preclude her from a traditional MFA. Welch felt like it was time for her to reenter a structured, community-based learning environment, and was looking for critical

5 https://www.darkstudy.net/.

engagement and feedback from peers, a "correcting experience," she says. She is in Dark Study class from 6 to 8 a.m., before going to work at the psychiatric office. At noon, she has an hour break and catches up with reading and class discussion over Whereby. After work, meetings, and class, Welch is usually home by 8 p.m. and able to put in some extra time studying. Typically, she expects to read about twenty pages of assigned reading per class, in addition to answering course questions and preparing for discussions. Recently, Welch has been reading sections of theory that seek to explore third spaces of operation within institutions, like Halberstam's *The Queer Art of Failure* and Rasheedah Phillips's essay "Communal, Quantum, and Afrofutures: Time and Memory in North Philly," from *Black Quantum Futurism: Space-Time Collapse II.*[6] Her practice involves actions and objects, and she is interested in the realities created by artificial hells. In her piece *Investment* (2019), the artist's partner poured casting plaster over her while she sat in a constructed box filled with sand, re-enacting the early steps in the process of bronze casting with her body. At the end of the three-hour performance, Welch stood up from the hardened plaster, leaving a relief where her body had merged with the fabricated landscape. Welch is planning two ambitious projects, in both scale and funding, and is seeking guidance on how to realize them materially and critically. The discussions in Dark Study have enabled her to question her work: whether she should use her own body in performance or invite group participation, the valences of class that the interactions of her performances involve, the audience it has addressed in the past, and who it will address in the future.

Dark Study hosts two courses in its first semester. "Art for Whom?" led by Maloof, is an overview analysis of empire that addresses class while developing a working definition of imperialism. The course will end with students producing analyses of class's influence on themselves and their art practice as a means of understanding their own identity through access (or lack thereof). "Divergent I," led by Cherry, discusses the art market and its influence on artists' studio practices and how nonprofits funnel money and influence through cultural institutions, or "why artists make work, how that work circulates, and the multitude of ways where the needs of the artist and the desires of a market-driven art economy diverge."[7] These externalities are explored through a series of student-led presentations and responses to Andrea Fraser's *2016 in Museums, Money, and Politics*, Martha Rosler's *Culture Class*, Denise Ferreira da Silva's *Toward a Global Idea of Race*, and Ben Davis's *9.5 Theses on Art and Class*, among others. Students have access to the whiteboard app Miro and are developing a sprawling map that traces nonprofits' capital and investments and the boards of major institutions through exhibitions and museum collections. Though we expect more from those in positions that are supposedly meant to protect our cultural heritage, trusteeship on American nonprofit and institutional boards is intended to keep

6 In which Phillips writes, "In our space-time mapping of the future, however, rarely do we take account of where the future is, who has access to it, its plurality, and whether we are all accelerating at the same rate and pace into that future.... The time dimension plays a crucial role in how people—particularly Black and poor people—are valued, treated, punished, or underserved by and within society." Rasheedah Phillips, "Communal, Quantum, and Afrofutures: Time and Memory in North Philly," in *Black Quantum Futurism: Space-Time Collapse II* (Philadelphia Afrofuturist Affair, 2015), 10.

7 Caitlin Cherry, Divergent I syllabus.

8 "Governed with little or no democratic input or oversight, they (nonprofit arts organizations) are part of a system in which public resources [...] are channeled to privately controlled organizations that operate with little public accountability; a system which [...] may serve to legitimize the economic inequality and privation that underlie so many of the social problems philanthropic organizations aim to solve." Andrea Fraser, *2016 in Museums, Money, and Politics* (MIT Press, 2018), 31.

the system in its current configuration as a strategic manipulation of the market, with the aim of using art and artists to circulate and concentrate capital.[8]

Contextualizing the art market and the imperialist project as objects of study within the structure of an advanced art program has the potential to facilitate practices that incorporate institutional critique into studio work. This shift, decentering artistic practice away from solipsistic analysis of the self and toward an ecological examination of culture and its systems, is significant. Dark Study fuses aesthetics with an investigation of and critical relationship with the structures aesthetics exists within, and, in doing so, it is seeking to enact a pedagogy informed by solidarity and intended to build community beyond those confines. This examination about circulation is further addressed by Dark Study's advisors, each of whom addresses the market and the circulation of art in their own practices, writing, and curation: Sondra Perry's *It's in the Game* questions museum acquisitions and their role in representation and the depictions of subaltern histories; Jesse Darling critiques the Ballad of Saint Jerome and the hierarchies of dependency and compromise that it establishes; David Xu Borgonjon evaluates cultural artifacts and the orientalizing of Chinese culture and artists, specifically in his critique of Asian Futurism in "Continental Drift: Notes on 'Asian' Art"; Che Gossett has written about trans cultural production and the violence against blackness; and Serubiri Moses, cocurator of *Greater New York 2021*, has long-term curatorial projects like *The Visual History of African Women's Liberation Struggles* (1989–) that deal with historical narration, African feminist theory, indigeneity, and their depictions. Cherry and Maloof made recommendations to advisors about whom they felt would benefit most from advising, but ultimately the mentors picked their mentees. "We really thought about who actually needs advising, and so when we speak about something like quality of work it's not a judgment of the work itself but more of where are they in their creative development," Maloof clarifies. "We chose based on who, in having an advisor, would have a significant impact on their work."

When evaluated as a whole—structure, ideology, and participants—it is clear that Dark Study is interested in developing visual artists who develop their practice as political entities and engaged critics of art-market institutions, scopic regimes, and cultural hegemonies. Because of its independence from endowment- and debt-backed programs, the school owes only its students. It presents a formidable anarchist/utopic engine: a free education that provides direct access to curators and critics working in the art world and an insurgent education that combines aesthetics with institutional and cultural critique. This critique, perhaps most radically, dissolves the individual liberal subject and replaces it with tentacular arrangements, collective thinking, and macroscopic pedagogical frameworks. As Moten says, "Like Deleuze, I believe in the world and want to be in it. I want to be in it all the way to the end of it because I believe in another world in the world and I want to be in *that*."[9] Utopic beauty is and always will be fugitive.[10] Dark Study proposes a reform not only of higher education but of the culture and world itself in hopes of creating a new one, and provides strength and solidarity in the spaces left to the divergent.

This text was originally published as Andrew Woolbright, "On Divergent Art Education: A Case Study in Dark Study," e-flux Education, March 24, 2021.

9 Moten and Harney, *The Undercommons*, 118.

10 Moten and Harney discuss the subversive intellectual's perpetual fugitivity. Though the university is a place of "refuge" it is also a place that cannot "bear what (the subversive intellectual) brings." She must "disappear into the underground." Moten and Harney, 26.

Fifteen Years of SOMA: Why Institutionality Can Be Its Own Political Act

Kim Córdova

In 2025, SOMA, the nonprofit alternative artist-run art school in Mexico City, celebrated fifteen years of operation. There is a macabre irony to writing about the project, which draws deeply on the legacies of arts-education programs in the United States, in the context of the all-consuming culture wars that have empowered a pro-nationalist US administration to vilify, attack, and defund higher education. MAGA's special reserve of rancor for liberal-arts education makes now a uniquely charged moment to write about the legacy of a radically generous project of collective work by a group of artists who use education as practice and who view national borders as provincialisms to be disregarded.

I could never write an objective essay about SOMA or the people who gave it form. It's had too big an impact on the direction of my life and work. I first participated in SOMA as a member of the second SOMA Summer cohort in 2011. Later that year, I was invited to enroll in the second generation of the two-year Spanish language PES (Programa Educativo SOMA), giving me the honor of being the first US citizen to enroll—and, far more dubiously, making me the reason SOMA had to institute a language-proficiency policy for future PES students. Sentimentality aside, I'm steadfast in the belief that the program has had an outsize impact not only on contemporary art ecosystems and practice in Mexico, but also throughout the Americas and beyond.

With the recognition that I would need help to wade through the muck of my memory and nostalgia to write an essay about SOMA in its quinceñera year, this essay reflects interviews with Eduardo Abaroa, Ricardo Alzati, Laura Cortés Hesselbach, Anthony Graves, Cuauhtémoc Medina, and Yoshua Okón. It goes without

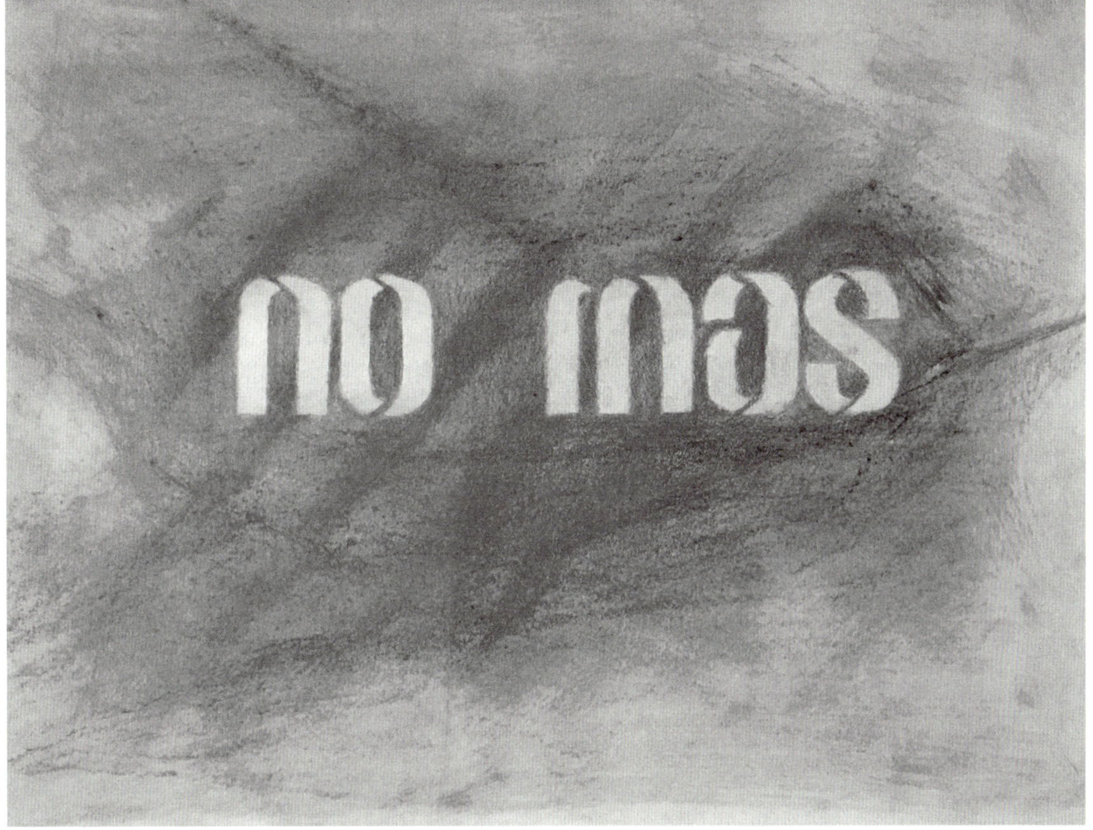

Bill Abdale, Untitled (no más), 2017. Graphite on paper, 8¼ × 11⅜ in.

saying that there are infinite ways to tell a story of SOMA, and this is just one.

The word "school," even if modified with a series of academic qualifiers, feels limited as a definition for SOMA given its scope and the breadth of its impact. A more precise descriptor might be a post-Conceptual artists' response to a set of social, cultural, economic, and political forces that coalesced into Mexico being a place with a rich artistic history and cultural life but with subpar graduate-level university studio-art programs. "I always have the feeling that one has to speak of SOMA both as an attempt to deal with the problem and as a symptom of the problem. Somehow the fact that these few artists with very little resources in a little house somewhere lost in Mexico City have such an influence is a sign of how wrongly the official [art education] system is being run," says Medina, the former chief curator of Museo Universitario Arte Contemporáneo and a researcher at Universidad Nacional Autónoma de México.

It's important to keep in mind that SOMA was born in the early 2010s, a time when "post-studio" and "post-Fordist" artistic practices were dominant. According to Alzati, SOMA intentionally "moved away from that more immaterial post-Fordist model of artist as a globetrotter with a video camera and a computer that lived between two or three cities, acquiring instead a focus on the local contexts and their implications for our discourse and outputs." To this end, a potent source of SOMA's strength is its rootedness in and its commitment to Mexico. According to Graves, SOMA Summer 2019 codirector and an artist, when SOMA started, in 2010, "artists like Eduardo Abaroa, Mario Garcia, and Yoshua Okón had international careers. SOMA and SOMA Summer planted them back in Mexico City."

As an institution, SOMA is situated in a shifting, mandala-like Venn diagram of antecedent and descendent networks of organizations within the city, across the country, throughout the Spanish-speaking world, and beyond. As Graves put it: "The networks of associations that SOMA and SOMA Summer created, and the other institutions that spun out of them ... it's exponential."

Founded in the early 2000s by a group of Mexico City artists led by Okón, the project draws inspiration from several institutions for advanced studies in art, including the UCLA and CalArts MFA programs, the Rijksakademie, and the Whitney Independent Study Program, from which members of the founding artist team graduated, as well as historical precedents including Joseph Beuys's work and Black Mountain College. This diverse set of influences created, for better or worse, a bridging effect that has developed, over time, a circuit of connection between Mexico and international art scenes. Most concretely, this circuit is evidenced by the formal agreements and exchange programs that SOMA has signed with universities including Yale, Harvard, Stanford, the University of Texas, Virginia Commonwealth University, CalArts, and Hunter College, among others.

There's perhaps room for criticism that SOMA has had its institutional gaze overly fixed on northern influences, but, according to Alzati, a faculty member, "the United States, unlike Mexico, has thousands of master's programs, or at least, it must be hundreds." SOMA, on the other hand, "arises because of the need, because of the failure of the national institutions to provide postgraduate study in the field of art." The number of foreign students who have come from across Latin America to study at SOMA suggests the program responds to needs that are more regional than national in scope.

SOMA was started by seventeen artists in Mexico City who are roughly grouped together as "the 1990s generation." Their largely post-Conceptual and often dematerial approaches toward artistic practice made study abroad necessary because neither of the city's main university programs offered MFA curriculums informed by postwar developments in art. Reflecting the mismatch between artists' practices and the local higher-education offerings, only seven of these founding artists have MFA degrees. Those that do earned them abroad, mostly in the United States. Graves recounts how Carla Herrera-Prats used to talk about "what it was like to be an artist in Mexico in the 1990s. There wasn't any real North American exchange pre-NAFTA. So if a friend came and brought an art magazine it would be a very big deal; artists would look at magazines together and trade them. That restrictiveness is what Carla sought to correct" with SOMA.

Okón received his MFA from UCLA and would teach his mentor John Baldassari's famed *Class Assignments* material at

SOMA, while his critique class draws notable inspiration from Michael Asher's legendary marathon critiques and process. SOMA's founding academic director, Eduardo Abaroa; Herrera-Prats, founding SOMA Summer Director; and artist board member Mario Garcia Torres all earned their MFAs at CalArts. Abaroa's pedagogical approaches were in a way also influenced by Asher, who was his mentor during his MFA, but he cites other CalArts artist faculty, Charles Gaines and Leslie Dick, as more direct influences on his teaching. Other artist board members include e-flux cofounder Julieta Aranda, who received her MFA from Columbia, and Carlos Amorales, who attended the Rijksakademie. Herrera-Prats notably also graduated from the Whitney ISP, on which she based the design of SOMA Summer, going so far as to "always dress like [ISP director] Ron Clark during the program. She wore brown shoes, light stonewashed jeans, and a blue striped Oxford. It was her way to settle into the position that she created for herself. She had to sort of be him first before she could really be Carla running the program," explained Graves, himself an ISP graduate and Herrera-Prats's partner in their artist collaboration Camel Collective.

An often-overlooked aspect of SOMA is that of the founding artists who received MFAs in the United States, all but one did so on Fulbright scholarships. Notably, the Fulbright stipulates that students are required to return to their home countries for two years after graduation. The Fulbright is not the reason SOMA was founded. But in a moment in which the program is being dismantled as part of a broad policy of US disengagement and discrediting of soft-power programs, I have to wonder if there's an argument that the scholarship's terms created an overall context of return in which artists who studied abroad were looking for community as they processed the experience of their studies abroad and thought about the next steps in their careers and practices.

While SOMA's influences are numerous, its heritage flows most directly from local artist-run exhibition and gathering spaces La Panaderia (1994–2002), which was founded by Okón and Miguel Calderón, and Temistocles 44, founded by Abaroa, Sofía Táobas, and Abraham Cruzvillegas. "The art institutions in the '90s were very flimsy, they were not functional. So our generation, we didn't have to demolish anything. It was already destroyed. We had to build something," says Abaroa. Okón also cites the art classes that Abaroa and Laureana Toledo (daughter of Oaxacan artist Francisco Toledo) were giving at El Centro de Imagen as foundational for SOMA and why he approached Abaroa to be SOMA's first academic director. At the risk of overly distributing credit for SOMA's origin, there's also an argument for the project's ancestors to include a more expansive list of artist-run projects in the city, including the Museo Ex-Teresa of experimental and performance art, Francis Alÿs and Melanie Smith's Mel's Cafe, and La Quiñonera. SOMA's board president, philanthropist Aimée Labarrere de Servitje, was writing her dissertation about the history of alternative artist-run arts spaces in Mexico City when Okón approached her with the idea to start the school.

Notably, Gabriel Orozco's Friday workshops are never mentioned as an influence in SOMA's founding. But they do emphasize an overall context of artists returning from abroad and self-organizing opportunities for communal study in response to gaps in the Mexican arts landscape that they identified based on their observations of other global cities' art ecosystems. Moreover, several of SOMA's founding artists are still represented by kurimanzutto, by far the most powerful gallery in Latin America, which Orozco co-founded in 1999, and which was more or less born from his Friday studio workshops. Even SOMA's founding director, Barbara Hernandez-Rosas, was recruited by Abaroa from the gallery's staff.

Reflecting on why he started SOMA, Okón instinctively begins by pointing to the societal conditions that drove him to start his previous artist-run space, La Panaderia, which lasted from 1994–2002: the devastating 1985 earthquake in Mexico City and the rise of neoliberal ideology, symbolically represented in Mexico by the 1994 signing of NAFTA and the Mexican Peso "Tequila Crisis." This was an era that prioritized markets, private enterprise built on debt leverage, a move to the suburbs, and the rhetoric of individual responsibility. These ideologies contrasted starkly with the destruction and semi-abandonment of neighborhoods like Roma, Condesa, Juarez, and Centro that were decimated by the earthquake and whose process of rebuilding was slowed by a brutal economic contraction when President Ernesto Zedillo devalued the Mexican peso as a response to the debt crisis caused by neoliberal reform of the Mexican banking sector, triggering local banks to over-leverage. "The art world in Mexico was completely crushed. Because we had the error de Diciembre, we had the Zapatismo, and we had a terrible economic crisis. Mexico started to have these waves of violence, especially in Mexico City," said Abaroa. It was against the ruin of neighborhoods damaged by the quake, the generalized sense of isolation that neoliberalism and recession fomented, and the lack of local opportunity to exhibit post-Conceptual contemporary art in local museums that La Panaderia took root as an experimental space for exhibition making and, perhaps most radically, institutionalized intergenerational artists hanging out.

According to Okón, the decision to close La Panadería in 2002, despite its success, had to do with how the Mexico City art scene had changed. Local museums had begun showing and collecting contemporary work, and other alternative spaces had begun to emerge. "So the space just wasn't quite needed in the same way." He himself was packing up to start his MFA in California. That said, "Every time I came back people asked when I would reopen La Panadería. It signaled to me that there was a community need still unattended in Mexico City. By then neoliberalism, along with its hyper-individualistic ethos, were fully established and the scene we had managed to build throughout the '90s had begun to fall apart. That's what got me thinking about starting the project that would become SOMA."

It's also relevant to highlight how there has been "a certain synchronicity, even symbiosis, between Soma and SITAC," said Medina. SITAC is a biannual art theory conference and is the flagship public program of the Patrocinato de Arte Contemporaneo (PAC). PAC is a consortium of private collectors and philanthropists who, under the nonprofit PAC umbrella, fund artistic production, exhibitions, and publishing projects through a set of open calls. Both founded in 2000, PAC established SITAC at a time in which global cities faced a "keeping up with the Joneses"–type pressure to have a biennial, something that to this day Mexico City notably lacks. Rather than respond to the impulse to start a biennial to exhibit art objects, the PAC elected to organize a "biennial" institution whose focus was on conversations about critical theory. Like SOMA, SITAC responded to a moment driven by the logic of markets with a staunchly anti-market and anti–art object proposal.

Over the years, many of SOMA's artist-professors and leaders have directed or spoken at SITAC, including Abaroa, who directed SITAC 9, and Jesse Lerner and Ruben Ortiz Torres, who directed SITAC 15. SOMA's board president is also the president of PAC's board. Today, SOMA's founding director, Hernandez Rosas, is the general director of PAC. Both institutions facilitate artist conversations, but in different ways.

SOMA's move this year to a new location has provoked significant institutional reflection. The new building emphasizes a new chapter in the project's history. Yearly rent increases had made the school's original home, a former cinema in the middle-class San Pedro de los Pinos neighborhood that has been synonymous with the institution since its founding, too expensive to sustain. SOMA, it seems, like the artists who have graduated from the program, can be seen as a victim of the project's success—which is itself tangentially connected to Mexico City's radical soft-power transformation over the last decade. In the last fifteen years the city's international reputation has radically evolved from a place foreigners feared and thought of as synonymous with street crime to a place synonymous with culture and taste that they aspire to visit. This has had real impacts on the city, including making it more expensive to live in and to operate a program like SOMA.

This moment of reflection and renegotiation points to how radically and rapidly transformative the 2010s have been for Mexico, for the art industry, and for the world. I often think about how, when I first arrived in Mexico City in 2011, my goal was to improve my Spanish so that I could comfortably order a "sitio" taxi from a radio dispatch service on my Nokia burner bar phone. These days, not a word of Spanish is needed to zip around the city as Uber and the logic of the markets have eradicated speaking local languages as a "friction" of international travel. The externalities created by Mexico City's enviable status in the attention economy became noticeable in SOMA Summer first. "The image of Mexico City became so big and so popular, it became very trendy. In 2018 and 2019 it was really obvious that applicants just wanted to come and see the hip cool stuff. And then we started to see these differences among the group. Participants were coming with other economic possibilities; they were more interested in going to Pujol, or in drinking natural wines," explained director Cortés Hesselbach. It might sound absurdly bobo to mention the Michelin two-star restaurant and natural wine in the context of the educational turn in contemporary art, but the large July 4, 2025 protests against gentrification and digital nomads, which called for gringos to leave Mexico and left several businesses in Roma and Condesa vandalized, emphasizes the magnitude of the issue and local communities' frustration with it. It also highlights how radically the sociocultural and economic contexts in which SOMA operates today have changed, and how they oblige the project to adapt as much as its changing internal dynamics do.

Cortés Hesselbach again: "Everything is changing. That understanding has really allowed us to understand how to adapt the programs. For instance, SOMA Summer. Obviously, after Carla passed away, the program changed. There was a lot of resistance at first to changing the program because it was her program and it was perfect. But it was tailor-made according to her personality and her energy.

"Looking back, I think that we were, in a way, really lucky that COVID happened. It really made us think how the program could continue by understanding the core of the program under new circumstances." She continued, "With COVID, it was obvious that the program could not run the same way as it was happening before, two months in Mexico City with the low-vaccination process happening here and, yes, the inflation in prices that COVID created. The format of the program in 2021, a three-week summer camp outside of Mexico City, really helped to change the profile of the people that were applying. I'm not saying that the previous participants were wrong or anything, but the program recovered the sense that it was a thematic program; people were not [any longer] applying to SOMA Summer just because of the Mexico City art scene."

As SOMA settles into a new house and grounds in the lovely, leafy, and central San Miguel Chapultepec neighborhood—the ten-year lease from local collector Moisés Cosío gives the institution some medium-term stability—it also highlights how the school is rethinking the tensions, opportunities, and dynamics of making art today to understand how to serve emerging artists. This has included questioning everything from confronting the role of art and artists in gentrification at a moment when Mexico City is straining under the effects of rapid migration by digital nomads, to rethinking the ideal hour to schedule public lectures for Gen Z artists who don't really drink and therefore don't relate to the dynamics of bars and beers the way that previous generations do. "One of the great things about SOMA is that the programs are constantly being studied and being evaluated. I mean the [PES] program changes every three months, and no generation has had the same program as the generation before," explained Cortés Hesselbach.

Some dynamics remain constant. SOMA remains committed to keeping tuition as affordable as possible. And they still refuse to pursue accreditation from Mexico's Secretary of Education (SEP) because doing so makes the program more accessible to artists that might not have had access to formal education like undergraduate university programs or even high school. Moreover, having SEP accreditation would add burdensome bureaucratic requirements that don't necessarily fit the needs of an art school. For example, though all the faculty are known and respected artists, they do not all have MFAs or PhDs, which SEP accreditation would require. The tradeoff to this is that as SOMA attracts artists to Mexico from other countries, it cannot sponsor their visas, a critical gap in their integration into the Mexican art system by which artists "rise" through selection for public grants like the FONCA or the Carillo Gil, which require formal residency status. "We support them as much as we can, for example with letters. But we are not an accredited school, so I think there is an implicit understanding by the students who come that they have to be a bit resourceful and solve those issues as individuals," said Alzati, a SOMA faculty member.

So what exactly is SOMA?

First, it's independent and artist-run. Second, it's nonprofit, noncommercial, and nongovernmental (it receives no government funding). Formally, it comprises four main programs: the heavily subsidized Spanish-language two-year PES or Programa Educativo de SOMA, which is roughly analogous to an MFA (albeit without studios), and has over the years graduated 167 students from fifteen countries. This program grants 90 percent scholarships to all students and, in cases of extreme hardship, grants full tuition scholarships. There is the English-language SOMA Summer for international students, which has graduated 361 students from sixty-eight countries. There is a residency program for invited artists, and a public lecture series called Miercoles de SOMA [SOMA Wednesdays], which has now run, with precious few exceptions, every Wednesday for the last fifteen years and is archived on the SOMA YouTube channel.

After a handful of interviews and reflecting upon my own experiences with the institution, SOMA emerges as a bit of a paradox. "I have a feeling that one good thing about SOMA is that it's not necessarily creating a 'school,'" said Medina brightly. By this he meant that it has not created a group of artists that produce or think in a cleanly groupable way. This signals the school's pedagogical approach is elastic enough to serve many kinds of practices rather than impose a kind of aesthetic or ideological tribalism. "It's a very functional sort of schema rather than an ideology of what we want to do or what we want you to learn from SOMA," Aboaroa reflected.

At the same time, it's an institution built to respond to a context of institutional and market failures that in turn has sprouted other institutions—both internally and externally. SOMA houses programs that have evolved to become institution-like: there is the Cuarto de Proyectos [the Projects Room]; the Campeonato Mundial de Ceviche [World Ceviche Championship], which we started as an end-of-term celebration for a class taught by artist Rubén Ortiz Torres and is now an annual community-wide gathering run by artist Ling Sepulveda; an art book library that is open to the public and which responds to how hard and expensive it is to access art books in Mexico; the annual benefit auction, which began (arguably) as a 2011 SOMA Summer participant-led initiative to help offset the cost of the school's stolen laptop when two members of our cohort and SOMA's then coordinator were mugged; and the Hymno de SOMA, which, somehow fittingly, is to the tune of New Order's "Bizarre Love Triangle."

These days there seems to be a dip in the number of alternative and artist-run projects in the city. "It's something that always goes in waves," commented Okón, sounding unworried. Nevertheless, participants of SOMA's programs have started their own institutions, including, in Mexico City alone: Taller Tajo, a production studio and artist residency; the Croma artist collective; the Local1 residency, bar, and exhibition space; the currently dormant Biquini Wax collective; and Canalla, in nearby Ciudad Neza. Outside of the capital, other projects include the Almendro artist residency in Culiacán and Bruma Laboratoria in Veracruz. I'm unaware of SOMA Summer students starting artist-run institutions in other countries but, statistically, the odds seem high.

The program seems to attract those doggedly committed to art. According to Cortés Hesselbach, "93 percent of SOMA's graduates still primarily identify as artists, even if that work doesn't earn them their living." And a majority of them stay in Mexico

City for at least a few years before moving on—myself among them. I stayed for ten years before personal circumstances obliged returning to the United States. I do what I can to maintain a connection to Mexico, but admittedly it waxes and wanes based on life's circumstances. Do I still identify as "an artist"? That feels harder to say. To the extent that I do, my definition of artist is radically expansive, but this is thanks to the influence of SOMA and studying under faculty like Abaroa, Herrara-Prats, Okón, and Minerva Cuevas.

The current context of censorship and institutional collapse—at least in global north contexts—makes for a charged climate for writing an essay about the past, present, and future of SOMA. As of this writing, the future of one of SOMA's antecedent programs, the storied and admired Whitney ISP, is shockingly in question. Former SOMA Summer codirector Sara Nadal-Melsió was the first ISP Associate Director appointed after ISP founder Ron Clark's retirement. She was fired and the whole ISP program was "paused" by the Whitney Museum's new director, Scott Rothkopf, in retaliation for her and the students fighting to maintain the program's academic independence from the museum. Prior to the ISP, Nadal-Melsió had been hand-picked by Herrera-Prats to codirect SOMA Summer 2019 with Graves when Herrera-Prats's health declined. The unclear fate of the ISP alludes to how many cultural institutions today find their leadership's (boards, donors, directors) interests at odds with those implementing programs—staff, artists, and audiences among them. The institutional schisms at programs like the ISP make SOMA's determination to operate as a rigorously noncommercial and independent space feel particularly trenchant.

As SOMA symbolically becomes an adult, or at least a teen, in its quinceñera year, the challenge is balancing how it conceptualizes itself as an elastic artistic response to a set of societal dynamics with its need to build organizational stability and institutional permanence. "It's starting to acquire the responsibilities of an institution. There's an awareness that it has to respond to more requirements than just having a multi-generational conversation about contemporary art. It begins to assume more responsibilities because there are so many people involved. There are the students, graduates, and people who support it with resources, and they all expect to see certain outcomes, right?" says Alzati.

At a certain point, all institutions, even radical communal ones, have to confront the unsexy and often treacherous trade-offs of institutional administration and sustainability. SOMA is no exception. Our present has become so destabilized it's impossible to say what the future will hold. But for now, SOMA's determination to find ways to continue to exist as an artist-run space independent of the art market and government funding may emerge as its most miraculous and political act.

Unifying Agents: Emancipation and Art Education in the Caribbean

Pablo Guardiola

For the vast majority of the people who inhabit the Caribbean Basin, moving between the countries that comprise it presents a difficult challenge: mobility in the region is determined by existing colonial structures, and travel visas and high transportation costs depress the circulation of the area's inhabitants. The economies associated with tourism have contributed to this deadlock, and the movement of foreign visitors and investors is generally more fluid. Through many strategies, over centuries, the Caribbean has been a brutal laboratory for the implementation of capitalist economic models: first, in the sixteenth century, through colonial exploitation by European powers, and later, since the nineteenth century, by the United States. What we in the Caribbean are today was forged from pure violence, both historical and contemporary. Many of these frameworks still manifest in manipulations to local sovereignty, such as France's indemnity against Haiti for its independence (repealed only in 2016), or in direct colonial policies, as is the case of the United States's control of Puerto Rico and some of the Virgin Islands, to name only some. Despite these adverse political and economic circumstances, cultural production in the region is extremely interesting, complex, and powerful, and despite differences in history and language, certain idiosyncrasies are common among the populations of the Caribbean. I do not wish to repeat homogenizing perceptions or clichés, but it is true that the people of the region share much in common, including ways of being, thinking, working, and living. Against colonial impositions, much of the thought produced from the Caribbean considers the body of water that defines our region not as a border but as a "unifying agent."[1]

1 See Reniel Rodgríguez Ramos and Jaime Pagán Jiménez, "Interacciones Multivectoriales en el Circum-Caribe Precolonial: Un Vistazo desde Las Antillas," *Caribbean Studies* 34, no. 2 (July–December 2006): 99–139, https://www.jstor.org/stable/25613538.

Figuring the Caribbean as a site of exchange and emancipation is just one starting point of the educational program RAY | RAYO | RAYON.

The organizers of RAY | RAYO | RAYON define the initiative as an interdisciplinary and experimental art education program operating from the insular and continental Caribbean that places the relationships among and emancipation of the region's constituents at its center. Convened by the Dominican curator Yina Jiménez Suriel and the Puerto Rican artist Beatriz Santiago Muñoz, the project had its first face-to-face meeting in Santo Domingo, Dominican Republic, in October 2022. In this meeting, participants from the Caribbean with various art backgrounds took up as their primary goal the responsibility of imagining the future form of RAY | RAYO | RAYON (hereafter RAYO).[2] The first day of this meeting was held at the National Botanical Garden in Santo Domingo, a deliberate decision by the organizers to discuss art education in a space not necessarily linked to the art world or higher education. Our sessions coincided with the National Festival of Plants and Flowers, an event that had been on hiatus for two years because of the pandemic, and the Botanical Garden was packed with people attending the festival, creating an environment quite rich in human activity. It was fortuitous that RAYO coincided with this event, considering that the program aspires to be in constant contact with other cultural manifestations: in the Caribbean, thinking about art should never happen in a void. The first day we met in an open pavilion with a thatched roof, where we not only made use of a public facility but also worked within the tropical context of the space—with the trees, the breeze, the heat, the humidity, and the sound of the birds inevitably becoming part of the collective thought process.

Beginning with a self-ethnographic exercise, this first meeting focused on the participants' reflections on their education in art and life. From sharing their formative experiences in a kind of educational *détournement*, certain elements of art and humanities education that intertwined with life itself arose as critical links among many participants' practices. This exercise also explored what elements were common among art education programs across different islands and what were not. For instance, conversations in a bar were understood as being as important as those in a classroom, and it was also pointed out how the importance of working together, whether in a studio or in organizing events or projects collectively, could sometimes go underrecognized, despite being fundamental to art education. Serendipity was understood as another element that should be protected within the participants' analyses of art education in the Caribbean. The idea of RAYO was determined in part from these experiences, drawing on what had already been interesting and what should be changed; it was a common thought that the current educational opportunities in the region do not completely satisfy the potential of a program focused on the region and its context.

Within this exchange, the lack of solid institutions for education in the arts and the

2 The following persons participated in the October meeting: Iberia Pérez González (curator, Caribbean Cultural Institute Coordinator, Pérez Art Museum, Miami), José Rozón (artist), Julianny Ariza Vólquez (artist), Luis Graham Castillo (curator), Madeline Jiménez Santil (artist), Marily Gallardo (artist, choreographer, and director of the Kalalú dance school), Mario Sosa (public policy expert), Maurice Sánchez (artist), Pablo Guardiola (artist and codirector of Beta-Local), Sharelly Emanuelson (artist), Tessa Mars (artist), Tony Cruz Pabón (artist), Yolanda Wood (art historian), Victor Torres (artist and researcher, RAYO administrator), Beatriz Santiago Muñoz (artist, co-organizer of RAYO) and Yina Jiménez Suriel (curator, co-organizer of RAYO).

colonial dependence that still exists in the Caribbean were raised as explicit conditions for RAYO to address. In some of the islands, there are no proper BFAs, and graduate programs are basically nonexistent. Further, some programs do not necessarily address the conditions informing cultural production from the region. The United States and Europe are, for many, the only options for higher art education, thereby enforcing still-existent colonial dependencies. It is necessary to note the economic and political costs that studying abroad might have for people who want to educate themselves in the visual arts: the increased expense creates a significant economic burden for students, which in many cases prevents them from returning to work in the Caribbean; this dependency in many ways presents unequal relations, in which the inhabitants from the region will end up as immigrants or second-class citizens in different countries. It is also interesting to note how several RAYO participants who studied outside the region, mainly in the United States and Europe, shared processes of unlearning or adapting their training experiences to the Caribbean context and almost always underwent processes of experimentation and self-direction to build other exchange opportunities and workspaces when they returned to the region. For example, when artists from the Caribbean study in the United States, much of their preparation is directed toward working in a generic big city modeled on New York or Los Angeles. That is not necessarily bad, but the contexts and resources are different, requiring adaptation, and it becomes necessary to build support structures that correspond to what is and isn't available in these locales.

RAYO did not emerge from nowhere, which was clear from the first meeting. It is a project in relation to other past, present, and hopefully future efforts to address art pedagogy in the region, which unfold in institutions, official academic spaces, independent organizations, workshops, and self-organized support structures and exist in the work of many artists, art historians, curators, and writers. Here, the research work of Natalie Willis Whylly, who generated a list of art-related infrastructures across the Caribbean, including academic institutions, independent nonprofits, and everything in between, provided a starting point. The proposed plan is that her list will grow from contributions by the RAYO online community. Communication within the Caribbean is limited, and for people working in the arts, it can be very difficult to know what initiatives, past and present, shape our art milieu. It is therefore incredibly useful to have access to such an inventory, not only to be aware of what is happening, good and bad, but most importantly to find models of action produced by people working in the region. Another important proposal of the day was the call for a collective effort to identify those who are currently working on and in the region as possible collaborators. It was agreed that collaborations should take many different forms and varied scales, from big events to one-on-one work, and be open to the entire Caribbean and its diasporas. Despite persistently addressing how problematic many of the institutions in the region can be, the participants recognized that there have always been interesting people working within them. The relatively small scale of the region can be considered an asset, with histories of collaboration—not necessarily within institutional contexts—that can be expanded through interpersonal relations. Leisure spaces, for instance, are usually shared, and it is common to have people from different backgrounds interacting around the same project, such as a carpenter, an artist, and a biologist. This tends to open collaboration and possibilities for exchange, where sometimes friendship bonds come before working situations. One objective is to see how RAYO can catalyze these collaborations. It is also necessary to identify the existing physical infrastructure for art and learning. For example, if you need a theater and there is already one, you don't need to build a new one; on the other hand, the theater may not be necessary, and a corner store or a bar might work better as suitable venues for a talk or an exhibition.

To start a conversation about art and emancipation it is necessary to address what form of art participants are talking about and what disciplines, models, and curricula their ideas might apply to, if any. Participants in this conversion must also confront traditional roles and hierarchies associated with schools, students, and teachers. The purpose of this first RAYO meeting, and the ones that followed, was to think with time and as a collective about how this new program can exist and what it can achieve. For RAYO, the context is quite important and determines a large part of its mission. As an educational project, it draws from the tools we have, as well as our sensibilities. We must point out that our focus was on transcending what we might lack, so that adverse conditions do not become barriers. RAYO does not seek to operate only from resilience but from other ways of being, living, and working in the Caribbean. This position does not cancel working from a historical, political, and decolonial consciousness, where population displacement, racism, and the consequences of neoliberalism are not ignored. RAYO is the relationship of various pockets that currently generate emancipatory thought and facilitate making art in the Caribbean as an act of political presence. A series of independent initiatives have shaped these ways of working, such as Alice Yard, Trinidad and Tobago; NLS Kingston, Jamaica; Beta-Local, Puerto Rico; and Curando Caribe, Dominican Republic, to mention only a few.

More than definitions, the project proposes tones of work, a fluid ethos, in which work is done in and beyond the obvious categories of the contemporary art world. RAYO, as a project, intends to blur the lines between practices, disciplines, and fields of study and seeks to contribute to the study of historical figures who need more visibility and to be sensitively contextualized within local conditions and histories. For instance, Silvano Lora's work related to water transportation and Indigenous uses of canoes and exchanges between traditional crafts and visual arts in Dominican Republic during the 1980s is a significant antecedent. Against all odds, there are many important artists in the Caribbean who do not participate in the global contemporary art circuit or who are only entering it now after many years of disregard. In regard to anchoring our narratives and sometimes requiring alternative forms to narrate them, we must take these artists and their work into account. Similarly, we must also look to examples of how art can connect the many knowledges that traverse the region, as, for example, the practices of Los Tejedores, in the Dominican Republic, or Minia Bibiani, in Guadeloupe, make apparent. Roles are not necessarily fixed in this new kind of educational program proposed by RAYO, and the responsibilities of curating, making art, and teaching could shift depending on the project. That does not mean that these categories will be eliminated, but they will become lighter, alleviating some of the burden associated with disciplines and practices. This will be a pedagogical space where, for example, artists with no previous writing experience can propose an onomatopoeic writing project as a temporary educational program. As well, it is important to signal that in its core definition, interdisciplinarity transcends the art world, and collaborations between many fields are encouraged. To know the history of Caribbean sculpture or photography, it is equally important to know specific craft practices or species of trees native to the region. RAYO believes that thought can be produced from art practices in dialogue with other study fields.

The goal of imagining a concrete pilot project emerged from the first RAYO meeting. The challenge remains to inaugurate such a project, not as much from a defined plan but from a common spirit. This chronicle focuses on the meeting in the Dominican Republic, in which I participated, but it should be mentioned that subsequent meetings followed, one online in February 2023 and in-person in Port of Spain, Trinidad, in May 2023. In all these meetings it has been explicitly pointed out that RAYO is a process, and that it is necessary to give it time to develop. Of course, the project faces the problem that financing is generally tied to specific time frames, as well as the fact that many funds are designated to specific countries, which often block the access of others. Within this situation there is another important factor, that of not competing with the funds that other independent organizations in the Caribbean already receive. In conceptual terms, it was established that RAYO is already happening—its reflection is part of its becoming. Following this line of thought, the idea of routes emerged as central to the pedagogical project, where inevitably the journey is the methodology. The key is to find the right ways to connect different routes, even if they are at times created accidentally. A common fantasy among artists in the region, for example, is to do projects from a sailboat, but to do so, it is first necessary to learn how to sail. Learning can also be done in an exploratory stage, where a kayak, given its different scale, might provide a more navigable option.

There are several clear points that should be included in this narrative: RAYO promotes the exchange of different forms of knowledge, as well as new paradigms focused on the training of artists. These are open, flexible, and very broadly defined. The program will not have accreditations, diplomas, or degrees; it will try always to be free of cost. The program cannot be exclusive: if there are interested participants, they cannot be discredited for not having sufficient preparation or experience. This point is important, since there was a recurring discussion about what to do with young artists who are starting their careers or are enrolled in educational institutions in the region and interested in other forms of education. Within this situation, it is necessary to see how to address expectations related to paradigms of professionalization in the arts, which RAYO has not yet resolved to address. Another factor that has been taken into account is determining when to open the conversation to other cultural agents not coming from the visual arts, as well as to people with other backgrounds, whether from science or within other fields of knowledge and contexts, such as agriculture, fishing, and carpentry.

At the moment, RAYO is perceived as a generator of support structures, specific to contexts and moments. These, in turn, are expected to serve as catalysts for relationships and exchanges among artists. More than anything, the group expectations are that, in a kaleidoscopic way, the routes and meetings that promote working and learning together in and from the Caribbean can be multiplied. These exchanges will provide other opportunities for artists in the region to produce work together, ideally experimenting in forms of collectivity. In the long run, this could also develop a solid base for younger artists, providing them with other models for education, production, and experimentation in their art practices. RAYO is part of a common recent synergy of interest in the Caribbean, within the region itself and its diaspora. It is necessary to organize efforts like this when the ideal conditions align, especially in an area where the paradigm of fragmentation and disconnection has been the historical norm.

This essay was originally published in e-flux Education on June 30, 2023. https://www.e-flux.com/education/features/548164/unifying-agents-emancipation-and-art-education-in-the-caribbean.

From the Wobbly Scaffolding

lugar a dudas cofounders Oscar Muñoz and Sally Mizrachi in conversation with Karen Devia

Karen Devia To begin, I would like us to talk about the reasons that led you to create and to conceive lugar a dudas as a project.

Oscar Muñoz I thought that we could try out a project that would feature some aspects of what I had encountered in other places which I liked. The first of these was Ciudad Solar, active between 1971 and 1977, where I showed my work and was able to get a grip on how things worked. Later, Pedro Alcántara and I were involved with a group—Taller Prográfica—and there we did some work around print and graphics.

Another important moment came when I met Virginia Pérez-Ratton in the mid-1990s. Virginia was curator at the Museum of Contemporary Art and Design in Costa Rica, where I was invited to be part of a great exhibition called *Relaciones*, in 1996, and there we became friends. Years later, Virginia founded TEOR/éTica, and in 2003 she invited me to present a solo show curated by María Iovino. I became aware of the incredible value of that space.

In 2002, I encountered something similar at the legendary Galería de la Raza, a space for the Chicano and Mexican community that was actively devoted to resistance in San Francisco. That space was run by Carolina Ponce de León; their ways of working and their approach to relationships were more horizontal than you would find in more established institutions, where relationships between people are more hierarchical, complicated, and distant. I was interested in their way of doing things.

So I started to think about a space of this kind. I envisioned a space that would be simple and not too ambitious. At a certain point, things lined up, I invited a group of people, most of them women, to meet somewhat periodically and share ideas. There was Connie Gutiérrez, Elizabeth

Escobar, Carmenza Estrada, Judith Kuj, Andrea Valencia, and Sally, who at some point joined in with a lot of enthusiasm. Once we got together, we began to look for a location.

Sally Mizrachi The idea came as a response to the situation in the city at the time. In Cali during the 1990s things were pretty hopeless, the drug trade had an impact on institutions, and the museum [Museo la Tertulia] had shut down. I remember that we would go out with [photographer] Fernell Franco and Marta, his partner, and we would do nothing but gripe about the city, gripe about the museum—we were complaining all the time. Until one day, Oscar said: "That's enough. I have to do something." What Oscar wanted was to give back to the city everything that Cali had given him. In 2003, for the last time, the Salón Nacional had a prize, and Oscar won it. At that point he had already purchased the house together with his sister, so he used the prize money for renovations.

OM When we set out to look for a location, there was a neoclassical house that I really liked. It was completely in ruins, there was nothing left of it except for the façade, which was truly a treasure. That house was a metaphor for the city: the traces of a beautiful past on the outside but demolished on the inside. The group didn't like the idea, and I think they were right. It would probably have been too complicated; the place was a drug zone, a rough spot. One day Sally mentioned that she had seen a house in the Granada neighborhood and that it could be the right one for the project, and she was right. We already had some previous contacts with the person who owned it, and I was able to buy it in partnership with my sister, Stella. And so we began to meet here once a week to think about how to proceed. Sally had grown gradually more committed to the project. That gave us a very important push, because later Sally would become, without a doubt, the soul and driving force of the space. For a while Sally was preparing herself to oversee the development of the project, Connie was working as a manager, and Paula Agudelo was in charge of accounting; in the meantime, I focused on making whatever adjustments the house might need, and we aren't really done with that yet.

SM Before that, I worked in fashion design and I was running a restaurant. Then I heard [curator] Jaime Cerón explain the new forms of interaction between people that were being explored in the art context. It didn't all turn around the figure of the curator, so there were these other ways for audiences and artists to relate; you could have an exhibition where things were more about mutual understanding and horizontality. In Cali there was this one curator, Miguel González, the high priest running the museum [La Tertulia]; in Medellín there was Alberto Sierra; and in Bogotá, Eduardo Serrano. When I heard what Jaime Cerón had to say, I realized that you could work toward closer relationships with other people and with artists, and this made me take an interest in the project. We came to this house and, even as we first walked in, we felt an atmosphere that drew us in. Before, the house had been the site of the Martenot Academy, where many contemporary artists in Cali had studied when they were children.

In 2004, while we were at work on remodeling the house, two local art events, the Salón Regional del Pacífico and the Salón de Octubre, were getting underway.

Our proposal was to host a group of workshops on curating as a complement to the programming of these two events, and people started to get to know us. Then we began to collaborate with other organizations, and this is when lugar a dudas really broke into the scene. Oscar was always thinking collectively, looking for ways to bring in other voices and ways of seeing, so we got in touch with Michele Faguet, Jaime Iregui, Juan Fernando Herrán, Bernardo Ortiz, José Ignacio Roca, Carmen María Jaramillo, María Clara Bernal, Juan Pablo Velásquez, and María Clara Borrero, and we invited them to help us work out, without any expectation of reaching some kind of certainty, what kind of place lugar a dudas could be. Back then there weren't as many collectives as there are today, there was only Helena Producciones, which was very well known in the city and outside, because the Festival de Performance had become an international event. Collectives like Casa Tomada were getting started at Bellas Artes [the School of Fine Arts], and you could see that things were coming back to life in the city. Oscar thought that local institutions were very fragile, so our goal was to strengthen the local scene, and for this reason we didn't intend to work against these institutions, but rather to work alongside them and do things together.

KD When did you open to the public?

SM On April 9, 2005, and we had been holding meetings since 2003. From the start we meant to use a room for exhibitions, and where we now have the Living Room we originally housed Cedoc, the documentation center, with Oscar's books and a collection of *Arte en Colombia* magazines donated by Celia Birbragher. Artists then began to donate publications that they had, and in that way, we put together the Cedoc with a few shelves and a table in the middle. People would come over and we noticed that there was this desire to meet with others. That gave us a lot of encouragement.

OM When we opened to the public, we found people who were willing to come and volunteer their work, people who brought a lot of enthusiasm with them and who were very important to us, mostly friends, students, or graduates from Bellas Artes and the Instituto Popular de Cultura. One day I noticed that our traditional Monday meetings had grown quite large and, with that new group of collaborators, we set out to work on furnishings, we built tables, the film screen, and the shelves for the Cedoc. It was very exciting. We put together an amazing team with people like César García, María Eugenia Duque, Oscar Montoya, Luis Mosquera, Oscar Acosta, Jorge Sánchez, Juliana Guevara, Wilson Nieva, Natalia Cajiao, Paula Agudelo, Juan Pablo Velásquez, Lina Montoya, and many others.

SM That same year the Daros Foundation, which held a very large collection of Latin American art, organized an exhibition in Zurich called *Cantos Cuentos Colombianos*, featuring works by Oscar and other Colombian artists. When we traveled to the exhibition, I brought along a brochure explaining lugar a dudas, and the organizers decided to place it next to an urn, so that visitors could find out about the space and make donations. This was the first funding that we received, along with the money from the ticket sales, which Daros also donated to us. I showed them some photographs of the Cedoc and I told them: "This is the documentation center that we are putting together." The librarian at the Daros Foundation was touched to see those scanty shelves with publications, and she told me that we were free to take any books we wanted. They shipped them to us along with other materials and catalogues from all their exhibitions. This was a boost to the documentation center and one of our first exchanges with other organizations in the country and abroad.

KD Oscar, how did you distribute your time as an artist and as a person who was now in charge of a cultural project?

OM Back then I thought I had some leisure time—later I realized that laziness and leisure are crucial to our work—that I could use to work on something else. It wasn't easy. I had many things to learn. It was difficult for me because I had to make an effort to be social in a way that I have always avoided, but people were starting to come. I found that very exciting, and there was this sense that the city was going through a good moment. That year I worked exclusively on lugar a dudas and, little by little, I was able to adjust, to determine what tasks I should take on and what I was interested in accomplishing, which is for the space to be able to create its own dynamics and to flow. Obviously, I was able to accomplish this once we began to pay those people who were taking on new responsibilities.

KD I imagine that a lot of effort goes into looking for funding in order to keep lugar a dudas running under suitable conditions, and to allow it to grow and develop new projects. How has your approach to funding developed?

OM Daros gave us some money to get started, a one-time donation. Later, they referred us to Avina, a foundation for sustainable development which was backing many different causes in Colombia, such as journalistic research on paramilitary groups. They gave us some annual money for a while. Then came Hivos; they had given some funding to TEOR/éTica in Costa Rica, but they had no programs in Colombia. One day they told us that they would like to give us some support. With those funds we decided to bring in someone who could assist users at the Cedoc, so we were able to hire Mónica Restrepo on a fixed salary. Over time I have come to realize that those modest jobs that we have been able to offer people throughout the years have been very important, for lugar a dudas and for the artists who have worked here.

SM Since 2007 we have had the support of Arts Collaboratory. It is very important for us to be part of that network, and not just for financial reasons. We learn from one another. We know that funding is essential, since we are not a company producing commodities, we generate no capital, and, for this reason, we have to outline other strategies that may allow us to fund our projects. Nowadays the situation is difficult and foreign resources are scarce, so we are putting more of an effort to look for funding here in Colombia. Although it takes a lot of patience to work through the hurdles of bureaucracy, we have obtained funding for specific programs from the Ministry of Culture and the city's Office of Cultural Affairs.

There are also individuals in Cali who have believed in lugar a dudas and backed us from the start. In this regard, Mariana Garcés helped us fund our Production

Grants for Local Artists (known as BLOC, for its Spanish acronym); there is also a printing house, Feriva, who produced our programming booklets for many years; and María Clara Borrero, who did some management work for us. Many people have helped us or have wanted to do so, but I should take a moment to mention Mario Scarpetta, who believed in lugar a dudas and gave us his support for about ten years, with extraordinary generosity and without even asking us to credit his name in some way. Without his support we would not have been able to carry out many of our production programs for emerging artists.

KD Let's talk a little bit about the programs developed by lugar a dudas. One of these has been running from the start, namely the film program, right?

SM Yes, from the start we wanted to screen films. At first, Ramiro Arbeláez, a cinema buff and historian, was in charge of programming. Every Saturday we would screen films and, back then, I designed the fliers. Then we decided to hire a graphic designer. The screenings went really well; many people came. After Ramiro, Catalina Rayo and Luis Mosquera programmed the series, and then a collective from the Universidad del Valle, called Suburbia, made us a proposal and we decided to let them run it. We thought that it was important to let other people do things at lugar a dudas, people who might know more about a topic than us. In this way we also began to attract different kinds of audiences.

KD Another flagship program at lugar a dudas is the exhibition series installed on the Shop Window. Could you talk a little bit about how it was conceived and about your expectations?

OM In the early days we rented out that space to a store that sold local design products called Demodo, and it was open for about a year, and after that we decided to use it as an exhibition space that we call the Shop Window. We made that change because we thought that we could use an approach to exhibitions that would be more open to the public, and it would also allow us to expand the Cedoc by moving it into the room where we used to install the exhibitions. In this way, we were able to run a continuous program of exhibitions that directly engaged people passing by, on the street, and this was unusual here at the time.

SM Many artists told us that they would get invited to show their work somewhere and they would just get a wall, so the artists had to do everything by themselves. We wanted to change that, and to encourage institutions and exhibition spaces to conceive that relationship in different terms. You had to acknowledge the work of the artists, you had to pay them, and we think that we have been able to bring about some degree of change in this regard. Artists should know that if they are invited to show their work, they can expect a stipend for their work, for their production; in this way we have been able to get artists to be noticed. Although the institutions may not realize this, the artists who have shown their work here have gained awareness that these are things that they can and should demand.

KD In that sense, by creating the Production Grants for Local Artists you were also aiming to promote the professionalization of artists' labor and the demand for financial remuneration.

OM This has been a very special program, and this is why I fight so hard to keep it going.

It has so many valuable components, so it's disheartening for us to be forced to run it with resources that are insufficient in proportion to the number of artists who apply. The program opens many possibilities by allowing artists who are just getting started to develop a project, to try things out, to make mistakes; it's a grant that provides a studio space and a sum of money that allows artists to flesh out an idea, and to have a chance to discuss it with other people. Someone who receives a BLOC grant can show the results of their work at the Museo la Tertulia, our current partner institution for the program. This allows artists to explore how their work can be exhibited in a particular location, to discuss it with curators, and to be involved in the installation process and in all stages of the development of their own shows. What artists can learn through this process is as important as the exhibition itself.

In earlier versions, the project was developed in partnership with the Alliance Française, Proartes, the Centro Colombo Americano, Comfandi, La Tertulia, and La Sucursal. The Museo la Tertulia has remained as a partner until now, partly because the director, Ana Lucía Llano, and the curator, Alejandro Martín, are aware that BLOC is worth the effort; they have understood the program's impact and relevance.

SM When we created BLOC, we invited other institutions to contribute to the project because, at the time, there were no sources of funding for artists in Cali. At first, six institutions teamed up to offer these grants for artists, which included a production budget, an exhibition, a brochure, and advertising to help promote the artist's work. The grants from the city's Office of Cultural Affairs came after BLOC and, in part, as a result of our efforts; they were created three years ago, and for a blueprint they relied on a different proposal by lugar a dudas—and we had to do some pushing to convince them. The Office took up our idea again and put it to work.

OM BLOC has helped to redefine the ways local government interacts with other institutions and with artists. This is what BLOC has argued for from the very beginning: it's about relationships based on trust between those involved, but it is also open to other discussions that may arise. These relationships have improved gradually, but things are still quite difficult because it is hard to avoid misunderstandings and disagreements, which often stem from the fact that we don't have enough resources to fund more artists. Despite this, we are open to debate about the way the program works. The fact that there are some who go to the trouble of publishing texts—sometimes anonymously—voicing their objections to the program shows that they take an interest.

KD Talking about these efforts toward constructing a collective and the frictions they entail, how have your relationships been with other groups and spaces in the city during these years?

OM They have gone through different phases; lugar a dudas was one of the spaces hosting the Salón Nacional de Artistas in 2008. Not so much in terms of exhibition space, but rather in terms of logistics and labor. The organizational meetings were held here, and this is where the curatorial team was assembled. Most of the exhibitions were installed at the site of the school,

Sagrada Familia, Bellas Artes, the Museo la Tertulia, and other spaces around the city. Our contribution to the Salón left us with many good experiences, it had a strong impact on the art scene in Cali, and it allowed us to act on a wider scale than we were used to. Sometime later, we had the intention of working to consolidate a kind of coalition of projects that were run by local artists in the city. It was called La Colaborativa, but it was a short-lived experiment.

SM La Colaborativa was born in 2009, and the goal was to establish an association of spaces and projects, to share concerns and to enable processes that wouldn't be feasible if we worked separately. We achieved this up to a certain point, but we did not get very far, because the spaces didn't have the capacity or the interest to remain committed. Several collectives from the city were involved in the project, among them Casa Mata, La Plástica Rayada, Descarrilados, and La Cubeta Pentaprismática. The first assembly of Arts Collaboratory, in 2011, met here in Cali, after we pushed for it, because we wanted the members of this network to get a glimpse of the local scene. The people from Arts Collaboratory had a chance to hear about all the projects that were underway in the city, and they were amazed to see that there was so much going on.

KD What led to the idea of inviting a curator or artistic director to work at lugar a dudas?

SM For eight years we took on the task of organizing exhibitions that would allow emerging artists to make their work known, and we created open calls for artists from Colombia and from abroad, with the idea that there ought to be transparency in the way in which projects were selected. Each year we close our doors during the month of January, and we meet to go over the year that just ended—a self-evaluation of sorts—so we can gauge where we have failed and how we can improve. For several years we focused our activities on projects around three lines: exhibition, research, and residencies. We would come up with new projects through discussions with the team. So we thought that we could invite other people to make proposals and to develop their own projects here, as a way of making room for other voices.

OM We noticed that our outlook had become somewhat closed, and we thought that we should crack it open, that it would be good for us to seek out other points of view, because it would shake up this scaffolding we were on, the wobbly scaffolding that we had climbed on. This brought about some interesting situations.

SM This was our first approach to the figure of the curator, and for three years those who were interested in the position would apply with a project once we issued our open call. The first time, we chose Miguel López, who is currently at TEOR/éTica. Miguel outlined a project that he worked on for almost a year, and during that time lugar a dudas used this project as a point of departure for all of its activities.

OM Miguel López was involved with the network Conceptualismos del Sur, and with queer movements in Latin America, so he brought many people to give talks and new audiences. In conversation with him we came up with the idea of *Tertulias sobre el Museo* [Gatherings On the Museum], a series of talks and meditations on the phenomenon of Latin American museums, with a nod toward Museo la Tertulia, which we also brought into the discussion. Back then, the museum was going through a lot of problems, there were no clear guidelines, and there were issues with its programming and its way of engaging with the city. Nonetheless, people still felt affection for that museum, so what we did was to host a series of conversations which Miguel conceived and coordinated.

SM There were around nine talks at different locations, La Tertulia being one of them. Thus far we have only been able to make a publication based on one of the conversations, with Fernando Carrillo, who came from the Museo Reina Sofía [in Madrid]. Others who came were Pablo León de la Barra, Gabriela Rangel from the Americas Society, Osvaldo Sánchez from the Museo Rufino Tamayo, Marcelo Expósito, Pamela Desjardins, Víctor Manuel Rodríguez, and Paola Santoscoy, and they all had a lot to say about what museums are going through.

OM After Miguel, we chose Gris García. Her work drew a lot from the idea that curatorial practices could be understood as processes that go beyond exhibitions. Through a diverse range of projects and events, Gris wanted to work around the concept of the host, and she invited artists like Carolina Bonfim, Javier Peñafiel, and La Fulminante to contribute to a set of core themes by staging talks, workshops, and performances. Gris was here for four months at first, and then she was able to get some funding from the ITM, an art school in Medellín, so she came back to organize an exhibition with people who had never shown their work at lugar a dudas.

Marilia Loureiro was the last of our guest curators. Her system was to extend an open invitation to someone who would then in turn invite a second person, who would invite a third person, and so on. Her way of doing things grew out of the principle of creating a growing network of individuals and interests through indeterminacy. She also organized *dérives* and walks around the city in conversation with other people.

Her programming was continuous, and it was nourished by the fact that she had arrived with no previous knowledge, which allowed her to approach people from the city so that they could keep the project going on their own. She was not too interested in exhibition processes, although I think she did organize a few. Her work argued, above all, for a dynamic of play and discovery.

The presence of these curators allowed us to understand that there were these other kinds of interaction that we hadn't thought about before. Overall, we were able to get involved in a conversation that gave us a glimpse of these new perspectives that we were not aware of, and this helped us to introduce some changes in our way of doing things.

SM Three years ago we realized that it was important to invite a curator with whom we could work on projects together, from a position that would be proper to lugar a dudas, based on attentiveness to the context and an understanding of the art scene; somebody who would create the activities alongside us rather than a curatorial project disengaged from our daily experiences. We wanted it to be someone from Colombia, although not necessarily from Cali, so we invited Víctor Albarracín. We had other candidates in mind, but we chose Víctor because he was a person who did not follow conventional rules and who could bring something else to lugar a dudas.

We were also reflecting on what had happened when Marilia and Gris were here, since they brought these beautiful projects to Cali and worked with the local scene and with people from abroad, asking other artists to join in, and this made us realize that it was time for us to get rid of this inflexible and schematic way of making a decisions by way of open calls, and that we should focus instead on engaging in direct conversation with artists, to discuss face-to-face projects that they would bring to us and those that our team wanted to try out.

KD In terms of the axes of lugar a dudas, there is one worth highlighting and that is the concept of "an education without a school," which led the way to projects like (uncertain school).

OM Already when Miguel López was here we were working on this idea of an education without a school, it was a thread running through everything we did at lugar a dudas, although not too consciously, but rather as something that was always there, implicitly. Our replica project, for example, was pedagogical in nature, because we invited students from the art schools to make a piece that would be a copy of the work of an artist who was in some collection and who had never come to Cali, and to exhibit that piece in the Shop Window, so that people would envision an imaginary museum. Later, during one of our meetings, we recalled conversations we had with several artists who would tell us that, when they were students, they had tons and tons of photocopies, because books are so expensive here, or because they had only used a particular chapter, or because there were no copies of the book available at the university, or maybe only the professor's, so they had to make photocopies and many of them ended up with boxes and boxes of photocopies. This is how we came up with the idea of the Photocopy Library, where we would invite others to suggest a text that they would like to read and which they thought would be relevant, and then to share it as a photocopy, understood as a point of departure for the circulation of knowledge. For me, this was a form of education without a school, which also surfaced in many other projects.

SM One day, Víctor told us that it was time for lugar a dudas to have a project that would be more straightforwardly pedagogical. A year later, we launched the first installment of (uncertain school), which took place in 2017, with support from the Ministry of Culture, Jumex, and the city's Office of Cultural Affairs. The school is now heading toward its third installment, and so far we have welcomed a broad gathering of tutors and students, some from Cali and quite a few from elsewhere in the world, all of whom come together for six weeks to engage in productive thinking around a particular issue, and to share a moment of life in this city where we also have so much to do in the streets, a lot of partying and a lot of chaos.

KD As for the people who make up a regular audience at lugar a dudas, I guess it is difficult to maintain the same degree of interest through the years, to keep going and to bear in mind that the audience and the context of the city itself are always in flux. How have you dealt with the complexity of these processes?

SM I would say the house has changed, or at least its spaces, when we have adjusted to make them adequate to the projects that we are working on. The house was a traditional residential space, typical of this neighborhood, with columns and fences; we used to leave the fence open, and we noticed that people wouldn't come inside because it was a house. The Shop Window had an audience, since it was intended to get people to come by and to engage with an art practice without having to leave public space, but those people wouldn't come inside. We started to post a billboard with our programming on the outside wall, so that passersby could find out about what was happening during the month, and we put up a sign that said, "This space is for you." These were things that we would come up with as we came to get a sense of how we could relate to the public.

OM This question about how to deal with a public or with an audience has been a struggle from the start, but things have changed. When we fixed up the house to open it to the public, what I had in mind was to bring it back to the way it looked originally in old photographs. I wanted it to have that kind of spirit.

Our first exhibition after we opened was called *L.A. Freewaves*. It was a group show with works on video by Latin American artists from Los Angeles. We had screens and headphones, but very few people showed up. We realized that we had to break with this kind of exhibition as we moved forward, so that people might feel that this was a space that they could occupy, that they could sit anywhere and nobody would charge them for it or ask them what they were doing there.

We had to shatter the division between the public and the private, which takes a lot of work because there are people who would like to keep them strictly separated. So, this is when we decided to work with the topology of the sidewalk, as though saying that we were turning that space over to the public. When the space is open, anyone who feels like it can sit there, on a spot that could be a private yard but that is now open to all. I think that when we did this there was a change.

SM As I said earlier, there are still some people who are reticent about us, who see us as a place that only a group can have access to, and once they get here, they realize that it's not like that. But even so this prejudice lingers on—it's hard to change that, because of the way people relate to each other in the art world and because of preconceived notions. Some people just see us as a closed group. Even when we used to have open calls, people thought that lugar a dudas would only select people who we were friends with.

OM Here we have a small local scene of people who are interested in art, and they know lugar a dudas. Within this community you have a smaller group of people who might be interested in what we do. Now, a person who comes from elsewhere, or who studies efforts to bring people closer to art, she might think that there is something interesting about this place; I mean somebody working on a research project or who works for an institution that is looking at how to create spaces in countries where there is no state support, where institutions are weak, she may find here a rich source of hypotheses. Some people might be interested in us because this is a space that has a certain history of resistance within a particular context, and that has faced some adversity. In a city like Cali, where we have no gallery system to speak of, no collectors and a very small amount of artistic activity, it's not easy to knit a social relation around art, because art doesn't have a presence here.

SM Our audience is not huge; we are aware of that. We are part of a few networks and we have seen how things are for other spaces here in Colombia and abroad, so we know that this is an issue for all of us. Those spaces do not draw a lot of people; instead, they reach a few people who are interested in particular things and are eager to see something different. Of course, we would love it if people from many different backgrounds would come, and we have accomplished this, for instance in 2017, with the collective Ensortijadas, a group of Afro-Colombian women who have been using the house to meet and organize public events. It is important for us to get other people to come, not just artists, but people or groups who are doing things in the city, who worry about issues in the city and who are dealing with these issues somehow. Sadud a Ragul, the coffee shop, was also conceived with this aim of getting other people to come by; it started as a very small food stall and gradually it's beginning to attract more people. Many people come to eat there but they never come into the house. Others take their time to discover that there is something else going on here and, when that happens, their perception changes.

OM In the early days, we felt that our task was to strengthen the local scene, to give it materials to work with and to collect our strengths. Things were all very fragile and scattered back then. I think there is a particular generation of people who made this possible and who enjoyed that moment. Nowadays, the city has changed quite a bit. Collectives like El Camión, Casa Tomada, Casa Mata, Espacio Temporal, Cabaret Machine, and many others have disappeared or changed over the years.

KD Do people see lugar a dudas as an independent space or as an institution?

OM From its inception, lugar a dudas has been relatively independent and relatively dependent. On the one hand, we can say that lugar a dudas is a dependent space, because it requires financial support. The space cannot generate the money that it needs to survive and calls on others to contribute. What we do is to take that money and turn it into activities for people. On the other hand, it is independent, to the extent that, from the start, we have been charting the situation and deciding which path to follow.

For us, it is important to be open daily, since institutions in Cali haven't typically been run with a clear sense of procedure for responding to the needs of users. We want to be open to the public from 3 to 8 p.m. In that sense, we function as an institution. We want the service we provide to be good, warm, and close; we want to work through horizontal relationships, unlike other institutions that look from above and interact with people through coldness, distance, and hierarchy. We aim to work in a different way, not only with the public understood as something abstract, but concretely, with our community of artists in Cali.

The work that Víctor is doing is something that you will not find in any other institution. What (uncertain school) is trying to do is not something that you can get just anywhere. In the screenings you will find a program that cannot be found anywhere else in the city. Because we have this way of playing with the marginal and, and at the same time, we have a respect for film as a discipline. To dig around, to probe, to see what's underneath, this is all part of the spirit of lugar a dudas.

KD After that balance, could you tell us how you perceive lugar a dudas in the present and how you envision its future?

SM I think that right now what is happening with (uncertain school) is very important, and this is a project that lugar a dudas is betting on. We see this is a project that, as we conceive it, or as Víctor conceives it, diverges from the way in which thought is produced in academia, and that would like to help prepare people to work in the cultural context with resources that are different from those offered by academia.

OM Our image of lugar a dudas in the future is still that of a space that is open to trying things out, open to suggestions coming from outside. We believe in mistakes; we haven't made enough mistakes yet.

SM We are always thinking ourselves over, redefining ourselves, and if we get to a point when we don't find any meaning in what we are doing, when we feel that we have completed a cycle, then we are not afraid to consider that cycle as closed. I think we have been an important landmark locally, in Colombia and in Latin America, a sign of what an art space can be, of a way of doing things; for that reason I think that, if it came to that, other people could take up the project and develop new ideas using what we have done, and what others have done, as an inspiration. We have raised certain questions that we may keep working on; the point for us is not simply to survive, but to do something that is meaningful within the art context, which is what we have been doing. If at some point this meaning should fade out, then we might say: "this is as far as we go."

This text was originally published in Palmeras en la Tormenta: una historia de lugar a dudas *(lugar a dudas, 2018), ed. Víctor Albarracín Llanos.*

Don't Teach, Learn: The Educational Experiments at EspIRA

Patricia Belli interviewed by Miguel A. López

Miguel A. López In Nicaragua, the ways of producing art have drastically transformed during the last twenty years. We have witnessed a critique of systems of representation that breaks down the hegemony of traditional disciplines of painting and sculpture. This process has encountered resistance. Crucial to the successful diversification of artistic languages has been a new generation of young artists educated in programs that are alternative to those offered by the Escuela Nacional de Artes Plásticas [National School of Fine Arts]. You have been the driving force behind such programs and educational experiments, which have had a significant impact throughout Central America. I would like to discuss the effects of a critical education in art. In 2001, you launched the first installment of TAJo (Taller de Arte Joven) [Workshop of Young Art], a program that takes place in your house. How did this program come about?

Patricia Belli TAJo emerged out of the realization that a new generation of artists would not come about spontaneously. We needed an alternative educational structure. In fact, I understood this two years earlier, when, in July 1999, the second Bienal de Pintura Nicaraguense turned into a battlefield between contemporary artists and traditional painters. That year, my work *Vuelo difícil* (1999) received the first prize from the Bienal. This work was a montage of a dress on which tiny picture frames with images were hanging; it utilized techniques like painting, sculpture, and photography without fully embodying any of those disciplines. The fact that a nontraditional work of art won caused indignation among an important segment of local traditional artists and provoked an attack on those of us who were trying to elaborate art from other perspectives. For them, the contemporary art we were trying to make was a scam.[1]

Despite everything, the most revealing aspect of this debate was that the conservative side was being led by the Escuela Nacional de Artes Plásticas and its seventeen- and eighteen-year-old students. It was a testament to the disastrous state of artistic education in the country and became the main reason behind the creation of alternative teaching platforms. That's how I opened TAJo in 2001 with the intention of creating the conditions to discuss works of art by local artists, questioning collectively their reach and effectiveness. We delved into this process based on the premise that art produces meanings that enrich the audience's experience. We revised and interrogated the sensations and meanings generated by works—their proposed senses and the formal solutions that they constructed—while discussing the synergy between them.

MAL TAJo's existence paved the way for the creation of EspIRA (Espacio para la Investigación y Reflexión Artística) [Space for Research and Artistic Reflection] in 2004, which has been your longest, most active, and possibly most recognized educational project—at least among those outside of Nicaragua. I think in that moment, it was clear enough to you how important it was to fill the void of artistic formation in Nicaragua. How was the journey from TAJo to EspIRA?

PB While TAJo was a group of people congregating to talk about art, EspIRA was developed as an association of artists and cultural managers—a legally constituted organization that provided a judicial shield for the work we wanted to do. In their essences, the broad objectives of TAJo and EspIRA are the same: to generate formative and educational spaces from which a position that is both critical toward reality and committed to the present can emerge. The only difference was that the legal status of EspIRA facilitated fundraising, which, in the long run, allowed us to elaborate and broaden the scope of the workshops. We brought in professors from other countries and offered educational activities from theoretical, practical, and even art historical approaches. On a methodological level, there was a big change insofar as the TAJo critical workshops were provided solely by me, within my house, and free of cost. On the other hand, EspIRA's funding and varied artist roster allowed the activities to acquire a diverse quality rich in perspective and educational dynamics.

MAL What were the specific formative aspects with which you wanted to radically differentiate yourself from the education imparted by the traditional School of Fine Arts?

PB An important aspect to point out is that the learning provided at the traditional art school in Nicaragua is technical. That has begun to change this year [2016], with a graduate from EspIRA being named the director of the School of Fine Arts. But not long ago, the school taught painting techniques and very limited art history classes. The iconography present in the school had Surrealist, Cubist, Romantic, and Neoclassical influences, but with very little information and no reflection on why these influences happen. Not to mention the lack of information on contemporary forms of creation.

1 The jury members for this edition of the II Bienal were Celia Sredni de Birbragher (Colombia), Jane Cazalla (Spain), and Vivian Pfeiffer (Argentina). The newspaper articles and opinions about this controversy were distributed as an appendix to the catalogue of the event. See *II Bienal de Pintura Nicaragüense* (Fundación Ortiz Gurdian, 1999).

In response, EspIRA established a model well-recognized in the contemporary art world, though unusual at a local level: it sought learning processes that allow for artistic production to take as its starting point personal experience, which allows it to be aware of its location, the context it operates in, and the elements it interacts with. We also wanted to avoid having these creative forms respond to traditional disciplines, and preferred having them build their own languages, freely articulating and communicating forms, ideas, and emotions.

The simple strategy used back then was dialogue, which continues to be the prevailing practice today. We are interested in discussing how meaning is generated in public terms and why we make art. That is what we do with the works of the participants: we analyze all those mechanisms through which meaning comes out of form, including biological sensations, perceptions, and the historic and cultural associations of images and materials. We also question the established taste, the aesthetic genealogy, the ways desire and aversion are produced and ask ourselves about the ideologies underlying these concepts.

In EspIRA we don't teach techniques or disciplines; we actually don't teach anything, as our system is based on learning, not teaching.[2] With regard to the art disciplines, we also don't promote their learning, because they're prescriptive. More precisely, we encourage their unlearning. When an EspIRA student has experienced more technical learning beforehand—whether painting, audiovisual, or theater—he or she will need to frequently experiment with that same language to dismantle and re-accommodate it to a more sincere mode of expression.

2 The idea of "not teaching but learning" comes from Mexican artist Francisco Quesada, who came to Managua to teach a workshop with that name in 2006.

This is a difficult task, as education in traditional schools is purely technical and usually lacks critical thought. It becomes a corset that limits and disciplines you. Many times, we end up unconsciously reproducing those same restrictions. We constantly face this situation and therefore emphasize that students need to transgress certain established forms: they need character and position-taking to contribute to their work. These tools can't be used arbitrarily or autonomously, as their gesture is part of a collective meaning. We view this critical conjunction of analysis and deconstruction as part of a synergetic exercise.

We do this to stimulate honest and non-derivative production. From this same perspective, we don't drive students to politically correct paradigms because it would be like promoting another technique or formula. Instead, we push them toward the ethical positions encountered by questioning one's surroundings and through the intertwining of personal experience with theoretical discussion. Sometimes these crossing points converge into familiar paradigms that are nonetheless personal, conscious, and situated.

Education as a Transformative Practice

MAL I would like for us to talk more about the dynamics of EspIRA. What are its working methods and how is time employed? Did you have some sort of goals embedded in your educational work?

PB Depending on the workshop and the instructor, a work session lasts around three to four hours. It can include a theoretical text, a formal analysis, a historical period or practice. The exercises challenge the participants' creativity and force them to explore their own interests. We manage to give profound reviews face-to-face because we strive to create an intimate space where everyone has a right and commitment to frankness and attention. These dynamics are common in all the workshops at EspIRA, whether theoretical, practical, or critical.

The activities we call "critique workshops" are the spine of young artists' work. It's a way of learning by doing, either about art, human relations, affects, perceptions, ideas, or otherness. We began to formulate our version of how to implement a critique workshop with TAJo in 2001, under the conviction that it was necessary to provide an atmosphere of "horizontality." One basic principle is that in a critique workshop there are no observers: all who talk show their work, and all who show their work talk. The best moment in this process is when participants who have been interacting for several months are capable of expressing their opinions without fear while having developed stronger argumentative abilities. That is the moment of harvest.

Similarly, the objectives embodied in our pedagogical work have also emerged through our journey. More generally, we perceive of education as an opportunity: an opportunity to provide spaces for elucidation and debate; to encourage the learning of a subversive trade; to rethink established cultural codes, including those associated with artistic creation; to cultivate emancipation through the investigation of the prejudices we construct and are seduced by; to invite reflection, aesthetic joy, and individual and collective transformation; to search for the autonomy of thought and equality in gender, class, and all other types of social domination; and to inculcate sensibility and discernment so as to achieve skillfulness as artists and interpretative capacity as a public. All of these patterns are not words or personal ideas, but the result of a collective effort realized by Darwin Andino, Ricardo Huezo, María Félix Morales, and me, locking ourselves up for a week in 2010 to create the master plan for the organization.

MAL EspIRA shares the desire to see in art education the possibility of building not only artists but critical citizens. In other words, citizens who confront everyday conflicts through creativity and commitment. Clearly, nothing guarantees that an emancipatory education occurs or that education itself promotes critical stances. In many cases, authoritarian models of knowledge are implemented under these same premises. However, we cannot renounce the promise of education as a transformative practice. I would like to ask you about primary education: what is the role of art education in that process?

PB I am not familiar with the ministerial programs of arts education in elementary school, but I have witnessed art classes in schools and talked to some teachers. In Nicaragua, art teachers in public schools are also teachers of other subjects; if they are capable of drawing, they'll teach art classes. Evidently, this causes them to lack a proper methodology, a comprehension of the social benefits of fine arts, or any critical component of creative work. To make matters worse, no one takes art classes seriously—not the ministry, schools, or even teachers—causing them to become a sad representation of what could otherwise be a great opportunity to develop creative people. Arts education thus remains more of a fiction than a reality.

In fact, at EspIRA we launched a project called "Jóvenes creativos" [Creative Teens], which caters to kids and teens with artistic and graphic skills through workshops focused on improving their perception and creativity. We hope that in the future, when facing the possibility of pursuing the arts, they can make an informed decision. In "Jóvenes creativos" we work primarily with our own bodies, and the perception of the other. It is a program that assumes the challenges of working with participants from different socioeconomic classes. It addresses this mix through exercises (sometimes theater or play therapy) to learn how to look and know ourselves: to look at people and not just their genotype, clothes, or gender. We contribute, even a little, to their encounter with happiness in empathy for others.

MAL Do you think art education in Nicaragua has changed in recent years, when EspIRA has been so active? Has the work you have done generated critical tensions to the point of forcing traditional academic education to rethink its modes of function?

PB As I mentioned before, arts education, or the School of Fine Arts, has changed in the past few years. This is also due to the Bienal de Arte de Nicaragua, an exhibition project with the most resources, exposure, and recognition in the country. It has presented contemporary art for the past fifteen years. We, who are small but stubborn, have had a growing presence in the artistic scene, especially in the Bienal. We have encouraged others to think of education in different terms. This has turned the tables, making students more curious and less averse to contemporary modes of expression. It is also interesting that the Institute of Culture has begun to organize competitions and exhibits that encourage the use of nontraditional materials, for example, an exhibit of works done with tires. But generally, those pieces serve only as decoration and not as a starting point for complex debates. Clearly, a move toward an unconventional object or mode does not systematically contribute to enriching the critical field. However, indirectly, it accomplishes something as students feel more confident in exploring what is happening in the art world. They are no longer intimidated by contemporary art.

MAL Just a moment ago, you mentioned how important it was for you that educational processes emerge out of a revision of personal experience. This reminds me of the premises of feminist artistic education, not only because the personal is positioned as a place where political meanings are generated for creative work, but also because the type of interaction you propose destabilizes the traditional authority of the master in favor of more fundamental horizontal exchanges. It reminds me of what the US feminist artist Judy Chicago calls the "circle methodology." In other words, an educational dynamic in which the master is the facilitator within a structure where everyone participates and shares experiences.[3] There is even a healing dimension in these dynamics, allowing one to confront problems that cannot be addressed alone. I shed light on this topic of feminist education because the art field is still dominated by masculine perspectives. I would like to ask you how you think gender and sexuality play a role in your pedagogical work. Is it possible to fight against the patriarchal and heteronormative structure—which surrounds the sphere of culture—from your own educational dynamics?

3 See Judy Chicago, *Institutional Time: A Critique of Studio Art Education* (The Monacelli Press, 2014).

PB EspIRA's education is without a doubt feminist, especially in its interactive methodology and focus on healing and emancipation. We are using both sensitive and rational tools and are motivated to overcome historical and personal traumas. Correspondingly, we support artistic processes which generate pieces that are potentially transformative for the audience. There are a variety of dimensions that may be challenged: the low self-esteem generated by the history of colonization, cultural abduction, pressure to fit into emotional molds based on Catholicism (e.g., guilt, drama, sacrifice), the abnegation of the feminine, the absence of histories based on personal narratives, the casualties of war, earthquakes, and so on. The artists cover these traumas from their own positions and in tones ranging from pain without cynicism to crass satire. And the political aspect of trauma is addressed throughout the process: an earthquake is a natural phenomenon but how natural is the way its victims die? Who authorized the location of the construction or the density of the cinder block that killed them?

The circle method of Judy Chicago has important similarities to our workshops. These include the circle we form to look at each other, the honest reflection that comes out of trust, enabling encounters between different people, the search for diverse perspectives, and an emphasis on meaning. These are some strategies we use to subvert self-imposed patriarchal structures in interpersonal relationships and works of art. We constantly examine personal experience, identifying it as such to articulate our perspectives and provide feedback on processes by drawing attention to the obscure and overlooked, and enjoying ourselves in our humanness, humor, and perversions.

Linking One Thing to the Other

MAL I would like to ask you about the distinct formative programs that were created inside EspIRA, like RAPACES (Residencia Académica Para Artistas Centroamericanos Emergentes) [Academic Residencies for Emerging Central American artists] since 2007, or TACON (Talleres de Arte Contemporáneo) [Contemporary Art Workshops] since 2010. The program RAPACES, for example, is an educational residence for Central American artists. In conversations I've had over the past year with regional artists younger than thirty-five, the program always popped up. This program you created was fundamental to the growth of their artistic processes and it also promoted considerable mobility for artists, creating new networks of exchange, production, and affect that endure to this date. How were the academic residencies organized?

PB It was both intense and beautiful, as is everything EspIRA does. The Academic Residencies for Emerging Central American artists began in 2007. Initially, there were many artists: we had a month's worth of work and more than twenty artists. This became emotionally draining and thus lent itself to an atmosphere of partying that competed with our objective of retreat and reflection. That's why we transformed the parameters in each new edition, reducing the number of selected people to favor the more intimate dimension we had in mind. The selection process became more rigorous to guarantee the participants' dedication. Our latest residency happened last year [2015]: it lasted only nine days and gathered eight participants. Back then I thought we had found the right measure.

Another interesting aspect was the frequency of participation. Suddenly, it became important to follow up with the participants over time, allowing them to return for multiple residencies. Hence, some artists came back for three years in a row, and it was excellent; we could see their growth and it allowed for a high level of debate in each edition. Clearly, the artists who came two or three years in a row led the dynamics of the workshops and the rhythm of discussion. In that sense, the participants of RAPACES inherited an eye for self-criticality, developed important advances in their research, and built new networks born of cohabitation.

MAL As part of RAPACES and TACON, you also created the television program *La Casa Estrella* [The Star House], which used mass media to disseminate information and educate audiences about contemporary art. What was the process behind the development of this television program? What themes did it explore, and what effects did it have?

PB *La Casa Estrella* was a thirty-minute television program, produced between 2009 and 2010 (and broadcast in Nicaragua during 2010 and 2011), that tried to introduce the public to contemporary art. It had two main plot lines: interviews with contemporary artists and reports on creativity and popular aesthetics. In each program, we created introductions that linked one aspect with another: contemporary thought with popular creative expressions that aren't necessarily fine arts or academic. We tried to emphasize the connections with spaces or dimensions that were well-known and recognizable by the broader public. We wanted to expand the scaffolding of contemporary art to a bigger public, which allowed us not to feel as if we were only speaking to ourselves. However, such extensive effects were not achieved. Instead, we ended up exponentially learning about what we were investigating. But once again, this experience remains with us.

MAL What roles do notions of collectiveness and self-organization play in EspIRA's work? Do you think these are pertinent concepts for thinking about education in this moment of global crisis—a crisis where knowledge is being privatized and the competitive logic of the markets is dictating professional artistic models?

PB Now that we are revising EspIRA's work methodology from a distance, we realize that concepts like collectiveness, self-organization, experimentation (linked to organizational autonomy), and horizontality (tied to collectiveness) have been crucial. But it wasn't a previously established plan; it just happened. On the other hand, we don't preach against the market. Instead, we stimulate a deeper investigation into alternative interests seen in works of art, revise the models signaled by these works, question how we perceive them, unearth ulterior motives, and, because of this, paradigms start to crumble. General complacency, the mercantile model, the NGO model, the model of contemporary aesthetics, these things all crumble while other models replace them.

The education we promote is headed toward the production of risky and well-considered works. But, above all, it orients the sensibility of artists and educates us all for the life and the world we live in. This leads us to promote the search for a common good. Undoubtedly, these considerations are a motive for debate and reflection: not only within arts education but also within symbolic production in general.

Maternity, Learning, and Artistic Practice

MAL Coming back to a personal dimension, I'm interested in knowing how your work as an educator has replaced the time you once dedicated to your artistic work. This might seem to be a minor question. But before putting forward a false comparison between the two worlds, I'm interested in convoluting them. I believe the pedagogical work you've done has required a generous donation of your time and energy, and that might have had an effect on your artistic production. How do you evaluate this process?

PB Though my work as an educator has never sacrificed my time with art, my work as an arts administrator has. I must emphasize this difference. Since EspIRA encompasses both types of labors, the distinction might be obfuscated. For example, critical workshops take six hours a week, while managerial work consumes whatever time is left, leaving my artistic practice very sporadic. In this sense, my position as an arts administrator had a tremendous impact on my work, life, and person: it was erosive due to the time required and its incompatibility with my contemplative character.

On the other hand, the critical workshops have helped my emotional health and my work. They helped me grow exponentially and offer me a space for dialogue based on empathy, sincerity, and critical thinking. The diverse and sincere gazes of the others enrich my analytical capability. I learn to better perceive emotional, social, and artistic phenomena and to identify cognitive vices. That is the starting point of my process: I mentally converse with different points of view that incorporate themselves through listening.

A lot of people have participated in the workshops. Unlike the critical seminars I participated in as a college student—which served as the origin of my pedagogical proposal—the workshops at EspIRA host diverse people, some of whom are not even artists. Methodologically, this is very enriching since every participant has to make an effort to use a common language that hasn't been learned a priori. We generate this language on the road, testing it as we go.

The workshops require me to be more precise in my ideas and in the definitions I state: I have to better articulate my opinion regarding art, the whys and hows of a work, and the function of the audience. It forces me not to take any criteria for granted, insofar as inquiry breaches all clichés. Shaping my practice as an art educator makes me understand my process as an artist. This allows me to substitute the time I dedicated to countless intuitive experimentations for more conscious processes that require less time for execution. I think you can see how my work now is more rational. This is good; it alienates me from sentimental self-indulgence and moves me toward a more critical rigor. But sometimes, I overdo it. The method has instilled itself in such a way that my new challenge is to get back in the game. Now I have more free time, and my comfort zone is no longer the workshop but words, which I need to work on.

MAL My previous question also had to do with pointing out how working as an educator is a form of caregiving. It makes me consider how, inside the patriarchal social structure we live in, there exists a logic of systematic invisibilization of care work. This work—reproductive, domestic, but also educational—has been historically assumed by women. For example, it is telling that the cumulative dynamics of capitalism are based on the negation of maternity work and the social organization of care. "If there is no reproduction, there is no production," the Italian feminist Silvia Federici reminds us. I believe there is an imbalance in the time and energy required by caregiving, and that this imbalance (which also affects the economic remuneration) allows male artists to reach fame and exposure more quickly. How do you view this process?

PB Care is what the world is missing: care for others, for the planet, and foremost for ourselves. Although individualism should mean a profuse amount of self-love, this "love" is co-opted and only responds to external ideas. I am not just talking about the common image and aesthetics of mass media, but also of more profound values which are essentially kidnapped by power. We no longer know who or what we are outside of this system. I have a hard time discerning what I truly need; whether my desires and fears are learned or not, figuring out what is expected of me. Hence, self-care and caring about others; however, we want to understand these, start with a search for who we truly are, what we need, and how we can redefine the pursuit of happiness.

Care is fundamental, and because of that, it should be reserved for people who have a vocation and training for it. It's incomprehensible how this task has been reserved for women, adhering to it as a role of gender and underestimating its value and cost. It becomes a double-edge sword: it brings an opportunity for service and care while isolating you from power, taking over your time, and relegating your personal aspirations.

For better or worse, women have been in charge of "caring." I say for worse as it has frequently meant the reproduction of desires and fears, both unnecessary and counterproductive. This task is not accompanied by a manual of reflection or questioning about its own labor of caring. That poor division of labor has cost a world of pain to humanity. We could have had a different world had we decided to build it together.

I decided to care for the formation of emerging artists. Both educational activities and fund management are actions designated for the care of artists. While I have a vocation and the tools for education, I do not have the tools for management. I was forced into this situation and opted to go forward with it; it does not mean I was capable, or I knew what to do. Errors were made in the process, but at least decisions were made. Just as it was a personal decision to have a baby, which, despite being modeled after stereotypes of maternity, was neither an imposition nor an accident.

Certainly, in recent decades there have been male artists more renowned than me. Yet, they didn't gain the experience or knowledge I did. Combined with a propensity for learning, both my conscious decisions—maternal and educational—allowed me to learn a lot; I grew with these experiences, which multiplied and are amplified in me. I think this is an exceptional case that became fundamental in my life: experience crossed paths with reflection, experimentation, questioning, empathy, and love. Not everyone is that lucky.

MAL How do you relate your maternal experience with the educational labor you've done in recent years? What has maternity taught you about the formative labor and learning process?

PB Being a mother is infinitely more complex than being an educator. In that regard, through education, I learned lessons that helped develop the delicate task of maternity. My work with young artists has meant working very closely with them. They belong to generations that I wouldn't know anything about otherwise, or at least not as well. This knowledge has given me a closer view of my son's generation. I can situate him and his experience in a better-understood context.

What you previously said is true: having a son, facing his circumstances, trying to meet him halfway, exploring coincidences to go through them—this has all been a learning experience which extends itself to others, and modifies my capacity for negotiation and empathy.

I would like to recall an image from a poem by Khalil Gibran about how parents need to be like bows that shoot forth their children as arrows. My apologies for the metaphor, but it illustrates precisely a lesson that is difficult to grasp. Neither your children nor your art students are yours; "they belong to life, longing for itself," and we are just instruments for them to achieve their goals. As a mother of both my son and art students, I can tell you it's not easy to see them grow into something different than what I wanted. Ultimately, the reward is not to turn them into mini-mes but instead for them to find their own truths, yearned-for happiness, and to take care of themselves and others.

Originally published in Miguel A. López, ed., Patricia Belli: Equilibrio y colapso *(Balance and Collapse) (TEOR/éTica and Fundación Ortiz Gurdián, 2018), 196–203.*

This interview was conducted in 2016; translation by Thomas Patier.

The Post-Living Ante-Action Theater Manual: The Audience Is Always Right

My Barbarian

The following texts and images about My Barbarian's Post-Living Ante-Action Theater (PoLAAT) were originally published in a 2015 issue of Pastelegram, *edited by Ariel Evans and Allison Myers.*

PoLAAT was a series of workshops and performances that My Barbarian (Malik Gaines, Jade Gordon, and Alexandro [Xandro] Segade) conducted at the New Museum in New York City (2008); the Townhouse Gallery and Rawabet Theater in Cairo (2008); the Institute of Contemporary Art at the University of Pennsylvania (2012); El Matadero and ARCO in Madrid (2010); Yaffa 23 in Jerusalem (2013); and Creative Time in New York City (2011). They drew on historical models of theater being used as a social and political tool such as Augusto Boal's Theater of the Oppressed, Rainer Werner Fassbinder's *antiteater,* and Julian Beck and Judith Malina's Living Theatre.[1]

As a part of this *Pastelegram* issue, My Barbarian conducted a series of conversations with curators that they had worked with on PoLAAT. In Alex Klein's conversation with My Barbarian about their 2012 project at the ICA Philadelphia, Gaines notes that public programs, education, and performance have come to have the same value as curatorial projects, something they also experienced with Eungie Joo at the New Museum. Segade adds that those programming models lend themselves to a blurring between performers and audience and between museum and performance spaces.

Leah Abir, who was a curator at Yaffa 23, Bezalel Art Academy's exhibition space in Jerusalem, first invited My Barbarian in 2009; they finally arrived in 2013. Abir notes that the Arab Spring occurred in between

1 Judith Malina and Julian Beck founded The Living Theatre in New York City in 1947. Rainer Werner Fassbinder founded the theater company Anti-Theater in the late 1960s.

those dates, and the Boycott, Disinvestment, and Sanctions (BDS) campaign had grown in influence. She had originally invited them to create a "conceptual or actual relation" to the 2008 Cairo iteration of PoLAAT. But, in keeping with the BDS principle of resisting normalization and avoiding the cliché of multiculturalism or coexistence, they reduced the idea of connecting the Jerusalem iteration with the one in Cairo. She talks about the mandate to participate in relation to the principle of refusal, producing a productive tension in the context of Jerusalem.

In a 2015 conversation with Eungie Joo about their 2008 PoLAAT workshop at the New Museum, My Barbarian talked about its theme—"Inspirational Critique"—which was a pun on the term *institutional critique*. Joo says: "Your concept of inspirational critique—this commitment based in positivity and love, is what I would perhaps term 'investment'—something I might describe as critique by example. I have long believed that we can exact more influence by doing; by imagining and demonstrating what, where, and how things could be rather than critiquing in a reactionary way."

The song conceived in the PoLAAT "Inspirational Critique" workshops ends like this:

I could love you   Try not to be dismissive
I could love you   Try not to patronize
I could love you   Try not to be defensive
I could love you   Try to sympathize
I could love you   Try not to be solipsistic
I could love you   Try not to hystericize
I could love you   Try not to be overly simplistic
I could love you   Try to realize

I could love you!

The Five Principles of the PoLAAT
Alexandro Segade
February 4, 2010

Central to the PoLAAT is a performance lab in which participants are trained in the tactics and techniques of the Post-Living Ante-Action Theater. Classes are composed of exercises designed to educate the participants in the five principles: Estrangement, Indistinction, Suspension of Beliefs, Mandate to Participate, and Inspirational Critique. Songs based on these principles are taught to the group. What follows are notes on these five principles, using examples from the Living Theatre and *antiteater* to illustrate them:

Estrangement

The performer acts out the distance between themselves and what they are doing. An adaptation of the Brechtian *Verfremdungseffekt*, often translated as the Alienation Effect, Estrangement also incorporates elements of camp, which uses an ironic displacement or disidentification to critique the action represented. The audience, it is hoped, will be similarly engaged in an active critique of the performance and the questions it poses. Estrangement is evident in the antitheater's use of the Alienation Effect as a performance of an "attitude, not a character."

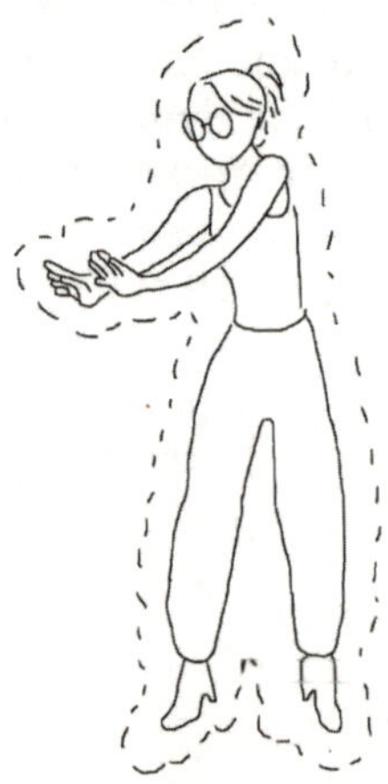

Indistinction

Contradictory formal and institutional distinctions are set in oppositional motion. The performer does two things at once, such as singing a love song and paying taxes. The play itself refuses to be a play and becomes a caucus, the narrative explodes with extraneous plot points and goes hyper-narrative or the signifiers of pop music are short-circuited by art historical classification, and so on. Theater as process is exemplified by the practices of *antiteater*. Plays were made into films and television series; films were adapted as plays, with cast members serving as both administration and crew for these various productions. This blurring of disciplines, forms, and roles provides a model of production in which all participants are expected to invest their talents in a group effort that may fail but do so spectacularly and with political commitment to democracy intact. Implicit here is a willful disregard of audience expectations, not to mention taste.

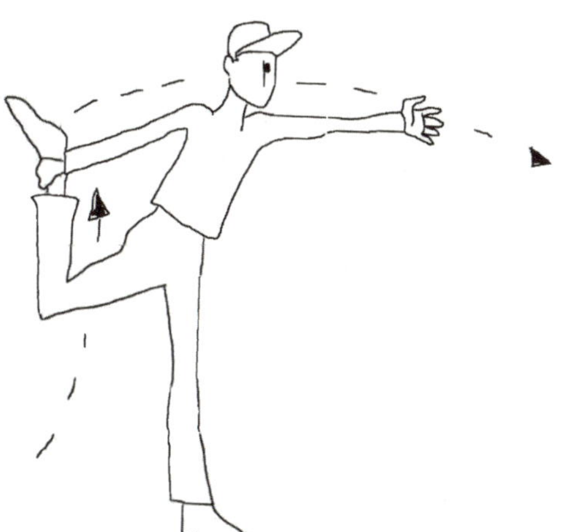

Suspension of Beliefs

A truism of theater is that it requires the suspension of disbelief, but the PoLAAT model questions ideological and aesthetic assumptions. The performer must consider all options. With so many contradictory political positions represented by the attitudes (not characters) onstage, the effect of their technique is the suspension of beliefs, when the actors and audience find their ideological and aesthetic concerns caught in a field of contemplation. This principle is exemplified by the Living Theatre's attempt to levitate a person in the performance of their play *Frankenstein* (1965).

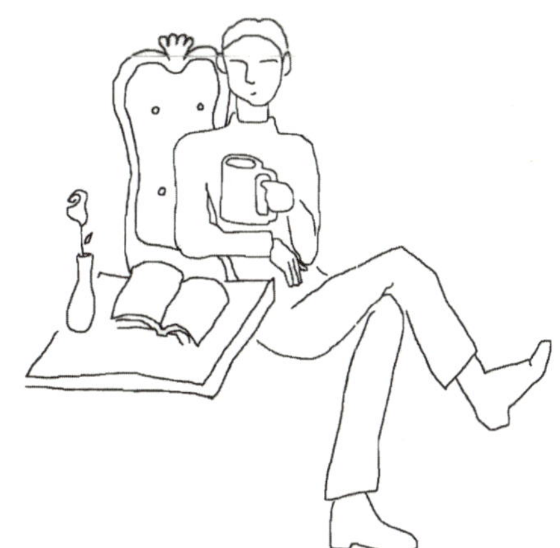

Mandate to Participate

Audience and performer are the same thing. All is rehearsal and rehearsal is all in a reconfiguration of event as process. The theater is made into an open system, disrupting the hierarchical structure of the stage, where the actor is speaker and public is listener. Structures for the inclusion of participation must be made clear; chaos can be managed. The audience becomes the cast and the cast gets naked with the Living Theatre. Democracy is alive again.

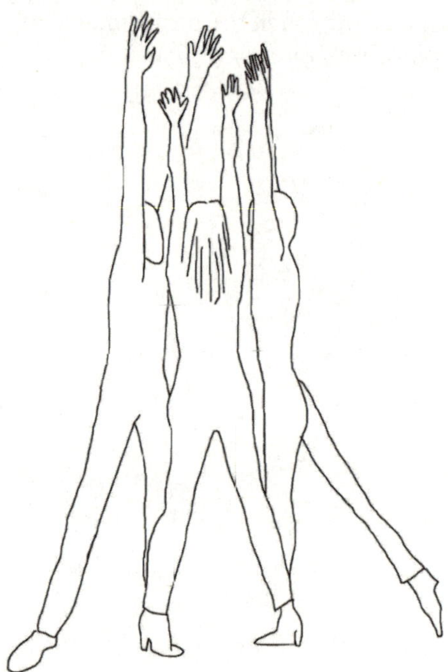

Inspirational Critique

When the structure of institutional thought is ruptured, an inspirational critique is the result: a moment in which, for a brief second, all is questioned, allowing for an understanding of the situation that opens itself up to new possibilities.

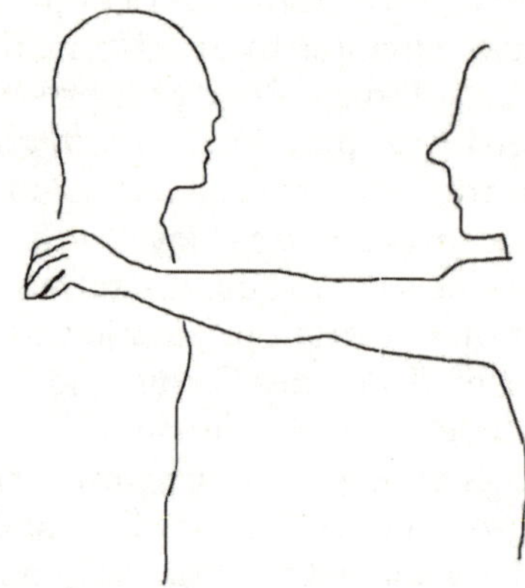

Inspirational Critique Exercises

1. Reflecting

Participants pair up. Facilitator asks each pair to decide who will be partner A and who will be partner B. B mirrors A's movements. A starts slowly then increases speed, shifts rhythm, plays with levels, moves around the space, dances, and so on. They reverse and B leads.

Variation:

1. Neither lead.
2. Close your eyes for thirty seconds, mirror, and then open them. Were movements synchronized?

2. Trusting

Participants form a tight circle, shoulder-to-shoulder, facing inward with both of their hands up, palms forward, in front of their chests. One person stays in the center of the circle, arms crossed across their chest with their eyes closed. Facilitator slowly spins them around. Trusting the group to catch them, they fall against the others. No one lets them fall completely. They are gently guided back into center. Work in silence.

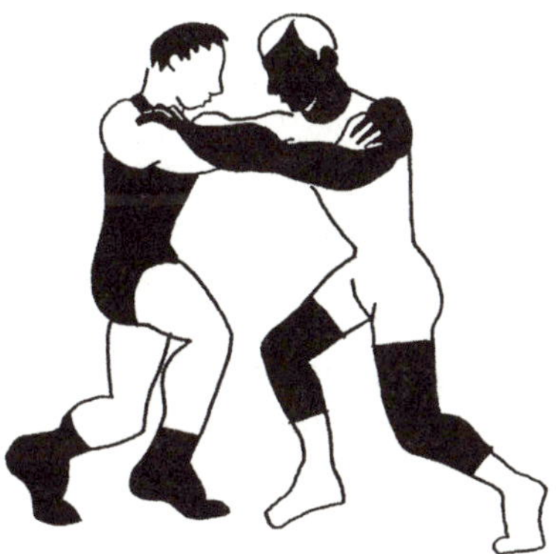

3. Pressuring

Participants pair up and push against each other's shoulders, face-to-face, trying "not to win." Both partners use equal strength but try to balance each other's weight so no one falls.

Variation

Back-to-back.

4. Truth-Circling

Sitting in a circle, performers tell each other embarrassing, confrontational, or otherwise truthful anecdotes and opinions about the performance that just happened.

Variation

Performers talk about embarrassing performance moments in their lives.

5. Audience Gets a Massage

To be performed with a live audience. The performers instruct the audience to rub the shoulders of the person seated in front of them.

Variation

The audience is guided through stretching exercises.

Alexandro (Xandro) Segade made the drawings that illustrate the PoLAAT exercises in the manual.

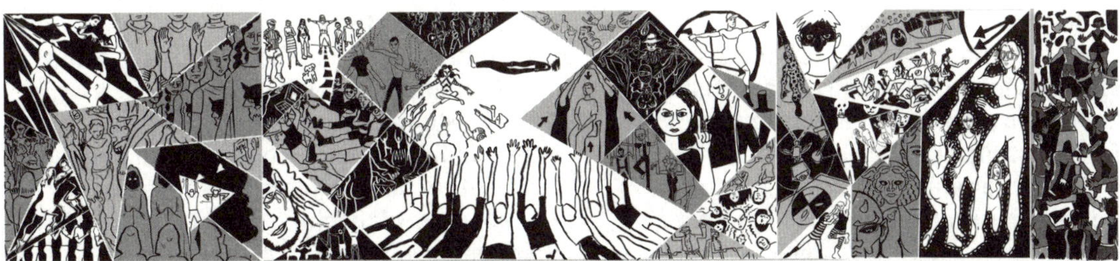

II. BFAMFAPhD

As of this writing, during the start of the second Trump presidency, I'm thinking a lot about tyranny and its relationship to higher education. As I outlined in the introduction, universities are never free from ideological constraints and the influence of power. But in the US context new political and economic pressures have created an environment that I haven't seen in my lifetime. I recognize that this is nothing compared to the necropolitics in the MENA region. But a new reality is unfolding.

The "regional context" of this section encompasses the United States and the Middle East. One reason for this is politics. On the one hand, after October 7, 2023, students in the US, mostly international, have been arrested, detained, and deported for Palestinian-solidarity activities. Meanwhile, the federal government is punishing universities for allowing these protests, withholding hundreds of millions of dollars and resulting in some institutions making further structural changes, constraining speech, and remaking their curricula beyond the Palestine issue. Targeting universities in this way is a long-term goal of the American right. At the same time, Gaza's universities have been physically decimated by Israel, which is funded by the United States; not only has the architecture and infrastructure been destroyed, but also the lives of faculty, staff, and students. In the United States, the specter of the "terrorist" is invoked to defend these actions, a claim that has its roots at the start of the twenty-first century when the repercussions of the Second Intifada and the military response to September 11 converged.

This context is addressed in several texts included here: A conversation between educators in the Middle East reveals the challenges of teaching within institutions at a moment when violence characterizes daily life. Ariella Aïsha Azoulay, who has a long history of writing about the intersection of art and politics in the region, talks about her experience within an American institution, applying her notion of "unlearning imperialism" to "unlearning Zionism" within higher education. A text by an anonymous Harvard senior, who posted it online after being threatened by the university for their activism, shows how Palestine reveals the limits of claims to free speech. Art historian Daniel Spaulding's essay "On Hating Students" reveals how institutional responses to Palestinian-solidarity activism have manifested as not only contempt but outright violence, underscoring a problematic structural relationship between students and university administration.

The specter of violence in learning environments is addressed by Cara Benedetto's 2019 exhibition *Blood from Stone*, which chillingly invokes the epidemic of school shootings and examines this threat to think about other forms of violence, pressure, and vulnerability that students face in school.

This section focuses on accredited art schools, colleges, and universities that issue degrees. It is titled after the organization BFAMFAPhD, cofounded by artists Susan Jahoda, Vicky Virgin, and Caroline Woolard and curator Blair Murphy. Their 2014 text "Artists Report Back," included here, illustrates the tensions between the challenge arts professionals face trying to support themselves after receiving high-cost degrees. It emphasizes that the privatization of school and the commodification of a degree in a capitalist context is often in tension with artists' creative goals.

While artist and filmmaker Jalal Toufic writes about being chair of an art department in Beirut (he now is teaching in Cairo), his contribution is less about the region and more about the structural limitations that hinder academic administrators from living up to their stated aims. Similarly, art historian Beatriz E. Balanta finds that claims of diversity and inclusion in liberal American academia are poisoned by white supremacy. Institutions have contradictions built into them.

Artist and writer Sean Dockray and philosopher Brian Holmes write about higher education in an American context, with particular emphasis on the legacy of the 2008 financial crisis. The ideas in these texts relate to the Occupy Wall Street movement and attend to the ways in which income inequality and the privatization of public education are inherently related, limiting the options for artists that graduate from these programs.

But beyond the political economy of debt, sometimes crises can produce a more productive environment of indebtedness. Critic and curator Anuranda Vikram talks about teaching during the COVID pandemic and the ways in which it revealed new, more flexible, forms of learning in tune with the rhythms and realities of students' lives. In a conversation with artists Steffani Jemison, Naeem Mohaiemen, and Beatriz Santiago Muñoz about art schools in the US, there was agreement that institutions inherently cannot allow for the influence of radical pedagogies advocated by bell hooks or Paulo Freire, but that faculty can take some of their lessons to find pockets of resistance. Something like what theorists Fred Moten and Stefano Harney would call the undercommons, which suggests that what seems irreparable may contain spaces for mutual aid and resource sharing.

Artists Report Back: A National Study On the Lives of Arts Graduates and Working Artists

BFAMFAPhD

As artists and art-school graduates, we often find ourselves in conversations about the difficulties of continuing our practice as writers, authors, artists, actors, photographers, musicians, singers, producers, directors, performers, choreographers, dancers, and entertainers. We struggle to support ourselves with jobs outside of the arts and we struggle to earn a living in the arts. Yet art-school administrators and "creative class" reports assure us that arts graduates make a living in the arts.[1] Loan officers insist that art students can afford art-school tuition, repaying student loans over time by working in the arts. This is not our experience. We decided that it was time to make our own report.

Connecting our lived experiences to national trends, we wanted to know: What is the impact of rent, debt, and precarity on working artists and arts graduates nationally? How many of us are there? If we are not supporting ourselves as working artists, what jobs do we work?

We looked at artists' demographics, occupations, educational attainment, field of degree, and earnings as recorded by the Census Bureau's 2012 American Community Survey (ACS). The ACS is the largest survey that collects data about artists, surveying roughly one out of every one hundred persons in the nation. With this data in hand, we made this report to reframe conversations about the current conditions and contradictions of arts graduates, and to make informed decisions about the ways we live and work. At the end of the report, please see our recommendations for organizational change and interpersonal action.

Susan Jahoda, Blair Murphy, Vicky Virgin, and Caroline Woolard (BFAMFAPhD), 2014

1 Creative Economy Report, Otis College of Art and Design, 2013, http://www.otis.edu/creative-economy-report.

Summary

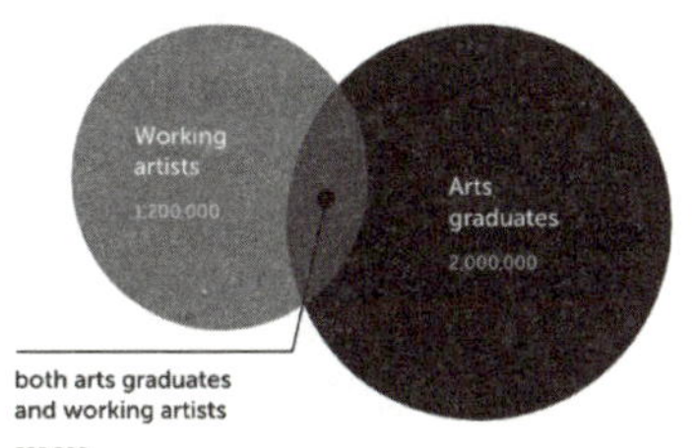

Most surprising was the lack of overlap between working artists and arts graduates. In the United States, 40 percent of working artists do not have bachelor's degrees in any field. Only 16 percent of working artists have arts-related bachelor's degrees. Though arts graduates may acquire additional opportunities and skills from attending art school, arts graduates are likely to graduate with significant student-loan debt, which makes working as an artist difficult, if not impossible. We acknowledge that some arts graduates are satisfied with work in other fields, but the fantasy of arts graduates' future earnings in the arts should be discredited. Since seven of the top ten most expensive institutions of higher education in the United States (after financial aid is taken into consideration) are art schools, the corresponding proportion of student loans are higher than those for graduates from non-art schools.[2] The majority of arts graduates work in non-arts fields. Out of two million arts graduates nationally, only 10 percent, or two hundred thousand people, make their primary earnings as working artists. Given the discrepancy between working artists and arts graduates, as well as the rising cost of tuition at art schools, we end this report with recommendations for policy makers, administrators, and educators in our field.

2 "How Does Your School Rank?" *The Wall Street Journal*, February 19, 2013, http://online.wsj.com/news/interactive/BORROW021620130216?ref=SB10001424127887324432004578306610055834952

Methodology

All statements in this report are based upon data collected by the Census Bureau's 2012 American Community Survey (ACS), unless otherwise noted. This is an annual survey that is designed to sample 1 percent or about three million households in the United States, gathering detailed data that was previously collected in the Decennial Census. A myriad of issues arise when using data to study artists. For this report we used two variables to identify this population: "primary occupation" (secondary occupation is not collected in this survey) and "field of degree," a relatively new variable directed at those who have a bachelor's degree. We will refer to people who have bachelor's degrees in the arts as "arts graduates" and to people whose primary occupation is writer, author, artist, actor, photographer, musician, singer, producer, director, performer, dancer choreographer, or entertainer as "working artists."

Arts Graduates

We looked at people with bachelor's degrees in music, drama and theater arts, film, video and photographic arts, art history and criticism, studio arts, and visual and performing arts living in the United States in 2012. The ACS does not collect the field of degree for master's degrees, so we define "arts graduates" in this report as people with BAs or BFAs in the arts who may or may not have an MA or MFAs in the arts. With only 15,929 MAs and MFAs graduating in 2012, compared to 91,222 BAs and BFAs in the arts that year, our focus on undergraduates represents a broad population of artists.[3]

Working Artists

We defined working artists as people whose primary earnings come from working as writers, authors, artists, actors, photographers, musicians, singers, producers, directors, performers, choreographers, dancers, or entertainers. We excluded designers and architects from both the data related to "arts graduates" and from the data based on primary occupation (working artist) because the higher earnings of designers significantly alter the median earnings of our field. We understand that "working artists" are often identified by their level of commitment, and not remuneration,[4] but we cannot track practicing artists who do not make their primary earnings in the arts using the ACS. In fact, no nationally representative data exists for practicing artists. While many artists are missed in our report, we chose to investigate the data we could isolate to learn more about working artists and arts graduates nationally.

Findings

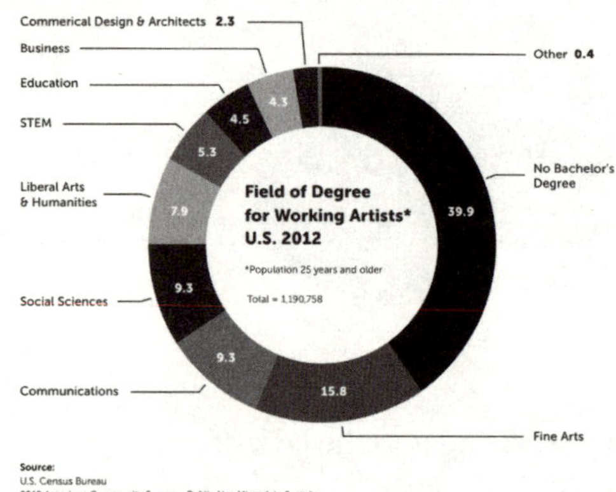

1.4 Million Working Artists

ACS data reveals that there are 1.4 million working artists. Of those over the age of twenty-five, or 1.2 million working artists, 476,000 did not get a bachelor's degree. That means that 40 percent of working artists over the age of twenty-five attended high school or got associate's degrees, but do not have bachelor's degrees in any field. Only 16 percent of working artists have an arts-related bachelor's degree.

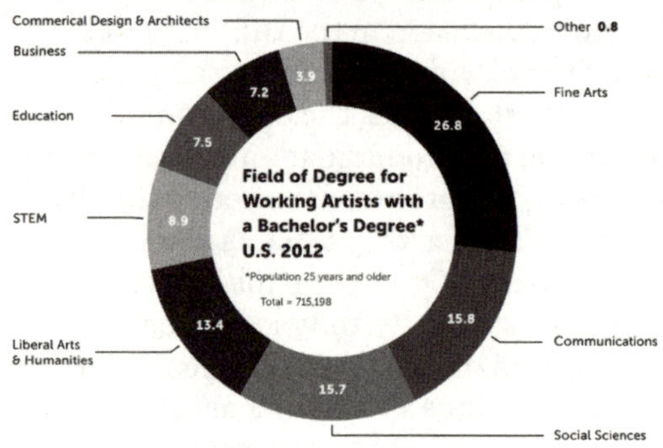

3 For more, see the National Center for Educational Statistics, https://nces.ed.gov/.

Of the 715,000 working artists who do have bachelor's degrees, only 27 percent have arts-related degrees. The rest studied communication, social sciences, liberal arts and humanities, science, technology, math, engineering, education, business, commercial design and architecture, or another field.

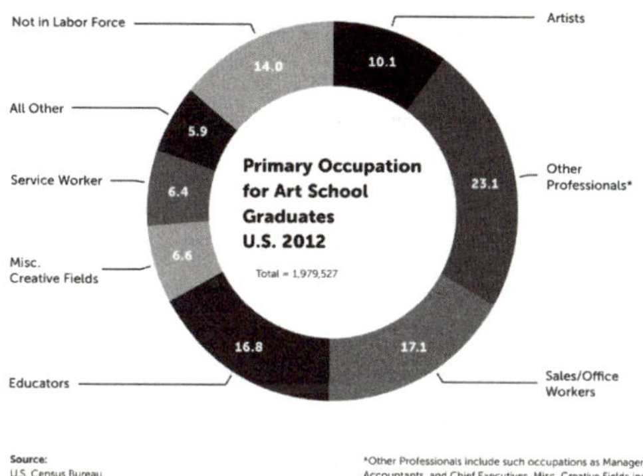

Source:
U.S. Census Bureau
2012 American Community Survey – Public Use Microdata Sample

*Other Professionals include such occupations as Managers, Accountants, and Chief Executives. Misc. Creative Fields include Architects, Designers, TV Announcers, etc.

Two Million Arts Graduates

There are two million arts graduates with bachelor's degrees in music, drama and theater arts, film, video and photographic arts, art history and criticism, studio arts, and visual or performing arts living in the United States. Fewer than two hundred thousand, just 10 percent, make their primary earnings as working artists. The rest are dispersed across other occupations: 23 percent work in professional and managerial occupations, 17 percent are employed as sales and office workers, and 17 percent work as educators. 14 percent are not in the labor force at all.

4 Notice to Applicants Re: Artist Certification, New York City Department of Cultural Affairs, n.d., http://www.nyc.gov/html/dcla/downloads/pdf/artist_certification.pdf.

5 Ruth Simon, "Loan Defaults Refer to the Three-year Cohort Default Rate on Federal Student Loans," *The Wall Street Journal*, Feb 18, 2013, http://online.wsj.com/news/interactive/BORROW021620130216?ref=SB1000142412788732443200457830661055834952.

Two Hundred Thousand Working Artists and Art Graduates

Although there are 1.2 million working artists over the age of twenty-five in this country, there are only two hundred thousand working artists with arts-related bachelor's degrees. The majority of working artists have median earnings of $30,621, but the small percentage of working artists with bachelor's degrees have median earnings of $36,105.

Default Rates for Arts Graduates

The US Department of Education data show that seven of the top ten most expensive schools in this country (after scholarships and aid) are art schools, and arts graduates' debt loads are higher than those of non-arts graduates.[5] The following percentages of students default on their loans.

— 6% of students from Cleveland Institute of Music default on their loans.
— 7% of students from the New School default on their loans.
— 7% of students from California Institute of the Arts default on their loans.
— 8% of students from the School of Visual Arts default on their loans.
— 8% of students from the Art Center College of Design default on their loans.
— 8% of students from San Francisco Art Institute default on their loans.
— 9% of students from Maine College of Art default on their loans.
— 10% of students from Pratt default on their loans.
— 10% of students from School of the Artist Institute of Chicago default on their loans.
— 10% of students from Minneapolis College of

Art and Design default on their loans.

- 11% of students from Berklee College of Music default on their loans.
- 13% of students from Ringling College of Art and Design default on their loans.
- 13% of students from Otis College of Art and Design default on their loans.
- 16% of students from Southwest University of Visual Arts default on their loans.

Predominance of White, Non-Hispanic Arts Graduates and Male Working Artists

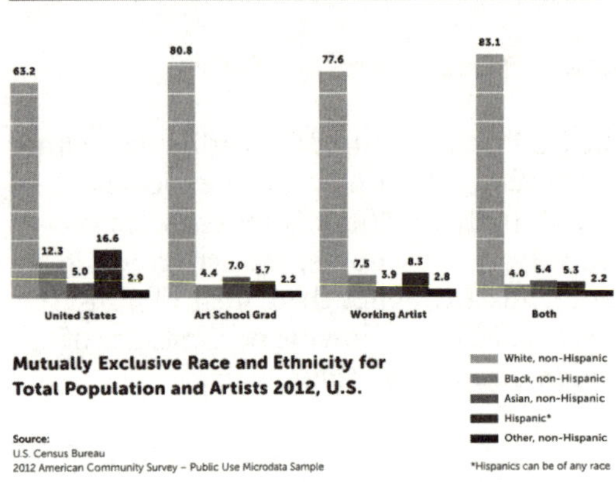

Mutually Exclusive Race and Ethnicity for Total Population and Artists 2012, U.S.

Source:
U.S. Census Bureau
2012 American Community Survey – Public Use Microdata Sample

*Hispanics can be of any race

The population of arts graduates and working artists is not representative of our country. The population of the United States is 63 percent White, non-Hispanic, but 81 percent of arts graduates are White, non-Hispanic. The population of the United States is 12 percent Black, non-Hispanic, but only 4 percent of arts graduates are Black, non-Hispanic and only 8 percent of working artists are Black, non-Hispanic. The population of the United States is 17 percent Hispanic, but only 6 percent of arts graduates are Hispanic and only 8 percent of working artists are Hispanic.

6 "How Does Your School Rank?" *The Wall Street Journal*, February 19. 2013.

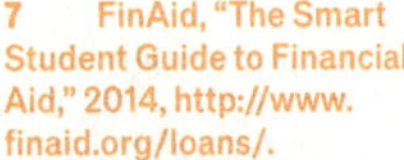

7 FinAid, "The Smart Student Guide to Financial Aid," 2014, http://www.finaid.org/loans/.

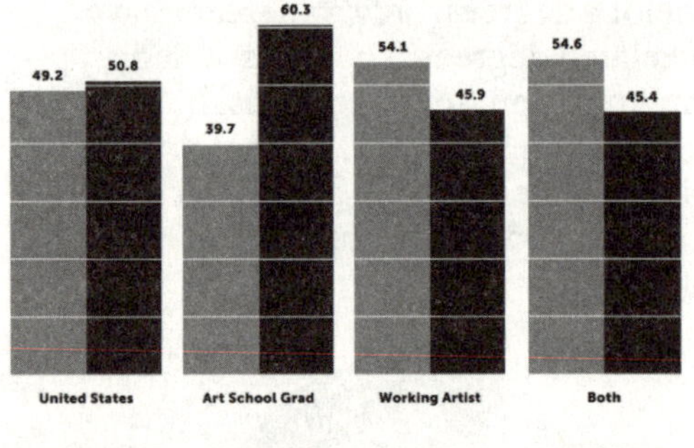

Gender for Total Population and Artists U.S. 2012

Male
Female

Source:
U.S. Census Bureau
2012 American Community Survey – Public Use Microdata Sample

While the United States is split evenly between males and females, males account for only 40 percent of arts graduates but over 54 percent of working artists. Females make up 60 percent of arts graduates but only 46 percent of all working artists. Of the two hundred thousand working artists over twenty-five with an art degree, 55 percent are male.

Recommendations

We have shown that seven of the top ten most expensive institutions of higher education in the United States (after financial aid is taken into consideration) are art schools, and that the corresponding proportion of student loans are higher than those for graduates from non-art schools.[6] With more student-loan debt than credit-card debt in this country, we are in the midst of an educational and social crisis.[7] We ask that artists, administrators, and teachers acknowledge the current financial and political economies in arts education: those of rising costs and student debt. To begin to imagine and enact economies of equity and cooperation in the arts, we must address the needs and capacities of both working artists and arts graduates. What follows are three recommendations toward the adequate nurturing of creativity in art education, visibility, and workforce development.

Art School

While this report reveals that an arts degree is not necessary for future earnings as a working artist, as 40 percent of working artists do not have a bachelor's degree in any field, the authors of this report believe that arts degrees remain valuable for critical thinking, skill-building, identify formation, and creative innovation that is necessary in the arts and beyond.[8] We acknowledge that some arts graduates are happy to work in other fields, but we hope to show that the fantasy of future earnings in the arts cannot justify the high cost of arts degrees. We know that expensive art schools leave arts graduates with high overhead in the form of student debt, making risk-taking and innovation after graduation more difficult, if not impossible. Still believing in the power of arts education, we point prospective art students toward low-cost and tuition-free arts programs and we defend the liberal arts as integral to higher education nationally.

Visibility

Knowing that 40 percent of working artists do not have bachelor's degrees in any field, cultural institutions should honor artists and culture workers who do not have experiences of formal higher education. Philanthropic and civic institutions should create programs to address the needs of working artists, looking beyond the written application, the lecture hall, the journal, and the museum for emerging talent. While working artists and arts graduates legitimate ideas and find rigorous debate in their spaces and distribution networks, cultural institutions could require that presenters, curators, and publishers look beyond networks of arts graduates. Programs to address the gap between working artists and arts graduates could create informal or formal channels for communication and could establish policies for evaluation and presentation of artists, regardless of educational status.

Workforce Development

We must close the gap between arts graduates and working artists, understanding that little overlap exists currently and that both populations have key insights to share with one another. We can provide opportunities for dialogue. Arts graduates have knowledge of elite social norms, shared jargon from lecture halls, shared regard for artists named in journals, and shared contacts at elite institutions. Working artists have an understanding of the market for their work, valuable business networks, and a familiarity with production and management. Both populations could benefit from worker and producer cooperatives, affordable arts institutions, and resource-sharing networks.

8 Frances Whitehead. "What Do Artists Know? The Embedded Artist Project," Artetal, January 2006, http://embeddedartistproject.com/What-do-artists-know.gif.

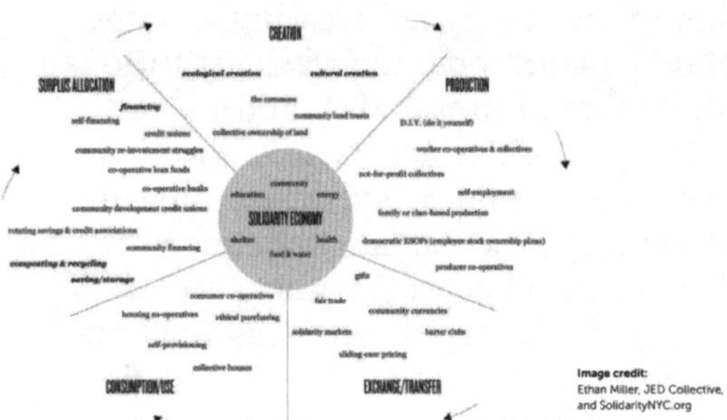

Image credit:
Ethan Miller, JED Collective, and SolidarityNYC.org

This diagram represents a solidarity economy of cooperation and equity that could be adopted more explicitly in the arts and could be supported intellectually and financially by arts institutions and arts schools nationally.

> Adequately nurtured, creativity fuels culture, infuses human-centred development and constitutes the key ingredient for job creation, innovation and trade while contributing to social inclusion, cultural diversity and environmental sustainability. —The United Nations Conference on Trade and Development's Creative Economy Report 2010

How might art education nurture culture? The majority of arts graduates work in non-art occupations to support themselves. Arts education should acknowledge and prepare art students for this eventuality. A disavowal of the connection between expensive tuition and future work and financial independence is no longer realistic or ethical. Preparation for artistic work in other fields, including arts management and administration, as well as training in artist-owned businesses, is essential. Arts graduates can prepare to see themselves as "artists in residence" in sales, education, service, and managerial jobs, while learning how to create an artist-owned business together with other artists, neighbors, and fellow low-income residents. We point prospective art students toward low-cost and free art schools, artist-run spaces, and independent communities of working artists, as we know that the time has come to speak openly about the political economies of art education.

There Is Nothing Less Passive than the Act of Fleeing

The Public School Los Angeles

What follows is a condensed and edited version of a text for a panel that was presented at UCIRA's "Future Tense: Alternative Arts and Economies in the University" conference held in San Diego, California on November 18, 2010. The panel shared the same name as a thirteen-day itinerant seminar in Berlin organized by Dockray, Waldorf, and Fiona Whitton earlier that year. The seminar began with an excerpt from Tiqqun's Introduction to Civil War, *which was co-translated into English by Smith; and later a chapter from Matteo Pasquinelli's* Animal Spirits: A Bestiary of the Commons. *Both authors have also participated in meetings at The Public School in Los Angeles and Berlin. Both the panel and the seminar developed out of longer conversations at The Public School in Los Angeles.*

Sean Dockray, Matteo Pasquinelli, Jason Smith, and Caleb Waldorf are founding members of and collaborators at The Public School. Initiated in 2007 under Telic Arts Exchange (literally in the basement) in Los Angeles, The Public School is a school with no curriculum. At the moment, it operates as follows: first, classes are proposed by the public; then, people have the opportunity to sign up for the classes; finally, when enough people have expressed interest, the school finds a teacher and offers the class to those who signed up. The Public School is not accredited, it does not give out degrees, and it has no affiliation with the public school system. It is a framework that supports autodidactic activities, operating under the assumption that everything is in everything. The Public School currently exists in Los Angeles, New York, Berlin, Brussels, Helsinki, Philadelphia, Durham, and San Juan and is still expanding.

The University, as I understand it, has been a threshold between youth and the labor market. Or it has been a threshold between a general education and a more specialized one. In its more progressive form, it's been a zone of transition into an expanding middle class. But does this form still exist? I'm inclined to think just the opposite, that the University is becoming a form for filtering people out of the middle class via student-loan debt, which now exceeds credit-card debt.

The point of the question for me is simply: What is the point of the University? What are we fighting for or defending?

The next question might be: Do students work? The university is a crucial site in the reproduction of class relations; we know that students are consumers, and are treated as such by the universities they attend; we know the student is a future worker who will be compelled to work, and work in a specific way, because she is crushed by debt contracted during her tenure as a student; we know that students work while attending school, and that for many students school and work eerily begin to resemble one another.

But asking whether students work is to ask something more specific: Do students produce value and, therefore, surplus value? If we can assume, for the moment, that students are a factor in the "knowledge production" that takes place in the university, is this production of knowledge also the production of value? We confront, maybe, a paradox: all social activity has become "productive"—captured, absorbed—at the very moment value becomes unmeasurable. What does this have to do with students and their work? The thesis of the social factory was supplemented by the assumption that knowledge had become a central node in the production of value in post-Fordist environments. Wouldn't this mean that the university could become an increasingly important flashpoint in social struggles, now that it has become not simply the site of the reproduction of the capital relation, but involved in the immediate production process, directly productive of value? Would we have to understand students themselves as, if not knowledge producers, an irreplaceable moment or function within that process?

None of this remains clear. And the question, moreover, is not only a sociological one. It is also a political one. The strategy of reconceptualizing students as workers is rooted in the classical Marxist identification of revolt with the point of production, that is, exploitation. To declare all social activity to be productive is another way of saying that social war can be triggered at any site within society, even among the precarious, the unemployed, and students.

There is a beautiful intuition by Mario Tronti that he expressed in a 1966 book seminal to the whole tradition of Italian *operaismo*: "Knowledge is tied to struggle. To truly know is to hate truly. This is why the working class can know and possess everything of capital, as it is enemy to itself as capital."[1]

Knowledge—and we could say education also—is coming only from conflict. Only she who grows up and lives along the tensions of the social fabric, perceiving and registering the field of forces of conflicts and frictions, can develop a proper knowledge, a sharp theory, a meaningful aesthetics—only she who lives conflicts on her own skin can run a "public school."

This is the lesson of the social movements of the 1960s and '70s and a lesson

1 Mario Tronti, *Operai e capitale* (DeriveApprodi, 2006 [Einaudi, 1966]).

we learned again in the punk age. Deleuze said once, in a dialogue with Foucault, "No theory can develop without eventually encountering a wall." That wall is the wall of conflict.

If art claims to be the very realm of radical gestures, it should also be able to initiate new forms of knowledge and new education practices. Knowledge is never neutral, but always an unconscious incarnation of power structures: here Foucault has already said everything. However, Foucault does not say much about the autonomous forms of counter knowledge. That passion mentioned by Tronti—hate for your own condition of exploitation—is suggesting something new. The political passion of hate becomes part of the backbone of a new counter-knowledge.

The relation between hate and knowledge suggested by Tronti stays on the opposite side of the cynical detachment of the new social figure of the entrepreneur-artist. In order to educate ourselves we should hate our very own environment and social network in which we were educated—the university. Knowledge production and education too should be based on the very hate for our existential condition, that is for a form of life hegemonized by capital.

Alternative Pedagogical Models

Let's consider the desire for "new pedagogical models" and "new forms of knowledge production." When articulated by the University, this simply means new forms of instruction and new forms of research. Liberal faculty and neoliberal politicians or administrators find themselves joined in this hunt for future models and forms. On the one hand, faculty imagines that these new techniques can provide space for continuing the good work while under the pressure of reduced budgets and standardization. They might even "engage with the community" or produce more timely research if these models introduce a mechanism to break through their inherited boundaries. On the other hand, investors, politicians, and administrators look for any means to make the University profitable. How can new forms of teaching and research use unpaid labor, eliminate non-productive physical spaces, and create new markets?

Symptomatically, there is very little resistance to this search for new forms and new models for the simple reason that there is a consensus that the University should and will continue. Given that we are speaking in an arts context, it's important to note that many of the so-called new forms and new models being considered lie beyond the walls and payroll of the institution and are therefore both low-cost and low-risk. They have been taken up for consideration by institutions across Europe to suggest "an educational turn" to art practice and again to propose "new forms of knowledge production." It is now a familiar story: the institution attempts to renew itself by importing its own critique. But what is the other side of this story? What happens to this "critique" as it is brought into the institution? The story is again familiar: the vampire institution extracts life from its critique, abstracts it according to institutional logic and history, and replaces its values with institutional ones—a familiar fate of "the alternative."

The Public School is not a new model and it's not going to save the University. It is not even a critique of the University any more or less than it is a critique of the field of art or of capitalist society. It is not "the next University" because it is a practice of leaving the University to the side. It would be a mistake to think that this means isolation or total detachment. After all, aren't most of us the offspring of the institution and some of us providing our labor to it? More than that, don't we parasite on it for materials, texts, and, if we're lucky, money?

Today the forms of university governance cannot allow themselves to uproot self-education. To the contrary, self-education constitutes a vital sap for the survival of the institutional ruins, snatched up and rendered valuable in the form of revenue. Governance is the trap, hasty and flexible, of the common. Instead of countering us frontally, the enemy follows us. We must immediately reject any weak interpretation of the theme of autonomous institutions, according to which the institution is a self-governed structure that lives between the folds of capitalism, without excessively bothering it. The institutionalization of self-education doesn't mean being recognized as one actor among many within the education market, but the capacity to organize living knowledge's autonomy and resistance.

One of the most important "new pedagogical models" that emerged over the past year in the struggles around the implosion of the "public" university are the occupations that took place in the fall of 2009. Unlike some other forms of action, which tend to follow the timetable and cadence of the administration to the point of mirroring it, these actions had their own temporality, their own initiative, their own internal logic. They were not at all concerned with saving a university that was already in ruins, but rather with creating a space at the heart of the university within which something else, some future, could be risked, played out, elaborated, prefigured. Everything had to be improvised from moment to moment, and in these improvisations new knowledges were developed and shared. This improvisation was demanded by the aleatory quality of the types of relations that emerged within these spaces, relations no longer regulated by the social alibis that assign everyone her place. When students occupy university buildings, here and in New York City and in Puerto Rico and in Europe and the United Kingdom, everywhere, they do so not because they want to save their universities. They do because they know the university for what it is, as something to be at once seized and abandoned. They know that they can only rely on, that is, learn from, one another.

The Common and the Public

One way to think of what we might recognize as an increasing bifurcation of the public and the common is to recast this split in terms that belong to the origins of the workers' movement. I am thinking in particular of the difference posited by Joseph Jacotot between what he calls a community of equals and the idea of society or the social bond. As recounted in Jacques Rancière's *The Ignorant Schoolmaster*, what is so "disconcerting" about Jacotot's theory of intellectual emancipation—his new "pedagogical model"—is that it is founded on a split, asymmetry, or incompatibility between the logic of community or the common and the dynamics of the social body.[2]

So, what is really so disconcerting about this antinomy between the logic of the common and the logic of the public? For Jacotot, it means the development of a communist politics that is neither reformist

2 Jacques Rancière, *The Ignorant Schoolmaster: Five Lessons in Intellectual Emancipation* (Stanford University Press, 1991).

nor seditious. It proposes the formation of common spaces at a distance from—if not outside of—the public sphere.

A communist pedagogy, to force the language of this figure of the early workers' movement, would not see its task as the transformation of a given institution, specifically the public universities and schools. The task, for Rancière at least, is clear: "whoever forsakes the workings of the social machine has the opportunity to make the electrical energy of emancipation circulate."

What does it mean to forsake the social machine? That is the major political question facing us today. Such a forsaking would require that our political energies organize themselves around spaces of experimentation at a distance not only from the university and what is likely its slow-motion collapse, but also from an entire imaginary inherited from the workers' movement: the task of a future social emancipation along with the vectors and forms of struggle such a task implies. Perhaps what is required is not to put off equality for the future, but to presuppose the common, to affirm that commons as a fact, a given, which must nevertheless be verified, created, not by a social body, not by a collective force, but a power of the common, now.

School is not University. Neither is it Academy or College or even Institute. We are all familiar with the common meaning of the word: it is a place for learning. In another sense, it also refers to organized education in general, which is made most clear by the decision to leave, to "drop out of school." Alongside these two stable, almost architectural definitions, the word gestures to composition and movement—the school of bodies, moving independently, together; the school only exists as long as that collective movement does. Perhaps this is a way to think of how to develop what Félix Guattari called "the associative sector" in 1982—"everything that isn't the state, or private capital, or even cooperatives." At first gloss, the associative sector is only a name for the remainder, the outcast, the already outside; but, in the language of a school, it is a constellation of relationships, affinities, new subjectivities, and movements, flickering into existence through life and use, not the word. Rather, this kind of school is a collective articulation, an "engaged withdrawal" that simultaneously creates an exit and institutes in the act of passing through.

Which itself might bring us back to school, to the Greek etymology of school, *skhole*, "a holding back, a keeping clear"—usually in the form of leisure or spare time—of space for reflective distance. On the one hand, perhaps this reflective space simply allows meaning, theoretical knowledge, and experience to shape or affect performative action; but on the other hand, the production of this "clearing" is not given, certainly not now and certainly not by the institutions that claim to give it. Reflective space is not the precondition for performative action. On the contrary, within the current configuration, it criticizes it, authors it, organizes it, and postpones it. Performative action is the precondition for reflective space—or, more appropriately, space and action must be coproduced.

Is the university even worth "saving"? We are right to respond with indignation, or better, with an array of tactics—some procedural, some more "direct"—against these incursions, which always seem to authorize themselves by appeals to economic austerity, budget shortfalls, and tightened belts. Perhaps what is being destroyed in this process is the very notion of the public sphere itself, a notion that is relatively less archaic than the university but which has no right to an eternal life either. It is easy to succumb to the illusion that the only possible result of this destruction of the figure of the public, of "publicness," is privatization, the transfer of public and socially or collectively produced wealth, knowledge, and even affective energies into the hands and pockets of tiny cliques of plutocrats and assorted vampires. But what if the figure of the public, which emerged in the context of the transition from the absolute to the liberal state, was to be set off against not only the private and property relations, but against a new and vibrant figure of the "common" as well? What if, in other words, the notion of the public has always been an unstable, mediating term between privatization and communization, and what if the withering of this mediation left these two processes openly at odds with each other? Perhaps, then, it is not simply a question of saving a university and, more broadly, a public space that is already withering away; maybe our energies and our intelligence, our collective or common intellectual forces, should be devoted to organizing and articulating just this sort of counter-transition, at a distance from the public and the "private."

Authorship and New Forms of Knowledge

For decades we have spoken about the "death of the author," but no one really believes it. The most sustained critiques of authorship have been made from the spheres of art and education, but, not coincidentally, these spheres have the most invested in the notion. Credit and accreditation are the mechanisms for attaching symbolic capital to individuals via degrees and other lines on CVs. That curriculum vitae is an inverted credit report, evidence of underpaid work, kept orderly with an expectation of some future return. All of this work, this self-documentation, this fidelity between ourselves and our papers is for what, for whom? And what is the consequence of a world where every person is armed with their vitae, other than "the war of all against all"? It's that sensation that there are no teams, but everyone has got their own jersey.

The idea behind the project The Public School is to teach each other in a very horizontal way. No curriculum, no hierarchy. But is the Public School also able to produce new knowledge and new content by itself? Can the Public School become a sort of autonomous collective author? Or is the Public School just a place of book exchanges, workshops, and social networking?

Recently some collectives started to refresh the idea of co-research, a form of knowledge that could produce new political subjectivities and new political organization.

If knowledge comes only from conflict, knowledge has to go back to conflict and to produce new autonomous subjectivities and "institutions of the common."

The UC Strike: At Long Last, the Shit Hits the Fan in California …

Brian Holmes

After the huge student movements in France in 2006, as well as last year's occupation of the Sorbonne by the staff and the professors; after the rolling and agitated "anomalous wave" of protests against the Bologna Process restructuring of higher education that swept Italy last year; after the astonishing refusal of tuition fees by Croatian students this spring and summer—to name only three arenas of an expanding transnational revolt[1]—the global crisis of the university has finally come home to the neoliberal heartland: the state of California. On September 24, a walkout of students, professors, and staff was called across the entire University of California system, in protest against draconian budget cuts decreed by the UC Regents, which is an extremely powerful and prestigious administrative body whose members are appointed directly by the state governor for twelve-year terms.

California is the state where, in 1979, the infamous Proposition 13 began choking off funding for public services while launching the "taxpayer revolt" of the rich and inventing the basic neoliberal campaign rhetoric that would bring Ronald Reagan to power. Since 1983 there has been only one Democratic governor of the state, Gray Davis, which means that the UC Regents have mostly been named by Republicans in order to represent multiple business interests in the fields of both research and education. The budget squeeze has been permanent, since the same Proposition 13 set the requirement of a two-thirds majority vote for any new local or state taxes. After Governor Davis was prematurely recalled by a Republican smear campaign following the "rolling blackouts" inflicted on the state by possibly the most corrupt corporation

1 "disOrientation 2.0: Global University Struggles—Google My Maps." Google My Maps, https://www.google.com/maps/d/edit?mid=1b902sVaNQrZaOb8FOZ-R7my3swto&ie=UTF8&hl=en&msa=0&z=2&ll=0.870412023411518%2C0.

of the dot-com era, Enron, it was the new "Governator" Arnold Schwarzenegger who signed the 2004 Higher Education Compact with the President of the UC Regents. In the context of the ongoing financial crisis and the resulting budget shortfalls across the US federal system, Schwarzenegger is now using the effective minority rule granted to the Republicans by the two-thirds majority requirement to be the "Terminator" of California's public education and research, which the compact redefines as a private good, to be produced by corporate investors and sold to clients on an open market.

There are now plans to raise tuition by 32 percent,[2] in addition to a 9.3 percent hike approved last May, as a consequence of the long-term withdrawal of state funding, further exacerbated by the current fiscal crisis of state governments.[3] The result will be the elimination of large numbers of economically disadvantaged students from the university and a shrinkage of the student population by as much as a third. In a videotaped speech[4] where he explains many of these issues, the award-winning Berkeley linguistics professor George Lakoff had to choke off his emotion as he recalled how glad he had been, thirty-four years ago, to come to teach at a public university: his own parents had been too poor to attend high school.

A wealth of information on both the budget crisis and the student/staff/faculty movement can be found by following the links at the UC Walkout website.[5] Among the more interesting bits is a talk by Wendy Brown,[6] the first American academic to understand Foucault's courses on the birth of biopower and to realize that neoliberalism means "the end of liberal democracy." For a wider perspective on the course and meaning of such struggles in the world, there is the Edufactory collective,[7] as well as The New School in Exile[8] and a highly subversive text on the protests at that institution in December 2008 titled "Preoccupied."[9] But if somehow you have not yet done so, the first thing to read—and certainly one of the most powerful student-movement texts since the Situationist tract "On the Poverty of Student Life"[10]—is this impressive and impassioned document, emanating from the "Research & Destroy" collective and prefiguring the events at UC Santa Cruz, where the Graduate Student Commons is still occupied as I write: "Communiqué from an Absent Future."[11]

This is a brilliant text for one simple reason: it says, flat-out, a large number of things which are simply true concerning the

2 "University of California May Raise Tuition 30%," *USA Today*, September 15, 2009, https://web.archive.org/web/20090923014724/https://www.usatoday.com/news/education/2009-09-15-university-california_N.htm.

3 Mitch Daniels, "The Coming Reset in State Government," *The Wall Street Journal*, September 3, 2009, https://www.wsj.com/articles/SB10001424052970204731804574390603114939642.

4 Jskoller. "UC Budget Crisis Teach-in at UCB 9/14: Prof George Lakoff Pt 5," YouTube, September 17, 2009, https://www.youtube.com/watch?v=FbZUJbc6vgk.

5 "UC Walkout and Beyond—Documents, Videos, and Photos from the UC WalkOut and Beyond," https://web.archive.org/web/20091103002611/http://ucwalkout.ning.com:80.

6 "Save the University: Wendy Brown, Part 6—UC Walkout and Beyond," https://web.archive.org/web/20091103034402/http://ucwalkout.ning.com/video/save-the-university-wendy.

7 Edu-Factory Collective, https://web.archive.org/web/20100405015255/http://www.edu-factory.org/edu15.

8 The New School in Exile, https://www.newschoolinexile.com.

9 Revolution by the Book, "Preoccupied: The Logic of Occupation," December 10, 2010, https://revolutionbythebook.akpress.org/2009/01/preoccupied-the-logic-of-occupation.

10 U.N.E.F. Strasbourg, "On the Poverty of Student Life: Considered In Its Economic, Political, Psychological, Sexual, and Particularly Intellectual Aspects, and a Modest Proposal for Its Remedy," The Situationist International Text Library/on the Poverty of Student Life, https://library.nothingness.org/articles/SI/en/display/4.

11 Research and Destroy, "Communiqué From an Absent Future: On the Terminus of Student Life | Revolution by the Book," December 10, 2010, https://revolutionbythebook.akpress.org/2009/09/communique-from-an-absent-future-the-terminus-of-student-life.

fundamental bankruptcy of the public university and of the society whose decay it has helped to perfect with a thousand sophisticated branches of knowledge and a thousand techniques of social engineering. The current economic collapse, the defeat of the US oil grab in Iraq after the needless loss of hundreds of thousands of civilian lives, and now the extension of the war in Afghanistan are only the most visible hallmarks of this decay, which has crept into daily life on every level, from the most pragmatic to the most subjective. Check this bit out to get the tone and the basic angle of attack:

> We work and we borrow in order to work and to borrow. And the jobs we work toward are the jobs we already have. Close to three quarters of students work while in school, many full-time; for most, the level of employment we obtain while students is the same that awaits after graduation. Meanwhile, what we acquire isn't education; it's debt. We work to make money we have already spent, and our future labor has already been sold on the worst market around. Average student loan debt rose 20 percent in the first five years of the twenty-first century—80–100 percent for students of color. Student loan volume—a figure inversely proportional to state funding for education—rose by nearly 800 percent from 1977 to 2003. What our borrowed tuition buys is the privilege of making monthly payments for the rest of our lives. What we learn is the choreography of credit: you can't walk to class without being offered another piece of plastic charging 20 percent interest. Yesterday's finance majors buy their summer homes with the bleak futures of today's humanities majors.

The anonymous text goes on to cover a long list of societal failures in excruciating detail. What it calls for—as you could guess from the short excerpt—is nothing less than a revolution. I'm not going to disagree. But because this moment and this movement are so important, I am going to take issue with one aspect of what I consider to be an otherwise perfect analysis. This criticizable aspect comes only after a series of remarkable arguments that have to be taken on board in order to get to the heart of the question:

> The university has no history of its own; its history is the history of capital. Its essential function is the reproduction of the relationship between capital and labor. Though not a proper corporation that can be bought and sold, that pays revenue to its investors, the public university nonetheless carries out this function as efficiently as possible by approximating ever more closely the corporate form of its bedfellows. What we are witnessing now is the endgame of this process, whereby the façade of the educational institution gives way altogether to corporate streamlining.

This is true. What we are witnessing with the current economic crisis and the collapse of state budgets is the culmination of the neoliberal program, that is the end of the welfare state that was instituted in the 1930s and strengthened again in the 1960s, and, consequently, the beginning of the full-scale precarization of the former middle classes in the US and in northwestern Europe, as it has already occurred in countless countries of Latin America, Eastern Europe, the Middle East, and Africa, after their subjection to bankers' techniques for the extraction of value from public institutions and infrastructures. To destroy any democratic critique of this process—and to open up another lucrative private market in the same blow—it is necessary for capitalist logic to destroy the public university. The real-estate bubble and its deflation, which finally delivered a wake-up call to the general public, is at the same time serving as the pretext for a decisive round of privatizations that seek to finish the job and eliminate any resistance to the appropriation of the entire public sector. That this extreme makeover of the former welfare state will undoubtedly be fatal to the entire system, threatened with climate change—and also with the looming revolt of all kinds of peripheries and underclasses—seems not to matter one whit to the people in charge. This is precisely because, to a large extent, there is no one in charge. The logic of capital has not only pervaded the hearts and minds of those who benefit in any way from it—the very middle classes produced during the postwar period by welfare-state entitlements—but it has also sedimented itself in a very large number of technologies, laws, bureaucratic procedures, organizational models, and operational goals whose inertial force is tremendous and still serves as a powerful tool in the hands of those elites who are, in small numbers, very conscious of what they are doing. Yet all this, immense as it is, hardly removes us from the obligation to think and to act intelligently, strategically, in what is clearly a dangerous situation.

The knot of the text comes when it attempts to define its own speaking subject: the students whom the university educates. Not coincidentally, this is the passage that introduces the call to insurrection—yup, that's the word, right here in Amerika—which takes up most of the third part of this extraordinary text:

> The university is subject to the real crisis of capitalism, and capital does not require liberal education programs. The function of the university has always been to reproduce the working class by training future workers according to the changing needs of capital. The crisis of the university today is the crisis of the reproduction of the working class, the crisis of a period in which capital no longer needs us as workers. We cannot free the university from the exigencies of the market by calling for the return of the public education system. We live out the terminus of the very market logic upon which that system was founded. The only autonomy we can hope to attain exists beyond capitalism.

Now exactly here, I want to ask the question: How can anyone accept this idea that the function of the university is to reproduce the working class without distorting every meaning of the words "working class"? The working classes of the university are the janitors, the food-service people, the maintenance men and women, the day-care staffers and receptionists, all the people stuck in increasingly exploited and precarious positions. Even when they do the same jobs at night or at odd hours scattered over the week, the students aspire to be trained as scientists, engineers, technicians, healthcare professionals, government officials, middle and upper managers, and cultural ideologists (a category in which I would include both artists and teachers). The difference between them marks the common consciousness, and it has to be addressed, even at a time when the objective distinctions between students and workers are blurring. It is true to say that the United States, like all countries that have undergone full-scale neoliberal regime change, no longer has any essential need for its traditional working classes, since industrial work has been largely outsourced, automated, or delegated to immigrants under conditions of extreme exploitation facilitated, in many cases, by lack of citizenship papers. But it is false to say that the neoliberal societies do not need the "human resources" produced by the university. They do, crucially, to maintain their advantages in what they themselves define as the Darwinian struggle of each country and, indeed, of each corporation against all the others. The present aim of the Republicans—the neoliberals—is to save money on taxes, to open up new markets for education and research while continuing to exploit the remaining (and hardly inconsequential) public budgets, and to exert further discipline over its future middle-management cadres by placing them under even more intense threats of joblessness and inability to pay their enormous student loans. In other words, they want to complete the program first launched in the age of Prop 13.

Why then, in such a brilliant text, do we get such a major mistake of class analysis? Undoubtedly because from that point forth, it is very easy to lapse into an outdated concept of revolution, wherein everyone dons a black mask and engages in a sweeping orgy of destruction that will send the existing system up in flames and allow the rise of a new one from its ashes. Now, does that appear likely? Has anyone studied what Homeland Security has been preparing for in this country for the last eight years? Has anyone observed the massive deployment of police, National Guard, United States Secret Service, and Army personnel armed with so-called less-lethal weapons at the recent G20 meeting in Pittsburgh, or at the RNC in Saint Paul last summer? Above all, has anyone noticed how successfully agents-provocateurs have been used at all these kinds of events since the anti-globalization movement brought street demonstrations back to the Western countries at the turn of the millennium?

The "Communiqué from an Absent Future" marks the return of an insurrectionist spirit to the United States, where it has not been seen on any large scale since the 1970s, with the brief exception of an important moment in Seattle. This spirit should be put to good use by everyone. If the current movement goes anywhere, some rioting in the streets is gonna happen, and a lot of occupations. But no one should kid themselves that student riots are going to change the system. What students can do, from their own class position, is both to reach out to the hyper-exploited working classes toward whom they are, in effect, precariously sliding, and, at the same time, to help to radicalize all those around them in what has become the central institution for the reproduction of the neoliberal hegemony, namely the contemporary research university. This will require inventing original techniques of radical action that can't be neutralized and made into a pretext for fascist reactions. Strikes that shut a university down—as has already happened for a day in the huge UC system—can also open up space for questioning what the uses of the university could be in a different society. Writers, media makers, performers, and artists, whether inside or outside the university, can use this moment to go further, to dig deeper into our hearts and minds and desires, and to lay the basis for a long-term, broad-based, constructive refusal of the literally insane and dangerous system that has taken root in the US over the course of the last three decades and especially the last ten years.

If the former role and glory of the public university under the welfare-warfare state is definitively over, then what can it become in the future? Wouldn't the best way to shut down its current operations be to convince all those inside it that the way it is operating is a travesty of all its potentials, including those inscribed at the heart of every academic discipline? Why not shut it down with an excess of transformative intellectual and artistic production that would have a huge insurrectional advantage, namely that it could not be stopped by police armed with truncheons and stun guns and less-lethal weapons that they are just dying to use? In the absence of a deep, problematic delegitimation of neoliberal capitalism and the invention of new ways to run a complex society, which transparently appears as the most urgent thing for all of us to focus on, the real revolution will never come. Yet the way things are going, with climate change and planetary civil wars looming on the horizon, all of us are mortally threatened by the absence of that revolutionary future.

This text was originally published as a blog post on October 1, 2009 at https://brianholmes.wordpress.com/2009/10/01/the-u-c-strike/.

The Hidden Costs of a Life of the Mind

Beatriz E. Balanta

The endless toggling between fascination and suspicion—or what I call my love affair with visual culture—began in Boston after I emigrated from a sun-drenched peripheral town at the edge of a sugarcane plantation. I was thirteen when I landed in the stuffy eighth-grade classroom commandeered by Mrs. R., a skinny white woman with boisterously curly red hair. Mrs. R. combined her instruction in English grammar and pronunciation with lessons on watercolor and entomology. She also taught us how to make pinhole cameras out of tin cans and introduced us, an energetic bunch of Black and Brown teens, to the Surrealist masters. I remember being in awe of the meticulous flamboyance of Salvador Dalí's landscapes and the visual antics of Pablo Picasso. In her class I became enchanted with saturated colors, the elegance of jagged lines, and the majesty of form. I was in search of the sublime, but Mrs. R. warned against such naive desires. She insisted that art was not about arousing the sensorium but a vehicle of ideological disruption.

In college I feasted on the delicious deceptions of trompe l'oeil, became interested in history painting, and staged dioramas that I photographed with my Konica C35. In spite of my sensitivity for the modes of speculation that art engenders, however, my formative experiences with art institutions were not pleasant. Museums and galleries were off-putting: wall texts and labels were abstruse, prices were out of reach, and these temples of contemplation required that the body be silenced in order to appreciate art in a reasoned manner. Above all, exhibitions were conceptually distant; they did not resonate with my experience or history. This sense of alienation was exacerbated by the ethnocentricity of art history. The survey courses that taught me to recognize genre conventions and the virtuosity of masters also taught me that art was the exclusive property of white men. These same courses taught me, by omission, that no creative ethos could take root in Africa, Latin America, the Middle East, or Asia. The lesson was simple and devastating: the genealogy of art began and ended in the West; Europe was both the center and the horizon of the aesthetic universe. My formal introduction to art was, therefore, predicated on the epistemological violence of exclusion.

A woman I never met taught me to distrust well-worn histories. I was still in college but had become suspicious of form and color and had begun to wonder about the sharp vestiges of colonialism. I abandoned photography and took up collage. I rummaged used bookstores for print materials I could destroy, reassemble, and re-signify. I found her tucked inside a book, a Taschen-like edition of Picasso's works. Her voice materialized as dainty inscriptions inserted between the lines, on the margins, and close to the book's gutter. She made heavy use of asterisks and brackets. Often she would encircle a phrase or draw an arrow to direct the reader's eyes toward her quick rejoinders and tart asides. She was angry. Resentment drove her to take possession of almost every blank space in the book, where she planted words that grew into a deliberate attack on the author's argument. Usually she penned long disquisitions, tightly packed at the top or bottom margins, that excoriated the editor for expunging Africa from the story of Picasso's genius. A lot of times, her rage was compressed in thunderous refrains. AFRICA!?! AFRICA!?! AFRICA!?! would bleed out of her pen and into my gut. Turn the glossy white page and there it was, AFRICA!?! AFRICA!?! AFRICA!?!, a triplicate indictment of erasure, desperation, and alienation hinged together by incensed exclamation points and saddened question marks. If the call, "Look, a negro!" plunged Frantz Fanon into blackness, the refrain—AFRICA!?! AFRICA!?! AFRICA!?!—pulled me out of alienation.[1] But I didn't know what to do with this flicker of freedom until much later. For years, it sat in my ear as low-frequency sonic disturbance.

The margins were her workshop, a place where she unveiled the grotesque figurations of Eurocentric accounts of art history and the ground on which she inscribed the primacy and centrality of Africa to the history of the West. The insolence of the alien scribe was earth-shattering. I had never come across the suggestion that art and Africa could be reflections of each other. And it had never occurred to me to question the authority of men who write. Her interlineal glosses and sideline agitations were an exercise in disfiguration that reordered the topoi of the book and revealed the fallacies of the canon. Years later, when I became a PhD student, I came to interpret her defacement of the mystifying history of Western art as the ethos of scholarship: to write in the margins, from the margins, and about the margins.

My encounter with the audacious scribe fueled my desire to salvage what had been deleted from the pages and landscape of history. More importantly, this fortuitous meeting forever changed my conceptualization of education. Until then, going to university was the ultimate in a series of utilitarian acts of survival. My mother held on tight to the belief that education was the only dignified vehicle out of poverty and the measuring stick through which society would ascertain my value. My mother buried herself in a mountain of debt to school me. Since those of us who struggle in

1 Frantz Fanon, *Black Skins, White Masks* (Grove, 1991), 111–12.

the peripheries of plantations, the ghettos of opulent cities, and destitute towns set against rolling prairies are only allowed to possess the bare minimum to sustain life, the luxuries—cultivation of the mind included—can only be purchased on high-interest credit. A photograph I keep amid other brittle mementos fails to document the transactions that underwrote my education, but it reveals the performative mechanisms through which the ideology of education as a serum that transforms the subjugated into a proper middle-class individual is ritualized.

According to the inscription on the back, written by my father in blue ink with self-assured penmanship, this photograph records the inauguration in 1979 of the Sacred Heart School in Puerto Tejada, Cauca, Colombia. The president of the Republic, Julio César Turbay Ayala, came to town to cut the ribbon—a ceremony that sanctified state power as benevolent. Four statuesque Black kids stand in the foreground; I am one of them. The other children on stage pay attention, they look at the camera. I don't. I squint and point my eyes somewhere beyond the crowd. Behind me, the handsome town's mayor, Miguel Gómez, clad in a suit and tie, gifts the photographer a flirtatious smile. To his left and at the center of the composition, the head of state stands. The bespectacled old white man does not look presidential; rather, in this snapshot, we see him as a priest. Caught in mid-motion, his hand looks as if about to anoint the child in front of him with the baptismal waters of wisdom. The other notable presence is the bodiless face of Mrs. Zolia, my preschool teacher. She smiles in admiration of the pupils. We, the chosen four, were the best crop of each of her classes. We were role models, we learned the ABCs dutifully, we sat still, we were polite and diligent. I, barely five years old, solemnly bask in the glory of being praised as the future of the race. There I am: a photo prop, a citizen in the making, the best student in preschool.

My solemnity, it turns out, had nothing to do with the state of my soul that day. I was in pain. That year, I attended school in flip-flops, but on the day of the Sacred Heart School inauguration I wore my cousin's shoes. According to my mother, I had been crying because they were too small and hurt my feet. The loan she secured to celebrate her daughter's learning aptitude was not enough. There was never enough—choosing which necessity to satisfy was the rule: uniform or shoes; arepas with or without eggs. This time the little money she borrowed was only enough to cover fabric for a new uniform and fees for the seamstress. So, there I stood, crisp and shiny, next to the president. I was publicly celebrated for my judiciousness and privately I agonized over the blistering pain of poverty.

By the time this photograph became part of my inheritance, my mother's total expenditure on my education was beyond calculation. I paid for college with a series of "promissory notes" that amounted to tens of thousands of dollars. This insurmountable string of zeros paid for the privilege of mastering the techniques of rhetoric, close reading, and formal analysis; bankrolled my introduction to Sojourner Truth, Karl Marx, and the massacre of El Mozote; funded my descent into the bowels of Elmina Castle; sponsored my discovery of Angela Davis, C. L. R. James, Patricia Hill Collins, Faith Ringgold, *This Bridge Called My Back*, Alma Woodsey Thomas, and *Borderlands/ La Frontera*. Through debt I financed my comprehension of the mechanics of colonialism. To learn that oppression is systematic, that it contaminates everything, reconfigured the chemistry of my eyes and the focus of my vision. My sight longed to be entertained, in the deepest sense of the word, by Black art, by Black ways of seeing the world.

I began to consider academia as a career because I wanted to understand how Blackness was made, how Black people thought themselves into being. I had no particular discipline in mind, the only thing I was sure of was that I needed to grasp the sociopolitical and ideological architecture of colonialism so that I could work to reverse its effects. I wanted to be an "enlightened activist."

Graduate fellowships and another string of zeros secured by "promissory notes" bought me a PhD. I learned to decipher the meaning of surplus and exchange value, enslaved labor, and the discourse of race in Latin America. As I reflect on my doctoral training, what I find most ironic is that while seminars were the testing ground of innovative theoretical approaches to oppression, the issue of class hierarchy in the university didn't make it into the syllabus. We spent hours criticizing the violent procedures of exclusion on which the Western literary, philosophical, and aesthetic canons depend, but I don't recall discussions about contemporary barriers that kept the university and thus knowledge itself lily-white and privileged. The financial, social, racial, and class systems that sustain the university were invisible and invisibilized.

I have inherited nothing except old photographs and my labor power. Most of my colleagues inherited the good manners, habits, and experiences that buy a red-carpet entrance into the ivory tower. Although a few subalterns have infiltrated the university, the number of interlopers remains stubbornly small. According to the National Center for Education Statistics, in 2016 there were 1.5 million faculty in degree-granting postsecondary institutions in the United States. The majority of those who teach are white: 41 percent are white men and 35 percent are white women. Not surprisingly, the number of faculty from historically marginalized ethnic and racial groups is painfully small. Polling reveals that 10 percent of professors in the US identify as Asian/Pacific Islander (6 percent are men, 4 percent are women). The remaining 14 percent is made up of: Black men (3 percent), Black women (3 percent), Hispanic men (3 percent), and Hispanic women (2 percent). American Indian/Alaska Natives and multiracial individuals are counted together; their presence is almost statistically insignificant, at 1 percent of the total number of people who belong to the profession.[2] Moreover, those of us who manage to enter the academic hallways are at an economic disadvantage. The 2015 US Survey of Earned Doctorates reports that "approximately half of American Indian or Alaska Native and Black or African American doctorate recipients and more than 40% of Hispanic or Latino doctorate recipients belonged to families in which neither parent had been awarded a college degree."[3] I don't need to cite these numbers to remind you that we are the minority.

I latch on to these numbers. These numbers confirm that we are unique; that we have made it. These numbers remind me that I am not alone. We dared to believe that reason could inhabit us and we could inhabit reason, and this unprecedented leap of faith has made a dent in the structure.

2 "Fast Facts: Race/Ethnicity of College Faculty," National Center for Educational Statistics, https://nces.ed.gov/fastfacts/display.asp?id=61.

3 "Survey of Earned Doctorates," National Science Foundation Report, 2015, https://www.nsf.gov/statistics/2017/nsf17306/static/report/nsf17306, 6.

Although our numbers are small, every day we produce scholarship that bends the rules, highlights the obscured, and shifts the terms of foundational debates in art history and visual culture studies. My current research project, for example, seeks to recover and situate a series of neglected projects of representation created by Afro-Brazilian cultural workers that unsettle ossified depictions of Black embodiment in the turbulent years between the abolition of the traffic in slaves (1850) and the official end of slavery in Brazil (1888). In the book, provisionally titled *Compromising Portraits: Visual and Literary Renditions of Black Subjectivity in Nineteenth-Century Brazil*, I show that the symbolic construction of Blackness was not a closed circuit of objectification but rather a charged enterprise contingent upon political environment, aesthetic genre, and modes of circulation. I track the ways in which portraiture, a genre that actively refused to depict subaltern subjects, was forced to accommodate a cadre of black men who became notorious popular figures and thus worthy of visual memorialization. I also foreground literary works like Maria Firmina dos Reis's *Úrsula* (1859), the first abolitionist novel penned by a Black woman in Brazil, that imagine multidimensional Black characters—characters who narrate their own histories, criticize the status quo, and thus provide a blueprint for the imagination of Black subjectivity. I argue that the visual and literary cultural objects under review exemplify what I am calling compromised acts of portraiture—that is to say, visual and textual performances that pierce generic conventions and provide complex lines of flight out of reified aesthetic and discursive typologies. Taken together, these projects of representation manage to alter the grammar of portraiture to reveal self-determined, although besieged, Black subjects. By undertaking an integrated reading of painting, lithography, photography, and journalism, I paint a more nuanced picture of insurgent programs of representation that sought to regenerate Black subjectivity. This is the kind of research I've always loved to do: excavating unheard narratives to complicate the picture of what we think we know.

Unfortunately, the meaning of the statistics I cited above always circles back to the sad reality that it is easier for a camel to go through the eye of a needle than for a person of color to inhabit academia. An exaggeration, perhaps. But the pithy numbers stare back at us; they haunt me. They're a source of conflict. They're a cruel reminder that universities are bastions of privilege. Do I encourage students of color to join the ranks and, little by little, tear down the walls that keep us out? Or do I use the numbers as a cautionary tale? And what do I caution against? After all, the university, like most spaces in US society, breeds microaggressions, tiny punctures into one's soul that build up slowly, like plaque, ultimately bending the back and exhausting the will.

I believe that the academic aspirations of people like me should be nurtured and strongly supported. Conversely, I would be remiss if I didn't acknowledge that to work at the university is to engage in a daily battle against institutional racism, marginalization, and misogyny. We subaltern academics who believe that the university should be a space inhabited by all should ask: What price are we willing to pay to be scholars? While I believe that we must actively engage in the production of knowledge, it has become increasingly difficult for me to devote my labor power to further enrich the white 1 percent. For me, the cost is too high in terms of psychic pain, isolation, and financial insecurity, to name a few. I am not naive; it is clear to me that most institutions in our society exist to sustain the status quo. In my case, however, the pleasure I derive from conducting research, writing, and teaching has stopped being an antidote to the nagging feeling that I am a mammy. Familiarity with "otherness," the geopolitics of the Global South, and the aesthetic languages developed by the oppressed, all of which I teach, have become required skills for the white-collar class that the management of transnational capital requires. As I see it, my labor is the milk that nourishes the younger members of the US bourgeoisie.

The suspicious optimism that sustained my academic aspirations has evaporated under the weight of a million microaggressions. For me, the time has come to take inventory and reassess how I/we should invest the assets I/we have gained in academia. Two decades have passed since the bald-faced scribe who lived in the margins of a book about Picasso changed the tenor of my existence by demonstrating the power of critique. I lost that book long ago, but I search the confines of my memory for her words. This time I want her to be my guide as I wander out of the ivory tower on my way back to the dusty town at the edge of a sugarcane plantation where my story began.

Editor's note: Balanta left her tenure-track position at Southern Methodist University in 2019 and moved to Cali, Colombia, where she founded Black Ground Lab, an organization dedicated to the arts and culture of the African Diaspora.

This text was originally published in Latin American and Latinx Visual Culture *1, no. 3 (July 2019): 78–82.*

Unstable Connections: University Teaching in a Time of Protest and Quarantine

Anuradha Vikram

Each week, for the twelve weeks that I met with my undergraduate students on Zoom, I got a window into their private lives and opened one into my own. After the UCLA campus shut down abruptly on March 10, my students scattered: some to too-tight quarters with their parents, some to deserted dorms on campus. Two travelled internationally and got caught in border quarantine for two weeks. I've always been transparent in the classroom about my life as a working parent. Part of my pedagogy is showing up as my whole self for every professional and personal endeavor. Even so, I never expected to be shielding my four-year-old's face from the camera that's recording in my home office.

The personal anxiety of inviting the public university into my home every day was paralleled by the greater anxiety the public as a whole has been feeling, to varying degrees, due to the virus and the financial catastrophe enabled by our national lack of response. In the university, though, despite the impression of normality, instability and fear were already apparent before the lockdown. On February 8, UC Santa Cruz fired fifty-four graduate-student workers who had organized a wildcat strike at the end of winter quarter. The first few weeks of spring had been peppered with solidarity actions across the University of California that foregrounded the high cost of living for teaching assistants systemwide. Graduate students at UC Santa Barbara and UC Davis threatened strikes to demand a badly needed pay increase to match the rising cost of rent near California campuses, including UCLA. My own course depends on four graduate TAs who run discussion sections and support student welfare and learning. They have more than demonstrated their essential value during the pandemic.

My first online art history lecture, which I had originally prepared for in-person delivery during winter quarter, included over fifty slides. I quickly learned that three hours of synchronous lecture is torture for instructor and students alike. The body needs more breaks during a video call. When my throat and my teacup ran dry, about every forty-five minutes, I came to recognize this as a sign that the students also needed to rest. For my first class of the (fully online) spring quarter, I gave a half-hour overview and a forty-five-minute lecture, had the students break out into discussion groups for twenty minutes, then gave them a forty-minute break to review the online resources and discussion boards I had compiled for the course. We met at the end for a twenty-minute Q & A. This weekly format broke the class up into lecture, independent research, and seminar components. I added a group assignment in the hope that the students would find some interpersonal connection despite the alienation inherent in the online setup.

Perhaps because the institution treated their comfort as paramount for once, the students mostly produced excellent academic and creative work. For some, immersion in contemporary art by artists who resemble them in complexion and personal history became a source of solace. I feel fortunate that, after two quarters covering two hundred years of global modern art history, my students had the broad perspective to click immediately with the works of contemporary artists. My undergrads responded to Arthur Jafa, ASCO, David Hammons, Tehching Hsieh, and Carrie Mae Weems in their final projects—artists who express race and embodied consciousness through elegant conceptual gestures.

The first four of Tehching Hsieh's *One Year Performance* works, made between 1978 and 1984, are particularly resonant as they anticipate facets of our strange moment of confinement and protest. In the first, *Cage Piece* (1978–79), Hsieh confined himself to a wooden cage constructed inside his apartment and lived removed from social or media stimulus, dependent on a cohabiting caregiver to provide his food, remove his waste, and document the daily action. This work reflected on the artist's then-undocumented status, but also on the social isolation felt by the immigrant, the invalid, or the prisoner. The next work, *Time Clock Piece* (1980–81), required Hsieh to punch a time clock every hour of the day as he went about his activities, including sleeping. The work includes a table listing all the artist's punches and the reasons he missed them, including sleep. As I go about my day, broken up into teaching, class preparation, writing, and homeschooling shifts, all in the same limited space, I think about how Hsieh regimented his mind to the clock. It's telling that the artist became less diligent as the year progressed, then reinvigorated in the home stretch.

Hsieh's third *One Year Performance, Outdoor Piece* (1981–82), gnaws at me as a person with the luxury of a home to live and work within. The artist remained outside for one year, never entering buildings or taking shelter. His voluntary homelessness may have been a cover for his genuine poverty, as Hsieh has spoken honestly about his financial and immigration challenges during this period. Joan Kee has argued that Hsieh's *One Year Performances* function as legal validations of a life lived extralegally, because the artist's instructions to himself in written form use the language of contracts to make his peripheral experiences into something concrete. Los Angeles's housing crisis has become even more apparent during the quarantine, as people living on the street lack access to hygiene needed to prevent the spread of COVID and have already been susceptible to typhus and other illnesses. It seems unlikely that we can return to normal activities downtown, where the unsheltered population numbers close to five thousand; meanwhile, fewer than eight thousand people statewide had been able to take advantage of vacant hotel room placements as of mid-May.

I do not know if any of my students are unsheltered. I know that less than half seem to have access to a stable enough internet connection and a quiet enough place to work that they are able to turn their cameras and microphones on during class. One student let me know that their parents are undocumented and fear deportation; another has been struggling with a violent experience. I don't require that the students be visible so long as they are making a good showing in our online discussion boards and in discussion section with the TAs. I know many colleagues who feel that audio and video should be mandatory for undergraduate students because their courses depend on having everyone's synchronous attention. I have had to accept that this may not be realistic given the instances of trauma I'm seeing.

Hsieh is perhaps best known for the fourth *One Year Performance, Rope Piece* (1983–84), for which he collaborated with performance artist Linda Mary Montano. Their art-life experiment is an inversion of our post-COVID future—two strangers, bound to stay within six to eight feet of one another for a whole year. Literally tethered together, the artists were forced to negotiate one another in all things. I think of them when my husband laughs heartily on a Zoom call from the desk a few feet over while I struggle to quiet my mind enough to write art criticism in the few short moments between requests from our two young kids.

I was blessed by Montano, the self-described "Art Saint," when she made an appearance in my graduate seminar for USC Roski in late March. Despite two separate meetings to troubleshoot tech issues, something went awry shortly into the class and Montano was no longer able to see me or the students (we could still see her). No matter. She had asked us each to prepare a one-minute performance for the camera based on studying one of her previous performance works. I chose *Three Day Blindfold/How to Become a Guru* (1975). "In this event," Montano has written, "I blindfolded myself because I didn't want to react visually or socially and thought that I could alter my perceptions and therefore drop habituation and judgement." I draped my head and face with a shawl covered in big gold sequins and meditated for sixty seconds. I named gold as my chakra color, which symbolizes the solar plexus. Vedic tradition calls this the center of confidence, dynamism, and will. This part of the body is associated with digestion and is also the home of "gut intelligence" in the form of the complex human biome. It seemed to me an inappropriate time to be guided by the head or the heart.

On May 1, UC faculty joined a May Day General Strike in solidarity with essential frontline workers and graduate students striking for cost-of-living adjustments. The night before, I recorded the lecture I would normally give in class and posted it online for students to review independently. From April 17 to May 1, discussion-board activity for the class dropped from thirty-five out of fifty-two students responding to twenty-two out of fifty-two. Three weeks later, there was little improvement. Our experiment with asynchronous learning seemed to have severed the already tenuous engagement of some students. Fortunately, toward the end of class, the students resurfaced, thanks to the group project, which served its purpose of maintaining connection beautifully. The genuine pride students felt for one another on completing the project and the class was matched by their excitement about their peers' inventive and creative presentations.

Scientific philosopher Giorgio Agamben has lamented how the shift to online learning results in "the disappearance of group discussion in seminars, which was the liveliest part of instruction." Mourning the loss of campus life, he describes how scholars in a community of knowledge are being replaced by atomized communities of learners dispersed across communities big and small. He imagines that university towns will be diminished by the disappearance of students. I feel his lament is bound to an old reality, one that maybe never existed, certainly not in my lifetime. In Agamben's world, students could afford tuition and housing without having to seek service jobs in town. What he forgets is that there were always students who were the first in their families to access higher education, they usually had to leave their communities to do so, and then they felt pressure to feint a lack of interest in returning with the knowledge they gained lest they lose their hard-won social legibility. An ideal community of scholars is one where every participant is secure in their legal status as a whole person and a citizen.

Online learning has its drawbacks, but many could be addressed with improved access to internet, shelter, and other basic amenities. One potential benefit is the loss of "town and gown" divisions that cast knowledge and service workers as different populations. Another is the end of elitism as a value, maintained by faculty who act as gatekeepers to private networks that undergird the ivory tower. These will likely lose influence absent extracurricular opportunities to curry favor with well-connected students. This is a cause for rejoicing. Students' relationships to peers and mentors, and to learning, will endure.

This text was originally published in X-TRA Online on July 20, 2020. See https://www.x-traonline.org/online/unstable-connections.

Art Schools in the Middle East

Gregory Buchakjian, Aissa Deebi, Walid Sadek, and Pelin Tan, moderated by Noah Simblist

Gregory Buchakjian is an associate professor at the Lebanese Academy of Fine Arts (ALBA), University of Balamand; Walid Sadek is a professor at the American University in Beirut (AUB); Aissa Deebi is a professor at Virginia Commonwealth University's campus in Doha, Qatar (VCUQ); and Pelin Tan is a professor at Batman University in Turkey and a cofounder of the online platform Urgent Pedagogies. All the speakers have experience teaching art in the Middle East and talk about the specific challenges of the current political moment, but also some of the larger tensions that have existed in the region for some time. This conversation was recorded October 30, 2024, during the attacks by Israel on Lebanon and Palestine, which sent shockwaves throughout the region and affected the participants in direct ways. The conversation has been edited for length and clarity.

Noah Simblist As the recent violence in Palestine, Lebanon, and elsewhere in the region has disrupted daily life, how do you see educational institutions responding?

Walid Sadek It seems to me that the devastation brought about by the current chapter of this ongoing war between Zionism and Palestinian liberation movements and their allies has put individuals and institutions on the defensive.

Speaking from AUB, I see that this institution is not prepared for something of this scale. I mean, previous crises have taught us to develop certain techniques. But my experience is that the university is almost shut down. We are teaching online, but it's really not a university. We're just providing basic services, a modicum of continuity.

NS What about you, Gregory?

Gregory Buchakjian We live in a country that has been going through wars and wars and wars. All my teenage and college years were marked by the Lebanese Civil War. I moved from one school to another, and the second school had itself moved from somewhere else. So, I was, as a student, a refugee. And the school was a refugee inside another school. I think that this is some kind of fate.

Since October 7, there was the threat that Israel would also attack Lebanon, but we wanted to be optimistic. The previous Israeli invasions of Lebanon, in 1982 and 2006, came as a surprise. This time, the Israelis were saying, "We are going to attack, we are going to attack"—and they attacked. It was extremely violent. The first week, everything stopped. The second week, we at ALBA resumed by teaching online. And in the third week, we entered a hybrid phase, saying to the students, "Those who can come, please come to campus." Walid was saying that AUB is not prepared, but, I mean, who can be prepared for such a catastrophe?

The other day, I saw a student on campus who lives in a neighborhood that was bombed. She was sitting on a chair. She couldn't think. She couldn't say a word. Her face was completely white, she was completely traumatized, and she wanted to stay, because otherwise students like her are stuck at home and feel like they are going mad. So this young woman who didn't sleep at night was exhausted. Yet she didn't want to go home because somehow the campus is a safe space that's outside of the war arena.

NS Wow, that's very powerful. In this case, Lebanon has become intimately connected with Palestine. But I wonder about other networks within the Middle East and North Africa (MENA) region. First, I wonder how you each define the MENA region. Are there subregions for art and education? For instance, is there a relationship between cities like Beirut and Ramallah and Cairo and Marrakech and Tunis and Doha and Riyadh? Is there a relationship with non-Arab countries like Turkey or Iran? Pelin, do you want to start?

Pelin Tan In the case of Türkiye, it is difficult to answer because art education in Turkish universities is separated from the Middle East. There is almost no connection to MENA. The art academies are looking to Europe, to the West, as it is the heritage of a Eurocentric modernist Kemalist ideology from the 1930s. But not as much as Lebanon.

In Türkiye, art education was developed at the beginning of the Turkish Republic and in the late Ottoman Empire. It was very Francophone. Now I feel it's connected neither to Europe nor the rest of MENA. What is happening more is that artist initiatives or biennials are trying to get more in contact with the Middle Eastern art world. For example, while I have been researching Palestine since 2014, I see that art institutions, especially in the West Bank, or in Lebanon, or Amman, are connected to US institutions and Europe, much more than their counterparts in Türkiye.

Aissa Deebi First, I want to comment about where we started. I think institutions were not prepared for what has happened since October 7, but I'm not sure if they were ever prepared to deal with these issues. I think the main challenge that Western academia outside of the United States is dealing with is the crisis of the values that those institutions were trying to bring to generations of creative practitioners in the Middle East.

Of course, in Doha, we don't live in a war zone, but we are in the geographic range of one. We are very close to Iran, but our experience is different from the experience in Beirut or in Gaza. We are not living the genocide physically, but we are living the genocide mentally.

Since October 7, Western therapy has failed fantastically to deal with those issues by trying to direct students' issues into anger management, instead of in ways that help everyone to accumulate the anger around us and channel it positively. This new liberal phenomenon is problematic. I think the crisis, the main crisis of October 7, is the collapse of all these humanistic values that institutions have been trying to inject into the students in the region.

If you want to speak of how art schools are connected in the Middle East, I will say they are not connected. You know, our model in Doha is very different from the model in Beirut. It's different from the model in Cairo. It's different from the model in Amman or in Tunisia or in Algeria. Our universities have different histories. The American University in Beirut is more a Lebanese than an American institution. But VCU hasn't managed to become local even after twenty-five years in Doha, or the American University in Cairo after one hundred years of trying to integrate into Egyptian society.

NS Many institutions have been built in the Gulf over the last twenty-five years. How has this affected the educational opportunities for the region? There's VCU in Qatar and NYU Abu Dhabi, plus many museums and biennials and art fairs and foundations. Is there a relationship between museums and universities in the region?

AD VCU in Qatar is one of the oldest academic institutions to offer arts education in the country, which received its independence in 1971. It's a very young country. The Fine Art Academy in Kuwait in the 1960s is an earlier model. But for many years, the major influence on the Gulf came from Iraq. However, Western institutions that have been established in the Gulf in the last thirty years offered a different model of education that was not previously available to the people in the region: the American system of liberal arts, BAs and BFAs.

Most art academies in Egypt offer "Art Education" rather than "Fine Arts" programs. If we look at the United Arab Emirates, we can see that in the last twenty-five years it has been building institutions, mainly museums, but there was no real focus on building art academies. Outside of, you know, NYU, Abu Dhabi has not managed to have a major impact on the art scene in the region. It's different from Dubai's art-market influence.

WS Everything I've written lately seems to be guided by the idea of fragmentation, but I want to think of fragmentation as a critical and generative notion to think through. We are having difficulty using an acronym like MENA to somehow delimit or define a region; even the term "Arab world" is suspect. It's difficult to believe in any of these things. The systematic destruction of Arab nation states in the last five decades caused a serious fragmentation.

So you have fragmentation, destruction, and a petrification of the public sphere, right? On the other hand, you have a growth in art institutions and museums and collecting practices. Of course, the concentration of Arab modernism and museums in the Gulf provides an opportunity for research.

But the problem is that what's missing is a trajectory for these opportunities. Because whenever you think of a trajectory or direction, you think of something a bit more political—and that's where I think you hit a wall.

On the other hand, in the face of so much fragmentation it seems to me that the challenge for art academies is to rethink their relevance to their locality—to build critical relationships to places, without becoming provincial or turning their backs on others. I don't think you can begin a conversation if you don't know where you are.

NS Are there differences between American universities such as AUB, AUC, VCU, and others like ALBA?

WS The differences between the various universities in "the region" right now remain circumstantial. I would like, instead, for the differences to be intentional. I would like it if a student who wants to study in the region says, "I want to study at ALBA, not at VCU Qatar," because of a very particular conversation that's happening.

NS How do you all think that formal institutional art education relates to informal alternative models like the academy in Ramallah, Ashkal Alwan in Beirut, or MASS Alexandria in Cairo?

PT There are general curriculum problems with the art academy that come from the beginning of the twentieth century, especially in the case of Türkiye. The academy and the museum were part of building the nation-state; they are elitist, urban class–oriented. These institutions don't really develop much until the end of the 1990s, when artist collectives and other kinds of initiatives started to expand, especially in and beyond Istanbul. The need to come together and have alternative forms of learning and discussion has to do, firstly, with the criticism of the nation-state, its identity and modernity.

Most famous artists from Turkey who have international reputations came from these alternative initiatives. We see how the fine arts academy was useless in the '90s because it was so conservative. It wasn't interdisciplinary or focused on artistic research.

In the meantime, censorship or auto-control of curricula in Türkiye is very disturbing for me. For example, in Lebanon, at institutions like Ashkal Alwan, I can assign some readings that would be censored in Türkiye. I was at Ashkal Alwan a few times; it's like a master's program. Art education at that level doesn't really exist in the fine arts academies in Türkiye. Pressures are on both sides—the student and the teacher. The sense of freedom and the inter-regional connection in such a program as Ashkal Alwan generates a more advanced level of discussion. Due to the histories of dispossession of the twentieth century, current ambivalence about border politics as they relate to extraction and war, or the fragility of migration ... it all suggests to me a collective base for sharing and debate across the MENA region.

AD I want to echo Walid about how we redefine and think of the region. He and I started a conversation when I was in Beirut last year about why Beirut is so important for the future of the arts, despite all the political challenges that it is going through. In Doha and in Cairo we don't have what Beirut offers as a space. Mainstream institutions in the Arab world never managed to offer this freedom of creative space—a safe zone for artists to create, outside of censorship, away from secret police sitting in Middle Eastern classrooms.

Since I came to Doha, I've been asking myself, "What is the motivation to start an art program in Qatar? Why do we need the fine art program in Qatar? Why does Qatar need an Education City? What is the purpose of bringing an American academic model into Qatar?"

Of course, cultural diplomacy has a huge influence to create mutual political and economic interests between two countries. But at the same time, what's the power of Western education in a country as small as Qatar? Pelin was talking about the crisis of nation-building in Turkey and how academies became super conservative. During my time in Cairo during the Arab Spring, things opened up, but this moment of freedom, where you could really experiment and push the envelope, is not available anymore.

Why are we building institutions in the region and what is the purpose of those institutions? We are allowing young people's minds to be part of larger conversations. But how large are these conversations? Do we really have a region-wide conversation about the arts? Or are we a group of small bubbles in different cities?

After the Arab spring, those of us at the American University in Cairo tried to decolonize the curriculum. We tried to think about how we could create an art curriculum that belongs to the context of Cairo, to rethink how we teach art history in a place where you can take a car and go to the pyramids, rather than buying a book that was published in New York in 1968 and teaching the history of Egyptian art through an American scholar that came to Egypt for six months. But since October 7, maybe larger questions about the region are much more urgent.

I'm thinking about what's happening in Gaza and the demolishing of all academic life, about three hundred artists living in refugee camps. It's quite challenging to think about the purpose of art institutions and mainstream governmental institutions. Maybe it's a moment to rethink which kind of institutions we need, or if we need institutions at all.

GB I think that we all share this question. What does it mean to not have school now? In Lebanon, in the Arab world, in the Middle East, in the world, we all are pessimistic because the world is not going in the direction we would like it to go—in terms of governance, in terms of the environment. I had this conversation with myself. I'm running this department. It is the oldest place where art is taught in Lebanon, but so what? Does it need to continue to exist? What is its purpose? Is its purpose to give students skills like drawing and painting and sculpture and installation and sound and video? I think that the answer is that we are here to open up this conversation with the city, with society.

I didn't have the ambition to go to the region because, as everybody has said before, I think that it's very complicated to establish bridges across the region. We all have bridges with other institutions in the West, and this is very colonial or postcolonial. We have a relationship with the Beaux Arts de Paris and Les Arts Décoratifs, but we don't have any agreement with any school in the Arab world, nor in Turkey or Iran.

We will see what happens if we're still alive. Meanwhile, I think that, for me, the most important thing is to be with the city, with the people of the city. I've had the opportunity to do that because a year after I started my mandate, we had the revolution in 2019.

For three months, people were in the streets. Everything was closed and, of course, we were demonstrating with our students. One day a student said, "We need to sit down in the atelier and have a conversation, not in the street. We need to have a conversation between us." But the school was closed. So this happened in my studio, which is not very big. I had thirty people in my studio, students and teachers. It was like a mini demonstration. Now, I won't say that we changed the world, and I won't say that this was a historical moment, but I think that it was important to keep this connection.

Afterward, we had the COVID–19 pandemic and the entire world started to go online. And my students got completely mad and told me, "We cannot keep on like this. We need to have human contact." And the students started to work all together in one of their studios. They created a collective and they started doing exhibitions in abandoned spaces in the city. I was very happy to see that the students were somehow not being passive, but moving on, creating something new. I think these small things are lessons about how we can keep up, lessons about solidarity.

In Beirut, after COVID, we had the August 4 explosion. And now we have the war. So you have a cultural scene which has suffered a lot, but which is still standing.

I have a lot of students who are queer. In Arab countries this is very complicated. It's very dangerous, and we do everything possible to allow students to have freedom in their projects, in their discourse, in the conversations within the school. Now we are facing another situation.

We have other students who are conservative, who don't want to draw the nude model in the drawing courses, for instance. Now, these are a minority, but it is very important to address this in a civilized way. So today I had a drawing teacher telling me about these students who don't want to draw the nude, and I gave her the example of the Lebanese painter Moustafa Farroukh, who, a century ago, had a scholarship to study in Rome. He arrived in Rome. He was Muslim and he goes in to the academy and there is a nude female. He is completely shocked; he doesn't know what to do. Farroukh wrote his memoir in Arabic. It's exquisite. He says, "I'm a pious Sunni Muslim and I see this woman, like God created her." And he had his dilemma. So I said to my colleague, "You should read them the text Faroukh wrote, it could be a great example."

WS At the risk of generalization, we can say that the European and North American model for art education is dominant, and it's dominant because the history and the theory of art is primarily written in those centers. But things are changing. It seems to me that if we want to think of decolonizing or localizing art education, we need to produce scholarly work that provides new models of interpretation. And the good news is that it's happening. The other day I wrote down the relevant books that have been published through American university presses. But there are not many, actually. I wrote down five books. The earliest one is from 2013 and the latest 2022. So this is very recent despite the fact that artists in the region have been doing work and there are catalogs and scholarly work. I would like to mention the book by Kirsten Scheid published two years ago, *Phantasmic*

Objects: Art and Sociality from Lebanon, 1920–1950, where she develops a theory of *tasweer.* Last year, we organized a conference to think about this concept. So it's happening, but it's going to take a while, because you are working against the hegemonic canon, right? It's not an easy battle.

NS Thinking about this notion of the future, or, dare I say, hope for the future, can anybody offer a word or a phrase that imagines something that we can hold on to as we move forward? Or perhaps cast a spell for a hopeful future for art education in the region?

AD It's very complicated to think about the future outside of the present moment. But despite all the challenges this region's been dealing with, artists manage all the time to make really fascinating work. I think that we should focus on artists, not institutions.

WS This is my answer to this question: The future is as open as it appears foreclosed.

Why I Protest

A College Senior Having His Degree Withheld

I was asked by the *Crimson* to write this op-ed to reflect on my time as a Harvard undergraduate student. Today, I am forced to publish this article anonymously. For my involvement in the pro-Palestine encampment, I have been placed on probation and my degree is being withheld for at least a year. Retaliation from the Administrative Board is likely if they identify who I am, given that I am one of fourteen graduating seniors in this position. I will not be allowed to walk with a degree in hand for standing up, consistently and proudly, for *veritas*. My family, who have made innumerable sacrifices to see me in the place that I am today, will not be able to hang a college diploma on our living room wall. I am leaving Harvard infuriated, exhausted, and disgusted. I am appalled by the university's moral and material complicity in an ongoing genocide, and the conditions of apartheid in occupied Palestine which it aids and profits from. But also—and perhaps naively—I am surprised that Harvard would go to the extent that it did to distinctly suppress voices that call attention to this issue.

For all intents and purposes, according to university spokesperson Jonathan Palumbo, the university is "committed to applying all policies in a content-neutral manner and per existing regulations as outlined in college and university Guidelines." If only Palumbo read the *Crimson* alone. Just last week, professor Steven Levitsky wrote extensively about the ways in which Harvard's response to pro-Palestine protests breaks from precedent and demonstrates the university's longstanding exception to free speech when it comes to Palestine. Several student groups, particularly those representing predominantly Brown, Black, and Asian students, have since affirmed what they see as the university's neglect of its own precedent. It is not lost on us that these decisions were made as Harvard comes under fire from Congress and engages in meetings with the Anti-Defamation League—notorious for perpetuating racist and Islamophobic sentiment. There is plenty that undermines the university's claim to content neutrality. The injustice lies bare before the student body and the world.

Yet I want to make one thing clear: Garber's rescission of his promise to allow organizers to graduate should not be considered an anomaly. For anyone involved in pro-Palestine organizing on Harvard's campus—and, in particular, seniors—this is the most apt culmination of our time at Harvard. Just this year alone, we witnessed the university refuse to condemn the doxing truck that paraded our faces around town. We saw the university's abject lack of empathy when it ignored death and rape threats to members of our communities, including those that had nothing to do with political organizing on campus. We begged for conversations with university administrators about topics we felt were important to us, only to consistently receive empty words and an aversion to direct engagement with student concerns. The Palestine Solidarity Committee, the only recognized Palestinian student group in the College, was suspended for alleged violations of President Garber's "Rights and Responsibilities," a decision that has since been challenged by the ACLU. We witnessed a divestment referendum shot down.

While the administrative board loves citing its bible, the Student Handbook, to punitively charge many of us, it conveniently forgets this passage: "It is the responsibility of officers of administration and instruction to be alert to the needs of the University community; to give full and fair hearing to reasoned expressions of grievances; and to respond promptly and in good faith to such expressions and to widely expressed needs for change." The university has never engaged in good faith with our communities even when we play by the rules.

We protest because we condemn the way in which this university, and this country, functions in aiding and abetting genocide. We protest because our predecessors, in the Civil Rights Movement, the anti–Vietnam War movement, the anti-apartheid South Africa movement, the Living Wages Campaign, the Iraq War protests, the Black Lives Matter protests, and Fossil Fuel Divest movement, teach us that despite all odds, one day we can win. We protest because our faiths teach us to. We protest because our grandparents and great-grandparents sought freedom from colonialism—and it is only our duty to carry that legacy today. We protest because our mothers cry every time they read an account of yet another Palestinian child being brutalized by IDF forces. We protest because we come from places that are sensitive to histories of genocide, ethnic violence, and occupation. We protest because we have hearts that respond to images of bloodied dead bodies and the destruction of "safe havens," refugee camps, and hospitals.

A job offer, a fellowship I was awarded, and a diploma is not my metric for success. Speaking out for and winning justice is. And so, Harvard, if you want to charge me for being human, go for it. I will not apologize for having a heart. Do not dare claim me as your own in a few decades.

This text was posted on Instagram by @harvardundergradpsc on May 19, 2024. It has been condensed for length.

On Hating Students

Daniel Spaulding

Is there anything more contemptible than an undergraduate? Not if you believe the news. In recent weeks, thousands of students have been arrested, manhandled, banned from campus, evicted from housing, and attacked with rubber bullets, tasers, and chemical irritants at the behest of their own institutional leadership. Mainstream coverage of students protesting the war in Gaza regularly proclaims concern for young people's well-being while revealing a clear desire to do them harm. Social-media comment sections are full of impassioned calls to ruin lives for what are, objectively, minor transgressions. Somehow this is not felt to be in contradiction to the overriding imperative of student safety. This style of thought is currently shared by many members of America's political and economic ruling class, constituting something like a spontaneous ideology that crosses party affiliations. Meanwhile, Israeli forces have destroyed or damaged at least 80 percent of schools in Gaza, prompting experts at the United Nations Human Rights Council to suggest that an intentional "scholasticide" is underway.[1] Respected news outlets insist that the specter of student-led pogroms on elite campuses is worthier of attention. The anti-student imaginary is full of massacres that aren't happening, rather than the ones that are.

What accounts for this collective pathology? Or to put it differently: Why does everyone hate college students? In academic as in other counterinsurgencies, it seems that there are times when it becomes necessary to destroy the village in order to save it. To protect students from other students, it is necessary to put a large number of students behind bars. In a fine article entitled "The Campus Does

1 UN Office of the High Commissioner for Human Rights, "UN Experts Deeply Concerned Over 'Scholasticide' in Gaza," press release, April 18, 2024, https://www.ohchr.org/en/press-releases/2024/04/un-experts-deeply-concerned-over-scholasticide-gaza.

Not Exist," Samuel P. Catlin points out that the logic of campus security is structured around a fantasy figure that the queer theorist Lee Edelman calls The Child.[2] The Child is not necessarily an actual child; rather, it's an embodiment of innocence as well as an investment in the (heterosexual) future, even at the expense of people who need help right now. Edelman names this complex "reproductive futurism." (Another pervasive moral panic that orbits around The Child is the current surge in trans- and homophobia, focused as it is on high-school sports and the putative threat of "grooming.") College students conveniently enter and exit the category of The Child depending on the exigencies of the moment. So do literal children: it is, after all, in the name of the abstract Child that conservatives defend the rights of fetuses even as they eviscerate funding for schools and social programs. But the Republican Party has no monopoly on this libidinal deformation. For the most part, it has been liberal-minded administrators and college presidents bringing down the hammer on campuses.

As Catlin observes, universities present unusually harsh discipline as justified when student-Children are under threat.[3] Police and administrative violence can be applied to students themselves once they have been stripped of citizenship in the academic state and designated "non-affiliates." We have seen this happen in the mass arrests at Columbia, NYU, Yale, USC, Emory, UT Austin, Cal State Humboldt, UCLA, and many other institutions. (The list has grown so long that keeping track is difficult.) Catlin argues that this process of recategorizing certain students as "outside" agitators is part and parcel of how both university administrations and the culture at large construct the "campus." The campus is not so much a physical space as an imaginary one, commonly represented as a site that is forever in crisis. Notions of the crazy, dangerous things that happen on college campuses seem to live rent-free in the minds of many Americans, including, or especially, those who have no direct contact with institutions of advanced learning. Catlin notes that people like to get worked up about protecting Children on Campus even if they happen to be indifferent to students in the flesh.

Catlin, however, underemphasizes the reality that sadism directed toward students is a fundamental component of public discourse on higher education. The student is somebody to whom discipline is always rightly forthcoming. Even more so when students are already hateworthy for other reasons: being humanities majors, feminists, queers, critics of colonialism. Even more abhorrent are art students, surely the most frivolous of all. But anti-student sadism generally does not dare speak its name outright. Hence the search for an innocent figure to protect against the disaffiliated student. Jewish people under the threat of antisemitism have been adopted as a new Child, requiring protection at any cost. This scenario—vulnerable Jews under siege—is infantilizing, and, by extension, antisemitic. Invoking antisemitism is a way to enjoy real, potential, or purely hypothetical anti-Jewish violence by concern-trolling about it. We have witnessed congresspeople all but salivate as they ask questions about the supposed genocidal intent of slogans such as "from the river to the sea." Since these sanguinary visions have little correlation with what protesters say or do, their

2 Samuel P. Catlin, "The Campus Does Not Exist," Parapraxis, April 2024, https://www.parapraxis-magazine.com/articles/the-campus-does-not-exist; Edelman, *No Future: Queer Theory and the Death Drive* (Duke University Press, 2004).

3 Catlin here appropriately cites Jennifer Doyle's *Campus Sex, Campus Security* (Semiotext[e], 2015).

wellspring seems to be the questioners' own imaginary. The figure of the student in revolt becomes the vector for the self-proclaimed philosemite's bloodlust. This student inflicts upon Jews the fantasized violence from which only actual violence can provide protection. It has been said that every accusation is a confession; I wouldn't put it so categorically, but talk of rampant antisemitism on campus mirrors the logic of Biden's claim that, without Israel, "there wouldn't be a Jew in the world that is safe"—a statement that serves as an ostensible warning but rings more as a threat.

It's moot to speculate how much of this rhetoric is genuine conviction and how much is performance, or whether there is even a difference between the two. There are, of course, powerful material interests that ratify this fantasy. While donor interests might explain the economic and political rationale behind the crackdowns at universities, they do not account for the specific patterns of brutalizing discourse, which seem to be surplus to the demands of capital and the state. Businesses, after all, still need universities to deliver qualified labor power and subsidized research, both of which are under threat from disruption on the scale we have been witnessing. I propose instead that the ferocity of the antagonism must come from the dense overdetermination of higher education's role in class reproduction.

First: it ought to be self-evident that the paradigmatic function of universities is to reproduce class. Until recently, the point of the Ivy League was simply to produce Ivy League graduates who could serve as a prefabricated (wealthy, white, Christian) ruling elite. Whatever knowledge students obtained along the way was essentially decorative. In recent decades, this function has partly broken down as degrees have become little more than a sorting mechanism—even at the lower end of the labor market—rather than a ticket into the bourgeoisie. While Ivy League universities retain their class-reproducing function to a greater extent than other schools, the ongoing diversification of student bodies means that the white, Anglo-Saxon Protestant, the Ivy League student is now many things at once: privileged brat, liberal arts major turned barista, future finance bro, precocious tech entrepreneur, preppy legacy dullard, affirmative-action fraud, dupe of tenured radicals, coddled baby, violent militant. This is what a discourse of class looks like in ruins.

Some of these valences of the Student do connote class superiority; when these are made the targets of anti-student zeal, the fantasy is one of revenge. But the modality in which one imagines revenge converges with the Student's other incompatible roles in at least one key way. The Student is preeminently a subject of discipline. Arrogant snowflakes meet the real world, where facts don't care about your feelings; would-be radicals get job offers rescinded; would-be gender theorists get their dignity stripped in low-paying service jobs. In all these scenes, a real insight into the falling value of advanced education in the labor market is articulated as schadenfreude, with boss or dean serving as avenging angel. In this respect, administrative and police violence, in concert with labor discipline, produces the real unity of an otherwise incoherent category. I would suggest that the figure of the student in current discourse is not a set of empirical characteristics; rather, it is defined by susceptibility to discipline. A student is a person to whom an expanded range of disciplinary procedures can be applied, since they are at the mercy of multiple sovereignties. Thus, students can be simultaneously arrested by the NYPD, evicted from their homes, and suspended from academic programs. And in Gaza, they are being killed.

There is nothing all that unique about the discipline to which students are exposed. Outside campus gates, non-graduates and the working poor face arbitrary power in even more naked forms. But off-campus violence is naturalized by economic and governmental rationalities in different ways. Here, the "mute compulsion" of economic relations limits the moral responsibility of individual actors, including bosses themselves.[4] Getting fired may ruin your life, but that's just the economy, stupid. At the same time, police and the legal apparatus directly coerce and punish. Despite being unambiguous manifestations of state power, police and the law nevertheless appear as the de facto forms of violence through which any bourgeois society controls its underclass; there is nothing shocking about a poor person getting arrested or getting shot, and, accordingly, nothing like the same attention is paid to such events compared to happenings on the mythic Campus. To those on the receiving end of economic exploitation and state repression, the student's position is enviable indeed.

What accounts for this distinction is that the student is seen as a future worker, or a potential future member of the reserve army of labor—even if, empirically speaking, a large percentage of students work their way through college, and that ostensible future is increasingly a vanishing one.[5] The myriad ways in which students feed into capital accumulation are not directly visible, since, qua students, students are not exploited. In this sense, their activities are perceived as analogous to other kinds of "unproductive," unwaged labor, such as housework. This is to put things in categorical terms that do not necessarily correspond to reality. Graduate students, for one thing, are often clearly workers (as teaching and research assistants), and successfully organize as such. But "worker" and "student" are at least notionally meant to exclude each other.

The campus thus appears to be a zone in which economic necessity is suspended. A corollary is that violence against students appears to be divorced from the "normal" repression of proletarians. To witness the spectacle of anti-student discipline is to see the force of pure sovereignty, stripped of its economic naturalization. The student is the torsion point at which the mute compulsion of capitalist social relations meets Louis Althusser's two state apparatuses: the "ideological state apparatus" that reproduces labor power, and the "repressive state apparatus" that metes out discipline and punishment. That students apparently have nothing more useful to do than to learn (or, heaven forbid, make art) is a source of envy, admiration, and resentment, some of it merited, since the quarantining of students from everybody else is part of class society's logic of separation. But resentment from on high is never merited in the slightest.

A proper contextualization of the current campus protests should not only slot them into the legacy of previous student movements (for which the mythos of "the

4 The phrase "mute compulsion" is Karl Marx's. Søren Mau has recently brought it back to attention in his book *Mute Compulsion: A Marxist Theory of the Economic Power of Capital* (Verso, 2023).

5 The growing unlikelihood that today's students will ever get to join the ranks of the middle class is the main fact that has to be appended to a text that otherwise remains exemplary, the pamphlet *On the Poverty of Student Life* (published by the Situationist International and students of the University of Strasbourg in 1966; Mustapha Khayati was the principle author).

sixties" is now set in stone). It should also tie them to other recent episodes of mass social unrest in the United States, such as the uprisings for Black lives in Ferguson, Missouri in 2014, and then across the nation after the murder of George Floyd in 2020. During the Black Lives Matter protests, relations between segments of the college-educated but downwardly mobile middle class and racialized proletarians became acutely problematized. Two symmetrical but contradictory representations of these events proliferated across traditional and social media alike. On the one hand, the poor and people of color were subject to a familiar and often blatantly racist rhetoric of feral lawlessness. On the other hand, educated and largely white "riot tourists," who dared to betray their race and class by performing material acts of solidarity with the insurgents, found themselves called out for supposed hypocrisy, often by liberals and even leftists. The question of what actions other than pointless virtue signaling or grindingly slow institutional reform might be permissible for the "graduate without a future," a term coined during another cycle of global revolt,[6] was left unanswered. A solution wasn't found, of course. In any case, despite great efforts made by Diversity, Equity, and Inclusion bureaucrats to roll out new "woke" capitalism within academia, the most important instances of unity happened not in the seminar room or corporate office but in the streets, where shared outrage at the police occasionally bridged real and persistent inequalities between different camps of demonstrators.

These moments of collective action may have been just as chimerical as the cross-class alliances of older proto-revolutionary sequences, such as when French lycéens steeped in Lacan and Mao's Little Red Book descended to the factories in the 1970s. There is something inherently absurd about these scenes: students who play revolutionaries always seem to wear an ill-fitting costume, even when their revolutions are quite real. Yet something of this sort remains at the horizon of any student movement that has the potential to transcend the hoary rituals of campus protest. There is a chance that pro-Palestinian students, recognizing the treason of their elders (university presidents, police chiefs, and far too many professors), will ally their specific grievances with a more totalizing proletarian critique of the educational system's function as an engine of class dominance.[7] To the advantage of our ruling class, this critique too often tends to be conflated with reactionary anti-student propaganda that fills the airwaves with horror stories about the American youth wing of Hamas. To put it succinctly, poor people hate students for good reasons whereas rich people hate them for bad reasons. Is it possible to disentangle the rational hatred of the poor from the irrational hatred of the rich? Not in words. But the history of revolutionary movements is a history of attempts—often failed—to unify various groups, in practice more than in theory: peasants and soldiers in 1917, workers and students in 1968.

This was originally published in e-flux on May 28, 2024. See https://www.e-flux.com/education/features/610182/on-hating-students.

6 Paul Mason, "The Graduate Without a Future," *The Guardian*, July 1, 2012.

7 This may be happening. As I write, graduate students in the University of California system have just voted to authorize a strike in protest of rights violations during recent demonstrations.

The University Struggle to Unlearn Zionism

Ariella Aïsha Azoulay interviewed by Linda Xheza

Linda Xheza In your book *Potential History: Unlearning Imperialism* you trace the foundations in imperialism of institutions such as the museum, the practice of photography, and human rights. These days I am reading Maya Wind's book *Towers of Ivory and Steel: How Israeli Universities Deny Palestinian Freedom*, in which she demonstrates how Israeli universities are complicit in the oppression of Palestinians. I think it is important to extend the discussion of imperial institutions you consider in your work and ask you about the complicity of Western academic institutions in relation to imperialism. What are your thoughts on the role of the latter in the legitimization of the state of Israel and the dehumanization of Palestinians?

Ariella Aïsha Azoulay Our universities are part of these other imperial institutions (archives or museums) I'm talking about in *Potential History*. They were formed to normalize imperial plunder of all sorts: material, intellectual, spiritual, cosmic, and moral. Similarly to museums and archives, their raison d'être is to divert us from the truth of the colossal imperial plunder that has been part of the world-destruction enterprise. These are sites of temptations that attract people with a certain promise of knowledge about the world, while obviously omitting that this knowledge and this world are those imperialism shaped. They acquired this status and power through the destruction of other forms of education and transmission, and thus arrived to impose themselves globally as a key for mobility within this world. The imperial nature is not only of the institution—it is also of many of the disciplines taught within it. The discipline of history is a paradigmatic case since it was fashioned to produce knowledge and narratives that bury what imperial violence destroys and proclaims over.

Palestine, May 1948, is a telling example. The Zionists were in the midst of their attempt to seize Palestine, destroy it, deport its people (by May only half of the total of 750,000 Palestinian expellees had been deported), and proclaim the establishment of the state of Israel on its ruins. How did historians and the discipline of history respond to this catastrophe? They started to provide historical narratives in which Israel figured as a given, a sovereign power capable of proclaiming a state and erasing another while neither exists nor occurs only in the language. While the Zionists needed a few more years to deport the majority of Palestinians and to achieve on the ground this split reality where they are situated "within" Palestine-turned-into-Israel—and thus turning the expellees into "infiltrators" threatening the new state's sovereignty—for historians this was already a fait accompli. They rushed to describe a split hierarchical reality where Zionists were recognized as legally inhabiting "their" country and their actions as part of law and order, while Palestinians, deported from their country, were depicted as intruders and a threat, identified with the categories that the international organizations of the "New World Order" crafted for people like them. The Zionist narrative of the destruction of Palestine was invented as a story of liberation of the Jewish people. After the Holocaust, this story served the New World Order that the newly founded United Nations heralded. In November 1947, the UN provided the legal basis for this split history in the form of the partition resolution, issued against the majority of Palestine's population. This resolution, followed by Zionist violence to conquer Palestine, was enough for historians to transfer Palestine to "the past" and relate to Palestinians as the enemies of the citizens of the newly declared state.

Historians' addiction to documents is toxic. It is also contagious since in a world imperially fabricated, their narratives enjoy a symbolic power coming from their knowledge of imperial facts (written in these documents) and their "right" order in time and space. Documents-based history assists in defeating those formations, forms of life, and aspirations that imperialism seeks to destroy. Historians are trained to relate to imperial proclamations as manifestations of truth that they amplify and disseminate as obligatory scaffolding for any historical narrative. *Potential History* is the rejection of this orchestrated attack on common just truths. What are those just truths of 1948 sacrificed by history?

(A) Palestine was in the process of being destroyed and this destruction could still be stopped and opposed and justice reclaimed. The leaders of Western countries, however, who had interests in the success of the Zionist narrative, supported the continuation of destruction (like we see today in Gaza) until the majority of Palestinians were expelled from their country (a process that took several years) and the invention of a Jewish state in Palestine seemed normal.

(B) Many Jewish survivors of the European genocidal attack against them were forced to become part of the Zionist enterprise in Palestine (given the lack of other viable options for them as Europe and the United States closed their gates) and to accept a bargain of reconciliation with Europe, which instead of letting them rebuild their communities in Europe, "gave" them a state of their own in Palestine that was not theirs to give.

(C) Diverse Jews were forced to leave their worlds behind and embrace the European relation to Arabs and Muslims as enemies, while it was not the Arabs and Muslims who were their perpetrators—but rather Europeans. This new enmity was achieved quite instantly once the Zionists destroyed Palestine and proclaimed the establishment of Israel against them and their will, including against the will of the Jews who were part of the Jewish Muslim world for centuries.

(D) The destruction of the millennia-old Jewish Muslim world in the Middle East and North Africa, forcing the Jews to be incorporated into the myth of a Judeo-Christian tradition invented for them as part of Europe's absolution of its crimes.

LX Many university administrators around the world have decided to act against their own students and staff, often resulting in the latter being brutally attacked by the police. What are your thoughts about this?

AAA I propose to look at what is going on in and against our universities as a three-pronged movement: (a) against the genocide and the entanglement of our universities in it; (b) against the failure of our universities to fulfill their role in an imaginary contract with certain segments of society that recognize them as sites of knowledge production and actually enables their existence (more than the donors!); (c) against the expansion of a class of administrators whose job is to implement a condition of thoughtlessness in the daily life of the university. I borrow the term *thoughtlessness* from Hannah Arendt to describe the way the managerial framework that administrators imposed over the years under the umbrella term *reforms* limits the ways students, faculty, and staff can think, ask questions, account for the world, and act and interact with each other and with others. That we are punished for doing what we assume ought to be the heart of our academic work—thinking, that is, asking what is going on in Gaza and naming it genocide, interacting with the truth-tellers of Gaza, asking questions about the involvement of our universities in the genocide—exemplifies this. Arendt developed this term in *Eichmann in Jerusalem* to describe the failure of the capacity to think with and through others and to grasp the meaning of what one is doing through the ways it impacts others. Thoughtlessness is a direct effect of a world imperially shaped, where instead of acting and interacting with others who also act, people are trained and expected to operate technologies and abstain from thinking with others. What is being marketed today as the advanced technology of AI, where machines think for us, is something that we have been already experiencing for decades through the expansion of this class of administrators whose form of governmentality leaves less and less room for thinking, and thinking through others, without which resistance is eroded, and the world becomes destroyed. This condition of thoughtlessness in our universities became even clearer as from the beginning of the genocide not a single university initiated study groups or task forces dedicated to the genocide, seeking to understand the conditions that enable this horrible enterprise of violence to last for so long, to study the concerted effort to gaslight its occurrence while it unfolds in real time in front of our eyes (and not after the fact), or to disaffiliate the institution from it and express solidarity. Rather, many of these universities established task forces to punish those of us who dare to think and do it with others. Calling the police into the campuses was not unprecedented or surprising, but a means to terrorize us as we were revolting against the condition of thoughtlessness and acting against the genocide and its normalization.

In this sense, I propose to relate to this movement whose major sites are the campuses as a truth-telling movement, a revolt against thoughtlessness as the condition under which a genocide unfolds in Gaza and we are being commanded to move on with business as usual, while we know that our institutions and many of their programs are funding and are funded by the genocide and contribute to it on many levels. Hence, I find it necessary to recur to a certain imaginary contract between the society and the university in order to ground our struggle against what those who rule the university are doing and acting as if they have the right to determine what is right and what is wrong. This mass movement of encampments is not (or not yet) a walkout from the university but an attempt to take seriously our role as constituencies of these imperial universities and rehearse what we believe the university should do. This movement foregrounds the cleavage or incommensurability between the commitment of the class of administrators to protect thoughtlessness and the capital these institutions accumulate through their donors, and the commitment of segments of the constituencies of the university (among the students, staff, and faculty) to the truth and its telling, that is, to anticolonial justice. This police violence exercised against the constituencies of the university when they rehearse this contract with society is thus not surprising but is inscribed in the agenda of this class of administrators. Just to make it clear—rehearsing this imaginary contract is not shared governance with administrators whose mission is to trap us under the condition of thoughtlessness—but rather rehearsing a different condition as the outcome of our power as the constituencies of the university without which they will not exist.

LX You have argued that the strike should not be considered as the right to protest oppression but rather should be seen as a collective opportunity to "unlearn imperialism with and among others." Is this what we are witnessing at the student encampments? The media often frame these encampments as pro-Palestinian camps, but according to your conception of the strike, it seems to me that what is also equally important is the refusal of the imperial world that is emerging there.

AAA The biggest achievement of this movement is in its success to disrupt globally and publicly the narrative about Palestine and Israel that the Zionists and the West have imposed since 1948 by using different violent means—including through our universities—and to expose and amplify the truth about Palestine and the genocidal nature of the Israeli regime. Calling this movement "pro-Palestinian" is a symptom of the condition of thoughtlessness where denouncing violence against one group is being depicted as being in favor of another group rather than against this violence and the enduring injustice that allows its perpetuation. The demands addressed to our universities to divest from Israel and from arms companies should be understood as part of the actualization of this imaginary contract with the university. If there were not such a contract many of us would not spend many years of our lives there and would not try over the years to create a university-within-a-university that allows us to carry on part of what we believe is our mission. It is not surprising, though, that all the encampments were formed as a university-within-a- university in which people can come together to study, think, and respond to the genocide in Gaza with others, that is, with the truthtellers from Gaza who broadcast it daily despite the efforts to eliminate and silence them. I deliberately speak about a contract not only with us who are in the university, but with the society in which it exists. Otherwise, we won't see members of the society participating in the actualization of such a contract like the judge in Providence, Rhode Island, who in May found that the forty-one students arrested by Brown university are not guilty. His judgment supersedes the failure of the president of the university to act as a president of a university first by commanding their arrest and then by refusing to drop the charges despite the multiple demands from students, staff, and faculty.

LX Last year when I taught your book *Potential History*, some of my students thought that what you argue there is maybe "too radical," but this year the majority of them are protesting in the streets. Do you think we are now at a historical moment where the imperial shutters are being loudly and powerfully challenged and rejected—perhaps one of the very few times this has occurred to such an extent? How did the genocide of Palestinians manage to form a decolonial coalition with many of us around the world?

AAA Yes, we are at this important moment when the metanarratives generated and imposed with so much violence in the late 1940s as part of the "New World Order" as a way of ending World War II are collapsing. One paradigmatic example is the truth about the nature of the Israeli regime as a genocidal one, which can no longer be hidden behind the justifications Europe provided as a way of absolving itself from its responsibility for the genocide it perpetrated against the Jews, as well as for the termination of the Jewish Muslim world in the Middle East and North Africa. The state of Israel destroyed Palestine, dispossessed Palestinians of their lands and worlds, and destroyed the diverse forms of life of Jews everywhere. This genocide in Gaza opens up the two questions that the West invented in the nineteenth century and acted as if they could only be resolved through their fusion—the Jewish question (which should rather be described as the question of the Jews) and the question of Palestine. This fusion enabled the Nakba and the promotion of the genocidal regime of Israel as a Jewish liberation project, which is at the basis of the current genocide in Gaza. It is not a coincidence that the persecution of the growing number of anti-Zionist Jews, protesting against the genocide and against Israel, is especially expansive in France and Germany, which understand the danger of having Jews joining other colonized people in denouncing the European imperial enterprise and the monster it created in the form of the Zionist state as their compensation for the genocide. We anti-Zionist Jews, as well as others in this movement, state it out loud—we will not let any university administrator command us what we have the right to think or what we can say when we see genocide.

This conversation was originally published in New Politics *(Summer 2024).*

From the Unreviewed Writings of a Peerless Thinker

Jalal Toufic

Throughout my three-year stint as a professor at the Department of Humanities and Creative Writing (which would be far more accurately named Department of Cultural Studies) of Hong Kong Baptist University, I was dismayed by the very low educational level of many if not most of the third- and fourth-year students. And I found the stark discrepancy between the low educational level of these students and their inflated grades unacceptable, indeed smacking of corruption, since student evaluations loom large in faculty reviews: in one fifty-student class, only two received a C, and in an eighty-student class, only five received a C, all the others receiving As or Bs. In comparison, the midterm grades of my six honors-project advisees were C, C-, D+, D+, D, and D-, and my grades for the midterm assignments of the fifty-three students in one of my courses included thirty-five that were between C- and B-. Gilles Deleuze wrote in *Cinema: The Movement-Image*[1]: "Eisenstein suggested that the close-up was not merely one type of image among others, but gave an affective reading of the whole film." The following question students are asked to answer for HKBU's Course Feedback Questionnaire, "I found that what I learnt was what I had expected of this course," is not just one among others, let alone an anomaly, but rather the key to understanding all the other questions of

1 Given how difficult it is for a student to fail a class at HKBU, since students can opt not to attend even a single session and yet pass the class, according to a university policy introduced in 2017, and since the warped grading-scale equivalence between the letter grades and the percent grades at HKBU functions as a type of grade inflation, the letter grades A-/A, for example, spanning eighty to one hundred on the percentage scale (if the grade-inflation trend is not countered, I wouldn't be surprised if some years from now the letter grades A-/A would be equivalent to seventy to one hundred on the percentage scale at HKBU and at other universities, especially in Hong Kong); and given the outsized weight student evaluations play in faculty promotion and tenure, the real evaluation that matters at HKBU, and in an increasing number of universities, is, symptomatically, the students' of the teachers rather than the teachers' of the students.

the CFQ. I can easily imagine the evaluations of the Department of Humanities and Creative Writing's students of the teaching of Deleuze, Jacques Lacan, and Alexandre Kojève, whose seminars count among the most famous and influential in the "humanities" in the twentieth century, had these thinkers taught a semester at HKBU: unsatisfactory! Here's what I consider the most plausible ratings by the HKBU Faculty Review Panel had Deleuze been a faculty member of the university: teaching (based almost exclusively on student evaluations): unacceptable; scholarly work: excellent (that is, he would have been evaluated as no different from the university's least published and productive faculty members, since, the bar being set so low for scholarly work to be evaluated as excellent [one article published in a so-called tier-1 journal and another published in a "second-tier" journal], they too are deemed to be excellent in this regard); service: threshold.

Friedrich Nietzsche:

> Learning transforms us.... But at our foundation, "at the very bottom," there is clearly something that will not learn, a brick wall of spiritual *fatum*, of predetermined decisions and answers to selected, predetermined questions. In any cardinal problem, an immutable "that is me" speaks up.... In time, certain solutions are found to problems that inspire *our* strong beliefs in particular; perhaps they will start to be called "convictions." Later—they come to be seen as only footsteps to self-knowledge, signposts to the problems that we *are*—or, more accurately, to the great stupidity that we are, to our spiritual *fatum*, to that thing "at the very bottom" that *will not learn*.[2]

2 Friedrich Nietzsche, *Beyond Good and Evil: Prelude to a Philosophy of the Future*, ed. Rolf-Peter Horstmann and Judith Norman, trans. Judith Norman (Cambridge University Press, 2002), §231, 123–24.

One teaches neither those who are fully teachable (is there such a human? Would an entity be human or still human if it is fully teachable, or would it turn out to be, for example, a trainable deep neural network? Beware of those who are fully teachable) nor those who are solely unteachable, those who are, from a Gnostic perspective, devoid of any spiritual light, but those who have something unteachable, a spiritual fate. And one teaches them with what is unteachable in one—one's "stupidity," one's spiritual fate. One teaches them in part to counter the teaching that treated them as fully teachable. One teaches them to differentiate what is teachable in them from what is unteachable in them.

In July 2015, I was offered the position of director of the School of Visual Arts at the Lebanese Academy of Fine Arts (Académie Libanaise des Beaux-Arts [ALBA]). I accepted the offer and wrote the following mission statement for the school:

> Established in 1944, the Lebanese Academy of Fine Arts (ALBA) was the first national institution of higher education in Lebanon. Before long, it was playing an important role in the Lebanese art scene, through its faculty (a notable number of whom were former students) and alumni. Yet, for various reasons, not least the civil war, Alba's School of Visual Arts for the most part did not accompany, let alone play a leading role in, the flourishing art scene in Lebanon in the past two or so decades. Within a couple of years, the school will *again* be part and parcel of the Lebanese art scene. But beyond becoming part and parcel of the Lebanese art scene, the School of Visual Arts at Alba will have really mattered, not proved fully reducible to culture, only if it graduates at least one artist who manages to "fail better" (Samuel Beckett: "Ever tried. Ever failed.

No matter. Try again. Fail again. Fail better" [*Worstward Ho*]); and/or at least one artist who constructs "a universe that doesn't fall apart two days later" (Philip K. Dick); and/or one artist who sacrificially (since this would require exposing himself or herself to it in the first place) wraps the invasive *jouissance* that only recently was taking aback vast zones of the region (Syria, Iraq, etc.) into (Hölderlinian) song or (Rilkean) angelic, awesome beauty; and if it enhances if not reestablishes the connection of art and thought, more specifically of thought-provoking art and art-provoking thought, a connection that has for quite a while now been a paradoxical one, given that, according to a still valid diagnosis of Heidegger, "we are still not thinking—not even yet, although the state of the world is becoming constantly more thought-provoking," and although fresh thought-provoking artworks continue to be made (only to then be largely shrouded by the numerous mediocre works with which they are exhibited in biennials, triennials, galleries and museums).

Some of the school's additional objectives:

— To provide the students with a "temporary autonomous zone" (to use an expression coined by Hakim Bey [a.k.a. Peter Lamborn Wilson] in his 1991 book of the same title) in relation to those of this region's problems that are outdated, so that he or she would be spared wasting his or her time rediscovering variants of solutions that are often decades if not centuries old.

— To lead students to the realization that, regarding actual artworks, the issue is not to understand them but to acquire intelligent and subtle incomprehension with respect to them and to intuit and appreciate their rigor, thus desisting from correcting any seeming failing in them—a correction that impairs not only admiration but also possible criticism of these works.

— To develop in students a flair for differentiating between a painting, video, and so on, that falls apart even before it is framed or screened and one that does not.

— To make students keenly aware that artists collaborate in an untimely manner with future and past artists and thinkers.

— To give students the stark realization "I've never thought before"—not simply about art, but tout court. And then to confront the student with what forces him or her to think (for example: the realization that he or she has never thought before? A thought-provoking artwork?) and thus with the chance to think, whether he or she would use this thinking in his or her art practice.

— To boost students' intuition, including their "'shit' detector" (Hemingway: "The most essential gift for a good writer is a built-in, shockproof, shit detector"; Frank Auerbach: "I hope I still have what Hemingway called the 'shit detector,' that I'm still severe enough with myself if something is not finished to destroy it and start again"), in a period when it is increasingly easy for those associated with the production of works that might be exhibited in galleries, museums, and biennials to fool curators, collectors, audiences, indeed also themselves (Richard Feynman: "The first principle [of having utter scientific integrity] is that you must not fool yourself—and you are the easiest person to fool")—including while working on scatology (Sade, etc.)—so that when they graduate they can depend on it to unsparingly destroy those of their works that fall apart before the perceptive spectator blinks.

- To provide the student with at least as much art as necessary to counter culture, if not transmute it into tradition (possibly by sublimating it or pushing it toward a special abjection or using it as manipulable stereotypes [as in the novels of Alain Robbe-Grillet]). To expose the student to art and thought, which belong to tradition, rather than merely to culture, whether high (exhibited widely in museums and biennials, etc.) or low, both insidious enemies of tradition. Much of what starts as ostensible counterculture ends up as culture. It actually belonged to culture all along; tradition consists of that part of counterculture that continues to be counterculture, perennially. The real artist and the real thinker are not cultured, but countercultured (and thus have, among other tasks, to coin adjectives absent from the dictionaries of those who are cultured).

- To graduate a number of students who end up producing rigorous works of art—which is not to say ones that would usher in or contribute to a golden age of art and thought in Lebanon and beyond, since the metaphor of the golden age should have ceased to be used with the abolition by the US government of the gold standard (the golden age for the use of the metaphor of the golden age was the period when gold acted as the economic standard of value, from 1821 [the year England established it] to 1971 [the year the US government abolished it]). The downside is that such students might be at risk of dying of laughter when they come across a reference to a golden age of theater in Lebanon in the 1960s and '70s.

A caveat concerning the school comes from Deleuze, writing in May 1990:

> Foucault located the disciplinary societies in the eighteenth and nineteenth centuries; they reach their height at the outset of the twentieth.... Foucault has brilliantly analyzed the ideal project of these environments of enclosure, particularly visible within the factory.... But what Foucault recognized as well was the transience of this model: it succeeded that of the societies of sovereignty, the goal and functions of which were something quite different (to tax rather than to organize production, to rule on death rather than to administer life).... We are in a generalized crisis in relation to all the environments of enclosure—prison, hospital, factory, school, family.... The administrations in charge never cease announcing supposedly necessary reforms: to reform schools, to reform industries, hospitals, the armed forces, prisons. But ... these institutions are finished, whatever the length of their expiration periods.... The societies of control ... are in the process of replacing the disciplinary societies.

While Deleuze's prescient words have become more manifest in our day, a quarter of a century after he wrote them, they have been obscured in the context of ALBA's School of Visual Arts by the accidental problems that have beset this school from around the time he wrote his text. As the school's new director, I consider that by fixing the largely accidental problems that have undermined the school for several decades, the problems that cannot be fixed by any administration and faculty, since they are symptoms of the ongoing transition from disciplinary societies to societies of control, would come to the fore and become clearer, this making it easier to contribute to "new forms of resistance against the societies of control."

Toward the end of his introduction, addressed to the Faculty of Arts and to Hong Kong Baptist University's six interdisciplinary research labs, which include the so-called Augmented Creativity Lab and "promise to enable academics from different backgrounds [including philosophy] to work together on common sets of problems," Professor Yi-ke Guo, the then newly appointed, pompous Vice-President (Research and Development) of the aforementioned university, said, in response to a question and in an exemplification of Cioran's aperçu that "the essential often appears at the end of a long conversation. The great truths are spoken on the doorstep,"[3] "Make a machine equipped with artificial intelligence write a poem. That would be a manifest result. The rest is philosophy." (I am quoting from memory; although what followed cannot be deemed "the rest" in any interesting sense, the aforementioned response marked for me the actual end of the meeting.) With his misunderstanding of whatever reductive epistemology he might have read, this limited researcher in the field of artificial intelligence made sure to betray his unawareness of the insistence of various great scientists on the relevance, indeed cruciality, of philosophy for science in general and for artificial general intelligence in particular, for example David Deutsch in his aptly titled article "Philosophy Will Be the Key that Unlocks Artificial Intelligence."[4] From what perspective can one rigorously say, "The rest is philosophy," while still understanding these words in a derogatory manner? One could say it, indeed a rigorous philosopher (Alain Baidou) did say it, from the vantage point of Lacanian psychoanalysis and its pass:

> But, you'll say, what about philosophy in all this? Well, philosophy is that which *doesn't pass*. This is something Lacan was deeply convinced of. I'd even go so far as to say that the detritus of a pass must be entirely philosophical—the waste material of a pass.... Show me the trash cans of a pass sometime—I think they'd be full of philosophy. That's what doesn't pass! And why doesn't the philosophical aspect of an analysis pass? Because it consists of everything that turned out to be hermeneutics, banal interpretation, various and sundry types of bullshit, disastrous totalization, self-awareness in an intense cogito [*cogito concentré*], absolute false knowledge, the triumphant authority of the master who never criticizes himself, and so on. What is all that? It's philosophy, ultimately![5]

While rigorous, that remains a negative assessment and evaluation. From what perspective could we maintain that "the rest is philosophy" but in an affirmative, redemptive sense and manner, so that one could respond emphatically to that pompous researcher in artificial intelligence: "No—the rest is philosophy"?[6] (Let this tasteless person asking for a poem composed by AI be perplexed by this twisted, poetic rejoinder.) More generally, how to redeem an inanity in the form of "the rest is ..."? One can do so by considering it from a vantage point where it can assume a rigorous affirmative value and status: in relation to what is useful, the rest is being (Deleuze: "When Bruno [in Werner Herzog's *Stroszek* (1977)] asks the question: 'Where do objects go when they no longer have any use?' we might reply that they normally go in the dustbin, but that reply would be inadequate, since the question is metaphysical. Bergson asked the same question and replied metaphysically: that which has ceased to be

3 E. M. Cioran, *Anathemas and Admirations*, trans. Richard Howard (Arcade, 1991), 82.

4 *The Guardian*, Oct 3, 2012, https://www.theguardian.com/science/2012/oct/03/philosophy-artificial-intelligence; see also "Creative Blocks: The Very Laws of Physics Imply that Artificial Intelligence Must Be Possible. What's Holding Us Up?," *Aeon*, October 3, 2012, https://aeon.co/essays/how-close-are-we-to-creating-artificial-intelligence.

useful simply begins to *be*"[7]); in relation to the police in Rancière's understanding of this term,[8] the rest is politics[9]—fittingly, given politics' acknowledgment of and concern about an implied activism, if not militancy, regarding the part of the community that is not acknowledged as a part of it; in relation to the sphere of what Lacan termed, in a derogatory manner, the service of goods (*le service des biens*), the rest is desire (Lacan: "What is Alexander's proclamation when he arrived in Persepolis or Hitler's when he arrived in Paris? The preamble isn't important: 'I have come to liberate you from this or that.' The essential point is 'Carry on working. Work must go on.' Which, of course, means: 'Let it be clear to everyone that this is on no account the moment to express the least surge of desire.' The morality of power, of the service of goods, is as follows: 'As far as desires are concerned, come back later. Make them wait'"[10]); in relation to *jouissance* (one of the guises of) the rest is the saint (Lacan: "A saint's business, to put it clearly, is not *caritas*. Rather, he acts as trash [*déchet*]; his business being *trashitas* [*il décharite*].... The saint is the refuse of *jouissance*"[11]); in

5 Alain Badiou, *Lacan: Anti-Philosophy 3*, trans. Kenneth Reinhard and Susan Spitzer (Columbia University Press, 2018), 85. Don't these characteristics apply to some degree to certain aspects of his philosophy, or at least to some of his texts? Here are two examples, from 1977, of the bullshit of a philosopher: "There is only one great philosopher of our time: Mao Zedong.... All the rest disappeared into futility" (Alain Badiou, "The Current Situation On the Philosophical Front," in *The Adventure of French Philosophy* [Verso, 2022], 1 and 4; when he was not bullshitting, the same philosopher wrote in a text dated 2005 and that would become the preface to the same book: "Let us take the example of two especially intense and well-known philosophical instances. First, that of classical Greek philosophy between Parmenides and Aristotle, from the fifth to the third centuries BCE: a highly inventive, foundational moment, ultimately quite short-lived. Second, that of German idealism between Kant and Hegel, via Fichte and Schelling: another exceptional philosophical moment, from the late eighteenth to the early nineteenth centuries, intensely creative and condensed within an even shorter time span.... There was—or there is, depending where I put myself—a French philosophical moment of the second half of the twentieth century which, everything else being equal, bears comparison to the examples of classical Greece and enlightenment Germany. Sartre's foundational work, *Being and Nothingness*, appeared in 1943 and the last writings of Deleuze, *What Is Philosophy?*, date from the early 1990s. The moment of French philosophy develops between the two of them, and includes Bachelard, Merleau-Ponty, Lévi-Strauss, Althusser, Foucault, Derrida, and Lacan as well as Sartre and Deleuze—and myself, maybe" [I would replace Bachelard with Lyotard—moreover, if Lacan, whom Badiou considers to be an antiphilosopher, is included in his list of major French philosophers, why isn't Blanchot, who maintained a neutral relation toward philosophy? This omission indicates a major blind spot in Badiou, who is in denial of his mortality, of his condition of dead (in other words, undead) even while still physically alive]); and: "It is interesting to note that, in *Rhizome*, the cunning monkeys of multiplicities, the heads of the anti-Marxist troupe, Deleuze and Guattari, openly strike out at the central dialectical principle: One divides into two.... We will not take Deleuze and Guattari to be illiterate. We will thus take them to be crooks" (the quote is from the text "The Fascism of the Potato," *The Adventure of French Philosophy*, 193–94; when he was not bullshitting, he wrote: "For Gilles [Deleuze], 'to think' means: to make a section in the chaos. To be as close as possible to chaos, and nonetheless to shelter oneself from it. The power of a thought is its capacity to stay as close as possible to the infinite with the minimum thickness for shelter. A thought is all the more creative, the less sheltering it needs. A powerful thought stands, almost naked, in the fiery midst of the virtual.... Gilles Deleuze: creator, by way of concepts, of new links, of hitherto impossible connections," *The Adventure of French Philosophy*, 340–41).

6 One of the most fitting, humorous uses of the dash is to have the seemingly same statement on both sides of it, qualified or negated on one side and affirmed on the other, for example because it was understood exoterically on one side and esoterically on the other.

7 Gilles Deleuze, *Cinema 1: The Movement-Image*, trans. Hugh Tomlinson and Barbara Habberjam (University of Minnesota Press, 1986), 185.

8 "Two logics of human being-together must ... be discerned.... Politics is generally seen as the set of procedures whereby the aggregation and consent of collectivities is achieved, the organization of powers, the distribution of places and roles, and the systems for legitimizing this distribution. I propose to give this system of distribution and legitimization another name ... the police.... The word police normally evokes what is known as the petty police, the truncheon blows of the forces of law and order and the inquisitions of the secret police.... The petty police is just a particular form of a more general order that arranges that tangible reality in which bodies are distributed in community. It is the weakness and not the strength of this order in certain states that inflates the petty police to the point of putting it in charge of the whole set of police functions." Jacques Rancière, *Disagreement: Politics and Philosophy*, trans. Julie Rose (University of Minnesota Press, 1999), 28.

9 See previous note.

10 Jacques Lacan, *The Ethics of Psychoanalysis, 1959–1960: The Seminar of Jacques Lacan, Book VII*, ed. Jacque-Alain Miller, trans. Dennis Porter (Routledge, 2008), 315.

the context of psychoanalysis, the rest is, exemplarily, the *object a*, the object cause of desire, and, since he is to allow "the subject, the subject of the unconscious, to take him as the cause of the subject's own desire,"[12] the psychoanalyst; and in the context of messianism, the rest is the non-non-Jew (drawing on "St." Paul, Agamben wrote: "The division of the law into Jew/non-Jew, in the law/without law, now leaves a remnant on either side, which cannot be defined either as a Jew, or as a non-Jew. He who dwells in the law of the Messiah is the non-non-Jew"[13]). Anyway, how would AI know what a poem is when, for at least a century now, every poet worth anything has pondered, questioned, and experimented with what a poem is?

For matters that are unimportant, I register my contrarian response in the big Other, for example through a dissenting vote, while in matters of importance, particularly ethical ones, I treat the big Other as nonexistent.

As long as there is no full, exhaustive knowledge—and, one can argue, there is no such thing, even if we postulate the existence of God, since, while all-knowing, He is infinite and the creator ex nihilo par excellence—there is no proof of understanding some topic or field other than the creation of *new* knowledge in it.

There is no difference between thought and thoughtlessness except when thought is thought-provoking.

Most instances of plagiarism in academia, especially in the field of cultural studies, are of what is unworthy of being published in the first place!

How ironic and twisted to have a literature review in most academic books and almost all PhD dissertations (mine didn't), especially in the field of cultural studies, since they end up being in their entirety no more than an expansive literature review. Freud's *The Interpretation of Dreams*, which includes a literature review, is a rare exception, since it then moves on to be one of the most original books ever written on dreams. The literature review in Freud's *The Interpretation of Dreams* should have been placed, like every literature review in an original book, in the middle, because a good researcher is one who does not start with searching and researching but, like any creative writer or artist, by finding ("'I do not seek,' said Picasso, 'I find'"[14]), but then searches and researches to remove those things he was not aware others had already addressed felicitously and to elaborate some others.

Nowadays, most academics read *only* to do the formal *literature review* section of their articles and, occasionally, as reviewers for this or that "peer-reviewed journal."

In 1977, in his one-time intervention concerning the so-called New Philosophers (*nouveaux philosophes*), Deleuze wrote:

> "These New Philosophers ... do have a certain newness about them: ... they have introduced France to literary or philosophical marketing. Marketing has its own particular logic: 1) You have to talk about the book, or get the book talked about, rather than let the book do the talking. Theoretically, you could have all the newspaper articles, interviews, conferences, and radio shows replace the book altogether, it needn't exist at all. The work which the New Philosophers do has less

11 Jacques Lacan, "Television," trans. Denis Hollier, Rosalind Krauss, and Annette Michelson, *October* 40 (Spring 1987): 19–20.

12 Lacan, "Television," 19.

13 Giorgio Agamben, *The Time that Remains: A Commentary On the Letter to the Romans*, trans. Patricia Dailey (Stanford University Press, 2005), 51.

14 Quoted in Rachel Flynn, "I Do Not Seek Picasso, I Find ...," https://www.tate.org.uk/tate-etc/issue-24-spring-2012/i-do-not-seek-picasso-i-find.

> to do with their books than with the articles they can obtain, the newspapers and TV shows they can monopolize, an interview they can give, a book review they can do ..."[15]

Nowadays, according to the twisted order of priorities of an increasing number of universities, especially in Hong Kong SAR, what matters most is no longer the book or artwork or film but the award of a grant, which is no longer treated as merely a means to an end, the production of a book or artwork or film; hence, symptomatically, it is not the publication of a book, including one that was written while drawing on the financial resources provided by a grant, but the awarding of a grant that gets all the congratulations and plaudits, demonstrative ones at that. As a faculty member at Hong Kong Baptist University for the past two years, had I, as a result of receiving one or more emails per day from the Faculty of Arts and the Graduate School announcing or reminding faculty members of some coming grant or other, ended up applying for one instead of ignoring all of them, it would have been one that provided teaching relief for the duration of the grant period and that led to a book in the form of a collection of grant proposals, each of which would be the distillation of a book in ten sentences or would provide a summary of the proposed book that could be perfectly related orally in a few minutes—none of these books would end up being written and published since each of the aforementioned ten sentences would actualize Nietzsche's ambition, mentioned in his book *Twilight of the Idols*, "to say in ten sentences what everyone else says in a book—what everyone else does *not* say in a book," and each of the *avant la lettre* summaries would covertly function as a Borgesian reason not to write the book ("It is a laborious madness and an impoverishing one, the madness of composing vast books—setting out in five hundred pages an idea that can be perfectly related orally in five minutes. The better way to go about it is to pretend that those books already exist, and offer a summary"[16]).

Increasingly, health is promoted as an absolute and exclusive value, certainly in much of academia in Hong Kong and much of official culture in Singapore (here's an example from academia: Hong Kong Baptist University's Faculty of Arts' Niche Research Area "has three central topics, Well-being, Value, and the Public Good," and one of its sub-themes is "Chinese and Cross-Cultural Health Humanities," which is said to be "an interdisciplinary and cross-cultural research field that focuses on the relationship between arts, humanities, health, and well-being"). The resultant lack of a dual perspective of sickness on health and of health on sickness is itself a sickness, or at least a symptom of sickness. Nietzsche: "Looking from the perspective of the sick towards *healthier* concepts and values, and conversely looking down from the fullness and self-assuredness of *rich* life into the secret workings of the *décadence* instinct—this is what I practiced longest, this was my true experience; if I became master of anything then it was of this. I have my hand in now, I am handy at *inverting perspectives*: the foremost reason why for me alone perhaps a 'revaluation of values' is even possible."[17] The obscure motivation of every institution or culture that values health and well-being to such a degree that

15 Gilles Deleuze, *Two Regimes of Madness: Texts and Interviews, 1975–1995*, ed. David Lapoujade, trans. Ames Hodges and Mike Taormina (Semiotext[e], 2006), 141.

16 Jorge Luis Borges, *Collected Fictions*, trans. Andrew Hurley (Viking, 1998), 67.

17 Friedrich Nietzsche, *Ecce Homo: How to Become What You Are*, trans. Duncan Large (Oxford University Press), 88.

its goal is the exclusion of any sickness and the eradication of all diseases is to prevent, block, indeed eliminate altogether the very possibility of a revaluation of values.

Soon after joining the Department of Humanities and Creative Writing at Hong Kong Baptist University, I was assigned, as one of the department's three full professors, to be a member of the committee in charge of the "yearly performance review" of various faculty members and tasked to evaluate in particular the research component. I naively read the articles the faculty members under review published during the relevant period, only to discover that the expected so-called research evaluation was to be exclusively determined by the prestige of the journals in which these articles had been published and of the publishers of any recent books by these faculty members (1.5 points for an article in so-called tier-one journals, four to six points for a sole-authored book, etc.), and that the so-called teaching evaluation was determined by students' evaluations, and consequently that we were there solely to count points, since the evaluation had ostensibly already happened elsewhere. Were those who gradually designed this system of evaluation worried that someone who starts by evaluating may end up creating values? They shouldn't worry about this eventuality, since one cannot really, fundamentally, evaluate without having already created new values. The other two senior faculty members on the committee would not countenance actually reading the academic output of the faculty members under review and possibly deciding that an article published in a so-called tier-1 journal is worthless; for them, an article published in such a journal must *ipso facto* be excellent. Through reveling in or at least acquiescing to and collaborating in the maintenance of such a system in which evaluation is outsourced to so-called peer-reviewed journals (in other words, to the editor in chief of the journal, possibly also, if there is one, its associate editor, and the two or three reviewers who were selected by the former), (preferably academic) publishers, and students, and hence in which they are treated as elementary accountants, the current senior academics in most cultural-studies departments and communication departments (some of these departments masquerade as humanities and film studies departments) betray that they are not able to evaluate, let alone create, new values, but are dependent on others' evaluations, themselves based on already established mainstream majority or minority values.

Excerpt from *The Unreviewed Writings of a Peerless Thinker, 2020–2022*, in *The Collected Writings (1991–2024) of a Mortal to Death: Jalal Toufic*, vol. 1 (No Place Press, 2025).

Learning Is a Desire for Proximity

Steffani Jemison, Naeem Mohaiemen, and Beatriz Santiago Muñoz, moderated by Noah Simblist

This conversation was recorded on October 3, 2024. It has been edited for length and clarity.

Noah Simblist Can we begin with a little bit about how each of you have come to your recent experiences of university teaching? How did you come into teaching in a more formal setting?

Naeem Mohaiemen In earlier correspondence, you referred to Occupy Wall Street and Strike Debt, and I have an Occupy-related connection.

I was a working artist for years. With regard to my education, I had adopted an approach of, "I don't want to become excessively self-conscious about the underpinnings of my work." An urban legend used to circulate that artists entered the Whitney's Independent Study Program making work and then exited it making theory. 16 Beaver, in some ways, was our model of a space where we could theorize our practices. There was a general perception of an excessively intellectualized part of the art world that was losing touch with the pleasure of material practice.

During Occupy Wall Street, I remember clearly a strong contingent of artist-educators. For example, Fia Backström, who was at Columbia University, would bring her students. I had a very sharp sense of Occupy Wall Street as being, for art educators, a moment of praxis after years of theory. I was influenced by that moment to enter graduate school; I applied to graduate school a month after Occupy Wall Street collapsed. I received a graduate degree that trained me to teach in an anthropology department, so I had to navigate what it meant to be in a studio program. Earlier today, I had a conversation with [artist and educator] Matthew

Buckingham during which we raised the question of whether we are teaching *making* or teaching *pedagogy*. That's the lens through which I'm thinking about art education right now.

NS Thank you. Steffani?

Steffani Jemison Thank you for sharing that, Naeem. My trajectory is a little different. In your preparatory materials, Noah, you mentioned bell hooks's *Teaching to Transgress*. The journey hooks narrates has always resonated deeply with my experience. I've loved school since I was a child, and I always imagined that my life would unfold in relation to communities of learning—and therefore teaching. I have always loved my teachers, I have always loved being taught, I have always loved being in environments where teaching and learning was happening. As a young person, I saw those as joyful places, places for both thinking and community-building.

Of course, at a certain point, in parallel with what hooks describes, I became somewhat disillusioned. I began to suspect that the intellectual work I cherished as a student of Black literature and aesthetics rarely reached audiences outside of it. I learned that academe requires research and administrative functions that have nothing to do with teaching and learning and realized it would always be a challenge to balance the multiple roles of teaching, office politics, and corporate logistics required to succeed as a professor. Although I had been on a traditional academic track, intending to pursue a PhD and a career entirely within the academy (while writing and making films and music and photographs as a hobby), I realized that art could be a space of praxis—a discourse within which I could continue the work that I wanted to do and reach a wide range of intersecting audiences.

The nature of my work meant that sales alone were unlikely to sustain me. I entered graduate school not because I needed it for my creative practice, but because it was a prerequisite for teaching at the university level, a vocation which could sustain my life as a working artist. I knew that as an artist, I wold be able to calibrate the energy I devoted to the university, keeping one foot inside the academy with my students and colleagues and the other foot firmly planted in the wider world.

I'll add that my disillusionment about the possibility of reforming the corporate higher education containers in the United States—or at least softening the effects of these institutions on students—has led me to create contexts outside of universities where the kind of learning that excites me can happen. Cultivating these learning spaces is an important part of my life's work. I wouldn't necessarily describe it as part of my artistic practice; I see these efforts as different but continuous.

NS Thank you. Beatriz?

Beatriz Santiago Muñoz I keep searching my brain to remember how I got here. Maybe I'll start by admitting that I don't think I can create a narrative where it makes logical sense. The decisions that I've made are economic; they're often about survival, rather than about love. They're full of capitulations, or, as maybe you say in English, compromises. In any case, I grew up in Puerto Rico and went to school in the United States; I followed the path for the bright and privileged on the island. I stayed in the US for an MFA. I finished my graduate studies when I was only twenty-four years old, and I didn't really understand what I had gotten myself into in terms of debt.

But I always knew that I was going to make artwork that wasn't going to be very successful in a market. So I always imagined myself teaching, and I came back to Puerto Rico to teach. I got a job at the University of Puerto Rico, which is a public university. For context, I was paid $21,000 a year to direct a department with eighty students and no assistant whatsoever. I was the person everybody wrote to ... about everything.

And so at some point in the middle of austerity cuts to public education, I saw that $21,000 and what I had to repay for my education and said to myself, "I can't do this anymore." My first thought was that I'd just be an artist, that I could make more money, even if I wasn't making market-friendly work. Anything would be better than my current situation. So I worked as an artist and got together with another artist and a curator and created a space called Beta—Local, which had an alternative-education aspect to it. I was part of the center of Beta—Local, which made me feel like I didn't have to leave the Caribbean to think about art critically.

At some point thereafter I began teaching during the summers in the Bard MFA program. It too became extremely frustrating, and I ended up quitting because of all the reasons that are familiar to anybody involved with American universities, which were exacerbated during the pandemic. So I haven't ever had a full-time, year-round position in an American university; instead, it's been something I do to supplement my income. Now I'm teaching one semester a year at Bennington College. I feel a certain bitterness about not being able to survive in the public-education system in Puerto Rico.

NS These answers are wonderful context and span what I think we're going to discuss. Since bell hooks came up, I wonder how you all think about radical pedagogy—as defined by hooks, Ivan Illich, Paulo Freire—and whether or how it fits into American art schools.

BSM There's an interpretation that comes from Pier Paolo Pasolini's film *The Gospel According to St. Matthew*, that Christ is a punishing figure. Ivan Illich was kind of punishing. He's telling you you're doing it wrong. He delivered a beautiful and punishing commencement speech to students at the University of Puerto Rico in 1969—the year my dad graduated. He remembers Illich's speech, in which he tells the students something like, "It is your job to dismantle this university system. You are receiving so much of the richness of this country to join a structure that will not benefit your poorest neighbors. You are entering into an epistemology that is completely alien." At their moment of celebration, Illich asked those graduates to dismantle the system they had benefited from and to create another one that could not yet be envisioned.

I don't agree with everything Illich imagined, but it's impossible to think one could take those ideas into any kind of university system as it exists today, since they necessitate the dismantling of that system. That's true even of Beta—Local, which we began with Illich in mind, trying to envision a horizontal structure in which anybody can teach and anybody can learn.

Beta—Local has existed for about twelve years. It's a 501 (c) (3) nonprofit that receives funding from American philanthropic institutions that have their own programming priorities. We lose a lot of autonomy in that process. So it's not a perfect space to think about what education can be, but, again, I don't think it's possible for me to bring Ivan Illich's ideas into a classroom in the Bard MFA program or in Bennington College—at least without those ideas being turned into a product that can be sold as a discourse.

NS Steffani, you mentioned your early interest in bell hooks. Can you talk about how that interest, and radical pedagogy more generally, has been part of your experience as a teacher?

SJ Thank you so much for sharing that, Beatriz. I don't disagree with what Beatriz just said; the challenge is that simply teaching radical-pedagogy content might lead the students to think it's just another tool for their toolbox. And of course that is problematic. But I still believe that radical study can happen within conventional institutions.

I have the great privilege of teaching at a public university—a state university, a majority-minority university, where most students receive support and the MFA program is offered free of charge. That makes it possible to have certain kinds of conversations that have been more difficult in other institutions. My students come to the university as a refuge because they can't stay at home. My students were the weird kid in the corner, scribbling in a notebook, who never found traction anywhere else. These students look at the kinds of jobs they think are available to them and want to give up, so they postpone entering the workforce by going to college. School is a lifeline and opportunity for these students to finally do that thing that they love.

I enter the classroom with a great deal of humility. I actually don't even like to use the phrase "my students." They're not mine. They're just students, and we are sharing space and learning together. I recognize this sounds kind of idealistic. Interestingly enough, as a younger faculty member, I was much more traditional as a teacher; I had inherited pretty conventional ideas about what a classroom should look like. Over the years those ideas have changed so much.

With all of that as an introduction, I will add a few practical things about how I structure my classes in relation to radical pedagogy. I find *Teaching to Transgress* really helpful, in part because it provides a map for students to think about their own relationships to learning. hooks uses erotic language to describe what it feels like to be in love with growing, in love with learning, in a way that resonates with many students with whom I share space. I often invite students to trace a learning genealogy for themselves, to reflect on everything that has unfolded in their lives to bring them here, to this room, where we meet together.

I'll add that I tend to structure my classes so that a lot of what happens, happens in the room. I really believe in the power—the potential—of the classroom itself as an arbitrary collection of very different people who come together in one moment, in one space. It sounds silly, but, in 2024, when algorithmic logic prevents many people from encountering ideas that oppose their own in a meaningful way, learning to navigate difference is so critical, for myself alongside the students in class. One of my own graduate faculty, Gregg Bordowitz, taught me that all politics is the politics of the room. It's important to begin thinking about what we can do together in the room, then to expand outward, to imagine that room becoming bigger and bigger until it encompasses the whole world. I also think there can be something powerful about turning the classroom into a space that feels a little bit different than the rest of the world, then allowing that space to serve as a model for what can happen elsewhere. I'll add that I find it a little confusing how rarely the experience of learning is explicitly thematized in class. To me, taking students seriously as thinkers means also inviting them to take their own relationships to learning seriously.

Those ideas are almost always a part of the way I teach, whether or not I frame them in relation to a specific thinker. Sometimes I find it a little bit difficult. At Rutgers, where I currently teach, a good portion of our students are first- or second-generation college students. Many do not have a habit of reading. And sometimes it can feel a little patronizing to constantly refer to things they haven't read, to situate myself as this figure of authority who exists within a network they feel they can never access. Instead, I try to use what happens with us together, in the room, as the critical foundation for whatever it is we are trying to explore—without spending too much time introducing or framing other theorists or histories.

NS Thanks, Steffani. Naeem, do you have a thought on this?

NM I'm thinking of two ways this plays out in my experience. One is the idea of expanding the classroom to a wider public than the students at the university. The second is about what they do with that education after they graduate, which is maybe when more transformative possibilities can appear.

As I mentioned, during Occupy Wall Street I saw graduate students and teachers from all the major universities basically move their classrooms to the park, where they held classes for everybody. Instead of your twenty-five enrolled students, it's everybody who happens to show up at that time. Another big influence on me is this project called Youth Solidarity Summer. It was a radical pedagogical experiment specifically for first- and second-generation South Asian youth from across the country, who would come together in New York. The teachers were university professors who focused their energy all summer on this alternative-school experiment. If they found their day job inadequate, each summer they get to do their projects unconstrained by the Committee on Instruction regulations or whatever else. Many people who attended either Occupy or Youth Solidarity Summer did innovative projects afterward. I've never done a proper mapping, but I know anecdotally that many people who met or deepened their relationships at Occupy Wall Street then went on to form loose coalitions, like the Gulf Labor Coalition, May Day Space, and more formal organizations. The consequences of Occupy are felt much later. I've only been teaching for four years, but I've been trying to build relationships with places like the Bronx Documentary Center, which is relatively near us, or the Penumbra Foundation for Photography.

For example, at People's Forum a few days ago, Vijay Prashad was talking about his new book with Noam Chomsky. That's an extension of the classroom unconstrained by university regulations, in a way, but still part of their education. And one current student who doesn't make objects is trying to form an alternative-cooperativism project for their thesis exhibition. They are trying to supersede the university's limitations in ways I want to support. These are the first steps of trying to build a somewhat transformative project that uses some elements of the university context but also can supersede its constraints.

NS On the notion of superseding the institution's constraints, the past ten to fifteen years have seen attempts to diversify and decolonize art education. How, if at all, has this played out in your institutions?

SJ One distinction to make is between the curriculum and the faculty, staff, administration, and students. That said, I also have taught at ten or more different colleges, universities, and art academies—Cooper, Parsons, Columbia, Trinity, Wellesley, Rice, University of Houston-Downtown, I could go on. Each context is so different.

NS Well, I have found, and perhaps you've seen this too, that decolonization is now kind of a standard question in job interviews. From my perspective, it's structural—it involves everything—though you'll often see specific calls in terms of representation in the student body or the faculty, or how the curriculum relates to those populations. To me there has been a change in how these topics are discussed over the last twenty-five years. So perhaps you each can pick an example that sticks out for you and share how these calls for diversity and decolonization have been received and responded to.

NM Unlike Steffani, I've taught in only one place, not counting guest-lecturing. At Columbia, I've seen the diversification push be somewhat successful when it comes to faculty and administration. But I think one area where we can push is class diversity, which is not as readily apparent as racial identity in an application or on a CV. It shows up more readily once a student arrives. Sometimes I worry that racial diversity is easier for the university to "fix" than class diversity.

In faculty meetings about admissions, I find myself discussing how, today, international students paying full tuition make up for other shortfalls in revenue. This leads to a situation where universities recruit based on the ability to pay. I'm not saying that international students are uniformly well-off—far from it—but there can be complicated skews in the admissions cycle. You look around the campus and see different racial and cultural backgrounds, but that mix may not represent the world in terms of class.

Pushing on this point may lead to more radical politics in the classroom. This question resonates across institutions, too: consider the different experiences of the recent protests that students had at Columbia University versus, say, the City University of New York, a public university.

BSM While listening to Steffani speaking earlier, I thought about the contradictory experiences of teaching. I have first-generation students, I have refugee students, I have students with wildly different demographic profiles. Of course, one has different relationships with these students. I can also see that nearly all of us on campus are there for similar reasons, namely economic-austerity measures and US politics. That makes it complicated to sit in a faculty discussion about decolonizing the curriculum as an inclusion measure when the broader context is so brutally exploitative. I disconnect—even more so when global movements demand responses and you see who on campus puts their name on the line. It can feel ludicrous, absurd; that's why I say I disconnect from it, or that it's a bit schizophrenic.

SJ I don't know how much I have to add, but I have experienced some of the challenges that Naeem described in terms of optical diversity, this desire for a "United Colors of Benetton" rainbow campus—and how much that masks. At private institutions, I've experienced the overreliance on international recruitment to solve both financial and diversity problems. And what Beatriz described also resonates. I will say, though, that while Rutgers is so diverse, I'm not sure the university can handle that diversity. Faculty and students are given very few tools to manage the complexity of our classrooms and our communities. It is a huge challenge.

The university is diverse because New Jersey is diverse. Rutgers has the second highest enrollment of Jewish students at any public university in the nation, according to Hillel. In my own classroom, many undergraduate students come from families, communities, and education systems committed to Zionism. I've also been told that Rutgers has one of the highest enrollments of Muslim students among American universities; the state of New Jersey has a particularly high concentration of Palestinian immigrants and descendants. It's not uncommon for these students to meet in a single classroom. How do you model a space that enables conversation meaningfully and supportively and generously and in ways that also move toward truth? How can the institution support that?

I have thought a lot this past year, while on sabbatical, about how one of Rutgers's biggest failures has been its inability to be brave enough to help the community imagine and model a physical space for conversation. A space where students and faculty and staff and neighbors and allies can find—I'll use the silly word—respect. Why is this so difficult? It's ironic how universities claim to want diversity yet can't handle it when they have it—can't handle difference. They are designed for ideological homogeneity—or heterogeneity only within very limited channels.

NS I teach at Virginia Commonwealth University, which is also a public institution that draws in a diverse student population. It's also a majority-minority student population. And I've been here for seven years. The two moments when it was most clear that the institution was not ready to handle that diversity were the Black Lives Matter protests in 2020 and the more recent Palestine solidarity encampments.

This past spring, activism around Palestinian solidarity has hugely affected not only the discourse within universities, but also others' view of universities and their relationship to a public. People have increasingly talked about the limits of free speech and who is included or excluded from campus. What have you learned while navigating this moment? What has it revealed to you about the teaching environment itself?

BSM This stretches back to at least 2021. I remember Yazan Khalili taking it upon himself to organize a space for all of us teaching Palestine. He took on that burden because it was an important moment. Nobody then could imagine what would happen two years later. But one thing I think about is how it was possible that this could happen within this small community but not transform the larger institution. So we know we can create some teaching spaces that feel protected, but also that they have limitations.

At Bennington, some faculty got together to create a pop-up course that quickly had a hundred students and people took clear political positions. It was not a "both sides" environment. Then, two hours away from campus, a Palestinian kid got shot. I keep focusing on the contradictions: protected spaces surrounded by others where anything can happen. It's a reminder that the university cannot be separate from its neighborhood, from the state, from the country.

NM I think back to my own experience of being an undergraduate on the Oberlin campus and conversations then and it's clear how much has changed—especially the prevalence of "hyphenated Americans" among the student body.

There are many young people who will argue with their parents at the dinner table, or across similar age divides on campus. The demographic changes on campus are so dramatic that people in power today think campus protests will ripple outward in dramatic ways, certainly in New York City, where young people are thinking of electoral politics. In that light, you can see the intensity of the pushback on speech as a positive development. It's a form of acknowledgment. But it creates its complications; many of us have recently found that by agreeing to teach, we have actually signed up for certain rules or constraints.

Now we realize the hypothetical outlined in a point of our contract is now a reality. That's been profound, and I have seen many more professors join the American Association of University Professionals to start to organize. I realize the American Anthropological Association can release a statement that the university cannot. You can belong to the university, but make sure to show up for the professional association. This goes back to my idea that the university campus should not be the beginning or the end of your work.

You look for creative solutions. I see students publishing zines and distributing them outside of campus to avoid certain regulations. I'm looking elsewhere for positive examples, because otherwise we might think nothing is happening. You can teach Edward Said in class, at least for now, but you can't necessarily talk about the meaning of his work elsewhere on campus. I find it encouraging that students are planning lots of things and not telling faculty, since presumably we are more aligned with the institution. I appreciate that they can be far more nimble off campus and without looping us in.

BSM I want to underscore Naeem's point about second-generation students; I think that's huge. That might be what finally provokes real change. We're about to have an election in Puerto Rico in which, for the first time in my or my parents' lifetimes, the independence candidate might actually win. It's just a shocking turn of events, and it has to do with demographics, with young people. That's exciting.

SJ Thank you all for sharing. I have two additional small observations. One is that the Black Lives Matter movement, which reached an apex in 2020, overlapped with the pandemic. I was teaching a performance class in spring 2020; it moved online, and suddenly it felt as though the students' work became accountable in fresh ways to their homes and their communities. Students were working through ideas not only in the classroom, but in relation to their childhood bedroom. As challenging as it was to experience the violence of separation and isolation, I found there was also something powerful about the unexpected opportunity to re-embed our creative work within our homes, families, and neighborhoods.

Since it hasn't come up, I also want to mention that social media has transformed the politics of the classroom. Often, I learn that a situation or exchange that felt one way to me in the room was interpreted entirely differently by students because of their relationships and exchanges outside class, especially material they post and read—about each other—on social media. My own social media activity has been surveilled by students who reported posts I liked or accounts I follow, with negative intentions.

That said, I feel very protective of all the students with whom I work, even the ones with whom I disagree! I teach at a small art school within a larger institution and genuinely try my best to take care of everyone when I can. I know how confused students are as they navigate this political moment. I hope that even what seem clearly to me to be mistakes will, in the long term, be learning opportunities for them.

NM I keep being reminded of other events, other details. Toward the end of last semester, there were moments where the question of withholding participation and labor came up in conversations both in-person and online. And just the conversations about it had real-world, on-campus ramifications. We have had people cancel their talks, and we are therefore deprived of the opportunity for conversation. We moved a conference about decolonization in South Asian cinema, off campus, into a church, to not require anyone to cross the picket lines of striking university workers.

These are all things you navigate. You're trying to be there for all the students, which is also part of where the discourse comes from about institutional neutrality. It converges with questions of student safety, with legal conversations.

NS It's interesting how, Steffani, you opened this question of social media, which ties in to what Naeem was saying about how the university experience is not limited to the campus or the classroom, for better or for worse.

NM Adding to this, it was only during Congressional hearings that I found out the most popular chat, or social app, is one no student has ever shared with me. It's like a parallel university composed of our students; it's where they have real conversations. So someone on campus might be monitoring others' social media, but what they're monitoring may not even be their "real thing." The real thing is completely unknown to us, as it probably should be.

NS Near the outset, Naeem, you brought up Occupy Wall Street, and I can't help but think about how the university system was affected by the 2008 financial crisis, not least through mounting student debt. So, to reframe that for a moment, how have you encountered neoliberal patterns of privatization through your own institutions? I taught for many years in a private institution. I now teach at a public institution, yet I've found it often functions like a private institution, not least because there is now so little public funding earmarked for subsidizing public education.

BSM I can talk about the private universities where I teach, but I think we know how those work. At the University of Puerto Rico, funding gets cut and positions are frozen. But it was a tuition hike that prompted a huge, three-month student strike in 2010, the longest in the history of the university. Yet despite winning certain concessions, tuition has continued to increase. So the demographic profile of the students increasingly becomes one of privilege. At the same time, private philanthropy has increased; you see Mellon Foundation logos on institute research, collaborations, events—almost everything. It's wild.

And of course, this means that the university disinvests in other forms of research, which mirrors what happens in the arts and culture more generally. Twenty years ago, art spaces in Puerto Rico received enough local funding and could be structured differently than their counterparts in the US. Now that the Mellon Foundation helps sustain something like fifteen or twenty small organizations with multi-year grants, well, those institutions are going to respond to changing expectations. And it will be very difficult to regain what's lost—in terms of programming and attitude, but also in terms of public funds.

NM I've been looking at the way that the private university is removing from its remit the obligation to fund students with scholarships. Administrations are trying to push that responsibility onto the student's field of study, or even the students themselves. You end up with certain departments, certain areas of study, being more likely to get funding. Right now, there is funding for artificial intelligence. If you were to recruit an MFA student who is working creatively with artificial intelligence, you'll be more likely to find outside funding that will cover part of their education.

That increasingly structures what students propose to study. And also where universities go looking for students. The student from Qatar or from Dubai is more valued than the student from Egypt because the latter is not going to be able to secure external funding. I see this as a way the university is pushing off its responsibility to fund everybody and designing what kind of students can come. As teachers, we have an argument to make that certain admissions policies aligned with the market are changing the university.

SJ I'm reflecting on why I feel I have little to add, and part of it is that I'm only willing to allow my teaching job so much of my overall psychological space. I love my work with students, but at the end of the day, it's a job—it's one part of the tapestry of my life. When my involvement in some aspect of the institution is kind of limited, I don't spend a lot of time thinking about it. I recognize it's a privilege to have that option.

I will say, Naeem, that I experienced exactly what you're describing when I taught at private schools. At Rutgers, we handle admissions ourselves, for both undergraduate and graduate students. Most Rutgers students receive significant financial aid, but we don't see their financial need when they apply; it's truly a need-blind admissions process. I don't even get to review their high-school grades, which sometimes I would like to see. But grades and test scores are not a part of our admission process. We admit based solely on the portfolio and statements.

Teaching in an art school within a public university, we just don't receive that private funding you both spoke of. Our department has no endowment and very few direct donors. We have nearly nothing, financially speaking. On the plus side, this means we have a great deal of autonomy. We can do whatever we want with our nothing, and sometimes that's refreshing.

Again, I recognize what a privilege it is that I can choose not to battle with some aspects of the university; maybe in a few years my priorities will shift. When you have a job that is supposed to be "for life," sometimes you make strategic decisions about what to think about when.

NS Thanks for offering that, Steffani, because I think a lot of people toggle back and forth between the life of the artist and the enormity of what it means to integrate into an institution. You all have been generous to offer up hope in relation to many of these difficult questions, which I honestly wasn't expecting. I wonder what comes to mind when you think ten, twenty, thirty years into the future. I often hear administrators talk about the future solely through the lens of technology. Where do you see things going? Where could they go?

NM This is a bit of a science-fiction jump, but I am sensing a geographical shift in the center of people's thoughts about higher education. You see that a little bit already; there is a very respected photography school in Bangladesh–Parthshala South Asian Media Academy. I feel like there will be more of that. How will it play out? Will teachers in the West and the global north move to institutions elsewhere? Will students come to the US for an education and then immediately leave to build a future in their homelands? The phenomenon of going back and building—that's a trend that I would like to see.

BSM I go back to Ivan Illich's challenge to the 1969 graduates. His vision would be really beautiful to see come to fruition—a system of learning and teaching that is more open and horizontal, that doesn't cost what it costs now, that isn't concerned about accreditation. Just as we have health clinics in every neighborhood, a system that is decentralized and more open, could we have something similar for the process of teaching and learning?

SJ That vision is really beautiful. I will add that I often think about June Jordan's writings, recently collected under the title *Life Studies*, as a framework for thinking about education rooted in experience. What you describe, Beatriz, feels so necessary. Yet, for all its downsides, there are certain features of the American higher education system that work well for many students. For example, the community-college system makes it possible for someone who was a poor student in high school or who wasn't on a pre-college track to totally change their life.

My stepdaughter went to community college before finishing her undergraduate degree at a university. My husband went to community college, then to university, then got a PhD—all in a way that would've been difficult in a publicly funded context, because what state would invest in a student who didn't already prove their potential? So I think a lot about how we can preserve some of the good stuff, the stuff we cherish, as we make broader changes.

The public fetishization of "the campus" is rooted in the fact that the campus really is powerful. Physical spaces where people gather are also places where change happens. They can be transformative for many people who have the privilege to experience them. So how can we extend those spaces? How can we extend where that kind of learning can happen beyond the traditional definition of the university campus—in the way that Occupy Wall Street, for example, was able to do? And how can we preserve what works about universities—the way they make it possible to rewrite your own future? How can we preserve the magic I felt and many of us once felt in the classroom, the erotics of learning?

I love Beatriz's idea of the clinic, which makes me think of the neighborhood library, the community library, which gives people a lot of agency and makes possible horizontal exchange. Perhaps what I'm trying to preserve is something inherent to learning itself. Learning is a desire. It's a desire for proximity, a desire to be closer to the world, to be closer to others. Let's imagine a world that fosters and preserves that intimacy.

Teaching Between Worlds

Angela Dufresne, Gordon Hall, Arnold J. Kemp, Aki Sasamoto, Nato Thompson, and Rodrigo Valenzuela, moderated by Michael Jones McKean

This conversation took place via Zoom on May 28, 2024. The transcript has been edited for clarity and length.

Michael Jones McKean Being an artist might have something to do very simply with cultivating a critical yet still hopeful experience of living—of being *alive.* The tools we have to engage in this process are: witnessing, imagining, and making things. In addition to being artists, we're all teachers here. There are very few disciplines that offer up the possibility to imagine futures, apart from teaching—and, more specifically, teaching art. So, we're straddling two disciplines—teaching and art—where we're encouraged to imagine different kinds of spaces. Worlds, even. With teaching and mentoring young artists, does [it] still feel like a zone of possibility to you? Are you still hopeful, in the ways you might have imagined when you began teaching?

Arnold J. Kemp I always thought, "Not only am I going to teach theory, or teach a skill, I'm also going to model behavior of how to be a good teacher." But I'm coming across folks who, because of experiences they've had in school, negative experiences around race or gender or sexuality or the cost of school—they might never teach. That's a concern of mine.

Rodrigo Valenzuela I think something that is worth questioning is this idea of "dreaming" that you talk about, Michael. When you desire something, what is your foundation to want that thing? In my case, I studied philosophy, I studied art history. I didn't have critiques, so, later on, it was mind-blowing to me to go to a place like Skowhegan, where it's an exercise of utopia. I didn't know how to be an artist. I knew I wanted to make objects, video, and I was thrown off by sixty different ways of making work there. I didn't know what to expect, so I assumed that a lot of bad behavior in art schools was normal. But I'm glad I didn't have [an art school experience] because now, when I teach undergrads, it's very refreshing to be able to teach in the way that I would like to have been taught. But still there is that "image"—the image of a world when you think that being a successful artist means money. So, how do we consider success if there are very few models for how to *not* be successful? Or, how to be regarded as thoughtful or meaningful. This is problematic when we encounter how to run this dream machine.

Angela Dufresne Since the pandemic, there has been this constant draw with different community groups that I'm involved in to siphon me into these spaces that are like what Nato [Thompson] has produced: self-organized popups, ad-hoc structures that get past the bureaucratic quagmire that is academia right now. With most of the folks I speak to, there is a consensus that, in academia, there's so much bureaucratic weight coming from above to write benchmarks and create verifiable matrices for what it means to learn and to produce an intellect in a body as an artist. But [it's also coming] from below, with certain kinds of expectations about mentorship that make it increasingly difficult to do what Arnold said in the beginning, which is to embody an alternative—an embodied way of living as an artist that can leave space that's open enough for a person to imagine their own practice.

I agree with Rodrigo, and I think my department thinks that the most productive place for imagining and bringing up new modes of living is by the cohort model; by a bunch of people stuck together and, given enough time, where outcomes aren't made verifiable. Where people can actually experiment and develop unprecedented ways of being together. That becomes harder and harder in academia. Is this the kind of learning that we're talking about, where artists develop in a way that is not within the normative progressive capitalist model of how a human being develops "into their full self"? That it isn't so imposed on by bureaucracy, but [that it] allows them to become people capable of imagining new modes of community and interconnectivity.

AJK I think it's important for me to say that I have tried to model myself after certain teachers, like [John] Baldessari, or Mike Kelley, or Paul McCarthy. Angela [Dufresne], I think, was in San Francisco at the time when I was [there]. When Tony Labat was teaching, David Ireland, and the Kuchar brothers. When I started to teach, I was in Portland, Oregon, and I wanted to create that community among my graduate students—world-making.

I'd always say, "Don't wait for a curator or some gallerist. Just make your own space." My students, many of them, have done that. Three of my students from those days have gone through gender reassignments, and I scratched my head when they wrote to me, each separately, and said, "I wanted you to know this before I told anyone else, because your classes gave me the bravery to explore who I really am." I'm still not exactly sure what they meant; but the way I taught back then is not a way I can teach now. One of the things I did with all my graduate students during my four years in Portland was go to a woman-run, woman-owned, woman-operated strip club called Mary's.

AD I know that bar!

AJK Yes, we'd go there and talk about economics and gender and race and class and sexism and feminism. We'd talk about performance. We met amazing people there—one stripper who spoke six languages, and I really got to know her. She called me Professor Booty. She'd say, "Oh, Professor Booty is here with his students." I don't know if there's anyone teaching like that anymore, and I certainly cannot teach that way now.

MJM Perhaps one of our shadow roles as teachers, working inside very corporatized, and—in some cases—multinational university systems, might be to keep academic bureaucracy at bay. To push back at this growing behemoth or at least try to hide its ill effects from our students and classrooms so that school doesn't end up feeling, well, too much like capital-*S* school.

I think many of us might be trying to cultivate spaces that are more undefined. But in the increasingly professionalized context that is art school in 2024, one where we ourselves might also be allergic to defining what "success" means in this context, a tension emerges. As we create and maintain spaces that feel more and more nebulous, those values feel at odds with the corporatized logic of higher-ed. This feels like one of the issues that's at play. How do we maintain *school*, without debasing it?

AD I don't know. It requires leaps of faith. RISD had, until about two years ago—a program in Rome called the European Honors Program. I taught in that for a year. We did presentations in a bus with a mic. We all got into my hotel room and watched *The Leopard* by Luchino Visconti. I was in bed with eight different students, and there were students on the floor and in the chairs. There was nothing weird; it was just what we were doing.

I was doing a project with African refugees in Rome and collaborating with this group of punk architects called Ati Suffix. Ati Suffix asked them what they wanted, and they said, "Well, we're in a holding pattern in this airplane hangar built by Mussolini, waiting for our visas, and they won't let us cook." I said, "Great. We've got three kitchens in the Cenci." And they came, and they cooked. In the meantime, we got these emails through students mentioning stuff to their parents; just an onslaught of horrific racist assumptions and safety concerns. We did it anyway. We told them that there was a social worker in the house—which there was—and ... basically to fuck off. We had the event, and it was totally transformative. It was a weekend in exchange with them, but it was pathologically stressful; and it should have been something else.

Gordon Hall I want to come out in defense of school, and by "school," I don't mean an administratively driven bureaucratic mini state. I came up through different kinds of progressive educational contexts when I was a kid. This version of education is fundamentally a group of people consenting to become a temporary community, in which one person—the "teacher"—takes on the responsibility of creating the structure: establishing the deadlines and, with kindness and love, maintaining structure, a level of formality unlike casual life. This produces a situation in which every participant's ideas are taken seriously by everyone else in the group. This is what I try to do with my students. I take every single one of them seriously as a person, as a thinker; and then, hopefully, they start taking themselves and one another seriously, as well. By the end of the semester, I feel like I have succeeded if the class could continue if I were not there. Because what I taught them was just what they ended up creating—being there together, making their work and giving each other real feedback, agreeing to the structure.

MJM When so much of what is learned often occurs organically, messily, and through osmosis; this sort of learning environment can privilege students of certain educational backgrounds. So, there might be something important about structure, about clarity, about being able to establish hierarchies needed for classes.

GH When I was a student, I wanted my classes to have structure. I wanted the discussion to be moderated. I wanted us to focus on what we were doing. I didn't like it when it was a free-for-all. I think that, even within the progressive model, the freedom that education promises is found through self-discipline. I don't mean top-down discipline; I mean self-discipline that creates the possibility for really different people from really different backgrounds and perspectives to find ways to interact and learn from each other.

Nato Thompson When I was in junior high school, my dad went to grad school at CalArts, and we moved into the dorms—me and my brother—in 1981. There was a clothing optional pool, and that was my most formative educational moment by far, sitting around the pool with naked eighteen- to twenty-four-year-olds. It was the first time I thought adults might be cooler than kids. But what I thought art school was, was more than a place to produce; it was a space where a *way of being* was modeled. When I was an undergrad at Berkeley, I had an adjunct teacher named Kevin Radley. He let us do the craziest art assignments, and he loved everything I did. And that's all I needed: crazy art assignments and someone to believe in me. I wanted permission to be as rebellious and wild as I could, with everybody else trying to make a poor case for the world being rational, when I could clearly see it was a mess.

I turned fifty. I was a curator. I've worked for nonprofits my entire slovenly life. It became very clear to me that nonprofits are institutions that raise money for the purpose of raising money. That's just the nature of the world. And rather than critique it—I didn't want to be one of these people [who sit] on the sidelines and point at the problems of the world, and [complain] about higher ed, or museums, or whatever, because it's one thing to critique.

The tender act of building institutions is not easy. And our fragile institutions, whether it's art schools, or our museums—our colonial museums—if they get erased, they do not get replaced. If you tear down our art schools, new art schools don't just emerge out of the rubble. I think the bureaucratic, painful task of world building that is the yang to the yin of art making is a tricky task; like the anarchist task ... how do you make your shared economies? How do you employ yourself? How do you live?

How many of us are in institutions we don't believe in, but we've got people [who] depend on us? I think students see that, but they don't see any way out of it. With the Alternative Arts School, I don't think it's a solution. I just felt like, in this Black Panther way, how can we share our money to build a different thing, and who's going to be administratively on top of it, so it's not just some utopian dream artist project that fails in four years, but actually lasts? And money, insurance, legal claims, all those things that are really boring, literally are the things that are preventing people from doing it. For me, world-building is both a dream and then, somebody willing to be an old nineteenth-century socialist—willing to compromise and do the hard work to just get the stuff done.

RV So, how is your project finding ways to be sustainable, beyond the dream? Could you tell us more about the project?

NT Sure. The school is tuition-driven and soon to be membership-fee driven. Artists pay for classes, and then the classes pay for a teacher and a tiny administration. Our student body's average age is thirty-eight years old. It's 85 percent female. We take the money from the Global North and apply it to the Global South and marginalized communities, so that it is globally diverse, but it is subsidized through North American cash. The internet is global, and the US dollar spends differently in different parts of the world. We aren't interested in artists only being online and see our role as a part of a larger artistic life. The school has really come to reflect a larger portion of the artist community that we don't generally see. Greg Sholette talks about [it as resembling] dark matter; that 98 percent of the art world is held together by artists you don't see in museums or galleries or teaching positions. In general, what we offer is a critical community and skills. But out of the gate, artists don't want to pay for community, even though that is exactly what they need. [They'll] pay for *classes*, but that's not what they want. So, you trick them with classes, and then you actually provide a global community of relationships that holds it together. We say we're a school, but what we really are is more of a global YMCA for working artists.

Aki Sasamoto I think, working at Yale, I realize [that] my role is really to provide access, and, to "point." Basically, my job is being a pointer to different facilities, and [at] different fields of ideas. I believe [that] if I'm working in a research university, I'm making sure that the art school exists, but that art students don't just look at art. They have to look at something that's *not* art. I think, with every institution I work with, I'm trying to figure out what that institution can best offer. So, I change my teaching tactics depending [upon] the location.

I know students come into our program wanting to [use] the studio space, to be introverted, and to use the library. They're actually very clear on what they want. I'm not going to question that. The only thing I'm going to hold the community to is to discuss effective and respectful ways of communicating. That has been a new thing, because we host students from different countries and cultures and different backgrounds. So, how can we set that tone?

RV Yale and UCLA compete for the same grad students. Maybe for sculpture, some people go to VCU. Gordon is in a special condition, where they have really smart undergrads, and Vassar has an amazing financial aid system; [it's near] the number one school to provide financial aid, so they get smart students [who] are happy to be there. There is a certain amount of happiness that you have when you don't feel that burden of money. A lot of models require money; even [when] running your own gallery. The Core Program [in Houston] was started by people from RISD. That could happen only in the economy of the '80s. It's probably very, very hard [for such a thing] to happen right now.

I have noticed a big shift at UCLA. Rodney McMillian has worked really hard, really steadily, toward shifting the culture of the department. I have done my part, too, [by] trying to look more at the backgrounds of our students. We have, every year, more students coming from community college, or Arizona State. Since I [got] here, very few of our grad students come from Bard undergrad, or the Maryland Institute College of Art, or Cooper Union. That has generated a very nice cohort, where they feel the opportunity that has been granted, and they are so excited to take advantage of it.

But I am afraid now because the system of starting something like the Core Program or starting alternative residency spaces, where these students are going to have a place after school, is unsustainable with the economy of 2024. To get free tuition—we are a state school—we need to fundraise a lot, and then, as soon as people know where the fucking money comes from, you're fucked. There's no good money when you need twenty million dollars for an endowment.

It is *so* complicated. Do we launder money through well-meaning education, or do you just tell people, "Hey, we are going to give you a prime education, but you're going to have to be in debt and you're going to have to deal with predatory lending systems"?

AJK I work in a big corporate institution now, I'm always trying to give the students more than what they're paying for. When I applied for my job to be the dean of the School of the Art Institute of Chicago, I gave a lecture as part of my job talk in which I talked about the expense of graduate school, and the real competition for SAIC coming from free nonacademic programs that were started by artists to support artists, such as C.O.P.S., which was the Conceptual Oregon Performance School. It was a pretty crazy school and [was] run by some very talented artists and teachers. One of them went on to Bruce High Quality Foundation and just got his first teaching job in Florida.

NT The task of producing a space, a breathing room—[doing] that makes no sense in a world of hyper-capitalism, utilitarianism, and fascism; I think it's worth saying what a noble journey that is. What a fraught historic journey that is. It is not a guarantee; so many of the cool institutions that were started in 1968 are getting eaten up by the promise of the nonprofit system. This imperfect bureaucratic structure is meeting its own contradictions. It wasn't as obvious in '68 what a board was going to do to an institution back then. It's only become clearer fifty years down the road.

MJM My home institution, VCU, is a state school and, by most measures, deemed "affordable" for our undergrads, and, though on the chopping block every year, we've—against all odds—been able to hold on to full funding for our MFAs, at least within my department. But, even so, tuition, money are enormous issues. With this idea of very real debt lingering overhead, while we talk about crafting experiences in art school that might be more-or-less goal-undefined, purposely nonlinear, and very process-based—all sorts of tensions are bound to arise. Some related to student expectations, but also a new, emerging by-product may be forming: an allergy to risk. I want to linger here, thinking about the spaces that we're creating, these spaces we're holding, not just for more students but [also for] artists in the future. It's a conundrum, and sadly one [that], against our will, we might be complicit inside of.

GH I could offer a little bit of my own experience with this. When I got my current position at Vassar College, I had to adjust to no longer working with grad students, as we don't have any grad programs. I've been quite surprised, though, that I feel free from the guilt that I was carrying during the decade I taught MFA students. It got more intense toward the end, because I, myself, was deep in adjuncting, being underpaid, and with debt from my own grad degree. The MFA students would ask me, "Gordon, should I go into teaching?" Or: "I'm going to be an artist. How does this work, you know, financially?" Sometimes I was just brutally honest. "No. Unless you have family money, do not try to do this, because there's absolutely no way to adjunct teach and make art and make a living." And other times I'd try to be positive, like, "You can figure it out, and there still are some tenure-track jobs, and you just have to stick with it."

All those answers felt very unsatisfying to me, and so I do feel a certain relief from directly being the person ushering them into what very likely will be years of financial precarity. I guess I wonder for the folks who teach primarily MFA students, and ones, especially, where people take on a lot of debt to do them—how do you grapple with that? How do we balance the need for open-endedness and experimentation with the feeling that—and I say this hyperbolically—we're possibly ruining someone's life?

AS I don't feel like I'm ruining their lives. I pretty much have admitted that I work for money. Those kinds of boundaries, giving people my own manual, and then I ask my students for their manual and a plan: how to make their art sustainable toward the end of their two years? Because the goal is to be honest about our relationship to money. Because I don't want to think about how much privilege they have, because I can't really decide what privilege is bad.

A lot of things are so American to me, to defend a privilege one finds themselves with. As an alternative, I want to relax my defense, so that the students will not mirror [me]. I'm just going to meet you with what I can, and let's find the most effective route for our conversation. That's my new idealism. Instead of trying to think about a new structure, I'm really trying to think about how to, one-to-one, figure out what to work on, like a working plan.

MJM Yes, we have *jobs*. When we're talking about teaching, we're also talking about, at some base level, a gig.

At one scale, we can imagine the idea of school, and all the ways that it might become something *else*. We imagine how it might unfurl into something more beautiful, something better. But as our institutions become more bureaucratic, the possibility of structural change at the scale beyond our voice in the room of students becomes harder to imagine. But at the end of the day, we spend the majority of our time as teachers, speaking with students in small groups or individually, about work and ideas. The main technology we have is what we *say*. I'm curious about this working tension that, on the one side, balances the behemoth of the institution, and on the other, the more intimate scale that we operate on as teachers—with all the complexities and freedoms it affords.

AD I am going to chime in, just because I feel like Gordon was talking very specifically to me, because I work in the cult school that costs so much money. I'm implicated in that, and I do throw up in my mouth every time a student says, "Is there more financial aid available?" We do actually have more financial aid available, and it is, like all money, covered in blood.

I don't just work with grads. I also chair a department of 170 undergraduates, who come from all over the world and have, like Aki said, very different relationships with debt. I have folks coming from the Middle East who were, like, "Nobody ever expected to get funding to go to school. Yeah, my family's been bending over to be able to afford to have this opportunity, and I'm going to use it for everything it's worth." Aki, I just love everything you've said, in the sense that we just try to know them, listen to them, and get them pointed in the right direction, so that they can move forward.

One of the things I always tell them—and I think I'm quoting one of my colleagues, Kevin Zucker, here—is, if somebody makes their best work while they're in grad school with us, we've done a disservice to them. We need to make that environment of vulnerability and risk in the studios, the opportunity for people to reinvent even their perception of themselves. One of the ways to do that is vulnerability—to embody all the vulnerabilities and the ridiculousness that is the haptic body. Michael, it is a linguistic thing, but it is also a haptic thing. Right? It is a way of actually showing up for the students and listening to them but also bending toward and away from them in the room when they are going through some real shit. The way that you make that space is with great assignments, and then getting the fuck out of the way. But also showing that you're vulnerable and flawed and are still functioning in a way that could inspire them to invent something sustainable for their lives.

It's not just art school that is ruining people's lives. I think we have such huge systemic problems that are making it impossible for anybody but the top 10 percent of wealthy people to flourish in any meaningful way. It's ridiculous.

RV I have been thinking why art school is so interesting for us to examine. It's that, in most disciplines in a university, there is a very clear goal. If you're studying medicine, you want to get a job in the hospital. Right? I think that very few artists have the goal of selling their paintings. They just want to make a beautiful painting or show it somewhere.

Because the goal is nebulous, what do you want with art? Maybe it's easy for us to say, because we got the job in academia, which is not that sustainable. By the end of the month, I don't have a lot of money left. But I can afford to have health insurance, and a house, and pay minimum bills, which frees you in some way. That's the thing that's amazing; when you are going to a place like the Core Program or Skowhegan for a little bit, you're not worried about bills, and it frees so much space in your mind to not worry.

I think about Arnold having a poetry practice, and Gordon having a writing practice. And you, Michael, having this long-term project that is twelve years long. I think you have built resilience. There is another outlet, something they didn't teach you at art school, but there is something that makes your life resistant to this thing

That is the hardest thing: how to transmit the resistance. I teach a class about the history of punk in Latin America, and what is very clear every year I teach it is the lack of consciousness that peripheral movements have about how important they are. You just do it as a way of subsisting, and then that creates a ripple effect into modifying paternal cultures. It is maybe a question for the panel: how to teach them to be resilient?

NT At the Alternative School we have, basically, all these middle-aged, female avant-gardists. One thing that's beneficial is that everyone's worked crappy jobs by the time they've come to this school, and many of them have given up on a career. I feel like artists are very anxious, [whether] they've made it or not. It's the most career-ignoring—and career-obsessed—field, maybe because the goal is not clear. But the thing that I find most valuable is art as world-builder.

There was an artist in my class who had been sending postcards to her whole family her whole life and didn't think that was an artistic practice. It was a way she navigated social relationships. Some find art as a way to legitimate their weird lifestyle and to find community. It seems like those intangible things are the things that hold up the most over the course of a life. It's not the object. Sometimes I wonder how much art teaching is reifying the setup for failure. The object you make, the thing to display, but in fact it's the process of living non-utilitarian that is the actual tissue, that is the world building, that holds it together through a lifetime.

GH I agree with what Nato just said, which is that even with the precarity, even with the debt, even with the very unclear career path toward some kind of sustainable life—developing one's thinking as an artist; solving problems as an artist, of having an artistic community, of having art be your life, regardless of whether you find any quote unquote success. These things are, I feel, worth a lot of risk and precarity.

AD As a middle-aged lady who has done so many crazy jobs, from being a bike mechanic to [being] a line chef, I can concur. Seriously.

AS I remember, recently, a student came from Cuba with two kids and a wife; it was quite a risk that he took to come to the school. I had just become the director, and he told me, "Hey, I'll be watching how you do this director job," or something like that. I was, like, "Ooh." [*laughter*] I knew, as a concept, that yes, a teacher is a role model and whatnot, but I realized I wanted him to think that it's an easy job, rather than a difficult job. So, I tried really hard to work less. To model this idea of having fun, and approaching the job as a *job* when necessary, so that I could give a better picture of a teaching artist to him.

Another thing that really helped me was to start critiquing [the students'] teaching. So, I'll give an assignment for them to teach a fifteen-minute workshop. Then, afterward, everybody critiques their teaching. The students appreciate that because when they are asking about teaching jobs, it's usually so opaque. It's like a restaurant job. Everybody pretends [that] they have three years of experience when they [actually] don't, because every restaurant requests experience. So, it's impossible to start, and that jump is really stupid.

MJM I want to give space for a final thought from everyone, perhaps something optimistic to imagine.

AJK My naive question is: How do we get the institution to *look more like our classroom*?

Something else: When I was an undergrad, my graduation speaker, Nancy Spero, said, "I've been making art for a long time. I feel like I'm just starting to get noticed, and it's always been about resistance and persistence." I feel like I sound old, but it echoes some of what we've been talking about, resistance and persistence.

GH I'll just add a final thought, which is that having this conversation is great. Even in this short time, I've learned a lot from each of you. I wish there were more situations like this, because once you're linked to an institution, you tend to just be *there*. And when we're not at school, we want to be in our studios. So, it's hard to know where the time for this kind of thing would come from, but it feels valuable to me. And, speaking of learning, I also want to add that, for me, world-building in the classroom happens when I am learning alongside my students. Learning with them, from them. I teach a multidisciplinary, critique-based course where, each week, a different student selects the materials and leads the class, and I participate in the discussion having, often, also only read what they chose for the first time. I learn so much, and I try to model this for them.

NT I really feel, hearing from all you instructors, [that] there's a lot of young people very frustrated with the world right now—reasonably so. But it's really helpful to hear from those [who are] on the other side, navigating difficulties, in terms of your institutions. I think [we're] making a defense of art instruction, with a caveat that you're aware of the problems.

Maybe the arts need to make a better case for why they exist. This idea of world building, [this] idea of producing new paradigms, it's much bigger than making art shows for the museums. Maybe there needs to be a stronger case for why art is so urgent now. Maybe we're making it privately, to ourselves, but solidarity within the arts is hard to come by.

RV I totally agree. I think solidarity is a wonderful thing that I always liked about other disciplines, but at UCLA we've been getting better and better at it. For example, hiring the best fit for what we think the art world should be, and not necessarily hiring the most famous artist [who] applied to the job. I benefited tremendously because of that. I got this job when I was thirty-four, and I didn't have a career. Very fancy filmmakers will look at amateur films all the time. Stephen Spielberg is not [looking only] at James Cameron movies. That's the thing in the art world that has always felt so strange to me. It makes sense to me, as a teacher, to take students to some studio of an artist that will have the space to host seventeen students. But it's very hard to give them a tour at Gagosian or David Zwirner when the reality is that they're supposed to be going to a group show in *a house*.

AD I feel this all so deeply, that the real sustainability for life as an artist is a social one. I've just been working more collaboratively and asking my students to work more collaboratively. But I also think there's something haunting—Arnold brings this up in his question—how do we convince institutions, make the boards and higher leadership, understand and support what works in the classroom? This disconnect is massive. And that is jouissance.

These conversations are curatorially ubiquitous at museums now, this idea of self-care and self-organization. I think we need to acknowledge that this is also the manifestation of really, really big, bad, and ugly systemic problems in our culture.

I want to also make a shout-out for jouissance, for the fact that we are still in the front lines trying to do this unverifiable work, and I will die trying. I've seen many, many people's lives transformed—[their] values, in terms of how they define success, this need for validation, all those things that can actually be deflected by meaningful jouissance in a lived experience. This is becoming harder and harder to come by, on an institutional level. It can be fostered in the classroom. The students want it—to be able to play and experiment in unverifiable ways.

Originally published in Art Papers, *Spring 2024. See https://www.artpapers.org/teaching-between-worlds/.*

Blood from Stone, 2019

Cara Benedetto

Blood from Stone, exhibited at Chapter Gallery in New York in 2019, included a broken litho stone, lithography prints, a ransom note as a takeaway, wall vinyl, and a broken lockbox. The show highlighted the fragility of learning environments in the United States. Pressure and an unlevel printing surface caused the stone to crack, serving as a metaphor for the unequal distribution of resources in an unjust system of production (the public school system) that further produces violence upon vulnerable subjects.

Wrinkles in the paper came from too much pressure and the unlevel printing surface. Text and colored pencil soften the printed target—a symbol that represents a horrifying plan. The frame mimics purple heartwood denoting false notions of heroism and pointing to the origins of social harms that lead to alienated citizens. Text—typed, handwritten, traced, and drawn on works in the show—was written in the voice of a subject who was frustrated and trapped in an unstable learning environment.

The vinyl depicts a photo of my office at Virginia Commonwealth University. It read: "100 most influential people was the title of the new school where all the tongueless teachers taught. They were made to sit quietly while students sucked on their most private memories."

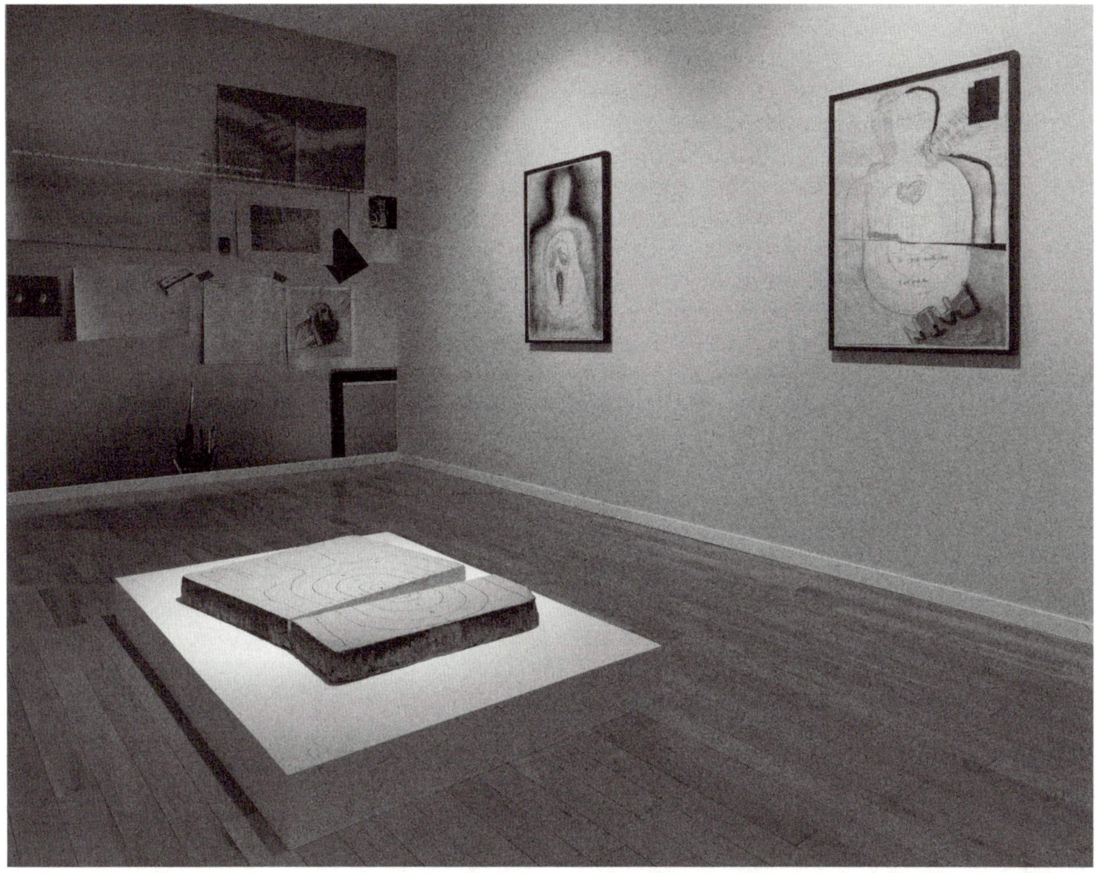

Installation view. Photo: Dario Lasagni

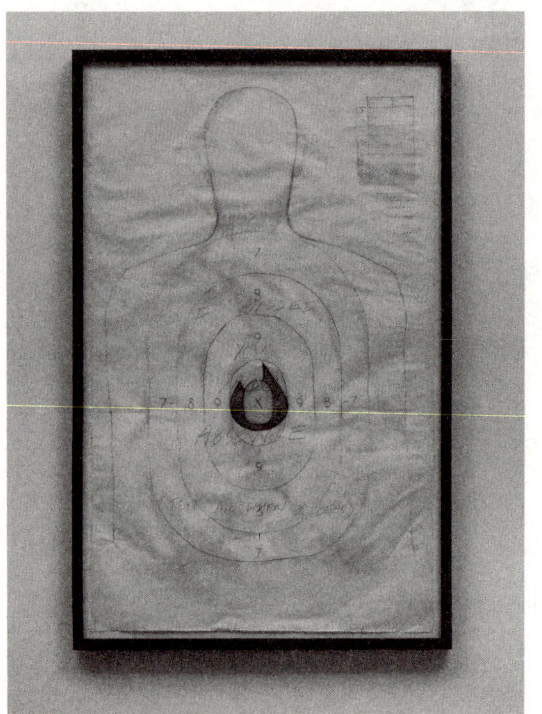

Missing, lithograph print with drawing, 40 × 26 in. (101.6 × 66 cm).

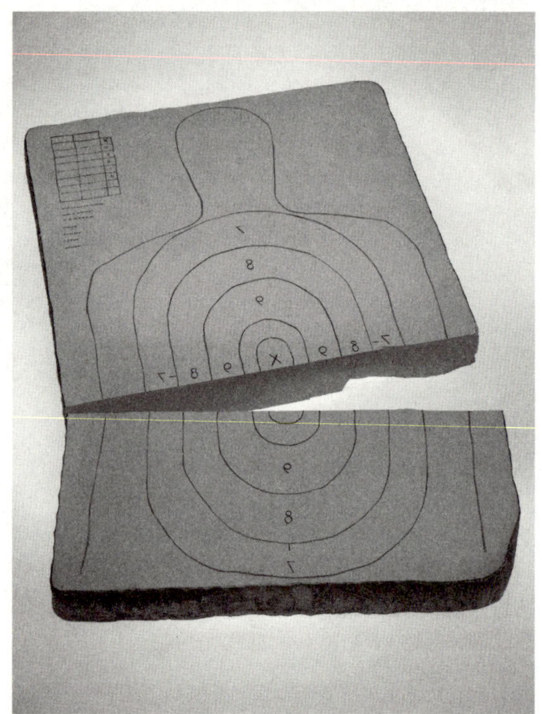

Lithography stone, 38½ × 30 × 3½ in. (97.8 × 76.2 × 8.9 cm).

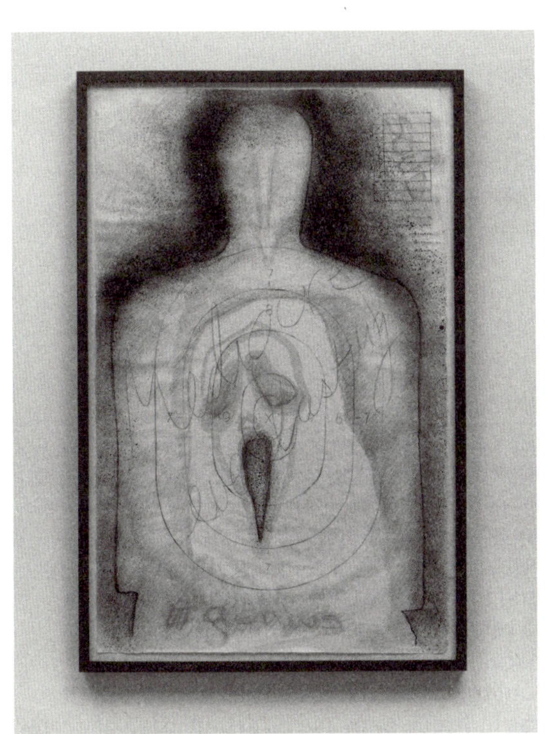

mediocre everlasting, lithograph print with drawing, 41½ × 27¼ in. (105.4 × 69.2 cm).

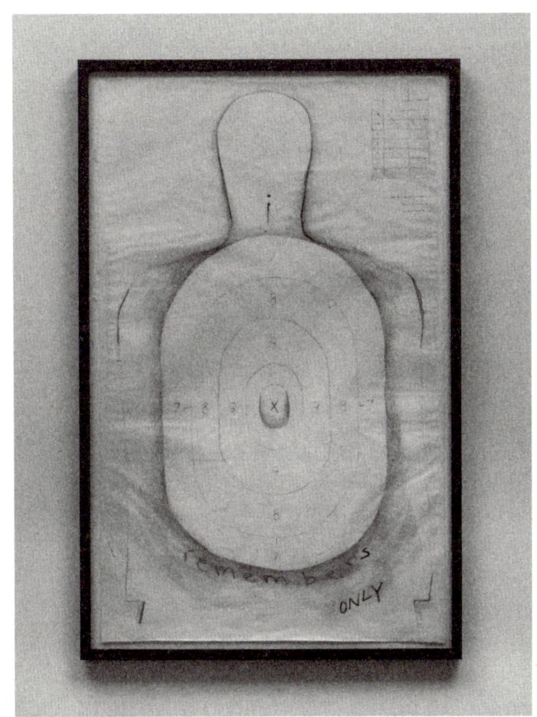

members only, lithograph print with drawing, 41½ × 27¼ in. (105.4 × 69.2 cm).

III. Practices

This section is dedicated to education as a medium, subject, or methodology in either artistic or curatorial practice or some hybrid of the two. The practitioners represented here have had multiple roles: as artists, as museum educators, as museum curators, as university professors, and as collaborators within alternative spaces. Artists Pablo Helguera and Luis Camnitzer have held many of these roles, and, as the conversation between them illustrates, blurring the boundaries between these positions can be fruitful but sometimes challenging in an institutional context. Thus, the point of view here does not focus upon the context of conventional or alternative institutions, but rather upon the perspectives of practitioners themselves. From a regional perspective, this section opens back out to the wider intersection of the Americas and the Middle East.

Artist Kameelah Janan Rasheed's interview reveals a teaching and advising practice centered on practical steps to help student artists succeed. Rasheed's artistic practice includes teaching in institutional and alternative settings, and centers learning in her artworks. Speaking about how a reader or viewer might understand her work, Rasheed says, "We have no choice but to be illegible. We have no choice but to be indirect, because an articulation of certitude is false."[1]

Artist Gordon Hall is also concerned with legibility and reflects on the 2016 Pulse nightclub shooting in Orlando, Florida, that killed forty-nine people. Hall describes a tension between the desire, joy, and unashamed presence of queer bodies and the targeting that visibility enables. Hall learns from an object that resists easy identification and asks how it can hold ambiguity through a lack of clear functionality. How can bodies or subjects be afforded this grace? How can an object

1 An artist project by Kameelah Janan Rasheed is included on pages 258–61.

teach us about the limits of legibility and help us learn how to see?

Curator and art historian Sarah Rifky's survey of her career condenses an enormous amount of social and political change into a six-year period (2009–15) in Egypt, during which she was at the center of initiatives that used art & education to attend to various crises.

Sociologist and art historian Pelin Tan's "Pedagogies of Commons as Transversal Methods" looks at Campus in Camps, an initiative by Decolonizing Architecture Art Research (DAAR), in the West Bank and Palestine,[2] and at the Terrestrial Cosmologies workshop in a Kurdish region of Turkey. She addresses decolonization through projects that sit at the intersection of art and design education initiatives.

Picasso in Palestine (2011), a project that turned a school into a museum, was a collaboration between artists and curators from different regions and institutions. It was also a political intervention into the context of Palestine. Included here is a conversation between curator Rasha Salti and artist Khaled Hourani, who is the former director of the International Academy of Art Palestine in Ramallah, in which he describes how the process unfolded, starting with a visit by students from the academy to the Van Abbemuseum in Eindhoven, The Netherlands. Also included here are selections from a graphic novel by the artist Michael Baers that tells the story from the perspective of multiple actors including Hourani; Jack Persekian, founder and director of Al Ma'mal Gallery in Jerusalem; and Charles Esche, former director of the Van Abbemuseum.

Artist and architect Yazan Khalili's essay discusses his experiences around limits to the supposed freedom of speech in museums and universities, especially regarding Palestine. In the last year, the freedom to gather, to hold flags or signs, or even to speak in many civic spaces has been stifled. A premise of the educational turn was the transformation of spaces from exhibition toward discourse—but when discourse is plagued by limits on freedom of speech, the formal structure of this discourse becomes even more important.[3]

2 An artist project by Campus in Camps is included on pages 336–55.

3 Grant H. Kester, *Conversation Pieces: Community and Communication in Modern Art* (University of California Press, 2004)

Of Workers and Trees

Luis Camnitzer and Pablo Helguera

Pablo Helguera At what point in your career as an artist did you become interested in the subject of pedagogy beyond traditional art education? Is there a particular moment in your life when education took on a special significance?

Luis Camnitzer I entered the School of Fine Arts in Montevideo, Uruguay in 1953 at the age of sixteen to study sculpture. It was a very academic school that focused on realism. The generation of students who were in "power" at that time, all anarchists, were already discussing how to reform the curriculum. The following year, all the union leaders graduated, and suddenly we were without a student association (AEBA). My sculpture teacher in the third year, a Stalinist-communist yet a great guy, pushed me to revive the association because he thought it was absurd that we weren't organized. Additionally, he hoped that we would fight to use the percentage funds for the arts in public buildings to create "Mexican-style" murals. So, I ended up as the general secretary of the association with no political or other experience. I reached out to some of the graduates to ensure continuity in the association's activities, such as re-affiliating with the University Student Federation, continuing the struggle to make the school independent of the Ministry of Education and integrated into the University of the Republic, and continuing discussions about the curriculum, all of which we achieved. This also included forgetting about Mexican murals. In 1956, I received a scholarship to study at the Munich Academy, and in 1957–58, I was tasked with an official mission (and the corresponding passport) to study curriculum structures. When I returned, there was a new generation in AEBA, and we continued working together on the development of a curriculum, which we managed to implement in 1960. The plan was inspired by the pedagogies of John Dewey, Maria Montessori, Ovide Decroly, and so on, and the models of the Bauhaus, Ulm School of Design, Kassel School, and the Chicago Bauhaus version. In this way, we were a decade ahead of many things that Joseph Beuys later proclaimed as his pedagogical revolution.

I tell you all this because my entry into pedagogy was not through direct teaching but through the anti-academic curriculum structure. Throughout the struggle to impose the curriculum, the Central Council of the University intervened in the School of Fine Arts and removed the director. Academic professors demanded that the director be reinstated and the intervention be suspended, with a threat of mass resignation if this was not done. With the help of the student federation, we managed to keep the intervention in place. The professors resigned, and therefore the University had to open positions for new teachers. The student assembly decided that three of us should apply for these positions, not to win but to serve as a reference for the other candidates regarding the new curriculum. Unexpectedly, three of us won the competitions. We were scared and returned to the assembly to see what to do, and it was decided that we should accept the positions for five years with the mission of helping to train new teachers. This is how I started teaching art (in printmaking), although my original and primary interest had been to help reorganize the institution.

PH We undoubtedly share an affinity for anti-institutionalism and anti-academia. But I think it's important to define exactly what we mean by these terms, starting with the term "academic." As you know, my formation as an artist took place in the education departments of various museums—indeed, a much more valuable education than the formal training I received in art school because my work in museums was not based on solitary work in the studio but on the daily task of connecting the public with works of art. Because of this, to me, the term "academic," beyond the conventional notion of nineteenth-century realistic art, generally represents the homogenization of terminologies and the transformation of every creative process into a series of recipes, whether it's the creation of a still life or a conceptual work. It's ironic that for thirteen years, I was the director of academic programs at the Museum of Modern Art—a period during which I sought to de-academicize the museum's pedagogy, much to the chagrin of academics.

As for the term "institutional," I'm afraid that I've always been much more institutional than you—a quality I admire in you. For me, working within existing structures is important, so I consider myself somewhat of a hermit crab, seeking to inhabit these structures in order to change them, even in my work outside of my museum work. My most extensive pedagogical project, *La Escuela Panamericana del Desasosiego* (The School of Panamerican Unrest), was precisely a simulation of the institution but with an experimental structure. I believe that you, on the other hand, are much more radical and aim to tear down existing structures to build new ones, but I'm not sure if I'm mistaken.

What is your interpretation of both terms?

LC Yes, we have to be careful with words, especially those with multiple meanings.

Here, I used the word "academic" in relation to the nineteenth-century French Academy. Most of the more contemporary professors at my school had studied with André Lhote, and they all believed that one had to start with copying from nature before attempting to break the rules. They used Picasso as an example, without understanding that the poor guy didn't have alternatives given the time he was educated. I think the difference between you and me, perhaps aside from temperaments, lies in where and how we were shaped. I've come to realize that, even though I was always very obedient to family rules as an only child, once I entered art school, everything came down to the location of power, its administration, and the interests it serves. In that sense, the generation that preceded me, which was openly anarchist and introduced me to the thoughts of Martin Buber and Herbert Read (i.e., an ethical and communal anarchism), found fertile ground in me.

The communist professor I mentioned, Armando González, who kept a bust of Stalin in his studio during the Khrushchev era, recognized this in me and, with great pain in his soul, told me not to try to be realistic and to follow my expressionist instincts. At the time, I was a terrible draftsman and always failed my drawing exams, but the liberation the professor gave me led me to analyze the distribution of power between me as the author and the pencil as a tool. Adjusting that distribution, creating horizontal teams of interlocutors for a common task, allowed me to adjust not only my art but my political ideology.

Today, in my very old age, I understand that I have always been more interested in education as an instrument of formation than art as a mechanism of production. In this sense, it's not about demolishing institutions but finding the fissures through which they can be guided to achieve that purpose. I believe this is where you and I are in strong agreement. By the time the institution operates, it generally adheres to plans that are already outdated and invalidate much of what they manage to do. But at the same time, they give us, those who disagree, the credibility to criticize them. Without institutions, this criticism is not effective because there is no sounding board.

One of the first museums that bought my work was MoMA, in 1962, but it was in a way that made me feel exploited. I decided then that my mission was no longer to get museums to collect me, and not even to try to destroy them. My mission was to collect museums. The bigger my collection, the greater my credibility, and therefore, the greater the echo of my criticism. I remain involved in art because it is the field that allows me to work with the fissures, and without institutions, there is no possibility of fissures. Today, for example, the famous "educational turn" has been institutionalized, and I believe it no longer serves to achieve an equitable distribution of power. That's why it seems to me that it's time to enter a period of an "artistic turn" that changes education to make it critical and imaginative. We want everyone to see and use the fissures, thus expanding the horizon.

I fear I'm compressing a lot in this response, but I don't want to abuse your space.

PH This conversation is starting to generate various facets I'd like to respond to; let's see if I can. Another difference between you and me is that I am the youngest of four siblings, them being much older than me. As a result, I believe I had an ideal situation: more freedom and many teachers (my parents, my brother, and my sisters), especially my brother, who was a philosopher and had me read the existentialists and a lot of literature. He wasn't really interested in political thought; this was an interest I developed due to my adolescent fascination with social realism (which was clearly anachronistic; one of my high school teachers used to make fun of me for being interested in 1930s art in the 1980s), but it evolved, especially when I moved to Chicago.

Regarding the idea of finding fissures and exploiting them and the artistic turn: indeed, the "educational turn" was a passing and somewhat brazen trend, using pedagogy as an idea to help validate curatorial reputations that weren't really committed to the transformative power of education that you describe. But of course, education is not a fad, and I believe that those of us interested in pedagogy have been doing it before, during, and will continue to do so after any trend.

As for your definition of the "artistic turn," I would like to know to what extent this is linked or equated with pedagogy as an artistic work in itself, and the difficulties that arise from doing so. Many of the pedagogical projects I've undertaken, I see them as artworks, but museums and contemporary art institutions struggle to see them as such. For instance, a few years ago, I led an experimental workshop in Mexico, titled *Theory and Practice of Limbo*, that I specifically requested to be presented as an artwork. The organization that supported me, which no longer exists, supported me in all aspects of the project, but, in the end, we couldn't present it (could I say, "package it"?) in a way that the entire workshop appeared as an artwork or performance. What I mean is that education is still seen as something external to art, not as art in itself. How do you see this relationship, and to what extent have you thought of your work as an educator as art?

LC I always missed not having brothers and sisters. The only child carries an overwhelming filial burden that in some ways distorts one's view of the environment. But that's a good question about accepting educational projects as artwork. My project *The Museum Is a School* is generally seen as an artwork, despite the contract that accompanies it. By calling it "art," its political function is dulled, which consists of making institutions enter into a contract with the public, where the public can file a lawsuit against museums adhering to the declaration but not fulfilling the "contract."

I often say that if I were the emperor of the world, I would prohibit the word "art" because it causes us more trouble than good. To me, art is fundamentally a way of confronting, processing, and generating information, in other words, a way of knowing. It is a meta-discipline of knowledge because it not only encompasses computable information but also does not necessarily adhere to existing codes or principles governed by logic. It allows us to go beyond the describable, create our own codes, and, more importantly, open up the imagination to the illogical, the absurd, and the impossible. Once we place ourselves in the realm of impossibility, we can evaluate the reasons for impossibility and the interests served by its definition and negotiate with the reality of what is possible. This is also an investigation into power: what are the obstacles, who put them there, which interests benefit from their existence, and how to remove them from the path. It is this aspect that makes artistic work essentially a political task (who has power, why they have it, and why we don't). From this perspective, art is a meta-discipline because it is not an alternative to scientific thinking but includes it as one of its branches.

If we understand art as the most complex and holistic way of the act of knowing or as a way to give a comprehensive (even if fictitious) order to the universe, this automatically defines how education should be in its entire process from birth to death, not just from preschool to postgraduate. It would also expose the danger of STEM education, which reduces education to what is applicable and profitable, gradually eliminating speculation and imagination. STEM makes us believe that education is training and that art is ingenuity rather than the exploration of the unknown.

I believe this identifies something on which we may possibly disagree: for me, politically, it's not about expanding the word "art" to accommodate educational projects but changing the educational process to accommodate and promote limitless imagination, regardless of the name we give to the results. Maintaining "art" as a separate disciplinary space fragments the act of knowing and allows the objectification of its results, isolating them from the process of social construction.

PH I'm not sure we disagree all that much, really. I wholeheartedly agree with the idea that art is a way of knowing and generating knowledge. On the other hand, I've always been aware of the danger of categories and labels, and I've also been convinced that what matters is not whether something is called art, education, or something else, but the effect it produces. When a person declares that something they see in a gallery is not art, their comment indicates that in their mind, this person has an implicit idea of what *is* art (e.g., academic art from the nineteenth century, for example). As an educator, I like to engage with these comments because they spark good discussions. As an artist, my attitude is usually one of acceptance because it's irrelevant to me whether the experiences I provide to a person are considered art, education, or something else. I believe that one's experience of a work cannot be truly articulated in words or any kind of definitive reflection.

But my perspective is that while terms may not matter, we also have no choice but to work within existing conventions and expectations because our ability to break, alter, and reimagine them helps us connect with the audience familiar with these conventions and allows us to help them generate new ways of thinking. Therefore, I believe I have to understand art as a language. That is, I think art operates in the same way as a language, albeit relying not only on words but also on physical elements (that produce sensory responses) and symbolic elements (that produce emotional, intellectual, and other responses). Hence, you and I have to accept being called artists because we use that language. Being an artist is a category that we need to do what we do, in my view. It's like Wittgenstein's ladder—it helps us get where we need to, and then we can discard it. But it seems important to me to defend the term "art" as a space to act freely according to the rules we deem appropriate. Perhaps it's a bad word, but it's necessary. I'm not sure if I'm making myself clear.

But my main question, definitions aside, concerns the role you see museums (or any other institution) playing in preserving your pedagogical work. Of course, your "art" works from the 1960s onward, including photography, printmaking, and so on, can be preserved in traditional ways, but your work goes far beyond the object. I have sometimes wondered if the art-education work I do is more of a methodology that should be continued like any other educational methodology (Montessori, Reggio Emilia, Freirean pedagogy, etc.) with its natural reinterpretations and adaptations that any methodology undergoes. Have you ever thought of your work in that way?

LC Certainly, in that sense, being described as artists doesn't bother me too much. What does bother me is, on one hand, that, as artists, we might end up believing ourselves to be such in the restricted definition, thus losing sight of our activity as "knowledge workers." On the other hand, it allows the word to reaffirm the artisanal production of the finished product. When you're asked about your profession and you say you're an artist, people always ask if you paint or what technique you use. If you were to say you're a philosopher, they would ask you about the ideas you work with and not whether you write by hand or on a machine. The point is that art is what I call a "craft plus," where it's the presence of the "plus," that something that doesn't fit into the traditional code offered by spoken or written language, that decides whether the activity is art or not. The only thing we can say is that precisely because it's indescribable, that "plus" (or the part that produces what you call "experience") expands knowledge. This is what sometimes frustrates me with some manifestations of "art as social practice." The results often exhaust themselves in description. Although they may improve a social situation, they do not affect or enrich the way of knowing. An imaginative social service remains a social service and can even become a political action. But the imaginative twist given to it only achieves a refinement of craftsmanship without transcending craftsmanship. And the fact that I'm an artist doesn't mean that everything I do is art, or that I should be protected if I do something unrelated to artistic pursuit that, if I were an ordinary citizen, could subject me to some form of punishment.

As for my work, since the sixties when I abandoned Expressionism and delved into Conceptualism (or "Contextualism," as we defined ourselves with Liliana Porter and José Guillermo Castillo before the term "Conceptual Art" was coined), I was always aware that I was working with problematizations, and these, secondarily, had to take on a "presence" to communicate. But precisely because I came from a craft background (first sculpture and then printmaking), and because my initial approach was to challenge the limits imposed by technical definitions, it was clear to me that it was about the interest in the problem rather than the perfection of the packaging. The interest in the problem, or its solution, is not in the literal but in the presence of the "plus." This conception of problematization defined that everything I did was fundamentally educational, and that the fetishistic collecting of the object was of no greater importance beyond economic benefits. It's about sharing the risk of speculation and thereby helping others explore the limits of their way of knowing. It's a collaborative effort where the artwork must retain its quality as a trigger rather than becoming an icon. This is where art and education are so closely linked. For me, the success of both the teacher and the artist is demonstrated by their becoming unnecessary.

Museums generally assume that the works they display are icons. If they were seriously concerned about education, they would understand that the icon represents an anti-pedagogical distribution of power. The icon demands admiration and submission, and it is the collection of icons that generally makes the museum a place of ostentation rather than education. The traditional and banal image of the museum as a church is not inaccurate. The canon does not like heresy, and yet it is heresy that allows us to question dogma. It's the challenge of the work through "miration"[1] rather than "admiration" and how this affects our daily decisions that gives educational value to a museum visit. An educational museum would underline this activity and measure its success not by the number of people who pass through its space, take selfies, and buy souvenirs. Instead, it would measure the impact that the museum experience had on the daily decisions of the visitors. Impact assessment would be much more useful than the usual measure of popularity. It would affect not only the internal policy of museums but also the external one. It would present the need to move away from the current model of an occasional open vault and instead work with schools to achieve curriculum revisions that complement STEM and ensure that people imagine before consuming. I believe that, as artists, this is the task we need to promote, not the personal fame of the artist.

PH I love your definition of artists as "workers of knowledge." I believe that many artists working in the social sphere implicitly identify with this notion without necessarily articulating it this way. I think this is why the term "social practice" is used in English, explicitly removing the term "art." Mierle Laderman Ukeles once told me that she despised this term because it made her feel as if an artist's profession was more like that of a therapist. But the use of the phrase reveals a discomfort, as you describe, with the word "artist," which indeed implies a craft-like production of objects. I'm not prepared to abandon the word because I believe we should redefine it rather than allowing others to use it in a way we consider wrong. Perhaps I'm an idealist.

Regarding your impatience with this type of work, which I sometimes share, especially in the case of many works that boast of being transformative more in their description than in the way they function in real life, one problem that arises from creating art that integrates into social or educational contexts is that it becomes elusive to criticism: if you criticize it as art, it is argued that it is education, and if you criticize it as education, it is argued that it is art, thereby seeking to become immune to analysis. The question we then have is how to evaluate this type of work, just as you talk about how we evaluate the impact of a museum experience on a visitor. As an educator in museums, where we always had to thoroughly evaluate each activity, initiative, and workshop and obsessively debate measurement parameters, I found it contradictory that an artwork presented as pedagogy was exempt from the same type of scrutiny as a regular educational project. I completely share your perspective about the emphasis given to STEM in the modern world, although in terms of science and technology, there is a focus on assessing and measuring results, which can be quite beneficial from their methods.

I don't want to overextend in this conversation, and you've already given me a lot of your time, for which I'm very grateful.

1 From the Spanish "mirar" (to see).

But I need to close a topic with you, which has to do with your legacy as an artist.

As you rightly point out, museums tend to turn everything into an icon or fetish, but I believe this is partly because artists don't offer them many alternatives. I recall that when I worked at MoMA on a retrospective of Lygia Clark, one of the most challenging issues the curatorial team faced was how to present her therapies—that is, the kind of activity that Lygia declared was not art because she had officially renounced being an artist when she decided to start doing therapies. They were, on the other hand, individual experiences and long-term processes, not spectacles or performances. In the end, we invited two of Lygia's former assistants who still conduct therapies, Lula Wanderley and Gina Ferreira, to train our educators to provide some kind of demonstrations to the public. It was by no means perfect, but, to this day, I don't know how else it could have been done if the goal was to share this crucial aspect of Lygia with the public. The therapies are not art, so they should not be subjected to the fetishistic treatment of something hung in a gallery, but the "demonstrations" were carried out in the last room of the exhibition, making it quite ambiguous.

So, my point is this question: What options can an artist provide to a museum to preserve and maintain their thinking beyond exhibiting their works? How can an artist keep their work alive without fetishizing it?

LC Lately, I use the simplistic image of a "tree of knowledge," where I place art as the root activity in its cognitive function, as language, in the trunk, and as a discipline producing "fruits" in the branches. For me, the important part is the root activity, but the word "art" is used for everything, making it unclear what we are talking about. Applying quantitative evaluation systems becomes even more confusing because they are not designed for the most important aspects of art, which are located in the spaces between the units and not within the units themselves. These spaces are what we lose with STEM, and, in the long run, we will end up failing to perceive them. However, this doesn't mean making the opposite mistake and ignoring the units. That would be confronting one form of knowledge fragmentation with another. I recall your quote about the group that did an educational project, and when you asked about the educational consequences of the project, they replied that they didn't know because it was a work of art, and they were artists.

Regarding Lygia Clark, part of the problem is the family, which encourages the fetishization of her work for their economic interests. I tried to reproduce one of Lygia's works in my *Didactics*, and they wanted to charge an absurd amount for rights, even though it was an obviously nonprofit academic book. I ended up using a page from a catalog that reproduced the work, presenting the catalog openly to evade the issue. I didn't find the Lygia Clark exhibition at MoMA very good precisely because it emphasized the works too much and ended up being dull. But the participatory aspect seemed well done to me. I didn't know it was your contribution, although I could have imagined it. That could have been the backbone of the entire exhibition, and then she would have appeared in all her power. But this is precisely the problem with museums; they get trapped in the objects and, in doing so, imprison the viewer's perception. The museum looks at the work, and it leads the spectator to do the same. When the museum is somewhat more progressive, it tries to enter the work and help the viewer do the same. But cognitively, this always uses the work as if it were a tunnel. I prefer the idea of going around the work to position oneself behind it, alongside the creator, to confront what motivated the creation of the work and see if it serves as a response to an interesting question or as a path of inquiry. This is where the "root" part of art is shared, and it initiates an educational process. The artist can revisit their own work in these terms and then help the museum do the same by demanding that this approach to accessing art is used. Along the way, the artist also learns to differentiate whether they are only navel-gazing or contributing to social construction. The fetish or economic value of the work corresponds to another field that has nothing to do with all of this. On the one hand, it's like confusing the beauty of calligraphy with the content of the text. On the other hand, it's like confusing the value of a manuscript signed by Simón Rodríguez or Paulo Freire with the cognitive consequences of what they are telling us. But in this confusion, artists are as guilty as museums, or at least we support each other in the same vicious circle.

This conversation was first published in the Beautiful Eccentrics *newsletter on January 15, 2024. See https://pablohelguera.substack.com/p/of-workers-and-trees.*

Translated by Eunji Lee.

On Gender, Sculpture, and Relearning How to See

Gordon Hall

I

I'm sunbathing on the beach in the Rockaways on a cloudless August day. It's blindingly bright and I have a T-shirt draped over my eyes to block the sun. I am overhearing a conversation between some of the friends around me and someone new who has walked across the sand to us. Whose is this voice I don't know? I think it is a man, someone I've never met. I uncover my eyes and see that it is one of my friends—a woman, a transwoman whose female-ness I have never questioned, whose voice I had always heard as a female voice. Had I never heard her before? How can my ears hear two different voices, depending on whether or not I know who is speaking? As I puzzle over this, I start thinking of other instances in which two or more versions of reality butt up against each other, two contradictory sensory experiences that are somehow real to me, depending on how I encounter them. What is going on here?

II

On March 23, 2016, the North Carolina House of Representatives passed the Public Facilities Privacy & Security Act, widely referred to as House Bill 2. The bill prohibits municipalities in the state of North Carolina from passing policies intended to protect LGBT people from discrimination, setting a minimum wage, and regulating child labor, and it dictates that transgender people must use the bathroom that corresponds to the sex printed on their birth certificates in all public facilities.[1] The bill was met with massive opposition from individuals,

1 This requirement is included in the law despite the fact that regulations governing the change of a sex marker on a birth certificate vary widely state to state. In North Carolina, such modifications are only allowed after the completion of sex-reassignment surgery, which many transgender people either cannot access or do not want.

corporations, and numerous other states that, as a result, banned non-emergency travel to North Carolina to protest the law. On May 9, the United States Department of Justice filed a lawsuit against North Carolina on the grounds that the bill violated several federal laws, including Title VII of the Civil Rights Act. At the time of this writing, the case is still open and House Bill 2 remains the law, although a lawsuit challenging its constitutionality will be heard at a trial scheduled to begin November 14, 2016.[2]

III

This winter I delivered an artist talk at Virginia Commonwealth University, where I've been teaching, about my investment in objects with open-ended or ambiguous functions—things that cause one to ask, "What is this for?" I discuss the studio as a place where I aim to make objects that frustrate even my own attempts to know them, once and for all, as one thing and not others. I make things that ask for nuanced, open-ended forms of reading that can accommodate this ambiguous functionality. Over coffee the following morning, one of the other faculty members in the department, Corin Hewitt, excitedly wanted to know if I had heard of a beloved object known as the "slant step." I had not, but since then an image of it has been following me around—in the studio, on the train, in and out of bathrooms—while reading the news. The slant step is a small piece of furniture that was purchased in a second-hand store in Mill Valley, California, in 1965 by the artist William Wiley and his then–graduate student Bruce Nauman. Costing less than a dollar, this one-of-a-kind handmade object, in wood and green linoleum, struck these two artists as puzzling and fascinating primarily because its function was a mystery. Though reminiscent of a step stool, the step part of the stool sits at a forty-five-degree angle to the floor, making it impossible to step up onto it, hence the name, the slant step. This unassuming, ambiguous object resonated not just with Wiley and Nauman, but also with a whole range of Bay Area artists in the 1960s, inspiring more than one group exhibition themed around it, a catalogue, and numerous articles as well as extensive use as a teaching tool by the painter Frank Owen. It is now in the permanent collection of the University of California Davis.[3]

IV

In 2012 I wrote an essay called "Object Lessons: Thinking Gender Variance through Minimal Sculpture."[4] In it, I proposed a way of reading sculpture as a form of embodied pedagogy—sculptures as objects from which we learn. Instead of thinking about artworks symbolically, metaphorically, representationally, or autobiographically, I wondered about the possibilities for treating objects as teachers who might be able to assist us in developing different ways of understanding and experiencing our bodies. Sculptures as dance teachers? As gym coaches? As lovers? I was

2 CNN, "Loretta Lynch's statement on North Carolina bathroom ...," https://www.youtube.com/watch?v=qGcurCOBrZo.

3 Visit *Art Practical* for a more complete history of the slant step. See https://wayback.archive-it.org/15633/20201224144457/https://www.artpractical.com/feature/the-linoleum-symbol-of-a-new-and-coming-faith/

4 Gordon Hall, "Object Lessons," https://gordon-hall.net/object-lessons.

5 For a book-length art historical exploration of some of these themes and a thorough bibliography, see David Getsy, *Abstract Bodies: Sixties Sculpture and the Expanded Field of Gender* (Yale University Press, 2015).

particularly interested in our tendency to understand art that relates to nontraditional genders and sexualities primarily in terms of representation, seeking evidence of LGBT subjects or authors in the work through depiction. Queer art tends to be thought of as art that announces itself as queer through a variety of tropes, ranging from documentary photography to material references such as glitter or leather. The "object lessons" framework was intended to eschew these tendencies in favor of an interest in phenomenological relationships with artworks, particularly sculptures, which could produce new, odd, or altered states of embodied being that might enable us to better develop, recognize, respect, and cultivate different forms of gendered living. Can objects help us rethink gender on a bodily level? Further, does the maker of an artwork have to be known to have been queer for their work to be meaningful in these terms? In whose art, both historical and contemporary, can we find beauty and sustenance, even if the artist did not explicitly frame their work as having anything to do with gender or sexuality? Since that essay's writing, I have come to think of the object lessons described therein as ways of approaching our variously felt struggles against hegemonic methods of taxonomizing, cataloging, and controlling bodies, as modestly offered resources toward imagining more expansive forms of embodied life.[5]

In being asked to write something in response to the North Carolina bathroom bill, I found myself returning to this work and wondering if this way of thinking might have something to contribute to our conversations around it.[6] I have written pages and pages of furious ranting prose directed at the many groups and individuals who support bills like House Bill 2 based on what is, in my opinion, an ignorant, cruel, and fear-motivated set of beliefs about transgender people's bodies and lives, only to realize that they don't care what I think. I am not real to them, and they very probably aren't reading artist writings commissioned and released by the Walker Art Center. These pages of writing will remain private, because what I actually do feel able to contribute, if anything at all, are some reflections I have had about the capacities for objects to teach us different ways to see. In this sense, I am not speaking to those that support this law, which, cynically, considering the adverse economic impact it has had on the state of North Carolina, and less cynically, the national trajectory to full legal equality for transgender people, will likely be struck down. It isn't a foregone conclusion, but what feels extremely sad to me is that the very necessary laws and legal protections that the government has to offer us do not have terribly much to do with changing the ways that we see, interpret, and react to one another's bodies.[7] What we require is a large-scale rearranging of the ways that bodies are classified and hierarchized along gendered and racial lines. This is largely a question of reworking our vision so that in the moments we encounter one another, we are actually able to see differently than

6 I have a troubling mix of conflicting emotions about being asked to write about House Bill 2. I both relish it and resent it. I think about gendered bathrooms quite a bit but also feel that I already think about them too much and am exhausted and humiliated by how I can't seem to get away from this very unglamorous topic. Simultaneously, I have thoughts that I want to share, so here we are.

7 As well as our own bodies, insofar as transgender people ourselves are often mired in an ongoing, and exhausting, labor of holding on to our own understandings of our bodies while living in a world that largely doesn't acknowledge or respect them and often, at best, corners us into pathologizing ourselves in order to access the medical and legal services we need.

the way we have been taught.[8] This is a form of aesthetic labor—relearning how to see and identify what we are looking at—and it seems to me that some of our best teachers might be things themselves.

V
Object Lesson: Slow Reading

The bathroom provision of House Bill 2 aims to "protect" non-transgender people from the experience of sharing a bathroom with someone of the "opposite sex." In this sense, it seems primarily targeted toward non-passing transgender people—those who are visibly transgender and gender non-conforming.[9] It would also be impossible to analyze the effects of bills like House Bill 2 without thinking through ways that they are likely to disproportionately affect non-white transgender people for a variety of reasons.

First, an intersectional analysis of gender policing acknowledges that fear is not doled out equally, and that a person of color is already more likely to produce anxiety for a nervous white person in a bathroom.[10] Being a non-passing trans person and a person of color works in tandem to increase the possibility of being read as a threat.[11] Many transgender people do not seek to pass, or do not identify as either one of the two available gender options. In situations in which a person does desire to fully transition, medical transitions are expensive and time-consuming. It is a luxury to pass. Even when insurance will cover sex-reassignment surgeries and access to hormones, it isn't necessarily an option for everyone to take weeks or months off from work to heal. Or people find themselves situated within community structures that they rely on, yet who will not accept them if they were to transition. There are numerous reasons why low-income transgender people are less likely to pass as the gender that they know they are. And in the United States, the legacies of slavery, segregation, redlining, and lack of access to quality free education has made it vastly more likely that people who are low-income are also people of color.[12] We must acknowledge that it is likely that many of those most adversely affected by laws such as House Bill 2 are both transgender and people of color.[13] We know that the legal changes of the past sixty years resulting from the civil rights movement have not led to the shifts in perception that we so direly need, with frequently deadly consequences. One of post–civil rights movement racism's main playing field is in the often-unconscious perceptual patterns of white bodies and ways that these play out in the mundane daily activity of interacting with and responding to

8 I'd like to add that this whole debate feels depressing to me because what is at stake is not even the outcome that I want, which is the abolition of the two-gender bathroom system and a general loosening of a world structured around the false idea that there are two genders, that same-gender spaces are "safe" and desexualized havens, and that all we need is to allow transgender people who clearly identify with one of the two options to go into the bathroom that "matches" their gender identity. What about gender-nonconforming people? Disabled people with other-gendered caregivers? Parents with children? But what I want is apparently so radical I am foolish to even hope for it in my lifetime. So, we will continue to agonize over who counts as a woman and who counts as a man and how we can continue using an outdated system. It feels bleak to be fighting for something that isn't even what one wants.

9 This is one of the reasons why some activists objected to the trend of passing trans men posting selfies of themselves in women's bathrooms to protest House Bill 2. Mitch Kellaway, "Casting Trans Men as Predators Won't Stop Bathroom Bills," *The Advocate*, March 29, 2016, https://www.advocate.com/commentary/2016/3/29/casting-trans-men-predators-wont-stop-bathroom-bills.

10 Visit the *New York Times* for an overview of recent research on perceptual bias in relation to race: Sendhil Mullainathan, "Racial Bias, Even When We Have Good Intentions," *New York Times*, January 3, 2015, https://www.nytimes.com/2015/01/04/upshot/the-measuring-sticks-of-racial-bias-.html.

11 Transgender people of color, particularly trans women of color, are murdered at the highest rate of any measurable demographic, and this number is increasing. Zach Stafford, "Transgender homicide rate hits historic high in US, says new report," *The Guardian*, November 13, 2015, https://www.theguardian.com/us-news/2015/nov/13/transgender-homicide-victims-us-has-hit-historic-high.

strangers, both within our institutions and on the street.

Supporters of bills such as House Bill 2 widely refer to them as "common-sense legislation." This moniker is, to my ear, accurate, insofar as those who deploy it rely on a particular version of common sense that puts its faith in biological essentialism. Much of the rhetoric used in defense of this kind of bathroom legislation seems to me to hinge on intense anxiety around the threat transgender people's bodies pose to this way of understanding sex and gender in which one can know what one is looking at. When I analyze this dynamic in this way, I am actually able to feel compassion for those who oppose the presence of transgender people in bathrooms that "match" their self-professed gender identities, because the idea that a person's gender could be self-determined and believed by others as a matter of faith is a legitimate shift into another perceptual system literally incompatible with one rooted in biological essentialism. We are telling you that what you see isn't true—a person may look like a woman or a man to your eye, but that does not mean that they are. This does go against what has long been widely held as common sense, a principle on which most of our medical and legal systems still rely. While the struggle for rights and recognition for transgender people is a legal battle, it is also a battle over whose perception is "real"—whose ability to read, interpret, and translate whose bodies should we consider credible? Given this, the functioning of our senses becomes a field of social negotiation, an ongoing push and pull around whose mode of seeing we want to put our faith in.[14]

I find that in the circles in which I move, I don't often encounter people who overtly espouse views on gender that disavow the realities of transgender lives. Most don't believe in biological essentialism in relation to gender and reject traditional roles for men and women while supporting transgender people's right to use any bathroom they want to. I wonder, though, if, despite this, many of us are still relying on this same version of common sense about gender as those who actively support bills that mandate bathroom access based on sex as assigned at birth. We wouldn't say it out loud, but we do it all the time—reading people as male and female, assigning them genders without their consent, expecting that we know something about each other based on these assignments. What would it look like for us to truly untether our genders from these original assignments that were given to us at the moment of our births? So much has changed so fast, I'm told, people need time to catch up.... For me, the time has arrived, and it goes way beyond arguing about bathrooms. I want to relearn how to see.

In the midst of all this urgency, the figure of the slant step comes to my mind. I feel embarrassed about it because what could this remote object have to offer when we are in need of such concrete changes? A useful object with no apparent use. A

12 The Pew Research Center shares the numbers on income inequality based on race: Eileen Patten, "Racial, Gender Wage Gap Persists in US Despite Some Progress," Pew Research Center, July 1, 2016, https://www.pewresearch.org/short-reads/2016/07/01/racial-gender-wage-gaps-persist-in-u-s-despite-some-progress/.

13 It has been striking to me that some civil rights leaders have condemned the link made by Attorney General Loretta Lynch between racial segregation and denying bathroom access, as in Pastor John Amanchukwu's statement that "a person's ability to self-identify as something they are not has nothing to do with civil rights." Watch a video of this rally in support of House Bill 2: "Black Pastors Rally Support for HB2, Saying LGBT Rights Are Not Civil Rights," May 25, 2016, https://www.newsobserver.com/news/politics-government/politics-columns-blogs/under-the-dome/article79515797.html.

14 Judith Butler, "A 'Bad Writer' Bites Back," *New York Times*, March 20, 1999, https://www.nytimes.com/1999/03/20/opinion/a-bad-writer-bites-back.html.

handmade thing of unknown origin, producing more questions than answers. An object that modestly requests a more effortful type of reading than what we normally engage in. We identify things in terms of their function and move on, reading passively. We learn only as much as we need to know. This object, compelling to so many in the past fifty years, is compelling to me as well, insofar as it encourages me to read more slowly. It makes me want to see it as more than one thing at once, or as many different things in quick succession. Looking to the slant step as a teacher, I want to learn what it seems to already know—I can't always know what I am looking at. Clearly already well used in the mid-1960s but for an inscrutable purpose, the slant step speaks of bodies without being able to name them. It has always seemed wrong to me to say that we see what is before us and then interpret it, because the idea of "interpreting what we see" implies an inaccurate linearity to this process and suggests that the things themselves are fixed while our understandings of them remain malleable. Rather, we understand what we are seeing at the same moment we see it; perception is identification. Understood in this way, changing our interpretations is literally synonymous with changing the functioning of our senses, initiating a pulling apart of the instantaneous act of assigning meaning to what we see. This slowness to assign identification in the moment of encounter lies at the heart of the slant step's curious appeal.

VI
Object Lesson: Object Kinship

On an overcast August day in 1995, Tyra Hunter, a hairstylist and Black transgender woman, got in a car accident while driving in Washington, DC. Adrian Williams, the emergency medical technician at the scene who began to cut away her clothing to administer urgently needed aid, is reported to have said, "This bitch ain't no girl ... it's a nigger; he's got a dick!" Hunter lay on the ground bleeding as Williams and the other EMTs joked around her, and died later that day of her injuries at a nearby hospital. A subsequent investigation into the events leading to her death concluded that it would very likely have been prevented had treatment been continued at the scene of the accident.[15]

In the fall of 2014, a grand jury in St. Louis County, Missouri, decided not to indict police officer Darren Wilson for the shooting death of eighteen-year-old Michael Brown. In the spring of 2015, the United States Department of Justice also cleared Wilson of all civil rights violations, deeming the shooting to be an act of self-defense. In Wilson's testimony in his grand jury hearing, he recounted looking at Brown in the moments before shooting him six times and described him as having "the most intense aggressive face. The only way I can describe it, it looks like a demon, that's how angry he looked."[16]

It's hard to stomach these statements, but I write them here because I am noticing the ways that both speakers managed to transform the person they were about to kill from a human being to a thing in the moments before their deaths. By a probably less-than-conscious twist of verbal gymnastics, both killers shift from using a pronoun

15 Account of Tyra Hunter's death found in Richard Juang, "Transgendering the Politics of Recognition," in *The Transgender Studies Reader* 1, ed. Susan Stryker and Stephen Whittle (Routledge, 2006), 712.

16 Quoted from NPR's coverage of Darren Wilson's testimony: Krishnadev Calamur, "Ferguson Documents: Officer Darren Wilson's Testimony," NPR, November 25, 2014, https://www.npr.org/sections/the-twoway/2014/11/25/366519644/ferguson-docs-officer-darren-wilsons-testimony.

generally used to refer to people (he/she) to using a pronoun generally used to refer to inanimate things: it. If murder is the act of permanently dehumanizing another, then it is as if, in order to give themselves permission to kill these two individuals, Williams and Wilson had to preemptively transform them from people into things. "It's a nigger...." "It looks like a demon...." Did these statements make it possible to turn a human being into a corpse? Maybe so, as a person turned non-consensually into a thing is already a person dangerously close to death.

Of the many protests in North Carolina over House Bill 2, at least one has ended with dancing. A video has been circulating on the internet of an activist and transgender woman named Micky Bradford voguing in front of a line of police officers guarding the North Carolina governor's mansion. The jostling cellphone video, taken by an unidentified member of the crowd, shows Bradford standing still in front of the line of police officers, seemingly lost in thought. She shifts slowly, taking off her bag, and gradually begins to dance for the crowd of demonstrators, who with their voices and a couple of drums provide an enthusiastic rhythmic soundtrack for her movements. The officers stand with blank faces as Bradford travels gracefully back and forth in front of them. For three minutes she dances, an outpouring of energy at the end of many hours of protest. Bradford recounts, "I was tired. The most I could do was dance away my anger, frustration, and sadness."[17]

In the 1966 slant-step show, William Wiley, the artist who originally bought the step from the thrift store, made a metal casting from it that bore the following inscription: "This piece is dedicated to all the despised unknown, unloved, people, objects, and ideas that just don't make it and never will, who have so thoughtlessly given their time and talent to become objects of scorn but maintain an innocent ignorance and never realize that you hate them."[18] For Wiley, the slant step was both an intriguing object of ambiguous functionality, while also serving another purpose as the object of certain recuperations. To treat a discarded object with care, to focus on it, show it to others, make copies and homages to it—to, in a sense, treat it with love—had a value for him on its own account. A small act of treating an uncared-for thing with care as an articulation of an ethos for encountering one another. Frank Owen, one of Wiley's friends and an original participant in the slant-step show, used the step as a model in his life-drawing classes for decades—producing innumerable depictions of its likeness and encouraging his students to think deeply about it through the slow and close looking necessitated by drawing. "This was its job—to pose on a model stand patiently (which it is very good at) and be drawn while also posing its eternal question: What is this thing, what is it for, and why do we attend to it?"[19]

I am writing this essay in the days and weeks following the mass shooting at Pulse, the gay nightclub in Orlando, Florida, in which forty-nine people were killed and dozens more seriously injured.[20] I read about it obsessively, as if knowing more about it could undo it, or at least help me

17 Raquel Willis, "This Radical Organization Has Been Fighting in the South for 25 Years," *Out*, May 29, 2019, https://www.out.com/out-exclusives/2019/5/29/radical-organization-has-been-fighting-south-25-years.

18 Regina Hackett, "William T. Wiley—Objects of Scorn," *Another Bouncing Ball*, December 8, 2009, https://www.artsjournal.com/anotherbb/2009/12/william_t_wiley_-_the_consolat.html.

19 Dave Jones, "The Slant Step Comes Home for Good," Dateline UC Davis, July 20, 2012, https://www.ucdavis.edu/news/slant-step-comes-home-good.

understand it, make it make sense. My grief about the present has woven its way into the writing of this piece, feeling rocked by the collective experiences of often unbearable vulnerability felt by many in my community, not just since this shooting but long before it. Recurring in the many posts, essays, and articles I have read are descriptions of the crucial importance that dance floors in queer nightlife settings have in mitigating these pervasive feelings of being threatened, marginalized, or objectified. Dance floors, at their best, have provided innumerable gay and transgender people with a momentary inversion of the conditions that govern their day-to-day lives—we can show off our bodies without shame. We can have a glimpse of what it feels like to be seen and recognized and celebrated, even if it is just for a moment in the midst of all the confusion and anxiety inherent to mixing with strangers. While thinking about this, I have revisited a piece of writing I did last summer for the catalogue of a retrospective of the Chicago-based DJ and art collective Chances Dances, whose parties I attended throughout the years I lived in that city. In it, I propose something called "reparative objectification" in which we collectively counteract the damaging effects of being objectified through mutually objectifying each other—interfacing with one another as bodies, but doing so in a way that supports rather than tries to destroy one another: "I found myself thinking about some other reparative process, one that countered this kind of damaging objectification with an even more powerful kind of objectification. I wanted [us] to treat each other like objects in profound affirmation, to learn to see each other, to look at one another as bodies and say YES."[21] This is much of what we do on the dance floor—embrace rather than disavow our object-ness in a space that allows us to do so without the risk of dehumanization that usually accompanies objectification. My thinking about this emerged in the months following the suicide in 2012 of our friend Mark Aguhar, who, moving through the world as both a transgender person and a brown person and a fat person, contended with a level of publicly expressed disgust, objectification, and policing that most of us can't imagine. Mark was unapologetic about her existence, and she arrived at the club looking gorgeous and ready to dance, which she did, incredibly and with conviction. I really sincerely hope that we were able to offer her some respite in these spaces, looking at her twirling body in a way that helped her live.[22]

In the months before she died, Mark took to tending to houseplants—usually small potted succulents that she arranged in artful compositions with decorative rocks and unique pots of different shapes and sizes. She had a special fondness for a plant called the ponytail plant, described by the artist Aay Preston-Myint as "frilly and frondy, and reminded Mark of her own ponytail." For an exhibition organized by Aay, Mark contributed a group of potted

20 During the editing stage of this essay, a series of additional fatal police shootings of Black individuals set off massive responses—including Paul O'Neal in Chicago, Philando Castile in Falcon Heights, Minnesota, and Alton Sterling in Baton Rouge, Louisiana. There were also two large-scale fatal shootings of groups of police officers, occurring in Dallas and Baton Rouge. The frequency of these tragedies prevents us from thoroughly responding to each one individually and causes them to fade into the past much faster than can be justified. I mention these new events here to acknowledge that they took place, but that they did so after this piece's creation.

21 Read my 2015 essay "Party Friends," https://gordonhall.net/party-friends.

22 Among the numerous pieces of writing about Mark Aguhar, the *Brooklyn Rail* recently published a beautiful essay by the artist Young Joon Kwak. "Critics Page: Mark Aguhar," *Brooklyn Rail*, July/August 2016, https://brooklynrail.org/2016/07/criticspage/mark-aguhar/.

plants and an ornate candy bowl filled with multicolored round hard candies (an homage to Felix Gonzales-Torres's candy-spill pieces from the early 1990s). Mark did not think of these pieces as artworks, per se, but referred to her work on them as "object styling." A post on her blog from 2010 titled "HOW TO STAVE OFF SUICIDE FOR ANOTHER COUPLE HOURS" consists of a list of fourteen points, including "cuddle with your friends as often and for as long as they are willing to stand you," "remember that you are worthy," and "consider the reality of hormones." She also added a note to "buy beautiful plants that remind you of yourself and that need careful attention."[23]

In thinking about Mark and her succulents, I am wrapping myself around the sustaining potential of relations of care with non-human things. I wonder about the role that the cultivation, protection, and recuperation of things might play in the day-to-day processes of healing necessitated by living as a body that is objectified, misread, or unrecognized. Can attending to objects with care be a labor of self-sustenance for us as well? Can the things of our lives be our companions, our children, our comrades?[24] What can we know or feel about our own bodies through the ways that we relate to objects? I want to propose the possibility that our relations with objects themselves might function as a means of remodeling our own often-fraught bonds with the materiality that is our own lived bodies. I sometimes joke that all I am doing in the studio is making friends. This joke is feeling more real by the day. I am thinking now about all the gorgeous nontraditionally gendered people I know coming back to their apartments exhausted from the daily labor of moving through the world and carefully watering their plants.

VII

I was disappointed to discover that the group of artists originally dedicated to the slant step does seem to agree about its original intended use. Both the poet William Witherup and Marion Wintersteen, the curator at Berkeley Coop Gallery that hosted the first slant-step exhibition, have stated that they believe the most likely original purpose of the object was to assist one while on the toilet, a footrest designed to create the ideal posture for having a bowel movement.[25] As much as I wish for the slant step to remain completely open-ended in its utility, and as embarrassing as it is to discover that it was probably originally made for use on the toilet, it also seems only right that it would have been placed in the bathroom, which at present is probably where we need it the most.

This essay was originally published on The Walker Art Center Blog, August 8, 2016. https://walkerart.org/magazine/gordon-hall-transgender-hb2-bathroom-bill.

23 See Juana Peralta and Roy Perez, eds., *Callout Queen*, 2012, https://issuu.com/poczineproject/docs/calloutqueen-zine.

24 The Russian Constructivists sometimes referred to objects as "comrades," as described in Christiana Kiaer, *Imagine No Possessions: The Socialist Objects of Russian Constructivism* (The MIT Press, 2005).

25 Cited in Christopher Knight, "Has art's Slant Step mystery finally been solved?" *Los Angeles Times*, June 9, 2014, https://www.latimes.com/entertainment/arts/culture/la-et-cm-slant-step-mystery-solved-20140609-column.html.

Six Years: We've Reached a Moment of Crisis[1]

Sarah Rifky

The countercultural infrastructure has collapsed. Since the late 1990s, contemporary art in Egypt has relied on international networks rather than state funding or private patronage. This funding model, once robust, has significantly weakened. These networks have positioned art as one facet of a broader philanthropic infrastructure, intertwining it with human rights, civic practice, journalism, and media, all supported by this underlying framework. Unlike Europe, where art is largely sustained by state and public institutions, or the United States, where art is embedded in foundations and museums, circulates as a market asset, and relies on both private patronage and state support, contemporary art in Egypt has developed around this foreign, fragile, and ever-changing infrastructural scaffolding.

This essay focuses on a six-year period (2009–15) during which rapid shifts in contemporary art's infrastructure altered the material and conceptual conditions of art making. Adopting a heuristic approach and drawing on my autoethnographic and situated historical analysis, I demonstrate how a nuanced understanding of art is inextricably bound to pedagogy, and both are grounded in our embodied knowledge of institutions and infrastructure.

One of the guiding principles of my work as a curator and writer is to consider every artwork as a school. While the relationship between art and pedagogy is more complex than this single assertion, the idea that "every artwork is a school" is one that is constantly tested and challenged through my work with contemporary art.

1 In some ways, this essay—tracing six years in the history of contemporary art in Cairo—nods to Lucy Lippard's *Six Years*. While not a direct parallel, her approach to chronicling Conceptualism's emergence through a mixture of discursive, thematic documentation and lived chronology informs my thinking on personal experience, contingency, and complicity in writing histories of contemporary art without archival anchors. See Lucy Lippard, *Six Years: The Dematerialization of the Art Object from 1966–1972* (Praeger, 1973).

At this moment of writing, I am employing this approach methodologically for the purposes of this essay, which unfolds as a series of stories tied to a specific moment in Egypt's recent political history. I will attempt to recapitulate this moment as a prelude to discussing my curatorial practice. Until the January 25 Revolution in 2011, which led to the ousting of President Hosni Mubarak, Egypt had long been governed under emergency law, a legal framework that granted the state sweeping powers to suppress dissent. State security vigilantly prevented any collective action in public spaces, treating even the smallest gatherings with suspicion and quashing any signs of insurgency.

Art was not exempt from control. Protests—whether led by civic groups, labor movements, or students—had been mounting steadily, especially since 2006, fueled by economic grievances, political repression, and the escalating frustration of our generation, which had known nothing but Mubarak's rule. Key movements, such as Kefaya (The Egyptian Movement for Change), had been challenging dynastic succession to the presidency, while the inspiration for the April 6 Youth Movement came from striking textile workers in Mahalla. Labor strikes were also appearing. Social media was strategically deployed and manipulated to craft the counter-image to state propaganda and mobilize a social movement. The spirit of resistance was palpable.

Between 2009 and 2015, Egypt experienced a rapid cycle of political change. The euphoria of the 2011 revolution was followed by a series of jarring reversals. Almost immediately after, Egypt's Supreme Council of the Armed Forces (SCAF) began orchestrating real-time historiographic erasure, actively antagonizing the 2011 revolution. By the time the June 2013 coup was underway, SCAF had effectively reset the clock—chronographically haunting the present and marking the beginning of a political unraveling with far-reaching consequences that continue to shape every facet of our lives, including contemporary art. We are still trapped in the aftermath of the counter-revolution. As the military consolidated power, it deployed its state-security apparatus to target human rights defenders, civil society activists, cultural organizations, activists, intellectuals, and artists, and continues to do so.

Since 2014, the state has imposed harsh penalties—including life imprisonment and substantial fines—on individuals and organizations receiving foreign funding deemed harmful to national interests. While the law primarily targeted NGOs focused on social justice, human rights, media, and journalism, cultural organizations that sustain contemporary art since the late 1990s have also become targets. One might plausibly argue that the state intentionally collapses the distinction between art and activism.

The state's interference in cultural spaces has taken many forms—raids, harassment of leadership, bureaucratic restrictions through permits and taxes, censorship, and direct crackdowns on artists. Townhouse Gallery serves as a stark example. At its height, it was one of the most prominent and singular spaces for contemporary art in Egypt. Nestled away in a downtown back alley amid mechanic shops, it occupied a distinctive position—both geographically and culturally—featuring, among other spaces, two expansive venues: the Factory and the Rawabet Theater, both opening directly onto the street. More than a gallery, in the conventional sense, Townhouse functioned as a vital place for coming together, one of the few—if not the only—spaces that, by virtue of its location, was a space where social interactions naturally crossed class divides, which remains rare in Cairo. In some cases, state repression has led to the dismantling of such critical institutions, and, in 2019, Townhouse was forced to close its doors.

In my curatorial practice in Egypt from 2009 to 2015, I was often explicit about the critical distinction between art and political activism, wary of their conflation. Understanding the political context is essential, not only to situate myself but also to frame the works I will discuss later in this essay.

The sequence of my analysis follows somewhat of a lived chronology, examining roughly six projects I was involved in. The central question guiding my thinking is one I intuit: What does it mean to describe contemporary art in Egypt as latent? When, how, and does art always appear, circulate, and operate as art?

By art's latency, I refer to the underlying, often unseen quality of the work—its potential or emergence—rather than its immediate, material manifestation. Focusing on art's latency means stepping back from the immediate concerns of value arbitration and legitimation. Instead, I aim to articulate the modalities these works present, their context, and their political resonance. The timeframes of these practices and their aftereffects overlap. Sitting with the latency of contemporary art also means acknowledging how the potency of its latent quality lingers—not only socially and politically, but also personally.

Spring 2009

The Twentieth Cairo Youth Salon, held at the Palace of the Arts in Cairo in the spring of 2009, was not just another entry in the Ministry of Culture's long-running initiative—it was an event that laid bare the fractures in Egypt's contemporary art landscape and an orientation point for my practice as an artist, curator, and educator. Founded in 1989, the Cairo Youth Salon has long been a volume-driven endeavor, packing hundreds of young artists into each edition. It follows a state-patronage model, akin to the Paris Salon and other state-run biennials, reinforcing Egypt's policy of prioritizing state-backed institutions over independent initiatives. Functioning as a juried competition, it relies on a selection committee of state-aligned artists and critics to determine who gets institutional recognition. More than an exhibition, the salon reflects the state's grip on artistic production, extending the reach of an art education system that, since the 1960s, expanded in step with socialist policies aimed at broadening access—without necessarily broadening possibility. But expansion came without the necessary scaffolding—no robust institutional networks, few galleries, limited avenues for critical engagement. Art schools multiplied, but what waited for graduates beyond them? Nothing.

Decades of imbalance—mass art education expanding without the infrastructure to support it—had led to stagnation. By the 1990s, the field had become increasingly insular, disconnected from both the realities of artistic production and the global circuits of contemporary art. Institutionally, it was rigid; intellectually, it lacked engagement with broader discourse; commercially, it remained limited.

Then, in the late 1990s, a shift occurred. It wasn't a sudden break but the result of conjuncture, which is often undertheorized. Economic liberalization, imposed through IMF and World Bank structural adjustments, brought along new avenues of philanthropic funding that reached the arts. At the same time, state-run cultural institutions, weighed down by growing bureaucracy and corruption, were becoming less relevant—not unlike the state of institutions across other sectors in the country.

A new infrastructure was taking shape. Private galleries like Karim Francis (established in 1997) and Townhouse (1998) offered alternatives, while institutions like the Goethe Institute and Pro Helvetia provided space and resources. Downtown Cairo became a focal point, marking a clear rupture.

Even then, the shift was undeniable. Egypt was being pulled into global contemporary art networks, moving beyond the state's grip on institutions and education. New platforms fostered new aesthetic-qua-political sensibilities, often backed by international support. By the early 2000s, the transformation was in motion. External funding—most notably from the Ford Foundation—helped sustain this new terrain, but the deeper shift was structural: a once-insular field had been forced into a broader conversation, shaped as much by economics and politics as by art itself.

It was around that time, that I, myself, became acquainted and then intimately involved with the field, first as an artist; then later shapeshifting my practice as a designer, writer, curator, and educator; and now, as an art historian. Around me, a generation of artists was emerging, looking for space to create and grow—bringing their work with them, showing it, traveling with it, knowing that movement shaped both their practice and themselves. The rise of some of these artists, which included Wael Shawky, Anna Bohighuian, and Hassan Khan, among two dozen others, coincided with a growing global interest in art from the Arab and Islamic world, a focus heightened by the political crises of the early 2000s—September 11, the First Intifada, the US invasion of Iraq. But this renewed visibility came with its own set of challenges. The Western culturalist framing of Arab/Islamic art reinforced essentialist narratives, forcing them on emergent contemporary art practices rather than expanding the possibilities of artistic production and discourse.

The Twentieth Youth Salon presented one volcanic rupture of these tensions. The Ministry of Culture invited contemporary artists and curators—Shawky, Khan, and Bassam El Baroni among them—who seized the opportunity to reconceive the Salon as an exhibition rather than an indiscriminate amassment of works. The selection process became a battleground, the show itself a sort of manifesto, a statement on what art is. The jury faction led by Shawky, Khan, and El Baroni represented a counter camp, intellectually and artistically vis-à-vis the state, and they mounted a defense of Conceptual art, radically reducing the number of participating artists to just ninety—down from the usual two to three hundred. To the old guard, this was an offense, a betrayal of the Salon's original function.[2]

What emerged was not just a dispute over numbers as a signifier of artistic merit but a deeper contestation of artistic meaning itself. The Salon exposed the fault lines in Egypt's cultural and countercultural

2 Omnia El Shakry describes this moment as "the arbitration of aesthetic judgment"—a rupture in the criteria that had long dictated artistic legitimacy. See Omnia El Shakry, "Artistic Sovereignty in the Shadow of Post-Socialism: Egypt's Twentieth Annual Youth Salon," e-flux Journal 7 (June 2009).

infrastructure. Core issues discussed during the symposium accompanying the Salon focused on what could be deemed "Egyptian" art, in an effort to locate art's authenticity. What interests me is what I perceive as a discursive fracture. The heart of the debate concerned what constituted art that was manifest, displayed, or exhibited. We were dealing with a form of aesthetic—and, as such, political—arbitration. In my early experiences with and around art, it often struck me that there was something else, something difficult to pin down, emergent, and potent, where the slip between reality and fiction was still malleable. I associated this quality with the counter-state institutional setting, or what I term countercultural infrastructure. The meaning, genealogy, function, and value of artworks—and how art works for me—always existed outside and beyond the state and its aesthetic arbitration.

Half a year after the Salon—which I hadn't attended—I returned to Cairo unsettled, fresh out of an MFA in Sweden, and in the midst of negotiating a divorce. Many of the same questions that had dominated the Salon were still preoccupying me; I was constantly thinking about how to do things with art. I had my eye on the directorship of the Contemporary Image Collective, an art space founded in 2004, but the position didn't work out. Instead, I joined Townhouse as a curator at a time when the space had already been around for a decade.

Townhouse wasn't new to me. As an undergraduate in the early 2000s, I had moved through its ecosystem in different roles—translator, archivist, graphic designer, audience member, writer, artist liaison, and, when needed, just an extra pair of hands. At some point, it dropped "Gallery" from its name, a small but telling shift. Townhouse was organic, chaotic, familial, welcoming—and always precarious. It was the heart of a fragile countercultural infrastructure that, eventually and perhaps inevitably, collapsed. The physical structure gave way in 2016; the institution itself shut down in 2019; William Wells, the gallery's founding director, was arbitrarily deported.

The fall season of 2009 was buzzing. Nikki Columbus, then resident curator at Townhouse, had been in extended conversation with the late artist Amal Kenawy, who was stepping beyond her usual mediums—painting, works on paper, installation, and performance within gallery walls—toward something more public. Kenawy herself was going through a transformational moment in her personal life, then recently divorced from the artist Shady El Noshokaty. Her work, which was often fragile yet violent, poetic, ethereal, was becoming more pointed, surreal, bolder.

1. Insurgent Forms (ca. 2009)
Silence of the Sheep (2009)

Amal decided to stage *Silence of the Sheep* as part of the exhibition's opening. She originally imagined it as the first in a series, however it ended up being a singular event. The original plan, as I recall it, was for her to hire her art students—she taught at the Faculty of Art Education—to follow her, crawling, as she shepherded them across a busy downtown intersection in the vicinity of several galleries. Not so much a critique of art education—though it could have been—but an act of civic disobedience disguised as "art." Amal was frustrated with the limits of what art did within the gallery space and was hoping that it would contribute to galvanize the public sentiment to do something. Her frustration was relatable.

The day of the performance, which took place in December, unraveled in chaos. That morning, I received a slew of distressed calls from the gallery informing me that the students had backed out. Should the performance be canceled? Unlikely. By midday, I learned that Kenawy had struck a last-minute arrangement with a group of day laborers to step in as performers. My immediate reaction was horror. A group of paid day laborers made to crawl through the streets of Cairo: The optics would be disastrous. But Amal insisted.

To remediate the situation, I volunteered myself to join. Partly out of unease, a sense of curatorial responsibility, and, I admit, partly out of thrill—when else would I get to experience something as crazy as crawling the streets of Cairo? Kenawy's brother volunteered to join. Two young girls from the neighborhood got excited and joined too. The three of us—three small women—were at the forefront of the herd, crawling on all fours, following Kenawy, who walked ahead of us. Noteworthy to mention was that we were all dressed in pajamas and wearing gloves.

By afternoon, the performance brought downtown traffic to a halt. The plan had been to enact a *détournement*: move through the streets without engaging, turn a corner, disperse. That was not what happened. The men lining the mechanic shops on Champollion Street—working-class men—began shouting profanities at us. There was so much anger. What was this? A humiliation of their dignity? It was a clusterfuck lost in translation, disrespect across lines of class, gender. The performance and its organizers were met with suspicion—we were a foreign provocation. The crowd grew volatile, and a fight broke out. I felt the work unraveling, its course lost. While I was in it, I hated it, but that's beside the point. The work then and after was doing something, and so I stuck with it.

In hindsight, there is a precise moment I want to bring back into focus: Kenawy, trying to explain to a mob of angry men, shouting above the rage chorus: "This is art!"

She likened it to the *aragoz*, the street-puppet show—familiar, local. But was it? The fight kept escalating, the crowd pressed in, a small international art world witnessing the event. The police became involved; it became a saga. For weeks afterward, what happened dominated discussions in Cairo's art-world circles.

The Cairo Complaints Choir (2010)

The following May I curated *Invisible Publics*—my first group show at Townhouse. For me, at the time and with shoestring resources, the scope was ambitious, but the premise was simple: What latent power might amass if an art audience thought of itself politically?

There were undertones of this in the works I selected, including ones by Sharon Hayes and Dora García. But one piece stood out: *The Complaints Choir*, a project by Finnish artists Tellervo Kalleinen and Oliver Kochta-Kalleinen. The idea was direct and open-ended. A workshop where community members—not professional singers—would be invited to come together to compose and perform a song of grievances. The results had been staged in Helsinki, Amsterdam, Berlin—each iteration an unfiltered expression of its own place and time. The lyrics were often funny, absurd annoyances of everyday life: Why is the vacuum cleaner cord too short? Why is the "meter pizza" only a half meter long? The outcome was straightforward; it was the perfect work to attune an audience to an aspect of the exhibition's premise—the collective vocalization of dissent and the power of coming together.

I was excited. The only problem—I didn't have the budget to bring the artists to Cairo. So, we improvised. The artists shared the work's framework, and I enlisted local musicians to help realize it here. An open call went out in April. The response was overwhelming. The interest exceeded anything we had imagined. Local newspapers picked up on it even before the performance had even taken place.

On opening night, Townhouse was overflowing. From the First Floor gallery—an apartment in a century-old building—where we were making final adjustments, William called me to the balcony. Below, the alley was packed, people spilling into the street. Inside, the Factory Space—a 650-square-meter former paper factory—was at capacity, standing-room only. Cameras, journalists, national news crews—an unprecedented level of attention.

The choir performed four songs. Each one landed like a spark in a pile of hay. The lyrics—sharper, sassier, more biting and raging than the typical choirs—took aim at the extension of emergency law, the exportation of gas to Israel, the failed garbage collection system "Europe 2000," the government's propaganda machine. "The workers aren't heard / Even the factory has been sold / The wheat is American / Our gas is being exported." The audience roared. The choir was unapologetically loud, cacophonous, and political.

By the time coverage of the performance spread, its framing had vanished. It was no longer just an artwork—or even an artwork at all. It had become something else entirely: a youth-led protest, a creative act of dissent slipping past the government's draconian grip on free expression. Maybe because it was wrapped in satire and avoided direct confrontation, it carried the weight of political humor, like newspaper caricatures. In every interview, I denied—sincerely and unequivocally—that the choir was "political." It was art.

That slippage, that departure from its original context, has lingered with me. Over the years, the project gave way to The Choir Project, led by Salam Yousry. By the time of the January 25 Revolution, it had taken on a life of its own.

It surprises me now how, for years afterward, I felt uneasy. Conflicted. As a curator, I had facilitated the work. I had received instructions from the Finnish artists, held the piece in my care. Had it been co-opted? Had I compromised the artists' authorship? Where was the boundary? When does an artwork end and something else, more akin to real life, begin? What happened with the choir in May 2010 was important, whether or not it was received or remembered as an artwork.

Both works, *The Silence of the Sheep* (2009) and *The Cairo Complaints Choir* (2010), were, in my view, subtly radical—one might even say political actions in disguise. Like Amal Kenawy, I could argue that the work was art, but, in reality, our exasperation with the public was irrelevant. As we each experienced these works in an embodied way (I, literally, at one point crawling on all fours), they did something. The paid laborers in Kenawy's project or the volunteers who joined the choir probably couldn't have cared less what we called the thing they had helped realize. My point is simple:

these works, authored by artists, curated, exhibited, and now recalled (art historically speaking), have manifested. But whether they did or not, something about the latency of the experience—irrespective of whether it was received as art—mattered.

2. Constitutive Practice (ca. 2011)

My interest in confrontational practices and works seen as insurgent forms gradually shifted toward something else: a desire to create my own art space. The objective was to establish a space for a closer, more critical, and meditative exhibition and study of art in practice. Still, newly graduated and navigating twentieth-century art history and critical theory, I felt something was missing. Beyond the singular artwork, performance, gesture, or exhibition, I began imagining institutions. This led to the creation of my first institution, the Cairo International Resource Center for Art (CIRCA), which, in reality, was the institutional equivalent to an imaginary friend.

MASS Alexandria

In the summer 2010 I started working closely with Wael Shawky. Shortly after, I was wrapping up my divorce; Wael and I became involved, personally and professionally. He had a studio in Miami, Alexandria—not the American city but a working-class neighborhood in the north of Egypt, overlooking the Mediterranean. He wanted to transform it into an art school. Shawky's mission clicked. All I ever wanted to do was to start an art school and a museum. Townhouse (or William to be more precise) was instrumental in helping Wael secure a grant from Foundation for Arts Initiatives (FfAI) to start up the school. By October 2010, we were busy recruiting our first cohort for a four-month pilot program. I aimed for twelve students; Wael insisted we take on twenty-four.

Every Friday, I traveled from Cairo to Alexandria to lead daylong seminars on art history and contemporary practice and host crit sessions—adapting as we went. Guest lecturers joined whenever they passed through.

And then, in January 2011, the revolution happened.

We were not going to disrupt the pilot program and break up the group. We decided to keep going until the summer. It was bumpy and inconsistent, but that was expected. Wael boot-camped the students, hurling them toward their first exhibition, Düsseldorf Academy–style.

Teaching at MASS was a portal to my understanding of the extent of the art educational crisis in Egypt. Many students had no exposure to contemporary art, period. We marathoned through art history, code-switching through material, bridging gaps where key texts simply didn't exist in translation. At the end of some sessions, we cut up photocopied readings into critical theory paper craft décor. Expanding the classroom became an act of creation itself—exhilarating, overwhelming. It always felt like we were sprinting up a learning curve; I was never quite sure where we would land.

In truth, it was never just about art or education. We spent a lot of time in the basement studio, but, in other ways, the program was a conduit for our students to the outside world—through us they were accessing the "art world," the countercultural network. Many of the students I developed strong relationships with were young women from conservative, middle-class families. My politically clownish pedagogical approach to them was riveting.

I juggled my teaching at MASS with adjuncting at the American University in Cairo. I was a proud graduate of the Visual Arts program's first cohort, a moment when contemporary art in Cairo felt like it was sensationally peaking—Larry Gagosian, Hans Ulrich-Obrist, and others gracing the city. By the time I returned to AUC seven years later, the program had gone to shit. Students—again, mostly women—had a shockingly limited grasp of contemporary art. Their work was aesthetic, superficial, and detached from history, discourse, or anything happening beyond their immediate environment. Anything that "looked like" art was art.

It became clearer to me: This was not just a higher-education problem, but a systemic pedagogical failure. What was missing wasn't just better teaching but an entire ecosystem: museums, critics, curators, art spaces, galleries, patrons, educators. The countercultural infrastructure was insufficient.

Beirut (2012–15)

I was hosting a birthday party on my balcony one evening when I stood with artist Iman Issa. We were leaning on the ledge, overlooking the neighboring 1930s villa through aging mango trees. Iman just looked at me and asked: "Why not turn it into an art space?" For about ten years, the villa had been the home to the Middle East Studies Program (MESP) run by the Council for Christian Colleges and Universities (CCCU). The unrest had sent them elsewhere, ironically to Jerusalem, where it was safer. The house belonged to distant relatives—not close enough for a discount on rent.

Jens Maier-Rothe, whom I had become close friends with in Malmö during my MFA, had just secured a short-term grant from the Institut für Auslandsbeziehungen (IfA) in Germany. In an entrepreneurial moment, Jens and I decided to establish Beirut. The world had become so intently fixated on Cairo that it felt natural to deflect that. There were at least three different stories as to why we called it Beirut. We announced it on May 1, 2012, before securing our first grant from FfAI. Support trickled in from the Goethe-Institut, the British Council, the Ford Foundation. Soon we were on the grid.

At the same time, I joined the team of dOCUMENTA(13)—somewhat reluctantly at first, but then I yielded to Carolyn Christov-Bakargiev's authoritative charm and was anointed as one of her "agents." On a car ride from Alexandria to Cairo, we drafted an agreement: We would host The Cairo Seminar in Alexandria, a CIRCA-dOCUMENTA(13) project. We haggled over the topic—not hope, as she kept suggesting, but sleep, I insisted.

In the midst of it all, I made the difficult decision to terminate a pregnancy. Days later, we announced Beirut, all while I was moving between Cairo, Alexandria, and Kassel, Germany. My experience of dOCUMENTA(13) was magically real—until it wasn't. Until the institutional pressures, the fractures, the impossibility of coherence took hold, and I found myself coming apart, my neurons fully diverged. The seminar on sleep made more and more sense: revolution had shattered sleep patterns; new waves of mental illness were surfacing all across my community. Alexei Penzin delivered his keynote on "sleeping politically." It was no longer theoretical.

Despite the divergence, all the work we were doing around that time felt urgent. Beirut became a space to host artists, stage high-caliber projects, and collaborate with leading international institutions. We registered Beirut as an LLC; a fictitious entity, it was an artwork contracted by Goldin+Senneby. A little-known fact: Egyptian art spaces often register offshore, usually in Sweden, sidestepping the draconian bureaucracy of the Ministry of Social Solidarity. It was a loophole that allowed us to receive foreign funding. Beirut was founded on the idea of institution-building as a curatorial act. Party on the scaffolding.

By 2013, the revolutionary energy had begun to curdle. The Muslim Brotherhood's election the year prior ushered in new tensions. We were exhausted, anxious. Funding became precarious. Then came the Rabaa Massacre: In August, the military killed nearly a thousand people protesting the ousting of the Muslim Brotherhood president Mohamed Morsi. The silence of progressives—the very community Beirut sought to exist within—was deafening. We had an exhibition to open in September, salaries to pay, a future to plan for. What was art's role after a massacre?

We were holding out hope for multiyear support from Arts Collaboratory—a Dutch philanthropic initiative geared toward supporting transcultural work in the global south. At one point, I was crouched under my grandma's heavy Art Deco dining table, quietly editing our proposal. We didn't get it.

I kept being haunted by the question: What is art's role after a massacre? Doing anything felt wrong, and so I was institutionalized again. My recollections of that fall are vague. My questions turned philosophical—on art, fascism, resistance, bodies, life, and death. To be playful felt dissonant.

This feels like a page out of a diary of a bad year.

The Imaginary School Program (2014–15)

We've reached a moment of crisis.

The Imaginary School Program (tISP) emerged from the work we had been doing at Beirut since the fall of 2013. With myself out of commission, the exhibition *Drawing with the Other Hand Is Imagining* was cared for by Antonia Alampi, who had joined us as curator in late 2012, not long after we had started programming. *Drawing*, the exhibition, reintroduced play, hope, and imagination—not as indulgences, but as prerequisites for artistic and curatorial thinking. It was poetic, and it became a prelude to the school.

One work that I recall is by Luis Camnitzer, who provided us with an instruction for children: "Pyramids have been outlawed. What alternative do you propose?" Since the 1960s, Luis's work was political in ways that were quite different from the politics/aesthetics of Conceptual art in New York. Luis affirmed that art was a means of possessing the world through intuition and that there was something radical about that, in a non-fussy way.

Artist Ashok Sukumaran from CAMP was also visiting that fall. Exuding his usual wisdom, he shifted the scale of my expectations of what art could do and how. In cities like Mumbai or Cairo, could art find new openings, persist like wild weeds, interconnect neural networks across the city? If art did not answer to the lofty goals of impacting broader societal change, what was it doing? Where did this leave us within the ecology of philanthropic infrastructure? Did we owe something to the countercultural infrastructure? I don't think I've ever phrased it as such, but the overwhelming feeling at the time was guilt.

The ISP launched in fall 2014 as an eight-month, practice-based theory program, an "institutional clinic." We were dissecting our practice, looking inward, dismantling Beirut. Could we turn institutional inertia into an object of study?

It had been a year since the coup. It was a bit like Sergei Tretiakov shouting at us, "Writers to the kolkhoz!" Sometimes writing (art) needed to be sublimated into another type of operation. For Tretiakov, this meant calling meetings, collecting funds, inspecting rooms—being an "operating writer," not just an "informing writer." Literacy, pedagogy—these felt like the heart of revolution.

Early romance is always real.

Looking back, hindsight is a privilege—but also a form of forgetting, thankfully. The program gathered an extraordinary group of thinkers, mostly from Cairo, deeply engaged in anthropology, Marxist studies, histories of education, and artist-led seminars. The emphasis was on the field: radical transparency in confronting institutions, exposing not just their (our) functions but their (our) fictions, their (our) urgencies, their (our) challenges, and their (our) failures.

Earlier this year, I worked with Engy Mohsen, who was writing on para-educational art institutes. While I served as a diligent reader, often it felt like a retroactive reality check.

Through the ISP we learned a lot about cooperative education, funding structures, the war on the future of the left, art, and social responsibility. But also, OMG, the "crisis emails," the flaring emotions, the curricular changes we were forced to implement. The first crisis email arrived in November, not long after the school had started. Its first words were, "We've reached a moment of crisis."

While we were designing the program—conscious of rejecting one-way learning, careful about integrating feedback, and committed to implementing our ideas of progressive pedagogy—participants wanted a clearer mission, more concrete goals. There were varying levels of commitment, dissatisfaction, and ennui. At times dysfunctional, it was always convivial; we built strong bonds. It felt like a rare point of stability within an otherwise precarious countercultural infrastructure.

Everyone agreed that in the end there was little left that was imaginary about the school—if anything it was "too real." Moments of clarity emerged: thought problems on funding, gentrification, and bilingual labor and their political, theoretical, economic contexts. At a certain scale, structure becomes essential—too much is suffocating, too little leads to tyranny. Jo Freeman's "The Tyranny of Structurelessness" was a case in point: informal structures do not eliminate power but render it invisible, unaccountable. We were learning how to organize, but also about leadership, accountability, decision-making, management. In practice, we grappled with this question: What is the relationship between structure and revolution?

Art can hold space for political imagination even as it soars, but it needs the scaffolding of organized movements. A few weeks ago, Engy sent me the first line highlighted in the preface of Hanan Toukan's *Politics of Art*: "The revolution, when it

3 Hanan Toukan, *The Politics of Art: Dissent and Cultural Diplomacy in Lebanon, Palestine, and Jordan* (Stanford University Press, 2009), i.

comes, is not going to be funded by the Ford Foundation."[3] Touché.

A cat meme: I will have spent my entire life trying to understand the function of remembering.

As the ISP concluded in 2015, I was knee-deep in bureaucracy—unraveling Beirut while carefully bringing the program to its end. The gap between imagining an imaginary school and actually building one was vast. A discussion, later transcribed in *Sunday Begins On Saturday: Notes from the Imaginary School Program*, captured this tension.

Some had previously attended MASS Alexandria and compared experiences: "It was experimental. All the rules changed. So if we now figure out a system ... I want to document everything because it was a disaster, and maybe someone can learn from it."

Someone else responded: "It's studied. You study what went wrong, hypothesize how to avoid it. Risk management, basically. So you come up with rules, not head in the clouds."

The reluctant consensus: there had to be a starting point, and this was it. The first cohort would inevitably test these programs and curricula. The critiques lingered in good faith. The community remains tightly knit, and these questions—about structure, experimentation, failure—continue to inform practices beyond ISP. This was unsurprising.

We were learning—something latent was at work, but it had yet to fully manifest.

3. Residual Practice (ca. 2014)

When *Egypt Independent*, a vital English-language newspaper, shut down in the spring of 2013, we lost more than a publication—we lost yet another outlet. From its collapse, Mada Masr emerged, founded on the eve of the coup on June 30, 2013. As the counter-revolution took shape, the urgency of our work at Beirut shifted. My theory-infused fixation on the question "what is an institution?"—through which I had staked a claim for the role of art institutions in times of crisis—gave way to our situated reality. In no uncertain terms, the pain felt most was that we were losing a revolution. We were well past the point of insurgent forms of practice. To make an institution was to aspire to form a constituency, a medium of political legitimation, a way of being, of saying: we are here.

By 2014–15, there was a shift to what I describe as residual practices—the chimeric traces of situations intended as art. A few months after Mada's founding, artist Adelita Husni-Bey planned a workshop with their team of journalists, editors, and copy editors. *On Difficult Terms* (2013) is a record of a dialogue session Adelita had planned, in which she illustrated a mind map of how language had transformed in recent years. The participants were grappling with the shifting meanings of words like revolution, coup, disillusion—words that had fractured, the memory of massacre still fresh. A mural—part mind map, part document—became a visual record of this linguistic rupture, moving with Mada's offices over the following decade.

Adelita was also working on *White Paper: The Land* (2014), a project that spanned Egypt, the Netherlands, and Spain and examined the relationship between land, language, legislation, and power. In Egypt, her point of departure was Cairo 2050, the state-backed, privately funded development plan that sought to redraw the city with little regard for mass displacement—dispossessing long-term residents of their land. Working in close collaboration with local filmmakers and activists, she gathered residents from Gezirat al-Qursaya and Ramlet Boulaq, communities that had long resisted state-driven, private investor–backed gentrification and violent eviction attempts. In 2012, Amr al-Bunni, a resident of Ramlet Boulaq, was shot and killed by a police officer following a dispute over unpaid wages. His death ignited widespread protests, exposing the volatility of the community's deep-seated struggle against government-sponsored dispossession and triggering violent clashes between residents and authorities.

Adelita turned to these stories, bringing affected residents into discussion. The people of al-Qursaya gathered around a model of their island—the same kind developers use to sell investors a vision of the future that excludes them. But this time, they had control. They debated, rearranged, tore pieces apart, rebuilt them. The model became a site of negotiation, a moment of agency in a landscape where they are so often denied one. The workshop wrestled with the language of land rights, ownership, and the legal frameworks that determine who gets to stay and who is erased.

Around that same time, Jasmina Metwaly and Philip Rizk were working closely with a group of nine workers from a demolished starch and glucose factory. *Out On the Streets* (2015) wasn't exactly a film about factory workers; rather, they were engaging the workers in an extended acting experiment. They filmed meetups in which they invited the workers to improvise and re-enact scenes they had experienced. The psychodramatic acts restaged state violence and police brutality, sometimes reversing power dynamics, other times unsettlingly having workers enact brutality on each other.

In some scenes, they pulled invisible ropes, became the machines their fathers once operated, and drew gestures toward an understanding that words failed to capture—somewhere between fiction, theater, and documentary—interwoven with mobile-phone footage recorded by the workers, initially as proof for evidence in court.

Jasmina and Philip's practice grew out of Mosireen, the activist media collective that had risen to prominence by documenting the revolution with urgency, amassing a critical visual archive of resistance. But they began to question their work: Was documentary, as a standalone form, still tenable? They moved away from short-form reportage and established an alternative space.

Out On the Streets draws a direct line back to labor strikes that helped set the stage for 2011. In February of that year, workers at the Starch and Glucose Company occupied their factory in protest against its closure. The factory had been privatized years earlier, and, under the pretext of renovation, was being systematically dismantled. Their struggle was one of many—an erasure of labor histories unfolding in real time. But the film, they insist, is not about this singular factory; it gestures toward something larger. It suggests that this is not just a labor struggle, but part of a broader, transnational process of privatization and dispossession, echoing the crises of Cairo 2050 and the relentless stripping of land from its residents.

When I think of the work Adelita did with journalists and communities, and the work Philip and Jasmina did with workers, I think of these moments as microcosms of something larger. Certainly, over time, as the artworks became manifest institutionally, one could say they preserved or indexed something of history for the future. But more importantly, for me, is how, for those who experienced it in their time, there is a chimeric transfer—something like DNA, residues. Whether the communities that partook in shaping the work considered them to be artworks—whether that designation mattered at all—remains an open question.

The intellectual genealogy of the works I discuss evokes the spirits of Bertolt Brecht and Paulo Freire—the modality of revolution beyond the insurgent form. Revolution is not a singular moment of rupture; it is the slow, arduous work of learning and continual restructuring. Our perception is unsettled—we become the audience, watching the mechanics of power at play until we begin to recognize ourselves within it, more and more, the feeling growing sharper, more lucid. Exercises in naming the world, in coming together. The cameras have left, the world has moved on, the revolution swallowed back into the machinery.

This mode of practice—what might be called residual practice—emerged not out of an aesthetic turn but out of necessity. After the coup, it felt like the only viable form of practice: one that did not monumentalize, did not presume endurance in the form of an object, but rather embedded itself in processes already unfolding, in the cracks and interstices of social and political life.

Spring 2025

Crisis, like revolution, is not necessarily momentous; it is not an event in itself. While this essay is, in essence, my own reckoning with past practice, the political, institutional, and artistic histories I engage with remain unstable and historically malleable. What is certain, as I look around now, is that what constitutes cultural infrastructure has fundamentally changed. The countercultural infrastructure that had a clear presence for nearly two decades—since the late 1990s—is now difficult to locate with the same clarity. There are only residues of it.

Hindsight carries the danger of essentializing, of neatly packaging assessments that we then teleologically unbox. My aim is not to "theorize" the past but to make sense of what is becoming. In a way, this essay itself is latent in what it is trying to express. The process I have undertaken—heuristic in nature—is an attempt to understand what remains from that time and how it carries forward after the collapse and retreat of a particular kind of infrastructural scaffolding. This is not to say that all civic and cultural practices have disappeared, but that they have been severely weakened, existing in a state of constant threat.

I consider contemporary art through this lens of latency—through the time of its making. To those standing by on Champollion Street, to the crowds and TV viewers witnessing the *Complaints Choir*, to the students (many of whom abandon art due to the absence of sustaining infrastructure), to the journalists doing their jobs, to the factory workers who have lost theirs, to the dispossessed residents, the work surely matters. But did it matter to them whether it was art?

Then, as with much of social and relational practice, I would argue that it might not—and that it doesn't need to. But the byproduct of this ambivalence is another problem. Art as latency means that it is not always immediately recognized as art. Its first life unfolds within lived necessity—embedded in resistance, labor struggles, and political urgency. It only takes on the formal designation of art in its second life, when it is lifted into an exhibition, a publication, or a discourse—when it is seen, named, and made legible within institutions. At the time, that designation did not matter to those at its center. Did the residents of al-Qursaya, fighting for their homes, concern themselves with whether their struggle took the form of contemporary art? This question, however, is not my end point.

I am not denying the arthood of these works, but their latency requires a more rigorous analysis. What are their consequences? There are no clear social or semiotic markers that distinguish them as contemporary art in their first moment of existence. I wonder: if the countercultural infrastructure had been robust, if we had sustainable institutions, archives, art critical practices, publications that lasted—a more visible stake, a stronger voice in public media—how would that have inevitably changed the nature of contemporary art's arbitration? I say this not to diminish the legitimacy of these works but to highlight art's bifurcated life: suspended between lived necessity and institutional recognition, between political urgency and aesthetic arbitration. This is not a lamentation of its marginality.

And yet, legitimation still seems to matter. The recession of Egypt's countercultural infrastructure after 2014 has ushered in neoliberal and neo-nationalist forces peddling yet another contested meaning of art—fixated on pyramids, glossed in French, gilded with "heritage," catering to luxury tourism and art-washing the state. The emergence of these new art scenes—marked by branding, investment, and profit—reflects a familiar global symptom: gentrification. These spaces physically and intellectually sanitize, commodify, and cater to new audiences. In this context, art has been stripped of the modalities I have outlined and replaced by a predictable counterfeit.

The latency of contemporary art is both its potential and its vulnerability. The loss of a countercultural infrastructure is not just the loss of a political space—it is also the loss of the mechanisms that once arbitrated aesthetic judgment. This presents a political problem. What is considered art—and I do not mean *good* art, but art in any form—is increasingly determined by forces beyond those that once shaped it. What remains to be seen is whether art's latent potential will find a way to reassert itself—not merely as a matter of institutional legitimation, but as something that continues to stake its ground, to resist the systems responsible for the erasure of an aesthetic and political sensibility.

Speech Beyond the Freedom of Speech[1]

Yazan Khalili

> America is actually a deeply totalitarian country, it's just entirely invisible as long as you stay inside the freedom of speech zones. The students have exited the free speech zone and now all pretense of this being a democracy is dropped. –@benfranklin2018 on X[2]

As I write this, the genocidal war on Palestine and the Palestinians in Gaza is putting the world in a confrontation with itself, making the whole political structure that we have been living under more vicious and clear, opening up the accumulated layers of normalized violence and political numbness, showing us, the political beings, our limits and lack of political agency as we are unable to interfere to stop the genocide that is happening in front of our eyes, on our bodies, and to our future.

Palestine, as a struggle, is the channel through which the new world is being born. What will emerge is the future morality of the world, either the dominance of a logic of power and destruction or a world where justice can still prevail. And between this and that, the structures of the world are being reconfigured.

This expanded genocide brings in questions about freedom of speech and the free agency of artists. In many western democracies, freedom of speech has been claimed as the main pillar, a claim preached to the world as the moral and ethical contract of modern societies. This claim is now being challenged by those speaking about freedom and justice for Palestine.

Here I will discuss how Palestine has been placed outside the realm of freedom of speech, and how we need to expand our understanding of how the structures of freedom of speech paradoxically exclude certain kinds of speech.

1 This text is an updated version of Yazan Khalili, "Freedom of Speech, Freedom of Noise," *e-flux journal* 97 (February 2019).

2 @benFranklin2018, X, April 24, 2024, https://x.com/benFranklin2018/status/1783272122720125048

I have dozens of stories about the way censorship functions within the public sphere. We are used to thinking of censorship as something limited to totalitarian dictatorships, where censorship is a mechanism of dominance. But here I will try to show that freedom of speech is itself a political structure of exclusion, a paradox that confronts politically engaged artists who speak to power, about power, and against its hegemony.

* * *

One lesson my father kept repeating to me: If someone publicly curses the president/leader/king/sovereign in front of you, don't say a word in response. "It's a trap," he'd say. "They're trying to trick you into confessing that you're with the opposition."

My father confessed that he'd learned this the hard way. In the early 1960s, he did his undergraduate studies in Syria at a time of great political turbulence. One day he took a taxi and the talkative driver began cursing the regime. My father, feeling a sense of camaraderie and relief, happily echoed the driver's opinions. Minutes later, the driver pulled into a parking lot that belonged to the secret service. My father spent the next few months in prison.

For him, speaking in a time of repression holds the potential of complicity with the regime. He always told me that only people who are backed by the regime can curse it. For him, the silent ones are those who are truly against it, and we should look for other forms of expression that can't be detected.

* * *

In "Democratis," the third part of Ziad Rahbani's famous radio show bearing the strange title *Tabi'a La Shi Tabi'a Shi* (Belonging to Something Belonging to Something Else), he tells the story of a playwright who writes a play about a playwright writing a play about censorship in his society. The playwright-within-the play takes his play to the censorship office for approval, and the play gets rejected. Now, the "real" playwright takes his play to the "real" censorship office for approval, and when it gets rejected, he asks, "But why?" The censor answers: "Look, there is nothing wrong with the play itself, except that you are lying about censorship. You see, we don't reject plays about censorship." Furious, the playwright responds: "But by rejecting it, you are proving that I'm right!" The censor: "This isn't true. We are only censoring it because you are lying and we can't let such lies spread around." This goes on and on, and the sound fades out and is replaced by funky jazz music.

Slavoj Žižek, in his lecture "The Need to Censor Our Dreams," talks about social codes and regulations in totalitarian regimes.[3] He explains that censorship always hides itself; it erases its traces because it has to be invisible, only showing a facade of freedom of speech. There are prohibitions that don't simply prohibit things, but which themselves are prohibited. One has to accept them, and also accept that they do not exist as prohibitions.

Before speech can be determined to be free or not, it first must be recognized as speech. For speech to be recognized as such, it has to be uttered by political beings.

In a well-known passage, Aristotle says that "humans are political animals" because they possess the power of speech,

3 Slavoj Žižek, "The Need to Censor Our Dreams," a lecture delivered at Sheikh Zayed Theatre, London School of Economics, London, on November 11, 2014.

which subjects them to common issues of justice and injustice. Animals, by contrast, can only express pleasure or pain. But how do we tell whether the person speaking is discussing matters of justice rather than just expressing their private pain?

In *The Politics of Aesthetics*, Jacques Rancière argues that there a crucial question precedes the problem of recognition. It is a properly political question: Who has the power to decide what counts as a voice, and what is mere noise? Rancière argues that politics is primarily the configuration of a space as political: "Politics first is the conflict about the very existence of that sphere of experience, the reality of those common objects and the capacity of those subjects."[4]

Plato argued that artisans, who were low on the social scale in his era, had no time for politics because they were too busy with their work. Obviously, this "lack of time" was not an empirical matter, but rather a naturalization of artisans' subordinate status. For Rancière, politics begins when those who have "no time" make themselves heard, when they prove that they can indeed utter proper speech instead of merely voicing pleasure or pain.

Hannah Arendt, for her part, wrote about the "rightless." She claimed that rather than being unequal before the law, for the rightless no law exists at all. It is not that they are oppressed, but rather that nobody wants to oppress them. They fall outside the regime of justice, and, thus, outside the freedom of speech. They are guilty of not even being worthy of oppression.[5]

An artist whose work was censored by the Israeli authorities once gleefully whispered to me: "Finally, they have taken my work seriously!" This is essential for understanding how censorship works. The dilemma of the speechless is that, in order to have their speech recognized as speech, they have to accept the possibility of it being muted. Being censored becomes a sign that your utterances are recognized as speech, and are therefore heard as political. The speechless kneel before the power structure, accepting its oppression in order to have their speech recognized as speech and then censored.

The power structure nowadays knows that censoring an artwork doesn't stop it from spreading, but rather makes it better known to the public with the attention that the act of censorship produces. What censorship does is take away the multilayered connections between its aesthetics and its political agenda and leaves it only to be read through the lens of censorship. Censorship tries to speak louder than the artwork, using the artwork as the medium for its own speech and hegemony.

Censorship isn't only about prohibition. It also works to divert and reshape meaning. It operates not only by preventing, but also by permitting, by opening the political structure to works that are fighting against it, in an attempt to corrupt the work by diluting and undermining its political agenda. This was the problem faced by the Russian art collective Chto Delat when they decided to withdraw from Manifesta 10 in 2014, which was being hosted in Saint Petersburg. In a statement, they said: "Manifesta has shown that it can respond with little more than bureaucratic injunctions to respect law and order in a situation where any and all law has gone to the wind. For that reason, any participation in the Manifesta

4 Jacques Rancière, *The Politics of Aesthetics*, trans. Gabriel Rockhill (Bloomsbury, 2013).

5 Summarized in Jacques Rancière, "Who Is the Subject of the Rights of Man?" *South Atlantic Quarterly* 103, no. 2–3 (Spring–Summer 2004).

10 exhibition loses its initial meaning."[6] Chto Delat's withdrawal sheds light on how freedom of speech, as a structure, creates situations in which participation corrupts speech by making it complicit with power, even if the work itself aims to expose the limits of speech.[7]

In 2014, artist Coco Fusco wrote about the detention of Cuban artist Tania Bruguera in her native country.[8] Fusco speculated that Bruguera's detention was linked to the renewal of diplomatic relations between Cuba and the United States. Fusco mentioned that the director of the National Council of the Fine Arts in Cuba, Rubén Del Valle, insisted that it was the state's prerogative to oversee all cultural activity and to keep politics out of Cuban art. Interestingly, Del Valle implies here that in a situation where the state monopolizes politics and political acts, art can be free of politics. Moreover, any artwork that tries to incorporate politics loses its status as art and instead becomes a political act seeking to deprive the state of its rightful role.

During this ongoing genocide, neither Coco Fusco nor Tania Bruguera nor Chto Delat has said anything about Palestine. In some cases, they even refused when asked to take a position. One has to think where Palestine is positioned within the liberal struggles for political and social freedoms and how the political movements against censorship have a blind spot when the struggle is against the models of freedom of speech provided by western democracies.

* * *

In the 2018 March of Return, when thousands of Palestinians in Gaza marched to the Israeli siege walls around the Gaza ghetto, demanding that the siege end and that they could return to the homes and towns that they were made to evacuate in 1948, the Israeli forces shot the demonstrators en masse, killing many and injuring many in their knees. The images of these demonstrations remind me of zombie movies, mainly the Hollywood ones, like Brad Pitt's film *World War Z* (2013), where the humans' last stand was Jerusalem. There they stood on the walls of the old city, killing the zombies en masse. One can't but think how the zombies are depicted by the living; speechless bodies coming in masses, without a context or a political demand, coming from death and only to be sent back to it, voiceless except for the sounds of their hunger and pain, and, eventually, like in all Hollywood movies, they disappear. As an audience we are trained to look at these masses from the position of the living, where the act of killing is made to protect the world from the savageness of the others.

We, the audience, are never able to engage with what the zombies want. Even though their speech is heard, it is not censored. Rather, it's meaningless. Arendt suggests that nonpolitical beings can thus practice absolute freedom of speech because their utterances aren't recognized as speech in the first place—they're just noise, in the eyes of the ruling political structure. Therefore, discussions about whether the speech of nonpolitical beings is "free" are

6 Mostafa Heddaya, "Collective Withdraws from Manifesta, Theater Director Denise Signature of Support for Putin," Hyperallergic, March 17, 2014, https://hyperallergic.com/115016/collective-withdraws-from-manifesta-theater-director-denies-signature-of-support-for-putin/.

7 Dave Beech, "To Boycott or Not to Boycott?," *Art Monthly* 380 (October 2014).

8 Coco Fusco, "The State of Detention: Performance, Politics, and the Cuban Public," *e-flux journal* 60 (January 3, 2015), https://www.e-flux.com/journal/60/61067/the-state-of-detention-performance-politics-and-the-cuban-public/.

meaningless. Their expressions of pain or pleasure can't be suppressed, because freedom-of-speech ideology doesn't regard the silencing of nonpolitical beings as suppression. This ideology rests on a universal distinction between what is speech and what isn't—what is human and civilized, and what isn't. For Islam al-Khatib, becoming monsters is an inevitable condition of embracing a more concrete and unapologetic narrative on freedom, a way of resisting the self-censorship and constrained visions of freedom that fulfills the Western frameworks that limit authentic expressions of resistance and refusal.[9]

Freedom of speech is the structure that either allows or censors speech—but this comes after that same structure recognizes what is speech and what isn't. Censorship, then, is a mechanism used by the freedom-of-speech apparatus to maintain its power to define what counts as speech, what is political, and what is civilized. In this sense, political struggle isn't only about overturning censorship, as this limits our struggles within the realms and contradictions of the existing power structures; we also need to bring our attention to where speech isn't recognized as such.

In 2019 the German Bundestag adopted the motion *Der BDS-Bewegung entschlossen entgegentreten—Antisemitismus bekämpfen* (Resisting the BDS Movement with Determination—Combating Antisemitism), a resolution that equated the Boycott, Divestment, and Sanctions (BDS) movement with antisemitism. When the German political parties worked on issuing this law against the BDS movement, using the International Holocaust Remembrance Alliance's problematic definition of antisemitism, the main obstacle was the constitutional protection of freedom of expression. Therefore the motion was only passed as non-binding, and the main power it has is the control of funding. The motion states that no public funding can be allowed to any institution or venue that invites, hosts, or allows any person or event that is involved in or supports BDS.

Funding becomes the power of the political structures outside the realm of law. It allows for strangling, censoring, and intimidating the cultural scene without a clear legal procedure. In other words, it is censorship without dismantling the structures of the freedom-of-speech apparatus. It is censorship outside the structures of freedom of speech. It eliminates Palestinian voices from the realm of political speech by connecting them to the terror of antisemitism. So, silencing it is not seen as censorship, but rather as protecting the civilized world from zombies.

Using funding as a tool of political suppression was tested in the peripheries before it was practiced in the centers of the freedom of speech. In Palestine itself, where the donor economy has become the main economy for cultural practices, creating cultural institutions became a tool to enable the dominance of this economy. Many international donors require Palestinian organizations receiving funds to accept "anti-terrorism" clauses, ensuring they do not have ties to "terrorist" organizations or work with individuals related to them. However, in practice, these donors often use the Israeli definition of terrorism, equating it with resistance and leading to a conflicted relation to conditional funding and the role of the donor economy in eliminating the culture of resistance from the cultural scene.

9 Islam al Khatib, "Becoming Monsters: What Happens When the Witness Becomes the Defendant?" March 13, 2024, https://www.versobooks.com/blogs/news/becoming-monsters-what-happens-when-the-witness-becomes-the-defendant.

* * *

Boris Groys has written that art activists do not want to merely criticize the art system or the general political and social conditions under which this system functions. Rather, they aim to change these conditions by means of art, in spaces outside of art.[10]

In his time, Walter Benjamin urged "advanced" artists to intervene, like revolutionary workers, in the means of artistic production, to change the "techniques" of traditional media, to transform the "apparatus" of bourgeois culture.[11] The engaged artists of today can also find in art the means to subvert the ruling power structure by interlacing a work's aesthetics, its political agenda, and its means of production.

But the engaged artist faces a double challenge: avoiding censorship and freedom of speech altogether. This is the paradox that today's politically engaged artists must deal with when exposing the power structure of freedom of speech.

* * *

The zombies might be the ones showing us the way, with their bodies that come out from the land, move together, demand a world where we are all recognized as zombies, and include us all in their collectivity. In the noise of their voices lies the political demands of the future.

10 Boris Groys, "On Art Activism," *e-flux journal* 56 (June 2014), http://www.e-flux.com/journal/on-art-activism/.

11 Walter Benjamin, "The Author as Producer," trans. John Heckman, *New Left Review* 1, no. 62 (July–August 1970), 83-96.

Occupational Hazards of Modern Art and Museums

Rasha Salti and Khaled Hourani

The Anecdote at the Origin

The group of visitors was being given a painstakingly thorough insider tour of the Van Abbemuseum that included the restoration ateliers, storage facilities, and the crate-making workshop. It was painstaking for Khaled Hourani, an artist and the director of the International Academy of Art Palestine in Ramallah, who knows how museums are structures that ultimately embody state sovereignty and self-determination, and who experienced the postponement of an ambitious promise by the Palestinian National Authority—but that's a whole other story. It's not that Hourani was disinterested, quite the contrary, but he is prone to allowing his mind to run astray and has a strong proclivity for finding inspiration from what seems to the rest of the world like a mundane convention or a basic principle for organizing civilian life.

As the tour guide listed countries across the globe, destinations to which works from the Van Abbemuseum collection had travelled, Hourani wondered whether there might ever be a time when Palestine would come up in such a list of places. The guide regaled visitors with incongruous anecdotes: a painting from the collection had once travelled to a museum in Greece in a military plane. At once mystified and bemused, Hourani tried to visualize the scene: the painting, crated with masterful craftsmanship, standing in the midst of the spartan interiors of an aircraft intended for the defense of a European democracy's national security.

For the remaining days of his visit, the image/anecdote stayed with him. Until the unthinkable crossed his mind: Could an acclaimed masterwork from the collection ever be allowed to cross the checkpoints that control access to the Occupied

Territories? To Ramallah? A genially absurd, comically surreal thought. Such thoughts are often the seed of Hourani's art practice.

In 2009, Khaled Hourani painted close-ups of a zebra horse, which he titled *Zebra*. That year, a Gazan was revealed to have painted live donkeys with black and white stripes and snuck them through the underground smuggling tunnels between Egypt and Gaza to showcase them as zebras in his zoo. When interviewed, he confessed that not only were real zebras too expensive, but also they would not fit in the tunnels. His zoo needed a new "sensation" to attract visitors and, considering Gaza was under siege, he had to come up with a novelty. Hourani's painting paid tribute to the man's creative genius, and interrogated, playfully, painting as an art form. In 2007, Kadima (Hebrew for "forward"), a "pragmatic" coalition of center-left and center-right politicians, was formed in Israel. Led by former foreign-affairs minister Tzipi Livni, the political party positioned itself as the more efficient bulwark against the rise of a radical right wing. The new party published its manifesto in Israeli newspapers. Hourani translated the text to Arabic and published it in one of the most widely read Palestinian newspapers ... only replacing every occurrence of Palestine and Palestinian with Israel and Israeli, and vice versa. It was an art project. The newspaper received many calls that day from enthusiastic readers with queries about how to contact the Palestinian "Forward" party.

The short and long of the story is that upon his return to Palestine he asked the IAAP students to select a painting from the Van Abbemuseum's permanent collection. They picked Picasso's *Buste de Femme* (1943). Hourani went back to the museum's directors and proposed that *Buste de Femme* be exhibited at the IAAP in Ramallah. Hourani recalls distinctly how the first discussions of the proposal were punctuated with guffawing and chuckles: Picasso in Ramallah! He could not tell whether his interlocutors from the esteemed museum would take him seriously. And yet, the signifying power of exhibiting a Picasso painting in Palestine was at once so captivating and explicit that, almost immediately, all those summoned to participate in making the project a reality were wholeheartedly enlisted.

The Making of ...

In the making of *Picasso in Palestine* the means are as interesting as the end. The means are, in fact, an end in themselves. The regime that governs the universe of museum practice and the administration of collections and loans is brought into an unimaginable engagement with the regime that governs the universe of military occupation. At the crux of collection loans is insurance. "The first insurance company we contacted studied the Oslo Peace Agreements and articulations of Palestinian sovereignty and concluded they could not be part of the project," Hourani said. "We were undeterred, and researched insurance companies that might be eccentric enough to partner with us." Eventually they found one: "The company, described by its director as 'adventurous,' insures tuna fish in Malta. The director and his deputy travelled to Ramallah to study the journey ... and came on board." Hourani paused, then exploded in laughter.

A legal team was assembled next. While existentially, poetically, and discursively, the question of the existence of Palestine and Palestinians is no longer a question, and neither is Palestinian political representation a question, Palestine is not—yet—an internationally recognized sovereign state. As such, it is neither a member of the World Trade Organization nor a signatory of the Global Agreement on Tariffs and Trade. Under the aegis of Israeli occupation, movement in and out of the West Bank and customs regulations are the dominion of the occupying state. Moreover, Palestine is not officially a place, a destination. After endless meetings in Eindhoven, Ramallah, and Haifa, it was agreed that regardless of the fact that the independent state of Palestine did not exist in the writ of international law, the International Academy of Art Palestine (IAAP) was, indisputably, an internationally recognized institution as well as a physical site. Effectively, it was the ultimate destination for *Buste de Femme*, and that was what mattered: the shippers had an address for their label.

"Discussions of the painting's itinerary produced a multitude of scenarios," explained Hourani. "One scenario proposed to bring it to Haifa and from there to Ramallah, but I did not want the painting to be spared the journey travelers to Ramallah are forced to navigate." So it landed by plane at Tel Aviv airport, travelled in a van to the Atarot checkpoint, and from there to the Qalandia checkpoint before entering Ramallah. "From Tel Aviv to Atarot, a private Israeli security company accompanied the van, and from Qalandia to Ramallah, Palestinian police. There was a three-kilometer section, a no-man's-land, where only civilians are allowed passage, Israeli private security cannot tread, and neither can Palestinian national armed security. The van was unguarded by armed security, instead protection was provided by some twenty international media cameras that accompanied the van and broadcast its passage on that road live." Hourani sighed. To resolve seemingly insurmountable obstacles, many such felicitous accidents had come up unexpectedly. "Often, things fell into place like magic, just when we thought we hit a wall and we might have to give up. A week before the painting was due to travel, I thought we would have to cancel the entire project ... and then, somehow, a resolution unraveled."

The amount of paperwork Hourani amassed (documents, permission slips, letters of support, evidence of this and that) and the process of translating, stamping, and certifying them all was nothing short of Kafkaesque. Adding to that, the volatility of the situation on the ground—whether a flare-up of violence in Gaza or an Israeli crackdown anywhere in the West Bank. "Needless to say, the Arab Spring, which made everyone in Palestine dream of a radically new political horizon, had its impact too." Hourani sighed again. This time, the tone of his voice betrayed the burdens he carried, the intense paradoxes he contended with. The euphoria at the prospect of the end of despotism in the Arab world and determining the fate of *Picasso in Palestine*, how could anyone predict any of the outcomes of the insurgencies in Tunisia, Egypt, Yemen, and Syria? And how would they translate in Palestine? "We considered the prospect of postponing the opening at several instances throughout the two years of working on the project. Timing was as significant as it was delicate. I realized, in discussions with the various counterparts, that *Picasso in Palestine* also brought regimes of time and their political economy into an uneasy confrontation: Europe's post-capitalist globalized time, Israel's military occupation time, and Palestine's contrived colonized time."

Two years in the making, *Picasso in Palestine* had to happen. Figuring out the most appropriate date or apt time was not unlike reading tea leaves. Finally, a date was set.

Picasso in Palestine

Over the decades of museum-collection loan practices, the regime of environmental conditions for the transfer of works has become stringent. Paintings are not only crated according to detailed and specific instructions, but the temperature and humidity levels must also be maintained within carefully controlled parameters. "Once it landed, the crated painting was transported in a van; it was essential that it not be opened until it reached its final destination," Hourani explained. "We had to extract a commitment from the numerous Israeli security instances that they would not do it." They promised to stick to their word if nothing 'suspicious' took place. "Anything could go wrong at any moment: if a child had thrown a stone at the van, if an Israeli settler had decided to pester a Palestinian, if any small, mundane incident had taken place—as they do all the time on the road from Tel Aviv to the Qalandia gate—the Israelis would have an excuse to stop the painting's journey and force open the crate. *Picasso in Palestine* was in many ways a series of orchestrated small miracles."

Hourani's tone changes radically when he recalls the moment of the crate's arrival to the IAAP space that had been specially constructed to house the painting. There, too, controlled environmental conditions had been secured. The crate's opening was an event attended by the various experts mandated to oversee the process, with every step documented. From that moment onward, and for the span of the month that followed *Buste de Femme*'s visit to Ramallah, *Picasso in Palestine* became a celebratory event. The opening celebration was an unprecedented success. Hourani, jubilant, is still surprised at the number of people who turned up. "I was expecting to see the usual suspects, Ramallah's art crowd, the faces I see at every opening or cultural event. The hundreds that flocked were faces I had not seen before, people, everyday people who were curious to see the painting and celebrate our feat. I stood in the courtyard receiving congratulations, like a groom at a wedding or some national hero who had achieved an exploit."

For the span of that month, people came from all over the West Bank to look at *Buste de Femme*. In order to maintain the temperature of the room and the humidity level, only seven people could be in the room at any moment, in addition to two private security guards. A conference took place, and philosopher Slavoj Žižek was brought in to give a lecture.

Beyond luring a new audience to an artistic event, *Picasso in Palestine* mobilized unprecedented interest from the media, both local and international. It took a few days for Hourani to take stock of the level of engagement from civil society, yet nothing prepared him for Amjad's letter. A week into the exhibition's opening, a courier from the International Red Cross (ICRC) delivered a letter to the IAAP for Hourani. He left it with the security guard on duty. It was from Amjad, a young Palestinian sequestered in the Jalbou' prison. Amjad had read about *Picasso in Palestine* and its resounding success; he wanted to congratulate Hourani and expressed his gratitude by tracing the drawing from a photographic reproduction in a newspaper. "My heart skipped a beat when I opened the letter. I was completely overwhelmed with an array of emotions—pride, humility, joy, awe. I could imagine Amjad in his cell, as almost all of us had been rounded up and jailed at some point in our—early or advanced—adulthood; that he was inspired to write to me was one of the most precious rewards of realizing this project. Part of the letter was yellowed from coffee; he had even cared to apologize for its untoward presentation." Hourani called the ICRC to find out how best to reply to Amjad and they recommended he publish whatever letter or message in a newspaper. Hourani did indeed, in the daily *al-Ayyam*.

A month after the exhibition opened, *Buste de Femme* was crated again and shipped back to Eindhoven. Its journey back home was different. It could not pass through Qalandia because the Israeli army mandates a thorough search of every vehicle, passenger, or piece of merchandise that leaves Ramallah and travels to Tel Aviv. Moreover, the search and examination process would have caused cumbersome delays and inconvenienced travelers. Instead, it went through Ofar, a checkpoint intended for the movement of goods. Hourani accompanied the van carrying the crate to Ofar, and so did the consul for the Netherlands. "The no man's land in this case is only six hundred meters long." Hourani laughed: "The next day the main page of the Israeli Defense Force's website featured a report (just before the news item on the renewed shelling of Gaza) that boasted about the excellent job the army had done in enabling the van's smooth journey." The Palestinian police report noted assiduously how there were no incidents on their end … except for a suspicious amount of empty beer bottles in the artists' studios at the IAAP.

Afterthoughts

The theoretical and analytical relevance or implications of *Picasso in Palestine* are rich, layered, complex, variegated, and genial. On the most immediate and mundane levels, a new audience in the West Bank was motivated to engage with art. On the other hand, an established museum in Europe has expanded the realms and political geography of its practice. On a more abstract scale, *Buste de Femme* now has Palestine written in its biography, and Palestine has *Buste de Femme* written in its modern historical script of enduring occupation. There are, of course, many deeper questions; in the guise of afterthoughts, two will be explored. The first is about Picasso and the prevailing identifications of his oeuvre. On the one hand, he is so widely known as a modern artist, his name is almost a brand for modernism in art, for the finest of its vanguard as well as for the most high-priced paintings. In other words, it is no surprise that the students of the IAAP picked *Buste de Femme* from the Van Abbemuseum collection. Other works may have spoken to them, but Picasso reigns supreme in the gallery of canons. Picasso is also known as a politically engaged artist; his *Guernica* is one of the past century's most epic works to denounce the horrors of war, to give a representation to the victims rather than the victors or warmongers. When I listened to Hourani's early explanations of *Picasso in Palestine* in 2009, I could not help thinking about Picasso in Israel. While *Picasso in Palestine* brought to the fore all the discursive and legal paradoxes of Israel's occupation of the West Bank and the international consensus that endorses it, as well as exposed the precariousness of the Oslo Accords, what would be the implications of Picasso in Israel? What would the set of identifications with his figure and oeuvre be?

Picasso in Israel

It is safe to assume that the various state and private museums dedicated to modern art in Israel have had a long and rich experience with loaning and lending masterworks of modernism from similar counterparts in Europe and North America, and that these transactions to have never come close to even prodding fundamental questions about the existence or legitimacy of the Israeli state, its constitutional writ, nor its military occupation of the West Bank and Gaza. It might be presumptuous, but harmlessly so, to assume that Picasso's works have travelled and exhibited in Israel's museums. The Israeli literati and cultural elite—as the rest of Israeli society—has always regarded itself as thoroughly European, by no means Middle Eastern, in spite of the geographical location of the country. As such, Israeli modern art embeds itself with extreme ease within the western canon, and thus Picasso's modernist proposals for visual representation and rendering have been in a "natural" conversation with Israeli artists. There might be strains in Israeli society that perceive their country as essentially peace-loving or not vested in the glorification of war and military culture, but the reality is obviously otherwise. Israel was born from a war, it has predicated its security on military occupation, and, in the past few years, it has built a massive reinforced-concrete wall around its borders to protect itself from the nation it occupies. It is a country in a permanent state of war.

In the summer of 2008, the German government brokered an impressive trade between Hezbollah and the Israeli government, of Israeli-jailed Lebanese and Palestinian prisoners in exchange for the remains of Israeli soldiers fallen on Lebanese soil. The event, showcased as one of Hezbollah's major victories, was broadcast with superlative fanfare on television. Cameras followed the prisoners from the main administration office in Hadarim Prison, where they signed their own official release forms, were handed over to the ICRC, and boarded buses to Lebanon. The prisoners were lined up against a wall, hands yet cuffed, to pose for a photograph. They stood, dressed in grey sweatshirts, against a reproduction of *Guernica*. In Israel, Picasso and his epic denunciation of war are appropriated to adorn the offices of prison administrators. How will that chapter be written in the biography of *Guernica*, and how will *Guernica* be written in the history of the Hadarim prison?

A little-known fact outside Israel is that its declaration of independence was first officially proclaimed on May 14, 1948, by the state's first Prime Minister, David Ben Gurion, in the main hall of the Tel Aviv Museum of Art. Photographs of the rally depict Ben Gurion standing against a wall with masterworks of Jewish art.

The site was not chosen for the "love of art," or to seed the Zionist state with a special connection to artistic practice. Or at least not consciously. The nascent Zionist council did not want to proclaim the state of Israel in a building that had any association with the British Mandate that was to end officially the following day, on May 15. The Tel Aviv Museum of Art was the Dizengoff House, an estate owned by a very affluent Jewish colonist who turned it into an art museum and donated it to the municipality after the death of his wife in 1930. In 1971, the museum was relocated to another site, and the building became a museum dedicated to the history of Tel Aviv–Jaffa that includes "Independence Hall." The day following that "museum declaration," Israel became formally at war with Palestine and neighboring Arab states. In the national chronology of Palestinians, that day is known as the first of their *Nakba*, or catastrophe.

This piece was originally published in a special issue of A Prior Magazine *in 2014 dedicated to* Picasso in Palestine.

An Oral History of Picasso in Palestine

Michael Baers

Picasso in Palestine, an Introduction

Noah Simblist

I first met Khaled Hourani, an artist and former director of the International Academy of Art Palestine, in Ramallah in 2011, just before the project *Picasso in Palestine* was to unfold.[1] I am interested in it for many reasons but, for the purposes of this book, what intrigued me is the gesture of turning a school into a museum—both institutions that must contend with the conditions of Israeli occupation and statelessness. In addition to Hourani's first-person narrative, related in conversation with Rasha Salti, I have also included selections from a graphic novel by artist and writer Michael Baers. He reappraises the project below; the earlier drawings presented on subsequent pages illustrate conversations between him and several protagonists in the story, including Hourani; Jack Persekian, director of Al Ma'mal Gallery, Jerusalem; and Charles Esche, then director of the Van Abbemuseum in Eindhoven, The Netherlands.

1 The International Academy of Art Palestine shut down in 2017 and transitioned to Birzeit University.

A Reappraisal of *An Oral History of* Picasso in Palestine

Michael Baers

I worked on the graphic novel and documentary *An Oral History of* Picasso in Palestine from July 2011 to May 2014, my intention being to present the complications behind exhibiting a single Picasso painting in Ramallah as completely as possible and in granular detail. My graphic novel's production coincided with a period that, from today's vantage point, now appears hopelessly optimistic. Not that it was a particularly good time to be alive in Palestine: rather, the conditions under which everyday Palestinians lived—their relationship to Israeli settlers' territorial ambitions, their negotiations of the temporal uncertainties of occupation, and the corruption and self-dealing of the Palestinian Authority (PA)—still offered some small space for hope. Salam Fayyad, a technocratic central banker whose brief was, as he himself put it, to build up Palestinian institutions in advance of a Palestinian state, was well into his tenure as prime minister. Benjamin Netanyahu was then, as now, the Israeli prime minister, and although never a proponent of peaceful coexistence with Palestinians, his ability to realize Revisionist Zionism's more radical policies was still constrained.

When, after a decade's absence, I visited Ramallah in the summer of 2022 to research why the Qalandiya International—an art biennial organized by a loose association of Palestinian cultural institutions—fell apart after only four editions (the last of which, entitled *Solidarity*, displayed a decided lack thereof), I found a city splintering under the pressures of occupation. It had also been transformed by a residential building boom—one result of the neoliberal economic policies foisted on the West Bank by the international community. From the balconies of new apartment blocks, middle-class Ramallah residents could watch the West Bank's territorial contiguity disappearing, as Israeli settlements, each with its hilltop observation tower like a capitation point along a necklace of sodium streetlamps, girdled the horizon. If, viewed from one angle, this most glaringly visible aspect of the PA's economic project was a response to the contingencies of the moment (i.e., the demands of donor nations), from another it appeared designed to prevent a repeat of the First Intifada (people tied to a mortgage being less likely to engage in protracted periods of civil disobedience), and from yet another could be considered a physical manifestation of the Oslo map, which by concentrating political and economic power in the cities had further disenfranchised rural Palestinians already made vulnerable by Israel's total control of Area C.

The aspirational lifestyle norms the PA had promoted earlier in the century, manifested now in limestone-clad apartment blocks, had also drawn the curators and cultural programmers I talked to into a double bind. The more they had bought into the international standards and practices of contemporary art, the further the art exhibited departed from being a form of resistance everyday people might relate to. Meanwhile, the short-term orientation of the policy objectives pursued by NGOs active in Palestine, along with the destabilizing effects of Israel's occupation strategies, made long-term strategic planning impossible for these institutions, a temporal corollary to the increasing fragmentation of the West Bank's territory, which made it increasingly difficult and time-consuming for cultural producers to meet face-to-face. As I wrote at the time:

> Everyone I spoke with talked of gaps and fragments: the gap between the institutions and the communities they were meant to serve, the gap between the artist's political imagination and the facts on the ground, the gap between the historical role of Palestinian artists as members of the resistance and the new, professionalized role of artists deploying art as the language of research. And finally, the gap between two historically relevant poles in

> art practice—the utopian dimension of art that tries to imagine a better world, and the critical dimension of art that holds up a mirror to society. And then there are the fragments ... the fragmentation of the society between rich and poor, left and right, believer and non-believer; the fragmentation of the land itself, because the mental distance between one town and another increases with the difficulty and inconvenience of getting from point A to point B, so that, in the end, from the perspective of Ramallah or Jenin, Hebron might as well be in China.

Picasso in Palestine was about testing the extent to which Palestine would be permitted to participate in the global cultural system. The paradox it gave expression to lay in its political and artistic ambitions opening a horizon the occupation could only foreclose. If, in retrospect, this bad situation is nothing compared to the horror of the present, it still serves to indicate the narrowing political horizon Palestinians, even those with good views from their apartments, have been living under for decades. Under certain conditions the transition from bad to worse does not happen incrementally but in clearly demarcated stages, just as water's transformation from solid to liquid to gaseous states occurs at distinct thresholds. By bestowing the appearance of complete impunity to a client state, the West finally vaporized the system of governance upon which *Picasso in Palestine* was based and to which it appealed.

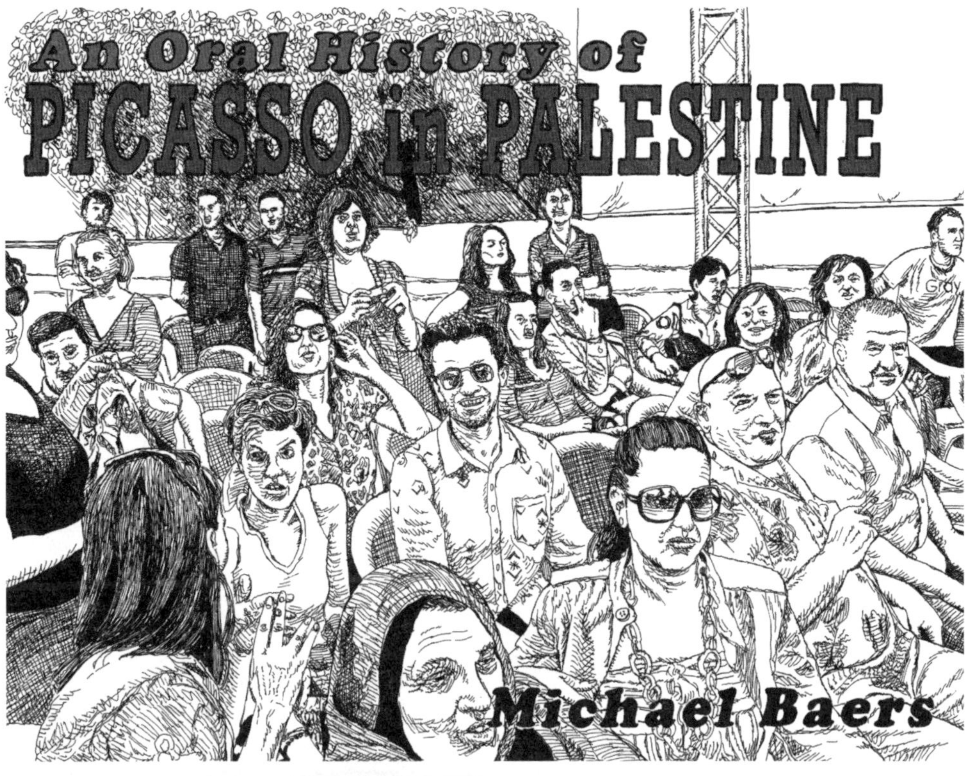
An Oral History of
PICASSO in PALESTINE
Michael Baers

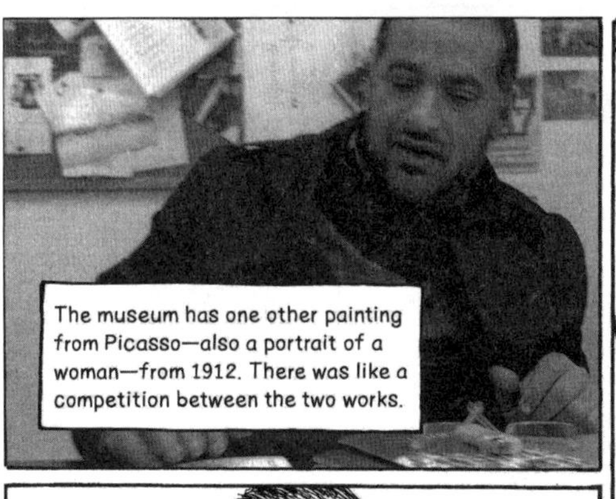
The museum has one other painting from Picasso—also a portrait of a woman—from 1912. There was like a competition between the two works.

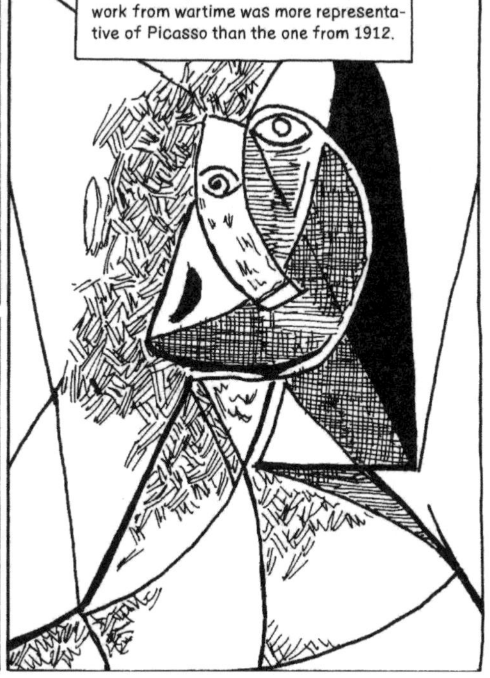
But this one, the *Buste de femme*, as a work from wartime was more representative of Picasso than the one from 1912.

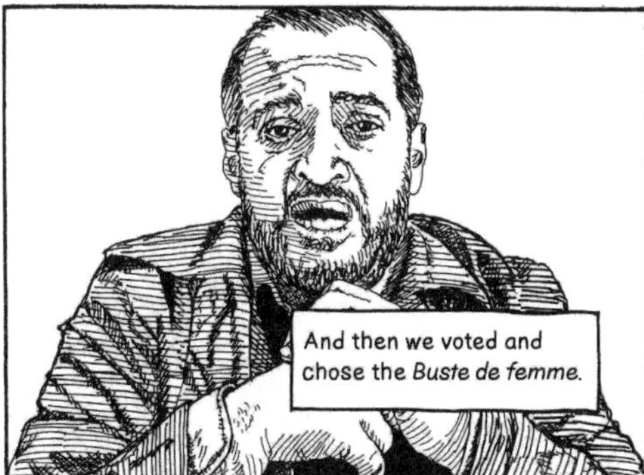
And then we voted and chose the *Buste de femme*.

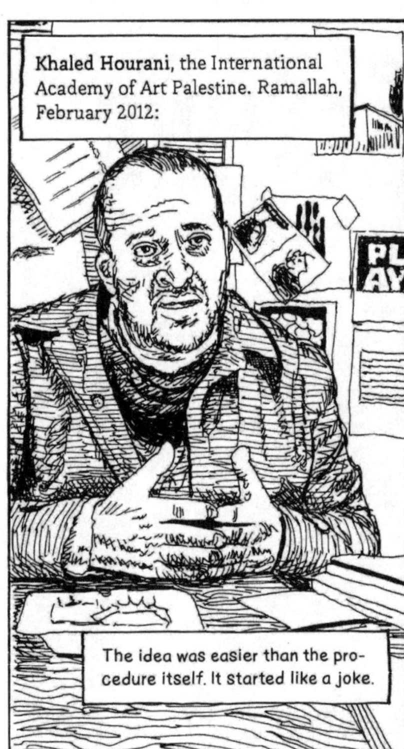
Khaled Hourani, the International Academy of Art Palestine. Ramallah, February 2012:
The idea was easier than the procedure itself. It started like a joke.

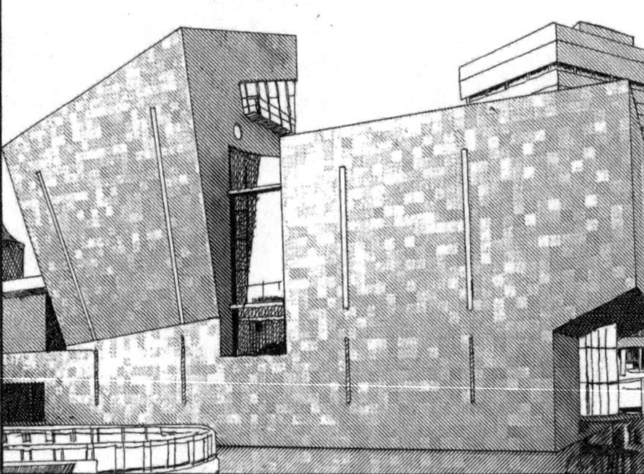
I was on a visit to the Van Abbemuseum three years ago, and we made a tour with the director and others of the rear of the museum. We were visiting the administration room, the collection, and they were explaining the policy of exhibitions—how they send artworks or parts of their collection to other countries, to other museums.

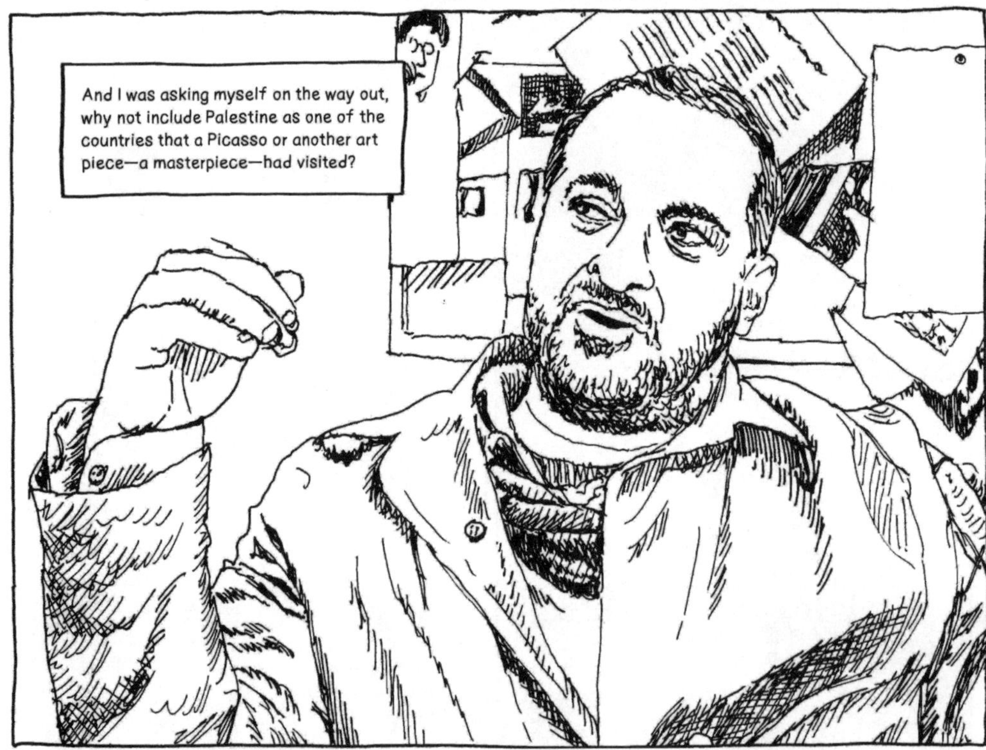
And I was asking myself on the way out, why not include Palestine as one of the countries that a Picasso or another art piece—a masterpiece—had visited?

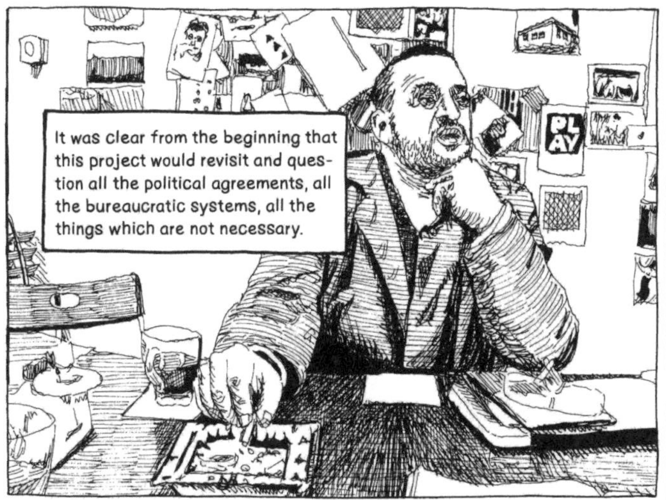

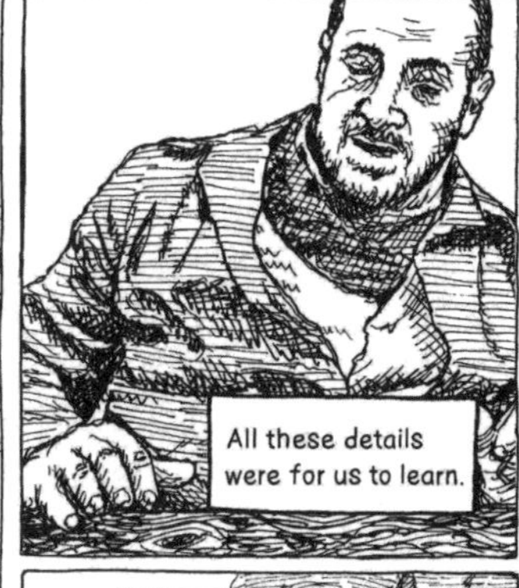

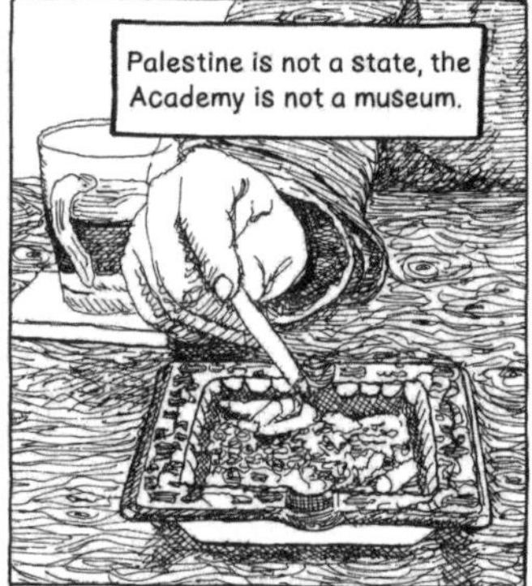

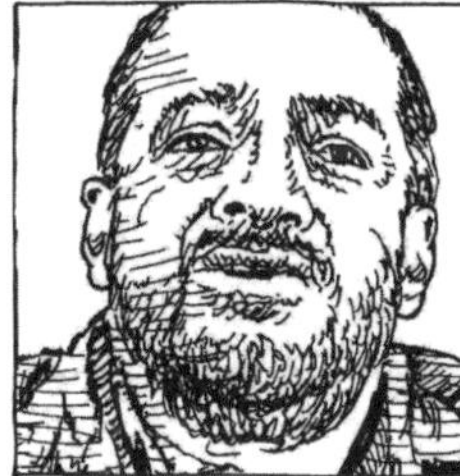

It was also clear from the beginning that for an insurance company to get involved in such a risky kind of situation... usually there might be a government invited or a connection with a museum who would bring some of their collection to be exhibited and guarantee the safety of the work, but in this case, this was not the situation.

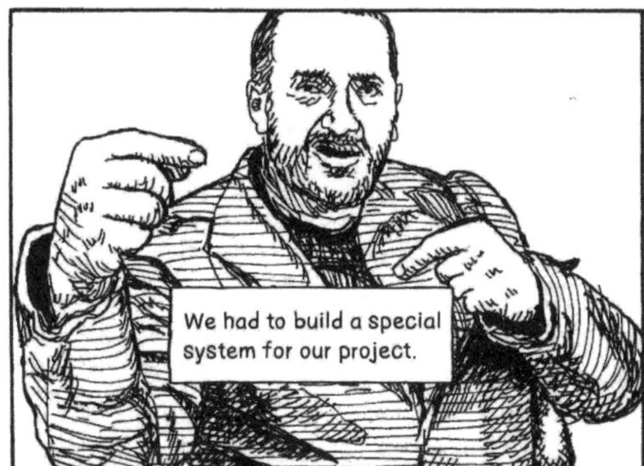

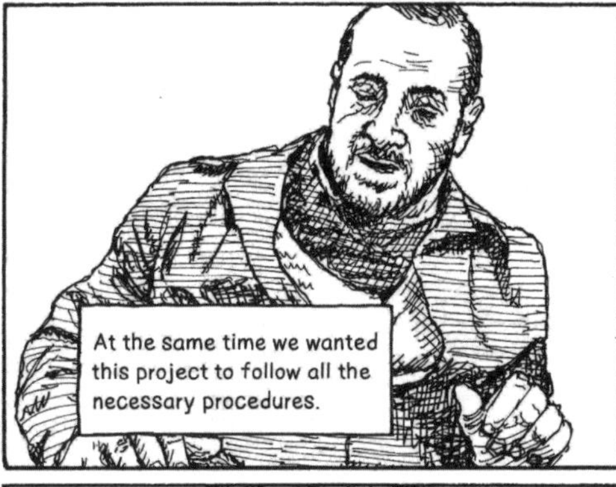

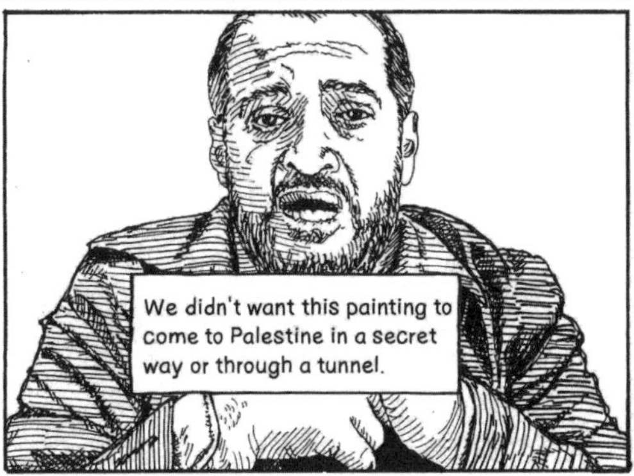

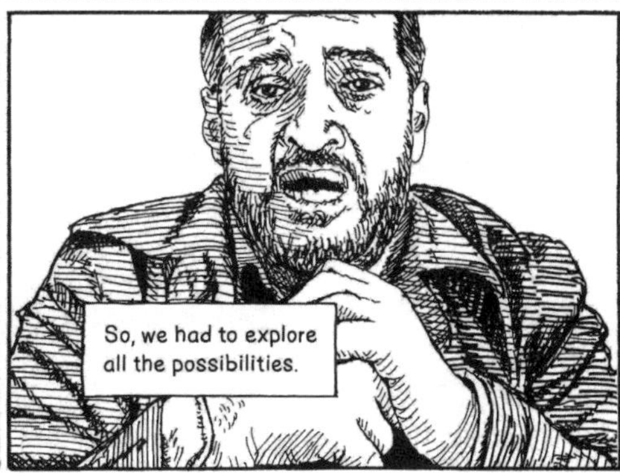

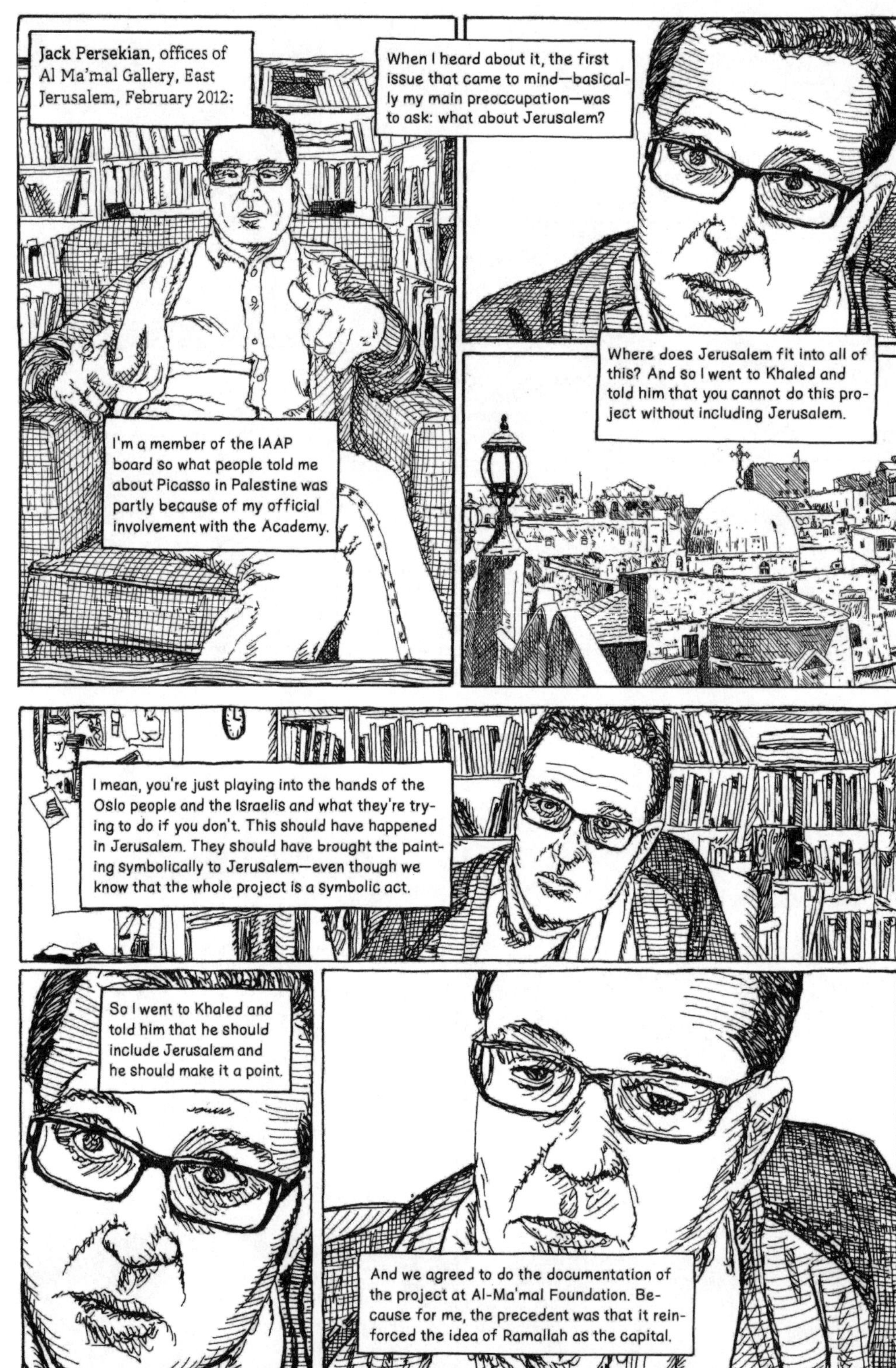
Jack Persekian, offices of Al Ma'mal Gallery, East Jerusalem, February 2012:
I'm a member of the IAAP board so what people told me about Picasso in Palestine was partly because of my official involvement with the Academy.
When I heard about it, the first issue that came to mind—basically my main preoccupation—was to ask: what about Jerusalem?
Where does Jerusalem fit into all of this? And so I went to Khaled and told him that you cannot do this project without including Jerusalem.
I mean, you're just playing into the hands of the Oslo people and the Israelis and what they're trying to do if you don't. This should have happened in Jerusalem. They should have brought the painting symbolically to Jerusalem—even though we know that the whole project is a symbolic act.
So I went to Khaled and told him that he should include Jerusalem and he should make it a point.
And we agreed to do the documentation of the project at Al-Ma'mal Foundation. Because for me, the precedent was that it reinforced the idea of Ramallah as the capital.

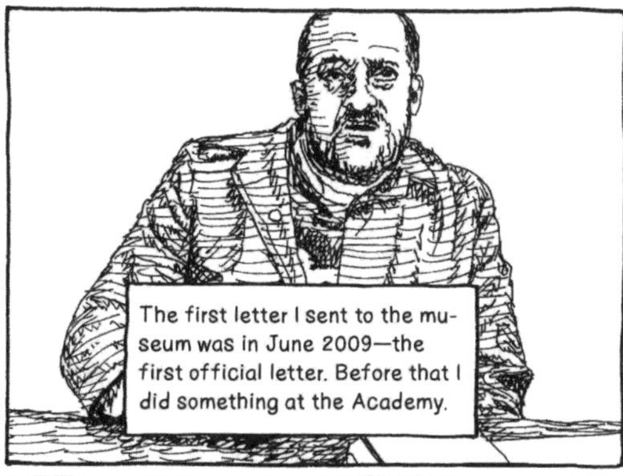
The first letter I sent to the museum was in June 2009—the first official letter. Before that I did something at the Academy.

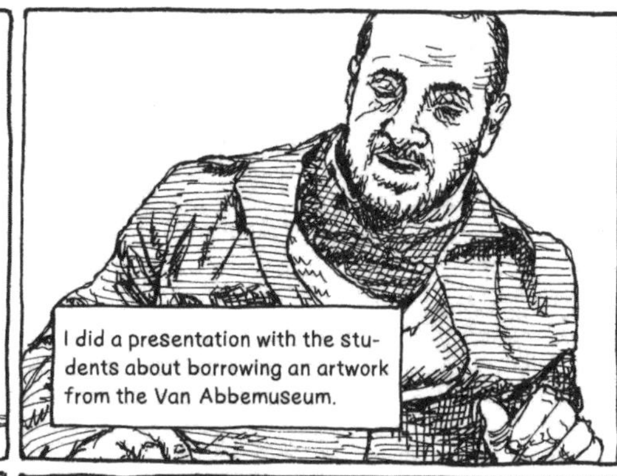
I did a presentation with the students about borrowing an artwork from the Van Abbemuseum.

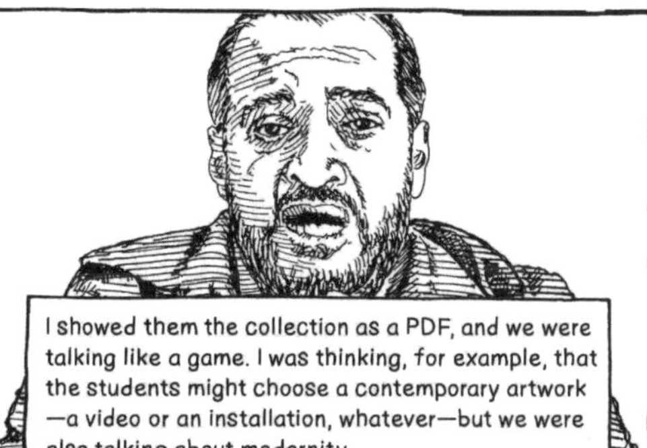
I showed them the collection as a PDF, and we were talking like a game. I was thinking, for example, that the students might choose a contemporary artwork —a video or an installation, whatever—but we were also talking about modernity.

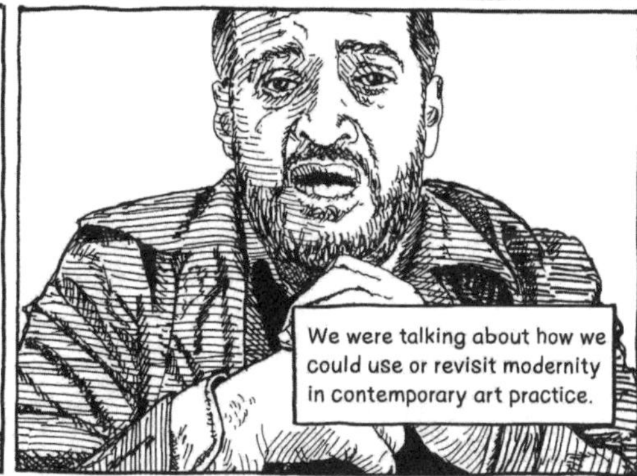
We were talking about how we could use or revisit modernity in contemporary art practice.

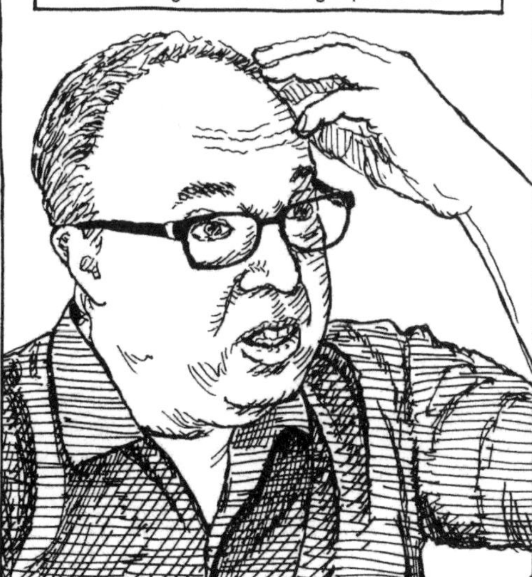
I think one of the crucial things that made me absolutely convinced that we should try and do it if at all possible was the absolute confidence with which Khaled and the students in Ramallah wanted to make this happen: to behave in a way as if the occupation was already overcome, and I think that was a huge and convincing aspect of it.

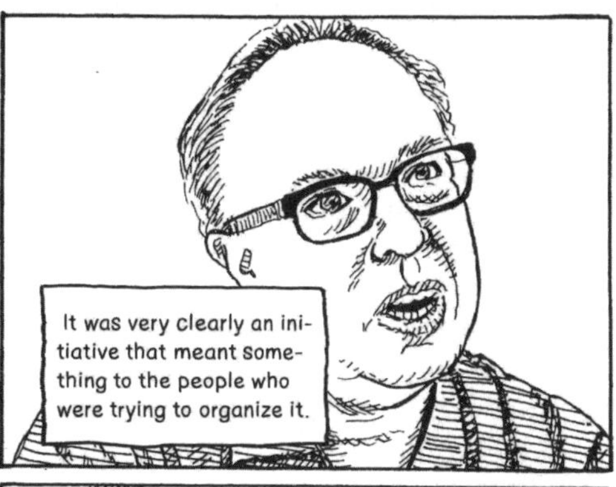
It was very clearly an initiative that meant something to the people who were trying to organize it.

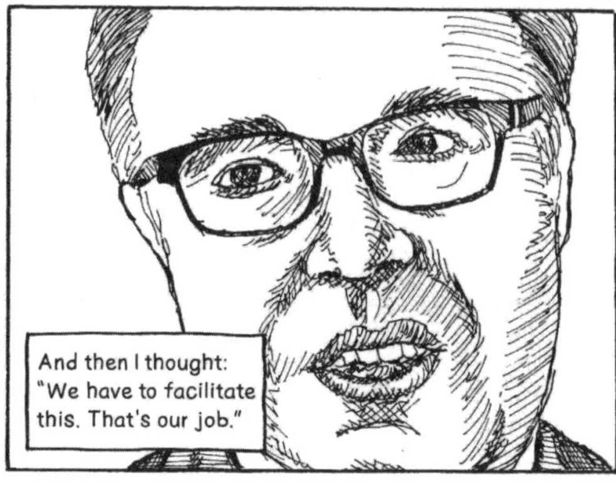
And then I thought: "We have to facilitate this. That's our job."

Pedagogies of Commons as Transversal Methods

Pelin Tan

Alternative learning and forms of knowledge sharing have expanded enormously in the last twenty-five years, creating transdisciplinary pedagogies of art, spatial practices, and architecture. The need to establish uncommon forms of institutional structures, modalities of unlearning, situations of commonality, and fresh artistic methodologies led to various pedagogical practices. Such practices stepped up to the threshold of institutions, applying diverse artistic research to trans-local territorial survival. Examples of these alternative pedagogies became rich and varied; as an annex of institutional expansion, as an artist initiative, as a field-engaged design studio, and as an active strike. Such a multitude of examples are reforming practice, pedagogy, and institutional structures (art/design institutions or academia) and responding to contemporary urgencies of sociopolitical struggles and coexistences. In this essay, I will first try to describe philosopher-activist Félix Guattari's "methods" and link them to pedagogies. An engaged artistic and spatial practice in socially engaged worlding needs a transversal method that cuts across interdisciplinary approaches and is in strike with/in the current climate crisis, active local communities, and the empowerment of human and nonhuman rights. Thus, the recent term *decolonial* focuses on alternative forms of artistic research and practice that push up against global extractivist geographies. Artistic methodologies and engaged pedagogies have become an affective practice transforming societies and communities.

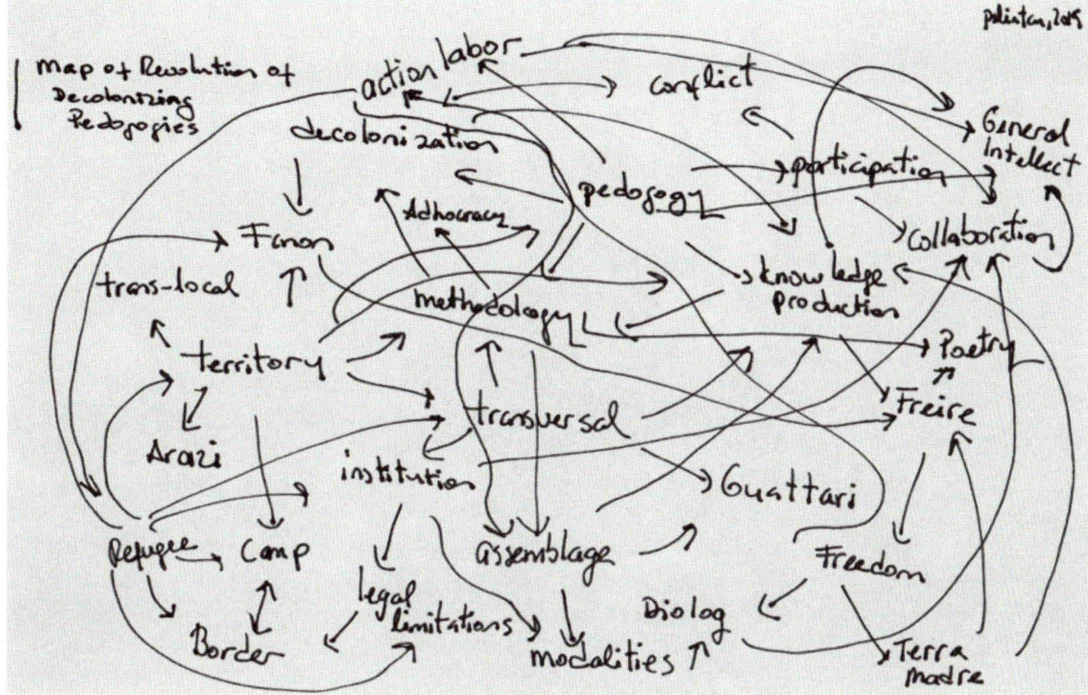

Diagram by Pelin Tan.

Transversal Methodology

A transversal methodology ensures trans-local knowledge production that rhizomatically reaches beyond topics of militant pedagogy, institutionalism, borders, war, refugee status, documents/documenting, urban segregation, commons, and others. This transversal practice mainly refers to Guattari. As he describes it: "neither institutional therapy, nor institutional pedagogy, nor of the struggle for social emancipation, but which invoked an analytic method that could transverse these multiple fields (from which came the theme 'transversality')."[1] I understand the notion of transversality as a practice where both epistemic and theoretical categories are transverse, replacing each other. Also, it is about a practice that is embedded in everyday life. The "institution/instituting" is part of it. Thus, creating such a practice also influences the political body of an institution and the way we are instituting it. When teaching architecture, different representations of knowledge, such as those related to small-scale design or to larger levels of integrated disciplines like sociology, the sciences, and art, I feel this practice is a powerful tool that could be carried further with students. Students' actions are part of this togetherness through a transversality of pedagogy.

The understanding of such a methodology is often affiliated with terms in alternative knowledge production and pedagogical practice, such as "assemblage methods" or "affective pedagogy."

1 Pierre-Félix Guattari, *The Guattari Reader*, trans. Gary Genosko (Blackwell Publishers, 1996).

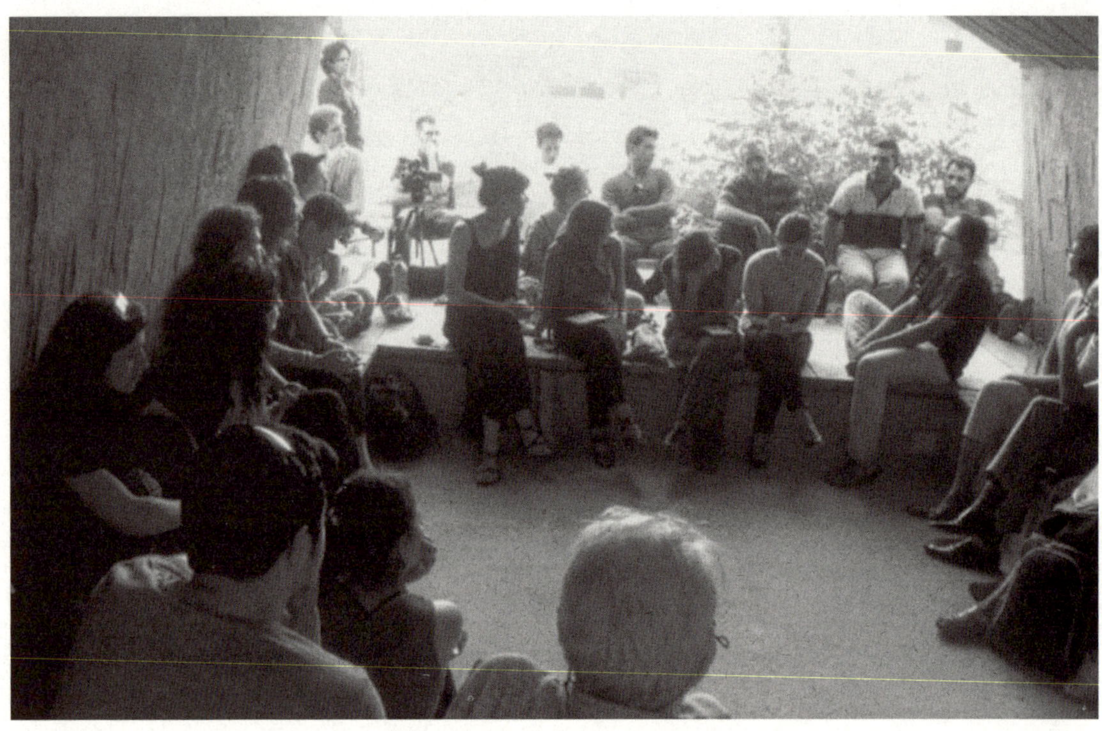

Concrete Tent at Dheisheh Palestinian Refugee Camps, West Bank, designed by DAAR. The first assembly was organized by Alessandro Petti, Sandi Hilal, Pelin Tan, and David Harvey in 2015.

Methodology is not only a tool in describing reality but also a political tool that takes part in the process of knowledge production. Thus, assemblage methods are described as "the process of enacting or crafting bundles of ramifying relations that condense presence and (therefore also) generate absence by shaping, mediating, and separating these. Often it is about manifesting realities out there and depictions of those realities in here. It is also about enacting Othernesses."[2] While John Law's statement in his book *After Method* mainly concerns critical approaches to methods in the social sciences, it also directly reveals the methodological problems in architecture research and its pedagogy. In the frameworks of both architecture and art, how can we as teachers understand the possibilities of creating such transversality that enacts Otherness? On the other hand, affective pedagogy refers to philosopher Gilles Deleuze's reference to seventeenth-century Dutch philosopher Baruch Spinoza's concept of "affect/affections" that are beyond the body and act as an assemblage of the form described in the context of aesthetics: "Affect is a starting place from which we can develop methods that have an awareness of the politics of aesthetics: methods that respond with sensitivity to aesthetic influence on human emotions and understand how they change bodily capacities."[3] Affective pedagogy is part of this research as it involves an instant involvement with the actors where there is local dispute and urgency as a social and political base. These local dynamics also affect pedagogical processes and products such as graduate theses, course actions, and themes.

Decolonial Pedagogy

There are two basic principles for decolonizing educational structures: constructing a non-hegemonic knowledge system through a collective process and creating an instituting practice without fully reaching the level of an "institution." Education defaults to a structure in which the institution becomes a machine to sustain itself. What is a collective process in education? It destroys the hierarchy of dualist structures between teacher and student, teaching and learning. Furthermore, it means collective self-teaching, learning by acting together, rejecting the gap between theory and practice, deconstructing terms in education that are sustained by institutions, and preserving traditional knowledge from earth and nature. The methodology, the syllabus, and any topic content are the bases for a pedagogy. Architecture education is often trapped between architectural genres of specific territorial conditions and global conflict of form-concept relations that conservatively inform the syllabus and design studio programs. So, I feel it always needs two processes: firstly, to decolonize architectural knowledge from a certain hegemonic territorial condition that the institution is attached to, and, secondly, to create a transversal methodology that goes beyond form and concept in design. An example of searching for an affective pedagogy is the Campus in Camps initiative by Decolonizing Architecture Art Research (DAAR) in the West Bank, Palestine. Decolonization methodologies in architectural pedagogy have specific contexts in disputed territories and cities. For instance, DAAR is "an architectural collective that is dedicated to speculating on the reuse and transformation of colonial architecture."[4] Founded by Sandi Hilal and Alessandro Petti, DAAR draws on the fields of art and architecture, focuses on Palestinian refugees creating common spaces and the dichotomy of public versus private space, and perceives the notion of the "camp" as a potential space beyond neoliberal citizenship. DAAR collaborates with diverse researchers, refugees, activists, and civil representatives to use militant urban and architectural research methodologies to identify common spaces in refugee camps and former military buildings. Working with the inhabitants of the Al-Fawwar Palestinian refugee camp, for example, they designed a small public space that was then realized by young Palestinian refugees and families. A space for the exchange of everyday experiences and local engagements can be the most important form of resistance against colonization. Campus in Camps, run by youth in the Dheisheh refugee camp, is an alternative pedagogical platform. This platform is based on several activities considering the refugee and urbanization of camp practices as well as global concerns about education and methods of decolonization. Using social-media tools as an expanding archive of sources for their activities, Campus in Camps enabled us to see a new vision of education employing critical spatial practices.[5] Campus in Camps

2 John Law, *After Method: Mess in Social Science Research* (Routledge, 2004), 122.

3 Anna Hickey-Moody, "Aesthetics and Affective Pedagogy," in Rebecca Coleman and Jessica Ringrose, eds., *Deleuze and Research Methodologies* (Edinburgh Press, 2013), 79–95. 4 Decolonizing Architecture Art Research, https://www.decolonizing.ps/site/.

4 Decolonizing Architecture Art Research, https://www.decolonizing.ps/site/.

5 Campus in Camps, http://campusincamps.ps.

set up participatory engagement in three camps. Firstly, it is based in the Dheisheh refugee camp, which was established in Bethlehem in 1948 and has since become urbanized. The third-generation youth and Hilal and Petti created the Phoenix Center, an initiative that includes the Edward Said Library and hosts talks and workshops with urbanists, spatial researchers, and architects from abroad. The center is where different researchers meet and introduce their projects about different geographies and methodologies. Campus in Camps produces readers on pedagogy, the commons, and other related concepts in relation to everyday life in urbanized camps. Fawwar camp is more like a village and in a rural area south of Hebron. Also established in 1948, Fawwar has a large population of women and children. Campus in Camps initiated a long-term participatory project led by Hilal to design a public space for women. The square is now a place for meetings, cooking, and assemblies organized by the women. As the camp is situated in a rural landscape, the women cannot easily access urban spaces and cultural activities. Domestic privacy is strong. Therefore, this square created a simple public space for these women, who took part in the design decisions, including the proximity to their domestic habitats. In his article "Decolonizing Knowledge," Petti explains that, during the First Intifada, basic educational infrastructure for children and young people was not available. Self-sufficiency and collectively maintaining the commons became an important life condition for Palestinians in the occupied territories. Self-education and collective teaching became a tool of autonomy: "Theoretical knowledge was combined with one that emerges from action and experimentation. Learning became a crucial tool for gaining freedom and autonomy. People discovered that they could share knowledge and could be in charge of what and how to study ... The classical structure, in which "expert teachers" transmit knowledge and students are mere recipients to be filled with information, was substituted by a blurred distinction between the two."[6] Petti adds that such an educational practice became a tool of empowerment and emancipation, which for Palestinians is vital for decolonization under the state of Israel.

Munir Fasheh, a mathematics teacher at Birzeit University in the West Bank, has been introducing new curricula since the 1970s. Influenced by Palestinian poet and scholar Khaili al-Sakkakini's methodologies, he works with schools throughout the West Bank region. During the first Palestinian intifada, when Israel closed all schools, universities, and other institutions for four years, he founded the Tamer Institute for Community Education, which stressed the need for

6 "Decolonizing Knowledge," Campus in Camps, accessed June 6, 2025, https://www.campusincamps.ps/democratizing-knowledge-production.

7 http://mujaawarah.org/en/; Fasheh: "A word that is used to describe how to deal with control and domination is *anarchy*. I suggest *mujaawarah* instead. Even people like [Noam] Chomsky could not find an English word that embodies what mujaawarah does. He uses *anarchism*, which he describes as 'a kind of tendency in human thought which shows up in different forms in different circumstances and has some leading characteristics.' Primarily it is a tendency that is suspicious and skeptical of domination, authority, and hierarchy. It assumes that the burden of proof for anyone in a position of power and authority lies on them." Munir Fasheh, "Reclaiming Learning as a Biological Ability," Urgent Pedagogies, accessed June 6, 2025, https://urgentpedagogies.iaspis.se/up-reader-006-fa-reclaiming-learning-as-a-biological-ability/.8
Munir J. Fasheh, "The Reading Campaign Experience Within Palestinian Society: Innovative Strategies for Learning and Building Community," *Harvard Educational Review* 65, no. 1 (1995): 66–93.

9 Fasheh, "Reclaiming Learning as a Biological Ability."

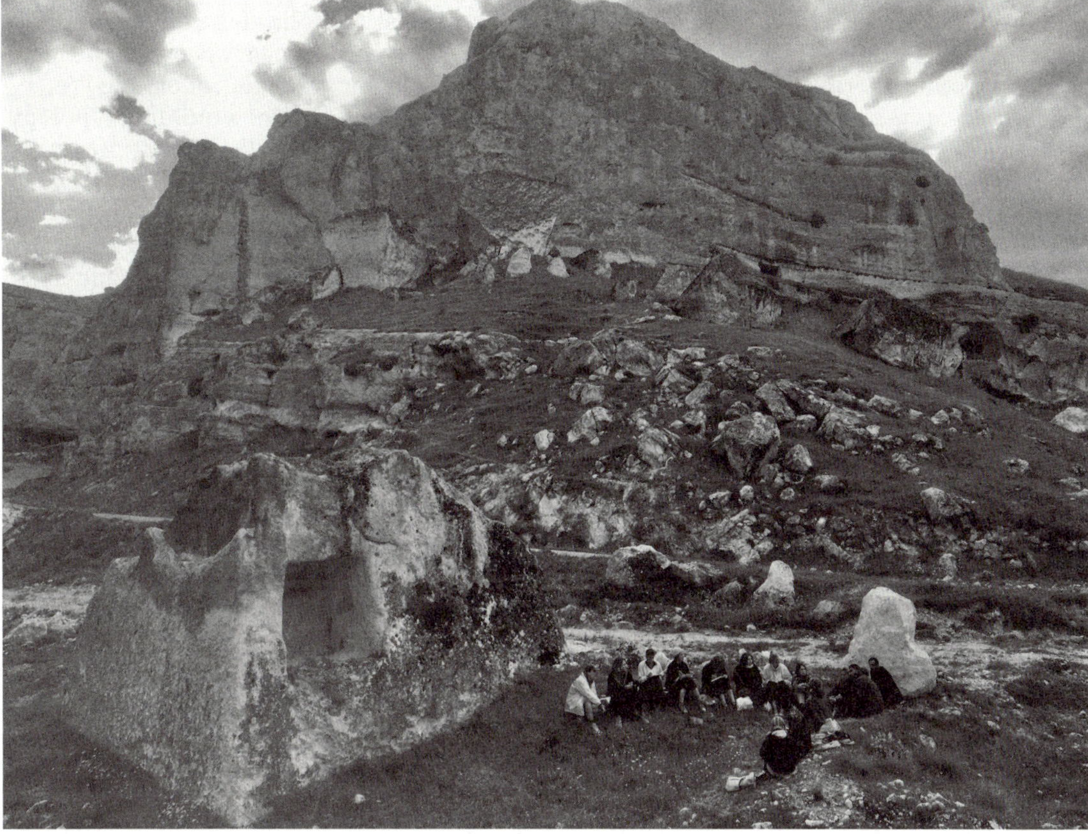

Terrestrial Cosmologies workshop in the water-dam area, Hasankeyf, Turkey, 2023.

learning environments where people learn without being taught. He became involved in *mujaawarahs* in the early 1970s, something he describes as a metaphorical community without authority or control.[7] Fasheh's experience formed the backbone of the First Intifada, where young people formed hundreds of neighborhood committees in the West Bank and Gaza Strip regions. During his teaching, he also inspired individuals including C. K. Ranju, Gustavo Esteva, and Ivan Illich, with whom he shared ideas on decolonial methodologies.[8] Fasheh worked mainly in refugee camps rather than in universities to develop his pedagogical vision, which rests on three pillars: *mujaawarah*, wellness, and nurturing soils.[9]

Diverse forms of education—either in a refugee camp or inside an institution in the heart of Europe—provide experiences of infrastructures that put the possibilities of alliances on our horizon. Scholar Henry Giroux mentions cultural theorist Stuart Hall's legacy on pedagogy: "For Hall, culture provides the constitutive framework for making the pedagogical political—recognizing that how we come to learn and what we learn is imminently tied to strategies of understanding, representation, and disruption."[10] Forming alliances as infrastructures of resistance, trans-territorial solidarities, and altering transversal methodologies is more urgent than ever in pedagogies of art and architecture. Yet it's important to remember that common methods of sustaining horizontal alliances through alternative economies and pedagogical modalities of unlearning vary in different territories.

The term "decolonization" in education is often discussed with reference to the legacies of Frantz Fanon and Paulo Freire. This term became important as an institutional critique and a search for alternative knowledge production in different colonizer-colonized structures. In the colonizer-colonized context, "decolonization not only resists territorial occupation and violence but also transforms institutions, cultural products, approaches, and values." Moreover, in pedagogy, "decolonization" basically signifies a non-institutional education where knowledge is produced and shared collectively. The university is commonly considered the main place for producing and disseminating knowledge. Alternative structures and new ways of producing knowledge such as collective research and its representation via social media are the main formation of non-institutional structures or "becoming" institutions. Transversality is the practice, in which knowledge is cross-created and disseminated.

Furthermore, such research processes and non-institutional structures can create a real effect and participate in the social-political transformation in the mainstream institutions and society. For example, water dams are expanding in Southeast Anatolia at the university where I teach. This reality is one of the main concerns in our graduate education. We take the "water dam" as a building typology and spatial reality, a colonizing strategy of the Turkish government to dispose of the land and create surveillance tools instead of welcome ecological outcomes. As graduate students (artists, architects, and planners) observe and analyze this forced transformation, they can develop a contra-knowledge of the role of such a spatial development that can encourage future acts of decolonization.

Eve Tuck and K. Wayne Yang argue that "decolonization" is a metaphor: "The easy adoption of decolonizing discourse by educational advocacy and scholarship, evidenced by the increasing number of calls to 'decolonize our schools,' or use 'decolonizing methods,' or 'decolonize student thinking' turns decolonization into a metaphor." The critical stance they elaborate in their article gives in-depth insight into why we use this term in the context of pedagogy. They continue: "Decolonization as metaphor allows people to equivocate these contradictory decolonial desires because it turns decolonization into an empty signifier to be filled by any track toward liberation."[11] For them, an anti-colonial critique and decolonization are slightly different. I think their critique is useful to understand the term better. On the other hand, the dualistic structures of colonizer-oppressed subjectivities are more complex today and are relative from territory to territory. In my opinion, using the word as a metaphor still has the emancipative power to reconsider our methodologies, our process-based research tools, the complex realities of territories, and the actors in the social production of architecture.

This pedagogical radicality gives us further knowledge production in architectural

10 Henry A. Giroux, "Public Pedagogy as Cultural Politics: Stuart Hall and The Crisis of Culture," *Culture Studies* 14, no. 2 (2000): 341–60.

11 Tuck, Eve and K. Wayne Yang, "Decolonization Is Not a Metaphor," *Decolonization: Indigeneity, Education & Society* 1, no. 1 (2012): 1–40.

education. But in what local conditions or extraterritorial constraints? And in which tradition of architectural history does this pedagogical radicality intervene? Especially compared to the social sciences and other fields, architectural education is more problematic because the market of the neoliberal urban arena is pressing young students and graduates. On the other hand, another problem is that referring to the social sciences, as we do in architecture, does not necessarily help create a radical method within architecture but rather keeps the focus on ... the social sciences. The radical questioning of the architectural discipline is deeply rooted in architectural education and still resists going beyond studio work, usual design methodologies, crossing multiple disciplines, and considering trans-local territories. From a Deleuzian perspective, today the gap between theory and practice is challenging. Trans-disciplinary thinking—borrowing cross-methods, using new media that provides performative visual representation tools, engaging as a militant researcher in everyday life—helps us to experience other "knowledge." Similarly, the multiplicity of knowledge production urges us to alter our research methods. Reformulating reactions in syllabi, design studios, or the politics of academic structures in architecture faculties will lead to inventing new pedagogies—not only in established architecture studios but also in many alternative collectives.

In April 2023, the Terrestrial Cosmologies workshop of design and anthropology brought together local students from the region with German and Italian students to work in a rural Kurdish village in Hasankeyf, near Batman, Turkey.[12] The workshop aimed to understand the terrestrial knowledge and local practices in Kurdish villages where residents are also currently resisting extractive projects devised by corporations and the state. Developed by Arazi Assembly Research Collective, which is based in Mardin, Turkey, the workshop considered the urgencies around pedagogical practices, or how such practices can take a more overtly engaged approach to scenes of conflict.

As a contribution to nurturing epistemic imaginaries, my focus is on emphasizing the urgency to create alliances within infrastructures of resistance through pedagogical practices and related research on critical spatial practices. Pedagogy, as grounded in processes of learning and unlearning structures, involves altering methodology, content, and tactics and, as such, needs the support of trans-local (planetary) alliances. The needs and tactics of what I understand as *urgent pedagogies* start from the entanglement of such partnerships of solidarity and mutual dependence.

"Alliances" of pedagogical practice are understood neither as permanent nor as formal structures according to Stuart Hall, who addressed the issue as a question of the decentralization of power and the capacity to speak across differences. Hall was speaking at a certain time and in a certain national condition, yet his understanding is vital for current pedagogies in art and architecture, and can help us appreciate the link between pedagogies and knowledge production, as well as their urgency. As Hall claims, "teaching" is a cultural practice and a process of activating knowledge in a social and political context. Layers of these contexts that are thick with colonial processes, hegemonic institutionalism, and extractivist capitalism prevent the transformation of dominant modes of the reproduction of knowledge.

12 Erasmus Triple Agreement workshop with Dr. Elizabeth Tauber and Dr. Jesko Fezer.

Systems of Grasping

Kameelah Janan Rasheed interviewed by Noah Simblist

Noah Simblist You have such a unique point of view because you're not just an artist who makes work about education and uses education as a medium. You studied education and worked as a social studies teacher in Brooklyn, and since then you've taught at museums, universities, libraries, and smaller initiatives like the School for Poetic Computation. You currently teach at Yale. How do you think that teaching is similar or different in these different contexts?

Kameelah Janan Rasheed Right before this call I was watering my plants and I was thinking to myself, "What has brought me the greatest joy in my life?" It's always been teaching. Of course, I love making and exhibiting art. But I think there's something about the discourse and community that gets built when you're teaching that doesn't necessarily happen in the context of making an art object and then leaving it behind. There's some type of corporeal presence that I really enjoy about teaching. When I was six or seven, I already knew. I helped my kindergarten and first-grade teachers write curriculum. I was not making a lot of friends by asking for more homework. I was very aware of that.

When I went into high-school teaching, the goal there was to think about things that I would have wanted from my educational experience as a young person. I was also thinking about the state of the world at the time that I was leaving college and grad school and wondering: How do I create space for young people to rigorously think through these things without imposing my point of view? So, when I work with high-school students, the joy for me is witnessing "Aha!" moments, witnessing young people become their own intellectual selves. Not parroting what someone else is saying, but having their own thoughts, arguing with one another with passion, and coming to a place of self-discovery. Those have been the most beautiful moments to witness because they are so intimate and private. I'm grateful to my students for allowing me to witness them.

In the college and graduate-school context, those moments are still there, but they're different because folks are at different stages in their lives. I find my role there is about supporting people as they go through transitional periods. I think that it's a really fragile time for people and I like being a support structure in that context.

In college and high-school settings, you get to be with people for a longer period of time, so you can build deeper relationships. Working in museums is different because it's a less longitudinal interaction. So you see someone enjoy the program, and you might see them in a couple years at another program, but it's a quick interaction. But a privilege that I've had over the years of doing public programming is that many people come back; there's a bidirectional witnessing. Them seeing me grow in my own practice and them connecting the dots between something they experienced in a workshop and then another. Yes, I enjoy making art objects, but my greatest desire is to create more spaces for people to be in relation.

NS That's a great transition into the next question, which is about your teaching a social-practices class. You were talking about how teaching is inherently mirrored with social practices and community-building, and you put those things together through this course at Cooper Union. Can you talk about your approach to that course?

KJR The first semester that I taught it there was a little bit of practicum, but it was rooted in theory. During the second semester we got a little bit more into practice because I was starting to feel a bit more comfortable with the idea that we could actually have a class that was about the fundamentals of teaching at an art school. And when I left, this past semester, the focus was on providing opportunities for students to reflect on their own learning experiences, to identify what an ideal learning experience looks like.

I did a lot of stuff around play and pedagogy, thinking through the relationships between safety and learning. We talked a lot about games as a low barrier to entry. One of my students said that the best invitations for play have a low barrier to entry. I think it was such a great encapsulation of what it means to really care about the people you're engaging with. Students created their own syllabi. And some students got practice by teaching their fellow students every few weeks.

This last semester we attempted to create a speculative school, and, within that, students proposed a series of courses. We had a meditation course that was about self-resourcing through ritualistic art practices. We had a course that was around gathering, and while I may be projecting here, felt like it borrows from the ideas of Ursula K. Le Guin and the Carrier Bag Theory that Mindy Seu's work introduced me to. We had courses that tried to get students to think about objects and sculpture. It was a really beautiful range of courses. And I think that it's a sneaky way to basically ask students what they're missing from their learning. That semester was really rough as the socio-political context of late 2023 came into focus. And I wish we would have had the opportunity to fully realize the school and the courses.

I also was teaching a class at Barnard called "Pedagogy of Play," which went more deeply into things like Dadaist or Fluxus approaches to pedagogy. Teaching social practice and pedagogy as play are attempts to think about the historical grounding of what it means to consider the language of action when it comes to learning, and then providing opportunities for people to make things.

The students at Barnard made Fluxus kits that had a range of activities inside of them, and the goal was to discover what type of learning experiences you can consolidate into a small container. And it was beautiful. Someone made a portable museum; someone else made a music box that had a bunch of things to play with to create music. Someone else created a series of Russian nesting doll–like boxes, and each time they were opened you encountered a set of questions. It was about trying to get people in their bodies to make work, but also to reflect on both their paths of learning and on future possibilities.

NS I love this idea of critique being a positive speculation that they could produce. You also have this initiative called the Orange Tangent Study, a consulting business that's centered on education. Can you say a little bit about how this came about, whom it serves, and what kind of projects it supports?

KJR During the first year of the pandemic, I was working at a nonprofit, and I remember telling someone about this idea. I was like, "I want to help people figure out this curriculum stuff, but in a different way than what I'm doing now." One of my first clients was a poet who was trying to figure out a chapbook. So I was like, "Okay, this actually is deeply rooted in pedagogy." My approach to talking to her about the practice, my approach to thinking with her about how she wanted this publication to be in the world ... these are all pedagogical approaches to thinking about relationality, insight, and the specificity of what we create.

And if you fast forward four years, I'm working with an architectural and environmental organization to support a group of fellows and their development of a curriculum that they'll teach next year. I've also worked with foundations that are supporting neurodiverse students. My main interest is supporting people who are working in any sort of learning environment and figuring out how to do the thing they're already doing in a more expansive way. I've also worked with a publisher who is releasing a set of learning aids. The most fun for me has been popping into places that I don't expect to be interested in a pedagogical approach and being able to use this developing skillset. I think so much of pedagogy helps me shape how I listen closely and also how I think about site-responsiveness.

Orange Tangent is a one-on-one learning experience, whereas the other things that I'm doing are more for larger groups over sustained periods of time. But in both contexts, I'm really interested in how we as humans relate to one another, how we relate to other species, and how the different systems that we come into the world with and create interact with one another.

I always tell clients that I never want to see them again. I am a very bad capitalist. I'm a very bad business owner. I don't want people to be dependent upon me. I want the sessions to be such that if they come back to me, they're coming back because they have a brand-new thing they want to work on. I'm interested in ensuring that there isn't a sense of dependence on me as a support; I'd rather be scaffolding for folks working toward a sense of independence and ownership over what they're doing.

NS The kinds of clients you're talking to don't fit a typical model of the student-teacher relationship in other institutions. We were talking about universities or high schools or museums and how teaching and learning happens in different ways. When you were talking about being a bad capitalist, that idea of the repeat customer, the repeat student ... it's not just a capitalist idea, it's built into nonprofit educational institutions.

KJR Yes, I agree.

NS I hear you saying that your work is an intervention into that system of treating students as clients.

KJR When I did nonprofit work, I found myself doing the same workshops repeatedly, working with the same people. I love everyone that I work with. I want that to be clear. But the concern I've always had is the progression narrative within education. You do a thing, you gain the skills, and you do the next thing. I don't want to impose a linear progression when it comes to learning.

But if we're trying to support students to be independent and curious learners, then we have to use the same principles when we facilitate adult education and actively think about the goal. The goal is to get them there, not to hold them in place doing the same things or waiting for me to tell them what to do.

NS Your formal education included degrees in public policy and education and not art; it seems to me that you have a really rigorous and deep understanding of the ways that these things work together. How do you think that informs your approach to teaching in art contexts? Do you notice that you have insight into some things that colleagues who have BFAs and MFAs might not have easy access to?

KJR I still find it hilarious at almost forty that people have hired me to teach in art schools. It's funny to me because, if I'm being honest, I came into my first graduate-level teaching experience feeling so intimidated. I was like, "I know how to teach, but will people presume that because I don't have a BFA or MFA that I should not be here?" I think what I'm bringing in is something about learning how brains work and pedagogy that helps you think about systems and organization.

I want to make the scaffolding apparent so that students understand a workflow that they can later replicate, modify, and expand. I spend a lot of time thinking about how artists develop systems, rituals, processes, and workflows that can be carried into other contexts.

I really do care about my students. It makes me sad when they're sad. I think a lot about Zaretta Hammond, who wrote about culturally responsive teaching and the brain and who talks about cognitive science. She says that "trust is the onramp to learning." When you develop trust with your students, as she notes, then they will trust that the pushes that you give them, the hard questions that you ask, are coming from a place of deep care and respect and not from a desire to embarrass them or to have a "Gotcha!" moment.

This is not to say that people with MFAs and BFAs don't know how to care about people. I just spent so much of my time prior to this in secondary education. There is knowing how to paint, and then there is knowing how to build a community where other people feel comfortable painting and experimenting in their practices. There's knowing how to make beautiful films, and there's knowing how to create an environment where people feel comfortable asking questions and taking the risks that they need to in order to make their own work.

Also, there were several times in the semester where I've been like, "What I just did was a terrible idea. Rewind, let's try this again." High-school teaching prepares you to be okay with being embarrassed and wrong, because high-school students have no filter. College and graduate students have a little bit more of a filter. So I say, "Guys, if you hate what we're doing right now, I will not be offended if you raise your hand and say, 'Wow, this is really boring. And I appreciate the time we took to put this together, but I think we all need a cognitive break.'" I always say, "I'm not offended. I'm not offended because this is not about me. This is about why you're paying tuition here." I'm trying to figure out how to make it non-hierarchical, because there will always be hierarchy when one person is giving grades. But I'm trying to create an environment where people feel safe to take risks. And I don't think that safety is being allowed to do whatever you want. No. Safety is to say, "I'm going to take a chance and try something wildly different." To be in an environment where people will be responsive and provide feedback.

NS When you talk about challenging people to take risks and creating safe spaces for people to push themselves beyond what they can do already, and that a certain degree of discomfort can be a possibility for growth, it makes me think about legibility in your artwork. You've talked about legibility in relation to your work as an artist, and how a viewer's understanding unfolds through looking or reading. How is learning something that you build into your process as an artist? How do you map how learning happens for a viewer encountering your work?

KJR One of the first times someone mentioned my work being pedagogical, I took a step back. I thought, "I don't want the work to feel didactic." I sat with the language for a long time to think about why that startled me. People have narrow notions of education in art; there's a desk or there's a talk—all these tropes. That's not what I'm doing. I am thinking about legibility as a part of pedagogy.

We presume that we can have information when we engage with a museum or gallery space—I'm here to understand what the artist is trying to say, and now I'm annoyed that I don't get it, right? There's a passive relationship between the viewer and the art.

You either look at it and say, "I got it. Boom." Or you take a picture with it: again, "I got it. Boom." Both are systems of capture. They're systems of grasping. When I was in Joshua Tree two weeks ago, I spent a little time studying the Buddhist principles of grasping because someone had mentioned it to me. And I was thinking a lot about grasping and how most of what we do as human beings is some attempt to contain, grasp, understand, codify, concretize—in some way hold the matter in our hands. I think my approach to legibility is a reminder that sometimes the best things we can experience in life may not be matter, may not be material. They may be immaterial; they may not be things we can hold in our hands. And so, for me, legibility is what I call the "jokey" part of my work—intentionally having someone turn a corner only for there to be a trickster moment. That has everything to do with my investment in the trickster as an archetype—a process of learning that plays with our perceptive capabilities, that plays with our relationship to certainty. That's how we learn. The trickster teaches us through illegibility and intentional indirection. I also think that it slows down the reading and learning process; the goal isn't to be expedient.

Capitalism requires that education be expedient. You go from grade one all the way to grade eight, and you're supposed to go in a straight line, with no time to linger in third grade and think about it. You need just to move. And I think that part of what I'm interested in is the cadence of a learning process and trying to think about that cadence in the way that I create work and then organize it in a space, which is to say that learning is a slow, circuitous, redundant, confusing, annoying, and never linear process. I think that coming to understand my own neurodiversity allowed me to understand why sometimes people's relationship to my work is one of confusion because it is based upon how my brain is building connections.

I'm interested in illegibility not as a performative gesture, but as literally what it is. We have no choice but to be illegible. We have no choice but to be indirect because an articulation of certitude is false. I don't think what I produce in my art practice has to be a final statement of anything.

NS You have talked about your family and your childhood as having a big influence on your relationship to education. One example of these early experiences is your father learning about Islam through annotating the Quran or other religious texts. I wonder if that annotation is part of a research experience for you. When you're reading something, you're annotating, you're underlining, you're taking notes. I see that as a kind of research, a process of teaching oneself. And then there's this practice of teaching others in a classroom. How do you see a relationship between research as a process of teaching oneself and education as a practice of teaching others?

KJR Yeah, there's osmosis. When I think about my dad and his annotations, they were for him, but the annotations were also to prepare this man, who eventually had five children, to be able to teach us. The way that someone comes to learn something leaks into a desire to impart it to others. Whenever I learn a new fact, my greatest joy is sharing it. This becomes connective tissue for many of the relationships that I've formed, whether they're lasting or not, around shared interests. I'm doing research so I can build connective tissue between things. I'm using connective tissue to then start building intimate relations with other people and other species. There's some research—a reaching or a yearning or an attempt to pull something together or pull things together. I'm thinking about the jellyfish that propels itself through grasping or contracting and opening or releasing. It's picking up and releasing, picking up and releasing. I think part of what you're doing as an educator is taking something that you picked up and you're sending it back out, because the letting go or the pushing out is the thing that propels you in other directions.

NS I think that's a beautiful metaphor. It relates to the Buddhist notion of grasping you mentioned earlier. Do you see a relationship between your teaching and social-justice activism? Do questions of legibility relate to activism as a practice? I'm thinking about bell hooks's text, "Theory as a Liberatory Practice," in which she talks about the tension within activist communities between theory and practice, and whether theory can make change, in part because of its perceived illegibility.

KJR Well, you decided to open the can of worms at the end, didn't you? I have so much to say about this. The first thing that I'll say is that when I decided to be a teacher, I was gaining more political understanding, and I said, "I need to teach the future leaders of America and the world because whatever I'm witnessing and experiencing right now is not it."

One of the tricky parts about teaching is that you are a human being, not a blank slate. You come in with your own stuff, your own beliefs, your own systems, your own perspectives on how the world should function. I think the duty of the educator is not to impose. The most important thing that I can do for a young person is to not tell them how I feel. It is to not tell them what *they* should feel. It is to not only give them books that validate a version of the world that I want to see. I think my responsibility is to expose them to all of it so that they can go about deciding—and understand that beliefs can change over time. The best that we can do as human beings is to sit with the mess that is the world and look at all of it together. I think that social justice in the educational context is about how much space and latitude I give students to figure it out.

In the past couple of years of regional, national, global strife and the pandemic, the interesting thing is the tension between urgency and slowness. Theory ... how do I phrase this? I'm trying to figure out the most diplomatic way to say this. I am curious about academia and the management of activism. But maybe it is more of a curiosity about our spoken and unspoken expectations of academics.

My parents told me about being a college student in the 1970s. And I am sure they have their own romanticizations, but folks were outside trying to figure stuff out. The professors were trying to figure stuff out too. Late capitalism, with the concern for how you're going to pay your rent and eat the next month, often makes it such that academia provides the financial support to just barely survive. We all need to be mindful of the intersections of our lives that are not visible to everyone. The student or the professor who doesn't go out to march is not more terrible than the one who does, because the one who didn't go out to march may have an immigration status that could jeopardize their ability to not return to a place that may not be safe for them.

It has never been a binary, it's never been, like, "theory is great, and activism is even better." We need both because theory allows us to take a step back and make sense of what has happened in the past. Activism gives us a sense of what it looks like in real time. They are connected. I think that we've seen, over the past few decades, they're being pulled apart. My romantic notion of being an educator and a professor had everything to do with what I had seen early on, watching professors, thinking they're engaged, they're involved, they're part of this. And then seeing that they're also scared. They're scared about losing their adjunct positions, which they barely got. That's a long way to basically say capitalism sucks. And we've always known that. But it's another way to say that the conversation around theory versus praxis is based upon people's access to safety and security under the material and spiritual precarity of capitalism.

NS The questions around the sustainability of universities, of nonprofits, of museums in relation to education can't exist separately from those larger questions around capitalism. And today, with the encampment movements and discussions about Palestine and divestment, that's become very obvious.

KJR One more thing. I think the hardest thing is that so many young people are told that college is the place where you get to grapple with all the messy stuff. You get to have tough conversations; you get to have important conflicts with one another. You get to really change and learn. And I feel like, in so many ways, the university has performed a bait and switch. They say, "This is not where you deal with hard ideas. This is the place where we tell you which hard ideas you can deal with and which ones you cannot."

Yet Another Score for Feral Translation, 2025

Kameelah Janan Rasheed

As Kameelah Janan Rasheed outlines in her interview on pages 250–57, she is deeply concerned with education as a multifaceted practice. In this artwork, Rasheed uses what she calls a "score"—as in guidance from composer to musician—to embrace the participatory nature of learning as an invitation to play. It is a set of drawings with prompts that guide the user to engage with writing through a series of interventions that result in a drawing to be given as a gift to a friend.

A SCORE IS AN INVITATION TO PLAY; AN ALGORITHM THAT CREATES GENERATIVE BOUNDARIES; A CONSTRAINT THAT LEADS YOU TO UNEXPECTED PATHWAYS; A PROMPT TO DO OTHER WISE.

Yet Another Score for Feral Translation, 2025

A Score for Feral Translation

2020

@ MASS MOCA
FOR THE 'KISSING THROUGH A CURTAIN' GROUP EXHIBITION CURATED BY ALEXANDRA FORADAS [COMMISSIONED PUBLICATION CONTRIBUTION]

During this last year, I would doodle oblong arcs and circles adorned with crooked tangent lines.

A tangent is a line that touches the circle at exactly one point without ever entering the circle's interior. The interior is sacred and thus prohibited. The tangent line kisses the circle, but only once. A fleeting and casual point of contact before a sudden departure. An itinerancy of sorts.

In March, I made an impromptu studio visit with an artist. In our conversations about translation, cryptography, and approximation, she mentioned Walter Benjamin's comparison of translation to tangent lines. After some digging, I found an excerpt from Benjamin's *The Task of the Translator* (1923) after he asks the question, "And what of the sense in its importance for the relationship between translation and original?":

> A simile may help here. Just as a tangent touches a circle lightly and at but one point, with this touch rather than with the point setting the law according to which it is to continue on its straight path to infinity, a translation touches the original lightly and only at the infinitely small point of the sense, thereupon pursuing its own course according to the laws of fidelity in the freedom of linguistic flux.

What follows is a score for feral translation. An invitation to kiss a sentence, gently, before finding another sentence to kiss. And another. And another.

2025

yet another score for feral translation

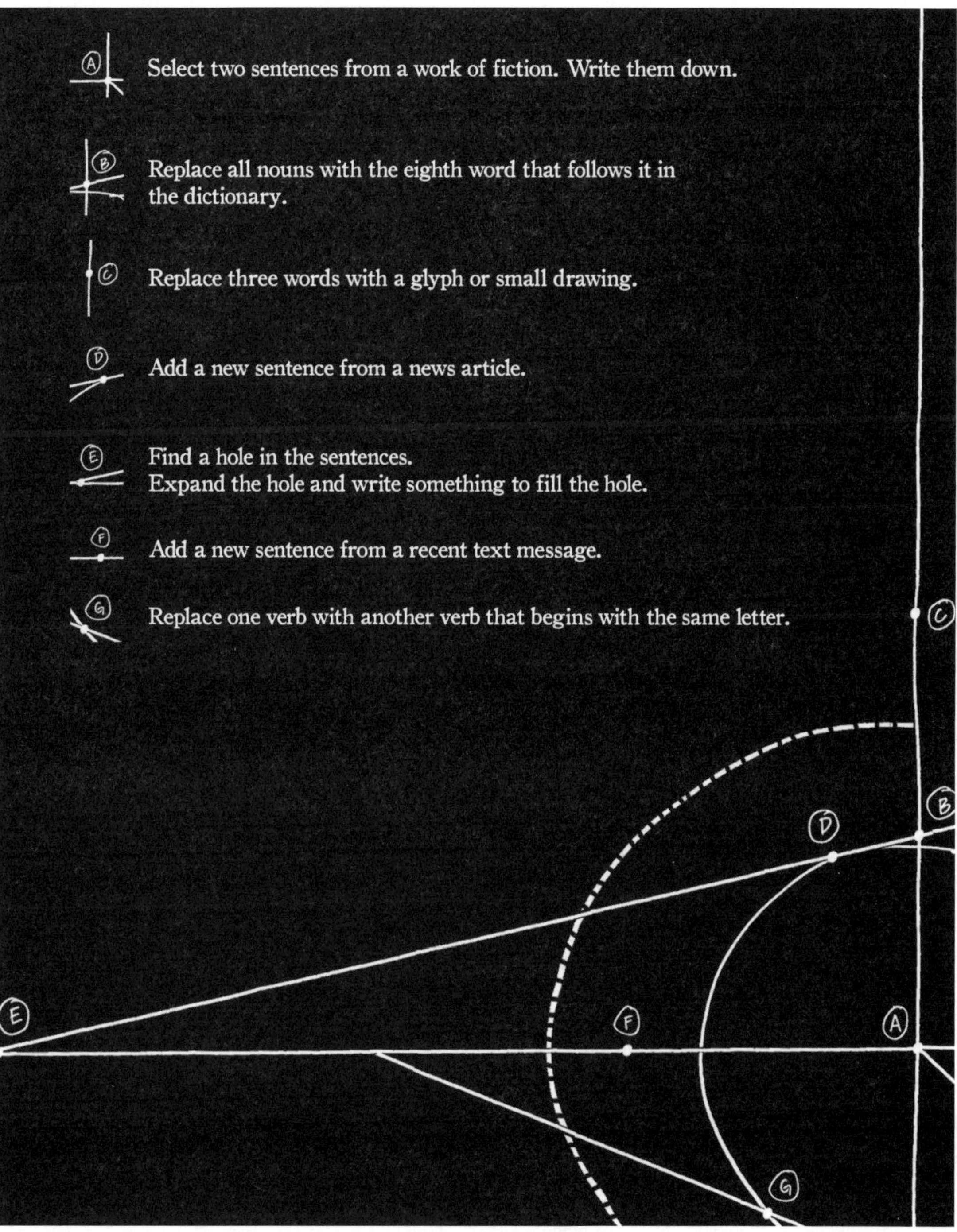
A Select two sentences from a work of fiction. Write them down.
B Replace all nouns with the eighth word that follows it in the dictionary.
C Replace three words with a glyph or small drawing.
D Add a new sentence from a news article.
E Find a hole in the sentences. Expand the hole and write something to fill the hole.
F Add a new sentence from a recent text message.
G Replace one verb with another verb that begins with the same letter.
C
B
D
E
F
A
G

IV. Museums and Biennials

Museums and biennials have a different relationship to the public than universities and alternative spaces. The tendency for collections or exhibitions to address a public creates an expectation of civic engagement that is far beyond what other kinds of education platforms like universities or alternative spaces practice.

In an essay that draws from his experience as an artist, museum educator, and university professor, Pablo Helguera talks about how museums and universities can learn from each other. He advocates for a merging of what he calls the *forum* and *temple* models of museums, along with formal and informal methods of education. Elsewhere, museum director Manuel Borja-Villel and artist and critic Marcelo Expósito discuss replacing an education department with one dedicated to public programs at the Museu d'Art Contemporani de Barcelona (MACBA). This emphasis on the public was meant to set up the potential for diverse groups to learn from each other. It's a notion echoed in curator Dominic Willsdon's essay, which refers to Borja-Villel's claim that education is an encounter between someone who knows something and someone who knows something else, a utopian model for what education can do. Willsdon's essay, narrating key moments in his experiences in museum education, emphasizes the idea of a public museum as a space where strangers meet, and his belief in institutions as structures that maintain that possibility within civic society. In a conversation between Willsdon, Magalí Arriola, Johanna Burton, and Sally Tallant, these museum directors, who all have deep histories in educational practice, talk about maintaining a belief in institutions at a time when there has been a crisis of belief in them.

In the introduction, I referred to the plan for Manifesta 6 to turn a biennial into a school. While this plan eventually failed, it was a model for education to function as an iconoclastic cudgel, to break the conventional mold with something radically different. This sentiment is very different from the belief that institutions must be maintained to serve a public. In Willsdon's conversation with artist and curator Mônica Hoff about the 9th Mercosul Biennial, it becomes clear that, in the context of Porto Alegre, Brazil, the biennial's long-term commitment shows that building and maintaining an institution dedicated to learning can indeed serve this purpose. As Hoff says, a teacher is an important agent in civil society, producing citizen subjects. In her interview, curator Manuela Moscoso notes that through her experience working in Brazil on the Bienal das Amazônias, she was reminded how different publics respond to the call for participatory educational projects differently. For example, she found that the public in Brazil was much more likely to respond than the public for a biennial in Ecuador.

Following this notion of context, in their conversation about biennials, curators and directors Sofía Olascoaga, Lucía Sanromán, Sally Tallant, and Willsdon underscore that perennial exhibitions often center on the life of a city. In a conversation about education at the Sharjah Art Foundation, educator Noora Al Mualla notes that the biennial has helped to develop the urban fabric. One example is a theater built for one biennial edition that has become a platform for other kinds of programming. In a conversation with Zeina Arida about her director's role at the Mathaf in Doha, she notes that the institution is located in Education City, a zone that invites collaboration between universities and museums. Finally, in a conversation with educator and scholar Thiago Gil de Oliveira Virava about the São Paulo Biennial as an educational context, he notes that schoolteachers were engaged with materials that helped them mediate the experience of the exhibition with their students, including projects by artists that were explicitly pedagogical. One of these, *The Tree School*, was a collaboration between Campus in Camps and Grupo Contrafilé. It is presented here on page 336–55.

These interviews and roundtables were an opportunity to assess recent history, ask about the present, and speculate about how we should move forward. Today, with the hardening of identitarian and nationalist sentiments, a social contract predicated on museums or biennials as open forums for discourse is neither self-evident nor universally assumed. Biennials emerged during a period of globalization that enabled them to become spaces for encounter and connection. As a new global order emerges, is this potential sustainable?

Cardinal Points in Art Learning

Pablo Helguera

As one takes on the task of understanding what higher education art programs can learn from museum education, I find it helpful to first understand the nuances of how learning occurs in both environments, to establish four cardinal points—two sets of opposite concepts, one associated with the notion of museum, and the other with the notion of school. While these categories might appear too broad and prescriptive at times, I believe they are useful to understand key aspects of the question at hand.

1. "Temple" versus "Forum"

From the time when the modern notion of the art museum was first developed, those who have built and run these institutions have implicitly or explicitly contended with the question of whether they should function as a "temple or a forum," in a characterization made in an essay in 1971 by the then Brooklyn Museum director Duncan F. Cameron.[1] The idea of the institution being a "temple" was rooted in the understanding that museums are keepers of culture and preservers of heritage, making that heritage available to the viewing public for educational purposes. The notion of the museum being a "forum" is predicated on the principle that museums should not be mausoleums of the past but active participants and brokers of a dialogue about the present. The "temple" position argues that the priority of the museum should be to display the history, whereas the "forum" position argues that museums lose relevance when they become mere repositories of historical material.

The "museum as temple" perspective is one where the institution prioritizes its role as a keeper of culture as well as a center and source for scholarship. From this perspective, the museum's relevance to the present often lies in its ability to serve as contextualizing interlocutor of the present through the presentation of historical material. The "museum as forum" perspective, which is more typically embraced by contemporary art museums, prioritizes a more journalistic, instead of historic, engagement with the current moment, presenting works by artists that represent present-day culture and concerns. The allegiance to the forum model tends to be invoked in grant proposals, mission statements, and any place where the institution is presented as a thought leader and a model for access and inclusivity in public discourse. The temple tends to be implicitly present in language that refers to the museum as a keeper of artistic treasures and cultural heritage, and even in instances where it emphasizes itself as a center for research and scholarship.

In my education museum work I often encountered how versions of the temple and the forum collided and also were interpreted differently, among both the education and the curatorial staff.

In 2007, when I was first hired as head of public programs at the Museum of Modern Art in New York, one of my roles was to oversee the gallery lecture program. The two dozen or so freelance gallery lecturers who worked in the program were very experienced and knowledgeable professionals, almost all of them with advanced degrees in art history and specialized in different areas such as architecture, photography, and early twentieth-century art. At the time, museum education had already moved on from the time when straightforward lecturing was considered best practice and it had been replaced by a much more interactive learning approach. In recognition of that fact, we sought to update our practices and, among other things, changed the term "gallery lecturer" to "gallery educator." This was a difficult shift for some of them, I believe because they saw the term "lecturer" as having a more respectable interpretation to the term "educator." On one occasion, at a meeting with a senior curator at MoMA to discuss an upcoming exhibition, we had a discussion regarding the gallery educator's role, emphasizing the importance of their role in interpreting the exhibitions. One of them said to the curator, "We are scholars." Our top curator took issue with that statement and tersely replied: "I want to let you know that us curators are also scholars."

It was a simple comment that nonetheless, at least to me, illustrated quite a bit about the subtle tension between academia and curatorial practice. Both curators and art historians often share the same initial academic path (such as obtaining a graduate degree in art history, although the curatorial field has expanded with the creation of specialized Master of Arts degrees in curating). However, curators truly cut their teeth working in museums, initially as curatorial assistants and eventually in more senior capacities. Curating is a hands-on practice that involves not just research, but institutional and administrative expertise, aside from its very public nature.

In reality, art historical scholarship and curating are complementary specialties, because both explore similar questions around art, be it through exhibition making or writing. For that reason, it is not uncommon for curators to seek the validation of scholars and vice versa, that is—for scholars to wish that their work had the same level of public visibility as that of

1 Duncan Cameron, "The Museum, a Temple or the Forum," in *The Journal of World History* special number, "Museums, Society, Knowledge" (1972). Duncan F. Cameron, "The Museum, a Temple or the Forum," Curator: *The Museum Journal* 14, no. 1 (March 1971), 11–24.

exhibition-makers, and for curators to wish that their work be seen, as the chief curator noted in that comment, as scholarship.

The exchange I previously mentioned also illustrates the way in which both curators and gallery lecturers often saw themselves: as individuals who could have the scholarship to accurately present and guard art history and, as to the gallery lecturers, their ability to create a framework of context and conversation to allow the public to understand and connect with the work. Yet in both instances (the curator and gallery educators), as I have observed over time, their primary aspiration was to be respected as scholars, not as popularizers of modern and contemporary art, as fine scholarship is what is most valued in the upper echelons of the art world.

One way to understand how they saw their respective educational and research roles is precisely by examining the concepts of formal versus informal education.

2. Formal versus Informal Education

Parallel to the temple/forum opposition, and somewhat related to it, is the question of how learning is complemented outside of formal structures, such as a degree-granting programs.

Informal education is generally defined as that kind of learning that takes place outside of the boundaries of our school life, from kindergarten to college; with the recognition that learning is an inherent aspect of being human and that never ends over the course of our lifetimes. According to a 2010 study, only 5 percent of an American's lifetime is spent in a classroom,[2] which means that anything else that we learn during the remaining 95 percent of our lives constitutes informal education.

Informal education is much more associated with leisure activities—ranging from watching a tutorial video or reading a book about a topic of interest to taking a continuing-education class. Because informal education does not have the assessment mechanisms typically required by schools or universities, the personal motivations and interests in learning (more than the need to fulfill an academic degree) are what often drives an individual.

However, informal education can also be understood as on-the-job training. The fact that art operates in the public sphere makes fieldwork experience paramount, and this can only be acquired by applying the ideas of art in the public sphere in public environments, such as museums and other exhibiting spaces. The proof of having successfully worked in these spaces (either by exhibiting, curating, or engaging publics) becomes a way by which an art professional's experience can be best assessed and measured; conversely, artists, curators, and educators who only hold a university degree and have no track record of applying their practice will have a much harder time gaining professional opportunities.

Both the concepts of informal and formal education also tend to be misinterpreted and stereotyped. For the last fifty years, formal (academic) education has been the target of fierce critiques, from Ivan Illich to bell hooks, primarily around the institutionalization of learning, followed by critiques in the 1990s around education as a for-profit industry (as referred to by the term "the education industrial complex"). As to informal education, this concept is often associated with hobbyism—a loosely

2 Lynn D. Dierking and John H. Falk, "The 95 Percent Solution: School Is Not Where Most Americans Learn Most of Their Science," *American Scientist* 98, no. 6 (November 2010), 486–493.

structured activity that has more of a social than a learning objective, which is not properly assessed and lacks the rigor and discipline needed to truly attain deep knowledge. In its most problematic forms, where leisure is privileged over critical thinking, informal education is derided as "edutainment."

While museums offer continuing-education programs, lectures, studio classes, and teacher and family workshops, and because the participation in their educational activities rarely involves a selection process beyond a registration fee, they are generally regarded as informal education spaces. My work over many years was to organize and offer such programs to the public. At the same time, I was often required to balance these offerings with more scholarly programs such as symposia, panel discussions, and academic lectures, often at the request of curators and senior leadership who wanted the museum to position itself as a leader in scholarship. And the key question my colleagues and I had to confront was how we could offer an array of programs that could fulfill the various content and audience goals before us: that is, to serve as an important source of research, reflection, and discussion about art at all the levels of specialization in the arts, from the general public and families to scholars.

As to higher education, it is understood that practical, real-world experience is a critical need for anyone pursuing a degree, which is the role that, ostensibly, internships and fellowships play. Such was the case of the beginning of my professional career as an artist, which took place in parallel, somewhat accidentally, with the beginning of a three-decade career in art museum education. I obtained my BFA at the School of the Art Institute of Chicago, a leading American art school that is primarily known for its connection to the eponymous, world-famous museum. It is not generally known that the school, founded in 1866, preceded the creation of the museum by more than two decades. The museum's collection, as with various other nineteenth-century art academies, served the dual purpose of being a study collection for students as well as a resource for the public.

At the Art institute of Chicago, the museum and the school's relationship has historically been uneasy in many respects, from the standpoint of governance and budgeting to administrative autonomy and the very subject of innovation. As an encyclopedic museum with a vast collection of art historically significant as well as famous and popular works, the Art Institute produces blockbuster, revenue-generating exhibitions that cater to both a tourist and local audiences; the school has its own reputation for experimentation and a rebellious stance against the status quo. I happened to straddle between the two institutions when, as an art student, I did an internship in the department of Africa, Oceania, and the Americas at the Art Institute; I would change my dirty studio clothes into office clothes and walk through the hallway and the pristine, climate-controlled galleries of the museum and into the museum's offices. Little did I know that my professional life would be an ongoing negotiation and balancing between the museum and the studio. Toward the end of my student years, I took on another internship, this time at what was then called the Mexican Fine Arts Center Museum (now renamed as National Museum of Mexican Art). This internship was important to me not just because I was able to learn real-life art education skills working with various publics, but because it allowed me to understand critical issues around community art and, more importantly, allowed me to connect with the Mexican immigrant community and confront questions about my own relationship, as both artist and individual, with my Mexican heritage.

In any case, the for-credit paid work that I pursued at the Art Institute and later at the Mexican Fine Arts Center Museum, unbeknownst to me, would later lead me to initiate a twenty-nine-year museum career. Furthermore, I learned over those years that while most of my colleagues and coworkers generally did possess art history or studio degrees, the vast majority of what they learned was through on-the-job training and the practical experience of working within an arts organization.

Thus, formal and informal education are complementary aspects of learning, and one can't be a replacement for the other.

3. Post-Studio Lessons and Productive Tensions

The multiple professional roles I have played in the arts (as a practicing artist, a museum professional, and more recently as university faculty) have helped me realize how both the museum and the university can learn from each other.

Higher education offers a privileged environment that is separate from the real world, which is why practical experiences (such as the museum internship I was able to obtain) are critical. The relationship between museums and art schools in this way can be very productive, as students can gain access to real-life understanding of how art engages the public. Education departments of university museums (I think of examples such as the RISD Museum and the ASU Museum, institutions with which I've had the opportunity to work as an artist) help students understand the role that art plays in society, outside of the bubble of academia. It is critical for studio programs to help art students reflect on how their artistic practices can engage with environments that go beyond the studio.

In addition, I learned that the benefit of doing public engagement in a museum goes beyond the ability to communicate and connect with publics; it is the opportunity of understanding what it means to work within an institutional context and learn the necessary skills to ideate, develop, and implement projects, often in teams, fulfilling institutional goals and understanding the needs and requirements of different publics.

In my current role as director of the Master's program of Art Entrepreneurship at the New School's College of Performing Arts, I work with emerging artists in the fields of classical music, theater, and jazz to help them expand their practices outside of the expected conventions of the stage, learning socially engaged art methodologies alongside administrative and management skills that will allow them to forge their own professional paths.

Conversely, an area where museums could learn from the art academy is in the presentation and experience of the artistic process. We consistently received feedback from visitors at MoMA about their interest and desire to understand how art works are made. Programs that display the artistic process help bring the artwork to life and dispel the idealized aura that works in galleries usually attain.

In 2009, the artist Luis Camnitzer created a piece consisting of a sign that is to be affixed to the façade of a museum. It reads, "The museum is a school: the artist learns to communicate, the public learns to make connections." The phrase embodies the extensive thinking by Camnitzer on the pedagogical mission of the museum, which he has sought to implement wherever he has worked as a pedagogical curator in institutions and biennials.

With the phrase "the museum is a school," Camnitzer is making a statement about how central the pedagogical function of the museum ought to be. This statement is even more meaningful for those of us who have worked in education in museums, where the (implicit or explicit) hierarchy is that the education department is primarily a support area for the curatorial program.

While Camnitzer's provocation has never been fully embraced by the art-museum world (although the piece has been installed on several museum facades and he has tested out his pedagogical ideas while working in various institutions), the implicit question that those of us who work or have worked in art museums (whether in education or curatorial or other programmatic areas) have dealt with over the years is how to make the museum fulfill the functions of interlocutor, documenter, contextualizer, and thought leader around the art of our time; in other words, how to truly transform the art museum into an educational institution.

And this pursuit can gain much from understanding the context of a place where formal versus informal pedagogy and temple versus forum intersect. Both the art academy and the museum need productive tensions to move forward. While we might define certain museums as following a "temple" or "forum" model, both perceptions coexist in practice, and in fact might need one another to function in productive tension.

I confess that over the course of my museum career I favored the "forum" and "informal" models of learning, with the belief that the museum has to be a platform for debate and take advantage of the unique space and create formats to include the views of individuals both inside and outside of art practice. Similarly, I am partial to informal learning, in part because this is how I learned about museum art education—through personal experience and professional practice, not through obtaining an education degree—which also led to my embracing pragmatism as a philosophy of education.

Because I was interested in experiential learning, I sought to break away from the classroom and auditorium, whose architecture tends to dictate the type of pedagogical experience that can be had (often of a hierarchical nature). My colleagues and I gravitated to galleries as the spaces where conversations and experiences could be had, given that, in the end, the original artworks are the reason for being (and the purpose of learning) in museums. However, over the years I also recognized that more traditional approaches (temple/forum) can also be useful to complement to the more experimental/experiential ones.

My eventual recognition of this fact began to emerge during a symposium I organized in 2002 at the Solomon R. Guggenheim Museum, "The Museum as Medium," on the subject of institutional critique in museums. During a panel discussion in this symposium, curator Lynne Cooke made an observation that has stayed with me until now: she argued, in broad strokes, that the notion of innovation in curating could sometimes be hollow, and that certain forms of traditional curating are not only appropriate but necessary. In other words, installing an exhibition of Minimalist art following the conventions of how it was exhibited initially (say, reconstructing Donald Judd's first solo exhibition in New York exactly as it happened) is very important in order to respect historical accuracy. To install those works in an experimental way could be interesting but would not give the public an accurate picture of the historical dimension of those early works, and, by extension, would not allow the visitor to form their own opinions around those works.

I belong to a generation of museum educators who came of age when teaching methodologies were prevalent, such as VTS (Visual Thinking Strategies), created by Abigail Housen and Phillip Yenawine in the late 1980s and early '90s. Methodologies are exciting to learn, and it gives one great satisfaction to implement them successfully; they often yield similar results and the more one uses and masters the methodology the easier it becomes to implement it. However, the more one applies it, the more it becomes the hammer for which everything looks like a nail—what is known as Maslow's hammer or the law of the instrument. This is true about education, curating, and art practice itself: experimental art forms undergo a period when they are new and exciting, then they enter the mainstream and become academic practices, following prescribed patterns. After that it is time to create new forms that will challenge the previous ones.

Today, no one set of principles dominates, but rather they coexist and intermix in various approaches. We have now grown accustomed to the idea that art genres blur and morph, and we celebrate the diversity of artistic languages instead of insisting on a uniform set of aesthetic and ideological principles—as early twentieth-century avant-garde movements tended to express in their manifestos.

What I started recognizing in my museum-education practice was that while this diversity of approaches and languages exists in contemporary art, we still sought to find and maintain unitary methodologies. This resulted in flattening the interpretive possibilities for art works that did not conform to certain expectations and conventions. (For example, it is difficult to use VTS to interpret socially engaged art as opposed to, say, an abstract painting.) The question then becomes, why not draw from the same philosophy of diversity of visual languages that artists employ? Why not emphasize using a diversity of interpretive tools instead of a single methodology?

So, without the pretense of outlining a methodology or manifesto, my humble suggestion is to consider the cardinal points of temple/forum and formal/informal education in both museums and academia to create productive tension. This was, in fact, an approach that I began taking in my own work starting in the early 2000s, drawing from elements of relational aesthetics and institutional critique to create pedagogical projects. In 2002, I created *El Instituto de la Telenovela*—a nomadic research center that studied the socioeconomic impact of Mexican soap operas in Eastern Europe. The project, which opened in Ljubljana, Slovenia, in 2002, took the form of an exhibition/installation, with a space evoking the modernist architecture of Luis Barragán, but doubled as a research and education center that offered information about the history of the Mexican soap opera and its cultural and economic influence around the world. The creation of a tongue-in-cheek "temple" (i.e., an institution devoted to the research of soap operas) merged with the more experiential (read: informal) ways in which audiences interact with exhibitions (with play being an important enticement for learning). A performance lecture I developed as part of this project, *Theatrum Anatomicum (or How to Dissect a Melodrama)*, which consisted in of two simultaneous/intertwining performance lectures on the subjects of Dutch anatomical theaters and the history of the Mexican soap opera, sought to merge academia and performance art.

Some of the projects I helped lead during my tenure in the education department at MoMA had a similar spirit of merging forum and temple, formal and informal methods. Sometimes they included the production of an event that would have all those qualities, as in a series of programs I organized termed as the Contemporary Art Forum. These events included formal auditorium presentations (lectures and panel discussions) but also more experimental components such as workshops, field trips, and performances. At the reception for one of those events we contracted a Colombian party bus, which broke away from the convention of the traditional cocktail reception after a professional gathering.

Perhaps a key element for freer experimentation in both museums and higher education institutions is the ability to recognize and consciously overcome self-imposed administrative boundaries of time, budgets, and other artificial parameters, but also understand how they relate to the environments and conditions under which learning takes place. But as I have also tried to show, museums and universities can learn much from borrowing from one another's approaches and productively altering the balance of temple/forum and formal/informal education. Such an approach can help revitalize knowledge production to keep learning institutions viable and vital resources.

Someone Who Knows Something... and Someone Who Knows Something Else

Dominic Asmall Willsdon and Mônica Hoff talk about the Bienal do Mercusol

Dominic Asmall Willsdon Hi, Mônica, good morning from San Francisco. I am happy to have the chance to correspond in this way. Let me ask you, first, what issues in education are currently most urgent in Rio Grande do Sul, Brazil. What kinds of questions are discussed—in the media, in government, among teachers—about the educational system? I ask this because the Bienal do Mercosul is an institution of informal education that works, in one way or another, to supplement formal schooling, so the conditions of formal schooling are our primary context. But more immediately, I am interested to hear whether educational concerns are any part of the current protests about public services that are taking place in Brazil.

Mônica Hoff Hi, Dominic, good morning from Porto Alegre. I'm also very happy to correspond with you. In the recent months of intense protests in Brazil, there has been much discussion about what kind of demonstration this is: Does it have to do with specific classes or civil society as a whole? In fact, it is impossible to separate one from the other—at least it should be, shouldn't it? A teacher, for instance, is not someone isolated. A teacher is perhaps one of the main agents in the context of society. From his or her classroom, there will emerge many citizens who invariably will be part of a political, economic, and social system already established. They will be employees or employers, parents, consumers, opinion-makers, customers, patients, managers, and even teachers.

In Rio Grande do Sul, the teachers' union is very strong and organized and has been taking to the streets regularly for many, many years. However, the rest of civil society neither supports nor participates actively in these demonstrations, that is, they don't take to the streets, occupy the city, search for improvement. Civil society does not give due importance to those claims, because it sees them as claims from that particular class, and therefore it feels released from the obligation to actively participate. After all, teachers are just "one class" of society and their issues don't affect the rest of it in a direct way.

I have been following the demonstrations closely and I have never seen so many people in the streets. I have never seen so many people experiencing and understanding, at the same time, what education and citizenship actually are. They might not even perceive that instantly, but that is indeed education. Arguing about it is education. Questioning it is education.

As for the most pressing question regarding education, from the point of view of teachers, it is category valuation. And, when I say *valuation*, I mean: first, respect for the minimum wage approved by the National Congress; second, better wages (the wages of teachers who work primarily in public schools are very low); third, better working conditions. At the same time, among the questions posed by other groups of civil society, that is, students, the self-employed, or retirees, we find: excessive expenses that the Brazilian cities—and, therefore, the public administration—are incurring by hosting the soccer World Cup, expenses that might as well be geared toward education, not to mention the lack of investment in public spaces and transportation.

These issues have grown like a snowball and are triggering a series of other movements of society geared toward organizing in assemblies held on the streets to discuss and define collective agendas, and demand that the public budget be directed to other services, for example.

DW Yes, it is an endless topic. I remember you talking last year about low pay for teachers as an issue in Brazil, and I said it was no less so in the United States. But I am interested in when the issue is not about money, or when a money issue expresses something else, perhaps something more abstract or fundamental. I would argue, for example, that the fundamental issue in the United States is one of competition—between students, between teachers, between schools, and ultimately between nations (in terms of economic performance).

I remember you talking, for another example, about *time* as a problem for teachers in Brazil. If we start to think about *time* and *space* as educational problems, we might already be saying something about why the pedagogical program of the 9th Bienal do Mercosul has evolved in the way that it has.

MH I remember that conversation, and especially about the presence of the figure of time in education (the pedagogical time; the teacher's time; saving time; the expected time). Actually, I can't detach one from the other, and, of course, the idea of competitiveness embedded in education is a crucial factor. Not only in Brazil, but with great emphasis here, children are educated to be successful (whatever that means). And this "to be successful" is closely related to a world whose metric is competition, related to the idea of productivity, and related to the condition of planned obsolescence.

Unfortunately, in Brazil, for some time now, education has to be measured by a productivity scale guided by the visibility of what is produced. This is the logic imposed by the Ministry of Education and federal programs upon graduate programs and, in a more veiled way, it seems to be addressed to basic education as well. Jerome Bruner, a well-known American psychologist and researcher in the field of children's development, states that education has to be fun. According to Bruner, a great part of the learning process takes place because of fun. The schools we have, however, are not fun places, they do not follow the logic of pleasure, they don't handle time so as to allow space for dialogue and curiosity.

The logic of education nowadays crushes time and obviously sets a rhythm that betrays itself from beginning to end. In this sense, non-formal educational initiatives, perhaps due to the fact that they don't follow curriculum and are more experimental, seem much more powerful. And I don't mean only those initiatives that come at the expense of a possible lack of formal education, but the initiatives that take place before that, in the public sphere: in classrooms without rooms, so to speak.

For years, much has been discussed about methods of teaching and learning processes. There is still debate about content and behavior. However, little is said about the form, that is, about the interference of physical and temporal structures in education, about how architecture and workload influence the real context of education. Educational theories are constantly imported and revised, but the architecture of schools and time allocated to classes in Brazil, in practice, follow the same educational logic of a hundred years ago, and there seems to be not much discussion about them. I tend to believe that there is no innovative pedagogy that will stand the school architecture of most Brazilian schools. Foucault enjoys high esteem here—the difference between them and the architecture of many prisons is virtually nil. And it really would not be that big a problem if the prisons were what they were supposed to be: spaces dedicated to education and "rehabilitation" and to socializing. But they are not and will never be, because it doesn't matter to civil society. It learned to work considering education as something out of reach, the function of others. *Ou topos*, utopia.

Regarding the issue of time, in the same manner, no pedagogy can survive as a living, pleasurable, and freeing process by conditioning learning to periods of fifty minutes. What are fifty minutes? Five units of ten minutes? Three thousand seconds? It's just one way of representing the quantification of time. Time spent in an art class is one and in a physical education class is another. The time employed to read a text is one and that employed to see an image is another. The time of a biology class in a closed room is completely different from the same class in a garden. On the other hand, there is the teacher's time—the (non) existence of that time (to think, to have fun, to experience)—that, for me, is completely related to the place education occupies in our lives.

It seems to me that one of the issues is that education wrongfully needs to be a "place of learning." And learning simply cannot mean fun, pleasure, and freedom.

DW Let me just note two things prompted by what you wrote before and now. One is about equality. Equality, the problem of inequality, the idea that inequality is a problem—this is central to this unexpected new era of protests. It goes beyond economic equality. In my city, people have taken to the streets in recent days, too, but it is to celebrate marriage equality, following two decisions by the Supreme Court of the United States. So how should we understand equality in education? The second thing is about visibility. One of the reasons why issues to do with public parks (or urban public spaces, generally), as in Turkey, and public transport can mobilize people, and for good reasons, is that these things are so visible, and embody so visibly what we seek to hold in common. Education is much less visible. Schools are turned inward on themselves. It is a big question: How can education be seen widely as a public good? Put the two together: how can equality in education be seen as a public good? How can we find some language, and some images, to represent equality in education now that education has become so much about individual achievement? There might be a role for art and cultural institutions in this, whether museums or biennials. Such institutions are certainly visible and public-facing; they are perhaps the most spectacularly visible sites of informal education. What can we do, in service of educational equality, with that visibility?

MH On the one hand, I think that the visibility of education is inherent to its effectiveness—in order to be seen, it has to be exercised. On the other hand, I believe that education is (and should be) invisible. That is its place. Perhaps art is the crux of it all, because it has the power to address education without apparently being it. There are a lot of projects and actions that can be examples of that, but I'd rather mention Colombia's case, particularly the administration of Antanas Mockus in Bogotá, which invested in seemingly simple poetic actions performed in public spaces to generate education. From an intentional urban quasi-chaos, he managed to address social and educational issues that were historically complex. It worked, to some extent. People learned when they began to see themselves as a significant part of a larger (and collective) context.

In the context of art institutions, yes, I do believe in the power of art institutions in the "rise" of education. Otherwise, I would not be at the Bienal do Mercosul. But I'm also afraid of it, because, for this to happen, there must be an inversion in the market logic of such institutions so that they begin to operate in the field of the real. Don't you think?

DW You have much more understanding of biennials than I do. It is only recently that I have been invited to think about what a biennial can be, specifically as an educational platform. I hear skepticism from many perspectives about the biennial as a form. Sometimes this has to do with how biennials promote an economics of the event. Cities have become landscapes of the event (cultural, corporate, sporting, etc.); they trade in events. Even people who are not so skeptical of biennials can seem exhausted by them. I have a sense (that is not based on much experience) that this exhaustion (shading back into skepticism) might allow for a reconsideration of what biennials are. It can lead us to think different things about how a biennial dwells in a city, how it abides in a place, not for a number of weeks and months, but over years. The Bienal do Mercosul already has something of this ongoing, longer-term identity—and, more than anyone, it has been your work that has created it. It struck me very much how, at the beginning of the process to create this ninth edition, so much was already in place: structures, a culture, an active legacy, a set of expectations. The Bienal do Mercosul seems already to be less a series of events and more like a single, continuous entity that pulses through the city, through the region, every two years. Something of this ongoing character is being proposed, right now, for example, by those who are rethinking the biennials in Santa Fe and Liverpool.

If a biennial is something supported by a city, what is it to think of a city as a whole as a space of learning—or even as an educator? Or a classroom without rooms, to use your phrase. Here is a whimsical thought that has been with me for a while. Like a lot of people, I was influenced, years ago, by Robert Venturi, Denise Scott Brown, and Steven Izenour's *Learning from Las Vegas* (1972). (As it happens, there seems to be a fresh interest in this; there have been a few recent publications reflecting on it: an edition by Supercrit and a couple of books coedited or authored by Aron Vinegar and an exhibition at Yale in 2009.) But I find myself thinking: What if we read *Learning from Las Vegas* not as a book about Las Vegas or about architecture, primarily, but as a book about learning? And how was Las Vegas, in 1972, a teacher? And is there a difference between its pedagogy and its curriculum? Can we think of the built environment of Las Vegas as its curriculum, and its social landscape as its pedagogy?

You talked about how school architecture disciplines educational experience. We know that for a hundred years or more, progressive educators have sought to pursue educational ends by architectural means. If there are affinities between education and architecture, there are equally affinities between deschooling (or unschooling) and anarchitecture. At the extreme, in this direction, might be the Forest Schools movement. Feeling constrained by the classroom? Go outside! There is some truth in this intertwining of educational and spatial planning. You only have to look at how the layout of classrooms has changed in the last century (from fixed rows of seating to collaborative islands, for example). I have some reservations, though, about how freedom is interpreted as the absence of constraint. (I am also skeptical about the progressive claims in favor of unschooling; in the debate last year across the publications Slate and *n+1* between Astra Taylor and Dana Goldstein, I'm with Goldstein.) Thinking about the city as a classroom might let us interpret educational experience architecturally, without this opposition of in school=unfree, unschool=free. There is nothing free about the space of cities, but their constraints and opportunities may be more expansive and multifaceted than those of the classroom. Certainly, our pedagogical program for this 9th Bienal, *Cloud Formations*, is an experiment with this larger landscape of the city, and beyond. How do you see the relationship, Mônica, between these citywide educational experiences and those of the classroom or lecture theater? And what kind of educator is Porto Alegre?

Also, one other thing in response to something you wrote earlier. I hear you asserting the importance of both pleasure and equality. Do you think these values are in tension at all? I would choose equality over pleasure any time. The worst thing that you can say about an education system is not that it is boring, but that it is unjust. This might be too large an issue to address here.

MH I see that *Learning from Las Vegas* has been a watershed for you. Perhaps it had on you the same impact that the book *Estetica da Ginga—an Arquitectura das favelas atraves da obra de Hélio Oiticica*

[The aesthetics of Ginga: the favelas architecture through the work of Hélio Oiticica] and some essays by Frederico Morais about the city as educator had on me a few years back. In the book, the author Paola Berenstein Jacques uses Oiticica's climbing of the *morro* [the hills, where the favelas are located in Rio] to take some sort of artistic, architectonic, and sociocultural inventory of this experience, evoking the voice of the community and the favela as a collective, as a space for social interaction, as an architectural landscape and political site. This helped me see the city as a space of expansion and contraction, as a "soft" and impermanent place, regardless of its massive architectural magnificence. A place in which pedagogy does exist, but the curriculum, as we devise it, doesn't.

This constitutes a "walking pedagogy" of sorts—an experimental pedagogy, which evolves on the way and has the size of the step. A sort of poor pedagogy, in the words of Jan Masschelein, or a pedagogy of the "bond." To me, the educational process of the Bienal do Mercosul lies in this imprecise micropolitics of the encounter. The biennial exhibitions are fundamental as a manner of "presentifying," putting on the agenda, in other words, lending visibility to the invisibilities of the present. And this per se is very important. But, nowadays, I see them as part of an endless process which takes place continuously in time and space in different ways, in which the exhibitions are no longer the pinnacle of the process, but one of the programs.

Thinking on the Porto Alegre context and, more precisely, about the Bienal do Mercosul, I sincerely cannot see it as a cultural institution that organizes a big art show every two years, but as an estuary, a liquid transitional environment between something apparently calm, permanent, silent, and necessary for a community (a river), and something big, external, wild, ravishing, notably geopolitical, and which allows for connections and contrasts with "distant lands" (the ocean). Perhaps that is why the Bienal do Mercosul isn't identified (outside the local context) as a large event of irreparable proportions. It is commonly seen as a biennial of more "human" proportions, perhaps as a broad pedagogical project—something that has a beginning but has no end.

Therefore I cannot separate the different editions, especially in terms of their pedagogical proposals. The curatorship of Luis Camnitzer, Marina de Caro, and Pablo Helguera don't seem to me to be in any way divergent; on the contrary, they only make sense together, overlapped, crossed over, in dialogue and having the city/community as mediator. In this sense, we cannot speak of different biennials, but one that, in the worst-case scenario, revises itself every two years, its inconspicuous permanence being, in fact, what sustains it and gives it breath.

In order to think about the educational issue in the 9th Bienal, I tried to focus on the more experimental beginnings of the pedagogical project's path (2006–2013), orchestrating what was already there, just removing its walls, allowing it to have rhythm and flow, to walk. I see myself "de-walking," in a certain way, that is, reviewing what has already been walked, pinpointing things here and there, reconsidering, putting old perceptions in dialogue with new hopes. Pedagogy seems to be that to me: not a metric, a proposal, but an organic process which walks the walk. If we return to the beginning of our conversation, in which we spoke of the demonstrations which are taking place in Brazil and across the globe, this will become even more evident. The city's occupation is, in fact, the occupation of a place called education—not only for those who occupy it physically and/or ideologically, but also for those who are occupied in not seeing it or escaping from it.

On *Cloud Formations*, the two initial steps toward that were: firstly, to tear down the physical walls (of the school, or the educational environment of the Bienal, two marks for behavior and perception), trying to look in the direction they do not always look to, making the actions and activities happen within the body of the city, in socialization spaces such as streets, squares, subway stations, public buildings; spaces unrelated to art or education, but to perspectives related to the relationship of man with nature, the public sphere, energy production, and the idea of the common good such as water-treatment stations, coal mines, wind farms, plantations, scientific and experimental laboratories, forests, power plants, taking place in different spots in Porto Alegre and other cities, in person and at a distance—through the activation of a network of mediators and educators, particularly; and, secondly, resulting from the first point, that the activities take place in transit, as in expeditions more than in classes, or as walking classes (peripatetic) in which mind and body, nature and culture, science and art are put into dialogue, or even against each other, all the time. I believe that what we could aim for is not for Porto Alegre to be this or that educator, but for it to perceive itself as such.

Finally, I don't think equality and pleasure are in tension. It seems to me that this is not the case of choosing one over the other, but of understanding one as an extension of the other. And that will always depend on what you mean by equality and pleasure. In Brazil, a boring class is never just a boring class—it is a mismatch, a disconnection of speeches (and narratives), and these discourses are never just plain linguistic ones. Maybe pleasure is missing because equality isn't the metric. Maybe equality isn't the metric because the idea of a hedonistic pleasure, in addition to being questionable, definitely cannot suit.

But speaking of education as encounter and equality: I would like to hear your thoughts on the closing symposium of the 9th Bienal and your expectations and forecasts for afterward. What should come after it? What is the meaning of (the project of) permanence in the case of an art biennial? Should the pedagogical curatorship continue, or have we reached a moment in which it doesn't need to exist anymore?

DW The term *symposium* still carries a memory of conviviality and Socratic dialogue, but contemporary symposia tend to be different. Thinking and talking has become professionalized. Symposia have become the performance of professionalized thinking. I am not against professionals. Ideologically, professionalism is rooted in the maintenance of the public good (doctors, lawyers, and teachers are among the original professionals), and that is not the case with the professional's historical rivals: the amateur and the entrepreneur. But professionalism does entail a conflation of status and value. Symposia can be performances of status. However, I was at a symposium in New York City two years ago, and Manuel Borja-Villel, the director of the Museo Nacional Centro de Arte Reina Sofía, said something striking which has become the impulse behind the symposium we will produce in November. He said that education is an encounter between someone who knows something and someone who knows something else. It is a simple, powerful definition—and it is both utterly ordinary and impossibly utopian. It provokes a variety of thoughts. It suggests, firstly, that before education is the acquisition of knowledge, or the formation of consciousness—or even instead of these things—it is an event in which people meet each other. The content of education is secondary; it is just something. Secondly, the term *encounter* suggests an element of surprise, of novelty, of estrangement, perhaps even of threat. Or if the other is not necessarily a threat, she is at least a stranger, or perhaps someone familiar experienced as a stranger. She is a stranger in as much as she knows something I do not know. I do not know what she knows and vice versa. Each possesses something that the other lacks. So, thirdly, and most importantly, this is an encounter between equals. I recall or imagine that Borja-Villel paused, for effect, momentarily after "someone who knows something," inviting the preconception that the other will be someone who knows nothing. One of the most pervasive and pernicious assumptions about education is that it entails the presence of knowledge in one, and its absence in the other. And so, in Porto Alegre, for the closing of the 9th Bienal do Mercosul, we are going to be a little contrary and attempt a symposium that performs, not professional status, but something else. It will be—we hope—a performance of the counter-assumption that education is an encounter between equals.

And after that? Well, Mônica, that might be more a question for you than for me! I will say one thing. I mentioned that at least a couple of other biennials are beginning to think of themselves as ongoing, abiding institutions for their cities: SITE Santa Fe and the Liverpool Biennial are the examples that come to mind. In each case, it is proposed that this continuous, year-round character should take the form of an educational initiative. I don't know whether this will take place, or whether other biennials will think similar thoughts. If it does happen, we might see the biennial form having two tempos: the faster, audience-centered tempo of exhibition presentation alongside the longer, slower, relationship-centered tempo of education. We might look back and see that the Bienal do Mercosul has set a certain precedent in this respect.

This was originally published in Weather Permitting: 9th Mercusol Biennial, *ed. Sofía Hernández Chong Cuy (Fondaçào Bienial de Artes Visuais do Mercusol, 2013).*

Can a Museum Contain Counterpublics?

Manuel Borja-Villel interviewed by Marcelo Expósito

Manuel Borja-Villel is among the most influential museum directors of the early twenty-first century. First at the Antoni Tàpies Foundation, then at the Museu d'Art Contemporani de Barcelona (MACBA), both in Barcelona, and later at the Museo Nacional Centro de Arte Reina Sofía (MNCARS), in Madrid, he has followed a different path from his colleagues, rejecting the neoliberal model of the art museum as a real-estate investment opportunity and refusing revenue-based exhibition choices in favor of politicized, critical, and experimental practices. At the same time, he has been able to balance a radical ambition for art to be a socially transformative medium with solid support from city and state bureaucracies and local publics. That this combination is understood as unusual says much about both his achievement and the state of play in museums across Europe today. While many museum directors are calling for less social or economic instrumentalization of museums and their collections, few are actually delivering something different from what the collector market or populist politicians demand of them. In Barcelona and Madrid, Borja-Villel did construct institutions that delivered difference. Each was not without its difficulties or opposition, but both museums under his directorship served as models that have inspired others to find their way around the narrow interests of the mega-galleries and their collectors and the predictable modernist artist–brand blockbuster shows that attract large enough crowds to balance the books.

The interview here is extracted from a longer exchange between Borja-Villel and the artist Marcelo Expósito, who is also currently a member of parliament in the Spanish Congress of Deputies.[1] *It explores how social critique can develop within an art institution, and focuses on Borja-Villel's*

1 See Marcelo Expósito, *Conversación con Manuel Borja-Villel* (Turpial, 2015).

time at MACBA, where he intended that the institution empower a grounded critique of current social conditions with different communities. Borja-Villel positions MACBA at the intersection of three relations: artists whose practices were increasingly entangled with social movements, especially from the 1990s onward, after the exhaustion of institutional critique; new social movements that were wary of traditional representative democracy and looking for different platforms for conducting critique; and the few art institutions open to reconsidering their social and political roles.

Marcelo Expósito Perhaps we can start by introducing your vision of the role of museums, and how you have set about shaping them to the demands you see as valid or relevant?

Manuel Borja-Villel One of the first things I turn my attention to when I take on a museum is the narrative we want to create, and the manner and context in which this narrative can be projected. Art history is an arena of political dispute among various narratives and images, and the narratives that issue from them are a battleground for hegemony. The war of images is also a war between conflicting visions of society. And it is fought out within an institutional system, not on an abstract plane. It is a system that determines the value of the work and the scope of its distribution. Historiographic narratives function as fiction even though they are based on reality. As a historian working in an institution, every story that you put together is a statement that has impact on reality in the present and also changes our collective perception of the past. Narratives and discourse don't just reflect the power structure, they are in themselves the power that is being fought over, particularly today. For instance, the resurgence of the importance of politics in our society takes the form of a struggle over which narrative will manage to achieve hegemony. The information and the historical remains are there; they are a fact. There is also a whole series of systems or mechanisms by which a narrative lays claim to the status of truth. But the way we tell the story changes the meaning of things. A work of art is an artefact, and a museum is a type of institution that can design and transmit a narrative, which can either create a sense of historical continuity or a change of direction. We know that works of art and utterances live several lives over the course of history. But it is important to bear in mind that the narrative is also linked to the structure of the institution from which you are operating. So if you want to make any substantial long-term changes, you must immediately start considering how to go about changing this structure.

ME When you arrived at MACBA in 1998, what did you find and what were your initial steps toward creating a new narrative? Were there specific measures you implemented toward transforming the museum in those early days?

MB-V Art centers began introducing accounting principles into their management as a result of the increasing influence of private investment. Educational activities increased the number of visitors to museums, helping to justify continued public funding. This "educational turn" sought to maximize audiences in order to secure revenue, sponsorship, and grants. However, what we did at MACBA was replace the education department with a public-programs department. The goal of the public-programs department was to contribute to making the museum a genuine public space. We wanted to reconsider the modern notion of education from the perspective of "radical pedagogy," which meant expanding our idea of the museum to make room for dissent and critique as well as the transfer of knowledge.

We wanted the museum to challenge people and be challenged by them; we wanted it to become an activating force. So the question was how to empower society, how to offer tools to allow citizens to exercise their political agency through the institution. And how the institution could become part of an instituting process and allow itself to gradually change as a result of those types of interactions.

ME That meant changing the notion of the public that was traditionally associated with the museum as an Enlightenment institution. You are saying that you wanted to open the museum to the dynamics of conflict that are intrinsic to civil society, instead of imagining society as a harmonious reality, with the institution contributing to its peaceful life. Your model also opposed the quantification of audiences that was imposed on many art centers under neoliberal globalization.

MB-V Michael Warner showed in his 2002 book *Publics and Counterpublics* how the concept of "publics" was a construction of modernity that has subsequently been naturalized, like other modern concepts such as "nation" and "market." But they are historical constructions, and in fact all those concepts—museum, public, citizenship, nation, and market—go hand in hand. Warner argues that the idea of the public as a universal category is a kind of "practical fiction," and suggests thinking in terms of a heterogeneous public sphere containing "counterpublics" with distinctive attributes that oppose this modern fiction.

The public-programs department was set up precisely because there was a need to change the way cultural institutions usually think about their audiences. If MACBA was really going to become a public space, then we could not merely think about audiences in numerical terms. We worked with the understanding that there was a society outside the museum that was not just diverse but made up of competing sectors, and that we had to think about how to build other audiences. In other words, that there is not a public but an ongoing construction of society that we wanted to participate in by providing critical tools. And this approach is based on the idea that cultural experience has to be an emancipatory activity.

We tried to incorporate other critical models, such as the figure of the "ignorant schoolmaster" proposed by Jacques Rancière, whom we also brought to work at MACBA. An ignorant schoolmaster is an educator who teaches without necessarily knowing, based on the idea that the uncertainties, doubts, and ignorance of everyone involved in the knowledge-production process are on the same level. The museum knows certain things that people may be ignorant of, but there are many other things that society knows and the museum doesn't. This approach to education is emancipatory because it means that everyone—the institution and its audiences—asks questions together, and participants have an active role. All parties involved learn from each other in different ways.

ME So, we could say that bringing the political into the museum was the second of your immediate measures after reforming the idea of the educational. But it seems to me you were also very concerned with the museological aspects of the institution.

MB-V When I was appointed, I decided to reorganize the collection around the unresolved conflicts of the sixties and seventies. It was not a whim based on my personal preferences—MACBA is a contemporary art museum, so the first question we had to ask ourselves was, "What does 'contemporary' mean?" Revising the history of twentieth-century art requires changing the historical narrative through a new collection policy, a new exhibition program, new public programming, and the connections between the three. An example would be our project with Jean-François Chevrier and Sharon Avery-Fahlström on the work of Öyvind Fahlström, an artist whose life reflected the vicissitudes of the twentieth century. Born to Nordic parents, Fahlström grew up in Brazil and was trapped in Sweden at the age of ten because of World War II. As an adult, he moved between Paris, Italy, and New York. He died in 1976 after a fragmented, hybrid life in which a fixed national or cultural identity was impossible. I found that very interesting when it came to questioning the relationships of local, national, and international identity, especially with respect to the kind of museum MACBA was expected to become. In fact, we were particularly interested in Fahlström's drawn and painted maps, in which he experimentally shifted global geopolitical borders through playful strategies and imaginative representations of reality. In the sixties, his work became more explicitly political, and he identified with the counterculture and social revolutions.

In 1999, we negotiated with Avery-Fahlström [his widow and collaborator] the long-term loan of his archive, setting it up in one of the MACBA offices so that we could proceed unhurriedly to classify and study his work in more detail. In 2000, during this process, we organized a major retrospective (curated by Chevrier, Avery-Fahlström, and me) that brought together works from collections scattered around the world. We also published a catalogue, for which we commissioned texts by two authors whose points of view were not usually found in art publications at the time. One was the American scholar Immanuel Wallerstein, a specialist in the relationship between waves of anti-systemic movements, global geopolitics, and the crisis of capitalism. The other was the Brazilian psychoanalyst and writer Suely Rolnik, who had led Félix Guattari on a kind of schizoanalytical tour of Brazil at the end of the military dictatorship. Rolnik had participated in the Brazilian counterculture of the 1960s and studied the clinical practice of schizoanalysis in Paris, which is one of the many ruptures of the that we were interested in bringing into the museum. So you can see that the Fahlström project was like putting together the pieces of a complex puzzle. We did not simply organize an exhibition by selecting a number of works and then commissioning articles about them for a catalogue, incorporating them into the collection and accompanying the whole process with a program of related activities. Instead, the project allowed us to develop a narrative that took into account twentieth-century political history, an analysis of global geopolitics, a critique of neoliberalism, and the history of the avant-gardes. These interrelated ideas revolved around the epicenter of the sixties and seventies, and the overall aim was to shed light on certain aspects of the contemporary situation. It allowed us to introduce an institutional model in which the public-programs, collection, exhibition, and publications departments worked together like cogs in a machine, based on a process of reflection, education, and critical thought. It is a model in which the various sections of the museum interact organically instead of the whole museum revolving around the fetish of collectable art objects.

ME I find it interesting that you do not simply add new names to existing narratives but actually rethink the historiographical canon from the point of view of these excluded artists and works. From the political perspective, it is fascinating to consider how the historiographical work of a museum can help to change common assumptions about history from the bottom up. Can you give me an example of how MACBA questioned established art history narratives without limiting itself to the political content of the artworks?

MB-V Another of our early thesis exhibitions was *Campos de fuerzas* [Force Fields, 2000], curated by the British art critic Guy Brett. The project, which spanned a fifty-year period, from 1920 to 1970, disregarded the usual distinctions between styles and brought together Kinetic art, Concrete art, and Informalism. The aim was to show artworks that modified their surroundings in real time, changing the way the viewer perceived the works and the reality around them. So there was no overt political content. But even so, we considered it to be closely linked to the type of art that explores social situations or engages in institutional critique. The way we saw it, the exhibition presented part of the story of how art had ceased to represent reality and started to physically intervene in it, offering viewers tools or models with which to change it. This break from traditional representation, along with the desire to transform the perception of the world, is not a marginal or minority practice. It was a major, central tendency that ran through the avant-gardes and did not respect the usual divisions by which museums classify twentieth-century art by mediums, styles, or movements.

ME There were claims that MACBA was not pluralist enough, and it makes me think of a certain multicultural notion of the inclusion of diversity—the kind of approach that paradoxically disables the political dimension by incorporating all differences within a preexisting value system or by celebrating the more superficial aspects of diversity. The institutions, policy frameworks, and narratives that shape the common assumptions of a society are not simply empty molds that can expand to make room for new problems. We cannot just add more subjects, more groups, more lifestyles. The crisis of a cultural paradigm is like the crisis of a political regime: it makes it necessary to question the systems that gave rise to the current situation.

MB-V There is a type of multiculturalism that is actually the cultural form of neoliberalism. It celebrates diversity almost as if differences were merely formal, as if they emerged naturally and simply had to be placed side by side in order to achieve some kind of universal harmony. Just like that, without political mediation and without revealing the social origin of the construction of these collective identities and the reasons why they have been treated differently. As a result, a pluralist idea that everything should be represented in a museum actually ends up hiding the problem of why a museum is an institution that leaves out certain things in the writing of history. You cannot simply put all the styles or movements side by side, because then you hide the conflicts between certain positions and ultimately reinforce the most conservative hegemonic visions of art history.

However, my idea of art history is by no means limited to a kind of activism. MACBA earned international recognition because of our capacity to rework complex historiographical narratives on a large scale as skillfully as any other important international museum. And the most interesting thing is that visitor numbers continued to grow. We were never a minority museum, and the figures show that our programming was very broad and not at all sectarian. But we never reduced ourselves to a "light" discourse, or to anything-goes pluralism. We did not turn our backs on presenting socially committed readings of art history and contemporary art. In fact, when political authorities became anxious about the critical nature of some of our activities, our best defense was an academically sound program that was recognized by our peers. If you decide to implement a model that is critical and conflictive, you have to be twice as rigorous and work twice as hard as those who operate under established parameters. You will always be subject to much greater scrutiny.

ME There is a widespread assumption that radical experiments begin "on the streets" and are then absorbed by art institutions or normalized in museums. That pattern has certainly been very strong historically. But during the 1990s, it was not uncommon for cultural practices, political critique, and social activism to move between the inside and outside of some institutions. From the museum's point of view, in retrospect, how would you evaluate this period? How can a contemporary art museum allocate resources to an activity that has both feet planted firmly in the streets and is closely linked to protest movements?

MB-V In 2001, our contribution to a city council triennial was *Las Agencias* [The Agencies] and the exhibition *Antagonismos* [Antagonisms]. They were designed to complement each other: the exhibition would offer a historical overview of the kind of art-activism experiments that were taking place at the same time on the streets. The title *Antagonismos* was a reference to Chantal Mouffe. She argues that accepting conflict is an inalienable dimension of democracy. We also have to accept that the construction of cultural identities is key to democratic politics. It follows that identities are not fixed or essentialist; they are dynamic, relational "subject positions" that are constantly redefined in conflictive relationships with each other. A museum can only participate in rebuilding democracy if it functions as a political space from which it is possible to express dissent. This does not mean that politics has to be the sole subject of all its activities. It means thinking about the museum's program as a whole from the point of view of how to radicalize democracy.

In parallel, the museum provided a space for *Las Agencias*. We agreed that it would operate autonomously and that museum management would not interfere, although obviously the idea was to review it together on an ongoing basis. Basically, it was intended as a practical experiment in actually building an in-between *agencement*, or assemblage, of institution and civil society. These practices were produced at great speed, and any contradictions were pushed aside. As a result, some collaborations were unsustainable in the long term. Some people later assumed that *Las Agencias* ended because the museum caved in to political pressure. But it must be said that social movements had a strong anti-institutional attitude at the time. The external pressure was less important to us than the fact that it was very difficult for the institution's own framework to sustain such a vertiginous dynamic of experimentation. It was one of the first experiences of this kind at the museum, and we still did not know how to create devices that could adjust to these kinds of assemblages. Unless you create appropriate measures that are flexible and able to adapt, it becomes impossible for the structure of the museum—which is usually rigid or has been designed for other purposes—to interact with the improvisation and urgency of social movements.

In any case, we need to rethink the meaning of success and failure in these kinds of collaborations. Their political nature means that some aspects inevitably take place through agreements, but there are also disagreements that are impossible to resolve. I also believe that the kind of experiments we were involved in ended up contributing to changing the city in ways that may perhaps be easier to perceive today. I think the work that was done at MACBA, particularly during the time of *Las Agencias*, is by no means unconnected to many of the developments that have taken place in the city between then and the obvious and profound changes that are in progress now.

ME Is it possible to avoid the split between the usual work of the museum and what we could call the activist side of your model? To what extent are the traditional museum activities open to influence?

MB-V I think a public museum should place itself at the service of the real complexity of society and help to radicalize democracy through culture. These processes that took place in the late 1990s and early 2000s—not just at MACBA—went on to have strong repercussions and are still very influential today. But they had their limits. Perhaps fifteen or twenty years ago we imagined that this experimentation between institutions and social movements would spread and continue more linearly over time. This has happened to some extent, but we are also seeing a rhetorical presence of politics in art that is counterproductive. I am not sure that the political rhetoric you can find all over museums and biennials these days measures up to the grassroots movements in countries in crisis. I often think that it is not capable of adequately criticizing or counteracting the neoliberal violence that still exists, or the rise of extreme-right political parties in Europe.

I would not want this self-criticism to be interpreted as a sign of agreement with those who think that politics should be removed from cultural institutions. My opinion is the exact opposite. Now that democratic institutions are being questioned, cultural professionals need to become even more deeply involved. The problem is that we do not really have much room for maneuver if we are just working from a single museum or only from the cultural sector. The alliances we started to create two decades ago need to grow and become more complex and larger in scope.

We organized *Antagonismos* and *Las Agencias* very early on, but we quickly became mired in pointless discussions about the differences between political art and art that is not political. We were constantly criticized for focusing on activist art to the detriment of other, non-politicized artistic traditions. We broke out of that frame of reference by organizing an exhibition titled *Arte y Utopía. La acción restringida* [Art and Utopia: Action Restricted, 2004], which revisited modern art using a work by the French poet Stéphane Mallarmé as the point of departure.

The decision to start with Mallarmé allowed us to get away from the clichéd idea of art history as two parallel lines that never meet: art for art's sake and socially committed art. With *Arte y Utopía*, we wanted to put together an alternative history in which the work of art resists the social order by defending the autonomy of both the work and the institution. The defense of the autonomy of art has been based on the idea of art as a space in which artworks only refer back to other artworks, without addressing the outside world. We wanted to present a history of the work of art that lays claim to autonomy but does so in order to resist the commercialization process that evolved into the cultural industry in the course of the century. In opposition to capitalism's exploitation of the subject through consumption, there are works of art that have sought to create a space that makes a different type of relationship with the spectator possible. The art that we considered to derive from Mallarmé was not uninterested in reaching spectators, it just declined to do so indiscriminately. *Arte y Utopía* presented a kind of art that sought one-to-one, specific engagement and opened up a relational space for each spectator. A space open to shifts, discontinuities, digressions. This was very important to us. That is precisely the kind of complexity that *Arte y Utopía* was about, the fact that there was not just one way of politically addressing reality through art in the twentieth century.

You may have noticed that we traced the history of the relationship between modern art and social change back to the late nineteenth century. This was not arbitrary. It was a key moment for these kinds of reflections. In 1902, Vladimir Lenin published *What Is to Be Done?*, his great work on the problem of revolutionary organization and political mass communication. [Leo] Tolstoy and Mallarmé considered themselves anarchists. Through their work, they were exploring different approaches to determining the relationship of the form of the work to the audience and the prospect of changing reality.

These reflections led us to conclude that our work at MACBA should also offer visitors a space for specific engagement with art—not so that they could turn away from reality, but to allow them to momentarily step back and critically reflect on it. It is an approach that differs from forms of artistic activism based on immersion in reality. We did not see it as the antithesis of activist agitation or of pedagogical dynamics based on debate. Our goal at MACBA was precisely to avoid having to choose between different options, to create connections between them instead.

ME So you are saying that a democratic cultural institution should favor a diversity of critical experiences, simultaneously bringing into play different ways of empowering its audiences and society in general. In the case of a museum, this includes having the capacity to politically reactivate the history of creative practices, to change the idea that art history is a narrative made up of lifeless objects with no bearing on today's reality.

MB-V That is why it was so important to set up a dialogue between the exhibition program and the public-programs department, which was more directly in contact with audiences, and to ensure that this dialogue helped to shape the collection, which is an important part of the museum's legacy. We believed that contact with art should as a matter of course lead to the empowerment of the spectator. We tried to achieve this goal in two ways. First, by opening up a space, through the public-programs department, where antagonism was expressed. Second, through an exhibition program and a collection based on presenting and creating the kinds of works and the kinds of devices that call for active engagement. Exhibitions like *Arte y Utopía* helped us to rethink the centrality of anti-monumentalist works in twentieth-century art. We shifted the collection toward more fragile kinds of works, in what are usually considered minor formats, on paper or perishable materials. Books and scale models were as important as "major" works of art in the traditional sense. The idea was to create a collection that was not authoritarian, a collection that generated the kind of relationality that we found in the work of Édouard Glissant, a French Martiniquan writer whose work combines poetics and politics and seeks to break down relations of colonial domination through a relational theory based on empathy and respect.

Originally published as Manuel Borja-Villel and Marcelo Expósito, "A Conversation between Manuel Borja-Villel and Marcelo Expósito," Afterall Journal *44 (September 4, 2017), 122–131.*

Translated from Spanish by Nuria Rodríguez. The authors would like to thank the Foundation for Arts Initiatives (FfAI) for their support.

A Museum in Education City

Zeina Arida interviewed by Noah Simblist

This conversation was recorded October 3, 2024. It has been edited for length and clarity.

Noah Simblist Let's begin with you introducing Mathaf. What is its mission? Can you tell us a little bit about its history?

Zeina Arida Mathaf is a museum dedicated to Arab modern art that also exhibits international contemporary art. It opened fifteen years ago, in 2010. I would say it was a pioneering institution when it opened; it was one of the first museums in the Arab world to focus on the region, and on supporting artistic production from the region.

Twenty years ago, we didn't even have the Arab Fund for Arts and Culture to support artists and institutions. Institutions could maybe get some support from the Ford Foundation if they were successful at fundraising. So when Mathaf opened, it represented a beautiful story of a private collection that H. E. Sheikh Hassan bin Mohamed bin Ali Al Thani had carefully put together in close dialogue with the artists he collected. Mathaf was the culmination of his vision.

Another thing that set it apart is that the museum opened as a place for research and education as well. It is located in Education City, Qatar, and its neighbors are universities. Although the museum is not affiliated with any of them, it was founded with an emphasis on the scholarly documentation of historical artists' practices, peer-reviewed research, and biographical writing. At the time it opened, I was still at the Arab Image Foundation. Mathaf commissioned artworks from a lot of my artist friends in Lebanon, Egypt, and elsewhere, and artists throughout the region saw the opening of the museum as a great opportunity. At that time, you really had no institutions in the region. More than twenty artists were given the opportunity to present their work at the opening. It was recognized immediately as a major event; there really was a buzz around the idea of regional self-reflection and the project of documenting and making accessible our visual culture.

I've now been at Mathaf for three years, and it has felt like the natural next step for my career. I've always worked in Lebanon. After I completed my studies, I went back to Lebanon and helped to found and build institutions. When I was ready to move out of Beirut, it made sense to continue the project of building Mathaf. It has a history but there remains much to do here in terms of institution-building.

So it represented a great challenge. For fifteen years, it has been presenting solo shows of mid-career artists. These were often major efforts, like Mona Hatoum, Kader Attia, or El Anatsui. Mathaf also broadened its understanding of the Arab world by exhibiting and collecting artists who may live elsewhere but whose practices are relevant to the region.

Arriving here in January 2022, just as museums were really reopening after the pandemic and just before the World Cup, made the moment seem one of change and opportunity. At that time, many museums needed to shift their relationships with their audiences.

More generally, it's a very interesting moment to be in Qatar and to be involved in the art scene because the museum sector and the creative industries are booming. This activity builds on strong foundations; there are several museums that have been here for a while, there is a lot of public art in the city and in the desert. At the same time, there are many new museums that are in the making or under construction, as well as the development of a creative scene that includes a photo festival and a platform called Design Doha. Mathaf, as the modern and contemporary art museum, has an important role to play. It can be the link between students and faculty at the universities, the public, and art and artists. We are working on many projects and programs that lead to us being more proactive and dynamic, being more directly involved in communities of local, regional, and international artists.

NS And how does Mathaf connect to the broader framework of the Qatar Museums?

ZA Mathaf is the fruit of a collaboration between Qatar Museums and the Qatar Foundation. The collection initially prompted the creation of the museum. When Sheikh Hassan bin Mohamed bin Ali Al Thani had given the collection to the Qatar Foundation, it prompted a conversation that led to the joint effort. Mathaf is hosted in a building that belongs to Qatar Foundation. We are also funded by the foundation, but we are operated by Qatar Museums.

NS I'd like to hear more about the relationship to Education City. I teach at Virginia Commonwealth University, and two years ago I visited its Doha campus. Tell me about the broader educational framework.

ZA The relationship has been active for years, but I would say that there is an opportunity to do more. I see this as part of my mandate. To give you an example of an older initiative, Mathaf has been collaborating with the Doha Institute for Graduate Studies on a yearly symposium open to scholars focused on very specific topics. That kind of thing, plus an internship program, was about the extent of Mathaf's engagement with these academic institutions.

In more recent years, we've been trying to find an alignment that goes deeper. We want the curators and artists who visit us to engage with faculty and students. For example, an artist that visited us last year did studio visits with students at VCU. And that was great; he enjoyed it, and they loved it. We have also hosted exhibitions of the alumni, students, and faculty associated with a school.

Now we are preparing for a survey exhibition of the multidisciplinary research group Forensic Architecture. We facilitated a nine-month master class for students from VCU, Georgetown University, and the Doha Institute for Graduate Study. These students worked on their own "forensic" investigation, which they will exhibit at Mathaf. We are very excited to see the result. Likewise, most of the public programs affiliated with the Forensic Architecture exhibition will be in partnership with other institutions and will be held at Georgetown University.

NS Fantastic. How does Mathaf approach education more generally?

ZA When Mathaf opened, I think the education and learning-and-outreach teams were the strongest; they hosted a lot of activities. Then, after some bigger restructuring at Qatar Museums, we still had our own educational team, but it was a bit more centralized. Today our education efforts are focused on programs with schools—with both teachers and school kids.

We help teachers to understand, and then build lessons around, upcoming exhibitions and collection displays. We also help them to think through how best to conduct art activities and workshops in their own schools. When students of any age—from three to seventeen—come for a guided tour, we also ensure they are given a hands-on workshop by one of our art educators. We've found that workshops are the format that works best.

NS You mentioned the sense of natural evolution in your career, from leading the Arab Image Foundation, which was established in relation to an archive of photographs from the region, to leading Mathaf, which is a collection of other kinds of artworks connected to the region. Can you tell us a bit more about the Arab Image Foundation and how these archives made their way into the public?

ZA The Arab Image Foundation was the idea of three artists, photographers then based in France, who came together, applied for a grant, and to their surprise received funding. This is when I met them and joined the group, helping them to open an office and build the institution. It's a conventional French nonprofit that has a general assembly composed of members that elect a board of directors every three years, with committee assignments if needed. Then there's the team. It was very exciting to think of the possibility of preserving material that no one else was really interested in.

And I have to say that each of us, at or near the beginning, had somewhat different visions of what the foundation should be. It took us years to understand this. What we all eventually agreed upon is a nonprofit that aims to collect and preserve photographic material produced in the Arab world by local photographers—images in some sense in opposition to those by eighteenth- and nineteenth-century travelers and

Orientalists. We did not come to the idea of treating the collection like its own artistic project until later. We began with preservation and making things accessible.

The other important idea was to rewrite the history of photography in the region, to elevate the stories of photographers who were completely unknown. Akram Zaatari, one of the three cofounders, would say that it is really an archive that helps to write the story of how society in the Arab world evolved. You can see, in some of the artistic projects he did, the modernization of the region. But also, for me, it was a way of reconnecting to Lebanon. We inherited an image of Lebanon from our parents, from earlier generations, that we really couldn't relate to—that it was kind of like Switzerland, that it enjoyed "The Golden Sixties." Of course, we had witnessed only war. So there was a consciousness about the responsibility we had, which informed our choices about what to exhibit and publish. This, plus the contributions of the various active members, may be what made the foundation such an interesting project, one that connected with audiences around the world while avoiding the cliché of being "the voice of photography."

It was important to me to build an institution, an archive, a history, and a language around a visual culture, but at the same time to resist being centralized or conformist in any particular way. It's a region, not a city or a country, and all the constituent countries that make it up are so different from each other. You know what I mean? That plus being demanding of ourselves about the quality of our research, the standards we aspired to, the collaborators we chose.

NS Thinking further, it's interesting to note the different kinds of institutional structures: one begins with a group of artists and a grassroots collaboration; the other emerges from a different context, with affiliations to Qatar Museums and the nation. That said, in the context of Lebanon, the artists you're talking about exemplified, and in some sense led, a kind of research-based practice, one that plays with the idea of the archive, that became globally popular.

ZA I think that's an important point. I really think the Arab Image Foundation and its work and activities influenced that development. Look at the artists who were part of it. When the foundation started, they were emerging artists; they "grew up" with the foundation. As their practices developed, they were nourished by, and in turn contributed to, the foundation. When Walid Raad was part of the board, he participated in all these debates around the definition of photography, as well as conversations about the foundation's organizational structure and processes. For instance, I know that he started working under the name The Atlas Group in part through the foundation's inspiration.

NS Oh really?

ZA Yeah. And of course, when he started working on The Atlas Group, he proposed to include in the Arab Image Foundation the collection he was building for The Atlas Group. The idea was brilliant, but we wondered whether it would jeopardize the trust of others we were trying to convince to donate their holdings to the foundation. We weren't ready at that time, so we told him no.

Anyway, these artists were all living abroad. And the artistic community is small in Beirut. When we had board meetings, all these artists would travel to Beirut and our other artist friends would know about it. It became the talk of the town. We had in common this recent violent history of the war. We were all dealing with the aftermath of the war, with postwar politics and social issues. There were a few other nonprofits at the time, and it created momentum and a fascinating context for artists.

NS And have you seen this notion of the educational turn impact artistic and curatorial practices in Beirut? Have people or institutions there explored how exhibitions can become educational spaces or how art making can center discourse rather than objects?

ZA It's interesting to think about Ashkal Alwan, who shifted the format of these public production platforms for contemporary artists. But it's not exactly answering your question because she [the director Christine Tohmé] never had an exhibition space. There were a few attempts in the postwar period, in the 2000s. There is the 98 Weeks Project Space, which presents materials pertaining to ninety-eight archives. I'm not sure if that counts, either. But 98 Weeks tried to transform a contemporary art platform into an educational one.

But in Lebanon and in countries where the museum sector is not so developed, you have to think proactively about audiences. You almost have to create your audience, will it into being. That makes more experimental work harder. The Beirut Art Center presented some exhibitions that had been, let's say, conceptually curated. And they suffered from a lack of an audience. In a sense, they only began consistently broadening their audiences when they built a café, a boutique where you can buy gifts, and an exhibition space in a nice garden. There were now several reasons why people would come together. Those kinds of gestures, plus the boom of collectors in the 2010s, helped. Several of those collectors wanted to open an art museum with their collections.

NS I hear what you are saying about the postwar context, the need to build institutions, and how different that is than in the United States or Europe, where an institution might have a big building, a collection, and a staff of curators. If you don't have that infrastructure, then perhaps you begin with conversation.

ZA Exactly. You just begin. We had no exhibition spaces; we did one show in a bank that was in downtown Beirut, a beautiful space. We all used these spaces downtown for years. It was a kind of educational platform, sure, but also it was a dialogue with the city.

NS How do you use that experience of building something from the ground up when you are working at Mathaf, in a very different context—one with resources that weren't available in postwar Lebanon?

ZA The resources are not necessarily what makes the difference. I have always been driven by building sustainable institutions because we are in a region that is not stable for so many reasons. In fact, I find a lot of similarities. Mathaf is not visible enough in the world. We're not fully online. Mathaf needs to further develop its community of artists. There is a lot of work ahead and a lot of opportunities. It's great to be in this, it's an opportunity for the whole region because artists in the region need support more than ever as they face attempts to cancel them or censor their work. We can play an important role. But we really need to activate the museum; today, this is how you are relevant as an art institution.

NS You mentioned artists being canceled, which is also an increasingly urgent question as political winds shift in Europe and the United States. It's interesting to think about the artists who came together for the Arab Image Foundation being expats who then came back to the region to build an institution. Because they and others did so, there is now an infrastructure in place that doesn't necessitate complete reliance on the United States or Europe to provide a platform for Arab artists.

ZA That's true, but again, it was based on these private initiatives. It is always related to individuals—people like Christine Tohmé [a curator and the founding director of Ashkal Alwan—The Lebanese Association for Plastic Arts].

NS Thinking ahead ten, twenty, thirty years, what is necessary to ensure that sustainability—for Mathaf or other Arab institutions? Is it just funding, or are other elements necessary?

ZA No, it's not only funding. It's preserving, working with, and making accessible both the collection and the institution's history. It's imperative to build an archive documenting the practices of all the artists who are part of the collection—and who are leaving us, one after the other, due to their age. It's important to also be up to date with emerging artists and their scenes. How can we ensure our work is relevant to both local and global audiences?

NS There are so many symposiums these days about the sustainability of art institutions, and they're often future-facing. It's interesting to consider how attending to the past and the present can be just as crucial.

ZA There are, of course, logistics to attend to as well. But it's so important to tell the right stories.

Education at the Sharjah Art Foundation

Noora Al Mualla interviewed by Noah Simblist

This conversation was recorded November 7, 2024. It has been edited for length and clarity.

Noah Simblist I'd like to begin with you sharing a bit about your role at the Sharjah Foundation and how it connects to education.

Noora Al Mualla I'm the director of learning research, so I lead an education team, a research team, and the publications team. Within the education team specifically, it's mainly segmented into two parts: adults and children. For adults, we have both bilingual art programs and programs based on specific exhibitions. Because over the years we've built a relationship with our audiences and we want to keep that going, we work year-round. For children, we have a good working relationship with schools; we host two or three school trips just about every day. Additionally, we have an in-house expert who makes sure all our programs are inclusive.

NS What is the research section?

NA We have in-house researchers whose efforts support the artists' works. At the same time, for the past few years we have focused on the urban landscape of Sharjah, specifically on the area where the foundation is located. It's a very special place in the old part of Sharjah, where most of the people now living here originally came from. We do a lot of research on the old houses, who lived in them, and what life was like in those early years. A related and important project is repurposing old buildings. Because we operate in a sort of heritage area, the Sharjah Art Foundation renovates buildings with support from the government, then turns them into community spaces or art spaces. We undertake the research that goes into that, too.

NS As for the biennial itself, what is the relationship between the educational teams and the curatorial teams?

NA One thing that is special about the foundation is that the education team is bigger than the curatorial team. We begin conversations with curators very early on, which I'm not sure is common in other museums. Once the concept, the participating artists, and the initial ideas of the works are being discussed, we are there in the room.

We also have special relationships with universities in Sharjah; our president is also on a board of the fine arts college. So we work closely with students and professors. For the most recent and the coming biennials, there has been a course in the American University in Sharjah about the biennial. We also help ensure students have full access to the artists. We encourage artists to work closely with students when they need assistance for their work. So the relationship between us and the curatorial teams is very close. We build on each other. Education is at the heart of everything we do.

NS I was lucky enough to go visit the Biennial during one of the annual March Meetings, and it was very impressive. One thing I noticed was that education was taken as a subject matter by many of the artists. Can you think of examples of how some of the biennial curators have thought about education within their curatorial practice?

NA I mean, Hoor al Qasimi's biennial was special to us on those terms, and she used site-specific works to focus on specific communities. She chose the works and their locations based on what she thought the local communities would be interested in. It also helps that we maintain long-term relationships with artists who participate in the biennial; they keep coming back, which also builds their relationship with our audiences. It turns into a mentorship-type relationship at some point.

Another special biennial was Christine Tohmé's. She was clear about her intention that it resonate beyond the art scene. She really wanted to work with craftsmen and craftswomen; the instructors who led workshops and events during that exhibition were not artists. We had weavers; we had fishermen teaching students how to make their own nets and to fish. I think it's valuable when curators try to bridge the gap between art and the people in the community.

People in the art scene speak a common language. It's like we're in a small bubble, imagining that everyone outside it understands what we do. We have to remind ourselves that's not often the case.

NS Yes, the discourse around education can mean different things to different people. And certainly the language used at the March Meeting, for instance, is academic. But it's also education to teach a skill.

NA Biennials require that kind of specialized language. Of course we try to bridge the gap here and there, but, for example, Okwui Enwezor's biennial had so much literature and so much information that it needed that kind of discourse. While other biennials might have the flexibility to be closer to different kinds of work, if you know what I mean.

More generally, our educators are always encouraged to be experimental, to be proactive, and to be part of the community. We are to listen, then go back and change our approach if needed. We're never rigid in the way we do our work. For example, after three consecutive March Meetings with weighty conversations in a lecture hall, people said, "Okay, it was amazing. But maybe something lighter, maybe?"

So for this past March Meeting, we thought collectivity was an important element of lightness, and we made that the theme. But also we created a setup where people can sit and discuss ideas comfortably. It wasn't a lecture. This responsiveness is common. One recent program was inspired by Hassan Sharif's *Semi-systems*. The series was developed while he was in London in the '80s, but during the formation of the education system in the UAE, the type of school was also called a "semi system" because students were part of the educational process. For this event and another forthcoming program, we wanted to focus on Arabic-speaking instructors and students for whom our usual English-language presentations are a barrier. It's been very interesting, and it has drawn out conversations that are relevant to what's happening now, politically and socially.

NS Who was involved in those early semi-systems?

NA When formal education started in the UAE, it involved people who are older than what we think of as student age. So programs were offered at different times—weekends, nighttime.

NS So it was almost like a civic program, a kind of educational imperative, educating the population.

NA Yes, but we mainly thought of it as an alternative school. So our semi-systems were three-day courses on weekends, for which we take a topic, read about it collectively, and then approach it in different ways.

NS And this was intergenerational, not just for young children?

NA It's mostly for adults but we encourage teenagers—we're not very rigid with our age segmenting. If a sixteen-year-old is interested and wants to join, I'm sure they'd get something out of it.

NS One of the subjects invoked during the educational turn in art is this notion of radical pedagogy, citing people like Paulo Freire or Ivan Illich, who wrote about how education can be used to transform society. This invocation of radicality was, again, very utopian. Has this notion of radicality ever been engaged through the biennial?

NA Well, the UAE is a conservative society, but at the same time we're progressive because it's mostly a young country. The population skews young. And the education system is honestly one of the best in the world. I think people are open and interested; they want to know more, to hear more, to be challenged. Also, we've gone through so many different topics over the years that it feels safe to say that the Sharjah Art Foundation is one the UAE's most progressive institutions.

NS One aspect of the educational turn was breaking down the boundaries between art production and interpretation. When thinking about the future—twenty, thirty years from now—how do you imagine the way education functions in the UAE in terms of that binary?

NA The educational part of the biennial will always be a tool to encourage discussion. The whole point of having this kind of platform is to bring people together, bring communities together, and think together about how we can build a better world.

NS As a final question, can you think of examples of something initiated in a March Meeting or a biennial that lasted beyond the specific moment, something that had or has an afterlife?

NA There are physical spaces. The Mureijah space built for Yuko Hasegawa's biennial was built on the footprints of the old Sharjah. Also, the Mirage City Cinema, designed by filmmaker Apichatpong Weerasethakul and architect Ole Scheeren for the eleventh biennial, is now where we host our film festival every year.

NS Interesting.

NA We have a cricket stadium also. It reactivates a 2015 artwork by Gary Simmons called *Across the Chalk Line*. We have a lot of Indian and Pakistani community members, and the artist wanted to build a cricket stadium for children; it's still used today. In terms of conversations, though I cannot remember the year off the top of my head, the conversation at one March Meeting led us to shift from having a "disabilities department" to having a person specializing in making sure everything is inclusive.

NS Is there something that I haven't asked yet about the approach to education that you want to express?

NA Only that exhibiting artists are always encouraged to hold workshops, hold conversations, and to speak to students. We feel it's important for people that young people hear the perspectives of those they don't normally have access to.

Education at the São Paulo Bienal

Thiago Gil de Oliveira Virava interviewed by Noah Simblist

This conversation was recorded November 5, 2024. It has been edited for length and clarity.

Noah Simblist How long did you work for the São Paulo Biennial?

Thiago Gil de Oliveira Virava I worked for the biennial foundation for twelve years and left the institution this month because I will be in Rome next year on a postdoctoral fellowship. I began my work there in 2013 as a research assistant for the curatorial and production teams. From 2016, I worked with the education team doing research and content production; for the last two years I managed the education team.

NS What is the biennial's approach to education?

TV The São Paulo Biennial has focused on education programs since its second edition, in 1953. Educators were called monitors at the time; they received groups, especially student groups, in the exhibition. Because the first six biennials were organized by the Museum of Modern Art in São Paulo, those monitors were trained by the staff of the museum—in particular the technical director, a German art historian working in Brazil called Wolfgang Pfeiffer. He provided these guides a short course in modern art history so that they could contextualize the biennial exhibition. I think that this model lasted until the eighties.

In that decade, especially when art historian and educator Ana Mae Barbosa brought her own theories of art education to the biennial, the foundation's approach to education shifted. There were new experiences: for example, educators created small studios within the exhibition space so that students could experiment with artistic materials. The idea was that in order for a student to be in relation with art, he or she has to be in touch with the materials with which it is made. Ideas like these have continued in the decades since. Of course, this is my view; I'm not speaking about on behalf of the biennial foundation. In 2010 the foundation created a new role, curator of education, which was first held by Stella Barbieri. It's around this time that what we call the "educational turn" started within the biennial. There was an increased understanding of education as an artistic practice.

NS Would you say it's at this moment that curatorial strategies began to integrate educational practices?

TV That question reminds me of something that I skipped: in 1998, in time for the biennial centered on the Brazilian notion of *anthropophagy*, the foundation changed its statute to introduce education as part of its mission.

That year's biennial, curated by Paulo Herkenhoff, was the first to publish and distribute, free of charge, educational materials for teachers working in public schools. The curatorial team, especially Herkenhoff, worked closely with Evelyn Ioschpe, director of art education for that edition. Together they made sure the curators' approach to anthropophagy could be translated for a student audience. This inaugurated a newly collaborative way of working that has only intensified in the past fifteen years. Every biennial since 2010 has included this type of educational material.

NS I've been to a few São Paulo Biennials. One was in 2014, when Charles Esche was artistic director. He and Galit Eilat invited the participation of Decolonizing Architecture, with Alessandro Petti and Sandi Hilal, who had previously created *The Tree School*. That project really used education not only as a method of interpretation but also as the work itself. Artists have increasingly joined curators in centering education in their practices. What other examples from the biennial come to mind?

TV Something that comes to mind is the 33rd Biennial, curated by Gabriel Pérez-Barreiro. He was interested in exploring attention in contemporary life. I don't think that was reflected in the *structure* of the exhibition, but it came through clearly in the education project, which involved what he and the education team called "attention exercises." Instead of explaining the curatorial concept or discussing artistic projects, these educational materials proposed exercises to help the audience sustain their attention by standing in front of an artwork for about ten to fifteen minutes while these experiments were mediated by educator-mediators. After the exercise visitors could discuss with the educator-mediator about what they saw in the artwork.

NS That biennial was in 2018. But it seems like the educational turn began growing in importance in the late 1990s. In 2006, Manifesta 6 took the form of a school. The Mercosul Biennial, in 2013, heavily emphasized its pedagogical program, even hiring Dominic Willsdon as a "pedagogical fellow" to advise the curatorial team. Documenta 15, in 2022, directed by the Indonesian artist collective raungrupa, likewise centered education. In some instances, curators even emptied venues of objects, focusing instead on conversations, on the relations between people. In your experience in São Paulo, did any curators think along similar lines?

TV Well, the 31st Biennial, in 2014, transformed the ground floor of the pavilion into what was called a "square"—it became a place for public programs. The artistic directors invited a cultural collective that had emerged in a distant neighborhood on the periphery of São Paulo, the Agencia Popular Solano Trindade, to take charge of the exhibition's public programs. They were to bring the cultural experiences of the city's edges to the center through these events. To me, this was a good example using the exhibition and its spaces to bring people with different experiences into a relationship with each other and with contemporary art.

NS That's a very prominent position, at the entrance—

TV At the entrance. But they didn't call it a school. As far as I can remember, no artistic director has thought of the biennial as a school like the exhibitions you cited.

NS In recent years, many in the art world have cited the radical pedagogy of Paulo Freire or Ivan Illich and tied it to a kind of radical politics. You could claim it's similarly radical to bring this collective from the periphery to the center; it's certainly a political gesture.

TV That's correct.

NS I wonder: the biennials that cite radical pedagogy often employ utopian language, which leads me to ask what works and what doesn't, what's realized and what's just potential.

TV That's an important question. I would say that we try to deal with curatorial provocations on two levels. First, we have a strong commitment to teachers working in the public-education system in São Paulo. So we offer them courses, and our educational publication is mainly conceived to be used in the classroom. We take the school board's official curriculum into account in this work. So our challenge is to connect this radical pedagogy with the reality of the schools, of the curriculum, of the teachers' everyday work. One of our roles is to find the topics in the curriculum that are progressive. And we are lucky in Brazil because our national curriculum is quite progressive. It was refreshed in 2017 after a decade of discussions with the educational community.

The other part of it is the mediated tools that we are in charge of preparing. These tools are conceived as a place for experimentation. We encourage educators to try new methods for discussing contemporary art with people who have no knowledge of the subject. The educators are free to create their strategies, their itineraries—even to confront the curatorial project and the curators' ideas during their tours.

NS In the last biennial, Denise Ferreira da Silva had a space for interaction that also included its own curriculum. I wonder how the teachers you speak of might engage with a project like that.

TV The educators really participated in the project because they used her space. They debated her ideas, and those of other Black authors like Brazilian philosopher Leda Maria Martins. These conversations were not part of the official public program, but rather part of the educators' own routines.

NS That's certainly different than pointing out details in a painting or a photograph. I wonder how you think the educational turn will affect the field in the future. Can this idea of education as a medium for artists or curators develop further in some way?

TV Well, even though an exhibition like the São Paulo Biennial is not directly connected to the art market, it's something that often crosses our path. I think that educational practices like we're discussing are not so easily absorbed by the art market. There is a potential for the attitude of "question everything" to be a source of conflict. What kinds of evolution are necessary to create and protect spaces of autonomy and independent critical thinking? I'm not sure that institutions are ultimately willing to put the educational turn at the center of their operations, to make it a foundation and give up their relationships with the art market, with sponsors, and so on.

NS Market questions are certainly pervasive, but I also had two thoughts earlier about ideology or ideological pressures. When you were talking about Brazil's progressive educational curriculum, I thought about the last political administration there and the many pressures it placed on education and culture. Did the Biennial feel any effects of that?

TV I don't think that the exhibition itself suffered from this kind of pressure, but I think that, as Brazilian society grappled with it, nearly every conversation could end up being a discussion about politics. The exhibition was politicized, at a very high level, because of everything that was happening. But the exhibition didn't suffer from direct pressure.

NS I was also thinking about the biennial that Charles Esche directed, which was planned at a moment of increasing awareness for the Boycott, Divestment, and Sanctions (BDS) movement. From the outside, it seemed like the curatorial group talked extensively about what it means to boycott, and who, and why. Was the education team involved in any of these conversations, or related ones about how to interpret this moment and movement for and with the public?

TV I remember that those of us involved in education were drafted into some of the conversations that artists were having. We wanted to know how artists were seeing, were interpreting, topics like this that were increasingly in the news. In particular, I remember a conversation in the Ibirapuera Park, where a group of artists had gathered on the grass, were discussing this topic, and were finding it difficult to reach any kind of collective position. The conversation itself struck me as very pedagogical. We were not involved formally, neither at the invitation of the curatorial team nor the artists involved, but it was in the air and to some extent unavoidable.

NS Is there anything that I didn't ask about that you'd like to share about your experience with education and the biennial?

TV I'll just add that education at the São Paulo Biennial works the way it does because of its long history. It started as part of a museum's activities, but since 1963 it has been an independent institution and not part of a museum.

That said, education can feel somewhat invisible because, historically, the artists and curators—the big names—are much more visible to the art world. But for the city and for the local audiences, the educators are really important. They help create the place that the São Paulo Biennial has in the imaginary of the city.

Back in the sixties, educators were even interviewed by the newspapers; they had almost a similar status as the artists, because journalists saw them as having the keys to the biennial's world. Of course, this understanding has changed. We don't see ourselves like this, nor do I think that people see us this way now. Nonetheless, we remain a link between people's everyday lives—their problems, their hopes, their references—and this big event that brings such interesting and often strange visual experiences and conversations to the city. We are still the link. To me, this is the essence of the Biennial.

Learning from the Medium

Manuela Moscoso interviewed by Noah Simblist

This conversation was recorded on October 29, 2024. It has been edited for length and clarity.

Noah Simblist After previously working on the Cuenca and Liverpool biennials, you're now working on the upcoming Bienial das Amazônias. One thing I have discussed with other curators is how curators and artists are centering pedagogy as a practice. Can you think of one or two examples from your experience where the curatorial strategy accounted for either teaching or learning as a practice?

Manuela Moscoso I think the idea of pedagogy is very expansive. I understand our practice as curators as ongoing learning that gets more sophisticated. I feel it is about learning by doing. You cannot just learn concepts in order to have your own voice as a curator; you have to be learning as an open person and develop through practice.

It also depends on the type of project. Pedagogy can appear in a project itself, if the work of an artist has a pedagogical tool. It is about creating a space where people share and learn from each other. One example from where I work at CARA involves producing a film by the artist Javier Téllez. The production of the film was the outcome of workshops between Venezuelan refugees looking at movies by Charlie Chaplin and producing their own movie inspired by one of them. So it was a collective tool where they talk about migration and about Chaplin and the structure of acting, and in a way that I feel has some pedagogy without having a classroom.

Another example that involved that exchange was during the 11th Liverpool Biennial, in 2021, when I worked with KeKeÇa, a Turkish collective. They work with percussion and how you can learn by doing percussion with your hands and clapping or touching something. They think about the history of percussion and how you can do it without any instrument. There were workshops for adults that were very collaborative; you create a piece of music together. We worked with a school that the Biennial had a relationship with. But this was during the pandemic. We had to switch to an online presentation, and then it became a tool that a lot of schools ended up using. Suddenly it became something completely different because it was easy to do it at home by delivering live workshops online.

Another recent example from CARA is that we worked with Octavia Projects, who do summer camps for femme, gender-fluid, or nonbinary BIPOC youth between the ages of twelve and sixteen. It's a free workshop created by artists. We invited them alongside another organization, Voluminous Arts, a record label that works with trans musicians that make experimental music and sound. We created a transgenerational project that amplified, supported, and created a queer space in the most expanded way. It was important for us to provide what they needed, a space of gathering and experimentation. They had a public program every Monday, which involved noise and sound performances. We had a faculty of trans scholars, activists, and artists who were giving different tools to the people from the record label and to the kids.

NS Sally Tallant, in another conversation for this book, talked about how the Liverpool Biennial was always modeled, from her perspective, on the city as a school and the ways in which the biennial participated in a direct intervention in the city. Do you think that there's a site specificity to the interventions in any of these projects?

MM It depends on the structure of the biennial. Does it have a budget? Does it have people that work there? Do they have political intentions? I don't think it's always about site specificity because the structure is given by the institution's relationship to the site. Cuenca is different from Liverpool and from Amazônia. You have to become site-specific because you cannot bring your own structure from the outside. I feel it is the first exercise as a curator to think site-specifically.

The other example that I was going to talk about is Jorgge Menna Barreto, who did a long-term project about food for the Liverpool Biennial. Again, because of the pandemic, we ended up doing a magazine instead of the restaurant we had planned. Barreto works on a non-discursive exploration of the world through the stomach, and we partnered with academics, chefs, and restaurants. It depends on the relationship you want to have with a city, but I think it's the structure of the biennial is necessary to create ambitious projects like this. As an institution, you have to be clear about breadth, about how far it can go. Maybe it can be very small but real. It's about matching the expectations from both sides to be site-specific.

NS The idea of impact interests me, because there were many claims of radicality during the educational turn. How do you assess the radicality of radical pedagogy?

MM I don't think these projects I've described are mainstream at all. There are many ways to approach a biennial. Again, it has to do with the structure. Biennials can be great or very bad. It's all about proximity. I think the radical is found in how we work with people, how we listen, how we create boundaries. It's more like a ground process than an air process.

NS Do you think that exhibition making in a biennial context has changed now that discursive practices have been normalized?

MM Yes and no. Because classrooms are not the same everywhere. Publics from Brazil will probably go for anything participatory, but this is not the same as in Ecuador. They will say, "Oh, no way José, I will not even enter the room." If you wanted that conventional classroom model but you turn the logic around, then I think it's an interesting project. Then it's radical. There is a word in Spanish, *tibio*—not hot, not cold. You don't have that in English, which is very annoying. I feel, just do it, cold or hot.

I also think about how image circulation happens and how traveling has become more accessible. Most young people know what Documenta is. I didn't know what Documenta was until later in my life. Now there is so much more access, not only visually, but textually through Instagram. Now there is greater circulation of ideas. You see a book or an exhibition about radical dance and you can find fifty more exhibitions at different scales about that topic. I don't know if it's good or bad, but it has created a different dynamic.

NS Do you think that these dynamics affect artists? If an artist self-identifies as "pedagogically" oriented, does that mean a certain kind of art production?

MM Yes, but I think it has always been like that. Maybe we're in an interesting moment because I feel like image circulation has led to an exhaustion. I also think that we are more intelligent about reading this proliferation of images.

NS On the one hand, people have more accessibility to what's happening in different places. But that also means that people are more likely to reproduce the images they see online, making the context more important to understanding each image. You could reproduce the image, but where is it coming from?

MM Yes, I believe that we need the whole experience of something: the smell, the people ... that's what makes it real. If we are talking about biennials as a format, I don't think any format is good or bad, it depends how you do it. We can be on Instagram looking at things elsewhere. But the biennial is a moment where people are together in a real space.

NS Have all of the biennials you've collaborated on have educational teams in addition to a curatorial team?

MM Yes, all of them.

NS If curators are thinking about education and the educators are tasked with education, how does that partnership work? Were there some tensions?

MM It depends. But this is not only a problem for biennials.

NS Also for museums?

MM Yes. It's a problem. I don't know how to break the spell. There are certain things that work as pedagogy that we curators just don't like. Let's say it's a coloring book. We will say: "This is not radical enough." But they work. On the other hand, sometimes a coloring book is what's expected and creating it involves no pedagogical experimentation. Sometimes pedagogical tools can be a little patronizing.

NS You mean prompts like, "What does this make you feel?"

MM Yes! When I encounter that, I say, "Take me out of here immediately." That's why I think kids are amazing, because they couldn't care less about this. Sometimes they're better students and much more straightforward than adults. They're not buying it. If they're tired, they couldn't care less what you're asking. But I think that this idea of correctness, what you're supposed to know, shouldn't apply when it comes to education in the arts. It could be much more fantastical.

NS You mentioned that participation is more of a challenge in Ecuador than in Brazil. How do you adjust between such contexts with your team?

MM In Ecuador, for instance, the biennial had a grant to develop the educational programs. This is exactly what I hate. But I cannot go to the educators and say "It doesn't work!" because then I patronize them. You have to let it go. And maybe you say, "Don't you think this would be amazing?" You introduce something else.

But we did another project with somebody that I admire so much, even though we lost him recently. It is Agency, an initiative founded by Kobe Matthys in Brussels. Agency deals with objects that resist the split between nature and culture and the ones that provoke authorship or other legal problems. We invited Agency to the Cuenca Biennial, and they came up with a question and then brought objects that responded to that question. In this particular case, the objects related to legal questions about authorship by phantoms or spirits.

For instance, there was a person whose kid had died. Someone said that they could invoke the child's spirit and let that spirit draw through their body. After a while, someone else wanted to do something with the drawing, but the person who had made the drawing said, "No, this is my drawing." And the father said, "No, it's not your drawing. It is my son's drawing."

NS That's amazing.

MM What used to happen in those scenarios is that experts adjudicated those competing claims. Agency has been so important for me as a curator. I've been in conversation with them for many years. This is pedagogy. In a situation like this, Agency would bring in different kinds of experts: one would always be a lawyer, while others depend on the objects under consideration. In this case, you have to have a medium, as well as an expert in drawing. Agency invites audiences to give their own perspectives about who is right and who is wrong. It was like a conversation. In Ecuador, people talked about a spirit's rights. It was an incredibly successful program.

NS Last question: Looking twenty, thirty, fifty years into the future, what do you hope for the trajectory of the educational turn in curatorial practice? What's the best way it can inform the way that we work?

MM Thirty, forty years is difficult; every sign in the world shows us a different path. For instance, when talking about the

Amazon Biennial, there is obviously a sensitivity around the environment and around other non-Western forms of understanding the world, and how both are being forcibly changed or erased. What is incredible about art is the power of materials, of finding language in solid objects, of finding other alternatives to those stories, of projecting history into the future. How can we let things speak for themselves? It's important to reconsider our position in the world. If we really take it seriously, the pedagogy could be really amazing. Even though the entire world is more connected, we need to find the points of solidarity, the points of specificity. That's what education should be.

Maintaining Belief in Institutions

Magalí Arriola, Johanna Burton, Sally Tallant, and Dominic Asmall Willsdon, moderated by Noah Simblist

This conversation was recorded on September 23, 2024. It was edited for length and clarity.

Noah Simblist I'd like to begin by looking at the educational turn and thinking aloud about how it affected museums. Do any of you feel particularly connected to or disconnected from this history? Do any of you feel as if you were an agent in introducing or moving education to the center of curatorial practice?

Sally Tallant I definitely do. I've spent my whole career, my working life, trying to change institutional structures so that they center civic, public, and educational values alongside—not above, but alongside—artistic values. I worked in Britain all through the 2000s and then more recently in the United States. I do think those contexts have different histories, even though we were all in dialogue. At the Serpentine, then the Liverpool Biennial, and now at Queens Museum, I've been trying to find ways to connect the institution to the people and communities that it serves. I feel I've been a part of these conversations right from the beginning—and I continue to be a part of them. And as I get more experienced, I am feeling more cynical. I am more skeptical about how this can work in such a volatile political environment. So yes, I feel very implicated.

Magalí Arriola I definitely relate to the educational turn in art institutions as I belong to a generation of curators (as I think most of us do) that grew as those changes were developing. Museums were heading toward a discursive shift associated with certain theoretical perspectives such as Maria Lind's New Institutionalism or Grant Kester's Dialogical Aesthetics, which generated heated debates. We're talking about a span of twenty years during which I've personally jumped in and out of the institution (public and private). At the outset of the 2000s I was working independently and then joined Museo Tamayo around 2010 in a curatorial position to later become its director. I think the context has greatly evolved since then.

One remark that struck me in the framework that Noah and Dominic set for this conversation was that curators used to work with objects and educators with audiences. That was indeed the first big change we might have performed and experienced as all of this history was taking place: a kind of transmutation of the object of curatorial practice that was meant to reshape the institution. However, that transformation was also related to how artistic practices themselves were changing. We as curators embraced the new ways in which artists were engaging their audiences, inside but mostly outside of the institution: A great majority of artists working in Mexico (that is where I started my career), and Mexico City in particular, in the late '90s and early 2000s, were deeply immersed in the urban context as a result of a huge lack of institutional support. As soon as the so-called dialogical or relational practices—here and elsewhere—became institutionalized, certainly contributing to an educational turn, they evolved into a legitimation strategy. So even though I relate to that story, I also became skeptical about it.

Johanna Burton I was trained as an art historian and thought I would be writing art history and teaching—really, education was always at the crux of what I wanted to do. I realized, though, that the mutual exchange I wanted led me to be a lot more proximate to artists. I wanted them to lead, to produce that space of exchange in real time. And so I moved into the curatorial sphere. I was Maria Lind's successor at Bard, where I ran the graduate program in curatorial studies after having taught there for many years.

When I look at my own trajectory, I feel I've made a clear set of decisions: I've been trying to find spaces that weren't very well defined and that allowed for new kinds of work and collaboration. And education was often that space. I was not trained as a classical museum educator. I'm trained as an academic and then a curator and then an administrator. But the space that could be both fine-tuned and re-ordered within those areas was most often via the portal of "education." The broad nomenclature of "education," which defines both so much and so little, is how I found some of my best colleagues. Dominic and I worked together, for instance, on a book that engages a lot of these questions. I tried to seek out the other people that do education in this expanded way; it's how I met Sally, too, as well as Sandra Jackson-Dumont, Hamza Walker, and many others.

After Bard, I ended up at the New Museum. The founder, Marcia Tucker, set that institution on its particular path, and then of course my predecessor heading the Education Department, Eungie Joo, laid the groundwork for a different kind of education program, one that was both at the center and at the edges of the institution. The New Museum served ostensibly traditional audiences and communities, which I think is necessary. But it also did totally radical, out-of-the-box stuff that had nothing to do with the exhibitions on view: Museum as Hub and Night School, for example, and then a number of residencies where artists led projects that they wouldn't be asked to do in museums otherwise, and books, like the *Public Servants* book I co-edited with Dominic, and the entire series I rebooted of which that volume was one. I've always heavily identified with these expanded, experimental modalities, but I didn't always know what to call it. And education is one word, but most people who use that word aren't talking about the same things. That became clear to me as I led an education department and then went on to try to lead institutions in the same ways I had led that department.

ST I started my job as the head of education at Serpentine in 2001. I moved from the curatorial track to do that. One thing that always goes missing from these conversations is that I love the work I do with children in schools, which is a lot of what we do. I think a lot of curators got interested in public programs as a way of extending exhibitions, but many are now genuinely engaging with people who feel the museum is not their space. And that is the majority of people. I love my work with seniors. We all want to work intersectionally, but I genuinely think that the most radical work I do is the work that I've weirdly found to be the most difficult to get into this conversation.

JB Yeah, I agree. I think people here are like, "Why are you spending so much time on K–12 programs?" But that work does have a radical effect. So when we're talking about education in an expanded sense, we shouldn't leave out the "unexpanded" sense.

Dominic Asmall Willsdon First of all, I'm so aware of the biographical parallels, particularly with Sally and Johanna. When I started at Tate Modern in the early 2000s, Sally was, I think, already at the Serpentine—she was on the other side of the city, but with a seemingly complementary temperament and philosophy. In the early 2010s, I was in San Francisco as curator of education and public programs at SFMOMA and Johanna was at the New Museum in the equivalent role—so on the other side of the country, and yet with a seemingly similar sense of what the role could be. I remember Johanna came to talk to my team sometime in the mid-2010s. Afterward, somebody said, "Oh, [Johanna's team] is like Bizarro us."

I came into this area of work, this institutional position, from academia. The thing that first engaged me was the unpredictability of encounters in the museum space. The sense of, I guess, the theater of strangers was energizing for me. There was a lot of creative opportunity in museum education because it was seen as essential that museums have education teams, but what those teams should do was not highly prescribed. I've found myself tasked with working at a large scale—and scale is really important to all of this. Instead of an audience, or a community, you are working for a public. There are four or five million people coming to the museum each year, and you want to know who is in these rooms, what do they know, and what kind of encounter can they have with each other.

I came almost straight from grad school, and a lot of people studying political philosophy as I was in the late '90s were interested in what could be radical democracy; [the philosopher] Ernesto Laclau was on my dissertation committee. At that time of Clinton-Blair consensus, there was that "end of history" sense that it's all democracy now, so the critical questions had become, "What kinds of richness, variation and depth can democracy have?" It seemed like a cultural question as much as a political one. It seemed like large cultural institutions could be the scene of the democratic encounter. Whereas today, when the fundamentals of democracy are at risk, it no longer seems like the time to study the forms of participatory affect and the nuances of democratic engagement. The early 2000s was a time for refining democratic engagement through cultural practice and institutions; that time has passed.

NS I think Magalí touched on this earlier, but in thinking about this twenty-year period in retrospect, what were the limitations of those educational tendencies in art institutions? Often the programs and projects came with a lot of utopian language.

MA Sadly I don't think we really got over those limitations, which I suspect result from the social rhetoric and political strategies that often accompany utopian language, and that are so difficult to implement. It sometimes feels like we're running around in circles, changing the wording to fight the same inertias—for the aspirations remain identical: to bring about a more egalitarian access to arts and culture. Johanna already mentioned the Museum as Hub, which was indeed a great initiative aiming to overcome the divide between centers and peripheries in the early 2000s. What some of our colleagues called back then "the local tango and the global dance" steamed from the assessment and critique of the identity politics behind the previous decades' multiculturalism. It seems that all that utopian language can now be summarized in a much simpler dictum preaching equality, diversity, and inclusion—a dictum that recent events have demonstrated can be erased in one go. While all of this has given visibility to individual voices from different communities (Black, native, Indigenous, Chicano, feminist, queer ...), we should still remain vigilant of how these identity divides are framed to avoid falling again into cultural sectarianism and favor, instead, a long-term integrated dialogue between those very same communities.

JB I do think when I came into this field, whatever this field is, there was a belief in the discursive platform, and that has gone away. We argued about texts, we read magazines. Frederic Jameson died yesterday and that's a huge loss in my world. But does Frederic Jameson still compute for people? I'm not saying that people are thinking less or that they're less interested in ideas, but it's different. Going into classrooms reminds me how fast things are changing.

There is no shared text, no four things we all read in *October* last week. There's no longer really a canon, a foundational set of texts. I want to be very mindful and clear. I'm not saying that's bad or good, but I think it changes the trajectory of how we talk about education—especially since, generationally, we are all basically in the same cohort and we have similar inheritances.

When I came on the scene, there were things like the Mountain School and Night School, and it felt like we could talk about everything. And, frankly, I thought all these projects were kind of ridiculous—at the same time that they seemed super cool. Each had ten people in their seminars or cohorts that weren't me; I just read about them. Even when I'd go to Passerby [the New York City bar owned by art dealer Gavin Brown], I didn't feel like I totally fit in. But it seemed both kind of symbolic and really important for a group of people in a social scene that I was proximate to.

And so the heyday of the educational turn that we're discussing was something I learned about and debated but wasn't necessarily something I participated in frontally. It seemed like there was an inside and outside. I wanted to go from being an art historian, where I was writing for four people, to curating for more people. And then it became interesting to administer an institution for even more people. But you become more and more invisible, especially as a woman, the better job you do clearing the stage for others. And so I wonder if we can talk a little bit about when something is rubber-stamped as an "educational turn" space versus when it just operates that way. I do think we're talking about style a little bit—or at least a period style.

ST Very interesting. I think there are different sets of limitations then and now, and we should separate those conversations out a little bit. I think in some ways what Magalí says is right, that some of the limitations that we thought we had dismantled have come right back. That's like feminist practice: if you don't do it every day, things just revert to how they were before. I do think politics is a practice.

I didn't come out of art history or theory at all. I came out of community art, and I was anti-institutional. I went into institutions to change them. The limitations I thought we'd managed to change were hardwired into people's professional paths. That hasn't happened. Everyone has a desire for change, sure, yet curators and educators don't often want to work together. This was a big learning curve for me. I assumed that everybody wanted to undo the curatorial hierarchy within institutions and to really think about education as a way to reimagine them. Not everybody's interested in that, which was a real surprise to me. Whatever changes we did make were unsustainable because every time an individual leaves an institution, it reverts back to how it was before. Biennials could be more flexible, but they're too production-oriented. It's very difficult to retain clarity and a position in a broader conversation around what the hell we think we're doing.

Our institutions reflect the world in which we operate; they're constructed through the conditions in which we operate. So in this moment of late capitalism, we have what we deserve, and market forces set the terms of the decisions we can make. In that context, how can I retain my belief that everyone should have access to the space? How can I encourage the staff to act differently?

NS Given what Johanna mentioned about style and the fact that each of you have worked with new generations of curators, how have exhibition-making practices evolved? How have younger people internalized this history? Do they take it for granted? Do they simply remake what happened before? Do you still sense that democratic impulse to engage audiences and create publics?

MA I don't believe there is a deep awareness of curatorial history nor exhibition making among my younger colleagues, but this is also probably particular to my context. There seems to be a complete blackout of art history—not just art history with capital letters, but also the recent history of exhibitions in Mexico and what they mean to our scene. The hard work performed by at least two generations before mine to make institutions available to contemporary art seems to have sunk into oblivion. I know different contexts move at different speeds and in very diverse directions as they're responding to different needs. However, my impression is that the new generations believe that, since they have a voice, it should be heard and spread out at all costs (maybe a consequence of social media?). That sense of entitlement sometimes overshadows the sense of respect and solidarity *for* and *with* which one works, even more so from the institution.

JB I may be seeking these people out, but I'm actually quite excited about generations that are coming up right now. I feel like there's a heavy weight on people's shoulders. And to Sally's point, I think in addition to what's happening in the present, they're aware that the structures they will inherit can revert to earlier forms. That said, I was interested to hear where you've come from, Sally. The reason I went immediately into the most high-minded academic environment I could find is that I come from lower-class rural Nevada, and all I wanted was to become part of the institution.

At the end of the day, we probably think the same thing, but my mindset was, "It exists so maybe if I can get in there, I can help change it, not tear it down." I tend to be on the reformist side of things, though maybe it doesn't sound as sexy as wanting to tear things down. But if you go back to, say, Dewey, reform can represent a lot of change.

Regarding younger people, there probably are some who aren't at all interested in engaging the history we're discussing. But there are also many I know who are really invested in carrying some of the tenets we're talking about forward—and I think pretty radically. Unfortunately they're having to be super diligent and hopeful despite the odds, because they see that the social systems literally won't be there to sustain or support them when they need it. When I'm working alongside young curators and artists, we often talk about projects that embody the issues that we're bringing up here, but it's hard to find the support for those projects—there is little philanthropy to support them. The pendulum swing that scares me most right now gets back to the individualism question, the representation question. Projects that are about really thinking through dialogic and critical questions are not so fundable right now. There's a pressure on museums to show they've checked boxes, but there's no money. I don't know if it feels like this outside of the United States, but from here it feels like it's happening everywhere. Funding for the arts in general is incredibly difficult right now.

DW I think about the generational question in terms of a big tent versus small tents. For decades we've hoped the institution can be a big tent. To use that political metaphor, one of the necessary characteristics of a big tent is that it needs to contain, and be resilient to, internal dialogue, even internal conflict. Those of us responsible for managing these institutions need to design them so that they can accommodate that conflict with a generation coming up.

Yet in younger generations I see less interest or belief in the big tent and a move toward a cultural space composed of small tents, with agreement expected *within* the institution and the conflict and dialogue happening *between* institutions. So you have less tolerance for differences of identity and opinion within the institution and a keenness to clarify the institution's positions so that it can be effective in its struggles with other institutions. It is a challenge to the liberal principles on which mainstream cultural institutions have assumed or adopted but may or may not have lived up to.

JB There may be less interest in a big civic tent, but I actually feel like, when you really get down to it, many audiences want big museums and spectacular shows. They want everything else too–there are artists who can and are showing in movie theaters, and they're working on AI projects and in collaboration with grassroots organizations, of course–but blockbusters are the mainstay and the focus. For better or for worse, at the end of the day, there's still some value inherent to museums, but it often reverts to the big exhibition as such and in its most conventional form. I'm trying to hold on to the fact that museums still hold value and interest because I think that's a good thing, but it's also important to be clear-headed about where most of that value accrues. And I think you're also right, Dominic; we can be our own worst enemies. The little tempests in the teapots that happen while running our institutions can be the hardest part of it. That's why, looking at all of you, I'm so grateful to have colleagues.

I call my colleagues all the time. We don't always agree, but it's usually very productive. And in general, we do ourselves a disservice by not projecting outward into society more than we do. While I think the legacies of institutional critique and looking inward are important, it's gone to a level where we can barely function. So I've been very interested in collaborations; we just embarked on three of them here. There's so much to be said not only for sharing resources, but also for keeping the institution limber and operating outside of its little lines.

ST I think that I don't fully agree with you, Dominic, because despite it all, I truly believe in the work that I'm attempting to do here. And I believe that the institution that we're trying to construct—for all of its flaws—is of value to the communities that engage with it. And I think the younger generation, brutal as they are, I admire the courage and conviction they have.

Even some people who are maybe only ten or fifteen years younger than me, rather than much younger than me, are very skeptical. They don't trust museums and institutions. But we have to construct something that's going to work. And I do think the flame of the market can destroy a lot of things, but, at the same time, maybe there's something productive there too. I do think that we are in a transitional phase. Finally, one thing I'm grateful for at Queens Museum is the ability to say we are "New York adjacent," or that we're in the center of New York and Manhattan is "New York adjacent." Whichever way it is, we are lucky to work closely with a generation of politicians in their twenties and thirties who are fighting for democracy in this country. They give me hope. They use our museum. As with our younger curatorial staff, we have to give them the tools. It's our job to make sure we construct an environment that can make what they need possible. And no, I don't know what that is. And no, I cannot get any funding. I'll never have the money I need, but I have a space, and we can do things together.

DW Sally, I still share your belief in institutions—you and I have certainly talked often about this. But for the first time, I'm conscious of that as a commitment that needs to be willed rather than something that's broadly assumed. I'm even more conscious of it now, running a film organization rather than I was at a museum of objects. Museums are where the art is. The physical objects anchor those spaces and organize the discourse around them. Film being more evanescent and immaterial doesn't warrant its institutions, such as festivals, to the same extent.

At a conference in Amsterdam recently, somebody from the Palestinian Film Institute, which is in that category of artist collectives that present as institutions, said to the director of the documentary film festival, "We don't need your festival. There are filmmakers who show their work on YouTube that want to ally with us. They want to be part of our collective because it embodies something: their values, their politics, their aesthetics. If this film festival doesn't do that any longer, then you'll be superseded as an institutional structure." This connects a bit to Sally's distinction between museums and biennials. Collections will continue to make museums more resistant to being superseded.

NS One topic we keep coming back to is how to define education, what is educational practice. We've talked about a theoretical educational practice, and about radical-politics education as a way to reach out to various audiences. We've talked about practices that are more dialogical or more discursive, that don't focus on artworks as commodities. I'm wondering, from your perspective as leaders in institutions, about the question of public versus private funding. Are there models that you think have worked, have been able to support these kinds of educational practices?

DW Well, we probably haven't talked enough about the role of the state in these matters and in different contexts. Two of us come from the UK but are in the United States now, Magalí is in Mexico, and Johanna's in the States—each presents a very different relationship between the government and cultural institutions. The presence or absence of government structure, never mind government funding, hangs over all these questions.

MA Even though Museo Tamayo is a government-run institution with a very restrained budget, I suspect that during my tenure there I probably had more flexibility than I could have had in any American institution—at least in terms of where I could place the money I raised through the private foundation associated to the museum. On the other hand, there was a whole range of topics, particularly those related to local politics, that could simply not be addressed. Interestingly, what suffered the most from that was our public and educational programing, which is where most social urgencies are voiced and discussed. However, I don't think that's unique to Mexican public institutions.

ST All funding comes with constraints, as you say, Magalí. I'm also in a city-owned building. There are limitations to what I can and cannot do. One change is the funders themselves: this new generation is less philanthropic; they want to do their own projects and want to own things in a different way. So we are part of an ecosystem that's changing.

People talk about being instrumentalized by the state, but I think being instrumentalized by funders and the market is a real thing, too. In New York, the state is the least of my problems. The people who get the most worked up about content are our funders. I don't mean that in a censoring way; it's more like they want to help tell us what we should prioritize. That applies to both private and public funding.

Another thing we haven't talked about is that more of us who come out of the education space are now directors. That wasn't the case until, what, seven years ago? Now there's a good number of us, but the ground beneath us is shifting. I think the foundations that most of us have spent decades building relationships with are also shifting gears to some degree. It's not a values shift; it's a structural change.

NS I want to see if we could end on a hopeful note, and if there are any projects in progress at your institutions or that you know about that are drawing on this educational turn in a productive and hopeful way.

ST We are still here. We are still here and doing this work. It's something.

DW I'm once again exploring partnerships with community colleges. Community colleges are one of the few institutional infrastructures in the United States in which I feel a completely unalloyed belief and hope. And so I find myself, time and again, looking for ways to enable whatever institutional structure I'm responsible for to add value to the community college system.

ST I see people all over the place doing incredible work. Magalí completed a whole administrative cycle despite no money, despite a political reality that's not going to support institutions. My friend Christine Tohmé is still running Homeworks despite what's happening in Lebanon. I feel like it's not the same, but I am building a children's museum. Johanna, you're making it happen, re-imagining MOCA. I do think we should find a way to celebrate those gains. And I also think that a lot of women who are feminists and educators have stepped into this space and it's hard as women. We are not all the same age here, but as you get older you become less and less visible and less relevant more quickly than the men around you. It is easy to become distracted by social media and everyday crises, but there is something of value to this.

MA The educational turn has definitely impacted my curatorial work over the years, particularly in terms of how in-depth research associated with artistic practice, whatever the topic, can unfold and expand to different contexts and disciplines. That is something which also permeated my term at Museo Tamayo, that I not only tried to transmit to my team but that we also implemented in our program and shared with our audiences. One of the things that I discovered and excited me the most was having a big diverse crowd following our program, ranging from kids—tons of kids—to teenage couples, extended families and, of course, the art-driven community. Perhaps because we lacked funding, and because we were understaffed, my team and I were obliged to turn the museum into one single organism in which the different departments (curatorial, educational ...) worked in very close collaboration. That's what kept us going. At least in the city and in the context of the park where the museum is located, it has been working.

JB I think what you just said is really important, Magalí. My understanding of what it means to serve this role has really changed. Before, everything had to be run through the lens of social- and self-reflexive critique. And now I'm interested in building a program that can accommodate that but can also accommodate somebody who just wants to come in because the building's open. There's something so interesting about letting go of my own ideas of what it means to serve the public. That has been liberating.

I was going to answer your question about what's coming up that feels really great. We're taking on this really intense show called "Monuments" later this year, which is co-curated with Hamza Walker and Kara Walker and our curator here, Bennett Simpson. It's showing decommissioned Confederate monuments from all over the country, alongside works by contemporary artists responding to the long arc of history that got us here. So this is all about education in one sense, and of course very heavy in a sense. On what would seem a different end of the spectrum of engagement, just last week we opened a beautiful Olafur Eliasson show about opticality and sensuality.

Both of those shows will serve publics, right? We can't necessarily predict what people need to have the kinds of experiences they're seeking or will respond to. I think that you just said it very well, which is to be open and have people want to come into the museum no matter what you have on view. Some of it they might want to interact with and some of it they might not. That's okay. You just want them to want to come back.

City as a School

Sofía Olascoaga, Lucia Sanroman, Sally Tallant, and Dominic Asmall Willsdon, moderated by Noah Simblist

This conversation was recorded on October 25, 2024. It has been edited for length and clarity

Noah Simblist In addition to your institutional roles, you've each worked on biennials in different capacities over the last fifteen years. Sally was director of the Liverpool Biennial from 2011 to 2019. Dominic was a cocurator of one of those editions of the Liverpool Biennial, in 2016, and worked as cocurator for the ninth Mercosul Biennial in 2013. Lucia was a cocurator of SITE Santa Fe's SITElines Biennial in 2014. And Sofía was cocurator of the 32nd São Paulo Biennial in 2016. So I'd like to discuss the ways in which your work on these biennials intersected with education in a traditional sense and in relationship to the "educational turn"—how either your curatorial strategies or the work of the included artists centered on pedagogy as a practice. Will each of you speak to one or two examples of how that played out in the biennials that you worked on?

Lucia Sanroman Well, to start with, SITE Santa Fe was not particularly focused on pedagogy in 2014; it focused on changing the form, function, and the territory of the biennial. Irene [Hofmann] and I started working three years earlier to conceptualize a Pan-American, rather than an international or cosmopolitan, biennial. So the work of pedagogy was left to the education department at the museum. But it characterized my dialogue with Irene, Candace Hopkins, and Janet Dees; we worked in a pedagogical way to figure out how to expand, to reconfigure, the model of the biennial. The pedagogy was internal; I can speak to that better than I can to public pedagogy, the form of engagement with audiences.

The other biennial I worked on, as a guest curator, was in Medellín, Colombia, in 2011, for which I invited eleven artists from Tijuana to come to Medellín and learn from the city. Literally: the motto was "to learn from." It was called *Projecto Coyote* in reference to the "coyotes" that transfer people through Mexico's northern border. We used the biennial to bring artists, musicians, poets, writers, architects, and urbanists to learn from specific people in Medellín. It was the most successful pedagogical program I have ever conceived, because it was specific about a transfer of knowledge between people who are in different localities but whose contexts might have similarities, namely the fragility of the state and the saturation of violence.

At that moment, Medellín's mayor was also implementing forward-thinking urbanist programs. It felt important to go and figure out what was happening as the city went from being known for drug cartels to being known for its park libraries and the quality of its schools. So we did research. Because I was managing the project, I was the only person who didn't actively participate in that research—and to be honest, that was a tremendously frustrating aspect of the experience. I was essentially a travel agent and a mother.

Anyway, it turns out there was a lot that people in these cities had in common. Another thing: I was very stubborn about there being no exhibition of this process. They ended up going against my will and making an exhibition about the act of connecting with one individual—but it was beautiful and interesting and lovely. One of the cocurators was my friend Bill Kelly, who emphasized pedagogy in that program. Interestingly, in the context of a city promoting its own social and public programs, Bill and his cocurators encountered resistance to their pedagogical ideas.

Our little program ended up receiving attention because it was hard to track. Colombia employed systems for tracking the social impact of projects. Because we reduced the exchange of information to only two or three people, we couldn't really track it, and it was useful for us to see our efforts that way. This project continues to impact my work. It gave me the taste for engaging in pedagogy within whatever structure I encounter. One strength of biennials is that they come and go and therefore can be reshaped. You don't have to conform to a particular structure.

NS Sally, given that you were responsible for the institution of a biennial and several of its iterations, what do you think about this?

Sally Tallant I ran the Liverpool Biennial, which is a specific model of a biennial, for eight years; I did five editions. Biennials are inherently linked to the conditions of the cities where they're located. Their structures emerge from what's possible and necessary in each environment. In Liverpool, I saw the city as a school. We used to reference [architect and historian] Denise Scott Brown and ask ourselves, "How can you learn stories from the city, from its particular places?"

Biennials are also attuned to people and economic history, not least because they are relatively precarious. Does a strong arts ecology surround it? I think there are three kinds of biennials. The first occurs where there's nothing else happening, there are no institutions, and it creates a kind of focus and brings an often-international conversation to a place. Think of the

Lubumbashi Biennale in the Congo or the Yogyakarta Biennale in Indonesia. And then you have biennials, like Lyon, Berlin, and Liverpool, that add to the cultural ecology of the place by bringing an international conversation rethinking the possibilities for artists and cities. Lastly, you have biennials that contribute to a city's tourism. A lot of the Asian biennials, as with Shanghai, are international exhibitions that happen within a museum's walls. One theme that can cut across these three types, and here I think São Paulo is important, is decentering where we're looking from and rethinking whose culture is valued and foregrounded. My drive was to build a biennial that genuinely thinks about what art can do in everybody's lives—beyond the art market.

It's also important to note that, with few exceptions, biennials happen in secondary and tertiary cities without a thriving art market. So it's important not to ask how art relates to the market, but instead how it relates to people. How can the biennial help to build that ecology I mentioned? I think the overproduction and spectacularizing nature of biennials that you refer to, Lucia, sometimes goes against the pedagogical intent. Perhaps that's because it's an exhausted format—something for us to discuss.

I tried to do what I called the "perennial biennial." I supported artists year-round. We did long-term commissions; Jeanne van Heeswijk's intervention was a multiyear commission that ended up taking the form of both housing and a bakery; it is its own business now.

At the same time, I did conceptual projects that garnered the attention of the international press. You need multiple entry points for biennials. You want to give the public an opportunity to think about how art can be part of their lives, and at the same time involve artists who maybe haven't received institutional shows yet, or who can maybe be more political and experimental than they can ordinarily.

In my mind, the multiyear projects created an underlying ethos, which was about seeing the city as a school and building education into the biennial. I think we learned a lot; I certainly learned a lot. Post-pandemic, in the face of the climate emergency, we have to question the excessive overproduction and travel associated with biennials. How can they operate both hyper-locally and internationally? The only other thing I'll add now is that I was part of the founding board of the International Biennial Association, which had twenty-one members and represented all the continents. The thing that I think the best biennials do is have a team on the ground that builds and holds all the relationships and then invite curators into those contexts. I met people working in impossible conditions all over the world who are trying to make biennials happen. They are courageous and visionary. And they're nearly all educators first, because they are trying to make something happen outside of the structure of museums and alongside people thinking about what art can do in the world.

NS That's a great start, Sally. Thank you. Sofía, could you speak to your own experience?

Sofía Olascoaga What Sally says resonates, not least because the São Paulo Biennial has a permanent structure and staff, some of whom work on the archive of the biennial. People there studied the Venice Biennale or the Museum of Modern Art as institutions with an educational purpose.

At the same time, there is the biennial exhibition, which actually began in the late 1940s with national pavilions and representation, drawing from the model of Venice. The biennial has changed over time; the structure is there but has not remained rigid or permanent. The political and economic turmoil in Brazil over the decades has also affected the structure of the biennial itself, even though it's not a state-funded institution.

In fact, it was launched by a board of businessmen—heads of industry, owners of companies. It's had different ways of existing over time, but the permanent staff and an institutional structure have remained. That staff grows, not least with the curatorial team, for every edition. When Jochen Volz began working on the 2016 biennial, I was surprised to be invited as an *artistic* cocurator and not specifically a kind of pedagogical curator. It was important for me that Jochen's invitation was not to consider only the formal educational elements of the biennial, as in the past, but also to partner with the curatorial team as a whole. In fact, this is how I understand my practice; I've decided not to honor strict categories of "curator" and "educator."

One thing that seems unique about the São Paulo Biennial is its scale. For the 2016 edition, we had eighty-one artists and about four hundred artworks. It's fascinating to think about curatorial positions and pedagogy and how they interact over short periods of time and yet deliver an installation that works at that scale. We had the resources to commission more than half of the works. And most of the artists I worked with were engaged with forms of pedagogy, but it was also a challenge to encourage the creation of works that could physically relate to the size of the exhibition space.

One example is [the biennial's title] *Incerteza Viva*, or *Live Uncertainty*. As a general framework, we approached the idea of inhabiting uncertainty in the midst of a crisis of paradigms, and the related need to live with different ecologies of knowledge, different narratives. As a curatorial team, we thought constantly about transdisciplinary and collective intelligence.

Part of our research involved five study days, as we called them. We were a team of five cocurators, all of whom lived in São Paulo during the preparations, so it was important for me that we got out of our meeting room and out of our heads. The study days were a way of researching in different territories; I was in charge of coordinating one focused on imaginaries of the Amazon that were not Brazilian. I organized a session with a local organization in Peru founded by someone who was a close collaborator of Ivan Illich. I asked them to think with me, and to host a session with guests that included some of the artists working toward the Biennial. It was five days of valuable deep listening.

Another intervention involved the educational components of the biennial, which had been traditionally located in the basement of the pavilion. We made a huge effort to ensure that the museum had educational spaces interspersed throughout the exhibition. The whole effort was translated spatially into an open plan, a kind of garden layout, you could say. The idea was to have educational toolboxes throughout the biennial; the activities were not separate from the artworks. We did receive critical feedback from some mediators and participants who felt they were being displayed in the exhibition, like in a fishbowl. That was really interesting and instructive.

LS The projects that you're describing are beautiful and complex and amazing. How were these curatorial and pedagogical ideas translated for educators who need to attend to potentially thousands of people? Especially when those people might be expecting, say, a painting workshop.

SO We never did a formal handoff. But there's something important to add here. For a long time, in non-biennial years there was an important theoretical seminar that trained most of the country's cultural agents—the future curators and directors of institutions. That ended sometime in the late 1990s. Then, in the 2000s, an educator ran off-year programs that connected with schools, with other institutions, with neighborhood organizations, and created what Sally was talking about—a sense of ongoingness.

By the time we arrived, even that had wound down. A big part of that permanent staff had been fired. We opened the mediation program to rehire them, at least for that edition of the Biennial. We tried to create a rich program as early as possible, one where the mediators' involvement could happen in a more organic way. We commissioned them to do research projects that aligned with their areas of expertise. The audience later signed up for guided tours that emerged from those research efforts. And, of course, the mediators were paid—for the study time *and* the mediation practice.

ST What you're saying links nicely to the precarity of the format, which is both its strength and its weakness. Curators come and go, but biennials persist in situ. This format allows for challenging the hierarchy and the privilege of curators, who must come in and join conversations that are already ongoing.

DW I arrived in Porto Alegre in 2012 to work on education programming for the following year's Mercosul Biennial at the invitation of Sofía Hernández Chong Cuy, who wanted to pair one local and one international pedagogical curator. My experience there and in Liverpool resonates with some of what has been said about place, time, and the encounter.

Sally, you and I began talking about the Liverpool Biennial when you presented your work to an audience in New York City at Independent Curators International. I think I was working on Mercosul at that time and trying to understand how to contribute in a place that was entirely new to me—and beyond my knowledge. And you started talking about Liverpool, the city closest to where I grew up. So joining you as a thought partner for the 2016 edition had the opposite appeal. I was interested in making the move from a location that was alien to me to one that had once been familiar, but with an overall model that was similar.

I returned to Liverpool, after decades away, as an American. My first art job out of college was as an adjunct teacher at John Moores University. Going back made me reflect on how you learn different things about yourself at different periods in life. That's one kind of encounter. But the model of the Liverpool Biennial, as was said earlier, is itself a meeting, an encounter. With biennals there's always that sense, unlike with museums, that these people have been brought together purposefully. This is a moment, an event, an assembly. What can we learn from each other in this meeting?

That's both the beauty and the limit of the biennial as an educational form. The difference between a biennial and a school is that the school is always there. Education is a long and slow journey; schools need to abide. In both the biennial and museum context, how can there be education when time is limited? I think we end up doing something that is an *experience* of the educational rather than education.

The other question that occurred to me was about research. What are we learning? What knowledge does this event yield? Each biennial contains a promise of something to be studied. It's like a collective assignment that we're going to submit to the teacher at the end, and something will be learned along the way. And I don't know if that always amounts to a lot.

ST Can I ask a related question: education for whom? I think for both artists and curators, biennials are great educational spaces. Dominic, to your point, if you really think about formal education, you can only really do that in partnership with education providers. It's the same for museums. I believe that it's not for us to reinvent the wheel, it's for us to get in the car and add something.

DW Today I run a documentary film organization, and it's interesting to see how the film festival is both the same as and different from the biennial. Sally, when you talk about artists and curators, the biennial offers them career development, the development of their practice. That's even more true in the film-festival context, because the film festival—in its industry role—provides opportunities for the development of film projects; it functions for professional development. What you actually want to achieve for yourself and your film is beyond the audience experience.

The festival is a step in making public a creative work, like the biennial in some ways, but in the film context it's much clearer. There are many details of this new context that fascinate me. For example, films can bypass censorship in some countries by being presented in festivals; they're not being screened enough to need to go through the censorship office. It's like the protected pre-professional status of art produced in art schools. I don't know if there are instances where the art world—perhaps in biennials?—provides explicit opportunities to see things that cannot be seen in the wider circulation of the work.

NS One topic I want to introduce is radical pedagogy. Dominic said two things that I think lead into this. One is the difference between the long duration of school versus the temporary intervention of a biennial or festival. The other is the idea of being able to evade censors because of the ephemeral nature of biennials and festivals. The educational turn in contemporary art generated so many propositions claiming radicality—the very gesture of turning an exhibition into a discursive space was claimed as inherently radical. So I'd like us to discuss for a moment how that appears in retrospect. What is the nature of that radicality, if indeed it can even be claimed as such?

LS I can offer, by way of example, the retrospective of Tania Bruguera's long-term projects at the Yerba Buena Center for the Arts. Tania espouses an educational philosophy in which the student—and by extension the exhibition visitor—must be made uncomfortable in order to generate a certain kind of disturbance in the field. The school we convened actually worked well because the students, from four Bay Area universities, came for sessions every night for six weeks. It was tremendously tough on the institution; all sorts of staff had to stay late, work extra hours. There were financial and staff-morale consequences.

And it was tough on the museum's regular audience, who came during the day and encountered an empty classroom with a bunch of chairs and some blackboards. Again, all of this is part of Tania's strategy at the time to create this kind of disruption in the field. It brings to mind a question a student recently posed to me: is it ethical to use a museum space as an education space, to deny the ticket-buying public the pleasure of having an aesthetic experience? My mouth dropped because it had never occurred to me that someone—a student at a New York University—would think like that.

ST There's such a different conversation around social justice and social practice in the United States compared to the intellectual tradition you emerged from in Mexico. In Britain, too, I found it important to acknowledge the conditions under which people are thinking and working because, well, we are not having the same conversations.

LS Exactly. And I think it's important for us to acknowledge there are actual demands from what we may call "audience" but can be a human being that comes into the space, or someone that learns about these projects by overhearing other friends, or someone who discovers them online. To be honest, I feel lucky to have been active, in the last decade, when we could be experimental with biennials and museums.

ST I'm hearing in what you say that the structure of education can feel alienating to an audience. This connects to what Dominic was saying earlier. There's a lot of highfalutin' public programming about education, and art that borrows from the aesthetics of education (tables, chairs, Post-it notes, and a lot of typing) but is not in fact part of a true learning process. I think that has really been our struggle for the last decade or so.

I've made some terrible exhibitions as well as some good ones. I think, at best, there needs to be a little more openness, kindness, and generosity on our part in terms of thinking for whom we are working, and who we are talking to. That too often gets lost. We're not just talking to the art world. We should not just be talking to ourselves. I've been doing cleanup here in Queens since Tania's project. It's hard work. There is damage in parts of the Queens Museum's community that may never be healed.

NS Wow, that's amazing.

ST It's fascinating. I wanted to do a project around how you end socially engaged projects because the endings are so often messy. Jeanne van Heeswijk's project is a good one. She thinks in such complex, unusual ways. With the bakery, she's still there. She still works. The biennial is not involved in that project, and now it's become housing. The community land trust she set up has built a whole street of housing. It employs people, it's a viable business. And that's thanks to the investment made by Jeanne, supported by the Biennial and all of the educators on the ground.

LS It's very hard work. And to be honest, I don't like when people who are more conservative than my very beloved curator friends say, "You guys, enough of your shit. We should just do beautiful things in the museum and not mess all of this up." I don't think that is the answer, but I must admit that the practices we have presented have not always taken audiences, taken *others*, into account. I went to one biennial in October; it wasn't one of the opening weekends, and it felt desolate. Simply desolate, like an empty party.

ST That's a great way to put it. So sad. The aftermath, the mess. It happened. You missed it.

NS Perhaps this notion of radicality was interpreted in a very particular way. Like Lucia, when you're talking about Tania—comfort wasn't the priority. There is discomfort in relationship to a pedagogical experience, discomfort in relationship to an art experience. Tied to that is also an anti-aesthetic impulse—or, from the inside, as Sally was saying, there are aesthetic assumptions in this work.

I presented the "educational turn" to my graduate students this week, and I was amazed by their disgust at the whole enterprise. They said, "What is this? It feels like a party I wasn't invited to—and maybe that I don't want to go to in the first place."

ST Are they close to the market? Do they understand how instrumentalized they are by the market? I mean, late capitalism has produced conditions that we all work in. We're trying to change something very big, very solid. And it's going to take more than a few years to shift things.

NS I think they don't realize that yet, which is a challenge.

DW Perhaps there was a way of thinking about these projects as "laboratories" in those days that has no currency, or a weaker currency, now. And Lucia, of course, your institution right now has the word in its name, but a laboratory is not supposed to be an accessible place. It's a closed space, for scientists, in which you experiment in order to learn. There is no audience. I think that if we've become less tolerant of those pedagogically inclined art experiences, it's partly that we are less tolerant of the laboratory experiment as an art move.

ST I'm remembering a dinner I had with Sofía in New York, during which we talked about how frustrated and disillusioned we felt. We were, and perhaps still are, struggling for language; the laboratory was and is a metaphor. We need artists to be involved in this struggle. And they are increasingly being educated to be closer to the market and less engaged with politics, with these questions. Given the rollercoaster of emotions in that conversation, Sofía, do you want to say anything about how you are feeling about these issues now?

SO I want to connect with something mentioned before around discomfort. This feeling also arises within institutions, whether a biennial or a museum. I remember the staff at MASP for example, a number of years ago, producing a Guerilla Girls exhibition. It raised a number of discussions among the staff that aired a lot of tensions within the museum about representation and gender and so on.

With regard to language and metaphors, I've appreciated the notion of learning webs, and that, in exhibitions, learning—and not necessarily education—can happen in ways that are productively different from schools. The audience an exhibition gathers is more like a group of amateurs or enthusiasts who don't necessarily come from the same age, class, or cultural background, but who come together guided by desire and interest. I think artworks can be tools that accompany an unstructured learning process, one that doesn't involve a linear curriculum. That doesn't make it less problematic, but it does give it a different organic element. You can have both sustained communities of practice or learning and more informal gatherings.

NS As a final gesture, I'd like us to think about a hopeful trajectory for the future. We've talked a lot about what has happened on the biennial circuit so far. What can be built upon or shifted about the way that education can have an impact in relation to biennials? Does anyone have hope?

LS I think we can learn to think about the ethics of what we are proposing. It's not because we're unethical, but that we must consider what we're attempting, how realistic are our beautiful desires for connection with underrepresented groups. I think humility, careful listening, and assuming less are good places to start.

ST I'm hopeful—as long as biennials can resist becoming trade shows, versions of art fairs, and can actually impact the situations where they're located. If they're done well, they give access to art and to new ideas to communities. We also have to invest in younger curators, the next generation that will take on these formats.

NS How about you, Sofía?

SO To me, the hopefulness comes from the act of situating, from a sense of grounding that comes from responding to local environments. I am also increasingly thinking about safety, about programming in public spaces. And, yes, I have hope for the new generations, for whom new ways of being together and creating cultural encounters may look very different to what we know. I think there's hope in that.

ST I agree and share the hope that they can reimagine these formats, do something that we can't see and build on what we've all learned.

Public Promises: Education, Architecture, Museums

Dominic Asmall Willsdon

In the West Midlands of England in the 1960s—not far from where I grew up, and not long before I was born—the architect and educator Cedric Price imagined a new kind of university that might emerge from the ruins of the nation's fading ceramics industry. Called the Potteries Thinkbelt, Price's proposal aimed to transform a dormant industrial infrastructure—abandoned factories, rusting rail lines, and idle rolling stock—into a dynamic network for learning, one that would reinvent higher education for a post-industrial age. He envisioned it as a new form of institution: flexible, cybernetic, anti-monumental, and integrated into everyday life. And he imagined it was for a new sort of public, one freed from England's rigid class hierarchies. As the Spanish art historian and curator Manuel Borja-Villel has said, education is not something transmitted from those who know to those who do not, but is an encounter between someone who knows something and someone who knows something else.[1] Less a traditional university campus than a mechanism for staging encounters between different forms of knowledge, Price's Thinkbelt sought to make that notion real at an enormous scale. Picture knowledge cars coupling and uncoupling across a vast post-industrial landscape made new through their congress.

Price is often cast as a visionary, a British Buckminster Fuller. But despite its extraordinary form, the Thinkbelt proposal was pragmatic. It wasn't a thought

1 Borja-Villel used the phrase during the panel discussion "Revisiting the Late Capitalist Museum," March 11, 2011. The discussion was part of the New Museum conference co-organized by the PhD program in Art History at the City University of New York, Independent Curators International, and the New Museum. I used an abbreviated version of Borja-Villel's phrase as the title for a symposium I co-organized with Mônica Hoff at 9th Mercosul Biennial, September 13–November 10, 2013, Porto Alegre, Brazil. See *Weather Permitting: 9th Mercosul Biennial*, ed. Luiza Proença, Sarah Demeuse, and Sofía Hernández Chong Cuy (Porto Alegre: Fundação da Bienal do Mercosul, 2013), 119–35.

experiment or a critique of existing institutions. It was a concrete solution for urgent social needs and was meant to be built. The project aimed to address postwar Britain's mounting challenges: technological stagnation, industrial decline, a shortage of skilled workers, and the persistent inequities of a higher-education system bound by class hierarchy. Price pictured the Thinkbelt as an integral component of the nation's welfare system, one that extended the postwar Labour government's commitment to public well-being. It would have stood alongside the National Health Service and British Railways as part of the nation's infrastructure of state-sponsored social progress.

The Thinkbelt was, however, unrealized—partly because it was overtaken by an alternative scheme: the "university of the air" that would become the Open University (OU).[2] The OU offered a more efficient solution at a greater scale, pioneering so-called distance learning through a synthetic program of courses offered via television, radio, and print media. Its architecture was, in other words, primarily virtual, taking physical form only during brief annual residential sessions. While I was in graduate school in the late 1990s, I taught art history during some of these in-person OU sessions. I taught Realism—that most pedagogical movement—from Gustave Courbet to documentary films. By that time, the OU had become the workhorse of democratic higher education in the UK. More art history students were enrolled in the OU than at all other UK universities combined. It aimed to deliver a high standard of education to a diverse student body that included working people, career-changers, and retirees whose experience and knowledge derived from their differing circumstances and experience in various fields. Two nurses attended my class at Birkbeck, University of London, on Michel Foucault's history of medical institutions, *The Birth of the Clinic* (1963).[3] A member of the European Parliament took my class on Jacques Derrida's 1991 book on the unification of Europe, *The Other Heading*.[4] These classes were encounters between their different experiences and my reading.

By illuminating the range of possibilities and realities for educational architecture, this pair—the unrealized Thinkbelt and the realized Open University—have shaped my understanding of educational institutions including museums, encompassing their relationship to technology, the phenomenology of encounter, and the space of teaching as an open arena. Both belong—or, in Thinkbelt's case, would have belonged—to the public sector; these were institutions intended to be for society writ large, not for specific communities. Both demonstrate how being part of the public sector—that is, being produced by the state—is not only a matter of administrative oversight and sources of funding, but a matter of forms, signs, affect, images, messages, and spaces. Both demand we interrogate how institutional spaces are structured, deployed, and experienced—that is, how they assemble publics.

2 Labour leader Harold Wilson proposed a "university of the air," intended as a remedy for the United Kingdom's system of educational segregation, in a speech, "Labour's Plan for Science," at the party's annual conference, held in Scarborough, England, on October 1, 1963. The speech was later published in pamphlet form and was widely memorialized on its fiftieth anniversary in 2023. After Labour's victory in 1964, the party's Minister for the Arts, Jennie Lee, led the founding of the Open University in 1969.

3 Michel Foucault, *The Birth of the Clinic: An Archaeology of Medical Perception* (Routledge, 1973; first published in French as *Naissance de la Clinique*, Presses Universitaires de France, 1963).

4 Jacques Derrida, *The Other Heading: Reflections On Today's Europe* (Indiana University Press, 1992; first published in French as *L'autre cap: suivi de la Démocratie ajournée*, Les Editions de Minuit, 1991).

* * *

I was diverted from a career in continuing education in 2000 when I became a curator of public events in the department of Interpretation and Education at the newly opened Tate Modern, London. Tate Modern wasn't intended as the Thinkbelt or Open University of art museums, but there are consonances worth marking. Like Price's proposal, Tate Modern reuses abandoned industrial architecture. Like the OU, it aims to provide a public service open to all as a benefit of citizenship.[5] This resemblance is figured in the museum's architecture: Herzog & de Meuron's transformation of the decommissioned Bankside Power Station, and its signature feature, the Turbine Hall, produced through the removal of the station's industrial boilers.

The Turbine Hall is a monument, not a Thinkbelt-like mechanism. But it is not just the museum's first and biggest space. The Turbine Hall sets the terms of engagement—the modes of encounter, comportment, and behavior—for Tate Modern as a whole. It assumed this role not in its first or second year—looking back, we can see how Anish Kapoor's domineering sculpture *Marsyas* (2002),[6] for example, misinterpreted what the space wanted to be—but arrived at its true function in 2003. It did so with two commissions: Rebecca Saunders's distributed music composition *Chroma I*, which filled the space with no materials and which was the first performance piece I worked to create;[7] and Olafur Eliasson's *The Weather Project*, which used simple means, including a screen, mirrors, and artificial haze, to transform the hall into an immersive and fictionalized environment.[8] The significance of *The Weather Project* is in how people began using the space. They put out blankets to bathe under Eliasson's cold sun and kicked footballs around the vast industrial interior. This communal use established the Turbine Hall as a public amenity like a park or pool and lent that character to the museum as a whole.

An image comes to mind. I am standing with Eliasson on the bridge in the Turbine Hall in 2003. We are waiting for the start of a public program, one of a series I co-curated with the OU's Doreen Massey of discussions with figures like N. Katherine Hayles and Bruno Latour.[9] We watch as a flash mob arranges itself on the floor to spell out the words BUSH GO HOME in the hall's mirrored ceiling, protesting the American president's invasion of Iraq. Both the space and the installation allowed, and perhaps encouraged, such improvisatory expressions. It was, in other

5 The two statuses, "open to all" and a benefit of citizenship, are not the same thing, though perhaps they seemed more similar in the optimistic flush of the early 2000s when the United Kingdom was part of the recently established European Union, which abolished border controls among its member states. UK citizenship has been given a more restrictive resonance after the nation's withdrawal from the EU in the late 2010s, and as the matter of who is a citizen—and therefore deserving of the state's benefits—and who is not, that is, immigrants, asylum seekers, and so on, has become increasingly politicized.

6 The Unilever Series: Anish Kapoor: *Marsyas* was on display in the Turbine Hall from October 9, 2002 to April 6, 2003.

7 *Chroma I* was performed in the Turbine Hall by Music Projects/London, June 16–18, 2003.

8 The Unilever Series: Olafur Eliasson: *The Weather Project* was on display in the Turbine Hall from October 16, 2003 to March 21, 2004.

9 Latour was a French philosopher and sociologist known for trenchant criticisms of scientific progress (*Laboratory Life: The Social Construction of Scientific Facts*, written with Steven Woolgar [Sage, 1979]), the false dichotomies of modernism (*Nous n'avons jamais été modernes: Essai d'anthropologie symétrique* [La Découverte, 1991], translated into English as *We Have Never Been Modern* [Harvard University Press, 1993]), and technocratic public-improvement schemes (*Aramis ou l'Amour des techniques* [La Découverte, 1993], translated into English as *Aramis, or the Love of Technology* [Harvard University Press, 1996]). Hayles is a scholar of science, literature, and technology whose book *How We Became Posthuman: Virtual Bodies in Cybernetics, Literature, and Informatics* (University of Chicago Press, 1999) is a key text among late twentieth-century analyses of technology and posthumanism.

words, a public space and an open situation, one the public made.[10]

This emergent mode of convening raised the question of what form of public education might suit that environment, and what it meant to be a curator of education in those circumstances. In the beginning, at least, all programming roles at Tate Modern had the title of curator. This was a feature, you could say, of the organizational architecture of Tate Modern. There were two divisions: Exhibitions and Collections (for art) and Interpretation and Education (about art). This was a traditional division of museum labor. But there were curatorial roles across both departments, which represented something like an upgraded status for the museum's educational functions, and came at a time when, as is noted elsewhere in this book, many artists and curators across contemporary practice turned to education's forms and modes.

Live long enough and history no longer seems like something inherited, a past that one might respond to or react against, but appears as something you witnessed and lived through, and in which you played a role, however small. This so-called "educational turn," a phrase meant to mark out as novel the increased adoption of educational values and tactics in art spaces in the late 1990s and early 2000s, is among the histories that I have lived. Put another way, I found myself beginning to work in educational roles in art institutions just as education began to be seen as something more than the mediation *of* art *for* the public, but rather as a curatorial and artistic practice in its own right—one dedicated to the formation of education-oriented publics in the vicinity of art.

10 *The Weather Project* was enormously popular, attracting wide attention in popular media and, according to museum reports, more than two million visitors. The artwork was also both an amenity and the performance of an amenity; the sun-mirage afforded no actual warmth.

The art history of this educational turn, however, has centered on anti- or extra-institutional experiments rather than on practices within institutions. Experiments give us a critical perspective and sharpen our sense of the problem; their proposals often entail symbolic and formal innovations in art or architecture. Experiments also often occur within an existing in-group, that is, people who have already found each other, circumventing the more open public character I have described above. This narrative of the educational turn therefore proceeds from outside-in, from galleries, alternative spaces, perennial exhibitions, and art practices, and only later arrives at working in more established institutions.

My own history runs in a different direction. I am, de facto, an institutionalist. My career and practice took shape within large-scale museums such as Tate and the San Francisco Museum of Modern Art (SFMOMA), which offered a different set of possibilities and problems. At Tate Modern, I was interested in the displacement of often-cloistered forms of academic discourse into the more public spaces of a major museum with a broad audience. The series I did with Massey was an example of that displacement, at scale. The discussions we organized with Latour, Hayles, and others drew packed, diverse, and non-academic crowds, who sat for hours participating in unpredictable group conversations about matters that usually don't leave the university. This was a profound encounter between different forms of knowledge and different ways of learning that are normally estranged from each other. We all felt a sense of risk.

What risk? Academia can be quite a closed system, one that inculcates a controlled argot and shared body of knowledge, and which addresses an audience it cultivates carefully and knows well. A museum like Tate, by contrast, offered the opportunity to take academic knowledge outside of this enclosure, into rooms where other forms of knowledge assemble, and into conversations with people who are not otherwise "supposed to" be together.

I see the public museum as a place for this sort of encounter, one where strangers meet. A public audience may be strangers to each other, and strangers to the subject matter. But each person within this public brings to bear their own knowledge. As with my case of the working nurses reading Foucault's history of the clinic, each knows something I and others around them do not. I saw my work as creating open-ended spaces to assemble such strangers around culture. That is something that working in institutions allows.

* * *

I left Tate to become the curator of education and public programs at SFMOMA in 2006. On the surface, and despite (at that time) dissimilar sizes, the two museums had the same purpose and position in their cities. But working in an American museum was different. Like other US museums of its type, SFMOMA does not make the same promises as museums like Tate. Unlike them, it is not a public amenity, a member of a set of public services; it is not primarily state-funded or governed. And this separation from the mission and support systems of the public sector is manifest in how the museum appears and carries itself.

You see it, for instance, in the museum's architecture, not only in the organization of spaces like its funereal black marble atrium, but in the choice of premium materials for building. This kind of value-engineering confirms the tastes of the museum's wealthy board members and plays out in its spatial forms, which convey luxury in line with the expectations of its donor class. This luxe experience is what it offers to its audience, too. Whereas Tate is adjacent to other public services, SFMOMA's competitive market includes other forms of commercial entertainment and leisure activities: movies, restaurants, and so on. The museum is one choice among many for how leisure time might be spent and competes for that time with everything else that the Bay Area has to offer. And like those activities, SFMOMA's budget relies significantly on earned income, that is, ticket sales, which creates a paywall around its exhibitions and collection.

The two factors, donor taste and audience, are, of course, connected. More than ninety percent of SFMOMA's collection is the result of gifts from private collections—again, little different from many other US museums. Its collection is therefore composed of the history of personal, or familial, choices. The museum's galleries can accordingly be read as extensions of the plush homes from which the art works came. The museum's audience traverses these spaces as guests—beneficiaries of the largesse of wealth—rather than as constituents or citizens. Indeed, the expansion of SFMOMA in the 2010s was driven by putting a family horde, the Fisher Collection, at the heart of the museum. And insofar as museums are machines for evaluation, even veneration, institutions like SFMOMA naturalize hierarchies of value around collectible works of art. The churchlike architecture of the Mario Botta–designed building conveyed this sense that we should see the museum's objects as holy.[11] We ascend into their light.

11 The Snøhetta-designed expansion in the mid-2010s, which preserved aspects of the Botta building, is another story; I address this briefly below.

What can it mean to perform the task of education under these conditions? In San Francisco, I inherited an existing job title—curator—and a particular organizational architecture. Unlike Tate, where the task of the education department was still to mediate what the curatorial department did, SFMOMA has five curatorial departments organized by medium: Architecture and Design, Media Arts, Painting and Sculpture (the biggest), Photography ... and Education and Public Programs. It was set up like a university faculty, where each department has its own area of expertise, and offered the possibility of education as one medium among others. I leaned into this opening as an opportunity to think curatorially: staging art events in educational contexts, presenting live and discursive art forms that did not generate collectible objects, and more.

From the beginning, I restructured the budget to reflect this relative autonomy. Rather than education being a line item within the budget of exhibitions generated by other departments, I combined those monies into a single budget and made choices about what we were going to focus on or do. Some of that activity was about exhibitions, some of it not. This autonomy, I ventured, could enable the pursuit of a program centered, curatorially, on education and the art of public encounter. Interpreting the role in this way wasn't necessarily what the museum expected or wanted—though it tolerated it, and the tolerance, almost till the end, was extraordinary. The education department often worked outside of the museum's main parameters and space, in peripheral and interstitial spaces not folded into the ticketed areas. But I was working against the museum's grain, rather than, as at Tate Modern, trying to deliver on the museum's promise, implicit in its architecture, as a public amenity.

My thinking on these matters owed something to Henry Urbach, who joined SFMOMA as curator of Architecture and Design the same year as me. His practice was animated by the impossibility of his task. You cannot, of course, put a building inside a gallery; there is not enough space. Alongside and often instead of the museum's traditional solution for curating architecture, such as displaying representations of it such as drawings, photographs, and models, Urbach curated the experience of "the architectural." One instance I remember is Alex Schweder's *A Sac of Rooms All Day Long* (2009), an apartment made of clear vinyl with its features—doors, windows, moldings—represented as if in an architectural drawing.[12] Powered by a fan, it inflated and deflated throughout the museum's open hours. It was an architecture that approached the state of being a building several times a day, falling short each time.

Curating education is likewise impossible. Education is cumulative; there is not enough time in a museum encounter to realize it, and especially not when the encounter is monetized per visit. The familiar units of educational experience are temporal and continuous: courses, semesters, and years. Schools are the environments that accommodate this longer duration. School time is cyclical and never-ending. Rather than just dramatize failure, as did Schweder's sac of rooms, I pursued two distinct modes: like Urbach, producing the experience of "the educational," and, more directly, serving the infrastructure of schools in the city's existing public sector.

Involving local schools is a staple of museum education. But the important step is to contribute within the school system

12 Schweder's sculpture was on display as part of the exhibition *Sensate: Bodies and Design*, organized by Henry Urbach and on view from August 7 to November 8, 2009.

rather than offer something "extra" and even subsidiary to it. Teachers are overworked; museums might help them do what is already required of them. At SFMOMA we developed in-service training for San Francisco Unified School District (SFUSD). And we collaborated with SFUSD to create an architecture program within Ruth Asawa San Francisco School for the Arts, the city's public high school for art. In working with public schools, however, we again ran against the grain of SFMOMA's inbuilt allegiances; several of the museum's board members were committed to private or charter schools (under the euphemism of "school reform"), and they saw the museum working with the public school system as a waste of time and resources. I had a sense of pride when, at an event celebrating the museum in Yerba Buena Park, a screen flashed the message, "Proceeds go to public schools."

* * *

The origin of this book was an imagined perennial art exhibition focused on education in art practice, envisioned between me—at the time, the director of the Institute for Contemporary Arts at Virginia Commonwealth University, where I arrived after SFMOMA—the institute's curator Sarah Rifky, and the artist and curator Noah Simblist, associate professor at the university. Like Price's Thinkbelt, it went unrealized. Had it been carried out as intended, its credo might have been Sarah's dictum that "every artwork is a school." To me, that never meant that every artwork is educational in its essence, but rather more literally, that each artwork might be a Thinkbelt-like architecture, figuratively occupied by teachers and students. I would like to have made that case, partly because it is at odds with the exorbitant interest I remember from the early 2000s in de-schooling and unschooling. What is education without its institutions? And what are those institutions without their architecture? "A school is a building with a school in it."[13]

The two cases I have articulated above, however, relate more to the matter of the museum's constituency and comportment: who a museum addresses, who it serves, and how, in its materiality and processes, it carries itself. Does a museum serve the wealthy collectors who support the museum financially and donate artworks to its collection? Or do they serve the public in its many visages: teachers, nurses, families, and so on? Should institutions of art be the scene of a detached celebration of beauty, one that aims to train observers in the cultural tastes of the ultra-rich? Or might they be spaces of civic debate, meeting places where strangers might exchange ideas—even, or especially, where common ground is hard to find? Might they serve children: subjects still being formed, whose experience with unfamiliar culture stands to authorize them to have thoughts and opinions, to express them, to participate?

Between 2013 and 2016, SFMOMA closed to expand its building. I thought of this hiatus as a time to design a reformatted function of art and education that would launch on reopening: a model for an educational department that would no longer be against the museum's grain. But the closure was a format of its own; perhaps ironically, it was during these years that the education program under my leadership best realized its public function. The most de-privatized version of SFMOMA might have been while its building was closed, and there were no

13 Paul Elliman, "A School Is a Building with a School in It," *Metropolis M*, August 23, 2006, https://metropolism.com/en/feature/een-school-is-een-gebouw-met-een/.

bounds other than the city itself. In 2014, for example, we staged the second *Chimurenga Library* at the main branch of the San Francisco Public Library (SFPL).[14] This project involved installations and systems for surfacing pan-African knowledge at a far edge of the African diaspora. Such projects were tentative and fragile, but extended the museum into urban public life in a way that the enclosure of the museum simply doesn't allow. The project with Chimurenga led to further projects with SFPL under the title *Public Knowledge*, which included recategorizing SFMOMA's education center as a branch of the city's public library.[15] Such efforts extended the museum into what remained of the public sector. When the museum reopened, however, its tolerance for such commitments was diminished, part of a new architecture that situated a family's collection at the museum's heart, more-or-less permanently.[16]

Is it still possible to imagine, and achieve, a public-sector architecture for art and education? In the United Kingdom and the United States, that time seems to have passed. The public sector is frail and in pieces; its symbols and images no longer have a constituency. This diminishment, even abandonment, of the public sector seems only about to get worse. I am writing this essay during the first weeks of the second Trump presidency, and from a new position responsible for supporting and defending documentary film—an art form educational down to its etymology, and where every work might really be a school. Reading this, you'll know better than I do now what becomes of public media and arts in the months and years to come.

Whatever happens, we know the contingency and vulnerabilities of the existing system. The public sector in culture and education was barely more than an episode across some decades of the twentieth century. We have seen how the structures we inherited from that era might need rebuilding. Technologies have changed; we don't lack for ways to disseminate art and education, but we need ways to discover and attend to it amid a torrential feed of other attention-grabbing information. If culture was once something we gathered around, if only to argue about it, now not even the enormity of climate and health crises figures as a shared reality, much less a collective orientation to the common good. Now our institutions of art and education are organized around commonalities and oriented to communities rather than publics. Yet the public sector can be rebuilt, with and without the state. The value of the public sector is that it is a space where you *don't* go to find people like you. It is a space estranged from family, from the enclosure of community. It is a space for strangers. Let's start there.

This text was written with the art historian and editor Julian Myers-Szupinska.

14 Chimurenga Library was featured at the San Francisco Public Library's Main branch from May 29–June 29, 2014, as part of the exhibition *Public Intimacy: Art and Other Ordinary Acts in South Africa*, coorganized by SFMOMA and Yerba Buena Center for the Arts, from February 21 to June 29, 2014.

15 *Public Knowledge* was a two-year project launched in April 2017 "in response to profound changes taking place in the San Francisco Bay Area due to the rapid growth of the technology industry," including rising costs, unaffordable rent, and a "fraying sense of community." Find a description and documentation of the Public Knowledge Library, as well as other projects and research engaged under its rubric, at https://www.sfmoma.org/artists-artworks/public-knowledge/.

16 The museum's acceptance of the Doris and Donald Fisher Collection as a hundred-year loan, alongside the Fishers' underwriting of the museum's expansion to display it, came with several restrictions, including galleries—really, an entire floor of galleries—dedicated to showing primarily works from the Fisher collection, recurring shows devoted exclusively to that collection, and more.

The Tree School

Campus in Camps and Grupo Contrafilé

The Tree School is a project by Decolonizing Architecture Art Research (DAAR) conducted from 2012–15 as Campus in Camps, an alternative school based in a refugee camp in Palestine. It also traveled in collaboration with various communities in Bahia, Mexico, Jerusalem, Hong Kong SAR, Melbourne, Zagreb, Dubai, and Cairo. It is predicated on the simple structure of gathering under the shade of a tree, using the tree as a metaphor for shared knowledge and connection.

DAAR describes the curriculum of the tree school as flexible and site specific with its length and structure adjusting to local needs and interests. They describe its activities as residing in the following areas: *rituals*, to share feelings or memories; *conversations*, the primary source of collective interaction; *dislocation*, designed to blur the boundaries between who is the guest and who is the host; *unlearning*, a process that questions what knowledge is considered valuable; *unpredictability*, with an emphasis on a temporary space that can hold doubt and the unknown; *Al-Atabeh*, an Arabic phrase that refers to a space that connects the entrance to the house to its immediate surroundings, emphasizing a process of transformation; *cooking*, emphasizing the process of eating together as a method of communal exchange; and *ritrovo*, an Italian phrase that refers to the joy of being together.

In this São Paulo iteration, Campus in Camps joined with Grupo Contrafilé to consider the relationship between the refugee camps in Palestine and the *quilombos* in Brazil. Quilombos were historically communities that were established by enslaved Africans and Afro-descendants who fled their oppressors as an active form of resistance. In both cases, self-actualized communities became spaces for collectivity beyond the nation-state. In this collaboration Campus in Camps included Sandi Hilal, Alessandro Petti, Ahmad Al Lhham, Isshaq Issa Barbary, David Konstwein, and Daniela Sanjinés. Grupo Contrafilé included Cibele Lucena, Jerusa Messina, Joana Zatz Mussi, Peetsa, and Rafael Leona, with Walter Solon.

The following is an excerpt from a publication presented on the occasion of the 31st Bienal de São Paulo in 2014.

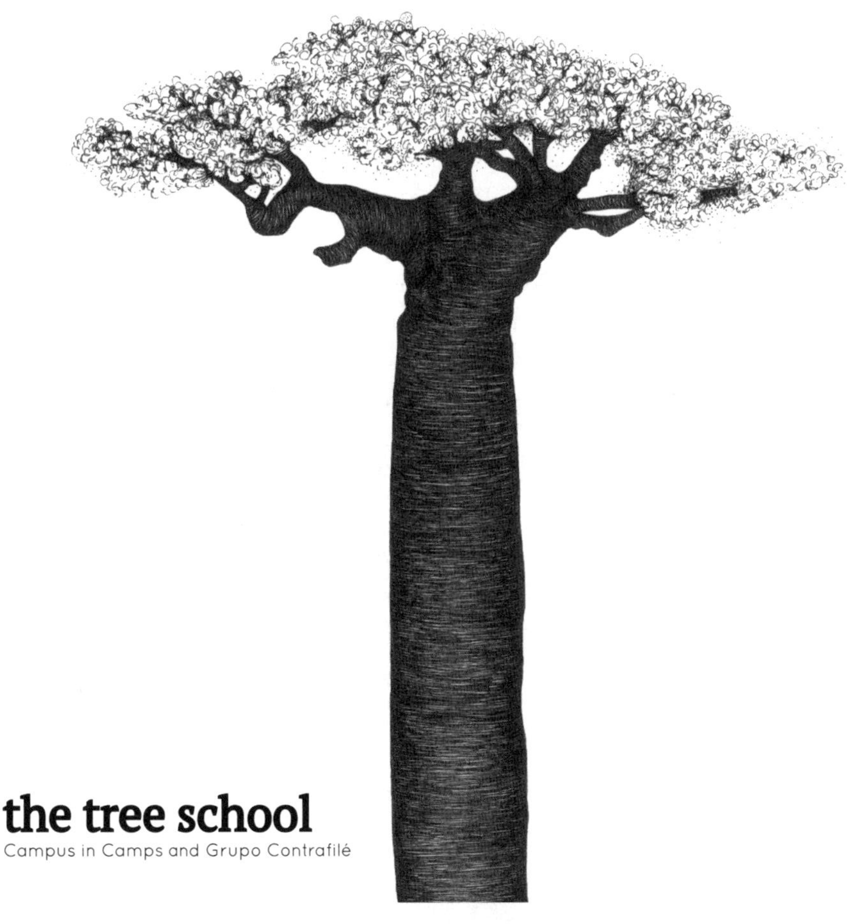

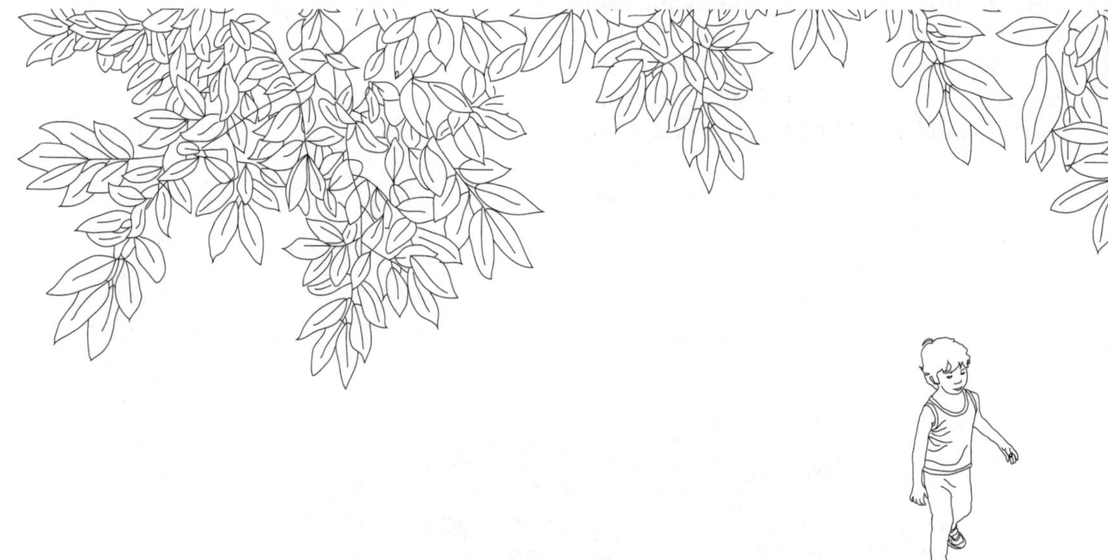

introduction

Contrafilé, a "Brazilian-based" art collective, and Campus in Camps, an experimental educational program based in Bethlehem's Dheisheh refugee camp, Palestine, have been invited to develop a common project on the occasion of the *31st Bienal de São Paulo*. Both groups share a common interest in decolonizing knowledge and aim to build a dialog from south to south, a direct exchange of thoughts and experiences rooted in common urgencies. They work around ambivalent questions concerning the relationships between *land, exile,* and *commoning.*

This project aims to cultivate and produce knowledge that emerges from regions of the world that rarely speak to each other, despite the fact they have very much to learn from one another. Particularly in this historical moment following the revolts in Arab and South American cities, these "two worlds" share similar urgencies in terms of social justice and equality. Though both regions have accumulated large amounts of wealth in recent years, its distribution remains dramatically unequal and power is still arrogantly detained by an elite. Colonialism is not just a ghost of the past. At the same time, the history of social movements in Brazil and the resistance to colonialism in Palestine are essential experiences to be shared and from which to learn.

Both groups are interested in drawing analogies and identifying differences between two exceptional spaces: Brazilian quilombos and Palestinian refugee camps. Quilombos were communities established by enslaved Africans and Afro-descendants who fled their oppressors as an active form of resistance. Later, they became spaces of refuge for many other groups in Brazil. Palestinian refugee camps were established in 1948 as a consequence of the *Nakba* (Arabic for catastrophe) in order to provide shelter for the hundreds of thousands of Palestinians who were exiled and had to flee their homes located in what today is Israel. After over sixty-five years, these camps have developed into semi-autonomous dense urban environments that are no longer simple recipients of humanitarian aid but rather active political spaces.

A shared interest in these spaces and communities provides a key for reflecting and understanding the relationships between community, territory, and politics beyond the idea of the nation-state.

In order to explore these questions, the two groups visited and conducted fieldwork in Southern Bahia, where important quilombola communities were historically established and where, today, new communities are experimenting different forms of life and knowledge production. Bahia is the "birth place of Brazil" manifesting and maintaining its fundamental link to Africa. They met with quilombolas, thinkers, artists, and activists from the Landless Workers' Movement (MST) in order to discuss the practice and theory of issues, such as displacement, exile, right of return, identity construction and subjectivity building, among others, that integrate the contemporary definition of collectivity.

In Southern Bahia, they formed a Tree School, where new forms of knowledge production are made possible, when teachers and students forget that they are either teachers or students.

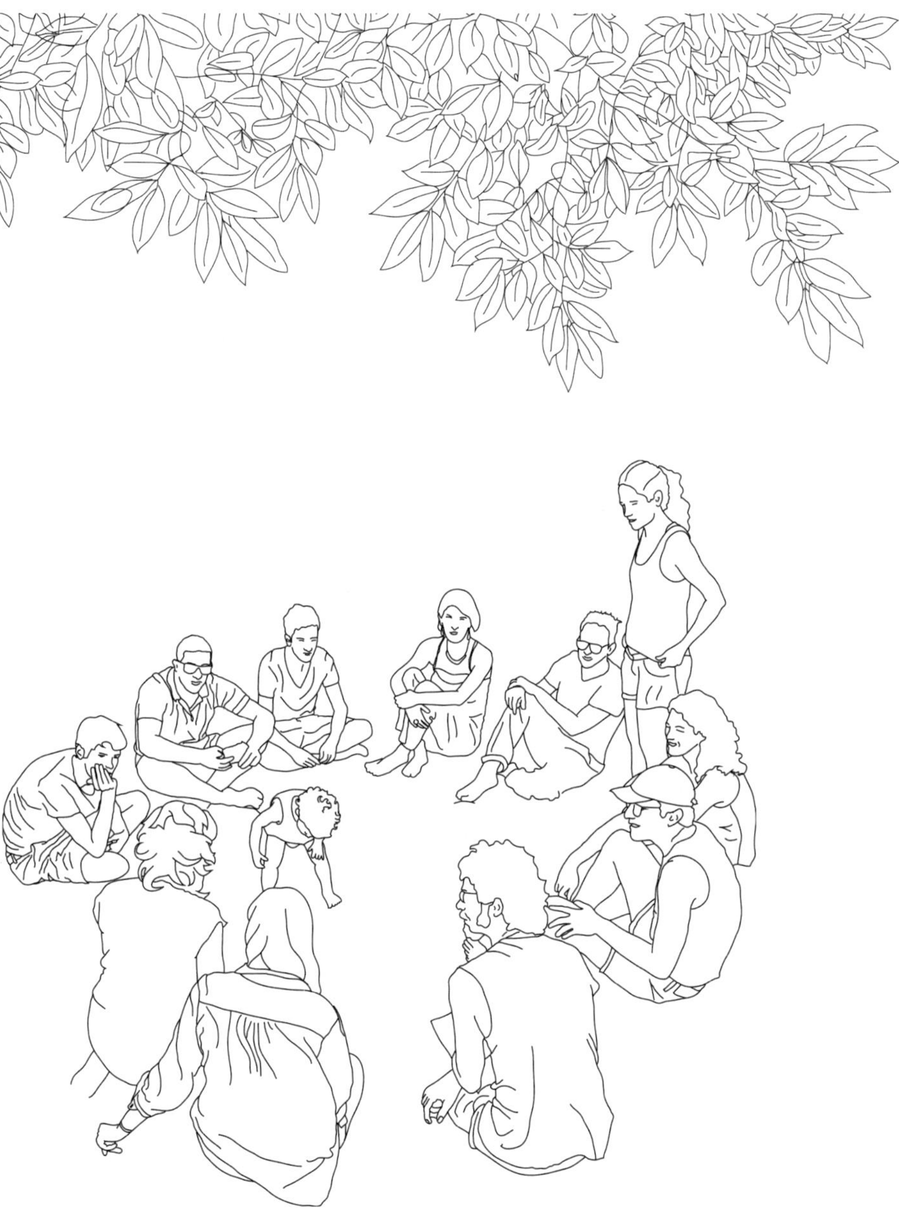

grupo contrafilé and campus in camps

The Contrafilé art group feels there is an urgency to create transgenerational spaces of critical production that try to overcome experiences where adults teach, children and youth learn, and elders are isolated. These new experiences open up an existential territory where everyone plays together, positioning themselves as bodies-in-manifest-state-of-creation. The projects *A Playground for Thinking* and *Playing* and *Backyard* were born of this desire.

When building a backyard in São Bernardo do Campo (a municipality located in the São Paulo metropolis), the group realized that, to many, the backyard refers simultaneously to an intimate and vast landscape (in which "the backyard is the world"). Generally, immigrants coming to the city from the Brazilian countryside, from the forests and farms, are met faced with presumably less honorable jobs and precarious living conditions. Yet, these are precisely the people who know how to work with "the land". One of the many effects of the exile of their deep skills is the forgetting of a possible bodily relationship with the city, which could be experienced as an art(e)fact.

Campus in Camps was established in 2012 as the first university in a refugee camp, based on the strong belief that refugee camps in contemporary Palestine are not only sites of suffering, marginalization, and political subjugation. Over sixty-five years of exile, an entire culture has been created in terms of communality, political struggle, and an absolute sense of hospitality. Refugee camps today are sites of a different form of knowledge that remains undetected and invisible. By bringing a university, a campus, to refugee camps the program intended to create a space where these forms of knowledge could flourish and interact with life outside the camps. What is at stake in this initiative is the possibility for the participants to realize interventions in camps without normalizing their knowledge and their conditions or simply blending the camps into the rest of the city. Campus in Camps brings together motivated and active young refugees from the West Bank in an attempt to explore and produce new forms of representation of camps and refugees beyond the static and traditional symbols of victimization, passivity and poverty.

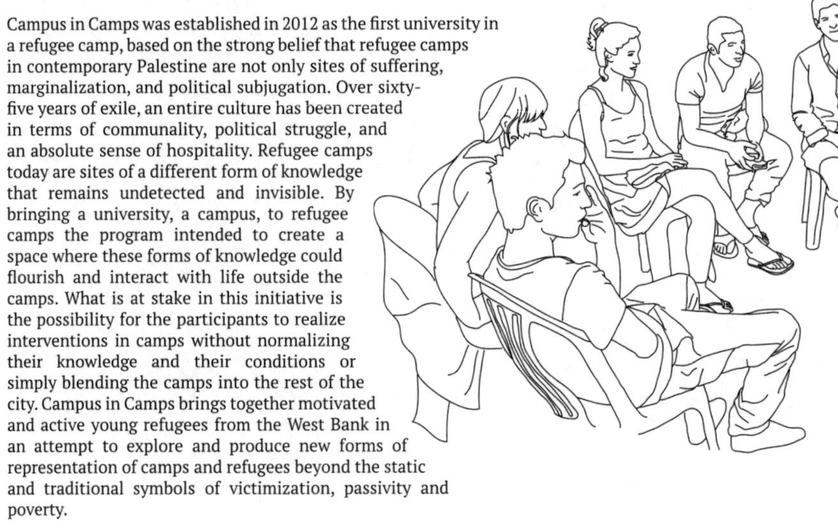

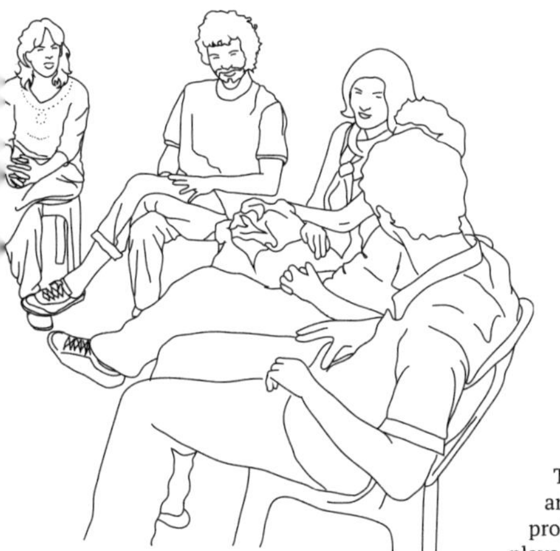

There are some points that link the experiences of quilombos in Brazil and Palestinian refugee camps. The first is that they are not utopian projects, but rather lived experiences and experiments where education plays a crucial role, enabling possible forms of decolonized knowledge to challenge dominant forms of political subjugation. In this sense, they allow us to imagine ways of conceiving a political community beyond the idea of the nation-state. It seems to us that this is the most relevant political discussion today, a time when the nation-state is in crisis but has not yet disappeared.

Therefore, how can we think of communality and individuality beyond the categories of the public (state) and the private (private property)? The "common" is hence a third productive category, which is sometimes independent and at other times partially coincides with public and private spaces. Consequently one could think about the political relation between people and space, not only in terms of citizenship, but also from the perspective of the refuge. The quilombos were originally built as places for people seeking refuge. Instead of always imagining how to become a good citizen, the question could be: Can we build a city and a territory today based on the notion of hospitality and refuge?

the tree school

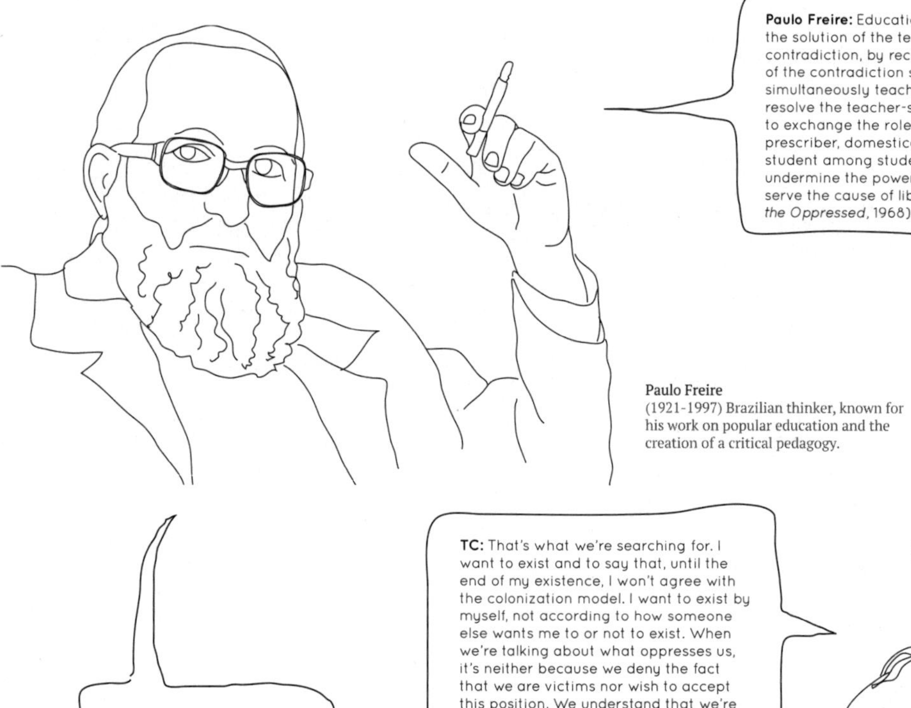

Paulo Freire
(1921-1997) Brazilian thinker, known for his work on popular education and the creation of a critical pedagogy.

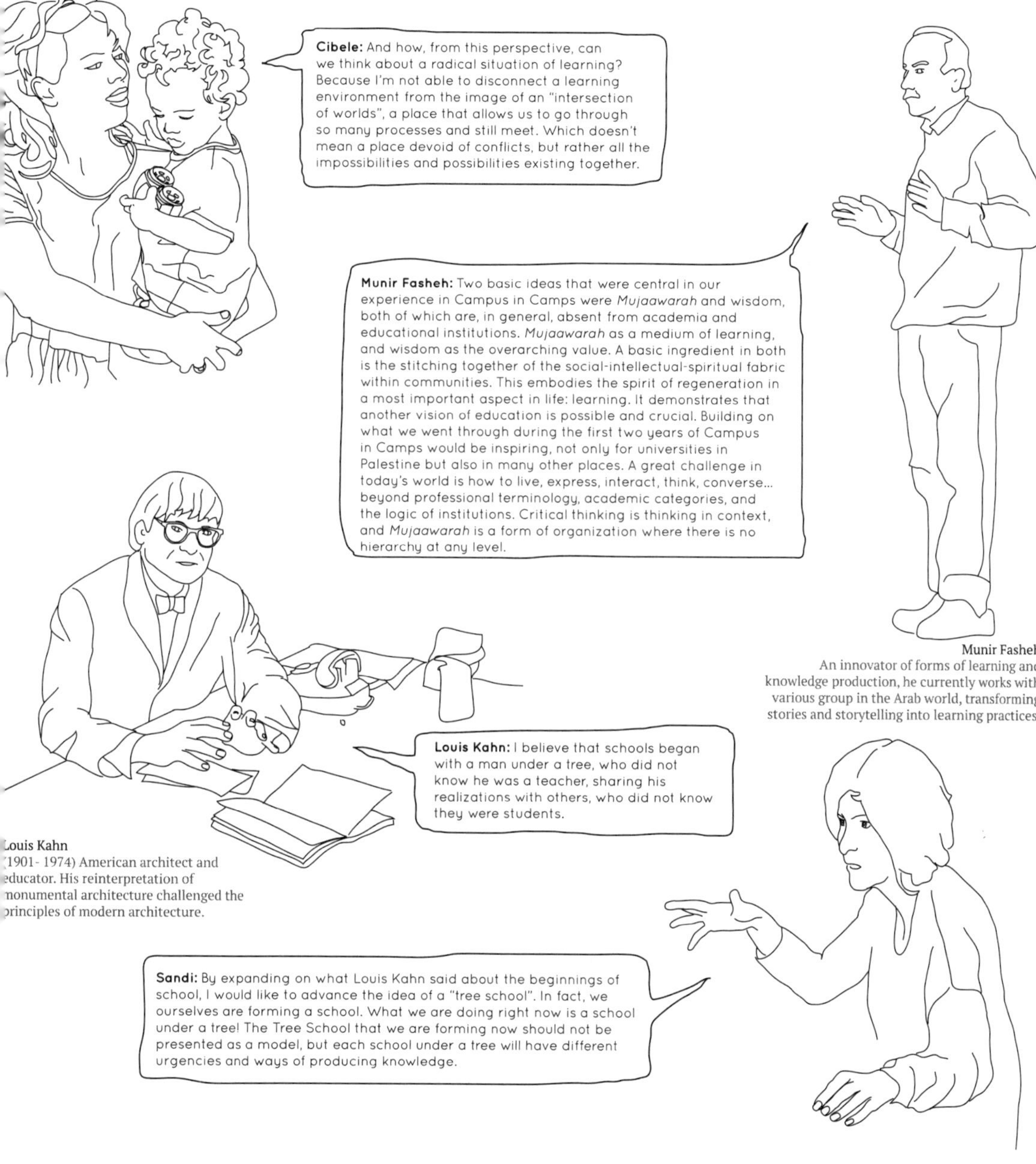

Munir Fasheh
An innovator of forms of learning and knowledge production, he currently works with various group in the Arab world, transforming stories and storytelling into learning practices.

Louis Kahn
(1901- 1974) American architect and educator. His reinterpretation of monumental architecture challenged the principles of modern architecture.

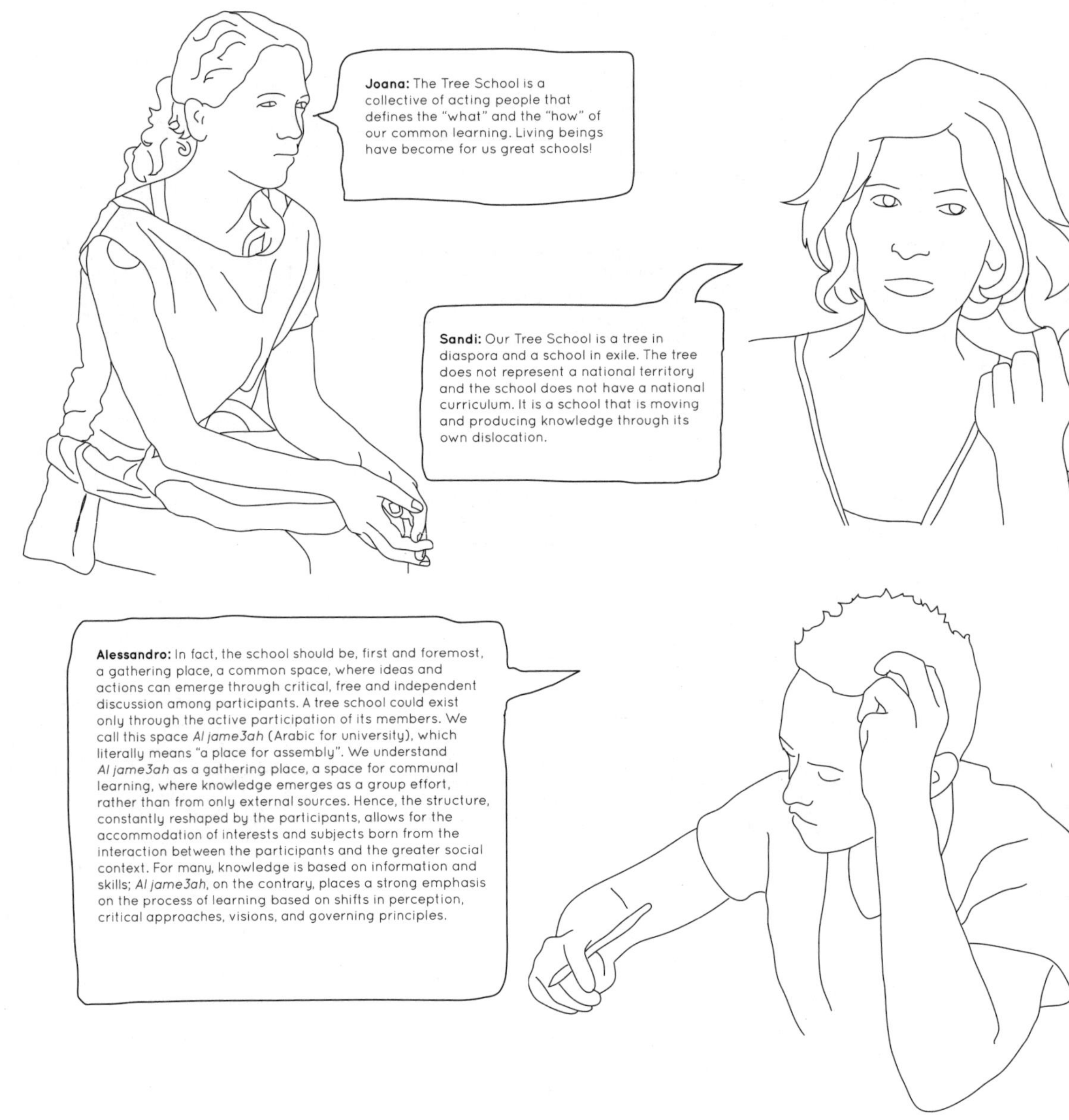
Joana: The Tree School is a collective of acting people that defines the "what" and the "how" of our common learning. Living beings have become for us great schools!
Sandi: Our Tree School is a tree in diaspora and a school in exile. The tree does not represent a national territory and the school does not have a national curriculum. It is a school that is moving and producing knowledge through its own dislocation.
Alessandro: In fact, the school should be, first and foremost, a gathering place, a common space, where ideas and actions can emerge through critical, free and independent discussion among participants. A tree school could exist only through the active participation of its members. We call this space *Al jame3ah* (Arabic for university), which literally means "a place for assembly". We understand *Al jame3ah* as a gathering place, a space for communal learning, where knowledge emerges as a group effort, rather than from only external sources. Hence, the structure, constantly reshaped by the participants, allows for the accommodation of interests and subjects born from the interaction between the participants and the greater social context. For many, knowledge is based on information and skills; *Al jame3ah*, on the contrary, places a strong emphasis on the process of learning based on shifts in perception, critical approaches, visions, and governing principles.

Rafael: In order to imagine this Tree School, one of the conditions is that there must be no pedagogic time measured in lecture hours. In this sense, the pedagogic time expands into our own lives. Just like in *Mujaawarah*, each person added into the group brings a possibility of destabilizing everything. The decision to not have a closed format also opens up the possibility of creating knowledge and building lessons within this destabilization. This means that the lessons don't start at a specific point, such as someone speaking, and they are not necessarily attached to a homogeneous and predetermined time. Rather, they correspond to a sequence of non-linear events that produce knowledge.

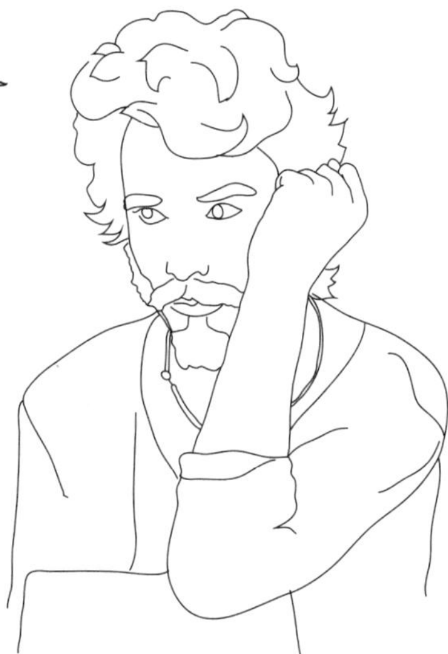

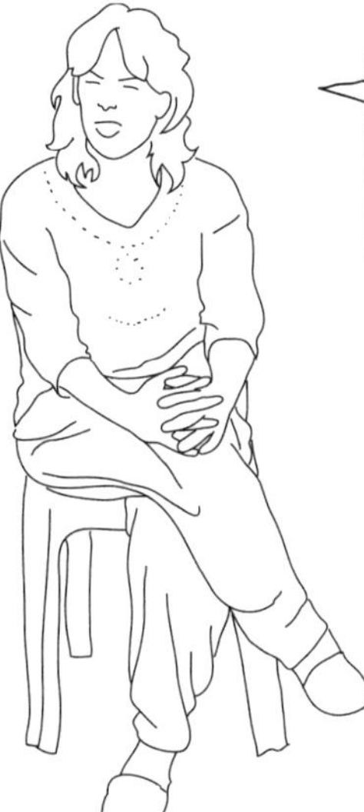

Cibele: We understand that obtaining a "space of collaboration" is significant since it by and large means having access to a "space of freedom." Games and playing reclaim a kind of *landscape-potency* within the body that has been lost in adults and children. And we believe that it is this same *landscape-potency*, which allows us to imagine and invent our own city, giving way to the unpredictable. Playing is understood as an exercise in smashing down the walls ingrained within ourselves and our society.

Joana: A tree school needs an interventionist character that not only "observes" a certain situation, but activates some "potentially rupturing" element in order to better comprehend the situation: a more pointed understanding of the social component therefore follows the assumption that it is necessary to actively stand in the center of a certain problem and to challenge reality according to the *sensations* it evokes in the body, building a shared understanding of it. Then the intervention occurs as evidence of a symbolic character, by triggering an "element" which, as it synthesizes a shared sensibility, causes the established situation to rupture. The result is ultimately evidence that there is a collective body sharing a new sensibility that makes itself known.

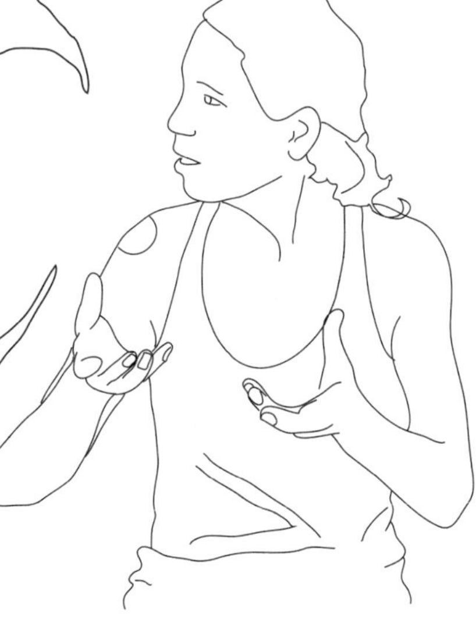

Alessandro: Not-normalizing knowledge production should be one of the principles of the Tree School. It is an important concept and practice in relation to the idea of diaspora and exile. We have to work with what we have and we have to do it now, without getting trapped in the messianic idea of future salvation, being either Communism or religion; we need to accept the idea of a continuous struggle for justice and equality, never being satisfied by the status quo and therefore never being assimilated or normalized.

Joana: What would it actually mean to transform our understanding of essential values, such as beauty, wealth and wisdom? The baobab could be the "great school" because it evokes the dimension of the common, of communication, community, as if it created a territory that isn't necessarily or simply physical, but also a symbolic territory of connection. I ask myself what knowledges are constituted, what institutions are formed "in diaspora." We do not have to be, as a rule, cured from the diasporas, since they are something that traverses us and can politicize us. What is this thought, school, lesson happening in this action and in this diasporic reality, be it Palestinian, black or Jewish?

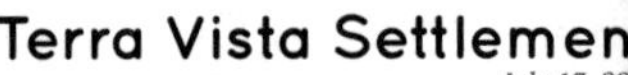

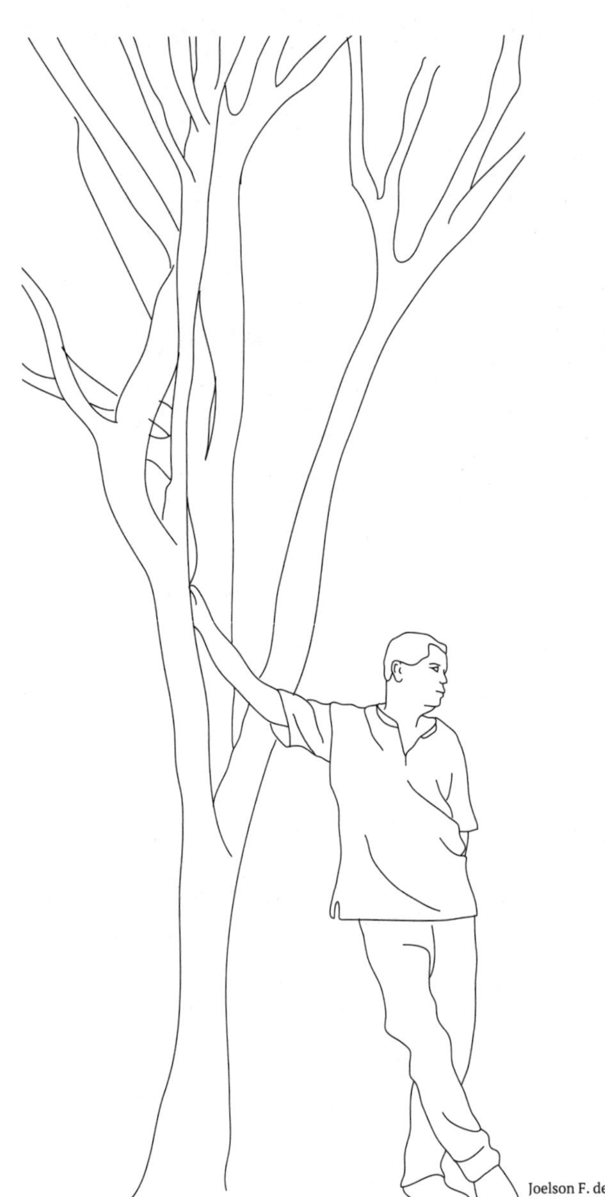

Joelson F. de Oliveira
Leader of the Terra Vista Settlement.

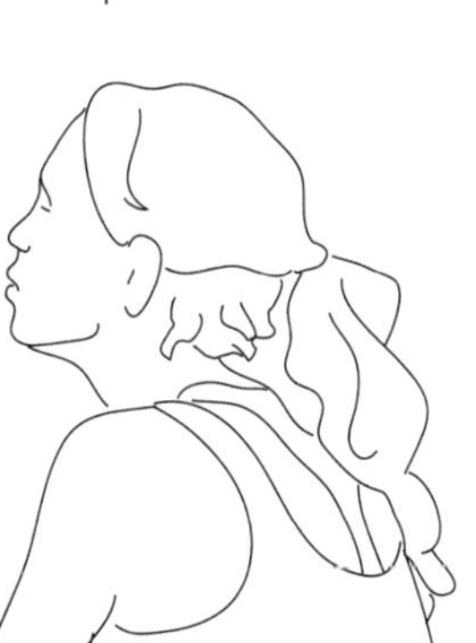
Joana: I've been thinking and have realized that the first thing Joelson showed us at the Terra Vista Settlement were two trees. This is how he welcomed us, not with a formal speech.

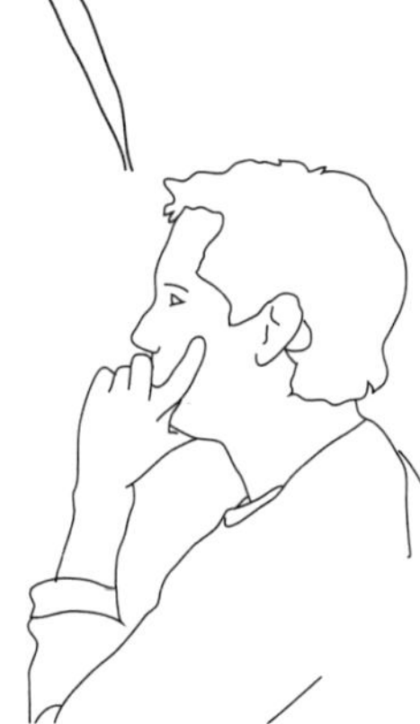
Pedro: This is a way of building a new spatial cartography, a new social memory. Yet this doesn't mean that trees are simply inanimate, external objects, which could only be understood as discourse devices. They are also sort of "almost-subjects" that move within distinct worlds. The outside world isn't only manipulated and directed by discourse, because the "almost-subjects" also have their own vitality and capacity of affection.

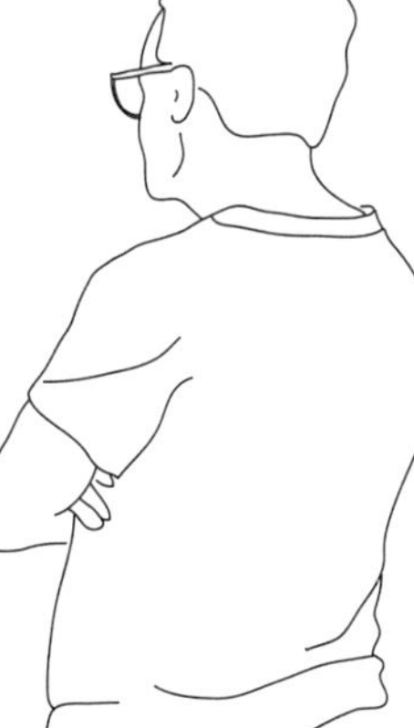
Alessandro: The first tree that Joelson showed us was a small baobab that the community planted to celebrate their connection with Africa and the quilombola movements in particular. The second tree, a pine tree, has a more ironic story. Joelson said that was given to the community directly from the hands of Yasser Arafat and the tree took his name after his death. It's quite a strange story considering that the pine tree has been used as an instrument of colonization in Palestine ever since the British Mandate. The pine tree was chosen because it grows quickly and does not need much maintenance and, most importantly, prevents other vegetation from growing nearby. This creates a virtual monoculture on the ground level that reduces the variety of wildlife and the possibility of grazing animals. The Jewish National Fund has massively used the pine tree for its forestation programs. In most cases, pine tree forests were used to create "fences" around Jewish communities and their surroundings. Also with the establishment of national parks, pine trees were used to hide the ruins of demolished Palestinian villages.

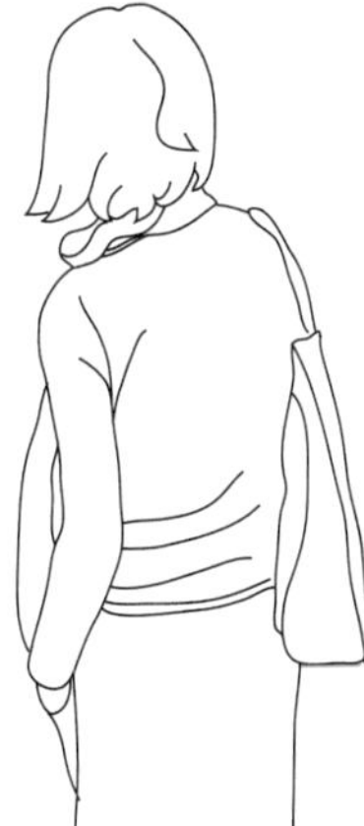
Sandi: I am wondering why Arafat would have given a pine tree instead of an olive tree, which is the symbol of resistance in Palestine.

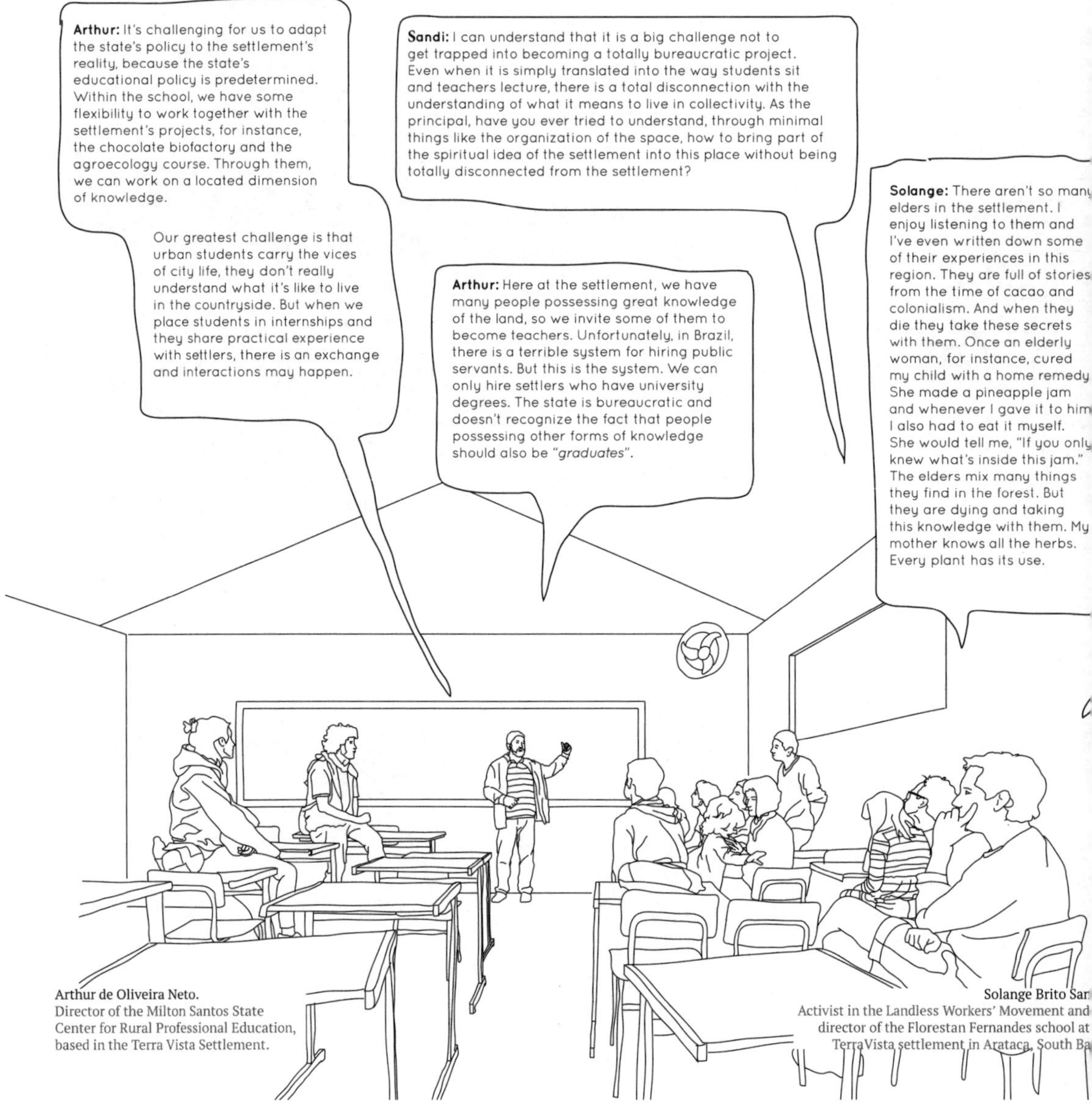

Arthur de Oliveira Neto.
Director of the Milton Santos State Center for Rural Professional Education, based in the Terra Vista Settlement.

Solange Brito San
Activist in the Landless Workers' Movement and director of the Florestan Fernandes school at TerraVista settlement in Arataca, South Ba

ibele: By writing down these ories and making them art of the school's projects, ouldn't this be a way of cknowledging them as forms f knowledge from the land hat "graduate" people, as rthur said? How do these orms of knowledge make heir way into the school? ow does the school relate to he knowledge of the elders? ome thoughts have emerged om the dialogue with the tudents. For example, how nportant is it to benefit om this already existing ntegration between young eople who are from the ettlement and young people ho come from outside the ettlement. Through this onnection, can they reduce nd reinvent bureaucracy om inside this gathering, *this* chool, which comes from a onnection "with the land", nd not from being "landless".

at the school

July 15, 2014
Milton Santos State Center for Rural Professional Education

Cibele: Hi! My name is Cibele, I came with this group to visit your school. We're working on an art project that will become a book and an exhibition reflecting upon issues like land, education, and spaces of collective construction. We come from São Paulo and from Palestine. Some of us live in refugee camps and we are very interested in the experience of the settlement. Do you study here? If so, which courses?

Female student: We study different subjects, some study zootechnology, others agroecology.

Cibele: Do you all live in the Terra Vista settlement?

Male student: No, most of us come from outside, from neighboring towns.

Cibele: Really? And what is it like to study in a school within an MST settlement? How does it impact your families and the communities where you live?

Male student: It's interesting. Nowadays we feel they respect it much more because this is one of the best schools in the region. But there's still a lot of prejudice. People don't understand what a settlement is. They say we study in "landless" schools, they think everyone here is violent.

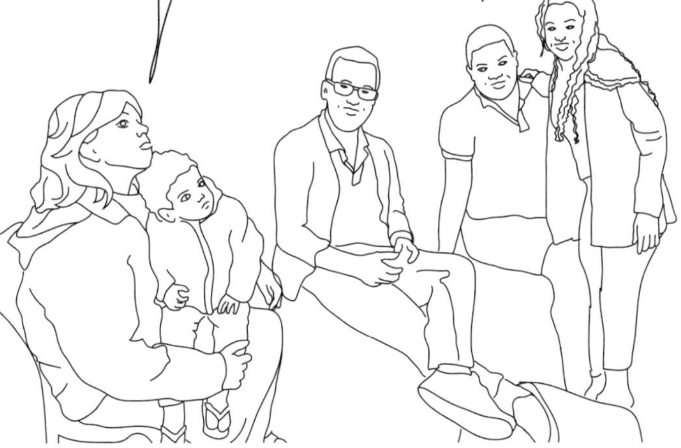

Female student: We learn many things about land in Brazil in a way we wouldn't learn elsewhere.

return to the sea

Solange: When it comes to "return", sometimes I think about my mother, who has a great knowledge of herbal medicine, but she denies her own culture. She is black and suffered a lot in her childhood, because her parents gave her away to a white family who always told her, "Never marry a black man!" So she internalized this and thought that her color was to blame for her suffering. And in order to relieve this pain, she became evangelical and started to deny her whole history. She loathes *candomblé* and drumming, for instance; she thinks paradise is in heaven. And I'm aware that my mother can't return, but I have to understand her own process, because after a certain age, for many, it doesn't seem to make any sense. Therefore, seeing people who were able to return makes me happy. I'm happy when I see Dona Maria Muniz, an indigenous woman from the Hã-Hã-Hãe ethnicity, who lives nearby and is the same age as my mother. As a child, she was expelled and had to live in the city with her mother. But recently she has reclaimed her land. She has returned, she had the privilege of returning.

Sandi: Yesterday, during Dona Ana's funeral, and listening to you, Solange, speak about your attempt to collect stories of the elderly, I reflected on the fact that Palestinians try to document as many stories of the past as possible, before the old people pass away. In 1948, Palestinian refugees were forced to leave their villages and cities in what is today Israel, and many lost access to the sea. The symbol of the Palestinian refugee became the key of his or her lost house. It represents the right to return to their homes. Now the key seems to represent only the lost private property. We lost much more that was not private but collective, such as cities like Haifa, Yafa and Akka. And the sea. It is time to think of the return to the Mediterranean Sea as a common right that all Palestinians, refugee and non-refugees, have lost. I'm not a refugee, I did not lose my home, but I lost the Mediterranean. The desire to return to the sea is a common desire among all Palestinians. A sea where your eyes are able to gaze beyond the closure and the borders that are all around us in our daily life. The sea is where all Palestinians go, when they finally have the chance to cross the border.

Sandi: Coming from Palestine, when we hear the word "occupation", it's strange for us that you, as the Landless Workers' Movement, are the "occupiers". We consider the Israelis occupiers because they took something that isn't theirs. This is something we reflected upon when those movements in Europe and the US called themselves "occupy movements". It made us feel uncomfortable. You can only occupy something that isn't yours. So when I hear you speaking, I feel it's not an occupation but a return. If indigenous people were in this land before colonization, then re-appropriating the land after so many years is a sort of return.

Solange: You can also use "return", I find it an attractive word, but I also like the word "occupy". Historically speaking, there was an inversion of facts. When you talk about invasion and link it to our movement, it's offensive to us, it hurts, because, in fact, the invaders were the colonizers who prohibited black and indigenous people from having land where they could live.

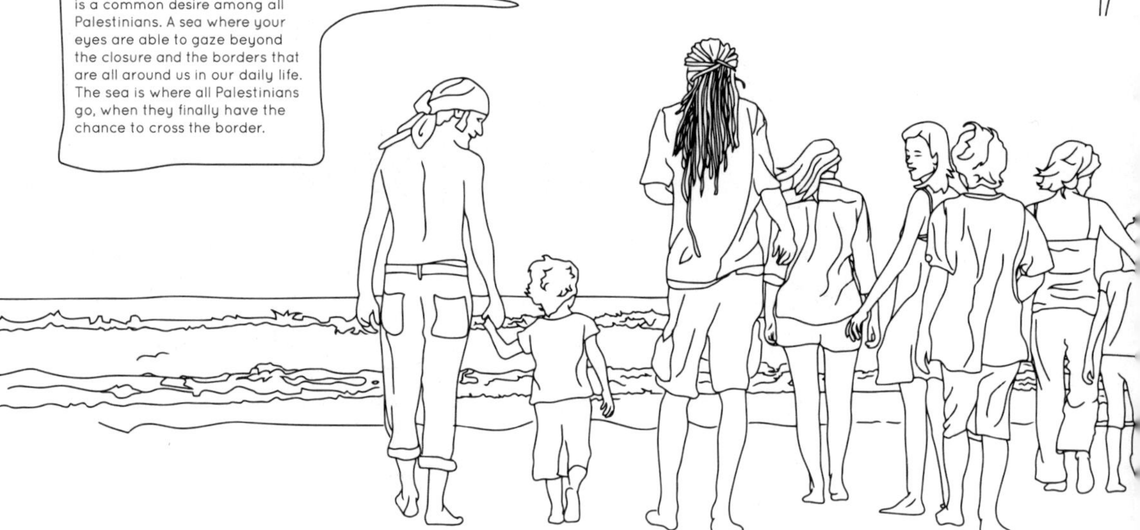

TC: I feel it's always about a return to the roots instead of considering return as the building of new roots. In quilombos, they do not want to return somewhere else, they feel that where they are is their place already. The quilombo is my place, I am attached to my memory and my roots are here. The process of colonization made us lose the African reference we had. We don't know where we came from so the desire to return to Africa died even if we still carried an African feeling inside us. But where in Africa would we establish ourselves now? The idea of return exists, but it's a different return, a return to a place within us. A return to the indigenous or African cosmic vision, so we can reconstruct our society.... It is not a return to a specific place.

Isshaq: In Palestine, return for some people means going back to a perfect past, for others it means going to a perfect future. But in between we say return to the common, return to the Mediterranean Sea. There's a search for identity.

Ahmad: This time... from this dialogue, I feel that our generation, the third generation after the *Nakba*, is like the new generation of the baobab tree. We both were born in exile and we both are trying to redefine ourselves now. We both know nothing about our original context, we both drank the water and ate the food of exile, built our entire lives in exile, so what does homeland mean to us? What does return mean to us? We both are asking ourselves: Return to what?

We both are asking ourselves what to do with our lives that we have been building in exile in the case of return. We both are asking ourselves if we have to take exile with us wherever we go and if exile should return with us.

Maybe the baobab tree in the Brazilian context did not really ask these questions but the Palestinian baobab did.

Eugênio: For me the baobab symbolizes neither a return to Africa nor the formation of Brazilian identity; the baobab is not a tree in exile, it's a world-creating tree.

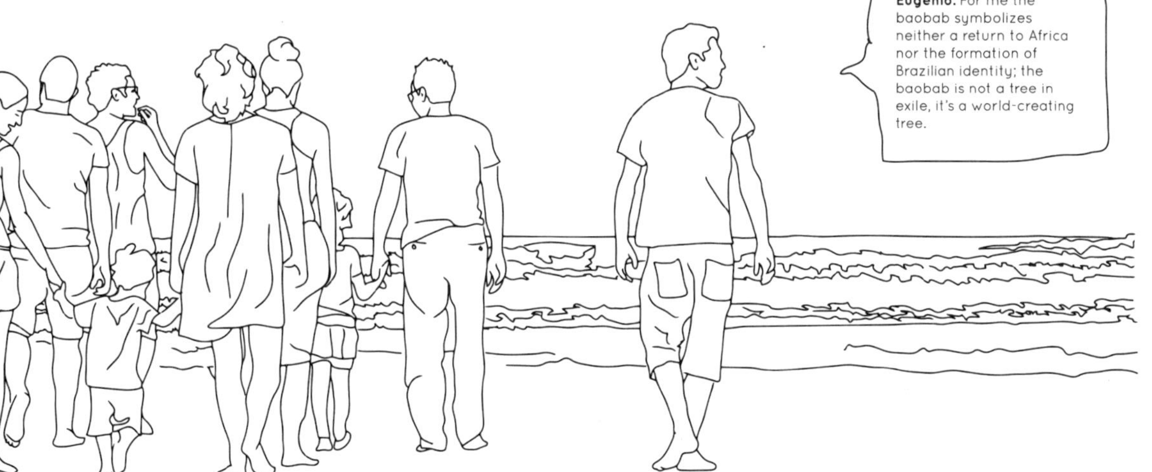

On listening...

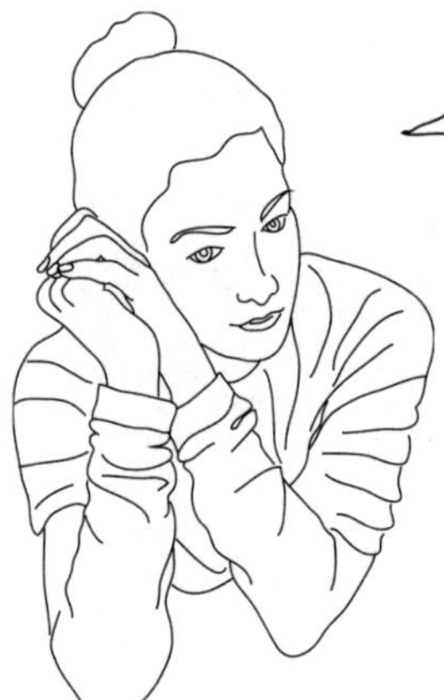

Jerusa: Actually, the most important lesson during this process of participating in the Tree School was that of listening, letting go of all preconceptions, of what I "thought", because I found myself in a place where I couldn't judge anymore. I had to start noticing the differences among all of us, the ways each person receives and processes things. I was totally committed to silence, to being able to see all those reactions or impossibilities of reaction and truly accept all forms of existence inside me.

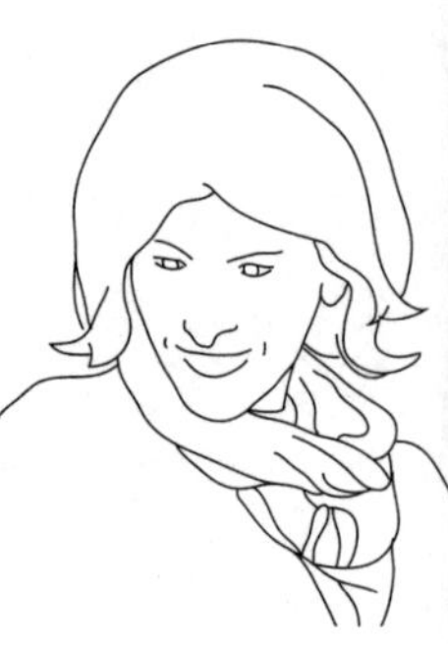

Sandi: One thing that happens in Palestine, or when you travel abroad and talk about Israeli colonization, is that people, in general, always say that they can only listen. They say they don't know anything about Palestine and, therefore, can't speak. So, Palestinians get isolated within a very local cause, even though the discussion is about the last form of colonization of the twentieth century. But what if you would participate not only by listening? This is something I'm slowly trying to understand. What did we do here? Even if I don't know anything about Brazil or you about Palestine, we kind of participate in each other's lives. We don't only listen to each other. This is a crucial aspect of this school; it asks me to give myself. I'm only part of it if I participate, and not if I expect only to listen.

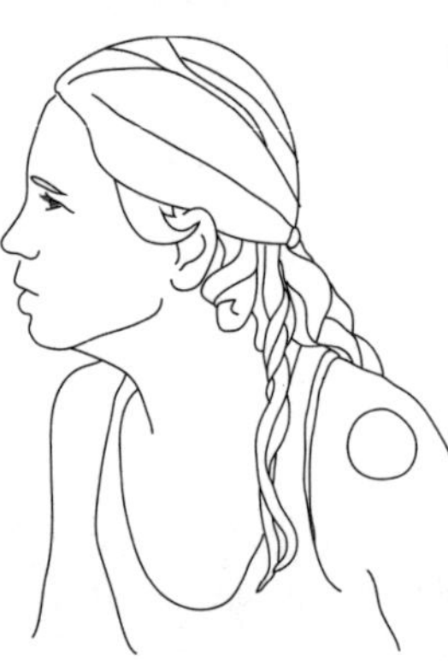

Joana: We worked for a long time with Fátima Freire, Paulo Freire's daughter, and we learned "void listening" from her. That is, how to empty yourself so that the other may fit inside you, so you don't always only listen and try to fit the other's categories within your own categories. It's very difficult. How can we avoid subjugating or underestimating the other by only listening from a position of guilt? Or even, constantly trying to find an equivalence that doesn't exist, out of the anxiety to participate and build something together, and therefore end up not actually listening to what is happening to this "other". Where is this space where we are neither apathetic nor impose ourselves on the other? What kind of listening is this? In fact, we were always talking about different kinds of listening, because listening has a lot to do with the place we come from. You were talking about some urgency to listen; we about another urgency to listen: you, about not withdrawing from political implication; us, about not imposing our categories on the other's categories.

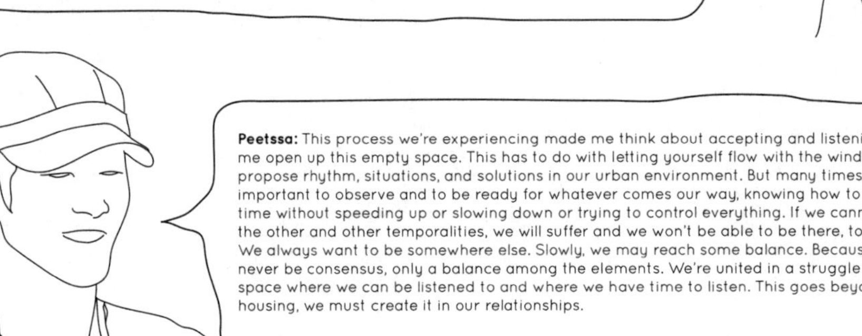

Peetsa: This process we're experiencing made me think about accepting and listening, it let me open up this empty space. This has to do with letting yourself flow with the wind. We always propose rhythm, situations, and solutions in our urban environment. But many times, it's more important to observe and to be ready for whatever comes our way, knowing how to deal with time without speeding up or slowing down or trying to control everything. If we cannot respect the other and other temporalities, we will suffer and we won't be able to be there, to be present. We always want to be somewhere else. Slowly, we may reach some balance. Because there will never be consensus, only a balance among the elements. We're united in a struggle for space —a space where we can be listened to and where we have time to listen. This goes beyond land and housing, we must create it in our relationships.

On knowledge...

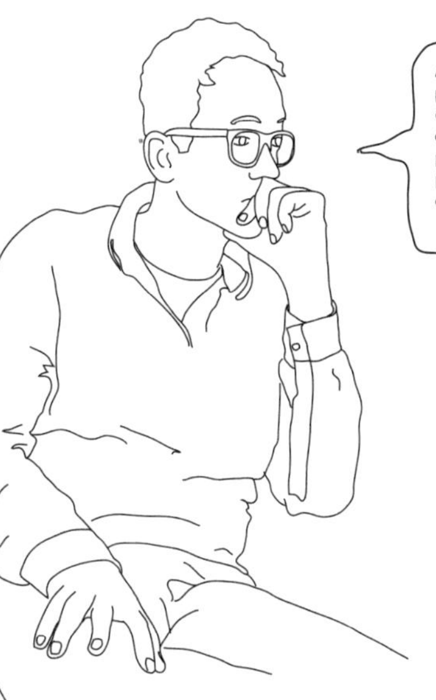

Alessandro: A lesson I feel was relevant for our school is that of always establishing the production of knowledge by including someone who can bring a radically different point of view. This Tree School is not aimed at standardizing knowledge and making people agree on things. Knowledge can only emerge when somebody brings a radically different point of view. People have the idea that knowledge is produced when you congregate and produce similar thoughts together, but I liked when we include diversities. Because these are significant moments when knowledge is added and produced.

David: It was very important for me personally to accept that I don't understand everything, but, at the same time, maintain my ability to be critical and reflect enough to enjoy this thing that I don't understand.

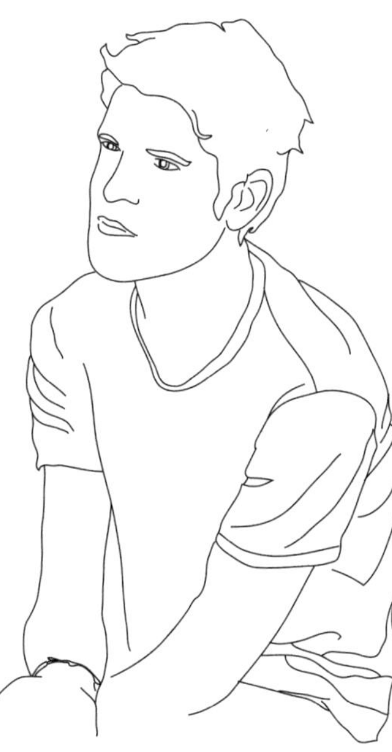

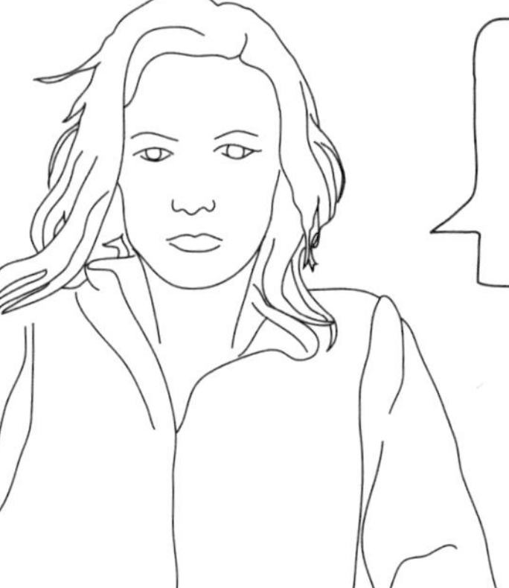

Floriana: A lesson I learned at the Tree School which could be important for its further development is the capacity of enduring the unknown, that is, allowing yourself to become permeable and, for a moment, not judging.

Alessandro: It is tragic that at the moment in which we are discussing the tree school as school in exile and place of refuge, six schools in Gaza have been hit, forty-seven people killed and hundreds wounded. UNRWA (United Nation Relief and Works Agency for Palestine refugees) schools in time of violence are usually transformed into safe havens, sanctuaries, where people can take refuge. However this does not prevent the Israeli army from bombing and killing innocent people there.

We always thought that our long-term task in Palestine is to not be following news of mainstream media production; not to make our own work just a reaction to military violence. But in front of this devastation I feel paralyzed, incapable of continuing, frustrated not to be in Palestine ...

More than 1.8 million people live in Gaza, the majority of whom were displaced between 1947-1950. They are originally from villages and towns very close to their site of displacement and refuge. Starting in 1948, their homes and villages have been destroyed by the state of Israel which has tried to erase them from the earth and from memory, in some cases covering the ruins with forests in other cases building new Jewish towns on top of them. This last assault on Palestinian refugees in Gaza is part of an ongoing attack against refugees, an ongoing *Nakba* that began over sixty-six years ago. For the Israeli state, Palestinian refugees are the worst nightmare, as their very presence problematizes the existence of a state based on ethnic cleansing and expropriation. Throughout all these years, Palestinians have not given up their right to return to their original houses nor their right to live in dignity. Israel is presenting their attacks and the killing of innocent civilians as a necessary evil that we need to accept. They want to convince the world that these horrible events are like a natural catastrophe, like a tornado or a tsunami, that we cannot stop and we must only endure, as cycles, one war after another. On the contrary, they are politically planned and executed by the military.

Gaza is a strip of only 360 km2. Imagine a rectangle measuring 40km x 9km, surrounded by walls, fences, checkpoints and military blockades on all its sides. Israel has erected concrete walls to the north and the east and crossing this border is only sometimes permitted for humanitarian cases. In the south, the current government of Egypt collaborates with Israel to keep the strip isolated. To the west, out to sea, Israel blasts Palestinian vessels if they dare to fish over 8 km from the coast, infringing Palestinian sovereignty. During the last bombardments, Israel has been "warning" the population to move. But move to where? There is no space in Gaza; no escape and no possibility to open the borders. At the time of this writing, almost two thousand Palestinians have been killed (the majority civilians). How is it possible for us to accept a situation of people being killed without even having the possibility to escape from the war?

I have just received this email from a very dear friend, Shourideh Molavi, who was supposed to join us here in Brazil to participate in the writing of this book. She just was in one the schools in Gaza that later was bombed.

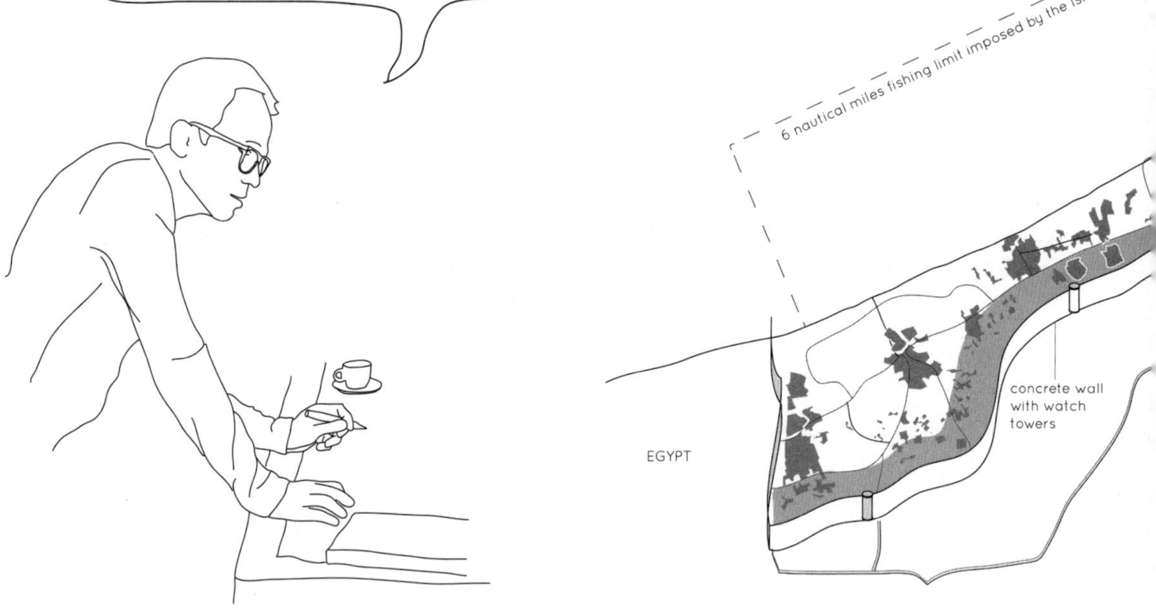

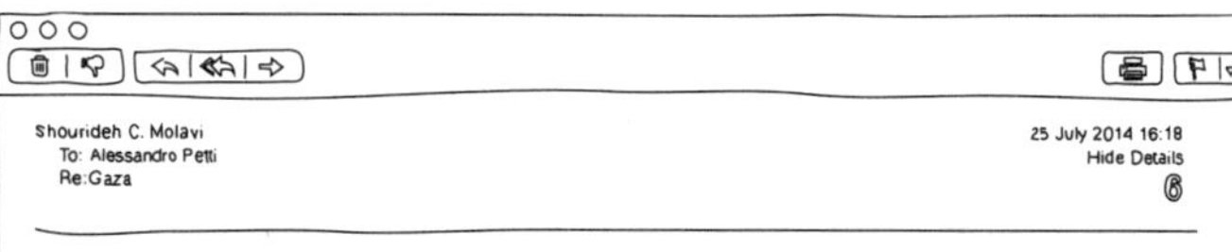

Hi dears,

I don't have much access to email and have been mainly texting with people. I've been in Gaza since last week and working with the Palestinian Center for Human Rights, taking to take narratives and documenting stories of displaced survivors in al-fakhura school in Jabaliya. Thousands here taking shelter. Just catastrophic. When people heard about the bombing this morning in Beit Hanoun school - not far from us at all - they began panicking, thinking that Jabaliya will be next. Some took their things and left, but to where, we don't know. One person said to me, "The best way to survive is to keep on walking and moving around and not sit still waiting for the bombs to hit you on the head. This is what Israel wants, to take away our roots, to have us keep moving and moving".

I try to get in as many interviews and then drive back to Gaza City and transcribe and summarize them - we are taking Israel to the International Criminal Court. I was in Jabaliya UN school all day again today and the interviews from today were very difficult to listen to. One mother described her son's superhero underwear to me when she found his body under the rubble, while another 15-year old boy described the purple color of his sister's skin when she was buried after dying when their house collapsed on them. It is mind-boggling that people are literally being killed by their collapsing homes. It does not give them shelter or comfort, the home is what is physically collapsing and killing people from the missiles. It is such a disturbing manner of turning people's homes against them.

Today one girl in early twenties started shouting at a French journalist who asked her whether she supports Hamas. "Do not ask me if I support Hamas. You see us suffering like this and you ask me if I support Hamas? Where do you see Hamas here? We are families, children, women suffering in this war." She ends saying, "I support the resistance!" It was powerful. The man was floored by her response.

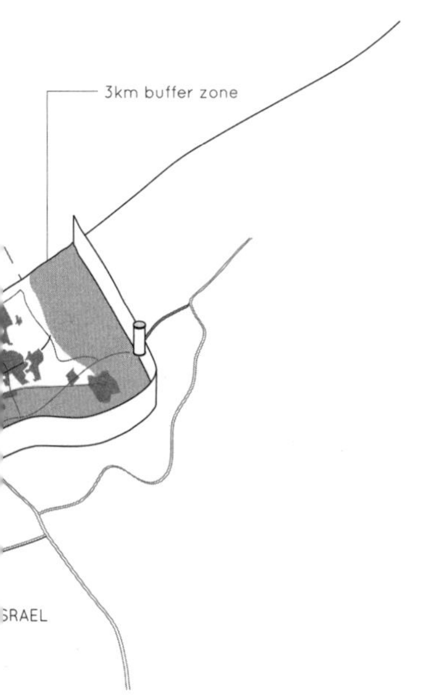

Allow me to describe things a little. I am sorry, dears, to paint such a picture, but I feel I must unburden myself a bit: The air is foul - the heat does not help the smells of sewage and maybe even bodies under the rubble that have begun to decompose.

The worst I heard from my friend Mohammad, who is also a journalist in Gaza is that animals started eating some of the dead bodies. I had to throw up when I heard this, really. Animals eating the bodies of dead people on the streets! Medical aid cannot get into the area either because Israeli tanks have blocked off the area, and Egypt still refuses to open the border at the end of the strip for any Palestinian, but is also blocking entry for internationals and even Egyptian citizens (!). I don't know what to say anymore - I don't think I will walk away from this 'normal'.

So you smell death and it's hard to get it out of your head and people carry lemons and vinegar with them to get the smell out. People are tired and they are broken. Enraged that Israel can bombard them like this, kill their children, and the world takes its time to break its silence. But in all of this there is also so much kindness. People take care of one another, comfort each other, and especially children who are looking for the best ways to support their parents. I've seen so many young kids, no older than 10 years old, hugging, comforting, trying to distract their younger siblings. They become caretakers of others so young. And all I think is that if Hamas grew out of the generation of the first intifada, where their young stones were met with bullets, then what is the generation that will grow out of the repeated onslaughts of the past seven years? What kind of teachers, parents, leaders will these kids grow up to be? By now, we can say that every single Palestinian child has lost an uncle or aunt, a parent or sibling, a grandparent, a neighbor, a school friend - someone they knew, someone who shaped their lives from war. No child is protected. I have not met a single child that has not lost someone violently and unnaturally.

I send you my hugs. I think of you often and wonder how differently the summer would have turned out if Israel had not launched another biennial war.

Love,
Shourideh

V. Sustainability

Thus far, this book has addressed contexts for education such as universities, museums, and nonprofit spaces and the perspectives of practitioners moving through them. Today a pressing question is the sustainability of these enterprises. How can institutions large and small sustain themselves? Should they be sustained indefinitely anyway? And how do practitioners sustain themselves and their work in relation to these platforms?

What is this sustainability anyway? I am defining it in terms of how we weather a crisis. If so, what kinds of crises? On the one hand I'm referring to economic sustainability. But that is never as simple as revenue. Future economic sustainability for institutions must also account for debt, investment, and risk management. I am also referring to ecological sustainability, and in this section artist Hope Ginsburg talks about her project *Meditation Ocean*, which is centered on encouraging sustained attention to the climate crisis. Her description of the video installation, originally presented at the Wexner Center for the Arts in Columbus, Ohio, an academic museum, suggests it was conceived in part as a node for educational programming that reaches beyond the university.

Artist and writer Gary Zhexi Zhang, in his text "On Financial Worlding," notes how the difficulty of forecasting connects the weather and finance. He talks about a worlding of risk, a measurable unknown, which is one way of thinking about not only the process of education but also the maintenance of institutions—or even smaller initiatives. One form of risk that has become paramount within American universities and museums is the discussion of Palestine. Students risk arrest, imprisonment, deportation, doxing, expulsion from school, or the revoking of their degrees. Faculty and staff risk harassment or losing their jobs.

Universities risk losing donor or government money. The epicenter of the student-encampment movement for this activism was Columbia University, where students were demanding the university's divestment from companies that support the Israeli occupation, in keeping with the Boycott Divestment and Sanctions (BDS) movement. Like almost all universities responding to this claim, Columbia officials said this was impossible. So, Adam Tooze, a professor there, conducted an analysis of the university's finances to address their claims. His examination reveals that, regardless of this political issue, universities are trapped in an unstable system of tuition, donor gifts and endowments, real estate investments, health and science research, and other factors. He makes it clear that this institutional model is just not working.

In her text "The Debt Collective," writer and filmmaker Astra Taylor tells the story of people with student debt organizing to collectively bargain for relief. Based on a union model, and informed by Occupy Wall Street, this initiative allowed ordinary people to gain power and leverage it in ways that previously had been afforded only to banks or corporations. This is a creative solution out of a broken system, spurred by a financial crisis.

While the war in Israel-Palestine revealed a crisis in higher education, COVID was a crisis that affected a range of nonprofit organizations throughout the world. Here, representatives from three Latin American organizations—Capacete, TEOR/éTica, and lugar a dudas—discuss the formation of Secue_LA, a collaborative online-education platform. This was not only a creative solution to pandemic-related challenges, such as the ability to connect in a moment when everyone was sheltering in place. It also addressed deeper systemic issues within the organizations' funding systems, which had recently seen decreasing support from European and American foundations. They worked together to find a way forward.

Working together across organizational, institutional, and even national borders has proven to be a progressive way to address a range of challenges. In a series of conversations about the RAW Académie residency at the Institute of Contemporary Art in Philadelphia, we can see how a Dakar-based organization, by coming to an academic museum in an American city, provoked new ways of defining both a museum and a university. Led by Linda Goode Bryant, who concurrently was developing a survey exhibition of the alternative space JAM [Just Above Midtown] at the Museum of Modern Art in New York, RAW Académie activated networks that included museums, universities, and alternative spaces and outlined how they represent different opportunities and challenges for collaboration. Like Secue_LA, RAW leaned into the collaborative and participatory nature of education as a condition of interdependence and indebtedness, strategies that are predicated on community and the common good.

Meditation Ocean

Hope Ginsburg interviewed by Noah Simblist

This conversation was recorded on August 28, 2024. It has been edited for length and clarity.

Noah Simblist *Meditation Ocean* addresses the representation of ecological impact and was presented in the context of an academic museum, The Wexner Center, last year. It also addresses education on several levels, including the ways that it seeks to educate a viewer through the video installations about particular ecologies and the challenges that they're facing, but also because you incorporated education so directly into the project. But before we get to *Meditation Ocean*, can I first ask you about some earlier initiatives like *Sponge*? How did *Sponge* come to be and how do you feel like it connected to education?

Hope Ginsburg *Sponge* was quite literally a knowledge-exchange project. That was its intention from the outset. It originated when I was in graduate school at the Massachusetts Institute of Technology and I was thinking about intervening productively into existing systems. That thinking came directly out of environmental work I was doing within the textile industry. The model of environmental intervention within industry was something I was inspired to apply in an educational context—what would it be like to make a school within a school? I proposed *Sponge* for the Independent Activities Period, the January term at MIT that encourages flexible models for learning. My "school within a school" was inspired by the sea sponge. I learned a lot about sponges doing this project.

The original idea was all about immersion. It was about how, even in my own art practice, I could not only take in information as a sponge absorbs water but also filter it and put it back out there in a way that catalyzed exchange, which is also what sponges do with nutrients. The original idea was a workshop model that would scramble disciplines and also flip hierarchies between experts and learners. Every participant in a *Sponge* workshop was both an expert and a learner. There was a model of taking in what the "curriculum" offered but then teaching something back to the rest of the group at the end, which, in the case of the first workshop, was on the fourth day.

NS You also applied this model elsewhere, right?

HG Yes, absolutely. I started the project with the knowledge that if you put a sponge in a blender, every little bit will grow up into an adult sponge. The idea was that *Sponge* would be replicable. There were a few workshops while I was in grad school. When I moved to Richmond to teach at Virginia Commonwealth University (VCU), I was invited to make a *Sponge* exhibition for which I programmed three weekend-long workshops. The first was "Feltmaking"; the second was "Water & Sound"; the third was called "Meta-Sponge" and it was quite explicitly about mixing disciplines. It included a curator, a biodynamic farmer, and so on. But this exhibition was also about making the space that would house these workshops. So there was still an interest in immersion, to get spongy about it, and installation. This exhibition led to the Sponge HQ, which was a space in the Anderson gallery at VCU that lasted six years. Sponge HQ was meant to be an interdisciplinary blender planted at a university, the way a sponge plants itself on a marine reef. And it was meant to do all of the filtering and collaborating. As I learned more about sponges by making this project, I found that sponges are known to be the first multicellular organism, which makes them a model of collectivity or collaboration. The Sponge HQ was meant to be a collaborative space.

NS On the one hand, you were choosing the sponge as a metaphor for flattening hierarchies. You begin by creating a school within a school as a student, then you have this job as a professor and are given an opportunity to embed this project within a different educational institution. As those things shifted did *Sponge* also shift?

HG There are many ways to answer that question. I continued to play with the question of hierarchy. For example, the first semester-long iteration of a sponge project was called *Colablablab*. I registered as a student at VCU, and I signed up for a biology lecture and lab. And then all of the students in *Colablablab* took the same biology lecture and lab. So the class took a class; and our class, which was an eight-credit constellation, responded to this new knowledge. On the other hand, there was a strong vector of participation in *Sponge*; it was collaborative but also participatory. The distinction I'm making is that when it was in participation mode, I took on a little bit of leadership. For example, if an opportunity came to me to make an exhibition like at the 9th Mercosul Biennial in Puerto Alegre, Brazil, then I could begin to imagine how the students and I might respond to such an invitation together. In a situation like that, I might take the lead, but then the students would be supported by class credit or artwork credit or school funding.

NS I'm glad that you introduced this notion of participation. Another way to think beyond the standard student-teacher relationship is in terms of leadership, opportunities, and facilitation. I also hear research implied in that process, like how you were researching sponges. And you're inviting other people to come along with you on that journey.

HG A catalyzing impulse for my own work is learning. And I think that art making has been a way of focusing and sustaining attention. There's also a social impulse to learn collectively with others, to receive, interpret, transmit, or exchange with others. So, in terms of research, maybe a pragmatic learning-by-doing ethos saturates the work. I also think that art can broaden what we mean by research, and, if so, I am swimming in that pool.

NS That's a great transition into your project *Land Dive Team*. What was it and how did it come about?

HG In *Land Dive Team* projects—which are live events, performances, or videos—a group of people meditates with scuba gear on land in a site that can be interpreted environmentally. For example in the video *Land Dive Team: Bay of Fundy*, three other divers and I meditated on the Fundy shoreline as its tide—which has the distinction of being the highest on the planet—rose on our bodies until we disappeared below. Another example took place in a formerly remediated wetland in the mud, allowing viewers to ask, what are these divers doing there? What if the water rises? In the case of a desert, the question might be, was this an ocean? Will this be an ocean? So again, a group of people meditating in scuba gear on land as a way of provoking questions about sites specifically related to the environment.

But to back up a little bit, I got there because of my interest in sponges. I learned to scuba dive so that I could see them alive on the reef. I attended an artist residency after I'd been working on the *Sponge* project for eight years. I was thinking more autobiographically and wanted to see what my work would do if I took a step back from *Sponge*. I was thinking in particular of an accident that I'd had in which I broke my sternum and a bone in my spine. I imagined making an underwater video reenacting that accident with scuba divers. And an image popped into my head of people meditating on land with scuba gear. So I invited my fellow residents to join me in a meditation with scuba gear. What happened was remarkable. Rather than just being a video production, it was actually quite an effective meditation. What I mean when I say *meditation* is practicing awareness of the present moment and meeting whatever is arising without judgement. The breath can be an anchor for finding the present moment because it's always there. So, when we were meditating with scuba gear, the meditation—that practice of returning to the breath every time the mind wanders—was augmented by the technology of the gear. Every inhale and exhale were amplified by the presence of the regulator in the mouth, by the weight of the gear. We were put right in our bodies and made aware of the other bodies breathing alongside us because of the soundscape.

After that first *Land Dive Team* practice in Florida, I realized that I was right back into a collective learning experience. I had to orient the participants in the "land dive" to the scuba gear, deliver an introduction to mindfulness practice, and then we had a collective experience. So, the original idea for the underwater video took a backseat and my attention shifted to the potentials of the *Land Dive Team*. It became an iterative project the way *Sponge* was. If *Sponge* was a series of workshops, events, classes, and hands-on making that was ten years in its expression, *Land Dive Team* was sixteen "land dives" in a variety of sites internationally from 2014 until 2021.

NS I hear you saying that facilitation became its own form of learning. This notion of participation, going from the individual to the communal, produced a specific experience of breathing that could be connected to mindfulness. What was the learning experience of breathing together?

HG I often learn about a project as I'm making it. By breathing together slowly my personal meditation practice deepened. It toggles back and forth between the individual and the collective. This is a new idea, so I'm working it out with you. When I began making the *Land Dive Team* projects, the role of meditation was to settle an individual anxiety about climate change and work with the regulation of the nervous system to be able to sustain attention to the climate crisis. What I learned is how settling into that place of awareness allows our individual being, our self, to start to dissolve. That is where that sense of interconnection entered the work for the first time. Learning with *Land Dive Team* deepened my own meditation practice and led to some of these deeper investigations of collectivity.

NS When I teach a class about contemporary art at VCU, I often show images of *Land Dive Team* together with *Flooded McDonald's* (2009) by Superflex. For viewers who encounter this and your work in a museum or gallery space, they are seeing an image of a potential future, of rising sea levels. There's something absurd about a group of people in scuba gear meditating on land, right?

HG: Absolutely, the project began with a kind of survivalist absurdity, asking "What peril is lurking for these divers?"

NS This is a good moment to transition into *Meditation Ocean*. Can you introduce us to the project?

HG *Meditation Ocean* is an accessible indoor ocean in the form of a video installation where viewers can have the experience of breathing with wildlife on the seabed, joined by divers that enter the scene to breathe with them. The first iteration of *Meditation Ocean* is also a platform for programming and reaching the public both within the ocean and in the field.

NS So then the question, who is *Meditation Ocean*? comes up because *Land Dive Team* implied a certain relationship between individuals and collectivity. And I think you've been very deliberate in *Meditation Ocean* being a kind of collective.

HG Absolutely. I have the honor of channeling *Meditation Ocean*, and the first iteration, *M.O. Turtlegrass Meadow*, on behalf of the Meditation Ocean Constellation, an expansive ecosystem of artists, curators, writers, musicians, meditators, divers, and scientists. The first instance of the Meditation Ocean Constellation comprised about fifty people who made the project happen. And that's not including all of the beings on the reef.

NS So, what was its first iteration?

HG As I mentioned, it was called *M.O. Turtlegrass Meadow*. The project was filmed during a four-day underwater meditation retreat in Biscayne National Park in the Florida Keys. The resulting six-channel video installation was installed as an exhibition at the Wexner Center in Columbus, Ohio. The score included ten commissioned guided meditations that played in the space, which also could be accessed outside of the exhibition. A series of public programs held by the Learning & Public Practice department at the Wexner Center and produced in collaboration with the Film/Video Studio Program, engaged high-school students, scientists in Columbus, and a university student group called Art & Resilience. It was an ecosystem on many levels: the makers, the participants, and the various departments at the institution with which I collaborated.

NS The presenting organization is an academic museum. Similar to a project that's tied to learning as a student at MIT, or as a professor at VCU, here you're embedding this project in a venue whose mission is to serve both the university and a general public. I imagine that some of those ecosystem nodes implicitly were tied to that mission.

HG *Meditation Ocean* came up through the Film/Video Studio, which is a post-production studio at the Wexner Center that filmmakers and artists move through to make their films. I had the opportunity to work with editor Mike Olenick on the *Land Dive Team: Bay of Fundy* video at the studio in 2016. Then I got really interested in the underwater coral farming that my collaborator and videographer Matt Flowers was doing on St. Croix. And so Matt Flowers, Joshua Quarles—who did the sound for the *Land Dive Team* projects and *Meditation Ocean*—and I made a multichannel video installation about coral restoration called *Swirling*. We edited that video with Alexis McCrimmon two years later in 2018 at the Film/Video Studio. In many ways, *Meditation Ocean* is a synthesis of *Sponge*, *Land Dive Team*, and *Swirling*. *Sponge* was a pedagogical space. *Land Dive Team* was embodied learning explicitly connected to an environment. For *Swirling*, to show viewers on land this underwater coral farming process, we wound up making a video installation. Sponge HQ closed in 2016, and, in the back of my mind, I was working through ideas for a new pedagogical space and a new space for environmental exchange. *Meditation Ocean* represents the notion of inverting the *Land Dive Team* and putting a group of actual divers on the seabed to breathe with the video's viewers instead of having participants schlep scuba gear to a given site. It occurred to me that this could be the new iteration of this idea, a new way to host environmental pedagogical work. All to say that *Meditation Ocean* was, in many ways, born at the Wexner Center in the Film/Video Studio in conversation with Alexis, Matt, Josh, and Jennifer Lange, who is the director of the Film/Video Studio Program and also the producer of *Meditation Ocean.*

NS So, how do you think the Wexner, as an academic *museum*, helped to support this work? One aspect of an academic mission is teaching and another is supporting research.

HG Yes, and knowledge production, which, in our field, is the production of artworks.

NS Museums often are thought of as presenting institutions: commissioned works are most often presented in an exhibition. New acquisitions are presented as a part of a collection. But this Film/Video program allowed you to research, to generate knowledge, to develop an artwork without necessarily presenting it at that institution. Some inherent learning existed within that without necessarily having to present it. That came later, right?

HG Absolutely. 100 percent yes to all of that.

NS So once the Wexner began discussing presenting the work, that introduced other questions about the engagement with the public and educational programming. Tell us about that.

HG As the opportunity to present *Meditation Ocean* at the Wexner emerged, more entities at the Wexner Center came online. The Exhibitions team became an important partner with Film/Video and Learning & Public Practice. It was a very collaborative project.

NS Were there specific conversations about engaging particular publics? How did you engage the undergraduate population? How did you engage the public of Columbus?

HG Under the leadership of Dionne Custer Edwards, Learning & Public Practice already had a robust educational program. When I came in as the artist/director of this collaborative project, I needed to understand how to engage with the systems and communities that were already in place. There were many conversations about who at Ohio State might be interesting to engage. The Byrd Polar and Climate Research Center became a partner as well as the Schiermeier Olentangy River Wetland Research Park, because I came with the notion that we were going to connect the Midwestern ecosystem of Columbus, Ohio with the far-flung location of Biscayne National Park in the Florida Keys. How do we learn about what's affecting local waters, what research is already on site, and how do we build a porous enough container for all of these ideas that the public can move through? We all wanted this ocean to be accessible and to touch on the guiding principles of the project, which were connections between individual and community wellbeing, human and more-than-human wellbeing, and also connections between the environmental and the social. We knew that everyone would come to the ocean with a different set of associations. We intended to make it accommodating. We also recognized that people might have fear or trauma around the ocean. A great deal of care and sensitivity was put into building programs that could meet people where they were.

NS With *Land Dive Team* you were talking about the feelings that one might have about rising sea levels and the way that you modulate, mediate, or prepare for those feelings. That aspect of this work relates to ways of thinking about climate change and the way that people deal with—let's call it—environmental activism or navigating climate justice. One way to look at climate change is to look at the facts: rising temperatures, rising sea levels. Another way is affective: a sense of fear or anxiety in relation to what the data implies. The way that feelings are mediated in relation to information reminds me of a pedagogical space. With this installation at the Wexner, and even in earlier projects, how did you think about the ways that learning functions within environmental activism and how you as an artist can invite a public to engage with this subject?

HG One proposal of this project is that we get our bodies back into the mix, get our felt-sense back into the mix. We're living in a very mental, above-the-neck, Western scientific culture. The data comes in through science, and that's very important. But one of many root causes of climate change, of the environmental catastrophe, is that we're cut off from our bodies, from our ability to feel connection to other people, to other species, to landscapes. We're unable to perceive the signals that our individual and collective bodies are sending up for us with great alarm. One of the informal pedagogies of *Meditation Ocean* is to start with a felt sense experience.

NS I wonder how you get a population that is in a landlocked location to think about this far-away space of the Florida Keys. Maybe *Meditation Ocean* is provocative by locating one space in another space.

HG Starting with the notion that wonder and awe are at the root of altruism,[1] a question is, how can you shift people's perception long enough for them to meet, get curious about, and connect with a site thatthey may not understand? Especially when such a connection may move viewers to engage with ocean justice. A pedagogical artwork does not need to literally transmit information. There are many ways to do that in the mix of the project's materials, like a site statement that looks at the social implications of Biscayne National Park and the Florida Keys, like writings in the gallery guide, like the content that moves through the guided meditation scripts that can be heard in the gallery. So, one can transmit the data or scientific research that supports a learning experience, but viewers are invited to take in their experience as it arises for them. I mean, I'm laughing at the idea of a meditation project that says: you will have this experience and leave with this specific new understanding.

NS You're laughing at it because it sounds absurd, right?

HG Right. Folks could approach *M.O. Turtlegrass Meadow* in many ways. And they did. There were many comfortable circular cushions of different heights and sizes all over the floor, and people built pillow forts and chilled all day. People started to use it as a meeting space or a workspace. At one point, a really provocative speaker was coming to campus, and a group of students and faculty held a counter-protest in the form of a workshop that took place in the installation. So you could come into that space and through the ambient score—which had reef sounds and musical elements made from synthesizing the human voice—experience the shifting light, the subtle movement of what was taking place in the videos, with no expectations. You could also sit down on a cushion and "dial in" a guided meditation on headphones or through a wall speaker and practice meditation more formally. This spectrum of informal to formal

1 The belief that awe and curiosity inspired by the natural world could motivate action on its behalf has been a driving force in Ginsburg's work. For the original research on the connection between awe and altruism, see P.K. Piff, P. Dietze, M. Feinberg, D. M. Stancato, and D. Keltner, "Awe, the small self, and prosocial behavior," *Journal of Personality and Social Psychology* 108, no. 6 (2015), 883–899. For further reading, see Dacher Keltner, *Awe: The New Science of Everyday Wonder and How It Can Transform Your Life* (Penguin Press, 2023).

meditation practice is analogous to the range of ways knowledge is transmitted in the project, from openly inviting curiosity to sharing very specific information about the site in the Florida Keys.

NS We talked about expanding the notion of what an educational space could be, how an artwork can function as a pedagogical framework, and, through that, how it can expand the definition of pedagogy itself. Pedagogy doesn't necessarily lead to certain outcomes like the acquiring of information or skills. But similarly, we were talking about how change is driven by a narrative of justice.

HG There's a helpful arc articulated by those working to address climate change: denier, accepter, supporter, activist. You're conjuring justice, and I want to return to that, but there's an interesting side question here about the relationship between activism and meditation, which is a practice of being and stillness. One useful way of thinking about the relationship between meditation and activism is the discernment of right action.

NS What do you mean by that?

HG By right action, I mean, how can we act in the world in a way that does not add to aggression or escalate a problem? What is the right action? And this is a moment-to-moment question, right? Action can be motivated by anger. Sometimes that's productive. Sometimes it may introduce harm. What I mean by meditating to train in right action is that one who has practiced meditative awareness gets a lot of intuitive information to help discern the right action in a given moment. It's interesting to unpack the relationship between a mindfulness practice and activism, because, in a way, the mindfulness practice is meant to decrease activation. You might say that through meditation, we learn when and how to act.

NS I hear you saying that you're trying, through your practice, to see how meditation and activism—which might seem to have nothing to do with one another—may actually be related.

HG Yes, but it's also important for me to say that I am learning. I am not a meditation scholar or a scholar of Buddhism, although what I'm referencing and learning about is Buddhist practice and specifically Vipassana, or Insight, meditation, in the Theravada tradition. I'm also not a scholar of climate policy or climate justice. I come to these spaces as a learner, and I hope that I'm transmitting these ideas with the appropriate humility. I think what artistic practice allows us to do is make these juxtapositions as a kind of public amateur.[2] In these projects, I learn in public with other people.

I think the question on the table is to do with meditation and climate justice.[3] I want to get back to this notion of the separate self and how harmful it is because I think it is so intrinsically tied to climate and climate justice. "I am a single being. I know and love a small group of certain other beings, and I want resources for myself and for these other beings that I love." Right?

2 Ginsburg cites the role of the artist as "public amateur" and more thoughts on learning in public as defined and articulated by Claire Pentecost, as an inspiration in her practice. See Claire Pentecost, "Beyond Face," *Continental Drift* 15 (May 2008).

3 While researching *Meditation Ocean*, Ginsburg participated in the Mind & Life Institute's 2021 Summer Research Institute, "The Mind, the Human-Earth Connection, and the Climate Crisis." The conference presentations are now an accessible online course. Ginsburg credits this program for deepening her understanding of the climate crisis, specifically Dekila Chungyalpa's presentation "Don't Look Down: How to Build Bridges with Unlikely Allies."

That sense of separateness and hoarding is partly about making resources and knowledge unavailable to other people. This is where root causes of the climate crisis—like globalization, neoliberalism, and colonization—come in, these acquisitive, grasping impulses that are colonial and supremacist. I'm referencing white supremacy, male supremacy, human supremacy. These are the justice issues bound up in climate, as communities of color, marginalized communities, and communities with fewer economic resources are bearing the brunt of the climate crisis.

NS You've talked about empathy for other species, paying attention to species other than our own. That interspecies awareness is important in relation to the conversation about a community in Ohio thinking about a community in Florida—and the awareness of what is similar and different between us. And that questions around climate justice have to do with the many factors that mean some people are more directly affected by the climate crisis than others. And there's also this simple idea that you were talking about with *Land Dive Team*: that there's one's individual experience, one's own breath, the breath of the person next to you, and the collective breath providing an easy way to move between the individual and the communal. But structural inequities make it difficult to move between contexts. I'm curious how you think about creating an opportunity to meditate on those differences. How do you account for different publics from a diversity of backgrounds encountering one artwork, one installation, one program? Some people may recognize something really clearly, other people may need it translated.

HG You make an ocean. This is a nod to the ocean and a thanks to the ocean. What space is capacious enough to hold it all, to allow all things to move through it? You make a sponge—in Latin, the *Phylum Porifera*—all pores, no inside or outside, no separate self. Everything that arises moves through. I think that what is proposed here are porous, vast, multivalent spaces that are full and layered and more than human.

More information about Meditation Ocean, *including collaborator credits, related publications, images, sound, and guided meditation scripts, can be found at meditationocean.com.*

On Financial Worlding

Gary Zhexi Zhang

Divined Fictions

The crimes of kings and the suffering of people will render universal this fatal catastrophe which must detach one world from another.

–Abbé Raynal, *A Philosophical and Political History of the Settlements and Trade of the Europeans in the East and West Indies* (1770)[1]

Finance and cosmology have long been conjoined as technologies of uncertainty. The "astronomical diaries," a collection of Babylonian cuneiform, presented astrological observations, political events, and commodity prices alongside startlingly accurate projections of celestial movements.[2] Like their ancestors, contemporary financial practitioners speak of the market in the language of the skies, "forecasting" the "turbulence" of a "risk universe" like anxious navigators in a weather system of their own making.

In a world intensively bound up with the consequences and cultural logics of markets, finance resembles an indexical engine, endlessly proliferating new linkages between creditors and debtors, investors and investees, prices and expectations. This engine is fueled by a fantasy of temporal capture, as in the notion of a "complete market," where "there is a price for every asset in every possible state of the world," where every risk is hedged and the "truth" or price of every asset is discovered, frictionlessly.

The fund manager turned anthropologist Philip Grant describes the "chains" of financial investment running throughout the system as an "architecture of constraint and enablement." "Chains bind," he writes,

1 Quoted in Michael Sonenscher, *Before the Deluge: Public Debt, Inequality, and the Intellectual Origins of the French Revolution* (Princeton University Press, 2009), 31.

2 John Grainger, "Prices in Hellenistic Babylonia," *Journal of the Economic and Social History of the Orient* 42, no. 3 (1999), 303–25.

"yet they are also (but not always) strong: through their binding they link, connect, enable, reinforce."[3] Like a catalogue of contractual fictions linking present knowledge to future desires and expectations, these chains bind a set of worldly conditions in place and form a lever of power over the opening and foreclosure of other possible worlds.

* * *

"Worlding," writes artist Ian Cheng, is the unnatural art of creating an infinite game by choosing its present, storytelling its past, simulating its futures, and nurturing its changes."[4] As a maker of simulations, Cheng's definition is willfully ambiguous as to *which* world is at stake. There is no definite article, no singular whole, only a constructive reality complicit in its own making and unmaking. In reality, worlding happens both *in* and *of* the world: Like the map that reconfigures the territory, it is both a production of new realities and reconfigures the world's ongoing transformation of itself and its subjects. As the late anthropologist David Graeber wrote, "the ultimate, hidden truth of the world is that it is something that we make, and could just as easily make differently."[5]

Through the lens of history, worlding could be understood in the transformations of ontological and epistemological categories such as "time," "nature," and "society" that order reality and hold it together in a relatively stable, coherent narrative for its subjects. This disorienting process can be felt acutely in times of catastrophic uncertainty, revolution, and narrative collapse, where the worlding of a world entails a new sense of time and an attendant reorganization of value. The architects of the French Revolution, for instance, marked their break with the old world by establishing a new Republican calendar and a new currency, the *assignat*, along with a proliferation of local currencies. As historian Rebecca Spang writes, "Time began again at Year One; the ten-day décade replaced the seven-day week; church bells, melted down to make small change, no longer rang the time for prayers."[6] The stability of a particular world depends on one's conviction in a particular socio-legal regime and its hold on the collective consciousness. If a regime is in question, the future can only be assured through the crystallization of other, incipient fictions. The turbulence of the revolution triggered a proliferation of local currencies. Unable to trust in the symbols of sovereignty stamped on their coins, revolutionary-era trade contracts started indexing a "deeper" layer of reality by specifying the purity of the metal they contained.

* * *

What sense of time emerges from our own era of contested narratives, ecological crisis, and socio-technological uncertainty? Our own time is often characterized by a "post-catastrophic" sensibility in which, to borrow sociologist Elena Esposito's phrase, we have "used up all our futures": where multiple endings are already being metabolized and redistributed by the temporal technologies of the present. Caught between

3 Diane-Laure Arjaliès, Philip Grant, Iain Hardie, Donald A. MacKenzie, and Ekaterina Svetlova, *Chains of Finance: How Investment Management Is Shaped* (Oxford University Press, 2017), 25.

4 Ian Cheng, *Emissaries Guide to Worlding*, edited by Joseph Constable, Rebecca Lewin, and Veronica So (Koenig Books, 2018). 5

5 David Graeber, *The Utopia of Rules: On Technology, Stupidity, and the Secret Joys of Bureaucracy* (Melville House, 2015), 89.

6 Rebecca L. Spang, *Stuff and Money in the Time of the French Revolution* (Harvard University Press, 2015), 18.

temporalities of plenitude and of scarcity, it is not that we cannot imagine the end of the world or the end of capitalism, but that they are unimaginable to one another.

Suhail Malik and Armen Avanessian characterize the temporality of financialization as the "speculative time-complex," in which linear time has been retooled into a plethora of alternate grammars, such as the preemptive, recursive, performative, cybernetic, memetic, and other nonlinear configurations of cause and consequence. For Malik and Avanessian, it is in the predictive logic of machine learning and the politics of preemptive military strikes that signify that time, as a socio-technical phenomenon, is changing: "you bomb somewhere and then afterward you will find the enemy you expected. You produce a situation that was initially a speculation."[7] Likewise, in the speculative logic of financial worlding, the future is not an inevitability, but a fiction to be indexed and occupied.

The Worlding of Risk

Whatever we mean by modernity [is] in some way linked with new attitudes toward the control of the future and life relatively secure from the disruptions of chance.

–Lorraine Daston,
Classical Probability in the Enlightenment[8]

Since the French Revolution [...] concepts no longer merely serve to define a given state of affairs, they reach into the future. Increasingly, concepts of the future were created. Positions to be captured had first to be formulated linguistically before it was even possible to enter and formally occupy them. The substance of many concepts was thus reduced in terms of actual experience and their aspiration to realization proportionally increased. Actual substantial experience and the space of expectations coincide less and less.

–Reinhart Koselleck,
"Begriffgeschichte and Social History"[9]

Between Koselleck and Daston's observations of post-Enlightenment temporality, two related models of the future emerge. For Daston, it is a future that can be controlled relative to the insecurities of chance, a statistical imagination of a world that can be insured, wagered, and hedged. For Koselleck, it is the emergence of a constructionist futurity which must exist in the virtual ("formulated linguistically") before it can enter the horizon of the actual. In economist Frank Knight's canonical definition, a "risk" is a measurable unknown, while an uncertainty is unquantifiable. In Koselleck's account, it is not risk (the known unknown) but uncertainty (the unknown unknown) which becomes a protagonist of a temporal politics. Where Daston's is calculated, risk-based time, Koselleck's is the time of prophecy and prefiguration. They are two sides of the same speculative coin. While the former assesses and negotiates the world of possibilities as they appear, the latter forces new worlds onto the horizon of possibility; while the former manages expectation, the latter collectivizes desire.

The modern risk universe emerged from a new relationship to time, via money, in the European Enlightenment over the seventeenth and eighteenth centuries. New

7 Armen Avanessian and Suhail Malik, eds. *The Time Complex: Post-Contemporary* (Merve, 2016), 11.

8 Lorraine Daston, *Classical Probability in the Enlightenment* (Princeton University Press, 1988), 164.

9 Rienhart Koselleck, *Futures Past: On the Semantics of Historical Time* (MIT Press, 1985), 78.

theories of probability, like the Swiss mathematician Jacob Bernouilli's law of large numbers, allowed uncertain phenomena to be measured in terms of their statistical distributions.

These numerical innovations had transformative ideological, legal, and moral implications. Usury, for instance, had been considered both sinful and illegal to Christian morality. As Thomas Aquinas had it, making money from lending money was tantamount to creating something from nothing, a privilege of God alone. With the emergence of new statistical frameworks, however, jurors argued that loans represented a calculable risk to the lender, be it a trading vessel's prospects of return or the anticipated length of an insured life.[10] In doing so, the temporality of risk summoned the once-intangible future expectations into the calculative world of the market, and, in turn, laid the foundations for finance as an arena for the control and contestation of time. As the novelist Daniel Defoe remarked optimistically of the new Friendly Societies for mutual insurance: "General peace might be secured all over the world by it [...] all the contingencies of life might be fenced against by this method (as fire already is), as thieves, floods by land, storms by sea, losses of all sorts, and death itself, in a manner, by making it up to the survivor."[11]

The reconceptualization of contingency also saw an explosion of financial innovations: lotteries, insurance schemes, tontines, and scams (many of which failed due to poor statistics). Life annuities, for instance, popular contracts which paid out fixed annual sums until the end of the investor's life, could be taken out on the "heads" of others, from family members to the Pope. In the decades before the French Revolution, life annuities had become so popular that Louis XVI used them to finance the indebted French treasury. In one scheme, the so-called "Thirty Virgins of Geneva," the bankers and noblemen of the Swiss financial center issued annuities on the heads of their daughters and spread the risk by packaging them into a financial security. As interest spread, the resulting investment offer was so popular that Voltaire complained that Geneva was becoming better known for annuities than for Calvin. As Rebecca Spang writes, "If, in some horrible conflagration, the entire female population of Geneva had perished simultaneously, it might have been as much as 40 percent of the French monarchy's short-term borrowing that was redeemed in an instant."[12] While turning young lives into a kind of mortgage security seems counterintuitive and perhaps dubious by today's standards, the episode is reflective of the way in which futurity was bound up with credit and the wider landscape of social security. With their exceptionally privileged status and the spread of risks across their numbers—in a volatile, indebted France a few years short of revolutionary upheaval—the prospects of the thirty children probably looked like one of the surest bets in Europe.

The speculative financial innovations of the eighteenth century also foregrounded a dialectic between money and narrative. The literary and economic scholar Mary Poovey argues that the emergence of paper money played a key role in the development and eventual breakup of the "fact/fiction continuum" in a developing print culture. The modern divide between fiction and non-fiction replaced a far more ambiguous

10 In 1662, the haberdasher John Graunt published a pioneering work of demography, a "life table" which surveyed causes of death across the population and demonstrated predictable patterns of life expectancy.

11 Daniel Defoe, "Of Friendly Societies: An Essay Upon Projects," ed. Henry Morley (London, 1887 [1697]), 144.

12 Spang, *Stuff and Money*, 20.

relationship to journalistic and literary narrative. Awash with newly valid and invalid forms of paper money, new modes of distinction were needed. These ways of "reading" grew in tandem with emerging literary forms, such as that of the shiller and the sales pitch, as opposed to the ostensibly sober analysis of the journalist and commentator.

Poovey observes that in moments of speculative crisis, such as the South Sea Bubble of 1720, the fact/fiction continuum ceased to matter, because "every share attained its value not (just) from some underlying gain by the company it represented but (also) from the desire of other buyers to purchase the company's stocks."[13] Like narrative fiction, speculative investment involves a suspension of disbelief, where the validity of an economic "fact" is upheld so long as others believe it too. Likewise, financial worlding can be understood as such a manifestation of collective belief: its struggle is not over the "facts" or underlying values but whether belief can be suspended until a new social reality takes shape—until the prophecy is fulfilled. As a fellow traveler on the fact/fiction continuum, money, it turned out, was the ideal vehicle for this journey.

13 Mary Poovey, *Genres of the Credit Economy: Mediating Value in Eighteenth- and Nineteenth-Century Britain* (University of Chicago Press, 2008), 82

14 Edward J. Oughton, Andrew Skelton, Richard B. Horne, Alan W. P. Thompson, and Charles T. Gaunt, "Quantifying the Daily Economic Impact of Extreme Space Weather Due to Failure in Electricity Transmission Infrastructure," *Space Weather* 15, no. 1 (2017), 65–83, https://doi.org/10.1002/2016SW001491.

15 "Solar Storm Risk to the North American Electric Grid," Lloyd's of London and Atmospheric and Environmental Research, Inc., 2013.

Fungible States

The disenchantment of one world was the revelation of another, in which a contingent universe of contingencies could be navigated by means of their fungibility. The underlying laws of this world, however, were by no means clear. Far from the control of the future imagined by Defoe, before long, the financialized market economy began to resemble something more like a turbulent world in which all were subject to the winds of mass psychology.

Nineteenth-century political economists such as Lord Overstone were preoccupied with understanding the business cycle as a pattern of commercial "moods," which evolved from "quiescence" into "growing confidence, -prosperity, -excitement, -overtrading, -convulsion, -pressure, -stagnation, -distress," before returning again to quiescence. Overstone believed that this cycle repeated roughly every decade, entering its lows with the emergence of "diseased credit," which effected a downturn of "faith in things unseen."

Others sought external causes for the forces that inexplicably haunted the market. The cofounder of the Marginalist Revolution in economics, Willam Stanley Jevons, spent years attempting to prove that financial crises were caused by sunspots, semi-regular cycles of electromagnetic activity on the surface of the sun. While a causal link was never discovered, solar storms and space weather continue to pose an exogenous threat to terrestrial economies. During the "Carrington Event" of 1859, the most intense geomagnetic storm ever recorded, witnesses reported sightings of the *aurora borealis* from Jamaica to Shanghai. The Carrington Event took place before the world became reliant on the electricity grid; a 2017 study suggested that a similar event today would cause over $40 billion of damage a day,[14] while the reinsurance market Lloyd's claims that such a rare but "inevitable" event could last between two weeks and two years.[15]

* * *

The age of financial crises was born at the height of European colonialism, and the collective fervor of speculation was also bound up with that most fundamental of narrative fictions, the nation. The "Panic of 1825," for instance, was tied up with speculation in London over the debt instruments of new nations such as Venezuela, Bolivia, and Peru, which had recently won their independence from the Spanish. As Romantic scholar Alexander Dick writes, "It was in the wake of the 1825 [financial] crisis that economists realized [...] that commerce operated according to rules and principles in which individuals had little direct, moral influence either as legislators or as managers."[16]

One notorious episode involved the conjuring of an entirely fictional nation, Poyais. Its "founder," Gregor MacGregor, was a British mercenary who had fought under the "Liberator of America" Simón Bolívar as well as the future president of Venezuela, José Paez. In 1812, MacGregor married Bolívar's cousin, Josefa, firmly cementing his position as an associate of the revolutionary elite of the fledgling South American states. MacGregor's uneven military record included capturing Florida from the Spanish and forming—for six short months—the independent Republic of the Floridas.

Having seen the outpouring of speculative capital from London's financial center into the new South American sovereignties, MacGregor developed a sovereign plot of his own. In 1820, he found himself in the court of King George Frederic Augustus, leader of the people of the Mosquito Coast, a British protectorate located in contemporary northern Honduras. The British-educated Indigenous king granted MacGregor custody of a stretch of Mosquito territory around the size of Wales, home to the "Poyer" people. MacGregor soon assumed the role of the "Cazique," or sovereign prince, of "Poyais." While his new nation was sizable, it was made of difficult terrain, unfit for livestock or cultivation.

MacGregor arrived in London in 1821, just as feverish investment into Latin American territories was taking hold. Enjoying some celebrity as an adventurer, he had arrived to sell Poyaisian assets, loans, and deeds in acres of Polynesian land to financial investors and would-be settlers alike. To this end, MacGregor set about constructing an elaborate alternative reality, almost entirely on paper. For Poyais, he designed a flag, army uniforms, and a currency; he drew up constitutional and commercial mechanisms, a British-style honors system, landed titles, and a coat of arms. In Britain, he set up Poyaisian offices in London, Edinburgh, and Glasgow and commissioned a lengthy publication titled *A Sketch of the Mosquito Shore* (1822), which detailed the illustrious natural riches of the Poyaisian territory, "chiefly for the use of settlers." The *Sketch* described its lush flora, fauna, and mineral wealth: the land was said to be so abundantly fertile that "a farmer could have three maize harvests a year."[17] It was an audacious investment pitch: by his account, plantations and settlements in such an "untapped" land could soon be worth millions of dollars. A charismatic publicist, MacGregor set up shop in a stately house lent to him by an aristocrat elite who wholeheartedly bought

16 Alexander J. Dick, "On the Financial Crisis, 1825–26," Branch, https://branchcollective.org/?ps_articles=alexander-j-dick-on-the-financial-crisis-1825-26, accessed February 14, 2023.

17 Thomas Strangeways, *A Sketch of the Mosquito Shore, Including the Territory of Poyais* (Edinburgh, 1822).

into his exotic fantasy. Framing his return to England as a state visit, a diplomatic letter from the "Cazique" was presented to George IV himself.

MacGregor could not have launched his scam at a better time. The lucrative world he fabricated proved irresistible to traders on the London exchanges. As investments in the newly established sovereignties of Peru, Chile, and Colombia soared, Poyaisian bonds and land grants appeared as similarly credible investments in a distant, resource-rich territory. The price of Poyaisian bonds joined Portuguese scrip and Chilean funds on the daily financial listings.

But MacGregor had bigger plans. Between 1822 and 1823, over two hundred fifty British settlers sailed for forty days to the Mosquito Coast, carrying fistfuls of MacGregor's own fiat currency, the Poyais Dollar, which he had printed by the Royal Mint of Scotland. On arrival in the Poyaisian capital, St. Joseph, the colonists found a small settlement on an unpromising land, with no sign of a royal palace nor the Poyaisian houses of parliament. The majority of the would-be colonists died of hunger, infighting, and tropical disease, and fewer than fifty returned to Britain.

The Poyais scheme was perhaps the most audacious securities fraud in the history of finance. It was also an exercise in financial worlding par excellence. MacGregor's scheme worked not simply because of his exceptional powers of persuasion, but because his desirous fiction hitched itself parasitically on a conjunction of other, even more powerful socio-historical narratives. From the hunger for returns on high-risk foreign debt assets in London, to the creation of new sovereign nations as new avenues of investment, to would-be colonists who dreamt of their new roles as the land-owning entrepreneurs of a faraway paradise, the mirage of Poyais was magnified by the convergence of multiple indexical imaginaries. Many of the settlers were themselves Scottish farmers who had been dispossessed by the highland clearances, the capitalist enclosure of rural land that began in the mid-eighteenth century.[18] Together, these vectors of financial, cultural, and affective investment were enough to bind an elaborate fabulation into a latent reality, a future terrain which had to be expected in order to be inhabited, and was soon enough bound in place by financial investments such that a reality otherwise would be unthinkable.

In particular, the scheme struck at the ambiguity at the heart of finance and nationhood, elusive notions whose "substance" elide legal fictions, social imaginaries, and material "facts." In the political scientist Benedict Anderson's well-known definition, a nation is "an imagined community": a fictional collectivity "moving steadily down (or up) history" despite the fact that a member of a nation will never encounter more than a handful of their compatriots.[19] Finance similarly speculates on the desires of others, converging a market of expectations into the figure of price, which becomes a mediator and determinant of collective desire. As sociologist Elena Esposito writes, a financial operation like the purchase of an option generates a "constraint," a constructive act that "influences the course of time and contributes to the creation of what will become true in the future."[20]

18 Alfred Hasbrouck, "Gregor McGregor and the Colonization of Poyais, between 1820 and 1824," *The Hispanic American Historical Review* 7, no. 4 (November 1927): 438.

19 Benedict Anderson, *Imagined Communities: Reflections On the Origin and Spread of Nationalism* (Verso, 2016), 26.

20 Elena Esposito, *The Future of Futures: The Time of Money and Society* (Edward Elgar, 2011), 4.

To the colonial speculators on the London Stock Exchange, during a period in which geo-imagination was transformed by imperialist expansion, was Poyais any more factual or fictional an investment than Venezuelan or Peruvian bonds? What if the disappointed colonists who arrived to Poyais had not fallen into turmoil, but found the limited resources they needed to establish a nation? Put another way, was Poyais a scam, or a suspension of disbelief, an exercise in collective worlding that is itself a prerequisite for any speculative collective project? Arguably, it was both. Having participated in the "fact" of new nations emerging from revolutionary fictions, MacGregor channeled the foment of colonial speculation into an operative fiction of his own. After attempting his scheme once more, unsuccessfully, in France, MacGregor eventually escaped to Venezuela, where he was retired with a military pension. For two years between the coronation of the "Cazique" and the arrival of British settlers on its shores, the nation of Poyais had been real enough.

Counterspeculations

Management scholar Gerald Davis argues that the postindustrial American economy has undergone a "Copernican revolution" in which it moved "from a social system orbiting around corporations [...] to a market-centered system in which the corporations themselves—along with households and governments—are guided by the gravitational pull of financial markets." After all, contemporary financial markets reign supreme as a horizon against which other social regimes rise and fall. When political uncertainty strikes, it is market moods which are reported as sober judgements on their possible consequences. And as demonstrated after the crisis of 2008, if global markets do in fact fail, it is up to states and their taxpayers, the investors of last resort, to prevent the unimaginable catastrophe of their demise.

The contemporary conditions of financial worlding pertain to a life in which financialization and the habits of speculation creep into every crevice of socio-cultural activity. In this speculative landscape, the philosopher Michel Feher argues that the site of contemporary class struggle shifts from the traditional strife between employers and workers to a society ordered by the relationship between investors and investees. As Feher observes of the financialized social order, the investor class, which wields power over future capital allocation in the market, takes precedence over the employer-owner of the capitalist firm. In this environment, Feher argues for an "investee activism" that shifts its focus "from the extraction of profit to the attribution of credit," that is, for investees to intervene in the speculative conditions of belief and expectation through which capitalist projects are rendered valuable in the future.[21]

Where traditional worker organization has become powerfully weakened, investee activism seeks leverage to alter the "conditions of accreditation" themselves. Feher compares the indexical politics of collective counter-speculation to the de-facto cartels formed by collective bargaining in the struggle between employees and owners over the price of labor. Likewise, counter-speculative strategies amount to the collectivization of investee desires toward common demands in the financialized field of expectation and creditworthiness. He identifies activist movements, such as Occupy Wall Street

21 Michel Feher, *Rated Agency: Investee Politics in a Speculative Age* (Zone Books, 2018), 52.

and the Dakota Access Pipeline struggle, as efforts to redirect capitalist projects by making their reputational and operational risks tangible to their investors.

In short, investee activism is about building collective leverage over investors and forcing them to re-evaluate their portfolios. Elsewhere, the emergence of "defund" movements from across the political spectrum, such as defund the police, #defundthebbc, or campaigns for climate divestment, build their leverage at the point where ethical legitimacy meets financial creditability, aiming to ignite reputational wildfires in order to realize new risks to their creditors. These strategies are symbiotic with platform capitalism, which monetizes the memetic forces of desire which give these movements their power. Nonetheless, with an increasing self-awareness among individuals as precarious stakeholders within a deeply financialized society, such strategies of counter-speculation offer potent and perhaps inevitable processes by which collective forces have already begun to mobilize.

Crowd Worlding

Media theorist Lars Ole Sauerberg identifies the sixteenth century as the beginning of the "Gutenberg Parenthesis," a period during which the advent of print media replaced a primarily oral culture.[22] The medieval form of cultural transmission in which information was spread through stories, rumor, and performance was disrupted by the emergence of the book, an infinitely replicable container of a canonical text. The period is described as a "parenthesis" because Sauerberg and the medievalist Tom Pettitt argue that this era is coming to an end with the advent of digital, networked culture. In the digital age, they posit, "the future is medieval": the textual authority of the book as a technology of "containment" is undone. Instead, what we see in the networks of "post-parenthetic" digital media is a culture of ephemeral communications, something more akin to the folkloric oral culture of the Middle Ages.

Whether or not this represents a "return" to an oral past, the Parenthesis offers a suggestive framework through which to consider contemporary techniques of cultural transmission. It is unlikely, after all, that anything that exists on the internet today will outlast a printed volume. The technological culture of the early twenty-first century is predominantly shaped on the memetic circuits of social networks, driven by viral trends in an intensely competitive attention economy monetized by digital platforms. Narratives come and go with multiple cycles of intrigue and outrage playing out on the feed each day. As an emotional arc ripples through the network, a liquid discourse is simmered down into meme formats, arguably the defining cultural containers of a post-parenthetic canon.

What does this have to do with financial worlding? Where contemporary culture shares with medieval times a folkloric network of transmission, it is powerfully accelerated by the incentive structures of an attention economy which monetizes (and crucially, makes fungible) these basic vectors of sociality. Concomitantly, the weakening of social institutions has blurred the boundaries between workers, states, and firms as both investors and investees in the financial economy. These developments

22 Lars Ole Sauerberg, "The Gutenberg Parenthesis—Print, Book, and Cognition," *Orbis Litterarum* 64, no. 2 (April 2009), 79–80.

are interlinked insofar as the processes of social participation are increasingly legible investable assets. Whether through the rise of self-employment, the precaritization of labor in the "sharing" economy, or the decline of social welfare, to participate in the contemporary social world is to be, at very least, an "entrepreneur of the self." Everyone speculates, albeit the returns on investment are powerfully asymmetrical.

Feher's insight here is that because investors speculate desires and expectations of the collective, investees must collectivize their desires in order "to participate, for its own purposes, in this game of self-fulfilling prophecies."[23] Its arena is the social domain of belief and reputation, rapidly diffused through cultures, fandoms, religions, political movements, and other communities of belief, all of which are increasingly self-aware of their agency as "assets" in a memetic economy. Encouraged by the platforms that monetize their acceleration, these forces resemble a speculative engine, a social machinery fueled by the propulsive forces of dopamine and FOMO, drawing ever more investors into its promise of latent capitalization.

Remortgaging the Master's House

people do not subscribe to my onlyfans because they want to see a random naked woman, they subscribe to my onlyfans because they want to see ME naked specifically based on a parasocial connection formed by following me on other social media platforms

–Tweet by @DarthLux, January 30, 2023 at 15:18[24]

23 Feher, *Rated Agencies*, 58.

24 https://twitter.com/darthlux/status/1620079014215057412?s=61&t=BlpomB7FAyE40avlTSXWbA.

Fandoms, in particular, have emerged in the platform era as powerful collectives in a financialized cultural landscape. While passionate fan communities have long been around, network culture has disintermediated and significantly tightened the feedback loops between fandoms and the objects of their investment. For instance, the business model for influencers, Twitch streamers and sex workers on platforms like OnlyFans has enabled individuals to cultivate personal armies of fans, patrons, and brand sponsorships, rendering social visibility itself a latently investable asset. In this context, collective desire (and the power to marshal it) is always already a vector of financial investment. Moreover, for many creators on the receiving end of attention and capital, the game is one of reputational arbitrage made possible by the fungibility of reputational assets between social worlds, platforms, and therefore, markets. A popular gaming streamer might make a lucrative pivot to being an MMA fighter or a political conspiracist, taking a vast following with them, while a podcaster might leverage their parasocial intimacy with a broad audience to sell nudes on OnlyFans.

Meanwhile, with an increasingly self-conscious sense of ownership over their chosen narratives, fandoms become analogous to "activist investors," intervening within and beyond the immediate world of their "avatar." In 2020, for instance, BTS "stans"—also known as Army—flooded the #whitelivesmatter hashtag with content related to their favorite K-pop band. When BTS responded approvingly, the army directed the power of its multitudes toward a Trump rally in Tulsa, Oklahoma, booking hundreds of thousands of tickets and leaving the US president speaking to a mostly empty stadium.

When Kamala Harris was featured on the cover of *Vogue* shortly before her inauguration as Vice President, dressed in a casual suit and sneakers, the magazine faced a backlash from the "Khive," who decried what they perceived to be an insufficiently edifying representation of the first Black and Asian Vice President. What seems striking about this episode is that the KHive was not defending Harris from a political angle, but condemning *Vogue*'s (ostensibly glorifying) editorial for failing to make good on the values they invest in Harris as an avatar of biracial female power in the economy: a collectively owned asset had been unfairly devalued, and after a clamor of outrage the magazine was forced to issue a new photograph.

Though these actions are but a drop in the ocean of public discourse, as investors and investees of cultural avatars by nature, fandoms and "stan" culture have demonstrated an innate capacity to mobilize their desires toward collective ends.

Avatar logic was also at play in the infamous Gamestop saga in early 2021, when a community of traders associated with a popular subreddit called r/wallstreetbets strategized to cause a 2000 percent stock-price surge in the flagging video games retailer Gamestop, resulting in a "short squeeze" on the hedge funds who had bet on the retailer's demise. Driven both by profit and righteous resentment, wallstreetbets fomented a particular surge of what Feher calls "stakeholder class consciousness." A debate ensued as to whether this bait-ball of self-fulfilling prophecy represented insider trading, as there was little precedent for the speed and scale at which such networked effervescence could be mobilized in the "rational" world of the market. By playing out on the financial markets themselves, the sabotaging of hedge funds' expectations by a swarm of Redditors was an episode of counter-speculative trolling par excellence. Retail investment activity is traditionally treated as background noise, mindless extras in a financial market "run" by professional investors with vastly superior knowledge and capabilities. As a revolt of the NPCs, wallstreetbets was galvanized by more than the mere prospect of financial gain—after all, most of its participants lost money as the pumped stock eventually plummeted. Their avatar was the vengeful underdog who spooked its financial masters. One viral post by a user called Space-peanut reflected on the devastating impact of the 2008 financial crisis on their family: "Taking money from me won't hurt me, because I don't value it at all. I'll burn it down just to spite them. This is for you, Dad."[25]

A Desire in Search of an Object

At inception, tokens are neither digital stores of value, nor equities—they are simply promises that attract an audience.

–Other Internet (Sam Hart, Laura Lotti, and Toby Shorin)[26]

The development of blockchain and cryptocurrency cultures since 2017 has been illustrative of the ways in which desire coalesces around the promise of alternative worlds in a memetic financialized culture. In that year, the speculative bubble in Initial Coin Offerings (ICOs) saw a proliferation of investment opportunities in crypto-token

25 Matt Taibbi, "'This Is for You, Dad': Interview with an Anonymous GameStop Investor," Racket, February 6, 2021, https://www.racket.news/p/this-is-foryou-dad-interview-with.

26 Sam Hart, Toby Shorin, and Laura Lotti, "Market-Protocol Fit," Other Internet, https://otherinter.net/research/market-protocol-fit/, accessed February 14, 2023.

projects, each backed by a "white paper" promising a technological fiction, most of which evaporated with the crash that followed.

The second crypto bubble of 2020–21 saw mainstream financial institutions like investment funds, hedge funds, and VCs ploughing into a market worth $2.4 trillion at the time of writing. As the crypto research collective Other Internet argue, the basic model for crypto projects is that of self-fulfilling prophecy: "The zeitgeist of an incipient token can be understood as a kind of decentralized branding, whereby permission-less narrative formation is driven by speculative desire." The meme-phrase "wagmi" ("we are going to make it") concisely characterizes the prefigurative condition of a desirous world which has to be animated by promise before it can be occupied in practice.

An NFT project that emerged in 2021, Loot, demonstrated how an open approach to collective worlding can be propagated by the engine of speculation. By that point, NFTs had already witnessed a speculative frenzy over the application of artificial scarcity to digital images, a dynamic analogous to traditional art-market investments. The Loot project first appeared as a series of eight thousand black squares, each containing a list of words ("Divine Robes," "Hood," "Ornate Belt") evoking the medieval world of fantasy role-playing games. Its creator, Dom Hofmann, stated that "Loot is the unfiltered, uncensorable building block for stories, experiences, games, and more in the hands of the community at no cost."[27] Due in part to its creator's existing renown, Loot gained instant notoriety, and bags of adventurer gear with varying degrees of rarity were soon trading hundreds of thousands of dollars in Ethereum.

To a culture composed largely of under-thirty-five-year-old males who grew up with the internet and MMORPGs, Loot only had to offer the briefest intimations of a lucrative metaverse before would-be players and creators piled in to populate it. Driven by surging prices and the promise of expansive adaptability, for a few months, Loot's growth was propitious. Discord channels proliferated, with some limiting access to owners of specific Loot bags; dozens of derivative projects, from character designs to pets, have been generated to cohabit Loot's world; entire playable universes have been proposed, although none have so far appeared. Even for a community as desirous and volatile as crypto, fueled by the boom and bust of "wagmi" energy and envious FOMO, Loot inspired a flood of laborious, emotional, and financial investment. Of course, none of this would likely have occurred if the scarce supply of Loot bags, originally free to create, had not accrued a $180 million market within days.

Arguably the first project of its kind, Loot had an alchemical quality in that it appeared to conjure a world from almost nothing more than a little metadata. To a multibillion-dollar NFT market desperate for a meaning to its explosive growth, Hofmann's project offered a skeletal garden of forking paths. For some, Loot was a nostalgic nod to the earliest text-based adventure games, evoking the "infinite game" of improvisatory storytelling, in which a narrative could be taken up and expanded by newcomers into a world of their own. Like other works of collective worlding, its claim to openness ("Feel free to use Loot in any way you want") is animated by the basic forces of sociality and speculation that motivates humans as time-bound communal and narrative-oriented

27 Loot, https://www.lootproject.com/, accessed February 14, 2023.

beings. Meanwhile, its existence as a scarce digital token established ownership as core to participation in its imagined community, rendering subsequent creators as stakeholders in a worlding enterprise: like a Ponzi scheme but also a little like a nation. Loot's derivative creations, like financial derivatives, functioned as promises on promises, games inside games, an expansive role-playing world that segued seamlessly into the market and back again.

The collective unconscious, it turns out, is structured like a pyramid scheme. In the ideal outcome, Loot's decentralized community of creator-investors would have proliferated an expansive metaverse unrecognizable to its genesis state. This imaginary superstructure depends on the crypto market at its base, the continuous promise of the financial returns, social imaginaries, and the influx of new capital and investible creations. As the NFT bubble deflated dramatically a year on from Loot's initial launch, a small community of developers have held onto its initial promise of decentralized worldbuilding, developing stories, characters, and multiplayer online games comprising what its followers call the "Lootverse," albeit for financial rewards a fraction of its initial trading values.

Amid the collapse of social and economic participation in the "ownership economy," catalyzed by the promises of blockchain and "Web3," Loot gave form to the growing continuity between labor and play, or between fictional and financial imagination. Following in the footsteps of the Poyais scheme, it produced a microcosm of financial worlding, in which a crowdsourced reality must be engineered by speculation before it can be occupied in practice. Socio-financial phenomena like Loot are only as real as the speculative imagination that keeps them afloat. While crypto cultures are inherently networked, their "limited and sovereign" territory is bounded by the dynamics of ownership. For its advocates, the ascendency of crypto is a social and institutional reckoning driven by hope, desire, and ressentiment over a power that has long been monopolized. As the media scholar Christian McCrea notes, "A thirst for reclaiming ownership in a world that doesn't let you own anything shouldn't be underestimated."[28]

28 Christian McCrea, "A Mind Forever Grinding," Beach Milk, October 10, 2021, https://beachmilk.substack.com/p/a-mind-forevergrinding.

Minimal Viable Worlds

Financial worlding in a post-parenthetic culture could be schematized in three interacting components: the pull of a speculative engine fueled by scarcity; a memetic network for growing its membership and generating cultic lore; and the seeds of a multiplayer narrative: an open and participatory teleology.

In the case of crypto, the advent of blockchain-based artificial scarcity instantiates a speculative dimension to digital information; its memetic culture-*cum*-marketplace provides the lore; underpinned by a narrative of techno-libertarian emancipation. Recalling Ian Cheng's definition of worlding, these parts are roughly isomorphic with the prerequisites of an agent-based simulation model: a resource, a ruleset for agents, and an environmental constraint.

With the viral convergence of different genres of investment, the potential of financial worlding derives from its capacity to operationalize desire; the reach of its temporal imagination; and the openness of its promise as a future to be occupied. Much like the paradox of nationhood, financial worlding is a collective fiction with a lacuna at its core, a belief held together by the beliefs of others. Nonetheless, it is an operative fiction that powerfully exerts its agency in the "factual" world through the increasingly fungible consistency of political, cultural, and economic processes: the alchemy that renders illiquid assets liquid. There is little to suggest a decline in this tendency; its emergent formations will be decided by the terms by which we choose to believe.

This text was originally published in Gary Zhexi Zhang, Catastrophe Time! *(Strange Attractor Press, 2023).*

Columbia University's "Crisis": A Political Economy Sketch Map

Adam Tooze

The tense standoff on Columbia University's campus between student protestors, the university administration, counter-protestors, and law enforcement has become the object of passionate engagement and moral opprobrium across the United States and far beyond. It has sparked movements on campuses across the country and repressive efforts including the deployment of armed police. The issues at stake are Gaza, Israel, the political culture of the United States, norms of behavior and free speech on campus, allegations of antisemitism, Islamophobia, and basic issues of control. But at Columbia, at least, the struggle is also about political economy. Indeed, to a surprising degree, questions of political economy are at the heart of the protest. At the same time, it is widely believed that financial anxieties are also influencing the cack-handed response of the university administration.

On Saturday last week, on a visit to the protest camp on the South Lawn, I was handed this flier:

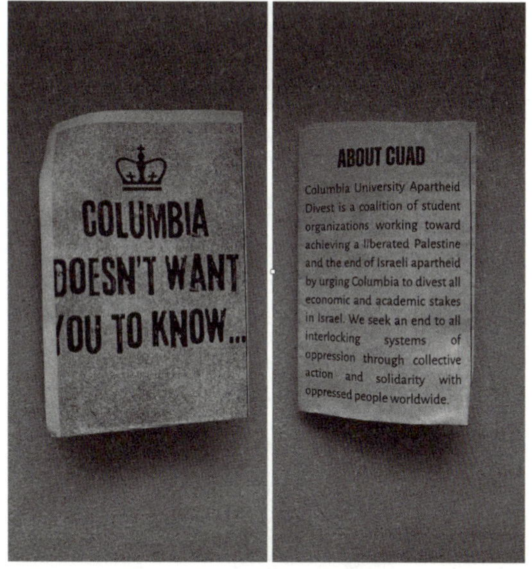

If you open the neatly folded paper square, inside you find this fascinating diagram:

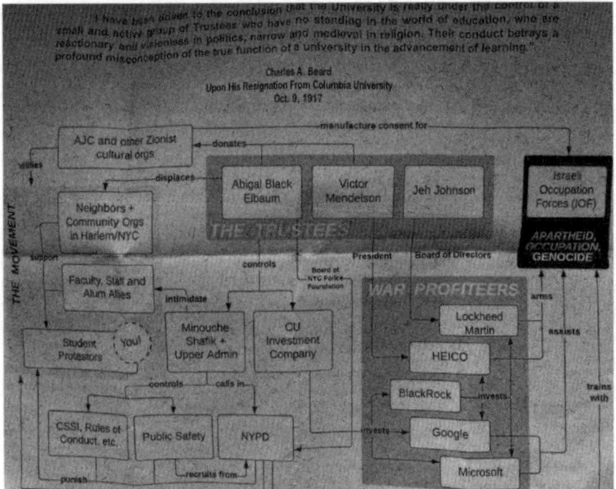

Emblazoned with a stirring quote from Charles A. Beard, the diagram seeks to capture the flow of power in the institution where I have worked since 2015. One of the interesting effects of the diagram is to contextualize some of the figures—notably President [Minouche] Shafik—who have become so central to reportage. Instead, the student analysts seek to focus our attention on corporate power structures and flows of capital and control that spread out beyond the university.

What the flier makes clear is that, at least for a substantial part of the protest, the issue at stake is political economy in the full sense of the term. What they seek to highlight is the way that a powerful educational institution like Columbia is embedded in networks of power and influence, which range from global high finance to the military-industrial complex, "Zionist cultural organizations," and local real-estate development in Manhattan and specifically Harlem, our immediate neighbor.

The team behind the pamphlet, Columbia University Apartheid Divest, is a coalition of eighty-nine student organizations that claim to represent three thousand students, a significant fraction of the Columbia student body. CUAD did not come into existence on October 7. It has been mobilizing on campus for some time. CUAD lobbied then-President [Lee C.] Bollinger already in 2016. And it does not operate only by means of protests and provocations. It seeks to combine analyses like the one in the flier with activism and electoral mobilization.

In 2020, CUAD conducted a referendum of the students of Columbia College, in which 61.03 percent of the 1,771 students who participated (1,081) voted in favor of divesting from Israel, 485 voted against, and 205 abstained. In response, President Bollinger announced the results would not alter university investments because "the University should not change its investment policies on the basis of particular views about a complex policy issue, especially when there is no consensus across the University community about that issue."

A new referendum was proposed by CUAD in March 2024, asking whether the University should divest financially from Israel, cancel the Tel Aviv Global Center, and end Columbia's dual-degree program with Tel Aviv University. The results were released on April 22 after the New York City Police Department, at the invitation of the university leadership, dismantled the first camp and arrested many of its organizers. When the results were reported on April 22, divestment was supported by 76.55 percent of voters, while the latter two propositions garnered 68.36 and 65.62 percent support. The election had 40.26 percent voter participation, with 2,013 students voting, which passed the minimum 30 percent voter participation threshold required by the Columbia College Student Council constitution.

The divestment proposal focuses specifically on publicly traded stocks and bond holdings.

- It is morally imperative, urgent, viable, and, most importantly, widely agreed upon in the University community that Columbia University must divest from and/or refrain from investing in the following companies and all subsidiaries: Microsoft Corp., Amazon.com Inc., Airbnb Inc., Alphabet Inc..
- For the same reasons as above, we urge the University to immediately withdraw assets from BlackRock's iShares ETFs which expose Columbia to Hyundai, Caterpillar Inc., Lockheed Martin Corp., Boeing Co., and Barclays Bank plc.
- Once again, for the same reasons as above, we also call on Columbia to refrain from investing directly and indirectly in: Elbit Systems, Sweden/China-based Volvo, UK-based JC Bamford Excavators, CAF, HikVision, and TKH Security

The particular holdings that they target are listed in a spreadsheet. The CUAD proposal was put to the university's Advisory Committee on Socially Responsible Investing in December 2023. The case was discussed twice by ACSRI, but the particular merits of the divestment proposal were not discussed because ACSRI focused on the question of whether CUAD had established a "broad consensus within the University community regarding the issue at hand." Ruling that they had not, in February of this year ACSRI rejected the CUAD proposal.

As ACSRI framed it, the issue turned on the definition of Columbia as a community. CUAD used referenda to establish the legitimacy of its demands within Columbia College—what might be called the core undergraduate program on campus. ACSRI's response was that this was far too narrow a base. ACSRI defines the "Columbia University community" expansively, including not only the huge population of postgraduate students, which takes the student total at Columbia to thirty-six thousand current students, but also 4,600 faculty. Nor did ACSRI stop there. It also insisted that the "Columbia University community" also includes all 385,000 living alumni. For a proposal to pass muster at ACSRI, what is required is not simply a majority but a "broad consensus" across this sprawling network.

To the tightly focused analysis of power and influence mapped by CUAD, the Advisory Committee opposed a definition of Columbia so encompassing and vague as to make the totality impossible to grasp, let alone to mobilize. How could one possibly hope to establish a broad consensus across the more than 420,000 people that ACSRI included in its idea of the "Columbia community"?

Neither definition is innocent. One seeks to lay bare hidden structures of power so as to challenge them. The other cloaks the status quo in an entity so amorphous that it is impossible to see the wood for the trees.

How might we go beyond both these options to produce an encompassing view of Columbia's political economy that was more inclusive than the CUAD version but not baggy and obfuscating like that offered by ACSRI?

On campus recently, another conflict that has forced self-definition has revolved around unionization. Union activists are concerned to take a holistic view of Columbia, so as to gauge what they may be able to extract in financial concessions. In 2023, CPW-UAW 4100, the Union of Postdoctoral Researchers at Columbia University, and the local chapter of the American Association of University Professors commissioned Professor Howard Bunsis of Eastern Michigan University, a specialist in the business operations of the American universities, to make a report on the financial conditions of Columbia University. His analysis offers us a third take on the question of Columbia's political economy that can be brought into an illuminating dialogue with the CUAD map.

Bunsis's conclusions were clear. Though Columbia routinely pleads poverty in denying claims by union organizers, it is in fact a truly wealthy organization which has huge resources and could have even more if it were better managed and less top-heavy in its administration. Compared to Columbia's ample resources, the claims by labor unions were modest and the opposition of the administration to those claims is therefore best understood not in terms of economic trade-offs, but as an assertion of power. The administration simply does not want to concede the power of employee organizations to make claims on their members' behalf.

Bunsis's analysis is comprehensive, but the first thing he notes is how opaque much of Columbia's financial reporting is. Bunsis has done similar reports on hundreds of American universities and colleges, and he has nothing good to say about Columbia's accounting. Specifically, compared to other Ivy League colleges, Columbia breaks out its costs far less comprehensively.

1. Comparison of the Natural Expense Categories of Columbia vs. 5 Ivy Peers
Sources: Each institution's 2022 audited financial statements

Columbia	Brown	Harvard	Princeton	Yale	Penn
Compensation and Benefits	Salaries and wages	Salaries and wages	Salaries and wages	Salaries and wages	Compensation and Benefits
Nothing separate	Employee benefits	Employee benefits	Employee benefits	Employee benefits	Nothing separate
None	Graduate student support	None	None	None	None
None	Purchased services	Purchased services	None	None	None
None	Supplies and general	Supplies & equipment	Supplies and services	None	None
None	Utilities and occupancy	Space and occupancy	Space and occupancy	None	None
None	Interest	Interest	Interest	None	Interest
None	Depreciation	Depreciation	Depreciation	Depreciation and interest	Depreciation
None	None	Scholarships/awards	Student stipends/prizes	None	None
All other	None	Other OH allocations	Other OH allocations	Other operating	Other operating
Total Expenses	Total Expenses	Total Expenses	Total Expenses	Total Expenses	Total Expenses

- It is clear that Columbia, with only two categories, reveals less information than every other peer.
- Both Yale and Penn report four categories;
- Harvard reports 9 categories, and Brown and Princeton report 8.
- Columbia and Penn combine salaries and benefits; the other four peers do not

Clearly, one demand that everyone concerned with the future of Columbia should make is for a far greater degree of transparency about what money goes where.

What Columbia does publish is enough to show us that, at least in financial and economic terms, Columbia is not one simple thing—an educational institution, or an alumni social network. It is a $5.8 billion-revenue organization consisting of at least seven main entities.

- A medical-industrial complex
- An externally funded research complex
- Very large professional schools: business, law, and so on
- Columbia College for undergraduates
- A real-estate empire: the original core of Columbia's endowment
- The fund-management organization that manages the financial assets of the endowment
- A development arm that raises money from alumni

The relative importance of these seven components can be judged from Bunsis's table on revenue streams.

Operating Revenue Distribution
Source: Audited financial statements

Amounts in thousands	2016	2017	2018	2019	2020	2021	2022
Medical faculty practice plans	1,125,031	1,199,364	1,235,032	1,300,863	1,306,121	1,480,146	1,511,543
Tuition and fees, Net	1,003,927	1,085,452	1,149,377	1,201,922	1,238,700	1,138,470	1,469,287
Government grants and contracts	800,463	901,057	932,464	957,447	1,018,877	1,095,862	1,212,635
Investment income	564,480	616,712	621,254	662,465	657,084	607,009	643,777
Private gifts, grants, and contracts	433,320	583,028	650,781	482,089	594,454	574,300	573,158
Educational and research activities	248,839	230,894	228,803	236,063	221,681	199,602	216,546
Auxiliaries	165,833	175,747	183,651	191,086	164,916	99,714	200,108
Total Revenues	4,341,893	4,792,254	5,001,362	5,031,935	5,201,833	5,195,103	5,827,054

Percentage Distribution	2016	2017	2018	2019	2020	2021	2022
Medical faculty practice plans	25.9%	25.0%	24.7%	25.9%	25.1%	28.5%	25.9%
Tuition and fees, Net	23.1%	22.7%	23.0%	23.9%	23.8%	21.9%	25.2%
Government grants and contracts	18.4%	18.8%	18.6%	19.0%	19.6%	21.1%	20.8%
Investment income	13.0%	12.9%	12.4%	13.2%	12.6%	11.7%	11.0%
Private gifts, grants, and contracts	10.0%	12.2%	13.0%	9.6%	11.4%	11.1%	9.8%
Educational and research activities	5.7%	4.8%	4.6%	4.7%	4.3%	3.8%	3.7%
Auxiliaries	3.8%	3.7%	3.7%	3.8%	3.2%	1.9%	3.4%
Total Revenues	100.0%	100.0%	100.0%	100.0%	100.0%	100.0%	100.0%

Total revenues were $5.8 Billion in 2022 The bottom panel reports that there are several significant sources

We will examine the distribution with and without the medical plans

The largest revenue driver is not the educational part of Columbia, but the medical-industrial complex. Tuition net of financial and "discount," at $1.469 billion, accounts for 25 percent of revenue. Of the students at Columbia, 27 percent are undergraduates. Columbia College undergrads, among whom CUAD principally organizes, make up 13.5 percent of enrollment in 2023, down from 15.5 percent a few years ago.

				Number Changes			Percentage Changes		
	2016	2020	2023	2016 to 2020	2020 to 2023	2016 to 2023	2016 to 2020	2020 to 2023	2016 to 2023
Columbia College	4,627	4,675	4,955	48	280	328	1.0%	6.0%	7.1%
Engineering	1,592	1,723	1,843	131	120	251	8.2%	7.0%	15.8%
General Studies	2,394	2,603	2,941	209	338	547	8.7%	13.0%	22.8%
Total Undergraduate	**8,613**	**9,001**	**9,739**	**388**	**738**	**1,126**	**4.5%**	**8.2%**	**13.1%**
Architecture, Plan & Pres	706	783	798	77	15	92	10.9%	1.9%	13.0%
Arts	852	862	850	10	(12)	(2)	1.2%	-1.4%	-0.2%
Business	2,207	2,281	2,396	74	115	189	3.4%	5.0%	8.6%
Climate	0	0	80	0	80	80			
Engineering	**3,263**	**4,176**	**5,512**	**913**	**1,336**	**2,249**	**28.0%**	**32.0%**	**68.9%**
Arts & Sciences	3,469	3,857	3,679	388	(178)	210	11.2%	-4.6%	6.1%
International & Public Affairs	1,333	1,298	1,526	(35)	228	193	-2.6%	17.6%	14.5%
Journalism	434	357	299	(77)	(58)	(135)	-17.7%	-16.2%	-31.1%
Law	1,547	1,617	1,717	70	100	170	4.5%	6.2%	11.0%
Professional Studies	2,514	3,709	4,021	1,195	312	1,507	47.5%	8.4%	59.9%
Social Work	900	986	1,185	86	199	285	9.6%	20.2%	31.7%
Total Grad and Professional	**17,225**	**19,926**	**22,063**	**2,701**	**2,137**	**4,838**	**15.7%**	**10.7%**	**28.1%**
College of Physicians & Surgeons	1,828	1,746	1,695	(82)	(51)	(133)	-4.5%	-2.9%	-7.3%
Dental Medicine	421	437	455	16	18	34	3.8%	4.1%	8.1%
Nursing	764	719	886	(45)	167	122	-5.9%	23.2%	16.0%
Public Health	1,433	1,570	1,789	137	219	356	9.6%	13.9%	24.8%
Total Medical Center	**4,446**	**4,472**	**4,825**	**26**	**353**	**379**	**0.6%**	**7.9%**	**8.5%**
Global Programs	**20**	**14**	**22**	**(6)**	**8**	**2**			
Total University	**30,304**	**33,413**	**36,649**	**3,109**	**3,236**	**6,345**	**10.3%**	**9.7%**	**20.9%**

All told, tuition revenue from Columbia College undergrads makes up at most 3.25 percent of Columbia University's annual revenue, likely less than that considering the higher fees charged in some of the professionals and the heavier "discount" on undergraduate tuition.

This puts in perspective the dilemma facing the Columbia management, but also their disastrous miscalculation of costs and benefits. One can see why management might be impatient with the demands of a few thousand students and perhaps a few hundred graduate students within a much larger university. One can see why they might fear a Congressional attack on over $1.2 billion in grant funding and federal Pell grants of perhaps one hundred million dollars (given to 20 percent of low-income undergrads). But why escalate? Why not defuse what it is a local incident even on Columbia campus? Why risk the "brand value" of degrees being conferred on tens of thousands of other students with a heavy-handed crackdown, vast media attention, and further protests? The impulse to coercively impose control on campus in the face of fierce outside criticism has disastrously backfired.

President Shafik was clearly under horrible pressure in the recent Congressional hearings and is no doubt being harangued by threatening voices from all sides. Some of these include the billionaire alumni of Columbia. According to the *Forbes* billionaires list, there are at least nineteen such people. Their names are Robert Agostinelli, Louis Bacon, Len Blavatnik, Peter Buck, Warren Buffett, Leon G. Cooperman, Noam Gottesman, Robert Kraft, Henry Kravis, Richard LeFrak & family, Daniel Loeb, David Sainsbury, Thomas Sandell, Shin Dong-Bin, Jerry Speyer, Henry Swieca, S. Robson Walton, Daniel Ziff, and Dirk Ziff.

Bob Kraft, the owner of the New England Patriots, has been particularly vocal, suggesting that he would withhold donations. "I am no longer confident that Columbia can protect its students and staff and I am not comfortable supporting the university until corrective action is taken," he said in a statement posted on X. Kraft is an alumnus and a longtime donor to Columbia, and he's also a supporter of Jewish causes: He helped fund the school's Robert K. Kraft Center for Jewish Student Life and started the Foundation to Combat Antisemitism. Already in November last year, Henry Swieca resigned from the Business School board.

Cooperman, Blavatnik, and Kraft are credited with donations worth nearly $100 million to Columbia. This is a lot of money. But in light of Columbia's endowment, which runs close to $15 billion, it is hard to see why such a contribution, split between three donors over many years, should move the dial. The fear, no doubt, is that where Kraft leads others may follow. Perhaps more ominous are trends in the school's "annual fund," which covers the cost of scholarships, student life, and internships, and where participation among donors may be down by 25 to 30 percent this year.

The extraordinary data combined by the Altrata group allow us to gauge how big is the donor pool beyond the billionaire elite.

The top twenty US universities churning out the most ultra-wealthy alums (with a net worth in excess of $30 million):

1. Harvard University 17,660
2. Stanford University 7,972
3. University of Pennsylvania 7,517
4. Columbia University 5,528
5. New York University 5,214

Altrata also compiles data on business leaders and their university affiliations; again, Columbia has a big network and much to lose. If these data are to be believed, approximately 2.3 percent of all senior executives in the United States appear to have some Columbia connection. With 1,557 alumni serving as senior executives in major global companies, Columbia comes in fourth place behind Harvard with 3,879, Penn with 2,387, and Stanford with 2,017.

So fundraising and development concerns may be driving the administration's efforts to silence the protests. But when one looks at the accounting data, it is not obvious why this should be the priority that it is often taken to be. Investment returns on the existing financial endowment are, generally speaking, far more significant than the relatively modest flow of new gifts.

Endowment in thousands	2016	2017	2018	2019	2020	2021	2022
Beginning Balance	9,639,065	9,041,027	9,996,596	10,869,245	10,950,738	11,257,021	14,349,970
Investment return	(218,226)	1,099,487	822,037	418,416	562,702	3,364,720	(997,276)
New Gifts	121,262	192,307	514,408	232,577	282,586	187,334	211,205
Appropriation for expenditures	(556,166)	(555,776)	(589,430)	(644,460)	(657,405)	(637,997)	(661,439)
Transfers/Other changes	55,092	219,551	125,634	74,960	118,400	178,892	377,386
Ending Balance	9,041,027	9,996,596	10,869,245	10,950,738	11,257,021	14,349,970	13,279,846

The imbalance would be even greater if Columbia actually achieved a better rate of return on its endowment. Since 2016, the rate of return has been remarkably poor. In every single year since 2016, Columbia's endowment has underperformed the S&P500.

	2016	2017	2018	2019	2020	2021	2022
Investment Return	(218,226)	1,099,487	822,037	418,416	562,702	3,364,720	(997,276)
Average Balance	9,340,046	9,518,812	10,432,921	10,909,992	11,103,880	12,803,496	13,814,908
Columbia Return	-2.3%	11.6%	7.9%	3.8%	5.1%	26.3%	-7.2%
S&P 500 return	1.7%	15.5%	12.2%	8.2%	5.4%	38.6%	-11.9%

If Columbia had simply put its money in a widely based index fund, it could have achieved its current endowment level and more without attracting a single cent in new donations from alumni and other donors. How, you might ask, can a fund as large as Columbia's manage to underperform the S&P500 index so badly? The answer is that most of Columbia's money is not in fact invested in public markets.

	2016	2017	2018	2019	2020	2021	2022
Level 1	1,069,460	1,254,710	2,024,210	1,884,993	2,168,867	2,293,740	2,143,396
Level 2	333,809	670,141	421,095	425,351	806,153	638,835	947,758
Level 3	93,871	107,200	115,283	143,365	220,239	226,094	162,769
NAV (Net Asset Value)	7,457,856	8,006,325	8,633,844	9,108,882	9,128,753	12,496,988	11,517,286
Total Investments	8,954,996	10,038,376	11,194,432	11,562,591	12,324,012	15,655,657	14,771,209
Other		0	0	0	0	96,696	(495,778)
Check total investments	8,954,996	10,038,376	11,194,432	11,562,591	12,324,012	15,752,353	14,275,431
% distribution	2016	2017	2018	2019	2020	2021	2022
Level 1	11.9%	12.5%	18.1%	16.3%	17.6%	14.7%	14.5%
Level 2	3.7%	6.7%	3.8%	3.7%	6.5%	4.1%	6.4%
Level 3	1.0%	1.1%	1.0%	1.2%	1.8%	1.4%	1.1%
NAV (Net Asset Value)	83.3%	79.8%	77.1%	78.8%	74.1%	79.8%	78.0%
Total Investments	100.0%	100.0%	100.0%	100.0%	100.0%	100.0%	100.0%
NAV Breakdown	2016	2017	2018	2019	2020	2021	2022
Global equities	706,709	940,126	876,462	1,174,241	1,705,137	2,366,699	2,105,044
Fixed income	287,284	287,639	287,343	322,184	280,953	281,470	0
Absolute return strategies	2,965,256	3,039,484	3,494,651	3,621,495	3,363,353	4,387,264	4,055,448
Private equity	1,901,644	1,980,967	1,972,357	2,056,544	2,219,528	3,415,388	3,139,022
Real Assets	1,596,963	1,758,109	2,003,031	1,934,418	1,559,782	2,046,167	2,217,772
Total NAV Assets	7,457,856	8,006,325	8,633,844	9,108,882	9,128,753	12,496,988	11,517,286

Columbia is a victim of the hype around alternative investments, private equity, hedge funds, and the like. And yet, for lack of any more public information about Columbia's endowment allocation, it is precisely on the minority of funds that are invested in publicly traded assets and exchange traded funds that the student activists are forced to concentrate their fire. And the assets that they would like to see divested are correspondingly tiny. A few million here or there in relation to an endowment of almost $15 billion.

So, from the point of view of the political economy, the whole dispute has the feel of shadowboxing. A small group of students camped on one lawn in a very large university complex, calling for relatively minor financial rearrangements in a baggy and poorly managed endowment, are turned by the repressive action of the the university administration, under pressure from politicians and donors, into a global news story, putting in doubt the standing of a multibillion-dollar educational, research, and medical organization. It is a case study in panicked control-freakery gone wrong. If the cause that the students are protesting were not so serious, if the slander heaped on them were not so manifestly unjust, the whole affair would have the feel of a dark comedy. One thinks of that 1980s New York classic, Tom Wolfe's *Bonfire of the Vanities*.

No doubt experts in university finance will find the treatment I have given here simplistic. They will call into question the complacent analysis of Columbia's riches and question whether the management really has the scope for independent judgement and action that I am implying. There are no doubt complex issues of budget management and fund allocation. Columbia is not one big well-organized corporation that the accounts paint it as. It is split into many fiefdoms, each with their own financial accounts and constraints. And yet, in the end, a summative financial judgement on its underlying position and the freedom of action this implies is not merely an abstract exercise. There are agencies divorced from campus politics that make precisely such assessments all the time. And tens of billions of dollars of debt depend on those judgments. I am talking about the ratings agencies that evaluate the bonds issued by America's universities.

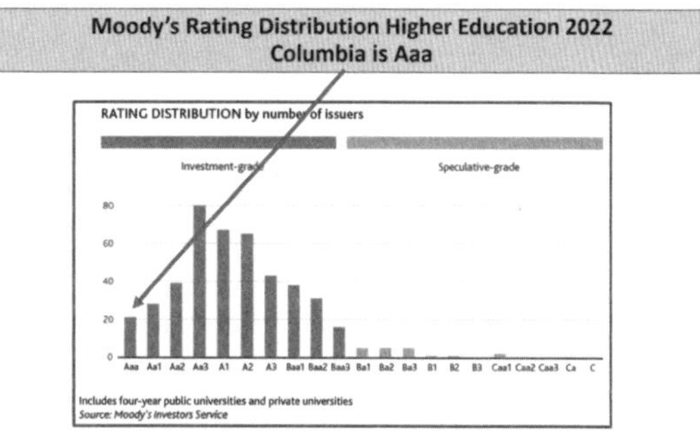

As the graphic makes clear, the judgement of Moody's on Columbia's financial situation is resounding. Columbia is not just investment grade. It is squarely situated in the top tier of American universities that issue debt that is triple-A rated. Very few private-debt issuers enjoy such a high standing. As Moody's makes clear, that rating depends on a comprehensive assessment of Columbia's balance between revenue flow and costs. That calculation includes its relations with alumni and donors. If Moody's issues a downgrade warning, Columbia would be miles away from serious financial stress, but it would mean that the current crisis had entered a new stage of seriousness.

This text was originally published in Adam Tooze's newsletter on April 26, 2024. See https://adamtooze.substack.com/p/chartbook-279-columbia-universitys.

The Debt Collective: An Introduction

Astra Taylor

In 2008, around the same time Lehman Brothers collapsed and the mortgage market began to melt down, I got a call telling me my student loans were in default. I remember trying to grasp the logic as I spoke to the collector. Because I didn't have money, they were increasing my principal by 19 percent. My balance ballooned, as did my monthly payments, which meant I was even more broke than before. My credit score tanked, further compounding my financial woes.

When I got involved in Occupy Wall Street a few years later, I realized my situation was hardly unique. Most people drawn to the encampments were also in the red. To talk to fellow protesters during the first few weeks of Occupy Wall Street was to talk about student loans that couldn't be repaid, medical bills that were piling up, houses that had been foreclosed on by bailed-out banks, and insolvent communities forced to endure austerity measures, with people of color hit hardest. Millions were homeless and jobless, delaying starting families or losing hope of ever being able to retire, while bankers got massive bonuses. Perhaps organizing around indebtedness, some of us thought, would be worthwhile.

That's what those of us who wrote *Can't Pay Won't Pay: The Case for Economic Disobedience and Debt Abolition* have been working to do ever since. The book includes a jointly authored record of insights and ideas developed over years with various collaborators too numerous to name individually. Our efforts kicked off in April 2012 when the Occupy Student Debt Campaign (OSDC) organized a protest marking "1T Day"—the day outstanding student debt hit one trillion dollars—and demanding full debt cancellation and free public college. (The 1T protest was the first time I ever heard anyone make the call for student-debt cancellation, and I was enrapt.) Over the coming months, OSDC merged forces with Strike Debt, a decentralized initiative focused primarily on public education. Strike Debt hosted debtors' assemblies, where strangers gathered and shared personal stories, and collaborated on a pamphlet called the *Debt Resisters' Operations Manual*, which combined practical financial advice and a radical overview of our economic system. A little over a year after Occupy began, we launched the Rolling Jubilee, a crowdfunded project that erased more than $30 million of medical, tuition, payday-loan, and criminal-punishment debt belonging to thousands of strangers. We acted just like debt collectors, buying portfolios of debt on shadowy secondary debt markets for pennies on the dollar, but instead of collecting on them we erased them, sending people letters notifying them that their obligations were gone, no strings attached. In 2014 we formally launched the Debt Collective, a union for debtors.

Over the years we have developed a shared understanding of the central role debt plays in our economy and the way debt might be wielded as a form of power, an analysis we share in the following pages. Debt, we realized, bridges the individual and the structural, the personal and political, binding each of us to a broader set of financial and political circumstances—circumstances that have emerged over centuries of racist, colonialist, and capitalist exploitation and wealth accumulation. Our goal has been to devise new creative ways to organize. Specifically, turning our individual indebtedness into a source of collective leverage in order to transform those broader conditions. As Marx famously said, the point isn't just to interpret the world but to change it.

Taking inspiration from the labor movement, we believe debtors organized in a union can exercise material power over their common circumstances. The two modes of organizing have different targets but complementary aims. Where labor unions focus on sites of production, debtors' unions focus on circulation, or how money and capital flow and to whom. Labor organizing targets the employer, demanding higher wages, benefits, and more. Debtor organizing, on the other hand, targets the creditor (which, in the era of neoliberalism, is also often the state). Debtor organizing fights against predatory financial contracts and for the universal provision of public goods, including healthcare, education, housing, and retirement, so that people don't have to go into debt to access them. These public goods and their access must be structured in ways that remedy long-standing and ongoing social inequalities. The Debt Collective believes that it is not enough for public goods and social services to be universal, they must be reparative, too.

One of the upsides to debtor organizing is that, unlike worker organizing, there have not been decades of class war aimed to suppress the tactic. Since the Labor Management Relations Act, typically known as Taft-Hartley, was passed in 1947, a lot of seemingly sensible union organizing strategies are simply illegal. The war on labor unions helps explain why only a small percentage of workers are organized on the job (about 6 percent in the private sector and 30 percent in the public sector). The core activities of organizing debtors have not been overtly regulated or restricted in the same way, leaving room to experiment. Debtor organizing has the potential to bring millions of people who may never have the option of joining a traditional labor union into the struggle for economic justice.

What follows is a document of collective thinking and an invitation to collective action. Like employers, creditors have enormous power over people's lives. We are forced to debt-finance healthcare, education, housing, and even our own incarceration. When we can't pay, debtors are disciplined with steep penalties, high interest rates or loan denials, and damaged credit scores, not to mention poverty, as unpayable bills come due. State power is often deployed to enforce unfair financial contracts through court judgments, garnishments, and even jail time. This book does not advise financial suicide but coordinated and strategic campaigns of resistance. An individual default is not a debt strike. As with any organizing campaign, there is no guarantee of success. Bosses retaliate against workers, and creditors can be expected to do the same to debtors who dare to throw down the gauntlet. But it is worth the risk, because the present is unbearable. Although many older people are also deeply indebted, the rising generation is the first in a century to face more dismal economic prospects than their parents, in part because they are being crushed by debt. In the United States, for example, student debt now surpasses $1.7 trillion. In better news, that's $1.7 trillion of leverage to use in the fight for a different economic system.

If we don't get organized, debtors will keep getting pushed deeper into a financial hole. In the throes of the pandemic, some payday lenders are charging close to 800 percent interest on short-term loans, taking advantage of people who have no other way to keep a roof over their heads or put food on the table. Mass unemployment in the absence of a functioning safety net intensifies mass indebtedness, fueling the already vastly unequal distribution of wealth along predictable racial lines. Meanwhile, financiers are becoming more powerful. When the stock market tanked, the Trump administration put the world's largest asset manager, BlackRock Inc., in charge of a multitrillion-dollar federal fund tasked with buying up corporate debt. Yet the tens of millions of people who lost their jobs are expected to continue making monthly payments to banks and bill collectors.

We've entered unprecedented territory, but we're not powerless. Over the last decade, once fringe left-wing ideas have become mainstream. Free higher education, universal health care, a Green New Deal, defunding and abolishing the police, and debt cancellation are now popular policies, thanks to grassroots pressure. I'll never forget how, back in 2012, 1T Day organizers were met with derision from the mainstream press when they called for student-debt relief and free college. "They want all student debt in the country forgiven. All $1 trillion of it. And if the government would be so kind, they'd appreciate it if it would pay for higher education from here on out, as well," Reuters' Chadwick Matlin snarked. "What has happened to this proposal? Hardly anybody has cared." NPR's All Things Considered also covered the action, reporting that "most experts believe there's little chance the government would ever forgive student loans." Those so-called experts were dead wrong. Over the last five years Debt Collective members succeeded in forcing the government to cancel more than a billion dollars' worth of student loans and put student debt at the center of the 2020 presidential primary cycle.

The moral of the story is that we have to keep organizing. If we don't, the crisis of indebtedness will only become more acute in the years to come. Personal debt has reached historic proportions, totaling $14 trillion, and staggering rates of unemployment and a decimated social safety net only raise the stakes. The chant that rang out at Occupy—"Banks got bailed out, we got sold out"—resonates in 2020, only it wasn't just the banks that got a lifeline when COVID-19 crashed the economy. The cruise and hotel industries, the fossil-fuel sector, meatpacking plants, private-equity firms, and more all lined up to receive public money while regular people were hung out to dry.

We need an organized, militant debtors' movement now more than ever. Given the way capitalism isolates and divides us, we have long needed to find a way to organize across physical distance and social difference, and debtors' unions offer one promising approach. Debtors who share common creditors are rarely confined to a single geographical location. Unlike workers, debtors don't share a factory floor or office but are connected nevertheless, bound by the same creditors and an economic system that forces them into debt for basic needs. Coordinated campaigns of debt renegotiation and refusal can include people who live on opposite sides of the country, opposite ends of the city, or, in some cases, on the other side of the world.

I write this in the midst of intersecting crises. A public-health crisis coupled with an economic crisis have intensified and exposed longstanding racial inequities, catalyzing a global movement against police brutality and white supremacy. With huge numbers of people newly out of work and vital social services being slashed, one thing is certain: many households, disproportionately households of color, will be forced to take on massive debts to survive the next year. Life was already difficult before COVID-19 crashed the economy; things are now becoming untenable. Racial capitalism is a centuries-long pandemic. We cannot afford not to rebel.

These days, the words *crisis* and *apocalyptic* couldn't be more apt. The first term comes from the Ancient Greek and means the turning point in an illness—death or recovery, two stark alternatives. The root of apocalypse means to reveal or uncover. This is the truth unveiled by this apocalyptic moment: to truly cure ourselves and survive this crisis we are going to need way more than a vaccine. We will also need more than debt write-downs or even debt abolition to heal what ails us, though that would be a welcome start. We need to completely transform our economy and society so that millions of people don't have to live in perpetual financial and physical peril. We offer our thinking, research, and proposals as a resource for everyone struggling to build a better world.

This essay was originally published as a foreword to The Debt Collective, Can't Pay Won't Pay: The Case for Economic Disobedience and Debt Abolition *(Chicago: Haymarket Books, 2020).*

RAW Académie at ICA

Linda Goode Bryant, Marielle Ingram, Alex Klein, and Marie Hélène Pereira

I Is for Institute
Alex Klein

I Is for Institute began with the underlying premise that institutions are mutable because they are shaped by people. The name is a prompt, an explanation, a declaration, and an interrogative position. Even as it simply articulates the definition of the "I" in an acronym such as "ICA," it underscores the belief that institutions are made possible by the workers who power them, while also offering a critical lens onto the way that institutions become imbricated within the identities of the very individuals who have the agency to change them. It is this tension that is at the root of both the problem and the promise of institutions—as it were, the "I" is inside of us.

In 2013–14 the Institute of Contemporary Art, University of Pennsylvania (ICA) in Philadelphia (where I was a curator from 2011–22), celebrated its fiftieth anniversary with a multifaceted, yearlong celebration that looked back at an incredible roster of exhibitions and artists that had shaped its history: Andy Warhol's and Joan Jonas's first museum exhibitions, Paul Thek's only US museum show, and the infamous Robert Mapplethorpe exhibition that launched the culture wars of the 1980s, to name just a few. Still, after revisiting the many names, brilliant ideas, and radical thinking that had shaped ICA's past and set the stage for its next chapter, I was left wondering if we had really gotten to the structural essence of the institution: what it had been, what was it now, and how it could be reimagined for a future yet to come.

What came next was a three-pronged approach to begin to reflect on the infrastructure not just of the ICA, but of a broad range of arts organizations. In order for us to begin to see ourselves more clearly, we felt we needed to look not only at our past, but also outside of ourselves. Alongside my colleagues, curatorial fellows Gee Wesley, and, later, Tausif Noor, and with the help of several interns and research assistants, we embarked on the project, which was documented on a website given shape by the design studio Other Means: iisforinstitute.icaphila.org.

We began by asking "what's in a name?" How does the actual name ICA resonate with the publics it serves, and how does it connect (or not connect) to the histories of other ICAs? As one of our key thought partners and collaborators, Koyo Kouoh, founding director of RAW Material Company, asserted, "dig where you stand." So, we hunted for clues by scanning through the small shifts in language throughout ICA's previous mission statements and recorded in closed-door university proceedings alongside questionnaires circulated to the general public. These findings allowed us to inhabit the space of the organization as a reciprocal organism—as a collective body that is in constant evolution.

The second facet of the project was a series of informal interviews with colleagues from differently scaled international contemporary arts organizations reflecting on the structures of their workplaces. While not comprehensive, the hope was to engage colleagues in frank discussion and reflection on *how* they do their work rather than the content of their latest exhibitions: What agency do we have within institutional structures? How can we make those underlying structures more visible? And assuming that those structures are heterogenous, how might we learn from each other in the hopes of building a better field? The website catalogues over fifty conversations reproduced in the form of lightly edited, print-on-demand PDFs and a podcast. In some cases, these are now an important record of institutional building, such as our first official interview with Bisi Silva, director of the Center for Contemporary Art, Lagos, Nigeria and Àsìkò, a platform for artistic and curatorial pedagogy across Africa. Many of the individuals interviewed no longer work at the same organizations, and in some cases the organizations no longer exist. The interviews also spanned major sociopolitical cataclysms, from the COVID–19 pandemic to devastating hurricanes, and the ways that individuals and institutions responded and adapted to them.

Looking back from 2024 on this multiyear, multiplatform project, it is hard not to read it through the lens of the seismic political events, climate crises, racial injustices, global health emergencies, horrific wars, constant attacks on trans and women's rights, censorships, and the destabilization of higher education that have fundamentally punctured our faith in institutions in the United States across the board. However, back in 2015, in the final years of the Obama administration, much of this was still to come, or at least could be said to still be repressed. Instead, the moment that forged the project was fomented by the post–Occupy Wall Street mobilization of equity work within the arts that challenged pay structures, hiring practices, workplace ethics, greater awareness of accessibility, diversity, gender dynamics, community engagement, and the relevance of organizations to their publics. Indeed, at the time, ICA was the first museum of its scale to become W.A.G.E. certified.

As our colleagues at the Kuntshalle Lissabon reminded me at the outset of the project, the word *institute* is both a noun that describes a place of knowledge production and a verb that means "to effect change." And thus, the third node of the project revolved around an invitation. Returning to the "I" in "ICA," I was interested in the double identity of an "institute" of contemporary art housed in a major research university. On the one hand, we could be aligned with a museum model in the traditional sense of an exhibition program, and, on the other hand, the ICA could be articulated along the lines of the other "institutes" and "centers" that populate higher education in the spirit of think tanks. What if our colleagues on campus understood the work we pursued not just in the service of cultural capital for the student population, but as a kind of research laboratory with living artists that could bridge gaps between different scholarly disciplines and departments on campus? In light of this double identity, we invited two thought partners on board who could help us to reflect and challenge our understanding of our structural mission: the Kunsthalle Lissabon in Portugal, whose experimental exhibition program and publications revolve around the notion of "performing the institution" and, on the pedagogic side, RAW Material Company in Senegal, whose Pan-African, horizontal, pedagogic framework challenges the Western hierarchical approach to learning through its prompt: "How do we learn from each other?" The outreach began with a reciprocal residency in which we would be in residence in Lisbon and Dakar, and each collaborator would spend time in Philadelphia. After the exchanges had happened, both partners were invited to propose next steps.

Kunsthalle Lissabon was then approaching its ten-year anniversary and its founders decided to mark the occasion through an act of disappearance. They invited ICA, along with three other organizations, to each take over their space for a season. The invitation was not just to curate a show, but to refashion their infrastructure and to hire the directors back as employees in service of another organization's mission. And so, in November 2019 the ICA Philadelphia's logo appeared on the front door of a small contemporary arts program in Lisbon, whose stated mission is rooted in "radical hospitality." The ICA's institutional design was imported and the very American exhibition *Trevor Shimizu: Performance Artist* was staged, accompanied by a brochure and wall labels. None of these formalities were customary for the KL, not to mention ICA's bureaucratic administration, programmatic requirements, and communications strategies. However, more than an absurdist gesture, by performing our own institutional customs in a different context, we were forced to confront ourselves and to reflect on what constituted our identity, values, and ethos as an institution beyond the implementation of our style guide.

This exercise partially prepared us for what came next. Following our residential exchange between Dakar and Philadelphia in 2017, Koyo Kouoh proposed that RAW in turn take over the ICA for a season. She imagined that we would both be put to the test: Would RAW Académie's culture of hospitality and collaborative creative generation work outside of the unique ecosystem they had built for themselves? Could ICA relinquish control and undo some of its hierarchies and bureaucratic systems in an act of open resource sharing? A project like this necessarily moves beyond the will of the "I" and is dependent upon the buy-in of the "we"; it required institutional approvals and collective participation from colleagues across the organization. What ensued was five years of false starts, massive logistical hurdles posed by the dense bureaucracy of the university and the xenophobic culture of the Trump presidency, changes in leadership in both organizations, and a global pandemic that made it near impossible to imagine how we would physically bring a Dakar-based art school and its international group of fellows and faculty to Philadelphia for two months, and in the place of a regular exhibition season.

The artistic director for the session was Linda Goode Bryant, who had themed the Académie around the idea of "Infrastructure." The fundamental idea was that over the course of the session the fellows would work together with the faculty to learn and imagine new ways of organizing an arts infrastructure, and that the galleries at ICA would be the location of the experiment. With an initial class of fellows selected and guest faculty invited, we were prepared but got off to a rocky start. When the pandemic struck, we hit the brakes and regrouped. We all agreed it was necessary to continue, but that something was off. Working remotely for two years, we had the opportunity to get to know each other better and to shift some of the decision-making processes from the institution to the people. "This is the way we do things here" became "let's try and build something else together." This realignment in the project benefited from the emergence of the greater reassessments that were happening organizationally in response to the Black Lives Matters movement and DEAI work that was taking place across the country. And programmatically it was building on decolonial precedents such as the Wood Land School's 2017 yearlong exhibition and institutional takeover of the SBC Gallery in Montreal and was synergistic with contemporaneous initiatives such as ruangrupa's ambitious artist-centric and participatory Documenta 15 and Goode Bryant's Just Above Midtown survey at MoMA. Here was an opportunity to not just bring more colleagues into critical roles in the process, but to ask the institution to undergo a transformation that relied on it, relinquishing control of its own authorship.

The project launched in March 2022 and, short of handing over the keys to the building, RAW Académie effectively took up residence in all of the behind-the-scenes and public-facing aspects of the ICA. On the exterior of the building were prompts inviting onlookers to imagine alternative infrastructures for the arts as well as a video with a live view of the street in Dakar where the Académie is located. In the lobby were mobile planters in a test of whether the museum could foster life and growth. The lobby desk was permanently dismantled and turned into a terrarium that was placed in the entrance to the gallery, while the lobby itself became an open resource center and lending library. Upon entering the gallery space, a wall of clocks displayed the time zones and locations where the participants were based, and all staff names across both organizations were listed on the wall alongside a weekly program of events. Numerous moments envisioned by Goode Bryant were meant to underscore temporality and to take you outside of yourself by disrupting the assuredness of the ground under your feet. The "exhibition" would be responsive to the learnings of the fellows and to the responses of the publics, with the galleries housing the public programs, the session room, and a continually changing footprint of the exhibition that featured contributions from all of the fellows. In an effort to make the architecture more adaptive, flexible screening spaces and mobile furniture units were placed in the galleries, so that the space could be responsive to the ideas that evolved over time. In some cases, the walls were stripped down to their studs in an act of ultimate transparency. At the far end of the gallery was what Goode Bryant described as a three-dimensional "video quilt" that grew over time to reflect the collective contributions of the Académie participants. And finally, there was an Académie room that was closed to the public when the fellows and faculty conducted their sessions and opened to the public when it was not in use.

To run the course, RAW Académie relocated two of its staff members, Marie Hélène Pereira, curator and director of programs, and Dulcie Abrahams Altass, curator of programs, full-time to Philadelphia alongside Goode Bryant, Marielle Ingram, and a local assistant, Gabrielle Bing. Over seven weeks the Académie fellows worked with a visiting faculty member on a specific topic and their findings spilled out into the public exhibition space. Each guest also gave one public talk that bridged the space of the session room with public dialogues. The lecturers included Gudskul, Arthur Jafa, Louis Massiah, Bonaventure Soh Bejeng Ndikung, Bryant Wells, and Sarah Workneh. In the spirit of RAW Académie's practice of creating more concentric rings, outreach to community members and Penn professors and students created more counter-pedagogic models. The fellows had breakfast and lunch on the premises daily, and staff and invited guests would often join them. A local chef was hired to cook special meals, and local businesses were engaged as regular caterers. As the first project to be staged right after the ICA staff returned to in-person work, and considering the different ways the COVID-19 pandemic had been experienced globally by the participants, this was both wonderful and stress-inducing.

What unfolded over the next seven weeks was intense. The speakers were brilliant, the conversations were rich, the issues were urgent, and the public response was electric. But the resulting "exhibition" and the internal dynamics were complicated and messy. Looking back, there is still much to learn and process from both the broader *I Is for Institute* initiative and its culmination with *RAW Académie at ICA: Infrastructure*. What follows is an excerpt of a conversation between some of the core organizers of *RAW Académie at ICA* reflecting on the project a few months after its conclusion.

The following is a conversation between Alex Klein, Marie Hélène Pereira, Linda Goode Bryant, and Marielle Ingram. It was originally published as a podcast on the I Is for Institute *website. The conversation, which was held online on December 13, 2022, provided the participants with an opportunity to reflect on their collaboration. They connected the work between RAW and ICA with Goode Bryant's larger project as the founder and president of Project EATS and her exhibition at MoMA,* Just Above Midtown: Changing Spaces, *organized by Thomas (T.) Jean Lax with Lilia Rocio Taboada, which revisited the gallery and culture that Goode Bryant fostered at Just Above Midtown or JAM from 1974 to 1986.*

Marie Hélène Pereira How was the JAM show and experience, Linda? I felt the joy and pride when we spoke about it when it was in preparation, when we were in Philly.

Linda Goode Bryant All of us who were involved at JAM, all the artists who were fortunate enough to be there ... none of us had seen each other in forty years. It was as if we had had breakfast that morning. It was as if no time had passed. We were just as in sync at the opening as we were when we were all living together. What we created is a kind of love I've never experienced. It was just really special. I am so appreciative of that. Dulcie told you about the Senegalese drummers?

MHP The drummers! I saw some videos online and I saw you were dancing with Thomas [T. Lax].

LGB Thomas can dance Sabar. He's taken lessons, but he would never do it. I was like, "Come on, Thomas, show us some sabar!" So there we were; the drummers were playing. And I said to myself, "The only way I'm gonna get Thomas to do this is to try to dance." He really got into it. It was a side of Thomas that was so great to see. Because he's really buttoned-down in certain ways. And it all came out. The goal was: can JAM at MoMA be JAM? JAM was in the house! MoMA did not exist that night, and it was most apparent with the drummers and the dancing. I could see the images of my ancestors in the rafters having a ball, just smiling. MoMA was transformed. MoMA was completely fucking transformed.

Alex Klein And it continues to be so. You are there stewarding the show. I think that was what was so impactful. The other day, when we came to visit for a tour, you said, "I'm just here, I'm here all the time. I'm seeing things through, I'm animating things, I'm leading programs. I am present." In the way that you were present in Philadelphia. I think, Marie Hélène, that this feels like the start of the conversation, because so much of the journey that we were on together was also leading up to this big question that you had about how relationships could come into a space. How can they change the space? Maybe Thomas dancing was letting the institution fall away for a second.

Mari, how are you feeling? It was a lot going from the ICA project into JAM. I don't even know if you two were able to have separation because there was a moment when the MoMA team was coming down to ICA and interviewing everybody, looking at the installation, and having lunch with us. You were just going from meeting to meeting and from Philadelphia to New York. I can only imagine what a trip of time and space and emotion it must have been for you all.

Marielle Ingram The transition didn't really exist, because we were working on both projects at the same time, really. But what became really clear was the difference between ICA and MoMA as institutions, and how the people within those institutions operate. It made us think a lot about how to bring everybody along for the ride when working on a collaborative project. It makes me think about the nature of collaboration between artists and institutions. When we were in Philly, it felt so much like a space that I was welcomed into, because of the way that the people in the institution engaged with us. That was in contrast with the way that we ended up working with MoMA.

AK That's a really poignant observation. When we started this project five years ago with Koyo and Marie Hélène and Dulcie, who we have to acknowledge is unfortunately not able to join us today, we discussed the idea of not just having a colonial import-export model, but thinking about what it would mean for one infrastructure to inhabit another so that we would both see ourselves in a different light. When one institution inhabits another, you would see yourselves more clearly as much as you would learn from the other organization.

MHP You see yourself more clearly as an institution, but you also see yourself more clearly based on where you come from. The idea of the Académie was that it would take Dakar as one of its main protagonists. In this session, we thought, "What will the Académie be if it is hosted in another institution and also in another city?" When we came to Philly, we really wanted to engage with the city, and I think we did so.

LGB I have become more aware of what I meant when I had the tagline for Project Eats: "Art, Food, Life." People have been saying: "What is the art?" The experience at ICA and the experience with the show at MoMA and then reconnecting with people where we built this thing. There's something about how that family got built. Bill Valerio, who was an intern at JAM and now is the director of one of the museums in Philly, said people at JAM hated each other and they loved each other. I don't know what those words are, respect doesn't seem like enough, but there was a connection. For me, Project Eats, while we grow food, while we make plant-based meals, while we are involved in providing support so that residents in the community can operate these farms in their communities, bottom line, Project Eats says, "Let's take elements of those relationships, put them in communities, and see what kind of ties develop. Let's make it possible for communities to have connection as neighbors." This is key to the kind of change we talk about—the social, economic, environmental, and human changes that we'd like to see happen. It really is tied to both experiences at ICA and MoMA. It ties back to us just being human with one another.

MI What you're saying is so relevant to something that I talked about with Sarah Workneh, who was a faculty member in the RAW Académie. We were talking about JAM, about what happens when you do extremely radical things and put them in MoMA, in the art historical canon, how that translates, how it is important for people to know that a space like that existed, that somebody like Linda exists. But we also talked about how it can never be a replica, how it always is a trace of something. Because JAM was such a special place, a constitution of people, right? To try and replicate it would be completely impossible.

Exhibitions about nostalgia often result in thinking about spaces as utopias. Sarah and I were talking about the problem of a utopia and how the JAM show, especially with the wall of bills, disrupts this idea that something was utopian. The problem with a utopia is that it doesn't capture the question of agonism. Agonism is a political and social theory that emphasizes the potentially positive aspects of certain forms of conflict. To bring this back into the question of the Académie, I wonder if institutions think about utopia as a way of operating. There's something inhuman about utopia. There's something that doesn't allow for relationships. Should we think about institutions as being able to support these kinds of relationships that Linda is talking about? Can an institution be a space that supports humanity?

AK This was the project at ICA in connection with *I is for Institute*, the idea of individuals, of humans, powering these organizations and making them more human and having the agency to do so. We talked a lot with Linda, leading up to the Académie, about boxes. What boxes do we put ourselves in? I see that also as the metaphor for the institution, the infrastructure that we allow to shield our vision, control our bodies, control our minds. What boxes do museums create? Linda, at one point you said, "This wasn't the Académie that I imagined, but it's the Académie that it needed to be." For me, that was really about success being bound up with failure. Collectively, we were part of a project where an institution was made vulnerable. Vulnerability is connected to the unpredictability of humans and relationships. I think it's also that positioning of antagonism versus agonism—with agonism being when humans are *productively* coming into conflict while still working toward something. I saw that in the organizational relationships leading up to the Académie. And then when we actually embarked on the Académie itself. On the topic of boxes: Do you feel that there was a moment when the boxes were penetrated? Or do you think that we actually just reinscribed the boxes with the hindsight we have now?

MHP I believe the boxes were there when we began trying to have this Académie together and working toward a collaboration, as we were thinking about how to meet as institutions and how to create a collective moment of mutual learning in Philadelphia. I consider ICA as one box, I consider Philadelphia as one box, and I consider RAW as one box. Thinking about the first conversations we had, and how we wanted to weave all this together, that's how we got to the point where we invited Linda. I think that we've managed to penetrate different boxes at different moments. But I also believe that we've left the boxes there. I believe that having boxes or creating boxes is not a bad thing. It's about what box you create, and all these relationships, and putting the human at the center.

LGB I love that phrase, "putting humans in the center," because it really is about that.

AK It's true. I think we all agreed that having that extra pandemic time that we had, while traumatic and difficult and logistically complicated for so many reasons, gave us the benefit of developing deeper relationships and working through things in advance of the session. I mean, having two years to forge relationships over Zoom was just incredible. It would have been amazing for the ICA team to have gone to RAW as well, for us all to go and to understand it. I think it would have been very impactful for my organization to come along because it was abstract for them.

Linda, I'm wondering if you could reflect on what you proposed pre-pandemic, which now feels so visionary. How was that desire met with reality?

LGB It's interesting that you asked that. I agreed to be a mentor at Columbia for the MFA students. I bring that up because the box of being an artist today means that you go through certain MFA programs and you then take residencies, post-MFA temporary positions, and then that allows you to move into a gallery. There is a list of things you do to get a gallery and become successful. They're following that path. I don't know if they're as connected to their work and what they're making as they are to making sure they're checking all the boxes at the highest level possible, given the competition around them. And so, on the heels of doing the ICA, I feel even more that there's a crisis of creativity in the world today. All forms of art, no matter the medium, are increasingly commodified. There's an imbalance in understanding. There's an imbalance between creativity needing to be supported financially and in terms of the ability to be creative and imaginative. There's such an atmosphere of discontent, frustration, and disappointment and yet people keep doing that every day. I feel like curators are more and more project managers. It's shaping how we're creative. It's shaping how we're supporting creativity to mimic the economic model of producers and suppliers. Artists aren't fucking producers and suppliers. That's not what we do. I believe in creativity. I believe in the human imagination. I believe in our need to communicate with one another, and communicating through art, when it's not a product, is one of the most honest forms of connecting with one another.

MI What you're talking about, Linda, is the professionalization of artists, right? It's like going to med school. You get into medical school, you get your residency, and then you have a job. And like being a doctor, it involves a lot of risk, a lot of debt. But to me, an artist is somebody who refuses to accept the current conditions under which we live. It's somebody who creates despite those conditions, somebody who has an orientation toward the world. That's what we're talking about with this project, right? We're talking about the ICA and RAW coming together and trying to build a new type of institution.

AK The structural level impacts everything we are able to do, which was made visible to me when you stripped everything down and saw the harshness of the structure in the United States: how you get paid, all the bureaucracy. One structural thing we did is ask every fellow to sign a form that said they were not making "art" in the space. That allowed us, as an institution, to give permission within that space for all kinds of things to happen—including ones that are surely art. But they didn't have to be treated as such institutionally. It was very open and flexible, as opposed to how things might be done at MoMA, or at the ICA under normal conditions. But as soon as the fellows came, they saw the boxes we had created. They couldn't let go of the institution, even despite our great efforts to create something different. The specter of what was outside kept coming into the room. I also want to mention that the RAW Académie is specifically posited not as an MFA program. It is a different culture, for example, than the university that is outside of the RAW Académie's walls in Philadelphia, the University of Pennsylvania.

MI I want to return to what you said about the art, Alex, because that's super important. It's really blowing my mind right now. And it goes to one of the questions around value systems that Linda posed for the Académie. What you did by allowing the fellows to sign that contract is to say, "What I'm doing here doesn't need to be ascribed value within the current art system." You're able to do more than if something carried that monetary value. With JAM, Linda talks about having no opportunity costs. It has me thinking about classic David Hammons works, which can be made out of hair, or barbecue bones, or things found in the trash, and his ability to create art out of something that, as you say, has "zero value."

AK To clarify a bit, this was a structural problem that was solved internally with colleagues to help us be supportive and caring. Because when value comes in, at least in our institution, it's not just, "Are we going to get sued if something gets damaged?" Our job, first and foremost, is care—curators are caretakers. So what does care look like in that respect?

LGB One of the hardest things to deal with during the MoMA show was the installation. I was told I could not touch the work. There are art handlers. I have never curated a show where I can't move the work around. That's how you become intimate with a piece. You pick it up, you move it, you look at it, you look at it next to something else, you put it real close so they're kissing, you are getting intimate. They said, "You can't touch anything. You have to ask somebody else to move it." How do we work around the rules? What we do is let the rules force us to work to work around them.

MHP The proximity starts in the creation of the work. It seems like the institution now is erasing the possibility of proximity between the artwork and someone who is not the artist. And that is funny because when you exhibit a work, you can see it might affect someone else. In a museum, the minute you approach a work, it goes "beep!" It creates stress for the viewer because you don't know how close you can get. How can we do it differently? How can we do it in a way that this proximity you're talking about is still there? Alex, the fact that the fellows were invited to sign a paper saying "I'm not doing art" was also a way of saying "I think what we are doing is more important than what you see." It's not about money; it's not about insurance. It's way more than that. Of course, all the conversation brought us back to the institution.

MI To complicate that a bit, if I stick with my definition of an artist as somebody who refuses to accept the current conditions of society, we essentially said to them, "Build a society you want to see in this space." But no matter what we did, the productive thing might have been for them to find the rules and the problems with them. Something productive comes out of that, ideally. But I think about whether or not it's always helpful for people to have something to push against. The fewer restrictions we made, the more of a challenge it became for the artists and curators. I wonder if the question of success or failure within that is moot, because there was supposed to be a kind of agonism. Because that's what artists do. But just to be the devil's advocate, should artists always be upset at institutions? Should revolutionaries always be pissed off at the government? What if institutions were friends of artists? Would we lose a lot?

MHP Yes, but what if we *are* the institutions? The individuals who were in those sessions were all institutions themselves. I have the impression that often we are battling with our own positions as individuals, on top of our position as institutions.

LGB You know, it takes me back to the common denominator of everyone who found their way to JAM. The thing that they shared was that no one would show their work except in the community they lived in. I keep saying if JAM could be created, why do we have to break it down? We all have our own boxes. What is the box we share? And maybe that's the work, identifying the box we all share.

AK It's also worth remembering that this was a moment at ICA when everyone was coming back to the office for the first time. Like every arts organization, we had lost about a third of our staff, who had gone on to other jobs. It was a moment within our institution when we were feeling a little fragile about being back together, being back in the organization. And there was a way that the RAW Académie helped us reacclimate to each other and to the building. But it was difficult at first. I know that I personally felt that quite viscerally. I brought it up a few times, feeling both a sense of a shift in my own body of being in the Académie room, and then being up in the office taking care of day-to-day things. So when Marie Helène talks about that individual perspective of infrastructure, I saw that in myself.

One thing we also talked about learning together was that words don't mean the same things to everybody. And it's such an obvious point, the term *infrastructure*, or a term like *hospitality*, or even *artist*. These mean different things to different people, and people hold and actualize them in different ways. I think that we really saw that coming into tension and fruition in the Académie.

MI Everybody wants to build new infrastructure. That assumes that the infrastructure isn't working for everybody currently. I wonder if it's about defining, for all of us, our discontent. We tried to do that by starting with the question, "What is the problem with the current infrastructure?"

LGB I think the individuals that were most consistently resistant to imagining the current infrastructure were those that most benefit from it. There was an assumption that everyone thought there needed to be a different infrastructure. And even if they thought that it is likely that they benefit enough from that infrastructure, it wasn't worth the effort.

MI I think this goes back to organizing social movements, which is making even the richest person realize that a system doesn't actually work for them. Because it's not about if that person is rich. It's not about how they benefit if they're white, Black, Hispanic, whatever. It's about getting them to understand that because the system doesn't benefit everybody, it actually benefits no one. And so in the Académie and with young artists today, people may think they're benefiting, but we're all not benefiting in some way.

LGB That could have been an interesting conversation, in hindsight, for the group, and early on. Because remember, within the first twenty minutes of us being together on that first day, members of the group were saying, "Tell us the rules." If we could rewind that, I think that that would have been a great time to ask: How does the current system benefit you? If it doesn't benefit everybody, it's not of benefit.

MI The benefit thing is also a rethinking of values, right? Having money can be a benefit, but it also can be detrimental in some ways. I feel like it's rethinking that kind of value shift.

AK The big questions that I actually came into this with were: Are new organizations possible? Are the old ones that we have able to be rehabilitated? Do new organizations need old organizations to survive? We're in a moment when we're all talking about institutional infrastructural change across society at large. What you're demonstrating is the way these things are entangled. Even radical new propositions are still somehow attached to older infrastructures. I'm really curious to hear your thoughts on institutions and organizations, and your individual work after this experience—which I think for you, Linda and Mari, in particular, is probably compounded by the experience that you've also had with MoMA and JAM. And Marie Hélène, thinking about Dakar and Philly. And maybe we'll talk more about our personal transformations as well. But it feels like the big ghost in the room, in a way. There are certain identifiable things within ICA that are different afterward. And it took the entire team to do them. So it's also really important that I mention all of the colleagues that got on board, were part of the conversations, brought ideas to the table, and participated in the Académie. Whether it was having lunch, or our director, Zoë Ryan, saying "yes," or dismantling the lobby desk and seeing what happened. It's still not there. So real, visible infrastructural change has happened; we will never be the same after the experience. So I throw that out to you.

MHP I want to start with what Mari said about the definition of value. How do we define value? The idea of creating a new infrastructure should have been put in the plural. We are creating infrastructures, many of them; it's not just one infrastructure that works for all of us. We realized in the process of the Académie that, depending on our goals or where we're coming from or where we're creating them, our infrastructures will be different. One of the main investments for this institution has been people, the value of those people in terms of their ideas, what they're seeing, what they've been putting forward, and also where they come from. The main questions are: why are you doing it? Who are you doing it for? How do we highlight the multiple worlds we are from? How do we not just put everybody in the same box? How do we create a space that is open for everybody to come and recognize themselves? It's also about opening doors for voices that we believe should be heard, and that are not necessarily validated by academia or these kinds of hegemonic institutions.

AK I think you just spoke really beautifully to the connection between institutional transformation and individual transformation and how it's hard to separate them. When I went to Documenta 15 this summer, seeing such resonances with the things that we were working out in space between people, I thought about other models that privilege relationships. Not that they devalue making, but they're not putting pressure on the end result. Maybe it's something about process and relationships, which I think was very palpable at Documenta 15.

MHP We've been working with ruangrupa [the curators of Documenta 15] since 2014. What they've proposed for this Documenta, the role of school, the role of so many collectives from all over the world, has disrupted the whole institution of Documenta, the politics that are embedded in it. In terms of understanding this type of institution and the role they play, and also how they often neglect human value. This is a Documenta that we will remember in ten, twenty years;

it will stay in our minds. The energy in the city, the energy of the artists who took part in it, the visitors, there was something so wonderful about just being there and witnessing the proposals and seeing how people are united around their own practices in very human ways. I found that very beautiful.

AK It's such a key point that you started a conversation with ruangrupa back in 2014. It really struck me that the entrance of Documenta included a timeline of the relationships and the whole journey. How did our Académie start? In the gallery here we also have a wall with the timeline of the relationships: RAW and ICA, and Linda and Mari, and the fellows. Our friends at the Kunsthalle Lissabon have talked about the exhibition being the place where a relationship gets made public, and that everything afterward is the maintenance of that relationship. There's some synergy there in terms of thinking about these things as living. And the way that Linda talked about being reunited with people she hadn't seen in forty years, because that was all based on relationships instead of relational conditions. It wasn't prefaced on a check-list of objects. The relationship is what generated everything.

Story of a Marriage: Secue_LA

Helmut Batista, Marilia Loureiro, Lola Malavasi, and Sally Mizrachi, moderated by Noah Simblist

This interview was conducted on July 31, 2024, over Zoom. It has been edited for length and clarity.

Noah Simblist I am interested in the models that you have created for alternative forms of art education that build on the pedagogical traditions of Ivan Illich or Paulo Freire. But first, I'd like each of you to introduce yourselves and your organizations. Let's start with Lola.

Lola Malavasi I'm Lola Malavasi. I am codirector of TEOR/éTica. I've worked here for almost thirteen years. TEOR/éTica started in 1999. This year we are celebrating twenty-five years of work, which is quite a feat in our context. It was founded by Virginia Pérez-Ratton; her wish was to create a platform for art from Central America and the Caribbean. Eventually that expanded to a network of agents from around the world, especially Latin America. We work along four axes. We have what we call *curatorial experiments*, working with the exhibition format. We have the Lado V—Center for Study and Documentation, where the archive and the library are. That space nurtures study, which is more related to our educational initiatives. We don't have a publishing house, but we do publish books. Finally, we offer grants and support through open calls, and we think about sharing resources like our houses and our knowledge.

NS Helmut, do you want to go next?

Helmut Batista Capacete started as an artist-run program and has had a winding journey, in part because we haven't had a constant logic guiding our way of working. It then turned into an international residency program with a pedagogical orientation, not in the sense of a school, but rather the exchange of information through professionals coming through Brazil or in residence with us. Because the program used to be one year long, each resident comes with different expectations. He's somehow part of the city and the community. So I'm not so sure if it's really pedagogical, though I think exchanging information is always pedagogical.

But we have been pedagogically oriented since 2010, when Capacete participated in the São Paulo Biennial. That year we started a one-year program for twelve participants. Because the Biennale, at that moment, had a lot of money, we could do a huge program. Since then, with some breaks in between, we have continued with this model. In the last four years before the pandemic, Camilla Rocha Campos was director.

The pandemic was a disaster for all of us here. Capacete was broken financially because we are fully financed by international partnerships. We have no local money. In response, we built this Secue_LA program, which was virtual, and when the pandemic was over everybody was happy to meet again. Since then, Capacete has joined forces with a different local program called Xow.Rumi. This is a one-year program with thirteen participants, all of them from Rio. It is pedagogical because we have seminars every month. We have studio visits, talks, and all kinds of activities. What the future looks like? I have no idea.

NS Sally, can you talk a little bit about lugar a dudas?

Sally Mizrachi The story of lugar a dudas is also long. First, one of the inspirations for lugar a dudas is TEOR/éTica. We are celebrating our twentieth anniversary this year. We started with one idea from Oscar Muñoz: sharing with others. It became a collective effort that many people from different perspectives added to. A space in Cali, Colombia is very different from New York or Rio. We started with some exhibitions, albeit in collaboration with other institutions already working toward similar goals. In doing so, we saw that the acts of investigation each exhibition produced are very important. So we opened a documentation center that is now the heart of lugar a dudas.

We also started the program we have kept up through the years. We say that it's "education with no school" because we approach our exhibitions, talks, and seminars in a pedagogical way. And then we opened a residency program with Helmut and three other organizations across Latin America. It was very important for the local context for us to create some dialogues with the neighbors that we have. Now we have a curatorial micro school, which has five participants. And our artistic director, Erica Flores, is both curator and the manager of this school. The school's participants propose the exhibitions. We have no other exhibition program other than the one emerging from the micro school.

NS Thank you all. Helmut said, "I'm not sure if what we do is education, unless sharing of information is education." How have your organizations approached education as you have defined it? And how does it relate to more traditional forms of education in universities or art academies that give accredited degrees?

HB I think that the beauty of the art context is that you can do whatever you want. You can experiment and if this experiment turns into an education program, then great! I think universities are very stiff. We don't have the European concept of an art academy in Brazil. We have some art schools, private schools, private universities, and, of course, art programs in universities, but from my point of view they suffer from a lack of money and a lack of international exchange. Our program is international and driven by exchange. I find it difficult to define it as a pedagogical system because, in the context of Brazil, what is an educational system? It is what the ministry tells you. We don't give out diplomas. Participants' experience with us might define them in the future, but it's not a diploma. They will never get a job in a Brazilian university, because you have to have a master's and a doctorate. Which is also ridiculous because in other countries you can qualify just by being a good artist. I think we have always been a midcareer program. They're already coming from schools—although not necessarily art schools, sometimes architecture or philosophy or dance. We are a place where people have time to think if it makes sense to make art. And this is where education happens for me.

LM For me, it has to do with our context. We inherited academic systems, like Helmut was saying, and they're quite outdated. For example, students at universities don't even study contemporary art, nothing from the eighties onwards. It's not given attention unless there's a specific professor interested in it. The context really dictates what we can do and what we want to do and how we can work from there. There's also the lack of resources: no public funding for arts, no public funding for arts institutions like ours. Only one public museum dedicated to contemporary art. For us, pedagogy is a way of healing that colonial path that we carry from our history.

For us, art is a tool. How can we use art to provide educational opportunities that go beyond the artists themselves? We talk about study a lot at TEOR/éTica, because for us that's the way of changing the language around education. I think *education* is quite a loaded word, like *pedagogy*. We came across the idea of *study* through [Fred] Moten and [Stefano] Harney's discussion of the undercommons, with study defined as a way of being with others to learn. The educational spaces that we open up through TEOR/éTica are about study. How can we use art to be with others, to learn with others, to propose spaces that will ultimately result in learning?

NS This idea of a colonial past that Lola introduced is interesting because, as she described the ministry of education defining education, he invoked the weight of a political structure. I wonder if some of the stiffness and limitations of funding or viewpoint in the more traditional institutions like universities is informed by that postcolonial context.

LM I think yes, in all of our contexts. We inherit these institutions. We inherit these systems from our colonizers from Spain and Portugal, from Europe. Obviously, there is a way of doing things that doesn't necessarily fit with our context, our social and political histories, and our communities. Many things were imposed very early on but don't necessarily work for us. That's where we try to look for other ways, to experiment with or learn from other systems, or just try to invent them.

NS And Sally?

SM I agree with Helmut and Lola and yes, all of us navigate our colonial heritage, but I think the wonderful thing is that we can change paradigms. We are always thinking about how to break the rules. In Cali, we have five art departments, five universities, and many students that graduate in "art," but there are no other specializations or a master's degree. Still, we try to work with the universities. We invited students and their teacher from one university to study an artist, and we wanted to create a collection of artworks that we cannot see in Cali because there's just one art museum. So we tried to envision a "museum collection" with art pieces that we have no opportunity to see. We invited the student artists to study figures like Warhol. They learned about the contexts in which Warhol lived and worked and then duplicated Warhol's work, and we exhibited it. We have a collection of these copied artworks.

NS Marilia, maybe you could introduce yourself as a way to introduce Secue_LA, since it builds on the histories of lugar a dudas, Capacete, and TEOR/éTica.

Marilia Loureiro Yes, but Lola, please jump in because Secue_LA was made by all of us. I am Marilia Loureiro, and I have worked with these three organizations at different moments. My first curatorial project was realized through an open call at lugar a dudas. It was a totally crazy project and, even now, I don't know why they accepted it because it had no formal exhibition, no conference, and it was made with local artists, but not only artists. It was a public program connecting food and territory and creating a space of being together. And it was a really important moment for me; I can see now that becoming a curator has to do with this project.

And then I met Lola and we had a great conversation. As for Helmut, Capacete had done a really amazing public program for the 29th São Paulo Biennial, which was my first job in the arts. Capacete enabled conversations and reflections on art by curators and artists in a really horizontal way. They moved the biennial to downtown São Paulo cultural spaces known from the time of the dictatorship in Brazil. The Left and the resistance to the dictatorship used these spaces. Years later, I went to Rio to do the Capacete program and there I met Helmut.

NS How did the pandemic affect the organizations and how did that crisis lead to the creation of Secue_LA?

SM This morning, as I thought about this meeting, I thought too of a 2015 film by Luis Ospina, a director from Cali, called *It All Started at the End*. Helmut interviewed Oscar and many other directors of art organizations during the pandemic. We talked about not knowing what to do with lugar a dudas and that it might be over for us, and Helmut shared the same perspective for Capacete. Then, at the end of 2020, Helmut contacted us again and said, "Hey, let's not close. We can think about one [collective] virtual program." I now see the pandemic not as a dark moment but as a great moment to stop, to think, to reflect about our spaces. So then we thought about other organizations that also address pedagogy. We already had a close relationship with TEOR/éTica. So we called and we proposed a marriage.

LM Literally proposed, like a marriage. We decided we were going to have a polyamorous marriage. For us it was also a moment of great uncertainty; I don't think our houses were even open at the time, which was especially difficult because part of our work is offering these spaces for the community. If we didn't have physical space, we had to think, "Okay, how do we build other spaces?" We started thinking about how to do this, and eventually we did some scouting for another curator; I wanted to work with somebody else. We did a round of interviews and eventually Marilia proposed this building a school from the idea of care. Not just because we were going through a pandemic, but also to ask what care means in Latin America. That's when the program started to take shape.

ML I thought of doing a project connected with care because I listened to them. Being together and looking after each other was a kind of care, them saying, "I don't want to close, but I don't know what to do." They were connecting as an effective network. I realized this was already a gesture of care and a gesture of sharing vulnerability, sharing how fragile we were at the moment personally, but also institutionally. And then when they told me that they were doing this project and why they started and this story of the three-way marriage, I realized that this was a different way of connecting and that it was totally a care practice. And then I said, "Okay, these three spaces are not museums, they're not huge art institutions. Inside these spaces we can think about care in a different way." We can also remember that art has a really important function of social healing, of political healing, of subjectivity healing. Care is a really big issue, one we have been dealing with for a long time, but we don't normally name it in art institutions.

NS How was the curriculum structured to think through care? Was it through reading about care? Was it through workshops? How do you actually introduce this as a subject?

LM It's important to say that we wanted to go beyond it being a subject and have it be a practice. For example, we instituted this thing that we called El Fondo, which is the common care fund, basically a common pot, an idea that comes from Arts Collaboratory. It's a network that lugar a dudas and TEOR/éTica are part of. There are people that can pay for the program and there are people that need funds to participate in the program. So we asked the people that were selected: how much do you need to participate, or can you contribute something? And some of them told us, "Oh, I would need fifty or seventy-five dollars." And some people actually said, "I can contribute thirty dollars." That monthly contribution would go toward the common fund, which could be used by the other participants; it was a way of caring for each other through a collective project. With that fund, for example, some participants made a publication. For us that was very important. And even though we were meeting virtually, we tried to create a space of closeness, to get to know each other a little bit more. Through that, some really interesting and lovely relationships developed. We had always planned that we would meet in person, and we thankfully got funds from the Foundation for Arts Initiatives to arrange that.

But traveling expenses added up. Marilia and I came up with an idea based on our travels to other countries. Hosting is staying with the people that receive us because they can show us their context in a more authentic manner. We thought, "Why don't we propose to the group that each person can be a host for somebody else in the group, and they can visit each other based on interest or shared projects or curiosity?" We would support them with money for the week of the visit, but it was really more about creating connections and having others stay with you in your home. And, like Marilia said, that was also an exercise in vulnerability. The group embraced the idea in such an enthusiastic way. I think that traveling was one of the strongest aspects of the project. We asked people to keep a journal, to answer four or five questions together, and the results were very moving. It was really interesting to see how their practices were impacted and how they learned from locals. At the same time, they expanded their networks. It cemented relationships, but also friendships.

NS Mutual aid was often discussed during the pandemic. In the United States, as things seemed to get back to normal, the more radical ways that people were willing to think about mutual aid started to fall away. Secue_LA began out of crisis and a lot of optimism, but I wonder how it has shifted over time.

ML One thing we were conscious of from the beginning was not wanting to be in front of a screen all day. We didn't want to have a school with three hours a day of meeting and talking. The rhythm that we established included more intense moments when people presented their own research, a lot which had to do with care. Someone presented on a rural school in the countryside of Costa Rica, another person on a group of performances in the northeast of Brazil that asked, "What is love and how can I translate it into public love?" The projects were connected with pedagogy in a really broad sense. There were really profound exchanges.

LM There was a sense of enthusiasm at the beginning. That's usually the case, then, as time goes by, there's this wave; sometimes more people are involved and sometimes less people are involved. We tried to ride those waves even in terms of how we managed the project. Sometimes there were moments of intensive work, and then sometimes people were more focused on their local projects. We tried to be conscious and respectful of how much people could give. All in all, most people were quite involved. And sometimes, of course, aspects of the program resonated more with some people than others, which is also part of it. Care was at the center, but we tried to think of care focused on the body, or on the land—different ways of approaching care. Those waves are very important when you try to build collective projects, both practically and creatively.

ML I wanted to offer to these twelve participants what I had: a community beyond borders. At some point I realized that I had this network, including people that weren't Brazilians or people that weren't physically close to me. There are so many amazing artists in Latin America that could totally connect and form a community beyond national borders. I think this group is on the same radio frequency. Now that Secue_LA is over, it's so nice to see how they're doing projects together and how they have each other as not only friends but as partners in art, people that they can conspire with. This was one of the amazing legacies of Secue_LA.

NS Did this project help develop a certain kind of "Latin American" context? I remember talking to Helmut about the question of language, too. What language did you use? Was it Spanish, Portuguese? Portuñol? What became common in Secue_LA that speaks to a kind of common identity or way of thinking?

SM Portuguese or Spanish or Portuñol, we didn't impose—but we didn't want English. It's another trauma in Latin America, another heritage. So we also have to heal from that.

LM Everybody would speak their language. Portuguese or Spanish. Some of the Brazilian participants spoke Spanish, so it was probably easier for them. I don't think any of the Spanish-speaking participants spoke Portuguese, but I don't know. We had this idea, unfortunately unrealized, of a glossary to translate some texts between the languages. I think that translation happened a little bit more through culture than language. People would send each other songs. It was fascinating; Latin America tends to be seen as one big block, but our contexts are completely different, even between the three organizations.

We had to learn how to work together, because doing cultural work is different in each country. We realized, though, that there are certain ways of doing things that relate; I can think of certain traditions in Mexico that suddenly resonated with things in Chile or Costa Rica. This common ground, like the topic of land, really connected people. We discovered similar struggles and similar ways of approaching these issues. That really created community among the participants.

NS How did this initiative, based on coming together, filter back into the individual organizations?

HB Well, most directly, one of the participants is now in my program. But, as organizers, we still haven't gotten together to reflect on what happened. Not everything was perfect. Maybe we had bad luck with timing: we started basically when the pandemic was over, but nobody knew that it was going to be over. I had been pretty sure that we would find a lot of money for virtual programs, but then suddenly the physical world came back, and everybody cut money for virtual programs.

Also, it was a two-year program, a very long program. It was the first-ever attempt to do such a long program in South America, I think. It was very demanding, maybe too much. For me, the longer the project, the better, but maybe that's not true for everyone and I'm still thinking about doing it again in some different way. Now we are doing it locally; Capacete is not doing curatorial work anymore. We are a platform that only uses our knowledge and contacts, and our participants make their own programs. I think this is an outcome of Secue_LA, because even though our three organizations initiated the project, everything else was Lola and Marilia.

More generally, I'm stepping back from making artistic choices. I cannot keep up. There are too many new questions on the table, especially in Brazil, with gender issues, racial issues, or colonial issues. And being a white man, you have to step down and let it go. I let it go already with Camilla Rocha Campos almost ten years ago. And now also with this program. That's how I see Capacete now: It supports other programs. For the moment it's a local program in Rio called Xow.Rumi. It's as experimental as Secue_LA. I have no idea where it's going to lead us because now the whole responsibility is on the thirteen participants, which is very complex; it's not easy. It might not work, but, for the moment, we're having a lot of fun. I think we are always learning from these experiments. I'm very grateful that we did Secue_LA.

NS Sally, what do you think?

SM As Helmut said, we learn from every project that we develop. Even if we have similar programs, we have different ways of approaching them depending on the context, the capacity, the sustainability. And I think that when we joined forces, we became stronger. For us it was very significant.

I also think that the networks are very important. Like with Arts Collaboratory, which brings together twenty-five organizations. It's a network not just of organizations, but also of caring. And our spaces, as Marilia said, are spaces of caring. With Secue_LA, all these artists that participated now work in and affect their local contexts. We helped them to do that.

HB We forgot to divorce. [*laughter*]

LM I was going to take that metaphor and bring it back.

I think it's still too early. It's been a couple of months since the last trip, and we haven't even had our last meeting with the participants. We're meeting with them next week. I can't believe it's been two years. But thinking about that whole marriage metaphor: things start to come up when you're in a long-term relationship that wouldn't have otherwise. And because you want to continue the relationship, you're willing to work on it. For us, it was important to understand what happened, for example, during certain disagreements when we were doing things in a different way than lugar a dudas or Capacete. We want to continue to be in these partnerships. So how can we work better? How can we understand others and ourselves, and how do we understand the limits of each organization? There's a desire to continue that I think that needs to be honored and understood.

ML And I think that if we knew before how difficult it is to be independent organizations, now we realize how difficult it is to be *inter*dependent organizations. It's hard, but worth it.

All That You Touch, You Change. All That You Change, Changes You.

Prem Krishnamurthy and Sam Rauch (Department of Transformation)

It's a fractured, fractious world out there. Institutions are failing or betraying us, infrastructures of sustenance are fraying to the point of collapse. The rapidly disappearing commons, both digital and physical, is increasingly polluted and exploited for the benefit of a small few. A livable future on a shared planet sometimes feels like a receding horizon. In this moment of individual and collective uncertainty, the prophetic words of Octavia Butler animate our initiative, which aims to fundamentally reorient our cultural and pedagogical networks around the need to *cultivate communities*: of creative practice, critical inquiry, mutual care, and collective repair.

Department of Transformation (DOT) is an artist-organized group and multimodal research project that develops and shares new tools to help effect the changes—personal, relational, and societal—we urgently need to survive and thrive in these unstable times. Through residencies, publications, exhibitions, workshops, and courses at art and design schools, as well as experimental public gatherings with artists, designers, therapists, organizers, facilitators, and practitioners from other fields, we test out new methods for how the arts can be a vector for connection, collaboration, and community.

Much of our work functions para-institutionally, embracing the opportunities and challenges that emerge from operating simultaneously within, beside, and beyond existing cultural and educational structures. In recent years, DOT has traveled to art and design schools, museums, and nonprofit organizations to create experimental, participatory programming at different scales. This trajectory began with the *2023 Spring Teaching Tour*,[1] which included workshops and events from Rome to Richmond, Virginia, with over a dozen other stops

1 See also https://dept-of-transformation.org/gatherings/spring-2023-teaching-tour, accessed March 12, 2025.

along the way. In fall 2024, DOT followed this with *It's the Time of the Season*, a series of "jamborees" with interdisciplinary faculty and student cohorts at public universities in the United States and Canada. Combining reflective and somatic practices, generative conflict-resolution strategies, and the co-creation of experimental group artworks, installations, and programs, our ongoing teaching seeks to reframe interpersonal skills as an essential extension of traditional artistic tools.

These pedagogical experiments are critical venues for DOT's core work of prototyping and documenting various methods drawn from a wide spectrum of practices and disciplines. In the course of our research, we've been working on *The Cookbook*: a compendium of methods, frameworks, reference texts, individual exercises, and group activities that anyone who is interested can apply within their own contexts. Our plan is to publish this in the coming years in various states of (in)completion and across a multitude of platforms for transparency and broad access.

Accessibility and openness are not incidental to our mission. As design historian Robin Kinross argued decades ago in his book *Modern Typography*,[2] the moment when printing began to document and share its methods—moving away from its guild-controlled character as a "dark art"—is also the moment in which it became "modern": self-reflexive about its methods, open about how to practice it, democratizing in its scope and effect. The formal skills of teaching and facilitating (not to mention therapy and more) are often transmitted behind closed doors, in selective, opaque, literally "disciplinary" processes that silo different forms of knowledge production and practice. At DOT, our goal is to mix it up, make these bodies of knowledge available to any who are interested, and allow people to draw upon, refute, extend, and transform these methods. We are learning out loud, prototyping in public, attempting to model and manifest—through collective experimentation and play, plus, sometimes, karaoke!—the kind of porous, vulnerable, and interdependent art ecosystem we want to live in.

DOT believes that in a society that values care and the common good, leadership looks like hospitality. With this in mind, we invite you to join us in trying a handful of the "recipes" from our cookbook. These are not final pieces but rather works in perpetual progress. Think of them as instructions for experiments that you or anyone else can try out, in order to create a sense of community and connection between humans. We welcome your tasting notes, your regional variations, your inspired combinations. Like the best recipes, these are precious parts of the commons, something that everyone needs and anyone can access. As Octavia reminds us: The only truth is change. We hope these recipes bring you pleasure, nourishment, and shared strength to face the changes still to come.

2 Robin Kinross, *Modern Typography: An Essay in Critical History* (Hyphen Press, 1992).

Letter to Yourself from the Future

Adapted by DOT from Liz Magic Laser, Debbie Millman, Milton Glaser, and others

A short individual assignment in future visioning

Ingredients

— Participants: yourself
— Optional: a group of friends or colleagues
— Pen & paper

Preparation Time: 15 minutes

Spend fifteen minutes responding to the following prompt:

> Close your eyes and imagine your ideal life in fifteen years. How has your life and the world transformed? From the perspective of your future self, write a letter to your present-day self describing your life. Where are you when you wake up? What does your day look like? Describe your surroundings, the colors, the textures, the smells, the temperature. What have you learned over these years? Describe your growth to yourself.

Additional: Try this with a partner or group of friends, writing individually. Then share with each other and discuss!

Interwoven

By Stephen Hanmer D'Elía (documented by DOT)

A physical exercise to explore interconnectedness, entanglement, and our dependence on one another.

Ingredients

— Participants: 6–20
— Materials: Large spool of colored yarn or thread

Preparation Time: 10–15 minutes

Instructions

1. Form a circle with all participants.
2. As facilitator, begin by holding the spool of yarn and grasping the end of the thread.
3. Toss the spool to someone else in the circle while keeping hold of the yarn.
4. The next person holds onto a piece of the yarn and tosses the spool to another participant.
5. Repeat this process until each person is holding a piece of the yarn, creating a web that connects the whole group.

Exploration

— Once the web is complete, experiment with movement while still holding onto the yarn:
— Lean back as far as possible without letting go.
— Move together toward the center of the circle.
— Walk in a circle while maintaining the web.
— Crouch underneath the yarn and see how it shifts.
— Play with movement and observe how the web responds.
— One participant remains outside the web, moving around and under it while the rest of the group interacts with the yarn. Observe how this changes the experience for both the individual and the group.

Reflection

After experimenting, drop the web to the ground and discuss:

— What did this exercise reveal about interdependence?
— How did it feel to be physically connected to the group?
— What surprised you about the way the web moved?
— How did it feel to be part of the web versus outside of it?
— What did you notice about the movement of the web when one person wasn't connected?
— How does this exercise relate to real-life relationships and communities?

— What challenges did you face in maintaining the web, and how did you adapt?
— What surprised you most about this activity?

On (Collective) Connection
By Prem Krishnamurthy
(riffing on Kae Tempest)

A short group exercise to connect through reading together

Ingredients
— Participants: up to 20
— The first chapter, "Set Up" from Kae Tempest's book *On Connection*[3]
— Optional: computer or screen with internet connection and speaker
Preparation Time: 15–20 minutes

— Start with a collective reading of the first chapter of *On Connection*. One method for this is to have each participant read one paragraph and then pass the book to the next person to continue reading.
— Optional: Try this standing! Try this while walking around a room! Movement and bringing the whole body into the act of reading can be great.
— Read aloud in this manner until you've finished the chapter.
— Watch the official music video for Kae Tempest's song "More Pressure" together.[4]
— [Optional] Dance!
— Finally: Discuss! What was that experience of reading together like?

3 Kae Tempest, *On Connection* (Faber & Faber, 2020), 3–9.

4 Kae Tempest, "More Pressure (lyric video) Ft. Kevin Abstract," https://youtu.be/S8gymPzmtZs?si=fJYjAhX7WGgcJx85, accessed March 12, 2025.

Ways of Reading
— Some alternative formats for running a reading group
— Next time you participate in a reading group, test out some different ways of reading together:
— Practice a collective reading of the book's first chapter or significant section. In a circle, invite each person to read a single sentence or paragraph aloud. Continue until you've finished the chapter or it feels like enough.
— An even more experimental form of this: invite people to read only a single word or several, as they feel it.
— Ask everyone to bring a sentence or paragraph from the book with them to read aloud. Start the group with people reading their selection, "popcorn style," with people simply piping in when they feel it fits. Leave space and silence in between.
— Stand up and discuss while walking around the room.
— Choose a word or sentence. Take a minute to embody this piece of language through movement and gesture.
— Break into smaller groups to discuss specific sections and then return to the larger group.
— Test out your own methods for reading together and send them back to us!

I Want / I Fear
By Prem Krishnamurthy

A short alignment exercise for a group of people who will collaborate together on a project

Ingredients
— A group of people who will work together on a project.
— Pens & paper or notetaking devices for everyone.
Preparation Time: 15–20 minutes

Part 1: I Want

Ask everyone in the room who will be involved in the project to complete a quick exercise: everybody has one minute to write down all the things that they "want" from this particular project. These can be personal or professional, individual or institutional wishes.

Then, proceeding round-robin style, each person in turn shares one thing they want. This circle continues, with each person sharing a second thing, then in the next round a third thing, and so on for as many rounds as is necessary until the whole group has added all that they would like to contribute.

Part 2: I Fear

Ask everyone in the room who will be involved in the project to complete a quick exercise: everybody has one minute to write down all the things that they "fear" about this particular project. These can be personal or professional, individual or institutional concerns.

Then, proceeding round-robin style, each person in turn shares one thing they fear. This circle continues, with each person sharing a second thing, then in the next round a third thing, and so on for as many rounds as is necessary until the whole group has added all that they would like to contribute.

See also:

Prem Krishnamurthy, "Troika," in *Tools for Collective Learning*, ed. Sofía Hernández Chong Cuy (Kunstinstituut Melly, 2022), 131–151.

5 "Troika Consulting," https://docs.google.com/document/d/18xb0N-3Z8iqpFkTKIZMEO2zO-gkSCvrnKVrqaRUBLhJ3c/edit?tab=t.0, accessed March 12, 2025. Adapted from https://www.liberatingstructures.com/8-troika-consulting via The Hum, thehum.org.

Troika[5]

A quick-fire method for generating feedback on individual challenges in a small group.

Ingredients

— Participants: Three
— Arrangement: Sit in chairs without a table in between you

Preparation Time: 60 minutes (45 minutes for core exercise, 15 minutes for debrief / reflection)

Begin with a brief moment for each person to reflect on these questions:

"What is your challenge?"
"What kind of help do you need?"

Tip: Keep it specific

Roles

— "Client": shares a challenge
— "Consultants": ask questions and provide feedback

Step 1: 4 minutes

— Client shares their challenge and what kind of help they need
— Consultants ask clarifying questions

Step 2: 5 minutes

— Client turns around to face away from the consultants and does not speak
— Consultants generate ideas, suggestions, and coaching advice together

Tip: Client can take notes or record the feedback for future reference

Step 3: 2 minutes

— Client turns around to group and shares what was most valuable about the experience

There is one minute between rounds to switch clients. Take a deep breath, shake it out, reset, recenter, and so on. Cycle through clients in alphabetical order.

At the end of the rotation, spend a couple of minutes sharing how the overall experience was. Make sure that everyone has a chance to speak.

Each round: 12 minutes
Entire exercise: 40 minutes

Doodling During Difficult Dialogues
By Prem Krishnamurthy via Anja Lutz

An experimental method for talking through challenging subjects

Ingredients

- Two people with a difficult topic to discuss
- Large piece of paper
- Drawing implements (pencils, pens, markers, crayons, and so on)
- Other art supplies as available

Preparation time: 30–45 minutes

Sometimes looking another person in the eyes while talking is ideal—it can help to create a strong emotional and empathetic bond. But when talking about hard, emotional, interpersonal topics, it seems that *not* looking directly at each other (for example, as happens when sitting next to each other driving, watching TV, or lying on a couch) can be a better strategy.

This method plays on the value of not always looking at your conversational partner as well as the cognitive rewards that can come out of doodling and drawing.

Here's a way to try it:

- Choose someone with whom you'd like to have a (potentially difficult) conversation.
- Invite them to have a tea or meal with you.
- Lay out a large piece of paper on your table.
- Keep some drawing, sketching, writing, and craft materials at hand.
- While you're talking, use the paper to draw and doodle—especially when difficult topics come up.
- Discuss with your partner after; ask how you each feel it went differently than if you had conducted a "regular" challenging conversation.
- Take a picture of the resulting paper and keep it.

P.P.P.P.P.P. (People! Practice Participating in Participatory Projects, Please.)
By Naoco Wowsugi

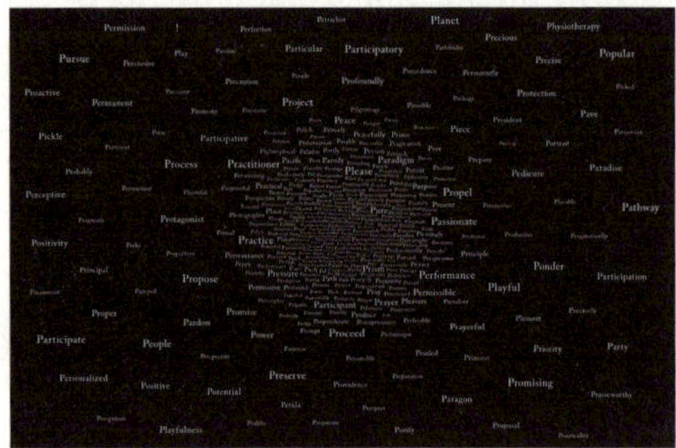

In 2016, artist Naoco Wowsugi pondered how to produce profoundly promising participatory projects and initiated *P.P.P. (Participating Participatory Practice)*. The project unfolded in secrecy because if the initiative were publicly revealed, the genuineness of the engagement might be compromised.

Through *P.P.P.*, Wowsugi experienced numerous participatory projects from the perspective of both a leader and a follower.

This participation involved activities such as writing contemplative comments and poems on a large quantity of Post-it notes; bravely mingling, singing, and holding hands with other attendees; tasting every article of food and drink in sight; applying skills gained from both BFA and MFA experiences to artistic workshops; and touring, rallying, and protesting—all while rocking an array of custom T-shirts. Wowsugi's enthusiastic participation made significant contributions to the success of these artworks.

P.P.P. informed Wowsugi's approach to community-engaged art by emphasizing hands-on experience, collective acts of care, and sharing resources with local communities. This transformation turned Wowsugi into a mutual-aid advocate within these communities, expanding the artist's role and thereby blurring the line between an artist and an engaged citizen.

Through Department of Transformation, Wowsugi now presents this project publicly for the first time and offers its example as a tool for others to use. *P.P.P.P.P.P.* invites people of all persuasions to practice prolific participation, paving productive pathways for their own particular creative powers.

TASK

Conceived by Oliver Herring; recounted by Sam Rauch

A group art making activity that can lead to collective chaos (and a lot of fun!)

TASK is many things—a Conceptual artwork and a framework for participatory performance and improvised collaboration, to name a few—but at its core, it is a simple set of instructions for a group activity that can be deployed in a wide variety of contexts and at virtually any scale.

In the words of TASK's creator, interdisciplinary artist Oliver Herring:

> TASK's open-ended, participatory structure creates almost unlimited opportunities for a group of people to interact with one another and their environment. TASK's flow and momentum depend on the tasks written and interpreted by its participants. In theory, anything becomes possible. The continuous conception and interpretation of tasks is both chaotic and purpose-driven. It is a complex, ever-shifting environment of people who connect with one another through what and who is around them. It is also a platform for people to express and test their own ideas in an environment without failure and success (TASK always is what it is) or any other preconceptions of how an idea, a material, or another person should be engaged.

Ingredients

1. **Humans:** minimum of several, maximum of several hundred, dressed in comfortable and non-precious clothing
2. **Materials:**
    a. Clearly marked container (box, bucket, bowl, etc.) to serve as the "TASK pool," stocked with blank pieces of paper and pens
    b. Miscellaneous arts/craft supplies (various types of paper, pens, markers, tape, glue, cardboard, aluminum foil, string/yarn, etc.), to taste, roughly scaled to the quantity of humans
3. **Space:** sufficient to comfortably contain all participating humans, with ample room to move around

Instructions

1. Assemble all participating humans and begin by explaining TASK protocol, as follows:
2. Take a blank piece of paper from the TASK pool, write down a task for another person or group of people to perform, and place the task in the TASK pool.
3. Draw a task at random from the TASK pool and perform the task according to your own interpretation, using whatever materials and other people are needed and available.
4. Upon completing your task, repeat Steps 1 and 2.

Tasting Notes[6]

A "task" can encompass virtually any potential activity, but should adhere to basic norms of respect, consent, and safety.

The duration of TASK is at the discretion of its organizers. Depending on the space and quantity of participating humans, organizers may elect to convene an optional post-TASK reflection and discussion session.

6 See also: https://oliverherringstudio.com/section/363344-TASK.html, accessed March 12, 2025.

Karaoke Practice!
by Prem Krishnamurthy

A fun and easy method for synchronizing people's bodies, minds, and spirits

As a readymade format, karaoke can generate mild to serious discomfort in people, piggyback upon existing artistic excellence, and demonstrate the possible range of vocal virtuosity (or its complete lack thereof)—while also creating community through shared vulnerability, mutual support, and physical synchronization.

Many people think that karaoke is about singing. Wrong! Actually, karaoke is about *showing up*: if you cheer others on, then you're great at karaoke. If you sit quietly in the corner, nursing your drink while watching the crowd, then you are great at karaoke!

There's also a misconception that karaoke is about virtuosic solo performance. Of course, there's nothing wrong if someone wants to get up and tear up a song. But karaoke can be even more fun when people all sing together.

So, next time you have a moment, you can kick off some spontaneous karaoke by asking everyone to take a deep breath and answer the question: "What song would you like to *hear sung* in karaoke?"

Contributors

Jonathas de Andrade was born in Maceió, Brazil, in 1982. His work, often a combination of photography, video, and installation, focuses on topics such as labor, identity, and the legacy of colonialism in Brazil. He has exhibited extensively internationally, including in such exhibitions as the Brazilian pavilion at the 59th Venice Biennale, the Bienal de São Paulo, and the New Museum Triennial. His work is included in the collections of major museums, such as the Museu de Arte de São Paulo and the Museum of Modern Art, New York.

Zeina Arida is the director of Mathaf: Arab Museum of Modern Art in Doha. She was previously the director of the Sursock Museum in Beirut and, from 1997–2014, the director of the Arab Image Foundation, where she contributed to the development of the Middle East Photograph Preservation Initiative (MEPPi).

Magalí Arriola was director of Museo Tamayo in Mexico City (2019–24) and the lead curator for Latin America at KADIST (2017–19). Arriola curated the exhibition *Pablo Vargas Lugo: Acts of God* for Mexican Pavilion for the 58th Venice Biennial. Previously, she was chief curator at Museo Jumex (2011–14); chief curator of Museo Tamayo (2009–11); and visiting curator at the Wattis Institute for Contemporary Art in San Francisco (2006).

Ariella Aïsha Azoulay is a filmmaker, curator, and professor of Comparative Literature and Modern Culture and Media at Brown University. Her books include *The Jewelers of the Ummah: A Potential History of the Jewish Muslim World* (Verso, 2024); *Potential History: Unlearning Imperialism* (Verso, 2019); *Civil Imagination: The Political Ontology of Photography* (Verso, 2012); and, as coauthor with Adi Ophir, *The One State Condition: Occupation and Democracy between the Sea and the River* (Stanford, 2012).

Michael Baers is an artist and writer whose work focuses on the intersection of artistic practice, institutional and state policy, and national/international politics—the latter considered in its many guises. He has sometimes referred to this set of interests as "social art history by other means." His work often develops out of oral history collecting and other forms of research. Baers is an affiliated researcher at Leibniz-Zentrum Moderner Orient (ZMO) in Berlin.

Beatriz E. Balanta is a writer, educator, and cultural producer based in Cali, Colombia. She has published articles about orgasms and psychoanalysis, political speech, racism and classism in academia, and photography and the construction of Black identity. Balanta is the executive director and founder of Black Ground, a cultural production company based in Cali and focused on contemporary art of the African diaspora. Previously, she was assistant professor of Art History at Southern Methodist University in Dallas.

Helmut Batista was born in Rio de Janeiro. He is an artist and, since 1998, the founding director of CAPACETE.

As a multidisciplinary artist, a member of the group Artefacto, and the founder of the Space for Artistic Research and Reflection (EspIRA), **Patricia Belli** has been a central figure in art and feminist practice in Nicaragua for over thirty years. Her distinctive assemblages confront political and sexual oppression, death, and desire.

Cara Benedetto is an artist and writer. Her work has been exhibited at Metro Pictures, New York; MOCA Cleveland; MOMA Warsaw; and the Jewish Museum, New York. She was writer in residence at Callie's, Berlin (2023–25) and a fellow at Akademie Schloss Solitude, Stuttgart (2014). She is the author of *Origin of Love and Other Tales of Degradation* (2020), *The Coming of Age* (2015), and *Burning Blue* (2015) and is the founder of *Overflow Journal*. She is associate professor in Print Media at Virginia Commonwealth University.

Manuel Borja-Villel is an art historian and curator. He served as director of the Museo Reina Sofía in Madrid from 2008 to 2023. Previously, Borja-Villel was director of MACBA in Barcelona (1998–2007) and of the Fundació Antoni Tàpies (1989–98). More recently, he was one of the curators of the 35th São Paulo Biennial. In 2015, he was awarded an honorary doctorate by the Universitat Oberta de Catalunya and is also a foreign member of the American Academy of Arts and Letters. He received the 2024 Audrey Irmas Award for Curatorial Excellence.

Linda Goode Bryant has assumed many roles over her career: gallery owner, filmmaker, farmer, and entrepreneur. She founded Just Above Midtown gallery (1974–86), which was the subject of a 2022 exhibition at the Museum of Modern Art, New York. In 2009 she established the urban farming initiative Project Eats. She has worked at The Metropolitan Museum of Art and The Studio Museum in Harlem. In 2022 she was artistic director for RAW Académie at the Institute of Contemporary Art in Philadelphia.

Gregory Buchakjian is an art historian and interdisciplinary visual artist. The recipient of a PhD from Sorbonne Université, he is director of the School of Visual Arts and associate professor at Académie Libanaise des Beaux-Arts (ALBA). He lives and works in Beirut.

Johanna Burton is the Maurice Marciano Director of the Museum of Contemporary Art (MOCA), Los Angeles. Prior to joining MOCA, she held posts including executive director of the Wexner Center for the Arts, Columbus, Ohio; Keith Haring Director & Curator of Education and Public Engagement at New Museum, New York; and director of the Graduate Program at Bard College's Center for Curatorial Studies (CCS), New York. She currently serves as a trustee on the board of the Andy Warhol Foundation for the Visual Arts.

Luis Camnitzer is a German-born Uruguayan artist, educator, and writer who moved to New York in 1964. He was at the vanguard of 1960s Conceptualism, working primarily in printmaking, sculpture, and installations. For more than five decades, his practice has been marked by an enduring interrogation of systems of power, the intersection of art and pedagogy, and the deconstruction of language and other familiar frameworks.

Campus in Camps is a project of DAAR (Decolonizing Architecture Art Residency), founded by Sandi Hilal and Alessandro Petti and situated between architecture, art, pedagogy, and politics. Over the last two decades, it has developed a series of research-based projects that are engaged in the struggle for justice and equality. In Hilal and Petti's practice, art exhibitions are both sites of display and sites of action that spill over into other contexts: built architectural structures, the shaping of critical learning environments, interventions that challenge dominant collective narratives, the production of new political imaginations, the formation of civic spaces, and the redefinition of concepts.

Aissa Deebi is an artist, curator, and writer. He has held various academic leadership positions including the chair of the Department of Art and Design at Montclair State University, Montclair, New Jersey. He was the founder and director of the Visual Cultures Program at the American University in Cairo; a visiting reader in Contemporary Art Middle East at Birmingham City University, Birmingham, UK; and a visiting international faculty at Cedim, EstudiosSuperiores de Diseño de Monterrey, Mexico. He is currently the chair of the Painting + Printmaking department and an associate professor of art at VCUarts Qatar.

Karen Devia is a visual artist, writer, and tattooer. Her work explores the concepts of temporality and body. In 2015, she was part of the contemporary dance company Danzados. In 2013, she was a recipient of the Magis Scholarship from the Pontificia Universidad Javeriana. She has been part of the team of lugar a dudas since 2017.

Sean Dockray is an artist and writer whose work explores the politics of technology with a particular emphasis on artificial intelligences and the algorithmic web. He is a founding director of the Los Angeles nonprofit Telic Arts Exchange and initiator of the knowledge-sharing platforms The Public School and AAAARG.ORG. He is a senior lecturer in the Department of Fine Art at Monash University in Melbourne.

Angela Dufresne is a painter based in Brooklyn. Through painting, drawing, printmaking, performative works, and community building she wields heterotopic narratives that are both non-hierarchical and unapologetically perverse, conjuring the rage, piss and vinegar, and passion of being female in America. She currently serves as the head of painting department at the Rhode Island School of Design.

Hope Ginsburg is a maker of collaborative projects where art, ecology, and spirituality meet. She is the artist/director of *Meditation Ocean* (2023–), which focuses on human and more-than-human thriving and is realized by an evolving team of collaborators called the Meditation Ocean Constellation. Since the late 1990s, Ginsburg's long-term artworks have integrated video, installation, performance, and pedagogy.

Pablo Guardiola is a visual artist and curator with works in sculpture, photography, and text. His practice points to different modes of narration and how these are perceived and understood. He is codirector of Beta—Local, an arts nonprofit based in Puerto Rico.

Magnus Ericson is a Stockholm-based curator and educator working across design, architecture, urbanism, and art. He is currently head of IASPIS Applied Arts, leading the program related to design, crafts, architecture, and spatial and urban practice. He has, over the years, in different institutional settings and as an independent curator, combined curatorial and pedagogical practice with an emphasis on socially engaged critical practice, alternative pedagogies, and organizing spaces for learning.

Marcelo Expósito is an artist and cultural critic whose work has been shown in recent solo exhibitions at La Virreina, Barcelona; Museo Universitario Arte Contemporáneo, Mexico City; PAV, Turin; and Parque de la Memoria, Buenos Aires. He was an artist-in-residence at the Spanish Academy in Rome (2022–23) and a guest artist at the 60th Biennale Arte Venezia (2024) as part of the *Disobedience Archive* curated by Marco Scotini. In 2025, he is a visiting professor at the Faculty of Arts of the University of Chile and at the Nuova Accademia di Belle Arti (NABA) in Milan. His latest book is *Interrupciones y movimientos* (Metales Pesados, Chile, 2024).

Gordon Hall is an artist whose work encompasses sculpture, performance, and writing. Hall has had solo exhibitions at MIT List Visual Arts Center, Cambridge, MA; Portland Institute for Contemporary Art, Portland, OR; The Renaissance Society, Chicago; and The Kitchen, New York, among other venues. Hall is assistant professor of art at Vassar College.

Pablo Helguera is a visual artist living in New York. His work involves performance, drawing, pedagogy, installation, theater, and other literary strategies. He is often considered a pioneering figure in the field of socially engaged art and has been recipient of many awards including the Guggenheim and Creative Capital fellowships and the first International Award for Participatory Art in Italy. He is author of many books, including *Education for Socially Engaged Art* (2011) and *The Parable Conference* (2014). He is currently assistant professor at the College of Performing Arts of The New School in New York.

Mônica Hoff is an artist, curator, and researcher based in Porto Alegre, Brazil. Her work investigates the relations between curatorial, artistic, and educational practices and how they contribute, resist, or determine institutional politics. Between 2006 and 2014, Mônica coordinated the education department of the Bienal do Mercosul in Porto Alegre, where she also acted as part of the curatorial team for its ninth edition, *Weather Permitting* (2013). Recent projects include: *Laboratório de Curadoria, Arte, e Educação* (2014–19), in collaboration with Fernanda Albuquerque; *Embarcação* (2016–18); and *Pedagogia em* Público, developed with Fábio Tremonte.

Brian Holmes is an essayist and artist. He holds a PhD in Romance Languages and Literatures from the University of California at Berkeley.

Khaled Hourani is an artist, curator, and writer. He was the artistic director of the International Academy of Art Palestine from 2007 to 2010, and its general director from 2010 to 2013. He also worked as general director of the Fine Arts Department in the Palestinian Ministry of Culture (2004–06). In 2013, he was awarded the Leonore Annenberg Prize by Creative Time, New York. In 2014, his retrospective was presented at the Centre for Contemporary Arts, Glasgow, and Gallery One in Ramallah. Another retrospective was presented at Darat Al Funun, Amman in 2017.

Marielle Ingram is a writer based in Brooklyn. She has contributed to exhibitions and programs at the Art Institute of Chicago; Gallery 400 and the Washington Park Arts Incubator, both in Chicago; and the Museum of Modern Art and MoMA PS1, both in New York. Her writing and film projects have appeared in publications such as *Real Life*, *Artforum*, *Take Shape X-TRA*, and *MIT Thresholds*. She holds a BA in philosophy from the University of Chicago.

Susan Jahoda is an artist, organizer, and teacher who lives in New York and currently teaches at the University of Massachusetts, Amherst. A member of three collectives—the Pedagogy Group, BFAMFAPhD, and NYCTBD—she is working toward developing equitable methods of teaching and commoning within the context of arts education.

Steffani Jemison is an artist who lives and works in New York. Her solo exhibitions include Lafayette Anticipations, Paris (2025); Centre d'art contemporain Genève (2024); JOAN, Los Angeles (2022); Contemporary Arts Center, Cincinnati (2021); and the Stedelijk Museum, Amsterdam (2019). Jemison is a Guggenheim Fellow, a Radcliffe Fellow, a Herb Alpert Awardee, and a Creative Capital Awardee, among other honors. She is associate professor of Art & Design at Rutgers University; her first novel, *A Rock, A River, A Street*, was published by Primary Information in 2022.

Arnold J. Kemp has been concerned with artists, writers, curators, and educators working in art spaces founded by and in support of other artists for almost four decades. His artistic work and writing are rooted in research and process and engage ideas about the permeability of the border between self and the materials of one's work. Kemp lives and works in Chicago, where he is a professor and former dean of Graduate Studies at the School of the Art Institute of Chicago.

Yazan Khalili lives and works in and out of Palestine and Amsterdam. He is a researcher, artist, and cultural producer. His practice frames landscapes, institutions, and social and technological phenomena as politicized entities. He cofounded two platforms of infrastructure for cultural practices (The Question of Funding in 2019, Radio Alhara in 2020). He is currently a PhD candidate at ASCA, University of Amsterdam.

Alex Klein is head curator & director of curatorial affairs at the Contemporary Austin. For over a decade she served as the Dorothy and Stephen R. Weber (CHE '60) Senior Curator at the Institute of Contemporary Art, University of Pennsylvania, where she curated numerous exhibitions and created the multi-platform initiative *I Is for Institute*. Prior to joining ICA, Klein held positions in the Wallis Annenberg Photography Department, Los Angeles County Museum of Art; the Roski School of Fine Arts, University of Southern California; and The Metropolitan Museum of Art, New York.

Prem Krishnamurthy has directed design studios, established galleries and institutions, curated large-scale exhibitions around the world, and taught widely. He received the Cooper Hewitt National Design Award for Communications Design in 2015 and KW Institute for Contemporary Art's "A Year With" fellowship in 2018. In 2019, Bard College's Center for Curatorial Studies acquired his professional papers. His books include *P!DF* (2017–20), *On Letters* (2022), and *Past Words* (2024), an anthology of his writing and experimental curatorial projects. In 2022, Krishnamurthy founded Department of Transformation, an artist-organized group that prototypes experimental methods for togetherness, learning, and collective healing.

M. Paola Malavasi Lachner (Lola Malavasi) is a cultural manager and curator whose work centers on education, collective practices, and institutional critique. She served as codirector and curator at TEOR/éTica, an independent contemporary art space in San José, Costa Rica, from 2017 to 2025. During her tenure, she played a key role in developing educational initiatives, including curating and facilitating *Alter Academia*, a residency/school for young artists from Costa Rica, and, alongside Marilia Loureiro, *LasecueLA: escuela latinoamericana de cuidados*, an experimental online (de)school developed with Capacete, and lugar a dudas. Collaborating with Miguel A. López, she cocurated the 2019 exhibition *Virginia Pérez-Ratton. Centroamérica: deseo de lugar* at the Museo Universitario Arte

Contemporáneo, Mexico City, and coedited its accompanying publication.

Miguel A. López is a writer, researcher, and chief curator of Museo Universitario del Chopo, Universidad Nacional Autónoma de México, in Mexico City. He focuses on the role of art in politics and public life, collective work, and queer and feminist rewritings of history. He was cocurator of the 2024 edition of the Toronto Biennial of Art. From 2015 to 2020, he worked as chief curator, and, later, codirector of TEOR/éTica, San José, Costa Rica. He lives and works in Mexico City.

Marilia Loureiro is an art curator and researcher. She worked on the curatorial teams at Museu de Arte Moderna de São Paulo (2011–12), Museu de Arte de São Paulo (2016–17), and the São Paulo Biennial (2018), where she organized the public program *Des/Re/organizações Afetivas* at the 33rd Biennial. She has collaborated with several self-organized art initiatives, including lugar a dudas (2015) and Capacete (2016) and served as curator and program coordinator at Casa do Povo (2017–21). In 2022, she participated in Pivô Pesquisa and, from 2022 to 2024, cocurated Secue_LA, a pedagogical project by TEOR/éTica, lugar a dudas, and Capacete, with Lola Malavasi. She is currently a curator at Instituto Inhotim.

Sally Mizrachi is a cofounder of lugar a dudas, a place for artists to gather in order to work through ideas, as well as to participate in a dialogue and public debate about art and politics. Since 2005, she has been in charge of the executive direction and the general coordination of the space, generating initiatives and alliances with institutions and organizations at a national and international level for the benefit of the artists in Cali, Colombia. She is an active part in the work teams of the Arts Collaboratory network. She lives and works in Cali.

Michael Jones McKean is an artist and teacher based in the United States and France. His work has been shown extensively throughout the world and he has received numerous awards, including a Guggenheim Fellowship and fellowships at the Museum of Fine Arts, Houston's Core Program; the International Studio and Curatorial Program and the Sharpe-Walentas Studio Program, both in New York; the MacDowell Colony, Peterborough, New Hampshire; the Provincetown Fine Arts Work Center, Provincetown, Massachusetts; and the Bemis Center for Contemporary Arts, Omaha, Nebraska, among many others. He is an associate professor in the Sculpture + Extended Media Department at Virginia Commonwealth University.

Naeem Mohaiemen combines films, photography, drawings, and essays to research forms of utopia and dystopia and transnational collisions within families, borders, architecture, and uprisings. Art critic Murtaza Vali considers Dustin Hoffman in *Marathon Man* (1976) as "a hapless history student studying for a PhD, an erstwhile stand-in for Mohaiemen." Naeem is coeditor, with Eszter Szakacs, of *Solidarity Must Be Defended* (2023) and author of *Bengal Photography's Reality Quest* (2025, in Bengali), *Midnight's Third Child* (2023), and *Prisoners of Shothik Itihash* (2014). He is head of the Photography Concentration and director of Undergraduate Studies in the Visual Arts Department, School of the Arts, Columbia University.

Manuela Moscoso is the executive director of The Center for Art, Research, and Alliances (CARA) in New York. She is the curator of the 2nd Bienal das Amazônias (2025) and has previously served as curator of the Liverpool Biennial (2021); senior curator at Museo Tamayo, Mexico City; adjunct curator of the 12th Cuenca Biennial, in her native Ecuador; codirector of Capacete, Rio de Janeiro; and cocurator of the Queens International 2012, among other roles.

Noora Al Mualla is director of learning and research at Sharjah Art Foundation. Previously, she was art centers manager and curator of modern Arab art (2016–19), senior projects coordinator for the Sharjah Art Foundation curatorial team (2015–16), and exhibitions coordinator at Sharjah Art Museum (2010–15). Al Mualla is also a researcher and writer with a focus on Arab and Emirati art. Born in Umm Al Quwain, United Arab Emirates, she currently lives in Umm Al Quwain and works in Sharjah.

Beatriz Santiago Muñoz is an artist who works primarily through the expanded moving image. Her films and videos are populated by thoughtful *actores naturales* and developed through her writing, structured improvisation, and, at times, chance operations. This work is built upon intersecting histories—Boalian theater and experimental ethnographic film—and her recent work is focused on simultaneous narration, the anti-colonial unconscious, and the subjective experience of disorder. She is an educator and was the cofounder of Beta-Local in San Juan and has taught art at various institutions.

Colombian visual artist **Oscar Muñoz** is interested in questioning the notions of time and reality. His exhibitions, individual and collective, include the Institute of International Visual Art, London; the Gwangju Biennial; the Havana Biennial; the Venice Biennale; Hiroshima MOCA; Museo la Tertulia, Cali, Colombia; Museo de Arte Latinoamericano de Buenos Aires; Museo de Arte de Lima; and Jeu de Paume, Paris. He lives and works in Cali, where he cofounded and directs lugar a dudas.

Founded in 2000, **My Barbarian (Malik Gaines, Jade Gordon, and Alexandro Segade)** was the subject of a 2021 survey exhibition at the Whitney Museum of American Art, with a monograph published by Yale University Press. The group's work has been presented at the Institute of Contemporary Art, the Los Angeles County Museum of Art, the UCLA Hammer Museum, and REDCAT, all in Los Angeles; the San Francisco Museum of Modern Art; and the Museum of Modern Art, the Studio Museum in Harlem, The Kitchen, the New Museum, and Participant Inc., all in New York. The group was included in two Performa Biennials, the Whitney Biennial, two California Biennials, and the Baltic Triennial. My Barbarian has been supported by USA Artists, the Foundation for Contemporary Arts, the Mike Kelley Foundation for the Arts, and others.

Sofía Olascoaga is a Mexican artist, curator, and researcher whose work explores the intersections of art, education, and collective action. Raised in a self-organized community in Cuernavaca, Mexico, her practice is deeply informed by intentional community models and the pedagogical ideas of Ivan Illich. She has held prominent roles including cocurator of the 32nd Bienal de São Paulo (2016) and academic curator at Museo Universitario Arte Contemporáneo (2014–15) and received fellowships from the Whitney Independent Study Program and Independent Curators International. She has also worked with the alternative school SOMA and the traveling documentary film festival Ambulante.

Matteo Pasquinelli is associate professor of the philosophy of science at the Department of Philosophy and Cultural Heritage of Ca' Foscari University in Venice, where he is coordinating the ERC project *AIMODELS*. His book *The Eye of the Master: A Social History of Artificial Intelligence* (London: Verso, 2023) won the Deutscher Memorial Prize 2024.

Marie Helene Pereira is senior curator of performative practices at Haus der Kulturen der Welt in Berlin. She is a member and curatorial advisor of RAW Material Company in Dakar, where has she curated exhibitions and related discursive programs. Previously she was part of the artistic team of the 12th Berlin Biennale (2022) and cocurated a guest section of the thirteenth edition of the Dakar Biennale of Contemporary African Art (2018). She lives and works between Berlin and Dakar.

Kameelah Janan Rasheed is a learner and seeker from East Palo Alto, California. She is a full-time instructor in the Sculpture Department at the Yale School of Art. Additionally, she has taught courses and workshops at the School for Poetic Computation. Alongside her work within existing institutions, she experiments with institutional design and community building through the many projects she stewards through KJR Studios. She founded The Little Octopus School (est. 2024), a roaming learning laboratory, and a publishing imprint (Scratch Disks Full) rooted in play, curiosity, and collaboration. She is also the founder of Orange Tangent Study (est. 2020), a consultancy reimagining the design of learning experiences.

Sam Rauch is an independent curator, consultant, and cultural producer based in New York City. He has collaborated closely with some of the world's leading artists to realize their most ambitious works and engage diverse publics in contexts including traditional museums and galleries, iconic urban landmarks, and important civic sites. Through exhibitions, commissions, programs, and publications, his partnership-based research, curatorial, and consulting work focuses on experimental, interdisciplinary, and collaborative art practices and projects that foster relations of kinship, reciprocity, care, and repair.

Sarah A. Rifky is a writer, curator, and art historian. She co-founded Beirut, a contemporary art space in Cairo, and has led curatorial and academic programs internationally. Her PhD from MIT explores the entanglement of art, infrastructure, and institutional absence in modern Egypt. Rifky's writing spans contemporary art, politics, and speculative fiction in relation to the Arab world. Her guiding principle is that every artwork is a school.

Walid Sadek is an artist and writer living in Beirut. He is a professor and currently chair of the department of Fine Arts and Art History at the American University of Beirut.

Rasha Salti is a Lebanese researcher, writer, producer, curator, and international film programmer based between Beirut and Berlin. She began curating postwar Beirut cultural events such as Image-Quest (1995), has led major film initiatives including *The Road to Damascus* (2006) and *Mapping Subjectivity* at MoMA (2010–12), and has served as a programmer at Abu Dhabi Film Festival and Toronto International Film Festival. She has written extensively in outlets like the *London Review of Books* and *Afterall*. Since 2017, she has been commissioning editor for La Lucarne at *ArteFrance* and her exhibitions have shown at Haus der Kulturen Welt, Berlin; Museu d'Art Contemporani de Barcelona; Sursock Museum, Beirut; and Palais de Tokyo, Paris. She organized two editions of Homeworks at Ashkal Alwan and is an advisor for the 61st Venice Biennial to follow through on the curatorial vision of Koyo Kouoh.

Lucía Sanromán is chief curator of Museo Universitario Arte Contemporáneo. Prior to this she was the director of the Laboratorio Arte Alameda in Mexico City (2018–25). She served as director of visual arts for the Yerba Buena Center for the Arts, San Francisco (2015–18) and was associate durator at the Museum of Contemporary Art San Diego from 2006–11. As an independent curator, Sanromán was awarded a 2013 Warhol Foundation exhibition grant for *Citizen Culture: Art and Architecture Shape Policy*, presented at the Santa Monica Museum of Art in 2014. Also that year, she curated the retrospective exhibition *inSite: Cuatro ensayos de lo público, sobre otro escenario* at Proyecto Siqueiros: La Tallera, in Cuernavaca, Mexico, and was cocurator, with Candice Hopkins, Janet Dees, and Irene Hofmann, of SITE Santa Fe's signature Biennial *SITElines.2014: Unsettled Landscapes*.

Engy M. Sarhan is a writer and curator whose research explores independent art schools and para-institutional pedagogies in the Arab world. She cofounded K-oh-llective, a platform for art publishing and shared resources across the region, in 2020 and has been a curator at Les Complices*, a community-based art space rooted in activist and artistic interventions in Zürich, since 2022.

Aki Sasamoto works in sculpture, performance, video, and more. In her installation/performance works, Sasamoto moves and talks inside the careful arrangements of sculpturally altered objects, activating the bizarre emotions behind daily life. Her works appear in gallery spaces, theater spaces, and odd sites. Sasamoto is a professor and serves as the director of graduate studies in Sculpture at Yale.

As a curator, writer, and educator, **Noah Simblist** works on how contemporary artists address history, sovereignty, and the tensions between political forces and self-determination. He edited *Tania Bruguera: The Francis Effect* (Deep Vellum, 2022) and *Artist in Residence* (Publication Studio, 2021). His curatorial projects include *Commonwealth* at the Institute for Contemporary Art at Virginia Commonwealth University (2020), *Conjunctions and Disjunctions* at Black Ground in Cali, Colombia (2022), and *Aissa Deebi: Exile Is Hard Work* at Birzeit University Museum in Palestine (2017). He is currently working on *Cracks in the Edifice: Niemeyer's Futuristic Fairground in Tripoli*, co-organized with Suzi Halajian and supported by the Graham Foundation. He is associate professor of art at VCU.

Jason Smith founded The Public School with Sean Dockray, Matteo Pasquinelli, and Caleb Waldorf in 2007 under Telic Arts Exchange in Los Angeles. The Public School was a non-accredited school with no curriculum. It expanded to other cities including New York, Berlin, Brussels, Helsinki, Philadelphia, Durham, San Juan, and elsewhere.

Daniel Spaulding is an assistant professor of modern and contemporary art at the University of Wisconsin-Madison. He is completing a book on the German artist Joseph Beuys, and his other writings have appeared in *October*, *Radical Philosophy*, *Historical Materialism*, and *Mute*, among other publications. With Daniel Marcus and Jennifer Nelson, he is a founding editor of *Selva: A Journal of the History of Art* (selvajournal.org).

Sally Tallant is the president and executive director of the Queens Museum, New York. She was previously the director of Liverpool Biennial from 2011–19. From 2001–11 she was head of programs at the Serpentine Gallery, London, where she was responsible for the development and delivery of an integrated program of exhibitions, architecture, education, and public programs. She has curated exhibitions in galleries, museums, public spaces, and non-arts contexts. She is a regular contributor to conferences nationally and internationally. In 2018 she was awarded an OBE for services to the Arts in the Queen's Birthday Honors List.

Pelin Tan is a sociologist and art historian based in Mardin, Turkey and the head of the film department in the Faculty of Fine Arts at Batman University. She was the 2019–20 Keith Haring Fellow in Art and Activism at Bard College and is the cocurator of the project *Urgent Pedagogies* at IASPIS, Stockholm.

Astra Taylor is a writer, filmmaker, and organizer. She is the director of numerous documentaries and her books include *The Age of Insecurity: Coming Together as Things Fall Apart*, *Democracy May Not Exist but We'll Miss It When It's Gone*, and the American Book Award–winning *The People's Platform: Taking Back Power and Culture in the Digital Age*. Her most recent book is *Solidarity: The Past, Present, and Future of a World-Changing Idea*, coauthored with Leah Hunt-Hendrix. She was the 2023 CBC Massey Lecturer and she cofounded the Debt Collective.

Nato Thompson is an author, curator, and what he describes as "cultural infrastructure builder." He has worked as artistic director at Philadelphia Contemporary, Creative Time, and MASS MoCA. He is the founder of The Alternative Art School, an online art school matching established, top-tier artists with working artists around the globe.

Christine Tohmé is a Lebanese curator and the founding director of Ashkal Alwan, the Lebanese Association for Plastic Arts. Since its founding in 1993, Ashkal Alwan has been committed to contemporary artistic practice, research, and education. In 2016–18, Tohmé curated the 18th Istanbul Biennial and the Sharjah Biennial 13, *Tamawuj*. Tohmé is also on the boards of Marsa, a sexual-health center for at-risk youth and marginalized communities in Beirut; *Afterall: A Journal of Art, Context, and Enquiry*; Haven for Artists, a Beirut-based artist collective; and the International Biennial Association, a platform for contemporary art institutional knowledge production and exchange.

Adam Tooze is the Kathryn and Shelby Cullom Davis Professor of History at Columbia University. His most recent book is *Shutdown: How COVID Shook the World's Economy* (Allen Lane, 2021).

Jalal Toufic is the author of, among other books, *What Was I Thinking?* (e-flux journal/Sternberg Press, 2017); *The Dancer's Two Bodies* (Sharjah Art Foundation, 2015); and *Forthcoming* (2nd ed., e-flux journal/Sternberg Press, 2014). He participated in the Sharjah Biennials 6, 10, and 11; the 9th Shanghai Biennale; *Six Lines of Flight: Shifting Geographies in Contemporary Art*, San Francisco Museum of Modern Art; *A History: Art, Architecture, and Design, from the 1980s Until Today*, Centre Pompidou, Paris; *Theater of Operations: The Gulf Wars 1991–2011*, MoMA PS1, New York; and *Home Beirut, Sounding the Neighbors*, MAXXI, Rome. He was the director of the School of Visual Arts at the Lebanese Academy of Fine Arts (Alba) from September 2015 to August 2018.

Rodrigo Valenzuela is a Los Angeles–based artist working in photography, video, painting, and installation. Using autobiographical threads to inform larger, universal fields of experience, his work constructs narratives, scenes, and stories that point to the tensions found between the individual and communities. Much of Valenzuela's work deals with the experience of undocumented immigrants and laborers. At UCLA, Valenzuela teaches graduate and undergraduate students in photography.

Anuradha Vikram is a writer, curator, and educator based in Los Angeles. They work with process-based, public, and participatory art forms, with a focus on transcultural approaches to technology, social engagement, and the body. In 2024, they were a cocurator, with Victoria Vesna, of the Getty Pacific Standard Time: Art and Science Initiative exhibition *Atmosphere of Sound: Sonic Art in Times of Climate Disruption* and a cocurator, with Jackie Im, of the 2024 Portland Biennial at Oregon Contemporary. They were faculty in the UCLA Department of Art and from 2016–20 and were a member of the board of directors of the College Art Association.

Thiago Gil Virava is a postdoctoral fellow at the Bibliotheca Hertziana—Max Planck Institut für Kunstgeschichte. His academic career has focused mainly on the history of modern art and art criticism in Brazil during the first half of the twentieth century. Among the subjects of his research are the writings on art by Oswald de Andrade, the Monumento às Bandeiras at the Ibirapuera Park in São Paulo, and the history of the São Paulo Biennial. Between 2013 and 2024, he worked as a researcher and manager of the education department at the Fundação Bienal de São Paulo.

Caleb Waldorf is an artist living in Berlin. Collaborating with writers, artists, curators, educators, designers, and software engineers, he has initiated and helped develop publishing frameworks, educational platforms, and online archives. The spaces and systems he works on are designed to foster collaboration and reconsider how we approach learning, publishing, and collective engagement.

Dominic Willsdon is executive director of the International Documentary Association. Previously, he was executive director of the Institute for Contemporary Art at Virginia Commonwealth University, curator of education and public practice at the San Francisco Museum of Modern Art, a pedagogical curator of the 9th Mercosul Biennial, a cocurator of the 9th Liverpool Biennial, and curator of public programs at Tate Modern. His coedited books include *The Life and Death of Images* (2008), *Public Intimacy* (2014), *Public Servants* (2016), and *Suzanne Lacy: We Are Here* (2019).

Caroline Woolard, an artist and organizer, moved to New York City in 2002 to attend Cooper Union, the only tuition-free art school in the United States. Since then, her artistic work has been subsidized by day jobs as a graphic designer, teacher, and nonprofit administrator, and has been supported by low overhead due to labor-intensive collective living situations. After cofounding and coorganizing resource-sharing networks OurGoods.org and TradeSchool.coop for five years, Woolard is now a core member of BFAMFAPhD and NYCTBD, focusing on the impact of debt and rent on artists in New York, and options for affordable space stewardship for all New Yorkers.

Andrew Paul Woolbright is an artist and critic living in Brooklyn and is an MFA graduate of the Rhode Island School of Design. In addition to exhibiting, he is editor-at-large at the *Brooklyn Rail* and director of the gallery Below Grand on the Lower East Side. Woolbright was previously a resident at the Sharpe-Walentas Studio Program. In 2024, he received the Irving Sandler Prize, awarded to an artist who builds community as part of their artistic practice. He currently teaches at Pratt Institute and The School of Visual Arts in New York.

Linda Xheza writes on photography and immigration at the Amsterdam School of Cultural Analysis, University of Amsterdam.

Living and working between London and Shanghai, **Gary Zhexi Zhang** is a visual artist and writer whose work explores systemic connections between cosmology, technology, and the economy. He operates individually or collaboratively with organizations using a variety of media, including installation, film, performance, research reports, and software. In 2024 he exhibited in the 9th Asian Art Biennial, Taichung and at the Power Station of Art, Shanghai and EPFL Pavilions, Lausanne. He also toured *Dead Cat Bounce*, an opera cocreated with Waste Paper Opera, across the United Kingdom. He is currently working on a book about emerging technocultures in a multipolar world.

Acknowledgments

The story of this book began in summer 2021, when Dominic Willsdon, then the executive director of the Institute of Contemporary Art (ICA) at Virginia Commonwealth University, asked me to join him and Sarah Rifky on a new triennial with a focus on education. Rifky had just been hired as the senior curator at the ICA and soon the three of us were working together on planning this huge project, which was to include an exhibition, public projects in the city of Richmond, a symposium, and a publication. As they both indicate in their contributions here, their experiences in innovative art & education practices are both deep and wide and they brought that to bear on this project. We worked together until both of them left the ICA in December 2023. Unfortunately, this meant that the exhibitions, and almost all related programming, were cancelled. I am grateful for this invaluable and collaborative exchange of ideas with Sarah and Dominic and am glad that they were able to contribute to this publication.

The Teiger Foundation had generously supported the curatorial research for this project and our proposal was to host an online convening in the summer of 2023, followed by an in-person summit that fall. For the online component we brought together a diverse group of artists, curators, academics, and cultural workers: Inés Dussel, Malik Gaines, Gris García, Tom Holert, Adelita Husni-Bey, Naima J. Keith, Christian Nyampeta, Eriola Pira, Beatriz Santiago Muñoz, and Pelin Tan, along with me, Rifky, and Willsdon as moderators. This group helped us think through the most pressing issues in art & education today in a variety of contexts.

Many people from the ICA helped organize the online convening including Yomna Osman, who worked on curatorial support, and Hala Al-Tinawi, who helped with administrative support. Over the course of the project, the whole team worked on a series of workshops to collectively envision what this triennial might look like at the ICA and in Richmond. I am thankful to Traci Garland for administrative support regarding this book and to Jessica Bell Brown, who joined the ICA in fall 2024 as its new executive director and enthusiastically supported this publication.

Following the departure of Willsdon and Rifky from the ICA, and in consultation with the acting director of the ICA, Chase Westfall, we went back to Teiger Foundation in early 2024 to propose that we use the remainder of our funding for a book that would draw on the research and subject matter of the triennial and they kindly agreed. I am grateful to Larissa Harris and the team at the Teiger Foundation for supporting this transition and the overall project.

I am grateful to Inventory Press for their expert stewardship of the editorial, design, production, and distribution of this book. Special thanks to Adam Michaels, Shannon Harvey, and Zoe Kauder Nalebuff. Thanks to Brian Sholis for his expert copy editing and proofing. Thanks also to Gabby Blanks and Sanija Dowden, VCU students who worked as research assistants for the book.

I am grateful for the support of Beatriz E. Balanta, Cara Benedetto, Gavin Kroeber, and Robert M. Ochshorn, who acted as readers for my writing related to this project, and to Nicole Killian for feedback.

In the spirit of collaboration and participation that marks much of the work described here, Engy M. Sarhan provided editorial feedback for Sarah Rifky's essay and Julian Myers-Szupinska coauthored the essay contributed by Dominic Willsdon.

I am grateful to the editorial advisors Pablo Helguera, Beatriz Santiago Muñoz, Pelin Tan, Dominic Willsdon, and all of the contributors. Each contribution has a story, but I want to thank Alex Klein in particular for her enthusiasm and for reconvening the group that collaborated on RAW Académie at ICA in Philadelphia. I also want to acknowledge the profound loss in May 2025 of Koyo Kouoh, the founder of RAW in Dakar, whose work was so influential and impactful in the field of art & education.

I was lucky to have traveled for other projects and intersected with a number of the people and organizations in these pages—community and networks of connection helped build the texts gathered here. A few examples will have to suffice. In São Paulo, I met Ana Roman at Pivô, who helped connect me with Thiago Gil de Oliveira Virava, who was director of education at the São Paulo Biennial for many years. I also met Helmut Batista in Rio de Janeiro at Capacete when I brought students to Brazil. When I worked on the exhibition *Commonwealth* at the ICA in 2019–20, I met Pablo Guardiola at Beta—Local in Puerto Rico and he mentioned that lugar a dudas was one of his inspirations. I was lucky to visit Sally Mizrachi in Cali, Colombia, at lugar a dudas, in addition to Beatriz E. Balanta at Black Ground in the same city. When I was at the Sharjah Art Foundation March Meeting in 2023, I met Judith Greer, who generously connected me with Noora Al Mualla. In Beirut, I met Christine Tohmé at Ashkal Alwan's new building, and we talked about the evolution of education for that organization. Many other recommendations and connections were made by people such as Marilyn Boror, Sofía Olascoaga, Tan, Willsdon, Alia Farid, Stephanie Smith, Muñoz, Joseph del Pesco, and Prem Krishnamurthy.

Living to Learn:
Art & Education for the Common Good
is published by
Inventory Press
2305 Hyperion Ave
Los Angeles, CA 90027
inventorypress.com
&
Institute for Contemporary Art at
Virginia Commonwealth University
601 W Broad St,
Richmond, VA 23220
icavcu.org

This publication has been made possible by
Teiger Foundation

Copy editing and proofreading
Brian Sholis

Design
IN-FO.CO (Adam Michaels, Diellza Veliqi,
Clara Chirila-Rus)

Printed and bound in China through
Asia Pacific Offset

ISBN: 978-1-941753-81-1
LCCN: 2025942896

Distributed by
ARTBOOK | D.A.P.
75 Broad St, Suite 630
New York, NY 10004
artbook.com